WRITING NEW ENGLAND

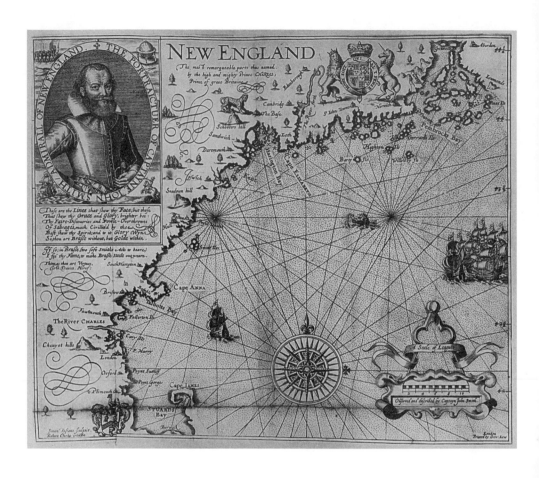

WRITING NEW ENGLAND

An Anthology from the Puritans to the Present

EDITED BY

ANDREW DELBANCO

The Belknap Press of
HARVARD UNIVERSITY PRESS
CAMBRIDGE, MASSACHUSETTS
LONDON, ENGLAND
2001

Pages 455–459 constitute an extension of this copyright page.

Library of Congress Cataloging-in-Publication Data

Writing New England : an anthology from the Puritans to the present /
edited by Andrew Delbanco.

     p.   cm.

  Includes index.

  ISBN 0-674-00603-8 (alk. paper)   974

    1. New England—Civilization—Sources. WR I

  2. New England—Literary collections.   10.01

  3. American literature—New England.

  I. Delbanco, Andrew, 1952–

  F4.5 .W75   2001

  974—dc21

  2001025779

Frontispiece: John Smith, Map of New England, 1616

CONTENTS

☙ DISSIDENT DREAMERS

☙ STRANGERS IN THE PROMISED LAND

THE ABIDING SENSE OF PLACE

PREFACE

Long before the modern dogma took hold that early childhood experience determines adult character, Alexis de Tocqueville applied the idea to America. Convinced that the childhood of the United States was to be found in colonial New England, he wrote, "if we would understand the prejudices, the habits, and the passions which rule" the life of the mature man, "we must watch the infant in his mother's arms." Today, however, not many Americans—not even, perhaps, many New Englanders—feel that in observing the strict Protestants who emigrated to New England nearly four centuries ago they are watching their younger selves.

And why should they? As New England expanded geographically from the scant coastal settlements with which it began, and as it grew more than commensurately in population, it was shocked, enriched, and transformed by the infusion of many traditions alien to its founders. One purpose of this book is to convey how New Englanders have come to live in different and distinct regions of cultural inheritance—as J. Anthony Lukas makes vivid in *Common Ground,* from which I have excerpted a chapter about a Boston family, the McGoffs, whose memories cluster not around Brahmin worthies with *Mayflower* names, but around such Boston Irish politicians as James Michael Curley and John Francis Fitzgerald, better known as Honey Fitz. By contrast, consider a remark the historian Bernard Bailyn once made about his predecessor at Harvard, Samuel Eliot Morison. A recreational sailor born to privilege who rode on horseback from his Beacon Hill home to his classroom building in Harvard Yard, Morison first discovered his passion for maritime history, according to Bailyn, in the "lore he had picked up from the old sailors whose memory went back to the days of the great clipper ships." McGoffs and Morisons lived barely a mile apart, but in utterly different worlds.

Imposing one unitary meaning on New England would be as foolish as it would be unconvincing. Yet one purpose of this book is to convey some sense of New England's continuities and coherence. I am persuaded that there does exist something that may be called, as Perry Miller called it some sixty years ago, the "New England mind." In pursuing that elusive entity, I have tried to avoid what Benjamin DeMott, with typical pungency, calls the "hallowing of New England," an attitude he summarizes with a list of symbols that tend to provoke automatic piety: "Pilgrims, Puritans, Boston Tea Party, Paul Revere, City on the Hill, Underground Railway, Massachusetts alone for McGovern, etc." The transience and diversity of cultural memory and the slippage of history into myth are among the reasons this book stresses both continuities and discontinuities, confrontations and accommodations—even as it remains committed to the idea that New England is more than merely a geographical term.

This having been said, a few words about the shape and contents of the book are in order. Soon after I accepted the invitation from Harvard University Press to edit a volume for the general reader covering the whole range, and whole history, of New England writing, I began to feel—as Howard Mumford Jones once remarked about an anthology of his own—as if I were "trying to sample the Atlantic Ocean with a tablespoon." Each piece has fought hard for its place against other contenders. Inevitably, the final cast and arrangement are expressions of personal taste; and so I imagine readers of this book as house guests spending time in the company of pictures and furnishings that matter to me and that seem to me to belong together. In making the choices, I relied on a principle of inclusion suggested by Helen Vendler in reviewing another anthology: "reading any major poet is an experience in how description may be renewed." Not all the writers in this book are major figures (a few are barely known), and only a minority of them are, strictly speaking, poets. But all are here because of the bracing freshness with which they describe places, people, ideas, and events, to which, even if the subject is familiar, we are reawakened by their words.

With the goal in mind of producing a relatively compact and readable book, I considered excluding altogether such writers as Emerson, Thoreau, and Hawthorne on the grounds of their ready availability elsewhere. As an opposite expedient, I also considered simply producing a book of ten or twenty "classics." In the end, I decided to include the major writers, but generally to represent them with less well-known instances of their writing—on the grounds that such standard works as *Walden* or Benjamin Franklin's *Autobiography* are widely accessible. The best way to read this book is in conjunction with these missing masterpieces. I should add that since novelists and historians suffer especially at the paring hand of the anthologist, I have excerpted sparingly from the former and, with regret, virtually not at all from the latter—favoring instead letters, poems, stories, and essays that can be feasibly printed without truncation. I hope that readers of this book will be stimulated to go to the full sources, and to other works by more authors than they meet here.

In short, I believe that the real challenge for the anthologist, who perforce deals in fragments, is to integrate the words of disparate writers into a new collaborative work that, despite its inevitably hybrid nature, has a coherence of its own. That is what I have tried to do: to make a book for *reading*—rather than for consulting, browsing, or leaving on the proverbial coffee table.

Finally, I should say that while this book has been assembled according to these literary standards, it is also meant to serve—to borrow a phrase Miller applied to a collection of his own essays—as "a rank of spotlights" on New England history. As Miller's metaphor implies, there are dark intervals between the lights. To provide a temporal frame for the readings, the book includes a chronology of developments in New England's political, economic, and cultural life; and each selection is preceded by a brief headnote intended to establish some context in which the selection may be better understood.

The test of all these principles and strategies will be each reader's experience. I can only hope that this book will prove as much a pleasure and challenge to read as it was for me to put together.

Andrew Delbanco
New York City
September 2000

INTRODUCTION

Nearly half a century ago, when the historian Samuel Eliot Morison sought to explain why anyone concerned with the New England present might care about its past, he went to his wine cellar for a metaphor. "The wine of New England," he wrote, "is not a series of successive vintages, each distinct from the other, like the wines of France; it is more like the mother-wine in those great casks of port and sherry that one sees in the *bodegas* of Portugal and Spain, from which a certain amount is drawn off every year, and replaced by an equal volume of the new. Thus the change is gradual and the mother wine of 1656 still gives bouquet and flavor to what is drawn in 1956."

My hope is that readers of this book, whether they sip from it or drink from it deeply, will come away with some sense of the bouquet and flavor of New England. Since the culture sampled here is not a true vintage but a mixture drawn from different grapes, readers will encounter in these pages not only Beacon Hill gentry and postcard-perfect villages, but also Charlestown Irish whose ancestors left behind a European famine only to serve in American kitchens, Vermont millworkers, immigrant Jews selling flavored ice on Revere Beach, and black migrants who, having fled north from slavery or sharecropping, discovered that the land of the abolitionists did not always live up to its proclaimed ideals.

This kind of human variety brings with it certain irrepressible questions: Can one speak of an enduring New England mentality that has somehow persisted from the Pilgrim fathers to the present day? Or is New England merely a collective name for six states—Vermont, New Hampshire, Maine, Massachusetts, Rhode Island, and Connecticut—a big parcel of real estate stretching from the Northeast Kingdom of Vermont to the New York suburbs of Fairfield County, bounded on the east by the Atlantic, on the north by Canada, and on the west and south by the Vermont, Massachusetts, and Connecticut state lines? In today's McWorld, is there still a discernible frontier dividing the coastal mega-city of Portland–Portsmouth–Boston–Providence–New Haven from its southerly extension through New York, Philadelphia, Baltimore, and Washington?

Regional differences do, of course, persist. When ordering a sandwich on a long roll, New Yorkers ask for a "hero" or a "sub." In parts of Massachusetts and Connecticut the same item may be known as a "grinder." In New York, a blend of milk and ice cream is called a milk shake, but if you ask for a drink by that name in Boston, you'll get nothing but frothed milk. If you're a Coca-Cola drinker, in New England you ask not for soda or pop, but for a "tonic."

Mastering such minor colloquial differences is helpful for negotiating everyday life; but one is left with the question of whether deeper distinctions mark New England as a place apart. In an America where most people live far from where they were born (not to mention from where their parents were born), what exactly do we mean when we speak of regional identity—as we seem to do the more we feel it slipping away? If "New England" means something, what is it? If it no longer does, what did it once mean?

Writing about the history in which his family played such a distinguished part, Henry Adams once answered this line of questioning by remarking that "resistance to something was the law of New England nature." The very founding of New England was, after all, an act of manifold resistance—to the perils of shipwreck, disease, starvation, and the hostility of wary "Indians," as well as to the dubiety and mockery of contemporaries, and indeed to the residual idea (not entirely refuted by Columbus) that the Atlantic Ocean marked the natural western boundary of civilization.

By the late sixteenth century, England was just beginning to enter the international competition to establish colonies in the New World. When English eyes finally turned westward in earnest, it was from a variety of motives: to mine gold or precious stones, to discover the fabled passage that would shorten the voyage to the Orient, to create new markets for finished goods, to establish colonies to which surplus or unwanted people could migrate or be banished. Some early propagandists also stressed the missionary motive of bringing the Christian gospel to American heathens. Others, mindful of the chronic imperial struggle with France and Spain, regarded the New World as an inevitable extension of the European theater of war.

Those who looked to America for any or all of these reasons were called adventurers, a word that had two pertinent meanings in contemporary usage: explorer-entrepreneurs willing to risk their lives, and investors willing to risk their money. The former ventured against the hazards of ocean voyages; the latter ventured the hope of realizing profits from timber and fur, and especially from the plentiful marine life that spawned along the North American continental shelf, where fish were "so abundant," according to one early observer, "that if a man step into the water they will come round about him; so that men were fain to get out for fear of biting."

These first adventurers had in mind no clear distinction between the vast territory that stretched between the 35th and 40th latitudes, called Virginia in honor of Britain's virgin queen, and the lands further north, extending to the 48th latitude, known simply as "northern Virginia." By the 1580s a number of wealthy merchants were looking to this mostly unknown and undifferentiated country with plans to emulate the profitable trade that had been achieved earlier with Russia, China, Turkey, and the East Indies through regulated trading companies, groups of investors to whom the crown granted monopolies for developing trade with some remote region of the world, in return for which a portion of the profits was to be paid into the royal treasury.

Early attempts to put this scheme into practice in North America were disastrous. Under the leadership of Sir Walter Raleigh—one of those Elizabethan hybrids who was half-statesman, half-pirate—scores of English lives were expended, most notoriously in several ill-fated attempts to settle the Chesapeake island of Roanoke just off the coast of the well-named Cape Fear. To this day it is not known if starvation, disease, or massacre by Indians was the primary reason for the Roanoke settlers' disappearance. What we do know is that with each shipwreck or failed treasure hunt, America confirmed its reputation as a place reserved for crackpots and dreamers, a reputation it had been unable to shake off since one explorer dispatched in the 1570s by Queen Elizabeth brought back a mound of yellow ore for deposit in the Tower of London—as "gold" that turned out to be nothing but worthless American dirt.

Yet through a combination of stubbornness, recklessness, unquenchable ambition, and cruelty to the hired men who faced the dangers personally and who often treated the native Americans with commensurate brutality, colonization efforts continued. In 1606, despite the dismal precedents, two groups of undiscouraged entrepreneurs—one centered in London, the other drawn from Plymouth and other port towns in Western England—formed a collective entity called the Virginia Company. The former group finally established a durable settlement in 1607 at Jamestown (named for Elizabeth's successor, James I), though it came close to failing when only 60 of the original 500 settlers survived the winter of 1609–10, some of them apparently by resorting to cannibalism. At about the same time, the latter group established a settlement near the mouth of the Sagadahoc River in what is now Maine, an encampment that lasted for barely a year, between the summers of 1607 and 1608, before poor management and the harsh climate forced its abandonment. Except for occasional fishing and fur trading, colonizing activity ceased in "northern Virginia" for more than a decade. It was not until 1616 that a veteran of several Virginia campaigns, Captain John Smith, whom two London merchants had hired to scout the northern shore for whales, gave the region the more grand and hopeful name that has stuck to it ever since: New England.

Around the time that New England acquired its name, developments at home were quickening interest in it. As tension rose between king and bishops on the one hand, and men of business and religious dissent on the other, New England became a plausible refuge for many sorts of restless people: well-born younger sons shut out by the laws of primogeniture from inheriting land; poor people forbidden to till, or scavenge on, lands which their landlords—intent on raising sheep for the expanding wool market—were enclosing with hedges and fences; and pious people to whom the clergy of the established church seemed scandalously ignorant of Scripture, indifferent to their parishioners' lives, and profanely devoted to ceremony and pomp.

With a mixture of such constituents in mind, a reorganized joint-stock company composed of members of the Virginia Company, along with some new investors, applied in 1620 for a royal patent for the New England territory. It was this new "Council for New England" that, in turn, granted a subsidiary patent to another group of investors led by a London ironmonger named Thomas Weston, who had negotiated a financial arrangement with a party of religious dissenters who needed capital if they were to realize their hope of removing to America.

These were the exceptionally disciplined and mutually committed people we now know as the Pilgrims. They were led by William Bradford, who as a boy had joined a congregation at Scrooby, a small town north of London. Members of the Scrooby congregation subscribed to a simple Protestant creed, from which they thought the established Church of England had strayed. They believed in the omnipotence of God, the sinfulness of man, redemption through Christ (whose saving love, they thought, was apprehended chiefly through the preached word), and subjection of the resurrected body after death to God's final judgment. Feeling that the clergy of the established church were, at best, paying lip service to these doctrines, they left England in 1607 for exile in Holland. There they grew concerned for their children, who they feared would stray from their customs and native language if the Dutch sojourn were extended. And so they decided—"not out of any newfangledness or other such like giddy humor," as Bradford later recalled, but "for sundry weighty and solid reasons"—to seek a new sanctuary where they might be free to worship as they wished.

"The place they had thoughts on," Bradford wrote, "was some of those vast and unpeopled countries of America, which are fruitful and fit for habitation, being devoid of all civil inhabitants, where there are only savage and brutish men which range up and down, little otherwise than the wild beasts of the same." One proposed destination was near the Amazon River, in Guiana; another prospect was raised by the New Netherlands Company, a group of Dutch investors who invited their English guests to settle along the Hudson River in territory claimed by Holland. But after arduous negotiations with

Weston and his partners, they chose Virginia, contracting to pay hefty dividends from the profits they hoped to make there in return for transportation and supplies. They shipped out in September 1620, planning to settle far enough from Jamestown to avoid interference from the church authorities that had begun to organize an Anglican establishment in America.

In early November, with winter bearing down upon them, they found themselves in shallow coastal waters off Cape Cod. Their trip, it seemed, had been watched over by Providence. Only one of the hundred voyagers had perished, and one baby, named Oceanus, had been safely born at sea. But now, while anchored in Cape Cod Bay, four more of their number died; and instead of turning south, they sailed into what is now Provincetown harbor and decided to seek a suitable site from which to face the future.

Embedded as it has become in layers of myth, the experience of these first New Englanders is largely unrecoverable. The myth-making began almost at once; it was given eloquent expression in Bradford's *History of Plymouth Plantation,* which he began writing around 1630, and with which he remained occupied for the remaining twenty years of his life. Like some who accompanied him, and many who followed, he paid swiftly and dearly for his enterprise. Upon returning to the *Mayflower* from a rowboat reconnaissance mission that included the legendary first landing at Plymouth Rock, he learned that his "dearest consort" had fallen overboard and drowned. (Morison speculates that she may have taken her own life after "gazing for six weeks at the barren sand dunes of Cape Cod.") Bradford's evocation of the Pilgrims' landfall, with its explicit parallels to the Israelites' pilgrimage through the wilderness, has become justly famous:

Being thus passed the vast ocean, and a sea of troubles before in their preparation . . . they had now no friends to welcome them nor inns to entertain or refresh their weatherbeaten bodies; no houses or much less towns to repair to, to seek for succour. It is recorded in Scripture as a mercy to the Apostle and his shipwrecked company, that the barbarians showed them no small kindness in refreshing them, but these savage barbarians, when they met with them (as after will appear) were readier to fill their sides full of arrows than otherwise. And for the season it was winter, and they that know the winters of that country know them to be sharp and violent, and subject to cruel and fierce storms, dangerous to travel to known places, much more to search an unknown coast. Besides, what could they see but a hideous and desolate wilderness, full of wild beasts and wild men—and what multitudes there might be of them they knew not. Neither could they, as it were, go up to the top of Pisgah to view from this wilderness a more goodly country to feed their hopes; for which way soever they turned their eyes (save upward to the heavens) they could have little solace or content in respect of any outward objects. For summer being done, all things stand upon them with a weather-beaten face, and the whole country, full of woods and thickets, represented a wild and savage hue.

The accuracy of this passage as a description of Cape Cod, of the Pilgrims' initial state of mind, or of their reception by the Indians, is dubious. One eye-witness account written much closer in time to the event describes an appealing landscape rather "like the downs in Holland, but much better," adorned by forest that was "for the most part open and without underwood, fit either to go or ride in" and inhabited by skittish Indians who, "when [they] saw our men following them . . . ran away with might and main." But this matter-of-fact report has been pretty much forgotten. It is Bradford's retrospective rendition that has found a permanent place in the nation's collective memory.

Among the many recapitulations of Bradford by later writers, here is one in which that resolute New Yorker, Norman Mailer, meditates on the strange Cape Cod mixture of desert barrenness and Edenic tranquillity that one still feels today when walking on its beaches and dunes:

> I contemplate the event on many a day. Those Pilgrims, having crossed the Atlantic, encountered the cliffs of Cape Cod as their first sight of land. On that back shore the surf, at its worst, can break in waves ten feet high . . . What fear those Pilgrims must have known on hearing the dull eternal boom of the surf. Who would dare to come near that shore with boats such as theirs? . . . They came around the point, and dropped anchor in the lee. It was a natural harbor, as protected, indeed, as the inside of one's ear. From there, they put down small boats and rowed to shore. A plaque commemorates the landing . . . [Here] is where they first landed with all the terror and exaltation of encountering the new land. New land it was, not ten thousand years old. A strew of sand. How many Indian ghosts must have howled through the first nights of their encampment. I think of the Pilgrims whenever I walk to these emerald-green marshes at the end of town . . . If I have a drink in me, I begin to laugh, because across from the plaque to the Pilgrims, not fifty yards away, there where the United States began, stands the entrance to a huge motel . . . Its asphalt parking lot is as large as a football field. Pay homage to the Pilgrims.

What Mailer captures in this juxtaposition of past and present is how deeply the Pilgrims have come to inhabit what might be called our national unconscious. We may degrade them with tawdry memorials, or invoke them as black-cloaked, high-hatted prigs. Yet somehow they defeat the caricatures. Every immigrant generation that followed has relived their mixture of guilt and exhilaration at leaving home, and has wondered with Bradford—"Ought not the children of these fathers rightly say: 'Our fathers . . . came over this great ocean, and were ready to perish in this wilderness'?"—if their progeny would vindicate or disappoint them.

Bradford's little band turned out to be the advance party of a much larger migration. With civil war looming in England, a human stream amounting to some twenty thousand persons followed the Plymouth pilgrims between 1630 and 1640, flowing across the "vast ocean" under the authority of a new trading corporation called the Massachusetts Bay Company. Led by a Lincolnshire gentleman named John Winthrop, several of its directors (or "assistants") made the shrewd move of physically taking their royal charter document with them, thereby establishing themselves as a virtually independent and self-governing community. After distributing themselves in several hospitable spots around the bay, they soon dispersed further west toward the Berkshires as well as south and east to Connecticut and Long Island. They founded towns to which they gave the names (Weston, 1642; Harvard, 1704) of investors or benefactors who, in some cases, never made the ocean crossing themselves. Or they appropriated Indian names—doubtless garbled in transliteration—like Scituate (1630), Narragansett (1657), and Massachusetts itself. Or they registered their hopes in names (New Haven, 1638; New Canaan, 1700) that were simultaneously memorial and prospective.

Why did these people make the voyage in such numbers and at such risk? Schoolbook answers like "religious freedom" or "economic opportunity" are not especially helpful. Like all immigrants since, they came for many reasons. Some—notably daughters and wives—came unwillingly or half-willingly, as did the poet Anne Bradstreet, whose "heart rose" against the "new world and new manners" to which her filial and spousal duty (her father and her husband were prominent figures in the first wave of emigrants) compelled her. A minor poet named Thomas Tillam, who stayed only briefly in the New World, was one of those convinced that they were heeding a call from God:

> Methinks I heare the Lambe of God thus speake
> Come my deare little flocke, who for my sake
> Have left your Country, dearest friends, and goods
> And hazarded your lives o'th raging floods . . .

Notwithstanding the tentative "methinks," here is the note of righteous zeal that angered many who remained behind in the old country—not only Anglican conformists whom one emigrant denounced as "irreligious" and "lascivious" persons who had "spread [through England] like grasshoppers," but also fellow Puritans (the very term Puritan was a mocking nickname given by opponents) who felt obliged to stay and fight at home for church reform.

Such disputes took place within a context of widespread expectancy that God was about to reveal his true purpose in unveiling America to English eyes, a purpose much larger than rewarding a few adventurers or lining the king's coffers. Many pious people believed that the last days prophesied in the Book of Revelation were at hand, and that the opening of the New World was a sign that the end was near. Some expected Christ's Second Coming to be preceded by a thousand years of sweet serenity, while others looked for him to descend in a burst of purifying fire that would consume the wicked world. Writing around 1650, one militant New Englander, Edward Johnson, gave a vivid account of England on the eve of the exodus in which one can almost hear the trumpets blare, as Christ "stirs up his servants as the heralds of a king to make this proclamation for volunteers . . . 'Oh yes! oh yes! oh yes! All you the people of Christ that are here oppressed, imprisoned and scurrilously derided, gather yourselves together, your wives and little ones, and answer to your several names as you shall be shipped for his service, in the western world, and more especially for planting the united colonies of New England, where you are to attend the service of the King of Kings.'"

Here we arrive at a keynote of New England literature, and one of its chief legacies to the development of American culture. Today we think of New England as a region radiating out from the Hub of Boston encircled by the corporate ring road known as Route 128—a land of think tanks and secular universities, far removed from "backwater" places where evangelical religion still matters. But 350 years ago, New England was the throbbing heart of Christianity in the New World, the consecrated birthplace of the idea that God had appointed Americans (a word that begins to be applied toward the end of the seventeenth century to colonists rather than Indians) as his holy army selected to prepare the way for Christ's enthronement. "The English Puritans," as one of their true heirs, James Russell Lowell, put it more than two centuries after the Great Migration, "pulled down church and state to rebuild Zion on the ruins, and all the while it was not Zion, but America, they were building." This theme of America's special mission, or Manifest Destiny, as it would be renamed in the nineteenth century, was reprised during the Revolution in many patriot sermons, as when the Boston minister Samuel West declared in 1776 that the "savage disposition of tyrants [is] exhibited to view by the Apostle John in the Revelation," and again during the Civil War, when the Boston abolitionist Julia Ward Howe declared, in what became the unofficial Union anthem, "Battle-Hymn of the Republic," "Mine eyes have seen the glory of the coming of the Lord!" The literature of early New England announces this enduring belief in America as the New Israel—as (to use the biblical phrases that Puritans often invoked) a "city upon a hill" or a "light unto the nations." Just "as one small candle may light a thousand," Bradford mused in the closing pages of his *History*, "so the light here kindled hath shone unto many, yea in some sort to our whole nation," for which "let the glorious name of Jehovah have all the praise."

But what, exactly, was the Old World darkness that the first New Englanders hoped to dispel? Why did they cull images of doom and damnation from the Bible (Babylon, Shiloh, Sodom) as analogies to the land they were leaving?

Many agreed with the minister Thomas Hooker who, in 1628, before he decided to join the exodus from England, was drawing dire conclusions from the departure of civic and religious leaders for the American wilderness: "England has seen her best days . . . God begins to ship away his Noahs, which prophesied and foretold that destruction was near; and God makes account that New England shall be a refuge for his Noahs and his Lots, a rock and a shelter for his righteous ones to run unto; and those that were vexed to see the ungodly lives of the people in this wicked land, shall there be safe." Around the same time, John Winthrop was gathering his own will to leave because he thought that England had become a place where "children, servants, and neighbours . . . are counted the greatest burthen, which if things were right . . . would be the chiefest earthly blessing." Winthrop spoke from the experience of the landowning class, many of whom had lately expelled (or were considering expelling) tenants from their land to make room for the more lucrative business of raising sheep. In the receding feudal past, a tenant's right to occupy and cultivate a particular plot on the landowner's estate had been inherited from his father and secured with symbolic offerings of crop or livestock. But in the new world of the emerging marketplace, men of Winthrop's standing who hesitated to charge real rather than nominal rents were jeopardizing the future of their own sons. With every qualm they felt at pressing their tenants for more, their sons' inheritance grew smaller. Propertied men had to choose between defending their moral convictions at cost to their worldly interests, or abandoning them at cost to their souls.

Many migrants to New England were people of lower social rank who would have liked to have had Winthrop's problems. But as England embarked on its long transition into modernity, from a country inhabited mainly by subsistence farmers to one where more and more rural folk raised crops and livestock for market, even men of modest means found themselves facing similar dilemmas. With the dislocation of landless people and the beginnings of a market economy, towns and cities were growing rapidly, as were the number of middlemen—"higglers, badgers, poulters, [and] fishmongers," as one writer enumerated them—who bought produce at local markets in order to hawk it from town to town. According to traditional ethical standards, such merchants were usurious meddlers who drove up prices for their own benefit. But nothing much beyond local barter could exist without them. In fact, the whole social landscape of England was changing: the professions of lawyer or merchant were becoming attractive options for younger sons excluded from land inheritance; poorhouses were filling; bandits and vagabonds (the entrepreneurial poor) were roaming the country and crowding the cities. In this context, men of property had to ask themselves whether they were contributing by their own business practices to the proliferation of such "noisome" people. And men of lesser means had to ask themselves if they were destined to join them.

This is also the context in which one may appreciate a remark D. H. Lawrence made seventy-five years ago in a searching little book called *Studies in Classic American Literature*. With a writer's instinct for the inner life of strangers, and a foreigner's feel for the chronic restlessness of Americans, Lawrence asked, "What did the Pilgrim Fathers come for, then, when they came so gruesomely over the black sea?" To this rhetorical question, he had a ready answer: "They came largely to get *away*—that most simple of motives. To get away. Away from what? In the long run, away from themselves." Lawrence got it right. To use a phrase that, in the 1960s, served as the shorthand term for all sorts of malcontents, the founders of New England were drop-outs—with all the indignation, idealism, and wounded righteousness that the term implies.

If these restless people left hints of their experience in letters, poems, and histories, their chief form of expression—and therefore a form to which this book gives some space—was the sermon. While they remained in England, one of the ways the Puritans had exasperated church authorities was by constantly complaining of being cheated of the spiritual gift of the preached word. Puritans took very seriously St. Paul's injunction that "faith cometh by hearing" (Romans 10:17); they believed that the saving grace of God—the infusion of the spirit without which the soul was doomed—was most likely to occur while a penitent sinner listened to a gospel preacher. Yet according to Anglican canon law, only four "homilies," or sermons, per year were required on the liturgical calendar, and these might be delivered by a clergyman visiting from some other parish speaking on abstruse theological points to which local folk felt little personal connection.

Puritan sermons were different. For one thing, they were abundant. Every congregation in New England included at least one "preaching elder," and sometimes two: a "teacher" who elucidated points of doctrine, and a "pastor" whose charge was to address the issues of daily life (responsibilities to family, neighbors, nation) that had become so vexing in England. In addition to preaching two sermons every Sunday, most New England ministers preached once more during the week; and all significant public ceremonies—anniversaries, elections, funerals, celebrations, days of thanksgiving or mourning—featured a sermon by a preacher especially invited for the occasion. One modern scholar, Harry Stout, estimates that in New England during the colonial period, the average weekly churchgoer attended "something like seven thousand sermons in a lifetime," which, since a sermon might last two hours or more, amounted to nearly "fifteen thousand hours of concentrated listening."

Imagining today what it was like to live in this culture saturated by sermons is not easy. It is hard to conceive how it felt, in a drafty meetinghouse silent except for the sound of the preaching voice, to be pinned to your pew by the eyes of a clergyman who seemed somehow privy to your secret sins. In addition to delivering partly memorized, partly improvised talks twice on Sunday and once on "lecture day," ministers held private conferences with those who wished to join the church—half-pedagogic and half-therapeutic sessions that culminated in a public profession of faith in which the aspiring communicant described how he or she had come out of sin into a life of Christian rectitude. Such public "relations" were a kind of initiation ceremony for admission to full membership (the right to partake of communion) in the church—a word that meant something quite different from what it had meant in old England. To the Puritans, a church was neither a physical structure made of wood or stone (which they called the "meeting house") nor a national ecclesiastical organization. A church was a group of believers who gathered together voluntarily—as Bradford's church had done at Scrooby—to keep the sacraments and to hear God's word.

Relations between preacher and hearer in such churches were intimate. Sermons sometimes took on the back-and-forth structure of a question-and-answer session, as if the preacher were recounting a recent conversation with a troubled member of his flock—as in John Winthrop's famous lay sermon, "A Model of Christian Charity," preached to his fellow emigrants just before they sailed for the New World. When Winthrop asks, "What rule must we observe in lending?" the sermon becomes a form of collective self-interrogation; and when he answers his own question—"Thou must observe whether thy brother hath present or probable or possible meanes of repaying thee, if there be none of these, thou must give him according to his necessity"—he gives voice to the utopian dream of a society in which love vanquishes greed.

Of course, Winthrop's dream that the people of Massachusetts Bay would be "knitt together in this worke as one man" could never be fully achieved in this world. No one knew this better than the Puritans themselves, who, following Augustine and Calvin, regarded unsanctified human beings as creatures motivated by greed, lust, and self-love. Even those whose affections had been redirected by the holy spirit toward God were susceptible to backsliding and needed to be on guard against the resurgence of sin. But if the Puritans' pilgrimage did not mark the Second Coming, it did bring to America a soaring aspiration that, when it inevitably fell short of realization, was transformed into self-criticism of the most stringent kind. And here, I think, we come as close as we are likely to get to the genesis of what Henry Adams called "New England nature."

Adams had in mind a certain quality of moral imagination that took distinctive shape as the first New Englanders recognized—but never quite accepted—the inevitable discrepancy between their ideals and their experience. One of the leading emigrant ministers, Thomas Shepard, recalled his former life in England, where the dissidents were "persecuted by enemies, driven into corners, or to towns six miles off to find a sacrament or hear a sermon." Under such conditions, faith burns at high heat. But when the migrants robbed themselves of their chance for martyrdom by voyaging to a place where there were "no enemies to hunt you to heaven, nor chains to make you cry," their fervor seemed to cool—at least according to the clergy, who were scolding them for their "frowardness" almost before the soil of old England was off their boots. Here begins a theme of chastisement that runs throughout American literature, provoked by the feeling that a great promise has been betrayed.

This promise was nothing less than the hope that in New England (to use a phrase from that half–New York, half–New England writer, Herman Melville), the "social acerbities" that afflict all human communities would be muted, if not extinguished, by a combination of shame and love. It was the task of the ministers to foster both: to reveal the pride and greed that infect the souls of even the most upright persons, and to hold up for worship and imitation the immaculate example of Christ, who, in order to save human beings from themselves, had lived among them without a shred of self-love. No true Puritan believed that any person could achieve such moral perfection in this life; indeed it was rank heresy to think so. But Puritans were committed to the idea that the Christian life literally begins—hence the metaphor of being "born again"—with the recognition that all human beings are helpless and doomed unless, and until, they obtain a glimpse of what it means to love without regard to self-interest, as Christ loves them. To convey some hint of man's peril and God's mercy was the duty and charge of the preacher, whom God was pleased to employ as his "mouth to the people."

Sermons were not the only weapons against pride. Sacraments, too, were part of the arsenal. Unlike in England, where the state church offered baptism and communion to virtually anyone who sought them, these privileges were at first restricted in some New England churches to those who had professed their faith before the whole congregation. Being received into the baptismal covenant was an expression of hope for one's soul under the stewardship of the church; but it was never a guarantee that God will find you "comely" in his sight.

Here was an expression of what Adams calls New England "resistance"—in this case, resistance to what might be called New England's incipient tribal pride. Ministers were at pains to rescue their listeners from the self-serving idea that their pioneer virtue somehow signified that God was satisfied with them. If New Englanders were blessed, it was not for any virtue of their own, but by God's inscrutable whim; and many of the most famous (or infamous) sermons are reminders that, dangling helplessly over hell, human beings can be dropped into the pit at any instant by a flick of God's finger.

Of course, New Englanders—like all human beings—seized opportunities to avoid this kind of exigent confrontation with themselves. In fact, their continual preaching against pride is proof that pride abounded; and it is one of the ironies of their history that these refugees from persecution quickly became expert persecutors themselves. From the hanging of Quakers and "witches" in the seventeenth century, to the execution of Sacco and Vanzetti in the twentieth, New England has never lacked for designated demons.

The first to fulfill this role were Pequot and Algonquian Indians, with whom the Puritans engaged in two bloody wars within fifty years of their arrival. Later, the role was assumed by Anabaptists and Quakers, later still by Irish and Italian immigrants, something of whose experience is evoked by writers included in this book in the section entitled "Strangers in the Promised Land."

Yet—and this is among the reasons that New Englanders succeeded early in creating a reflective and morally complex literature—their relation to the dissidents they hanged or banished, and even to the Indians whom they fought, cajoled into submission, or drove into the interior of the continent, was never psychologically simple. As they exercised their righteous virtue against these devils and deviants, they were often prodded to scrutinize their own deficiencies. Here is the founder of Rhode Island, Roger Williams (in 1643), writing about the Narragansett Indians, who by their example of gravity and mutual devotion seemed to him to rebuke his own people for their flagging discipline and love: "Their manner is upon any tidings to sit round, double or treble, or more, as their numbers be: I have seene neer a thousand in a round, where *English* could not well neere halfe so many have sitten: Every man hath his pipe of their *Tobacco,* and a deepe silence they make, and attention give to him that speaketh; and many of them will deliver themselves, either in a relation of news, or in a consultation, with very emphaticall speech and great action, commonly an houre, and sometimes two houres together."

This inward turn toward self-admonition is the hallmark of what Henry James called "the New England conscience"—a phrase that remains, I think, the best shorthand name for the sensibility that arises from Puritanism and that, transmitted by those mysterious mechanisms we call tradition, ultimately unites the disparate writings gathered in this volume. In an excellent book on this theme, the scholar Austin Warren summarized the effect of the emigration by which New Englanders gained a new world but lost the psychological advantage of having their virtue confirmed by persecuting enemies: "The 'New England Conscience' is not the mark of those who . . . are the objects of persecutions, but of those who suffer interiorly *from their own consciences.* They are tormented by doubts and scruples, feel the mixed—and hence impure—motives which prompt them to perform 'good works.' However many 'duties' they have performed, they feel they have never adequately done their Duty. However penitent for their Sin, and their sins, they never feel their contrition adequate."

To hold the self strictly accountable for its impurities and imperfections can be deforming. The diaries and poems of early New Englanders are redolent with self-disgust: "Ah Lord! Teares of blood cannot wash away the guilt," writes the minister and poet Michael Wigglesworth in his diary in the 1650s, "Lord I am vile, I abhor my self." But there is also in the New England conscience a candid and even stirring recognition that perfect justice and love, while beyond the capacity of human beings to achieve, are ultimately the only worthy aims of the well-lived life.

In the early 1640s, with foreboding and paradoxical humility, the great first-generation minister John Cotton, preaching on the Book of Revelation, articulated the tremendous sense of self-importance that attended the New England experiment—as if it were mankind's last chance for redemption in the eyes of God. Rarely has so much urgency been concentrated in the simple preposition *here:* "Beleeve it, you will find this true, and remember it while you live: If you be corrupt in *New-England,* if you be unfaithfull here, if you be worldly minded here, false of your words and promises here, injurious in your dealings here . . . you cannot poure fourth a Viall of more wrath on religion, as it is here reformed and established, through the blessing of God, you cannot load it with a heavier Viall of Gods wrath, than if here you shall grow worldly and covetous, deceitfull and contentious, and unbrotherly!" With the ever-present possibility of its shading into self-love on the one hand or self-hatred on the other, this moral scrupulosity—whether we prefer to call it New England nature or New England conscience—is the fundamental legacy of Puritanism to New England and, more generally, to America.

One aim of this book is to register the fate of that conscience in the place to which it was first carried from the Old World. Long after the specific doctrines (predestination, original sin) and ecclesiastical practices (public professions of faith, strictly independent congregations) of Puritanism had evolved into new forms, something that may still be called the Puritan conscience continued to animate many of the writers represented here—as when John Quincy Adams, speaking in 1841, asks God to bear him out in his work of defending the liberty of fugitive slaves, or when Theodore Parker inveighs in 1854 against the moral perils of prosperity. Several of the figures whom readers will meet in these pages (Henry Adams, Oliver Wendell Holmes, Jr.) write and speak with a familial sense of loyalty to this lineage, and, not infrequently, in order to chastise their fellow New Englanders for betraying it—as when Harriet Beecher Stowe, in 1852, constructs a portrait of a chilly Vermonter who confuses fastidiousness with Christian love, or, closer to our own time, in 1960, Robert Lowell holds his fellow Bostonians to account for abandoning the ideals of their predecessors.

One hazard of such devotion to the sacralized past is self-righteousness, a danger that not all writers in this book entirely escape. But there has also been in the New England tradition a salutary self-doubt—a certain wry self-deprecation exemplified by John Adams when, in a charming letter of March 2, 1816, having asked his old Virginia rival and late-life friend Thomas Jefferson, "Would you go back to your cradle and live over again your 70 years?" he goes on to make him an honorary New Englander: "I believe you would return me a New England answer, by asking me another question, 'Would you live your 80 years over again?'" This playful yet strenuous habit of incessant interrogation is a vestige from a church-centered society in which the clergy was charged with searching out and extirpating all traces of pride, an obligation passed on to the jurists, orators, social reformers, and writers of fiction, poetry, and social criticism who succeeded them and who constitute the *dramatis personae* of this book. As Adams indicated to Jefferson with his epistolary equivalent of a smile, no question in New England should fail to lead to another question (here is the essence of William James's "pragmatism"); no chain of interrogation should be allowed to come to an end.

This questing, disputatious quality of mind was summed up by the great English cultural critic Matthew Arnold in a single word—"Hebraism." Though Arnold was not writing specifically about New England, he had in mind the kind of religious passion that accounts for the creation of New England—the sort of imagination that "seizes upon certain plain, capital intimations of the universal order, and rivets itself . . . on the study and observance of them." It is the sort of mind that, with an acute sense of its own fallibility, seeks moral knowledge in the wisdom literature of the past. For New Englanders, this meant the Bible, the church fathers (chiefly Augustine), reformers such as Calvin, and, in due time, their own secular sages such as Emerson and Holmes. But if the New England mind has been inclined toward ancestor worship, it has also been intent on reaching a future worthy of its prophets. It is preoccupied with human weakness; placing "under the name of sin, the difficulties of knowing oneself and conquering oneself which impede man's progress to perfection," it insists that while no one can fully overcome these impediments, everyone has an obligation to try.

Writers who exemplify this New England mind tend to seek the future through a dialectical process of debate with themselves—which is why, for example, Emerson and Wallace Stevens often leave us feeling suspended between seemingly contradictory truths. It is a mistake to try to summarize the "position" staked out by such a writer. John Winthrop, for instance, begins his great sermon on Christian charity by noting that "God hath so disposed of the condition of mankind, as in all times some must be rich, some poor, some high and eminent in power and dignity, others mean and in subjection." But readers who would glean from these words that Winthrop was complacent about the inequalities of the human world will have missed a powerful countertheme in the sermon: his cherished ideals of humility and mutual obligation. "No man," he wrote, "is made more honorable than another or more wealthy, etc., out of any particular and singular respect to himself." In other words, it is a sin for a highborn man to think he deserves his advantages.

Sometimes the dialectic breaks down, and contending ideas once held in balance within a single mind are expressed singularly by separate antagonists. More than two hundred years after Winthrop, for instance, we find two New England writers, Charles Sumner and William Graham Sumner (no relation), taking up again the ancient question of equality vs. hierarchy. The former makes a passionate case that equality is mankind's destiny under the watchful eye of God; the latter makes the opposite case that human beings have been, and always will be, arranged along a scale from strength to subjection, and that there is something aesthetically satisfying in this natural order. It is as if Winthrop has become the common ancestor of two descendants quarreling over their patrimony.

Here, then, is one way to read this book: as a kind of family history. Of course, family must be understood as a metaphor, since one of the remarkable features of the New England tradition is how its themes and preoccupations have been disseminated far beyond the original lineage of English Protestants—to New Englanders of Irish Catholic or Italian descent such as John F. Kennedy or A. Bartlett Giamatti; to African Americans such as W. E. B. Du Bois; and to latter-day inheritors of the New England moralist tradition, from Felix Frankfurter to Jonathan Kozol, who might be called "Jewish Puritans." There are others in this book (Jean Stafford, John P. Marquand) who speak authoritatively about the exclusionary clubbishness of New England. And still others (E. E. Cummings, Shirley Jackson) mercilessly expose the cool disregard or fierce animosity that outsiders can feel in a New England town.

Yet in its early commitment to universal public education and its fundamentally liberal politics, New England has remained impressively true to its originating principle that the worth of individuals has nothing to do with their circumstances of birth. The founder of the first church at New Haven, John Davenport, put it this way more than 350 years ago in admonishing his congregation not to think their children worthy merely because they were born into Christian families: "Grace is not capable of being propagated . . . in a lineal succession by natural generation." Here is the most abiding, and most radically democratic, idea that runs through New England thought from the Puritans to the present day: the idea that the wellborn have no special claim on God's favor, and that divine grace may inhabit and animate the mind and heart of anyone who seeks and loves truth.

Finally, it should certainly be said that there are less insular and reflexive ways to read this book. One way is to read it as testimony to the inestimable contribution by one region to what once might have been called the American national character. There are clues in this book to the process by which an American national consciousness emerged out of sectional allegiance—as when Charles Sumner, in his impassioned argument against segregated public schools in the city of Boston, transforms that resonant phrase from Acts, "God is no respecter of persons," into "the State is no respecter of persons." Here, we see the force of New England religious piety being channeled into political feeling. A decade later, Julia Ward Howe's "Battle-Hymn of the Republic" registers that same transformation, only now the sacralized entity is not the state of Massachusetts but the United States of America.

As I read and re-read the works from which this book has been assembled, it struck me that perhaps their greatest salience for contemporary readers is their refutation of the idea that America has always been a culture dominated by the marketplace values of self-aggrandizement and competitive strife. Many of these writers give voice to countervailing ideas of charity, mutuality, and responsibility to others as well as to oneself. And so I venture the hope that this book might help dissuade readers from believing that Americans possess no traditions opposed to the seemingly ineluctable triumph of marketplace values in our own time.

Chronology

1697   Royal African Company's monopoly on the slave trade is broken—Britain allows all merchants to engage in trade, leading to a rise in slave imports

1700   General Court of Massachusetts orders Jesuit priests and popish priests to depart the province; Massachusetts and Connecticut allow all Protestant denominations to worship openly

1701   Students at Harvard, dissatisfied with its drift away from theological orthodoxy, found a new college, Yale, at Saybrook, Conn.; moved to New Haven in 1717

1702   Cotton Mather, *Magnalia Christi Americana*

1704   French and Algonquins raid New England frontier towns; Deerfield Massacre—captives taken to Canada

1704   First regularly published American newspaper, *Boston News-Letter*, begins

1708   Saybrook Platform—churches of Connecticut declare governance by councils of ministers that supersede the authority of local congregations

1710   Cotton Mather, *Bonifacius*

1711   Descendants of those executed during Salem witch trials awarded compensation

1712   Nantucket fishermen capture a sperm whale, sparking whaling industry

1713   "Bread Riot" in Boston Common to protest grain export

1714   First pipe organ played in an American church at Boston's King's Chapel—denounced by Puritans

1715   Lighthouse erected at Boston harbor

1720   Fires in Boston and New Haven blamed on blacks; Boston Council rules that gatherings of 2 or more blacks are punishable by whipping

1721   Cotton Mather, with Zabdiel Boylston, institutes smallpox inoculation in Boston; New England *Courant* started by Benjamin and James Franklin

1724   Fort Dummer built in northwestern New England, first permanent white settlement in Vermont

1730   First Presbyterian church formed in Boston

1731   First public concert of secular music in the colonies takes place in a Boston home

1734   Series of revivals known as the Great Awakening begins—Jonathan Edwards emerges as leading preacher

1737   Edwards publishes his *Faithful Narrative* of the outbreak of conversions in Northampton, Mass.

1738   English evangelist George Whitefield tours the colonies, rekindling evangelical fervor; controversy intensifies between "New Lights" devoted to the Awakening and "Old Lights" alarmed by its excesses

1740   First incorporated company, the Land Bank, established in Massachusetts

1741   Jonathan Edwards, *Sinners in the Hands of an Angry God*

1742   Charles Chauncy, *Enthusiasm Described and Caution'd Against*

1744   First American law school founded in Litchfield, Conn.

1746   Jonathan Edwards, *A Treatise concerning Religious Affections*

1747   Riot in Boston over impressment of citizens by British Admiral Knowles; mob burns home of Royal Governor Thomas Hutchinson

1749   Black woman burned to death and black man hung in irons for poisoning their master in Cambridge

1752   First maple sugar and syrup made by whites in Vermont

1754   French and Indian War (1754–63) begins (American theater of Seven Years' War, 1756–63); Indians aided by the French are driven back to Quebec by Roger's Rangers, famous raiders attached to the British army

1754   Dartmouth College established in Connecticut as Moor's Indian Charity School

1755   First whaler outfitted at New Bedford, Mass.

1757   Jonathan Edwards becomes president of the College of New Jersey (Princeton)

1760   Jared Eliot's *Essay upon Field Husbandry in New England* published, first major treatise describing modern farming techniques for the colonies; blacks are 20 percent of the population of Newport, center of slavery in the North; port dominates midcentury slave trade

1762   First church in Vermont established at Bennington

1763   Treaty of Paris—French give up efforts to control Maine; Touro Synogogue dedicated in Newport, R.I.; Rhode Island College, named Brown University in 1804, incorporated

1764   Sugar Act, Currency Act; *Hartford Courant,* country's oldest continuously published newspaper, founded; "Triangle trade": Rhode Island imports molasses from West Indies to make into rum to trade for African slaves to send to West Indies; New Hampshire and New York fight over jurisdiction in Vermont

1765   Mutiny Act; Stamp Act; Massachusetts assembly refuses to vote mandated supplies to British troops; Governor Samuel Ward of Rhode Island refuses oath to enforce Stamp Act; Custom House and Board of Commissioners established in Boston; Boston Riots—Sons of Liberty terrorize stamp agents and burn stamps (Rhode Island and Massachusetts collectors resign); Lieutenant Governor Hutchinson's home destroyed; Rhode Island stamp tax collector's Newport home wrecked by mob, prompting his resignation

1767   Townshend Duties; Boston merchants lead boycott on British imports until they are repealed

1768   Rioting on Boston docks causes Britain to send soldiers to protect customs officers

1769   Dartmouth College moves to Hanover, N.H.

1770   Boston Massacre—British troops fight Boston laborers; Harvard stops ranking its entering students according to the social prominence of their fathers; Ethan Allen forms Green Mountain Boys to protect Vermont from New York control

1772   First Committee of Correspondence organized in Boston by Samuel Adams; Rhode Island residents board the British ship *Gaspee,* setting it on fire in Narragansett Bay

1773   Tea Act and Boston Tea Party; itinerant preacher Isaac Backus's *An Appeal to the Public for Religious Liberty*

1774   Enslaved Africans in Massachusetts petition Britain for freedom; Boston port closed; Rhode Island prohibits the importation of slaves; New Hampshire militia at Portsmouth captures first British military post to be seized by Americans

1775   Parliament declares Massachusetts in rebellion; battles of Lexington, Concord, and Bunker Hill; Ethan Allen and Green Mountain Boys of Vermont take Fort Ticonderoga; Benedict Arnold leads the Kennebec Expedition from Augusta to Quebec; British fleet destroys Portland, Me.; New England Non-Resistance Society forms; out-migration from Massachusetts begins, to continue into the 19th century, first to northern New England, later to New York and Ohio

1776   Thomas Paine's *Common Sense* sells nearly half a million copies; John Adams, *Thoughts on Government;* Abigail Adams asks John to "remember the ladies" at the Continental Congress; New Hampshire first state to declare itself independent of Great Britain, 6 months before the Declaration of Independence; Nathan Hale, of Connecticut, hanged by British in New York; British evacuate Boston; first 13-stripe flag raised over Prospect Hill in Somerville, Mass.; Rhode Island is first colony formally to renounce all allegiance to King George III

1777   Vermont declares itself an independent republic, adopts first con-
            stitution forbidding slavery and allowing all men to vote without
            regard to property (universal manhood suffrage); battle at
            Bennington; Isaac Backus, *History of New England* (1777–96)

1778   Rhode Island guarantees freedom after war to all enlisted slaves;
            Ethan Allen petitions the Continental Congress for Vermont's
            statehood; Phillips Academy established at Andover, Mass.;
            Continental Congress divides Massachusetts into 3 districts,
            one being Maine

1780   American Academy of Arts and Sciences established in Boston;
            Shaker settlement established at Enfield, Conn.

1781   Benedict Arnold leads British troops in burning New London;
            Phillips Academy established at Exeter, N.H.

1783   Massachusetts Supreme Judicial Court declares slavery a violation
            of the state constitution; first African American Congregational
            minister ordained in Litchfield, Conn.; Webster's *American Spell-
            ing Book* published

1784   America's first law school founded at Litchfield, Conn.; Connecti-
            cut legislation provides that every black born after March would
            be free at age 25; Samuel Seabury, a Connecticut Anglican, conse-
            crated a bishop by the Scottish Episcopal Church; Ethan Allen
            (and Thomas Young), *Reason the Only Oracle of Man*

1785   Two-party political system begins in New Hampshire; King's
            Chapel, Boston, adopts an edition of the *Book of Common Prayer*
            without reference to the Trinity—first Unitarian congregation

1787   Shays' Rebellion

1788   New Hampshire's vote secures ratification of U.S. Constitution

1789   First published American novel, William Hill Brown's *The Power
            of Sympathy*, released in Worcester, Mass.

1790   First American crew to sail around the world returns to Boston in
            the *Columbia;* New York sells claims to Vermont for $30,000;
            Rhode Island is last of 13 original colonies to ratify Constitution
            after amendments recognize rights of smaller states

1790   Judith Sargent Murray's "On the Equality of the Sexes" printed in
            the *Massachusetts Magazine;* first federal patent granted to Sam
            Hopkins of Vermont for the manufacturing process of potash and
            pearl ash; first water-powered cotton mill in U.S. built in Provi-
            dence, R.I.

1791   Vermont admitted to the Union as 14th state

1792   First issue of the *Farmer's Almanac* appears in Boston; Joseph
            Harper arrested for first attempt to operate Boston theater; Sarah
            Pierce opens a school for girls at her home in Litchfield, Conn.

1793	Pottery manufacture begins at Bennington, Vt.
1794	Play prohibition repealed; theater opens in Boston; Massachusetts Historical Society founded, first of its kind in the U.S.
1795	Mutual Assurance Company of Norwich, Conn., is incorporated; Hartford becomes insurance center of U.S.; Connecticut sells the "Western Reserve" on the south shore of Lake Erie to fund its public school system
1799	Charles Bulfinch completes the neoclassical Massachusetts State House
1800	Middlebury College chartered in Vermont; semaphore (visual signaling) communication stations established on hills between Martha's Vineyard and Boston
1801	Boston Board of Health orders vaccinations, regulates burials, and quarantines the sick; nondenominational church founded in Lyndon, Vt.
1802	First canal built in U.S. at Bellows Falls, Vt.; Terry and Thomas Connecticut Clockworks mass-produce timepieces with interchangeable parts; Bowdoin College opens in Brunswick, Me.
1805	Henry Ware, a Unitarian, elected Hollis Professor of Divinity at Harvard; Daniel Webster pleads his first case in the courthouse in Plymouth, N.H.
1806	Noah Webster publishes first American dictionary at New Haven, Conn.; Massachusetts Congregationalists protesting rising liberalism found Andover seminary to preserve Calvinist orthodoxy; Kittery-Portsmouth Naval Shipyard established at Kittery, Me.
1807	Jefferson's Embargo Act, shutting off trade with England, brings economic distress to New England merchants that continues till the end of the War of 1812, in 1814; Boston Athenaeum founded
1808	Paul Revere begins the first U.S. copper rolling mill in Canton, Mass.; Roman Catholic Church built in Newcastle, Me.
1812	War of 1812 begins; Fort Cassin, Vt., defended against British; British embargoes on various American ports spur local manufacturing; *New England Medical Review and Journal* (later *New England Journal of Medicine*) begins publication; American Antiquarian Society founded
1813	Battle of *Chesapeake* and *Shannon* outside Boston Harbor; Colby College founded in Maine; Commodore Oliver Hazard Perry of Rhode Island defeats British in Lake Erie naval battle
1814	First completely mechanized cotton fabric production, from raw cotton to cloth, at first U.S. textile company in Waltham, Mass.

1815   New England delegates meeting in Hartford protest the commer-
        cial disruption of the War of 1812 and demand power for the
        states; *North American Review* begins publication

1816   "Dartmouth College Case" argued by Daniel Webster before the
        U.S. Supreme Court

1817   William Cullen Bryant, *Thanatopsis*

1818   Boston Handel and Haydn Society (est. 1815) gives first *Messiah*
        performance; Boston establishes public elementary schools;
        Benjamin Silliman, the first professor of chemistry and natural
        history at Yale, founds *American Journal of Science and Arts*;
        Hitchcock Chair Company founded in Riverton, Conn; Con-
        necticut Toleration Party ratifies new constitution separating
        church and state—disestablishing the Congregational church and
        extending the franchise

1819   Maine votes to separate from Massachusetts and adopts state
        constitution; William Ellery Channing, "Unitarian Christianity"

1820   Lunenburg Bibles printed by horse-powered press in
        Massachusetts

1821   First U.S. high school opens in Boston; Amherst College
        founded; Timothy Dwight, *Travels in New England and New York*
        (1821–22)

1823   Lowell, Mass., "the manufacturing city," begins operation;
        Catherine Beecher opens Hartford Seminary; Lyman Beecher,
        The Faith Once Delivered to the Saints

1824   Pawtucket, R.I., women textile workers strike—first recorded
        strike involving female employees; first public high school for
        girls opens in Worcester, Mass.; first black students admitted at
        Dartmouth College

1826   First rail line in the U.S. stretches 3 miles from the Neponset
        River to the granite quarries in Quincy, Mass.

1827   Massachusetts is the first state to use taxes for public education

1828   Nathaniel William Taylor, *Concio ad Clerum*

1829   William Apess's *A Son of the Forest,* first published autobiography
        written by an Indian, appears; first modern hotel, Tremont
        House, opens in Boston

1830   Thaddeus Fairbanks (Saint Johnsbury, Vt.) invents platform scale
        for which he is knighted by the emperor of Austria and which
        kicks off the city's economic growth

1831   Wesleyan College founded at Middletown, Conn.; New England
        Anti-Slavery Society established; Mt. Auburn Cemetery estab-
        lished in Cambridge, Mass.

1831 William Lloyd Garrison starts abolitionist newspaper, *The Liberator,* in Boston

1832 Perkins Institute, first U.S. school for the blind, opens in South Boston; Samuel Francis Smith composes hymn "America" at Andover Seminary

1833 Hartford and New Haven Railroad incorporated; Prudence Crandall of Canterbury, Conn., arrested for establishing a school for black girls; Congregational Church disestablished in Massachusetts—last New England state to do so; first steam railroad in New England connects Boston and Lowell

1833 Lydia Maria Child's *Appeal in Favor of That Class of Americans Called Africans,* calling for immediate emancipation, prompts the Boston Athenaeum to revoke her library privileges

1834 Abner Kneeland, a Free Enquirer who doubted divine origin of the scriptures and adopted pantheistic views, convicted on blasphemy charge in Boston; George Bancroft, *History of the United States* (1834–76)

1835 Omnibuses run on fixed routes in Boston; shoe factory established in Farmington, N.H.; first train runs between Boston and Providence; William Ellery Channing, *Slavery*

1836 Ralph Waldo Emerson, *Nature;* first meeting of the Transcendental Club

1837 Little, Brown & Company founded, Mt. Holyoke College founded; Emerson delivers his "American Scholar" Phi Beta Kappa speech at Harvard; Horace Mann begins Massachusetts Board of Education, reforms schools as Secretary of Education; in 1839 establishes the first state normal school to train teachers, in Lexington, Mass.

1838 Sarah Grimké's *Letters on the Equality of the Sexes* appear in the *New England Spectator;* English monopoly on screw manufacture broken with the founding of the Eagle Screw Company in Rhode Island; Ralph Waldo Emerson, "Divinity School Address"

1839 John Humphrey Noyes founds Putney free love and communist community in Vermont; Boston Academy of Music performs city's first instrumental concerts; Andrews Norton, *A Discourse on the Latest Form of Infidelity,* attacking Emerson; Washington Allston's exhibition at Harding Gallery, Boston—first retrospective exhibition in the United States devoted to an American artist

1840 Orestes Brownson, "The Laboring Classes"; first number of *The Dial,* edited by Margaret Fuller and Ralph Waldo Emerson; Adams & Company establish express parcel service between New

York and Boston; first nut and bolt factory opens in Marion, Conn.

1841   Brook Farm socialist community opened in West Roxbury, Mass., by George Ripley—disbanded in 1847; Catharine Beecher, *A Treatise on Domestic Economy;* Theodore Parker, *Discourse on the Transient and Permanent in Christianity*

1842   First free public art museum in the U.S., Wadsworth Atheneum, opens in Hartford, Conn.; Massachusetts child labor law mandates 10-hour day for those under 12; in speech before the Massachusetts legislature, Dorothea Dix calls for separation of the criminal and the insane

1843   Massachusetts passes law forbidding state authority to capture fugitive slaves; Methodist Episcopal church splits over slavery, with abolitionists forming Wesleyan Methodist Church; insane asylum opens in Dorchester, Mass.; Goodyear Metallic Rubber Shoe Company, later Uniroyal, begins in Naugatuck, Conn.; Elias Howe invents first practical sewing machine in Hartford; John Hickling Prescott, *History of the Conquest of Mexico*

1844   Amos Bronson Alcott establishes communal farm, Fruitlands, at Harvard, Mass.—lasts 7 months

1845   Severe potato famines in Ireland accelerate Irish emigration; Margaret Fuller, *Woman in the Nineteenth Century;* Rufus Porter's *Scientific American* founded; Horace Mann, *Lectures on Education*

1846   Nathaniel Hawthorne, *Mosses from an Old Manse;* the ballet *Giselle* makes its American debut at Boston's Howard Atheneum; William Morton demonstrates use of ether during surgery at Massachusetts General Hospital; Boston Stock Exchange founded

1847   Henry Wadsworth Longfellow, *Evangeline;* Samuel Colt receives federal order for guns and sets up factory city in Hartford, Conn.; Horace Bushnell, *Views of Christian Nurture*

1848   First chewing gum manufacturer established at Bangor, Me.; New England Female Medical School opens in Boston; James Russell Lowell, *The Biglow Papers* (first series) and *A Fable for Critics*

1849   Henry David Thoreau, *Resistance to Civil Government;* Francis Parkman, *The Oregon Trail;* Charles Sumner argues unsuccessfully for school desegregation before Massachusetts Supreme Judicial Court in the Roberts case—schools remain segregated for another 6 years

1850   Nathaniel Hawthorne, *The Scarlet Letter*

1850–51 The "Associates," 15 rich families in Boston, control 20 percent of the country's cotton spindleage, 39 percent of the insurance capital in state of Massachusetts, and 40 percent of banking in city of Boston; violent clashes in Boston as abolitionist mobs attempt to liberate fugitive slaves held in custody for remanding to their former owners

1851   Herman Melville, *Moby-Dick;* Maine is first state to prohibit sale of alcoholic beverages

1852   Harriet Beecher Stowe, *Uncle Tom's Cabin;* Massachusetts enacts compulsory school attendance law for children between 8 and 14; Rhode Island abolishes capital punishment

1853   *Fern Leaves from Fanny's Portfolio,* by Sara P. Willis, is an instant bestseller; Paulina Davis launches *Una,* one of the first feminist newspapers in America, in Providence, R.I.

1854   Attack on Boston Court House to free fugitive slave Anthony Burns; Henry David Thoreau, *Walden;* Massachusetts Emigrant Aid Society established to promote antislavery emigration to Kansas; Samuel Colt opens munitions factory in Hartford, Conn.; Boston Public Library founded, first free public library in the world to be supported by city taxes

1855   Boston public schools racially integrated

1857   *Atlantic Monthly* begins publication; Harvard botanist Asa Gray popularizes Darwin's *Origin of Species* in the *Atlantic Monthly;* shoeworkers strike in Massachusetts, New Hampshire, and Maine

1858   Oliver Wendell Holmes, *The Autocrat of the Breakfast Table*

1860   First formal kindergarten opened in Boston by Elizabeth Palmer Peabody; Christopher Spencer of Connecticut patents the self-loading repeating rifle, 200,000 of which are manufactured for the U.S. government before the start of the Civil War; one-third of Boston population is Irish

1861   First Ph.D. given in America granted at Yale; Massachusetts Institute of Technology (MIT) founded

1862   Julia Ward Howe, "Battle Hymn of the Republic" appears in *Atlantic Monthly*

1863   Wendell Phillips delivers Toussaint L'Ouverture speech as debate rages over enlisting blacks in the Union army; Travelers Insurance Co., pioneer of accident insurance, established in Connecticut; Robert Gould Shaw killed in attack on Fort Wagner, Charleston, S.C., as he leads 54th Massachusetts Infantry Regiment, first corps of African American troops raised in a free state

1864   Northernmost engagement of Civil War at St. Albans, Vt.; Bates College founded in Lewiston, Me.; Milton Bradley & Company begins manufacture of games in Massachusetts

1866   John Greenleaf Whittier, *Snow-Bound;* University of New Hamp-
        shire founded
1867   New England Conservatory of Music founded; 7-week shoemak-
        ers' strike and walkout at Lynn, Mass., longest in country's history
1868   Louisa May Alcott, *Little Women;* New England Woman Suffrage
        Association founded
1869   Last whaling voyage from Nantucket; Harriet Beecher Stowe,
        Oldtown Folks; Lucy Stone and others found the American
        Woman Suffrage Association—moderate group separate from
        Elizabeth Cady Stanton and Susan B. Anthony's more radical Na-
        tional Woman Suffrage Association
1870   Lorenzo Dow Baker of Wellfleet, Mass., founder of Boston Fruit
        Company, is first to sell bananas commercially in Boston; Boston
        Museum of Fine Arts established
1872   H. H. Richardson's Trinity Church, Boston, completed; Boston
        Daily Globe begins publication; Nansen, oldest ski club in the
        U.S., established in Berlin, N.H.; Great Fire devastates Boston
1875   Mary Baker Eddy publishes *Science and Health with Key to the
        Scriptures,* founds first Christian Science Church 2 years later
1876   U.S. Coast Guard Academy founded at New London, Conn.;
        Mark Twain, living in Hartford, Conn., publishes *Tom Sawyer;*
        Alexander Graham Bell invents the telephone in Boston
1877   First intercity telephone communication, between Salem and
        Boston; *Black Beauty* by Anna Sewell first published in America
        by Massachusetts Society for the Prevention of Cruelty to Ani-
        mals; Rhode Island School of Design founded; amendment to
        New Hampshire constitution abolishes rule that governor, sena-
        tors, and representatives must be of the Protestant faith; Charles
        S. Peirce, "Fixation of Belief"
1881   Boston Symphony Orchestra founded; University of Connecticut
        established at Storrs; Frank Munsey of Maine starts the nation's
        first illustrated general circulation magazine; Oliver Wendell
        Holmes, Jr., *The Common Law*
1888   First demonstration of an electric automobile, built by Fred W.
        Kimball Co., Boston; Edward Bellamy's *Looking Backward,* about
        socialist Boston in 2000, published
1890s   Maine and Massachusetts battle the gypsy moth; 3 million tons of
        ice cut from Maine's lakes and ponds to supply iceboxes in the
        U.S. and abroad
1890   Emily Dickinson's poems go through 7 printings

1891	Harvard neurologist P. C. Knapp writes the first paper in the U.S. on brain tumors
1892	Trial of Lizzie Borden in ax-murder case in Fall River, Mass.
1894	Boston Immigration Restriction League established—pushes for literacy tests to keep out "undesirables"; Radcliffe College affiliates with Harvard
1895	W. E. B. Du Bois receives Ph.D. at Harvard; Connecticut's Hart Rubber Works produces first American air-filled tires; player piano invented and manufactured in Meriden, Conn.; Oliver Wendell Holmes, *The Soldier's Faith*
1897	William James, *The Will to Believe*
1898	Anti-Imperialist League founded in Boston to protest military action abroad, specifically in the Philippines; first U.S. subway begins operation in Boston
1899	Biggest banquet in nation's history takes place in Boston—2000 diners, including W. B. Plunckett and President McKinley, and 400 waiters—to celebrate U.S. Senate's ratification of peace treaty with Spain
1900	Trolleys replace horsecars in Boston
1901	Boston Red Sox founded
1902	Helen Keller, *The Story of My Life*
1903	Red Sox win first World Series played, defeating Pittsburgh; New Hampshire licenses liquor sales, ending 48 years of prohibition; Massachusetts issues the first automobile license plates
1906	First radio program combining voice and music broadcast from Brant Rock, Mass.
1907	William James, *Pragmatism;* Henry Adams, *The Education of Henry Adams*
1908	Fire in Chelsea leaves 10,000 homeless and destroys $10 million in property; *Christian Science Monitor* begins publication in Boston
1909	New Hampshire adopts direct primary law
1912	Massachusetts becomes first state to enact minimum wage guidelines
1912–18	Red Sox win 5 World Series
1913	Robert Frost, *A Boy's Will;* George Santayana, "The Genteel Tradition in American Philosophy"
1914	Yale Bowl, first full-size football stadium, seating nearly 80,000, opens in New Haven; Robert Frost, *North of Boston*
1916	Birth Control League of Massachusetts founded

1917   Yankee Division of Massachusetts is first National Guard division
        to reach the battlefields of France
1920   Plymouth Rock moved back to water's edge from town square;
        Connecticut's KKK chapters have over 20,000 members, reflect-
        ing hostility to Roman Catholics, who since the war are the most
        numerous religious group in the state; Department of Justice and
        local police round up 600 aliens, many Russian, for deportation
        in early morning raids and march them through the streets
        in chains
1921   Sacco and Vanzetti, Italian immigrant anarchists, convicted for
        payroll robbery and murder in Braintree, Massachusetts; executed
        in 1927
1922   E. E. Cummings, *The Enormous Room*
1923   Robert Frost, *New Hampshire*
1926   Middlebury College Bread Loaf Writers' Conference founded in
        Ripton, Vt., with help of Robert Frost
1928   Massachusetts votes for Alfred Smith, a Roman Catholic, for
        president—first Democratic majority in the state's presidential
        election
1929   Massachusetts establishes its own unemployment program till na-
        tional government steps in with Depression relief
1930   John Cheever publishes his first story, "Expelled," about his ex-
        pulsion from Thayer Academy; Rockefeller Foundation endows
        Woods Hole Oceanographic Institution in Massachusetts
1932   Bennington College founded in Vermont; meteorological station
        begins operation atop Mt. Washington, N.H.; police drive 25
        hungry children away from a buffet for Spanish war veterans dur-
        ing a Boston parade
1933   First ski-tow in U.S. operates in Woodstock, Vt.
1935   Moose hunting banned in Maine
1936   First Berkshire Music Festival at Tanglewood, in Lenox, Mass.;
        Maine and Vermont are the only 2 states to prefer Landon to
        Roosevelt
1939   Perry Miller, *The New England Mind: The Seventeenth Century;*
        2nd volume, *The New England Mind: From Colony to Province,*
        published 1953
1941   Vermont declares war on Germany before U.S. does
1942   Fire in Cocoanut Grove nightclub in Boston kills 487
1945   Mayor James Michael Curley, one of the last big city political
        bosses, reelected in Boston while under indictment for mail fraud

1946   John Fitzgerald Kennedy elected to Congress; Rhode Island passes law requiring employers to pay women equal wages with men; Red Sox lose World Series in 7 games to St. Louis

1947   Composer Charles Ives, resident of Connecticut, receives Pulitzer Prize for his Third Symphony

1948   First chess-playing computer built at MIT; Brandeis University founded in Waltham, Mass.

1950s   Route 128, Boston's circumferential expressway, built

1954   First atomic-powered sub, the *Nautilus*, launched at Groton, Ct; Connecticut elects a Jewish governor, Abraham Ribicoff

1957   Boston Redevelopment Authority, in charge of urban renewal, formed

1959   Boston Celtics win the first of 8 consecutive championships (through 1966)

1960s   Busing in New Haven and Hartford, Conn., to achieve school integration; reform mayor, Kevin White, elected in Boston; John F. Kennedy elected president

1962   Boston experiences economic boom as its urban renewal program—first in the country—is a tremendous success

1966   Edward Brooke of Massachusetts is first black U.S. Senator since Reconstruction

1967   3 masked gunmen steal a Brink's armored truck carrying more than $600,000 from Brockton, Mass., shopping plaza; Red Sox lose World Series in 7 games to St. Louis Cardinals

1969   Race riots in Hartford, Conn.; collapse of the New York, New Haven and Hartford Railroad; Moratorium Day anti-war candlelight vigil in Boston; Newton College of the Sacred Heart, near Boston, displays huge red fist on its front door; at Brown commencement, two-thirds of students turn their backs on Kissinger

1970   Hampshire College founded in Massachusetts; Boston Bruins win Stanley Cup

1971   Boston Women's Health Book Collective publishes *Our Bodies, Ourselves*

1972   Massachusetts is only state to chose McGovern over Nixon in presidential election

1975   Mob violence after judge imposes school desegregation busing plan in Boston; Red Sox lose World Series in 7 games to Cincinnati Reds

1976   Boston's Quincy Market reopens (downtown urban mall movement); commemoration of the Boston Tea Party—an environmental counterdemonstration highlighted by the dumping of packages labeled Gulf Oil and Exxon overshadows the official tribute

1977   Justice Department supports Maine Indians in their suit against the state for the recovery of aboriginal lands; 2000 demonstrators march on Seabrook, N.H., nuclear plant construction site and state police arrest those who refuse to leave

1978   Red Sox lose pennant race to New York Yankees in playoff game forced after team squanders 10-game lead in last month of season

1979   Massachusetts first state to establish a lottery solely for the funding of the arts

1980   Following lead of California, Massachusetts voters approve Proposition 2.5, which limits property taxes; compromise settlement ends legal battle of Maine Penobscot and Passamaquoddy to recover their land in northern Maine—federal government pays tribes $81.5 million

1981   East Boston residents take to streets to protest cutbacks in funding for fire, police, and teachers

1985   International Physicians for the Prevention of Nuclear War, based in Boston, receives Nobel Peace Prize

1986   After coming within 1 out of victory in Game 6, Red Sox lose World Series to New York Mets after potential 3rd-out ground ball goes through first baseman's legs

1988   Yale alumnus sets fire to shanty erected by students to protest university investment in South Africa; Rhode Island is only state that celebrates VJ Day, commemorating victory over Japan in World War II

1990   68 percent of Vermont population is rural, highest of all states; Vermonters elect a democratic socialist as their only congressional representative; uninsured paintings worth $100 million are stolen from the Isabella Stewart Gardner Museum in Boston

1992   Last surviving member of New Hampshire's Shaker community, Ethel Hudson, dies at 96

1993   First mayor of Italian descent, Thomas Menino, elected in Boston

1990s–   The "Big Dig"—most ambitious publicly funded construction project in modern American history, designed to create system of tunnels and sunken roadways in Boston, runs billions of dollars over budget—sparking national debate over how to proceed with improving the infrastructure of American cities

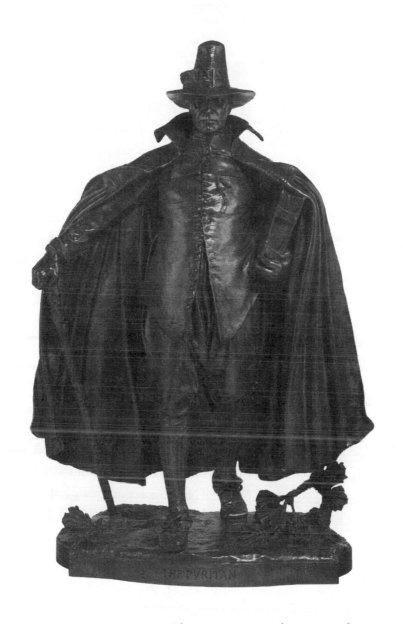

THE PVRITAN

The Founding Idea

IF PURITANS BROUGHT to these shores the conviction that God had chosen New England for the purpose of creating a godly community, their presumption carried with it a sense of responsibility that was quickly transmuted into guilt. Before the Massachusetts Bay settlement had completed its first decade, one of its leading ministers, Thomas Shepard, was lamenting: "O, New England! New England! that are now making a conquest of the world, and seekest for the spoil of it to enrich thyself . . . I dare not yet tell thee what Christ Jesus has to say unto thee!" This note of self-chastisement rose to a higher pitch as the first generation, waning in strength or dying away, turned over the pulpit to its children— who, following the Hebrew prophet Jeremiah, charged the chosen people of New England with backsliding toward sin.

The contrapuntal themes of this first New England literature— hope and disillusion, confidence and self-doubt—recur in many variations over the centuries, including in the work of writers with little interest in the theological categories of Calvinism. But never far from the heart of New England literature is the idea that if only humanity would awaken to the sinfulness and futility of self-love, the world could be redeemed.

Augustus Saint-Gaudens, *The Puritan,* 1887

John Winthrop

From A Model of Christian Charity

 1630

Sometime in the early spring of 1630, probably just before sailing from South-ampton aboard the *Arbella* as head of the expedition carrying the first wave of what became known as the Great Migration to New England, John Winthrop (1588–1648) preached this lay sermon (he was never ordained as a minister) outlining his vision of the holy community that he hoped would spring to life in the New World. For two centuries, the sermon circulated in various manuscript versions; upon its first publication, by the Massachusetts Historical Society in 1848, it became known as the classic statement of the Puritans' understanding of their place in history, their mission, and their ideals.

A Model Hereof

God Almighty in his most holy and wise providence hath so disposed of the condition of mankind, as in all times some must be rich, some poor, some high and eminent in power and dignity, others mean and in subjection.

The Reason Hereof

First, to hold conformity with the rest of his works, being delighted to show forth the glory of his wisdom in the variety and difference of the creatures; and the glory of his power, in ordering all these differences for the preservation and good of the whole; and the glory of his greatness, that as it is the glory of princes to have many officers, so this great king will have many stewards, counting himself more honored in dispensing his gifts to man by man, than if he did it by his own immediate hands.

Secondly, that he might have the more occasion to manifest the work of his spirit: first upon the wicked in moderating and restraining them, so that the rich and mighty should not eat up the poor, nor the poor and despised rise up against their superiors and shake off their yoke; secondly in the regenerate, in exercising his graces in them, as in the great ones, their love, mercy, gentleness, temperance, etc.; in the poor and inferior sort, their faith, patience, obedience, etc.

Thirdly, that every man might have need of other, and from hence they might be all knit more nearly together in the bonds of brotherly affection. From hence it appears plainly that no man is made more honorable than another or more wealthy, etc., out of any particular and singular respect to himself, but for the glory of his creator and the common good of the creature, man. Therefore God still reserves the property of these gifts to himself as [in] Ezekiel 16:17. He there calls wealth his gold and his silver. [In] Proverbs 3:9 he claims their service as his due, *honor the Lord with thy riches,* etc. All men being thus (by divine providence) ranked into two sorts, rich and poor, under the first are comprehended all such as are able to live comfortably by their own means duly improved; and all others are poor according to the former distribution.

There are two rules whereby we are to walk one towards another: justice and mercy. These are always distinguished in their act and in their object, yet may they both concur in the same subject in each respect; as sometimes there may be an occasion of showing mercy to a rich man in some sudden danger of distress, and also doing of mere justice to a poor man in regard of some particular contract, etc.

There is likewise a double law by which we are regulated in our conversation one towards another in both the former respects: the law of nature and the law of grace, or the moral law or the law of the gospel, to omit the rule of justice as not properly belonging to this purpose otherwise than it may fall into consideration in some particular cases. By the first of these laws man as he was enabled so withal [is] commanded to love his neighbor as himself. Upon this ground stands all the precepts of the moral law, which concerns our dealings with men. To apply this to the works of mercy, this law requires two things. First, that every man afford his help to another in every want or distress. Secondly, that he performed this out of the same affection which makes him careful of his own goods, according to that of our Savior. Matthew: "Whatsoever ye would that men should do to you." This was practiced by Abraham and Lot in entertaining the angels and the old man of Gibeah.

The law of grace or the gospel hath some difference from the former, as in these respects. First, the law of nature was given to man in the estate of innocency; this of the gospel in the estate of regeneracy. Secondly, the former propounds one man to another, as the same flesh and image of God; this as a brother in Christ also, and in the communion of the same spirit, and so teacheth us to put a difference between Christians and others. *Do good to all, especially to the household of faith;* upon this ground the Israelites were to put a difference between the brethren of such as were strangers though not of Canaanites. Thirdly, the law of nature could give no rules for dealing with enemies, for all are to be considered as friends in the state of innocency, but the

Gospel commands love to an enemy. Proof: If thine enemy hunger, feed him; *love your enemies, do good to them that hate you,* Matthew 5:44.

This law of the gospel propounds likewise a difference of seasons and occasions. There is a time when a Christian must sell all and give to the poor, as they did in the Apostles' times. There is a time also when a Christian (though they give not all yet) must give beyond their ability, as they of Macedonia (II Corinthians 11:9). Likewise community of perils calls for extraordinary liberality, and so doth community in some special service for the church. Lastly, when there is no other means whereby our Christian brother may be relieved in his distress, we must help him beyond our ability, rather than tempt God in putting him upon help by miraculous or extraordinary means.

This duty of mercy is exercised in the kinds, *giving, lending,* and *forgiving*—

Question: What rule shall a man observe in giving in respect of the measure?

Answer: If the time and occasion be ordinary he is to give out of his abundance. Let him lay aside as God hath blessed him. If the time and occasion be extraordinary, he must be ruled by them; taking this withal, that then a man cannot likely do too much, especially if he may leave himself and his family under probable means of comfortable subsistence . . .

Question: What rule must we observe in lending?

Answer: Thou must observe whether thy brother hath present, or probable, or possible means of repaying thee. If there be none of these, thou must give him according to his necessity, rather than lend him as he requires. If he hath present means of repaying thee, thou art to look at him not as an act of mercy, but by way of commerce, wherein thou art to walk by the rule of justice; but if his means of repaying thee be only probable or possible, then is he an object of thy mercy, thou must lend him, though there be danger of losing it, Deuteronomy 15:7, *If any of thy brethren be poor, etc., thou shalt lend him sufficient* . . .

Question: What rule must we observe in forgiving?

Answer: Whether thou didst lend by way of commerce or in mercy, if he have nothing to pay thee, [thou] must forgive (except in cause where thou hast a surety or a lawful pledge), Deuteronomy 15:2. Every seventh year the creditor was to quit that which he lent to his brother if he were poor, as appears [in] verse 8, *Save when there shall be no poor with thee.* In all these and like cases, Christ was a general rule, Matthew 7:22, *Whatsoever ye would that men should do to you, do ye the same to them also.*

Question: What rule must we observe and walk by in cause of community of peril?

Answer: The same as before, but with more enlargement towards others and less respect towards ourselves and our own right. Hence it was that in the primitive church they sold all, had things in common, neither did any man say that which he possessed was his own. Likewise in their return out of the captivity, because the work was great for the restoring of the church and the danger of enemies was common to all, Nehemiah exhorts the Jews to liberality and readiness in remitting their debts to their brethren, and disposing liberally of his own to such as wanted, and stand not upon his own due, which he might have demanded of them. Thus did some of our forefathers in times of persecution in England, and so did many of the faithful of other churches, whereof we keep an honorable remembrance of them . . .

Having already set forth the practice of mercy according to the rule of God's law, it will be useful to lay open the grounds of it also, being the other part of the commandment, and that is the affection from which this exercise of mercy must arise. The Apostle tells us that this love is the fulfilling of the law, not that it is enough to love our brother and so no further; but in regard of the excellency of his parts giving any motion to the other as the soul to the body and the power it hath to set all the faculties on work in the outward exercise of this duty. As when we bid one make the clock strike, he doth not lay hand on the hammer, which is the immediate instrument of the sound, but sets on work the first mover or main wheel, knowing that will certainly produce the sound which he intends. So the way to draw men to works of mercy is not by force of argument from the goodness or necessity of the work; for though this course may enforce a rational mind to some present act of mercy, as is frequent in experience, yet it cannot work such a habit in a soul, as shall make it prompt upon all occasions to produce the same effect, but by framing these affections of love in the heart which will as natively bring forth the other, as any cause doth produce effect.

The definition which the scripture gives us of love is this: "Love is the bond of perfection." First, it is a bond or ligament. Secondly, it makes the work perfect. There is no body but consists of parts and that which knits these parts together gives the body its perfection, because it makes each part so contiguous to others as thereby they do mutually participate with each other, both in strength and infirmity, in pleasure and pain. To instance in the most perfect of all bodies: Christ and his church make one body. The several parts of this body, considered apart before they were united, were as disproportionate and as much disordering as so many contrary qualities or elements, but when Christ comes and by his spirit and love knits all these parts to himself and each to other, it is become the most perfect and best proportioned body in the world. Ephesians 4:16, *Christ, by whom all the body being knit together by every joint for the furniture thereof, according to the effectual power which is in the measure of every perfection of parts, a glorious body without spot or wrinkle,* the ligaments hereof being Christ, or his love, for *Christ is love,* I John 4:8. So this definition is right: *Love is the bond of perfection.*

From hence we may frame these conclusions. First of all, true Christians are of one body in Christ. I Corinthians 12:22, 27, *Ye are the body of Christ and members of their part.* Secondly, the ligaments of this body which knit together are love. Thirdly, no body can be perfect which wants its proper ligament. Fourthly, all the parts of this body being thus united are made so contiguous in a special relation as they must needs partake of each other's strength and infirmity; joy and sorrow, weal and woe. I Corinthians 12:26, *If one member suffers, all suffer with it; if one be in honor, all rejoice with it.* Fifthly, this sensibleness and sympathy of each other's conditions will necessarily infuse into each part a native desire and endeavor to strengthen, defend, preserve and comfort the other . . .

The like we shall find in the histories of the church in all ages, the sweet sympathy of affections which was in the members of this body one towards another, their cheerfulness in serving and suffering together, how liberal they were without repining, harborers without grudging and helpful without reproaching; and all from hence: because they had fervent love amongst them, which only make the practice of mercy constant and easy.

The next consideration is how this love comes to be wrought. Adam in his first estate was a perfect model of mankind in all their generations, and in him this love was perfected in regard of habit. But Adam rent himself from his creator, rent all his posterity also one from another; whence it comes that every man is born with this principle in him, to love and seek himself only, and thus a man continueth till Christ comes and takes possession of the soul and infuseth another principle, love to God and our brother. And this latter having continual supply from Christ, as the head and root by which he is united, gets the predomining in the soul, so by little and little expels the former. I John 4:7, *Love cometh of God and everyone that loveth is born of God,* so that this love is the fruit of the new birth, and none can have it but the new creature. Now when this quality is thus formed in the souls of men, it works like the spirit upon the dry bones. Ezekiel 37, *Bone came to bone.* It gathers together the scattered bones, or perfect old man Adam, and knits them into one body again in Christ, whereby a man is become again a living soul.

The third consideration is concerning the exercise of this love which is twofold, inward or outward. The outward hath been handled in the former preface of this discourse. For unfolding the other we must take in our way that maxim of philosophy *Simile simili gaudet,* or like will to like; for as it is things which are turned with disaffection to each other, the ground of it is from a dissimilitude arising from the contrary or different nature of the things themselves; for the ground of love is an apprehension of some resemblance in things loved to that which affects it. This is the cause why the Lord loves the creature, so far as it hath any of his image in it; he loves his elect because they are like himself, he beholds them in his beloved son. So a mother loves her child, because she thoroughly conceives a resemblance of herself in it. Thus it is between the members of Christ. Each discerns, by the work of the spirit, his own image and resemblance in another, and therefore cannot but love him as he loves himself . . .

If any shall object that it is not possible that love should be bred or upheld without hope of requital, it is graunted; but that is not our cause; for this love is always under reward. It never gives, but it always receives with advantage; first, in regard that among the members of the same body, love and affection are reciprocal in a most equal and sweet kind of commerce. Secondly, in regard of the pleasure and content that the exercise of love carries with it, as we may see in the natural body. The mouth is at all the pains to receive and mince the food which served for the nourishment of all the other parts of the body, yet it hath no cause to complain; for first the other parts send back by several passages a due proportion of the same nourishment, in a better form for the strengthening and comforting the mouth. Secondly the labor of the mouth is accompanied with such pleasure and content as far exceeds the pains it takes. So is it in all the labor of love among Christians. The party loving, reaps love again, as was showed before, which the soul covets more than all the wealth in the world. Thirdly, nothing yields more pleasure and content to the soul than when it finds that which it may love fervently, for to love and live beloved is the soul's paradise, both here and in heaven. In the state of wedlock there be many comforts to bear out the troubles of that condition; but let such as have tried the most, say if there be any sweetness in that condition comparable to the exercise of mutual love.

From former considerations arise these conclusions:

First, this love among Christians is a real thing, not imaginary.

Secondly, this love is as absolutely necessary to the being of the body of Christ, as the sinews and other ligaments of a natural body are to the being of that body.

Thirdly, this love is a divine, spiritual nature: free, active, strong, courageous, permanent; undervaluing all things beneath its proper object; and of all the graces, this makes us nearer to resemble the virtues of our heavenly father.

Fourthly, it rests in the love and welfare of its beloved. For the full and certain knowledge of these truths concerning the nature, use, and excellency of this grace, that which the Holy Ghost hath left recorded, I Corinthians 13, may give full satisfaction, which is needful for every true member of this lovely body of the Lord Jesus, to work upon their hearts by prayer, meditation, continual exercise at least of the special [influence] of this grace, till Christ be formed in them and they in him, all in each other knit together by this bond of love.

It rests now to make some application of this discourse by the present design, which gave the occasion of writing of it. Herein are four things to be propounded: first, the persons; secondly, the work; thirdly, the end; fourthly, the means.

First for the persons. We are a company professing ourselves fellow members of Christ, in which respect only though we were absent from each other many miles, and had our imployments as far distant, yet we ought to account ourselves knit together by this bond of love, and live in the exercise of it, if we would have comfort of our being in Christ. This was notorious in the practice of the Christians in former times; as is testified of the Waldenses, from the mouth of one of the adversaries *Æneas Sylvius,* "mutuo [ament] pene antequam norunt," they use to love any of their own religion even before they were acquainted with them.

Secondly for the work we have in hand. It is by a mutual consent, through a special overvaluing providence and a more than an ordinary approbation of the churches of Christ, to seek out a place of cohabitation and consortship under a due form of government both civil and ecclesiastical. In such cases as this, the care of the public must oversway all private respects, by which not only conscience but mere civil policy doth bind us. For it is a true rule that particular estates cannot subsist in the ruin of the public.

Thirdly, the end is to improve our lives to do more service to the Lord; the comfort and encrease of the body of Christ whereof we are members, that ourselves and posterity may be the better preserved from the common corruptions of this evil world, to serve the Lord and work out our salvation under the power and purity of his holy ordinances.

Fourthly, for the means whereby this must be effected. They are twofold, a conformity with the work and end we aim at. These we see are extraordinary, therefore we must not content ourselves with usual ordinary means. Whatsoever we did or ought to have done when we lived in England, the same must we do, and more also, where we go. That which the most in their churches maintain as a truth in profession only, we must bring into familiar and constant practice, as in this duty of love. We must love brotherly without dissimulation; we must love one another with a pure heart fervently. We must bear one another's burthens. We must not look only on our own things, but also on the things of our brethren, neither must we think that the Lord will bear with such failings at our hands as he doth from those among whom we have lived; and that for three reasons:

First, in regard of the more near bond of marriage between him and us, wherein he hath taken us to be his after a most strict and peculiar manner, which will make him the more jealous of our love and obedience. So he tells the people of Israel, "You only have I known of all the families of the earth, therefore will I punish you for your transgressions." Secondly, because the Lord will be sanctified in them that come near him. We know that there were many that corrupted the service of the Lord, some setting up altars before his own, others offering both strange fire and strange sacrifices also; yet there came no fire from heaven or other sudden judgment upon them, as did upon Nadab and Abihu, who yet we may think did not sin presumptuously. Thirdly, when God gives a special commission he looks to have it strictly observed in every article. When he gave Saul a commission to destroy Amalek, he indented with him upon certain articles, and because he failed in one of the least, and that upon a fair pretense, it lost him the kingdom which should have been his reward if he had observed his commission.

Thus stands the cause between God and us. We are entered into covenant with him for this work. We have taken out a commission, the Lord hath given us leave to draw our own articles. We have professed to enterprise these actions, upon these and those ends, we have hereupon besought him of favor and blessing. Now if the Lord shall please to hear us, and bring us in peace to the place we desire, then hath he ratified this covenant and sealed our commission, [and] will expect a strict performance of the articles contained in it. But if we shall neglect the observation of these articles which are the ends we have propounded and, dissembling with our God, shall fall to embrace this present world and prosecute our carnal intentions, seeking great things for ourselves and our posterity, the Lord will surely break out in wrath against us, be revenged of such a perjured people, and make us know the price of the breach of such a covenant.

Now the only way to avoid this shipwrack, and to provide for our posterity, is to follow the counsel of Micah, to do justly, to love mercy, to walk humbly with our God. For this end, we must be knit together in this work as one man. We must entertain each other in brotherly affection, we must be willing to abridge ourselves of our superfluities, for the supply of others' necessities. We must uphold a familiar commerce together in all meakness, gentleness, patience, and liberality. We must delight in each other, make others' conditions our own, rejoice together, mourn together, labor and suffer together, always having before our eyes our commission and community in the work, our community as members of the same body. So shall we keep the unity of the spirit in the bond of peace. The Lord will be our God, and delight to dwell among us as his own people, and will command a blessing upon us in all our ways, so that we shall see much more of his wisdom, power, goodness, and truth, than formerly we have been acquainted with. We shall find that the God of Israel is among us, when ten of us shall be able to resist a thousand of our enemies; when he shall make us a praise and glory that men shall say of succeeding plantations, "the Lord make it like that of New England." For we must consider that we shall be as a city upon a hill. The eyes of all people are upon us, so that if we shall deal falsely with our God in this work we have undertaken, and so cause him to withdraw his present help from us, we shall be made a story and a by-word through the world. We shall open the mouths of enemies to speak evil of the ways of God, and all professors for God's sake. We shall shame the faces of many of God's worthy servants, and cause their prayers to be turned into curses upon us till we be consumed out of the good land whither we are agoing.

And to shut up this discourse with that exhortation of Moses, that faithful servant of the Lord, in his last farewell to Israel, Deuteronomy 30: Beloved, there is now set before us life and good, death and evil, in that we are commanded this day to love the Lord our God, and to love one another, to walk in his ways and to keep his commandments and his ordinance and his laws, and the articles of our covenant with him, that we may live and be multiplied, and that the Lord our God may bless us in the land whither we go to possess it. But if our hearts shall turn away, so that we will not obey, but shall be seduced, and worship other gods, our pleasures and profits, and serve them; it is propounded unto us this day, we shall surely perish out of the good land whither we pass over this vast sea to possess it.

> Therefore let us choose life,
> that we and our seed
> may live by obeying his
> voice and cleaving to him,
> for he is our life and
> our prosperity.

SAMUEL DANFORTH

From A Brief Recognition of New England's Errand into the Wilderness

 1670

Samuel Danforth (1626–1674) was born to a prosperous family in Suffolk, England, and migrated as a child to Cambridge, Massachusetts. Educated at Harvard College, he was ordained in 1650 at Roxbury, where he assisted the renowned John Eliot in ministering to the Indians. Beginning in 1634, one minister in the Massachusetts Bay colony had been honored each year by being asked to preach on the occasion of the opening session of the General Court. In 1670 the call came to Danforth, who responded with what has become the most famous of the New England "jeremiads"—a form of public utterance that, linking New Englanders with the chosen people of Israel, excoriates them for reverting to their sinful ways while exhorting them to renew their work of bringing humanity closer to the day of redemption. Danforth's sermon prefigures the premises and structure of many subsequent works of American oratory, committed as it is to the proposition that God's people in the New World must accept and live up to the work of cosmic importance for which they have been chosen.

"What went ye out into the wilderness to see? A reed shaken with the wind?

But what went ye out for to see? A man clothed in soft raiment? Behold, they that wear soft clothing are in kings' houses.

But what went ye out for to see? A prophet? Yea, I say unto you, and more than a prophet" (Matt. 11:7–9).

These words are our Savior's proem to his illustrious encomium of John the Baptist. John began his ministry not in Jerusalem nor in any famous city of Judea, but in the wilderness, i.e., in a woody, retired, and solitary place, thereby withdrawing himself from the envy and preposterous zeal of such as were addicted to their old traditions and also taking the people aside from the noise and tumult of their secular occasions and businesses, which might have obstructed their ready and cheerful attendance unto his doctrine . . .

Doctrine. *Such as have sometime left their pleasant cities and habitations to enjoy the pure worship of God in a wilderness are apt in time to abate and cool in their affection thereunto; but then the Lord calls upon them seriously and thoroughly to examine themselves, what it was that drew them into the wilderness, and to consider that it was not the expectation of ludicrous levity nor of courtly pomp and delicacy, but of the free and clear dispensation of the Gospel and kingdom of God . . .*

To what purpose did the children of Israel leave their cities and houses in Egypt and go forth into the wilderness? . . . Was it not to see that burning and shining light which God had raised up? To hear his heavenly doctrine and partake of that new sacrament which he administered? O how they were affected with his rare and excellent gifts! with his clear, lively, and powerful ministry! The kingdom of heaven pressed in upon them with a holy violence and the violent, the zealous, and affectionate hearers of the Gospel took it by force (Matt. 11:12; Luke 16:16). They leapt over all discouragements and impediments, whether outward, as legal rites and ceremonies, or inward, the sense of their own sin and unworthiness, and pressed into the kingdom of God as men rush into a theater to see a pleasant sight or as soldiers run into a besieged city to take the spoil thereof; but their hot fit is soon over, their affection lasted but for an hour, i.e., a short season (John 5:35) . . .

Use I. Of solemn and serious enquiry to us all in this general assembly is whether we have not in a great measure forgotten our errand into the wilderness. You have solemnly professed before God, angels, and men that the cause of your leaving your country, kindred, and fathers' houses and transporting yourselves with your wives, little ones, and substance over the vast ocean into this waste and howling wilderness, was your liberty to walk in the faith of the Gospel with all good conscience according to the order of the Gospel, and your enjoyment of the pure worship of God according to his institution without human mixtures and impositions. Now let us sadly consider whether our ancient and primitive affections to the Lord Jesus, his glorious Gospel, his pure and spiritual worship, and the order of his house, remain, abide, and continue firm, constant, entire, and inviolate . . . let us call to remembrance the former days and consider whether "it was not then better with us than it is now" [Hos. 2:7].

In our first and best times the kingdom of heaven brake in upon us with a holy violence and every man pressed into it . . . How diligent and faithful in preparing your hearts for the reception of the Word, "laying apart all filthiness and superfluity of naughtiness," that you might "receive with meekness the ingraffed word, which is able to save your souls" [Jas. 1:21], "and purging out all malice, guile, hypocrisies, envies, and all evil speakings, and as newborn babes, desiring the sincere milk of the Word, that ye might grow thereby" [I Pet. 2:1, 2]? . . . How painful were you in recollecting, repeating, and discoursing of what you heard, whetting the Word of God upon the hearts of your children, servants, and neighbors? How fervent in prayer to almighty God for his divine blessing upon the seed sown, that it might take root and fructify? O what a reverent esteem had you in those days of Christ's faithful ambassadors that declared unto you the word of reconciliation! "How beautiful" were "the feet of them that preached the Gospel of peace, and brought the glad tidings of salvation!" [Rom. 10:15] . . .

And then had the churches "rest" throughout the several colonies and were "edified; and walking in the fear of the Lord, and in the comfort of the Holy Ghost, were multiplied" [Acts 9:31]. O how your faith grew exceedingly! . . . O how your love and charity towards each other abounded! O what comfort of love! What bowels and mercies! What affectionate care was there one of another! What a holy sympathy in crosses and comforts, weeping with those that wept and rejoicing with those that rejoiced!

But who is there left among you that saw these churches in their first glory and how do you see them now? Are they not in your eyes in comparison thereof as nothing? "How is the gold become dim! how is the most fine gold changed!" [Lam. 4:1]. Is not the temper, complexion, and countenance of the churches strangely altered? Doth not a careless, remiss, flat, dry, cold, dead frame of spirit grow in upon us secretly, strongly, prodigiously? . . . Pride, contention, worldliness, covetousness, luxury, drunkenness, and uncleanness break in like a flood upon us and good men grow cold in their love to God and to one another. If a man be cold in his bed let them lay on the more clothes that he may get heat; but we are like to David in his old age: "They covered him with clothes, but he gat no heat" (I Kings 1:1) . . .

Now let me freely deliberate with you what may be the causes and grounds of such decays and languishings in our affections to, and estimations of, that which we came into the wilderness to enjoy . . . Surely it is not for want of fullness in the Spirit of God that he withholds comforts and blessings from any; neither doth he delight in threatenings and judgments, but his words both promise and perform that which is good and comfortable to them that walk uprightly . . . What then is the cause of our coolings, faintings, and languishings? The grand and principal cause is our unbelief. We believe not the grace and power of God in Christ. Where is that lively exercise of faith which ought to be in our attendance upon the Lord in his holy ordinances? Christ came to Nazareth with his heart full of love and compassion and his hands full of blessings to bestow upon his old acquaintance and neighbors among whom he had been brought up; but their unbelief restrained his tender mercies and bound his omnipotent hands, that he could not do any great or illustrious miracle amongst them . . .

But though unbelief be the principal yet it is not the sole cause of our decays and languishings; inordinate worldly cares, predominant lusts, and malignant passions and distempers stifle and choke the Word and quench our affections to the kingdom of God (Luke 8:14) . . . Some split upon the rock of affected ostentation of singular piety and holiness and others are drawn into the whirlpool and perish in the gulf of sensuality and luxury . . .

Use II. Of exhortation, to excite and stir us all up to attend and prosecute our errand into the wilderness. To what purpose came we into this place and what expectation drew us hither? Surely not the expectation of ludicrous levity. We came not hither to see "a reed shaken with the wind." Then let not us be reeds—light, empty, vain, hollow-hearted professors, shaken with every wind of temptation—but solid, serious, and sober Christians, constant and steadfast in the profession and practice of the truth, "trees of righteousness, the planting of the Lord, that he may be glorified" [Isa. 61:3], holding fast the profession of our faith without wavering . . .

But to what purpose came we into the wilderness and what expectation drew us hither? Not the expectation of courtly pomp and delicacy. We came not hither to see men clothed like courtiers. The affectation of courtly pomp and gallantry is very unsuitable in a wilderness . . .

To what purpose then came we into the wilderness and what expectation drew us hither? Was it not the expectation of the pure and faithful dispensation of the Gospel and kingdom of God? The times were such that we could not enjoy it in our own land, and therefore having obtained liberty and a gracious patent from our Sovereign, we left our country, kindred, and fathers' houses, and came into these wild woods and deserts where the Lord hath planted us and made us "dwell in a place of our own, that we might move no more, and that the children of wickedness might not afflict us any more" (II Sam. 7:10). What is it that distinguisheth New England from other colonies and plantations in America? Not our transportation over the Atlantic Ocean, but the ministry of God's faithful prophets and the fruition of his holy ordinances . . .

The hardships, difficulties, and sufferings which you have exposed yourselves unto that you might dwell in the house of the Lord and leave your little ones under the shadow of the wings of the God of Israel, have not been few nor small. And shall we now withdraw ourselves and our little ones from under those healing wings and lose that full reward which the Lord hath in his heart and hand to bestow upon us? . . . And do we now repent of our choice and prefer the honors, pleasures, and profits of the world before it? . . .

How sadly hath the Lord testified against us because of our loss of our first love and our remissness and negligence in his work! Why hath the Lord smitten us with blasting and mildew now seven years together, super-adding sometimes severe drought, sometimes great tempests, floods, and sweeping rains that leave no food behind them? Is it not because the Lord's house lyeth waste, temple-work in our hearts, families, churches is shamefully neglected? What should I make mention of signs in the heavens and in the earth—blazing stars, earthquakes, dreadful thunders and lightnings, fearful burnings? What meaneth the heat of his great anger in calling home so many of his ambassadors? In plucking such burning and shining lights out of the candlesticks; the principal stakes out of our hedges; the cornerstones out of our walls? . . . Is it not a sign that God is making a way for his wrath when he removes his chosen out of the gap? Doth he not threaten us with a famine of the Word, the scattering of the flock, the breaking of the candlesticks, and the turning of the songs of the temple into howlings?

It is high time for us to "remember whence we are fallen, and repent, and do our first works" [Rev. 2:5]. Wherefore let us "lift up the hands that hang down, and strengthen the feeble knees; And make straight paths for our feet, lest that which is lame be turned out of the way; but let it rather be healed" (Heb. 12:12, 13) . . .

"Alas, we are feeble and impotent; our hands are withered and our strength dried up . . . alas, our bruise is incurable and our wound grievous; there is none to repair the breach, there is no healing medicine."

The Lord Jesus, the great Physician of Israel, hath undertaken the cure. "I will restore health unto thee, and I will heal thee of thy wounds, saith the Lord" (Jer. 30:17). No case is to be accounted desperate or incurable which Christ takes in hand . . . When Christ came to Lazarus his grave and bade them take away the stone, "Martha saith, Lord, by this time he stinketh: for he hath been dead four days." But Christ answereth, "Said I not unto thee, that, if thou wouldest believe, thou shouldest see the glory of God?" (John 11:[39], 40). Let us give glory to God by believing his Word and we shall have real and experimental manifestations of his glory for our good and comfort.

"But alas, our hearts are sadly prejudiced against the means and instruments by which we might expect that Christ should cure and heal us." . . .

"But alas, the times are difficult and perilous; the wind is stormy and the sea tempestuous; the vessel heaves and sets and tumbles up and down in the rough and boisterous waters and is in danger to be swallowed up."

Well, remember that "the Lord sitteth upon the flood; yea, the Lord sitteth King forever" (Psal. 29:10) . . . "He stilleth the noise of the seas, the noise of their waves, and the tumult of the people" (Psal. 65:7) . . . Yea he can enable his people to tread and walk upon the waters. To sail and swim in the waters is an easy matter, but to walk upon the waters as upon a pavement is an act of wonder. Peter at Christ's call "came down out of the ship, and walked on the water, to go to Jesus" (Matt. 14:29), and as long as his faith held, it upheld him from sinking; when his faith failed his body sunk, but he "cried to the Lord, and he stretched forth his hand, and caught him, and said unto him, O thou of little faith, wherefore didst thou doubt?"

"But what shall we do for bread? The encrease of the field and the labor of the husbandman fails."

Hear Christ's answer to his disciples when they were troubled because there was but one loaf in the ship: "O ye of little faith, why reason ye, because you have no bread? perceive ye not yet, neither understand? have ye your heart yet hardened? having eyes, see ye not? and having ears, hear ye not? and do ye not remember?" (Mark 8:17, 18; Matt. 16:8, 9). Those which have had large and plentiful experience of the grace and power of Christ in providing for their outward sustenance and relieving of their necessities when ordinary and usual means have failed, are worthy to be severely reprehended if afterward they grow anxiously careful and solicitous because of the defect of outward supplies . . . Attend we our errand upon which Christ sent us into the wilderness and he will provide bread for us. "Seek ye first the kingdom of God, and his righteousness, and all these things shall be added unto you" (Matt. 6:33).

"But we have many adversaries and they have their subtle machinations and contrivances, and how soon we may be surprised we know not."

Our diligent attention to the ministry of the Gospel is a special means to check and restrain the rage and fury of adversaries . . . If the people cleave to the Lord, to his prophets, and to his ordinances, it will strike such a fear into the hearts of enemies that they will be at their wits' ends and not know what to do. However, in this way we have the promise of divine protection and preservation. "Because thou hast kept the word of my patience, I also will keep thee from the hour of temptation, which shall come upon all the world, to try them that dwell upon the earth" (Rev. 3:10). Let us with Mary choose this for our portion, "to sit at Christ's feet, and hear his word"; and whosoever complain against us, the Lord Jesus will plead for us as he did for her and say: "They have chosen that good part, which shall not be taken away from them" (Luke 10:42). Amen.

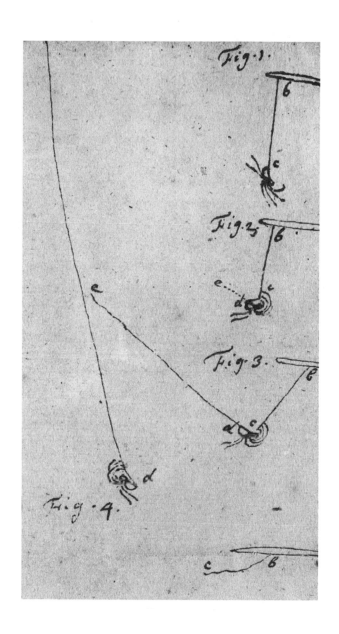

God Speaks to the Rain

FROM THE PURITANS to the Cape Cod nature writer Henry Beston, whose meditative book *The Outermost House* has become a staple work in our own time of heightened concern for the natural environment, New England writers have been engaged with the idea, as Thomas Hooker expressed it nearly four centuries ago, that "God speaks to the rain, and it hears; God speaks to the corn, and it hears." One of the burdens of New England writing has been to justify this claim, or to register the sorrow, wistfulness, or antic relief of living in a world where believing it has come to seem a vestige of childish credulity.

Jonathan Edwards, Spider Letter, 1723

Edward Taylor

Preface to God's Determinations Touching His Elect

 1680s or 1690s

Born in Leicestershire, England, in 1642, Edward Taylor came to New England in his twenties. After being graduated from Harvard in 1671, he took up the ministry at the frontier town of Westfield, where he served unflaggingly until his death at age 87 in 1729—though in his infirm last years he accepted assistance from younger clergymen. Taylor was a proponent of strict qualifications for church membership, and though he published no verse in his lifetime, he regularly composed devotional poetry as a preparatory self-discipline before officiating at the Lord's Supper, which he restricted to church members and regarded as his gravest and highest ministerial duty. When these "preparatory meditations" were discovered and edited by Thomas H. Johnson in the 1930s from manuscripts in the Yale University Library, American literature gained a poet of previously unsuspected power. Taylor also composed a long poem in the Miltonic mode, *God's Determinations Touching His Elect,* whose Preface gives vivid expression to seventeenth-century ideas about the origin and meaning of creation.

Infinity, when all things it beheld
In Nothing, and of Nothing all did build,
Upon what Base was fixt the Lath, wherein
He turn'd this Globe, and riggalld it so trim?
Who blew the Bellows of his Furnace Vast?
Or held the Mould wherein the world was Cast?
Who laid its Corner Stone? Or whose Command?
Where stand the Pillars upon which it stands?
Who Lac'de and Fillitted the earth so fine,
With Rivers like green Ribbons Smaragdine?
Who made the Sea's its Selvedge, and it locks
Like a Quilt Ball within a Silver Box?
Who Spread its Canopy? Or Curtains Spun?
Who in this Bowling Alley bowld the Sun?

Who made it always when it rises set
To go at once both down, and up to get?
Who th'Curtain rods made for this Tapistry?
Who hung the twinckling Lanthorns in the Sky?
Who? who did this? or who is he? Why, know
Its onely Might Almighty this did doe.
His hand hath made this noble worke which Stands
His Glorious Handywork not made by hands.
Who spake all things from nothing; and with ease
Can speake all things to nothing, if he please.
Whose Little finger at his pleasure Can
Out mete ten thousand worlds with halfe a Span:
Whose Might Almighty can by half a looks
Root up the rocks and rock the hills by th'roots.
Can take this mighty World up in his hande,
And shake it like a Squitchen or a Wand.
Whose single Frown will make the Heavens shake
Like as an aspen leafe the Winde makes quake.
Oh! what a might is this Whose single frown
Doth shake the world as it would shake it down?
Which All from Nothing fet, from Nothing, All:
Hath All on Nothing set, lets Nothing fall.
Gave All to nothing Man indeed, whereby
Through nothing man all might him Glorify.
In Nothing then imbosst the brightest Gem
More pretious than all pretiousness in them.
But Nothing man did throw down all by Sin:
And darkened that lightsom Gem in him.
    That now his Brightest Diamond is grown
    Darker by far than any Coalpit Stone.

Cotton Mather

From The Christian Philosopher

 1721

Once the pre-eminent intellectual leader of New England, Cotton Mather (1663–1728) is best known today as a zealous persecutor of "witches" who staked his reputation on the idea that the wild, presumably bewitched, behavior of several young girls in Salem in 1692 meant that Satan had chosen the town as the place to deploy witches into battle against God and the godly. In his own time, however, Mather was in the vanguard of advanced knowledge—a prodigiously well-read student of science as well as of theology. *The Christian Philosopher* is his late-life compilation of natural wonders in which he celebrated the mystery and genius of God the designer. At one point in the book's lengthy enumeration of natural phenomena (Cotton Mather was never succinct), he interrupts himself to explain, "These are some of the Songs, which God, the Maker . . . has given me in the Night."

Such an unaccountable thing there is as the magnetism of the earth, a principle very different from that of gravity.

The operations of this amazing principle are principally discovered in the communion that iron has with the loadstone: a rough, coarse, unsightly stone, but of more value than all the diamonds and jewels in the universe . . .

In every magnet there are two poles, the one pointing to the north, and the other to the south.

The poles in diverse parts of the globe are diversely inclined towards the center of the earth.

These poles, though contrary to one another, do mutually help towards the magnet's attraction and suspension of iron . . .

Iron receives virtue from the magnet, by application to it, or barely from an approach near it, though it do not touch it; and the iron receives this virtue variously, according to the parts of the stone it is made to approach to.

The magnet loses none of its own virtue by communicating any to the iron. This virtue it also communicates very speedily; though the longer the iron joins the stone, the longer its communicated virtue will hold; and the better the magnet, the sooner and stronger the communicated virtue . . .

The effluvia of a loadstone seem to work in a circle. What flows from the

North Pole comes round and enters the South Pole; and what flows from the South Pole enters the North Pole.

Though a minute loadstone may have a prodigious force, yet it is very strange to see what a short sphere of activity it has; it affects not the iron sensibly above an inch or two, and the biggest little more than a foot or two. The magnetic effluvia make haste to return to the stone that emitted them and seem afraid of leaving it, as a child the mother, before it can go alone . . .

To fall down before a stone and say, *Thou art a God,* would be an idolatry that none but a soul more senseless than a stone could be guilty of. But then it would be a very agreeable and acceptable homage unto the glorious God for me to see much of Him in such a wonderful stone as the magnet. They have done well to call it the loadstone, that is to say, the *lead*-stone: *May it lead me unto Thee, O my God and my Saviour!* Magnetism is, in this, like to gravity, that it leads us to God and brings us very near to Him. When we see magnetism in its operation, we must say, *This is the Work of God!* And of the stone, which has proved of such vast use in the affairs of the waters that cover the sea, and will e'er long do its part in bringing it about that the *Glory of the Lord shall cover the earth,* we must say, *Great God, this is a wonderful gift of Thine unto the world!*

I do not propose to exemplify the occasional reflections which a devout mind may make upon all the creatures of God, their properties and actions and relations; the *Libri Elephantini* would not be big enough to contain the thousandth part of them. If it were lawful for me here to pause with a particular exercise upon the loadstone, my first thoughts would be those of the holy Scudder, whose words have had a great impression on me ever since my first reading of them in my childhood: "An upright man is like a needle touched with the loadstone; though he may through boisterous temptations and strong allurements oftentimes look towards the pleasure, gain and glory of this present world. Yet because he is truly touched with the sanctifying spirit of God, he still inclineth *God-ward,* and hath no quiet till he stand *steady towards Heaven.*" . . .

For what is now before us, . . . Christian, in the loadstone drawing and lifting up the iron, behold thy Saviour drawing us to himself, and raising us above the secular cares and snares that ruin us. In its ready communication of its virtues, behold a shadow of thy Saviour communicating his holy spirit to his chosen people, and his ministers more particularly made partakers of his attractive powers. When silver and gold are neglected by the loadstone, but coarse iron preferred, behold thy Saviour passing over the angelical world and choosing to take our nature upon him. The iron is also undistinguished, whether it be lodged in a fine covering, or whether it be lying in the most squalid and wretched circumstances—which invites us to think how little respect of persons there is with our Saviour. However, the iron should be cleansed; it should not be rusty; nor will our Saviour embrace those who are not so far cleansed that they are at least willing to be made clean, and have his files pass upon them. The iron is at first merely passive; then it moves more feebly towards the stone; anon upon contact it will fly to it and express a marvelous affection and adherence.

Is not here a picture of the dispositions in our souls towards our Saviour? It is the pleasure of our Saviour to work by instruments, as the loadstone will do most when the mediation of a steel cap is used about it. After all, whatever is done, the whole praise is due to the loadstone alone. But there would be no end, and indeed there should be none of these meditations! . . .

What a great King is he who is the owner, yea, and the maker of all the magnets in the world! *I am a Great King, saith the Lord of Hosts, and my Name is to be feared among the nations!* May the loadstone help to carry it to them.

JONATHAN EDWARDS

The Spider Letter

 1723

In 1723, the nineteen-year-old Jonathan Edwards wrote this letter, apparently in the hope that it would be published in the Transactions of the Royal Society. (Recent scholarship has proposed that the recipient was Paul Dudley, a Massachusetts judge and member of the Society.) Like Cotton Mather, Edwards (1703–1758) tends to be associated with the darker side of Calvinist piety—the side that emphasizes God's fearful fury (as in his notorious hellfire sermon, "Sinners in the Hands of an Angry God"). But Edwards's writing always had a strain of ecstatic poetry that soars in praise of the intricate beauty of the natural world.

WINDSOR, OCT. 31, 1723

Sir;

In the postscript of your letter to my father you manifest a willingness to receive anything else that he has observed in nature worthy of remark; that which is the subject of the following lines by him was thought to be such: he has laid it upon me to write the account, I having had advantage to make more full observations. If you think, sir, that they are not worthy the taking notice of, with greatness and goodness overlook and conceal. They are some things that I have happily seen of the wondrous and curious works of the spider. Although everything pertaining to this insect is admirable, yet there are some phenomena relating to them more particularly wonderful.

Everybody that is used to the country knows of their marching in the air from one tree to another, sometimes at the distance of five or six rods, though they are wholly destitute of wings: nor can one go out in a dewy morning at the latter end of August and beginning of September but he shall see multitudes of webs reaching from one tree and shrub to another; which webs are commonly thought to be made in the night because they appear only in the morning by reason of the dew that hangs on them, whereas they never work in the night, they love to lie still when the air is dark and moist; but these webs may be seen well enough in the daytime by an observing eye, by their reflection of the sunbeams; especially late in the afternoon may those webs that are between the eye, and that part of the horizon that is under the sun, be seen very plainly, being advantageously posited to reflect the rays, and the spiders themselves may be very often seen traveling in the air from one stage to another amongst the trees in a very unaccountable manner. But, sir, I have often seen that which is yet more astonishing. In a very calm serene day in the forementioned time of year, standing at some distance between the end of an house or some other opaque body, so as just to hide the disk of the sun and keep off his dazzling rays, and looking along close by the side of it, I have seen vast multitudes of little shining webs and glistening strings, brightly reflecting the sunbeams, and some of them of a great length, and at such a height that one would think that they were tacked to the vault of the heavens, and would be burnt like tow in the sun, making a very pleasing as well as surprising appearance. It is wonderful at what a distance these webs may plainly be seen in such a position to the sunbeams, which are so fine that they cannot be seen in another position, though held near to the eye; some that are at a great distance appear (it cannot be otherwise) several thousands of times as big as they ought: They doubtless appear under as great an angle as a body of a foot diameter ought to do at such a distance; so greatly doth coruscation increase the apparent bigness of bodies at a distance, as is observed in the fixed stars. But that which is most astonishing is that very often there appears at the end of these webs, spiders sailing in the air with them, doubtless with abundance of pleasure, though not with so much as I have beheld them and showed them to others. And since I have seen these things I have been very conversant with spiders. Resolving if possible to find out the mysteries of these their amazing works, and pursuing my observations, I discovered one wonder after another till I have been so happy as very frequently to see their whole manner of working; which is thus:

When a spider would go from one tree or branch to another, or would recreate himself by sailing or floating in the air, he first lets himself down a little way from the twig he stands on by a web, as [in] Fig. 1; and then taking hold of it by his forefeet as in Fig. 2, and then separates or loosens the part of the web *cd* from the part *bc* by which he hangs; which part of the web *cd,* being thus loosened, will by the motion of the air be carried out towards *e,* which will by the sufferance of the spider be drawn [out] of his tail with infinite ease by the moving air, to what length the spider pleases, as [in] Fig. 3: And if the further end of the web *de,* as it is running out and moving to and fro, happens to catch by a shrub or the branch of a tree, the spider immediately feels it and fixes the hither end of it, *d,* to the web *bc,* and goes over as by a bridge by the web *de.* Every particular of this, sir, my eyes have innumerable times made me sure of, saving that I never could distinctly see how they separated the part of the web *cd* (Fig. 2) from the part *bc,* whether it be done by biting of it off or how, because so small a piece of so fine a web is altogether imperceptible amongst the spider's legs, and because the spider is so very quick and dexterous in doing of it all. But I have seen that it is done, though I have not seen how they do it. For this, sir, I can see: that the web *bc* (Fig. 3) is separated, and not joined to the spider's tail, while the web *de* is drawing out.

Now, sir, it is certain that these webs, when they first come from the spider, are so rare a substance that they are lighter than the air, because they will immediately ascend in a calm air, and never descend except driven by a wind: and 'tis as certain that what swims and ascends in the air is lighter than the air, as that what ascends and swims in water is lighter than that: So that if we should suppose any such time wherein the air is perfectly calm, this web is so easily drawn out of the spider's tail, that barely the levity of it is sufficient to carry it out to any length. But at least its levity, or ascending inclination, together with so much motion as the air is never without, will well suffice for this. Wherefore, if it be so that the end of the web *de* (Fig. 3) catches by no tree nor other body till it be drawn out so long that its levity shall be so great as to be more than equal to the gravity of the spider, or so that the web and the spider taken together shall be lighter than such a quantity of air as takes up equal space, then according to the universally acknowledged laws of nature the web and the spider together will ascend and not descend in the air. As when a man [is] at the bottom of the water, if he has hold of a piece of timber so great that the wood's tendency upwards is greater than the man's tendency downwards, he together with the wood will ascend to the surface of the water. Therefore, when the spider perceives that the web *de* is long enough to bear him up by its ascending force (which force the spider feels by its drawing of him towards *e*), he lets go his hold of the web *bc* (Fig. 4) and, holding by the web *de,* ascends and floats in the air with it. If there be not web more than enough just to equal with its levity the gravity of the spider, the spider together with the web will hang *in equilibrio,* neither ascending nor descending, otherwise than as the air moves; but if there be so much web that its ascending tendency, or rather the buoying force of the air upon it, shall be greater than the descending tendency of the spider, they will ascend till the air is so thin, till they together are just of an equal weight with so much air. But if the web be so short as not to counterpoise the weight of the spider, the web and spider will fall till they come to the ground.

And this very way, sir, I have multitudes of times seen spiders mount away into the air with a vast train of this silver web before them from a stick in mine hand; for if the spider be disturbed upon the stick by shaking of [it] he will presently in this manner leave it. Their way of working may very distinctly be seen if they are held up in the sun, in a calm day, against a dark door or anything that is black.

And this, sir, is the way of spiders' working. This is the way of their going from one thing to another at a distance, and this is the way of their flying in the air. And although I can say I am certain of it, I don't desire that the truth of it should be received upon my word, though I could bring others to testify to it to whom I have shown it, and who have looked on with admiration: But everyone's eyes who will take the pains to observe will make them equally sure of it; only those who would make experiment must take notice that it is not every sort of spider that is a flying spider, for those spiders that keep in houses are a quite different sort, as also those that keep in the ground, and those [that] keep in swamps upon the ground amongst the bogs, and those that keep in hollow trees and rotten logs; but those spiders that keep on branches of trees and shrubs are the flying spiders. They delight most in walnut trees, and are that sort of spiders that make those curious, network, polygonal webs that are so frequently to be seen in the latter end of the year. There are more of this sort of spider by far than of any other.

Corollary 1. Hence the wisdom of the Creator in providing of the spider with that wonderful liquor with which their bottle tail is filled, that may so easily be drawn out so exceeding fine, and being in this way exposed to the air will so immediately convert to a dry substance that shall be so very rare as to be lighter than the air, and will so excellently serve to all their purposes.

Corol. 2. Hence the exuberant goodness of the Creator, who hath not only provided for all the necessities, but also for the pleasure and recreation of all sorts of creatures, even the insects.

But yet, sir, I am assured that the chief end of this faculty that is given them is not their recreation but their destruction, because their destruction is unavoidably the constant effect of it; and we find nothing that is the continual effect of nature but what is the end of the means by which it is brought to pass: but it is impossible but that the greatest part of the spiders upon the land should every year be swept into the ocean. For these spiders never fly except the weather be fair and the atmosphere dry, but the atmosphere is never clear and dry, neither in this nor any other continent, only when the wind blows from the midland parts, and consequently towards the sea; as here in New England, the fair weather is only when the wind is westerly, the land being on that side and the ocean on the easterly. I scarcely ever have seen any of these spiders flying but when they have been hastening directly towards the sea. And the time of their flying being so long, even from about the middle of August, every sunshiny day till about the end of October (though their chief time, as was observed before, is the latter end of August and beginning of September). And they, never flying from the sea but always towards it, must get there at last. And it seems unreasonable to think that they have sense to stop themselves when they come near the sea, for then we should [see] hundreds of times more spiders on the seashore than anywhere else. When they are once carried over the water their webs grow damp and moist and lose their levity and their wings fail them, and let them down into the water.

The same also holds true of other sorts of flying insects, for at those times that I have viewed the spiders with their webs in the air there has also appeared vast multitudes of flies at a great height, and all flying the same way with the spiders and webs, direct to the ocean. And even such as butterflies, millers, and moths, which keep in the grass at this time of year, I have seen vastly higher than the tops of the highest trees, all going the same way. These I have seen towards evening, right overhead, and without a screen to defend my eye from the sunbeams, which I used to think were seeking a warmer climate. The reason of their flying at that time of year I take to be because the ground and trees and grass, the places of their residence in summer, begin to be chill and uncomfortable. Therefore when the sun shines pretty warm they leave them, and mount up into the air and expand their wings to the sun, and flying for nothing but their own ease and comfort, they suffer themselves to go that way that they can go with the greatest ease, and so where the wind pleases: and it being warmth they fly for, they never fly against the wind nor sidewise to it, they find it cold and laborious; they therefore seem to use their wings but just so much as to bear them up, and suffer themselves to go with the wind. So that it must necessarily be that almost all aerial insects, and spiders which live upon them and are made up of them, are at the end of the year swept away into the sea and buried in the ocean, and leave nothing behind them but their eggs for a new stock the next year.

Corol. 1. Hence [there] is reason to admire at the wisdom of the Creator, and to be convinced that it is exercised about such little things in this wonderful contrivance of annually carrying off and burying the corruption and nauseousness of the air, of which flying insects are little collections, in the bottom of the ocean where it will do no harm; and especially the strange way of bringing this about in spiders, which are collections of these collections, their food being flying insects, flies being the poison of the air, and spiders are the poison of flies collected together. And what great inconveniences should we labor under if it were not so, for spiders and flies are such exceedingly multiplying creatures, that if they only slept or lay benumbed in winter, and were raised again in the spring, which is commonly thought, it would not be many years before we should be plagued with as vast numbers as Egypt was. And if they died ultimately in winter, they by the renewed heat of the sun would presently again be dissipated into the nauseous vapors of which they are made up, and so would be of no use or benefit in that in which now they are so very serviceable and which is the chief end of their creation.

Corol. 2. The wisdom of the Creator is also admirable in so nicely and mathematically adjusting their plastic nature, that notwithstanding their destruction by this means and the multitudes that are eaten by birds, that they do not decrease and so by little and little come to nothing; and in so adjusting their destruction to their multiplication they do neither increase, but taking one year with another, there is always an equal number of them.

These, sir, are the observations I have had opportunity to make on the wonders that are to be seen in the most despicable of animals. Although these things appear for the main very certain to me, yet, sir, I submit it all to your better judgment, and deeper insight. I humbly beg to be pardoned for running the venture, though an utter stranger, of troubling you with so prolix an account of that which I am altogether uncertain whether you will esteem worthy of the time and pains of reading. Pardon me if I thought it might at least give you occasion to make better observations on these wondrous animals, that should be worthy of communicating to the learned world, from whose glistening webs so much of the wisdom of the Creator shines.

> Pardon, sir, your most obedient
> humble servant,
> Jonathan Edwards

William Cullen Bryant

Forest Hymn

 1825

William Cullen Bryant (1794–1878) was born in the western Massachusetts town of Cummington. After a brief period practicing law in Great Barrington, he left at the age of thirty-one for New York City in pursuit of a literary career. From 1829 until his death, he was editor of the *New York Evening Post* and a major figure in New York civic and political life.

"Forest Hymn" was the last poem Bryant composed before leaving Massachusetts. Notwithstanding its derivativeness from Wordsworth, and a certain provincial earnestness, it is a poem of authentic feeling that catches the growing doubt among New England romantics that church forms could express adequately their impulse to worship. He returned years later to the poem in order to revise it following suggestions by a friendly critic who objected to the "sarcasm" in the lines about jewels and "envious eyes." Feeling increasingly remote from the New England landscape that had once inspired him, Bryant remarked that "an alteration ought never to be made without the mind being filled with the subject." Nevertheless, he changed the lines, which became: "These dim vaults, / These winding aisles, of human pomp or pride / Report not." The text printed here is that of the first version.

> The groves were God's first temples. Ere man learned
> To hew the shaft, and lay the architrave,
> And spread the roof above them,—ere he framed
> The lofty vault, to gather and roll back
> The sound of anthems; in the darkling wood,
> Amidst the cool and silence, he knelt down
> And offered to the Mightiest, solemn thanks
> And supplication. For his simple heart
> Might not resist the sacred influences,
> Which, from the stilly twilight of the place,
> And from the gray old trunks that high in heaven
> Mingled their mossy boughs, and from the sound
> Of the invisible breath that swayed at once
> All their green tops, stole over him, and bowed

His spirit with the thought of boundless power
And inaccessible majesty. Ah, why
Should we, in the world's riper years, neglect
God's ancient sanctuaries, and adore
Only among the crowd, and under roofs
That our frail hands have raised. Let me, at least,
Here, in the shadow of this aged wood,
Offer one hymn—thrice happy, if it find
Acceptance in his ear.

             Father, thy hand
Hath reared these venerable columns, thou
Didst weave this verdant roof. Thou didst look down
Upon the naked earth, and, forthwith, rose
All these fair ranks of trees. They, in thy sun,
Budded, and shook their green leaves in thy breeze,
And shot towards heaven. The century-living crow
Whose birth was in their tops, grew old and died
Among their branches, till, at last, they stood,
As now they stand, massive and tall and dark,
Fit shrine for humble worshipper to hold
Communion with his Maker. Here are seen
No traces of man's pomp or pride;—no silks
Rustle, nor jewels shine, nor envious eyes
Encounter; no fantastic carvings show
The boast of our vain race to change the form
Of thy fair works. But thou art here—thou fill'st
The solitude. Thou art in the soft winds
That run along the summit of these trees
In music;—thou art in the cooler breath,
That from the inmost darkness of the place,
Comes, scarcely felt;—the barky trunks, the ground,
The fresh moist ground, are all instinct with thee.
Here is continual worship;—nature, here,
In the tranquillity that thou dost love,
Enjoys thy presence. Noiselessly, around,
From perch to perch, the solitary bird
Passes; and yon clear spring, that, 'midst its herbs,
Wells softly forth and visits the strong roots
Of half the mighty forest, tells no tale
Of all the good it does. Thou hast not left

Thyself without a witness, in these shades,
Of thy perfections. Grandeur, strength, and grace
Are here to speak of thee. This mighty oak—
By whose immoveable stem I stand and seem
Almost annihilated—not a prince,
In all that proud old world beyond the deep,
E'er wore his crown as loftily as he
Wears the green coronal of leaves with which
Thy hand has graced him. Nestled at his root
Is beauty, such as blooms not in the glare
Of the broad sun. That delicate forest flower,
With scented breath, and look so like a smile,
Seems, as it issues from the shapeless mould,
An emanation of the indwelling Life,
A visible token of the upholding Love,
That are the soul of this wide universe.

    My heart is awed within me, when I think
Of the great miracle that still goes on,
In silence, round me—the perpetual work
Of thy creation, finished, yet renewed
Forever. Written on thy works I read
The lesson of thy own eternity.
Lo! all grow old and die—but see, again,
How on the faltering footsteps of decay
Youth presses—ever gay and beautiful youth
In all its beautiful forms. These lofty trees
Wave not less proudly that their ancestors
Moulder beneath them. Oh, there is not lost
One of earth's charms: upon her bosom yet,
After the flight of untold centuries,
The freshness of her far beginning lies
And yet shall lie. Life mocks the idle hate
Of his arch enemy Death—yea—seats himself
Upon the sepulchre, and blooms and smiles,
And of the triumphs of his ghastly foe
Makes his own nourishment. For he came forth
From thine own bosom, and shall have no end.

    There have been holy men who hid themselves
Deep in the woody wilderness, and gave

Their lives to thought and prayer, till they outlived
The generation born with them, nor seemed
Less aged than the hoary trees and rocks
Around them;—and there have been holy men
Who deemed it were not well to pass life thus.
But let me often to these solitudes
Retire, and in thy presence re-assure
My feeble virtue. Here its enemies,
The passions, at thy plainer footsteps shrink
And tremble and are still. Oh, God! when thou
Dost scare the world with tempests, set on fire
The heavens with falling thunderbolts, or fill,
With all the waters of the firmament,
The swift dark whirlwind that uproots the woods
And drowns the villages; when, at thy call,
Uprises the great deep and throws himself
Upon the continent and overwhelms
Its cities—who forgets not, at the sight
Of these tremendous tokens of thy power,
His pride, and lays his strifes and follies by?
Oh, from these sterner aspects of thy face
Spare me and mine, nor let us need the wrath
Of the mad unchained elements to teach
Who rules them. Be it ours to meditate
In these calm shades thy milder majesty,
And, to the beautiful order of thy works,
Learn to conform the order of our lives.

RALPH WALDO EMERSON

From Nature

 1836

"*Nature*," the elder Oliver Wendell Holmes once wrote, "is the Book of Revelation of our Saint Radulphus." This shrewd remark suggests much that readers need to know when first approaching the leading figure of antebellum New England life and letters, Ralph Waldo Emerson (1803–1882). What Holmes captures is the quasi-religious ecstasy that animates Emerson's hymn to the fecundity and benignity of nature, his tone of prophetic fervor in reporting the mystical experience of feeling "the currents of universal being" flow through him as he walks in snow at twilight, and, not least, the slight pomposity (caught perfectly in Holmes's latinization of Emerson's first name) of his self-appointed role as blessed witness. But no critical summary can convey the giddy joy of Emerson's prose as he expresses his ultimately humble amazement at the beauty and unity of the world.

I. Nature

To go into solitude, a man needs to retire as much from his chamber as from society. I am not solitary whilst I read and write, though nobody is with me. But if a man would be alone, let him look at the stars. The rays that come from those heavenly worlds will separate between him and what he touches. One might think the atmosphere was made transparent with this design, to give man, in the heavenly bodies, the perpetual presence of the sublime. Seen in the streets of cities, how great they are! If the stars should appear one night in a thousand years, how would men believe and adore; and preserve for many generations the remembrance of the city of God which had been shown! But every night come out these envoys of beauty, and light the universe with their admonishing smile.

The stars awaken a certain reverence, because though always present, they are inaccessible; but all natural objects make a kindred impression, when the mind is open to their influence. Nature never wears a mean appearance. Neither does the wisest man extort her secret, and lose his curiosity by finding out all her perfection. Nature never became a toy to a wise spirit. The flowers, the animals, the mountains, reflected the wisdom of his best hour, as much as they had delighted the simplicity of his childhood.

When we speak of nature in this manner, we have a distinct but most poetical sense in the mind. We mean the integrity of impression made by manifold natural objects. It is this which distinguishes the stick of timber of the wood-cutter from the tree of the poet. The charming landscape which I saw this morning is indubitably made up of some twenty or thirty farms. Miller owns this field, Locke that, and Manning the woodland beyond. But none of them owns the landscape. There is a property in the horizon which no man has but he whose eye can integrate all the parts, that is, the poet. This is the best part of these men's farms, yet to this their warranty-deeds give no title.

To speak truly, few adult persons can see nature. Most persons do not see the sun. At least they have a very superficial seeing. The sun illuminates only the eye of the man, but shines into the eye and the heart of the child. The lover of nature is he whose inward and outward senses are still truly adjusted to each other; who has retained the spirit of infancy even into the era of manhood. His intercourse with heaven and earth becomes part of his daily food. In the presence of nature a wild delight runs through the man, in spite of real sorrows. Nature says,—he is my creature, and maugre all his impertinent griefs, he shall be glad with me. Not the sun or the summer alone, but every hour and season yields its tribute of delight; for every hour and change corresponds to and authorizes a different state of the mind, from breathless noon to grimmest midnight. Nature is a setting that fits equally well a comic or a mourning piece. In good health, the air is a cordial of incredible virtue. Crossing a bare common, in snow puddles, at twilight, under a clouded sky, without having in my thoughts any occurrence of special good fortune, I have enjoyed a perfect exhilaration. I am glad to the brink of fear. In the woods, too, a man casts off his years, as the snake his slough, and at what period soever of life is always a child. In the woods is perpetual youth. Within these plantations of God, a decorum and sanctity reign, a perennial festival is dressed, and the guest sees not how he should tire of them in a thousand years. In the woods, we return to reason and faith. There I feel that nothing can befall me in life,—no disgrace, no calamity (leaving me my eyes), which nature cannot repair. Standing on the bare ground,—my head bathed by the blithe air and uplifted into infinite space,—all mean egotism vanishes. I become a transparent eyeball; I am nothing; I see all; the currents of the Universal Being circulate through me; I am part or parcel of God. The name of the nearest friend sounds then foreign and accidental: to be brothers, to be acquaintances, master or servant, is then a trifle and a disturbance. I am the lover of uncontained and immortal beauty. In the wilderness, I find something more dear and connate than in streets or villages. In the tranquil landscape, and especially in the distant line of the horizon, man beholds somewhat as beautiful as his own nature.

The greatest delight which the fields and woods minister is the suggestion of an occult relation between man and the vegetable. I am not alone and unacknowledged. They nod to me, and I to them. The waving of the boughs in the storm is new to me and old. It takes me by surprise, and yet is not unknown. Its effect is like that of a higher thought or a better emotion coming over me, when I deemed I was thinking justly or doing right.

Yet it is certain that the power to produce this delight does not reside in nature, but in man, or in a harmony of both. It is necessary to use these pleasures with great temperance. For nature is not always tricked in holiday attire, but the same scene which yesterday breathed perfume and glittered as for the frolic of the nymphs is overspread with melancholy today. Nature always wears the colors of the spirit. To a man laboring under calamity, the heat of his own fire hath sadness in it. Then there is a kind of contempt of the landscape felt by him who has just lost by death a dear friend. The sky is less grand as it shuts down over less worth in the population.

II. Commodity

Whoever considers the final cause of the world will discern a multitude of uses that enter as parts into that result. They all admit of being thrown into one of the following classes: Commodity; Beauty; Language; and Discipline.

Under the general name of commodity, I rank all those advantages which our senses owe to nature. This, of course, is a benefit which is temporary and mediate, not ultimate, like its service to the soul. Yet although low, it is perfect in its kind, and is the only use of nature which all men apprehend. The misery of man appears like childish petulance, when we explore the steady and prodigal provision that has been made for his support and delight on this green ball which floats him through the heavens. What angels invented these splendid ornaments, these rich conveniences, this ocean of air above, this ocean of water beneath, this firmament of earth between? this zodiac of lights, this tent of dropping clouds, this striped coat of climates, this fourfold year? Beasts, fire, water, stones, and corn serve him. The field is at once his floor, his work-yard, his play-ground, his garden, and his bed.

> "More servants wait on man
> Than he'll take notice of."

Nature, in its ministry to man, is not only the material, but is also the process and the result. All the parts incessantly work into each other's hands for the profit of man. The wind sows the seed; the sun evaporates the sea; the wind blows the vapor to the field; the ice, on the other side of the planet, condenses rain on this; the rain feeds the plant; the plant feeds the animal; and thus the endless circulations of the divine charity nourish man.

The useful arts are reproductions or new combinations by the wit of man, of the same natural benefactors. He no longer waits for favoring gales, but by means of steam, he realizes the fable of Aeolus's bag, and carries the two and thirty winds in the boiler of his boat. To diminish friction, he paves the road with iron bars, and, mounting a coach with a ship-load of men, animals, and merchandise behind him, he darts through the country, from town to town, like an eagle or a swallow through the air. By the aggregate of these aids, how is the face of the world changed, from the era of Noah to that of Napoleon! The private poor man hath cities, ships, canals, bridges, built for him. He goes to the post-office, and the human race run on his errands; to the bookshop, and the human race read and write of all that happens, for him; to the court-house, and nations repair his wrongs. He sets his house upon the road, and the human race go forth every morning, and shovel out the snow, and cut a path for him.

But there is no need of specifying particulars in this class of uses. The catalogue is endless, and the examples so obvious, that I shall leave them to the reader's reflection, with the general remark, that this mercenary benefit is one which has respect to a farther good. A man is fed, not that he may be fed, but that he may work.

III. Beauty

A nobler want of man is served by nature, namely, the love of Beauty.

The ancient Greeks called the world [*kosmos*] beauty. Such is the constitution of all things, or such the plastic power of the human eye, that the primary forms, as the sky, the mountain, the tree, the animal, give us a delight *in and for themselves;* a pleasure arising from outline, color, motion, and grouping. This seems partly owing to the eye itself. The eye is the best of artists. By the mutual action of its structure and of the laws of light, perspective is produced, which integrates every mass of objects, of what character soever, into a well colored and shaded globe, so that where the particular objects are mean and unaffecting, the landscape which they compose is round and symmetrical. And as the eye is the best composer, so light is the first of painters. There is no object so foul that intense light will not make beautiful. And the stimulus it affords to the sense, and a sort of infinitude which it hath, like space and time, make all matter gay. Even the corpse has its own beauty. But besides this general grace diffused over nature, almost all the individual forms are agreeable to the eye, as is proved by our endless imitations of some of them, as the acorn, the grape, the pine-cone, the wheat-ear, the egg, the wings and forms of most birds, the lion's claw, the serpent, the butterfly, sea-shells, flames, clouds, buds, leaves, and the forms of many trees, as the palm.

For better consideration, we may distribute the aspects of Beauty in a threefold manner.

1. First, the simple perception of natural forms is a delight. The influence of the forms and actions in nature is so needful to man, that, in its lowest functions, it seems to lie on the confines of commodity and beauty. To the body and mind which have been cramped by noxious work or company, nature is medicinal and restores their tone. The tradesman, the attorney comes out of the din and craft of the street and sees the sky and the woods, and is a man again. In their eternal calm, he finds himself. The health of the eye seems to demand a horizon. We are never tired, so long as we can see far enough.

But in other hours, Nature satisfies by its loveliness, and without any mixture of corporeal benefit. I see the spectacle of morning from the hilltop over against my house, from daybreak to sunrise, with emotions which an angel might share. The long slender bars of cloud float like fishes in the sea of crimson light. From the earth, as a shore, I look out into that silent sea. I seem to partake its rapid transformations; the active enchantment reaches my dust, and I dilate and conspire with the morning wind. How does Nature deify us with a few and cheap elements! Give me health and a day, and I will make the pomp of emperors ridiculous. The dawn is my Assyria; the sunset and moonrise my Paphos, and unimaginable realms of faerie; broad noon shall be my England of the senses and the understanding; the night shall be my Germany of mystic philosophy and dreams.

Not less excellent, except for our less susceptibility in the afternoon, was the charm, last evening, of a January sunset. The western clouds divided and subdivided themselves into pink flakes modulated with tints of unspeakable softness, and the air had so much life and sweetness that it was a pain to come within doors. What was it that nature would say? Was there no meaning in the live repose of the valley behind the mill, and which Homer or Shakespeare could not re-form for me in words? The leafless trees become spires of flame in the sunset, with the blue east for their background, and the stars of the dead calices of flowers, and every withered stem and stubble rimed with frost, contribute something to the mute music.

The inhabitants of cities suppose that the country landscape is pleasant only half the year. I please myself with the graces of the winter scenery, and believe that we are as much touched by it as by the genial influences of summer. To the attentive eye, each moment of the year has its own beauty, and in the same field, it beholds, every hour, a picture which was never seen before, and which shall never be seen again. The heavens change every moment, and reflect their glory or gloom on the plains beneath. The state of the crop in the surrounding farms alters the expression of the earth from week to week. The succession of native plants in the pastures and roadsides, which makes the silent clock by which time tells the summer hours, will make even the divisions of the day sensible to a keen observer. The tribes of birds and insects, like the plants punctual to their time, follow each other, and the year has room for all. By watercourses, the variety is greater. In July, the blue pontederia or pickerel-weed blooms in large beds in the shallow parts of our pleasant river, and swarms with yellow butterflies in continual motion. Art cannot rival this pomp of purple and gold. Indeed the river is a perpetual gala, and boasts each month a new ornament.

But this beauty of Nature which is seen and felt as beauty, is the least part. The shows of day, the dewy morning, the rainbow, mountains, orchards in blossom, stars, moonlight, shadows in still water, and the like, if too eagerly hunted, become shows merely, and mock us with their unreality. Go out of the house to see the moon, and 'tis mere tinsel; it will not please as when its light shines upon your necessary journey. The beauty that shimmers in the yellow afternoons of October, who ever could clutch it? Go forth to find it, and it is gone; 'tis only a mirage as you look from the windows of diligence.

2. The presence of a higher, namely, of the spiritual element is essential to its perfection. The high and divine beauty which can be loved without effeminacy, is that which is found in combination with the human will. Beauty is the mark God sets upon virtue. Every natural action is graceful. Every heroic act is also decent, and causes the place and the bystanders to shine. We are taught by great actions that the universe is the property of every individual in it. Every rational creature has all nature for his dowry and estate. It is his, if he will. He may divest himself of it; he may creep into a corner, and abdicate his kingdom, as most men do, but he is entitled to the world by his constitution. In proportion to the energy of his thought and will, he takes up the world into himself. "All those things for which men plough, build, or sail, obey virtue," said Sallust. "The winds and waves," said Gibbon, "are always on the side of the ablest navigators." So are the sun and moon and all the stars of heaven. When a noble act is done,—perchance in a scene of great natural beauty; when Leonidas and his three hundred martyrs consume one day in dying, and the sun and moon come each and look at them once in the steep defile of Thermopylae; when Arnold Winkelried, in the high Alps, under the shadow of the avalanche, gathers in his side a sheaf of Austrian spears to break the line for his comrades; are not these heroes entitled to add the beauty of the scene to the beauty of the deed? When the bark of Columbus nears the shore of America;—before it the beach lined with savages, fleeing out of all their

huts of cane; the sea behind; and the purple mountains of the Indian Archipelago around, can we separate the man from the living picture? Does not the New World clothe his form with her palm-groves and savannahs as fit drapery? Ever does natural beauty steal in like air, and envelope great actions. When Sir Harry Vane was dragged up the Tower-hill, sitting on a sled, to suffer death as the champion of the English laws, one of the multitude cried out to him, "You never sate on so glorious a seat!" Charles II, to intimidate the citizens of London, caused the patriot Lord Russell to be drawn in an open coach through the principal streets of the city on his way to the scaffold. "But," his biographer says, "the multitude imagined they saw liberty and virtue sitting by his side." In private places, among sordid objects, an act of truth or heroism seems at once to draw to itself the sky as its temple, the sun as its candle. Nature stretches out her arms to embrace man, only let his thoughts be of equal greatness. Willingly does she follow his steps with the rose and the violet, and bend her lines of grandeur and grace to the decoration of her darling child. Only let his thoughts be of equal scope, and the frame will suit the picture. A virtuous man is in unison with her works, and makes the central figure of the visible sphere. Homer, Pindar, Socrates, Phocion, associate themselves fitly in our memory with the geography and climate of Greece. The visible heavens and earth sympathize with Jesus. And in common life whosoever has seen a person of powerful character and happy genius, will have remarked how easily he took all things along with him,—the persons, the opinions, and the day, and nature become ancillary to a man.

3. There is still another aspect under which the beauty of the world may be viewed, namely, as it becomes an object of the intellect. Beside the relation of things to virtue, they have a relation to thought. The intellect searches out the absolute order of things as they stand in the mind of God, and without the colors of affection. The intellectual and the active powers seem to succeed each other, and the exclusive activity of the one generates the exclusive activity of the other. There is something unfriendly in each to the other, but they are like the alternate periods of feeding and working in animals; each prepares and will be followed by the other. Therefore does beauty, which, in relation to actions, as we have seen, comes unsought, and comes because it is unsought, remain for the apprehension and pursuit of the intellect; and then again, in its turn, of the active power. Nothing divine dies. All good is eternally reproductive. The beauty of nature re-forms itself in the mind, and not for barren contemplation, but for new creation.

All men are in some degree impressed by the face of the world; some men even to delight. This love of beauty is Taste. Others have the same love in such excess, that, not content with admiring, they seek to embody it in new forms. The creation of beauty is Art.

The production of a work of art throws a light upon the mystery of humanity. A work of art is an abstract or epitome of the world. It is the result or expression of nature, in miniature. For although the works of nature are innumerable and all different, the result or the expression of them all is similar and single. Nature is a sea of forms radically alike and even unique. A leaf, a sunbeam, a landscape, the ocean, make an analogous impression on the mind. What is common to them all,—that perfectness and harmony, is beauty. The standard of beauty is the entire circuit of natural forms,—the totality of nature; which the Italians expressed by defining beauty "il più nell' uno." Nothing is quite beautiful alone; nothing but is beautiful in the whole. A single object is only so far beautiful as it suggests this universal grace. The poet, the painter, the sculptor, the musician, the architect, seek each to concentrate this radiance of the world on one point, and each in his several work to satisfy the love of beauty which stimulates him to produce. Thus is Art a nature passed through the alembic of man. Thus in art does Nature work through the will of a man filled with the beauty of her first works.

The world thus exists to the soul to satisfy the desire of beauty. This element I call an ultimate end. No reason can be asked or given why the soul seeks beauty. Beauty, in its largest and profoundest sense, is one expression for the universe. God is the all-fair. Truth, and goodness, and beauty, are but different faces of the same All. But beauty in nature is not ultimate. It is the herald of inward and eternal beauty, and is not alone a solid and satisfactory good. It must stand as a part, and not as yet the last or highest expression of the final cause of Nature.

IV. Language

Language is a third use which Nature subserves to man. Nature is the vehicle of thought, and in a simple, double, and threefold degree.

1. Words are signs of natural facts.
2. Particular natural facts are symbols of particular spiritual facts.
3. Nature is the symbol of spirit.

1. Words are signs of natural facts. The use of natural history is to give us aid in supernatural history; the use of the outer creation, to give us language for the beings and changes of the inward creation. Every word which is used to express a moral or intellectual fact, if traced to its root, is found to be borrowed from some material appearance. *Right* means *straight; wrong* means *twisted. Spirit* primarily means *wind; transgression,* the *crossing of a line; supercilious,* the *raising of the eyebrow.* We say the *heart* to express emotion, the *head*

to denote thought; and *thought* and *emotion* are words borrowed from sensible things, and now appropriated to spiritual nature. Most of the process by which this transformation is made, is hidden from us in the remote time when language was framed; but the same tendency may be daily observed in children. Children and savages use only nouns or names of things, which they convert into verbs, and apply to analogous mental acts.

2. But this origin of all words that convey a spiritual import,—so conspicuous a fact in the history of language,—is our least debt to nature. It is not words only that are emblematic; it is things which are emblematic. Every natural fact is a symbol of some spiritual fact. Every appearance in nature corresponds to some state of the mind, and that state of the mind can only be described by presenting that natural appearance as its picture. An enraged man is a lion, a cunning man is a fox, a firm man is a rock, a learned man is a torch. A lamb is innocence; a snake is subtle spite; flowers express to us the delicate affections. Light and darkness are our familiar expression for knowledge and ignorance; and heat for love. Visible distance behind and before us, is respectively our image of memory and hope.

Who looks upon a river in a meditative hour and is not reminded of the flux of all things? Throw a stone into the stream, and the circles that propagate themselves are the beautiful type of all influence. Man is conscious of a universal soul within or behind his individual life, wherein, as in a firmament, the natures of Justice, Truth, Love, Freedom, arise and shine. This universal soul he calls Reason: it is not mine, or thine, or his, but we are its; we are its property and men. And the blue sky in which the private earth is buried, the sky with its eternal calm, and full of everlasting orbs, is the type of Reason. That which intellectually considered we call Reason, considered in relation to nature, we call Spirit. Spirit is the Creator. Spirit hath life in itself. And man in all ages and countries embodies it in his language as the FATHER.

It is easily seen that there is nothing lucky or capricious in these analogies, but that they are constant, and pervade nature. These are not the dreams of a few poets, here and there, but man is an analogist, and studies relations in all objects. He is placed in the center of beings, and a ray of relation passes from every other being to him. And neither can man be understood without these objects, nor these objects without man. All the facts in natural history taken by themselves, have no value, but are barren, like a single sex. But marry it to human history, and it is full of life. Whole floras, all Linnaeus' and Buffon's volumes, are dry catalogues of facts; but the most trivial of these facts, the habit of a plant, the organs, or work, or noise of an insect, applied to the illustration of a fact in intellectual philosophy, or in any way associated to human nature, affects us in the most lively and agreeable manner. The seed of a plant,—to what affecting analogies in the nature of man is that little fruit made use of, in all discourse, up to the voice of Paul, who calls the human corpse a seed,—"It is sown a natural body; it is raised a spiritual body." The motion of the earth round its axis and round the sun, makes the day and the year. These are certain amounts of brute light and heat. But is there no intent of an analogy between man's life and the seasons? And do the seasons gain no grandeur or pathos from that analogy? The instincts of the ant are very unimportant considered as the ant's; but the moment a ray of relation is seen to extend from it to man, and the little drudge is seen to be a monitor, a little body with a mighty heart, then all its habits, even that said to be recently observed, that it never sleeps, become sublime.

Because of this radical correspondence between visible things and human thoughts, savages, who have only what is necessary, converse in figures. As we go back in history, language becomes more picturesque, until its infancy, when it is all poetry; or all spiritual facts are represented by natural symbols. The same symbols are found to make the original elements of all languages. It has moreover been observed, that the idioms of all languages approach each other in passages of the greatest eloquence and power. And as this is the first language, so is it the last. This immediate dependence of language upon nature, this conversion of an outward phenomenon into a type of somewhat in human life, never loses its power to affect us. It is this which gives that piquancy to the conversation of a strong-natured farmer or backwoodsman, which all men relish.

A man's power to connect his thought with its proper symbol, and so to utter it, depends on the simplicity of his character, that is, upon his love of truth and his desire to communicate it without loss. The corruption of man is followed by the corruption of language. When simplicity of character and the sovereignty of ideas is broken up by the prevalence of secondary desires,—the desire of riches, of pleasure, of power, and of praise,—and duplicity and falsehood take place of simplicity and truth, the power over nature as an interpreter of the will is in a degree lost; new imagery ceases to be created, and old words are perverted to stand for things which are not; a paper currency is employed, when there is no bullion in the vaults. In due time the fraud is manifest, and words lose all power to stimulate the understanding or the affections. Hundreds of writers may be found in every long-civilized nation who for a short time believe and make others believe that they see and utter truths, who do not of themselves clothe one thought in its natural garment, but who feed unconsciously on the language created by the primary writers of the country, those, namely, who hold primarily on nature.

But wise men pierce this rotten diction and fasten words again to visible things; so that picturesque language is at once a commanding certificate that he who employs it is a man in alliance with truth and God. The moment our discourse rises above the ground line of familiar facts and is inflamed with passion or exalted by thought, it clothes itself in images. A man conversing in earnest, if he watch his intellectual processes, will find that a material image more or less luminous arises in his mind, contemporaneous with every thought, which furnishes the vestment of the thought. Hence, good writing and brilliant discourse are perpetual allegories. This imagery is spontaneous. It is the blending of experience with the present action of the mind. It is proper creation. It is the working of the Original Cause through the instruments he has already made.

These facts may suggest the advantage which the country-life possesses, for a powerful mind, over the artificial and curtailed life of cities. We know more from nature than we can at will communicate. Its light flows into the mind evermore, and we forget its presence. The poet, the orator, bred in the woods, whose senses have been nourished by their fair and appeasing changes, year after year, without design and without heed,—shall not lose their lesson altogether, in the roar of cities or the broil of politics. Long hereafter, amidst agitation and terror in national councils,—in the hour of revolution,—these solemn images shall reappear in their morning lustre, as fit symbols and words of the thoughts which the passing events shall awaken. At the call of a noble sentiment, again the woods wave, the pines murmur, the river rolls and shines, and the cattle low upon the mountains, as he saw and heard them in his infancy. And with these forms, the spells of persuasion, the keys of power are put into his hands.

3. We are thus assisted by natural objects in the expression of particular meanings. But how great a language to convey such pepper-corn informations! Did it need such noble races of creatures, this profusion of forms, this host of orbs in heaven, to furnish man with the dictionary and grammar of his municipal speech? Whilst we use this grand cipher to expedite the affairs of our pot and kettle, we feel that we have not yet put it to its use, neither are able. We are like travelers using the cinders of a volcano to roast their eggs. Whilst we see that it always stands ready to clothe what we would say, we cannot avoid the question whether the characters are not significant of themselves. Have mountains, and waves, and skies, no significance but what we consciously give them when we employ them as emblems of our thoughts? The world is emblematic. Parts of speech are metaphors, because the whole of nature is a metaphor of the human mind. The laws of moral nature answer to those of matter as face to face in a glass. "The visible world and the relation of its parts, is the dial plate of the invisible." The axioms of physics translate the laws of ethics. Thus, "the whole is greater than its part"; "reaction is equal to action"; "the smallest weight may be made to lift the greatest, the difference of weight being compensated by time"; and many the like propositions, which

have an ethical as well as physical sense. These propositions have a much more extensive and universal sense when applied to human life, than when confined to technical use.

In like manner, the memorable words of history and the proverbs of nations consist usually of a natural fact, selected as a picture or parable of a moral truth. Thus; A rolling stone gathers no moss; A bird in the hand is worth two in the bush; A cripple in the right way will beat a racer in the wrong; Make hay while the sun shines; 'Tis hard to carry a full cup even; Vinegar is the son of wine; The last ounce broke the camel's back; Long-lived trees make roots first;—and the like. In their primary sense these are trivial facts, but we repeat them for the value of their analogical import. What is true of proverbs, is true of all fables, parables, and allegories.

This relation between the mind and matter is not fancied by some poet, but stands in the will of God, and so is free to be known by all men. It appears to men, or it does not appear. When in fortunate hours we ponder this miracle, the wise man doubts if at all other times he is not blind and deaf;

> "Can such things be,
> And overcome us like a summer's cloud,
> Without our special wonder?"

for the universe becomes transparent, and the light of higher laws than its own shines through it. It is the standing problem which has exercised the wonder and the study of every fine genius since the world began; from the era of the Egyptians and the Brahmins to that of Pythagoras, of Plato, of Bacon, of Leibnitz, of Swedenborg. There sits the Sphinx at the road-side, and from age to age, as each prophet comes by, he tries his fortune at reading her riddle. There seems to be a necessity in spirit to manifest itself in material forms; and day and night, river and storm, beast and bird, acid and alkali, preëxist in necessary Ideas in the mind of God, and are what they are by virtue of preceding affections in the world of spirit. A Fact is the end or last issue of spirit. The visible creation is the terminus or the circumference of the invisible world. "Material objects," said a French philosopher, "are necessarily kinds of *scoriae* of the substantial thoughts of the Creator, which must always preserve an exact relation to their first origin; in other words, visible nature must have a spiritual and moral side."

This doctrine is abstruse, and though the images of "garment," "scoriae," "mirror," etc., may stimulate the fancy, we must summon the aid of subtler and more vital expositors to make it plain. "Every scripture is to be interpreted by the same spirit which gave it forth,"—is the fundamental law of criticism. A life in harmony with Nature, the love of truth and of virtue, will purge the eyes to understand her text. By degrees we may come to know the primitive sense of the permanent objects of nature, so that the world shall be to us an open book, and every form significant of its hidden life and final cause.

A new interest surprises us, whilst, under the view now suggested, we contemplate the fearful extent and multitude of objects; since "every object rightly seen, unlocks a new faculty of the soul." That which was unconscious truth, becomes, when interpreted and defined in an object, a part of the domain of knowledge,—a new weapon in the magazine of power.

Margaret Fuller

Dialogue

 1840

This miniature erotic lyric by Margaret Fuller—simultaneously cocky about the human ability to attract the attention of the cosmos, and terrified of the shortness of its attention span—was published in the first issue of the Transcendentalist journal *The Dial.* Some 150 years after her death (born in Cambridgeport in 1810, she died in a shipwreck in 1850 with her husband and child while returning from covering the Italian revolution as a journalist), Fuller is now widely recognized as a major figure in American intellectual history. Above all, she was committed to the idea that no human being should be obstructed by circumstances of birth from the opportunity for self-fulfillment.

DAHLIA

My cup already doth with light o'errun.
   Descend, fair sun;
I am all crimsoned for the bridal hour,
   Come to thy flower.

THE SUN

Ah, if I pause, my work will not be done,
   On I must run,
The mountains wait.—I love thee, lustrous flower,
   But give to love no hour.

Richard Henry Dana, Jr.

From Two Years before the Mast

 1840

Born to a family of high social rank in a house that still stands adjacent to Harvard Yard, Richard Henry Dana, Jr. (1815–1878) is one of those writers doomed to be known as precursor to a genius. The figure by whose brightness his reputation has been dimmed is Herman Melville, who admired *Two Years before the Mast* and learned from its account of shipboard life as experienced by a novice sailor. The young Dana had that peculiar combination of restiveness (he was rusticated from Harvard for taking part in a student revolt) and vulnerability (a bout of measles weakened his eyes) for which the standard prescription in his day was an arduous ocean journey. The result was a compelling book about his two years' voyage around Cape Horn on merchant vessels chartered to bring back hides from California. In the short excerpt that follows, he meditates on his first encounter with sudden death, and captures the peculiar combination of superstition and stoic bravery with which seasoned sailors faced the terrors of the sea.

Monday, November 19th. This was a black day in our calendar. At seven o'clock in the morning, it being our watch below, we were aroused from a sound sleep by the cry of "All hands ahoy! a man overboard!" This unwonted cry sent a thrill through the heart of every one, and, hurrying on deck, we found the vessel hove flat aback, with all her studding-sails set; for, the boy who was at the helm leaving it to throw something overboard, the carpenter, who was an old sailor, knowing that the wind was light, put the helm down and hove her aback. The watch on deck were lowering away the quarter-boat, and I got on deck just in time to fling myself into her as she was leaving the side; but it was not until out upon the wide Pacific, in our little boat, that I knew whom we had lost. It was George Ballmer, the young English sailor, whom I have before spoken of as the life of the crew. He was prized by the officers as an active and willing seaman, and by the men as a lively, hearty fellow, and a good ship-mate. He was going aloft to fit a strap round the maintopmast-head, for ringtail halyards, and had the strap and block, a coil of halyards, and a marline-spike about his neck. He fell from the starboard futtock shrouds, and, not knowing how to swim, and being heavily dressed, with all those things round his neck, he probably sank immediately. We pulled astern, in the direction in which he fell, and though we knew that there was no hope of saving him, yet no one wished to speak of returning, and we rowed about for nearly an hour, without an idea of doing anything, but unwilling to acknowledge to ourselves that we must give him up. At length we turned the boat's head and made towards the brig.

Death is at all times solemn, but never so much so as at sea. A man dies on shore; his body remains with his friends, and "the mourners go about the streets"; but when a man falls overboard at sea and is lost, there is a suddenness in the event, and a difficulty in realising it, which give to it an air of awful mystery. A man dies on shore—you follow his body to the grave, and a stone marks the spot. You are often prepared for the event. There is always something which helps you to realise it when it happens, and to recall it when it has passed. A man is shot down by your side in battle, and the mangled body remains an object and a real evidence; but at sea, the man is near you—at your side—you hear his voice, and in an instant he is gone, and nothing but a vacancy shows his loss. Then, too, at sea—to use a homely but expressive phrase—you *miss* a man so much. A dozen men are shut up together in a little bark upon the wide, wide sea, and for months and months see no forms and hear no voices but their own, and one is taken suddenly from among them, and they miss him at every turn. It is like losing a limb. There are no new faces or new scenes to fill up the gap. There is always an empty berth in the forecastle, and one man wanting when the small night watch is mustered. There is one less to take the wheel, and one less to lay out with you upon the yard. You miss his form and the sound of his voice, for habit had made them almost necessary to you, and each of your senses feels the loss.

All these things make such a death peculiarly solemn, and the effect of it remains upon the crew for some time. There is more kindness shown by the officers to the crew, and by the crew to one another. There is more quietness and seriousness. The oath and the loud laugh are gone. The officers are more watchful, and the crew go more carefully aloft. The lost man is seldom mentioned, or is dismissed with a sailor's rude eulogy—"Well, poor George is gone! His cruise is up soon! He knew his work, and did his duty, and was a good shipmate." Then usually follows some allusion to another world, for sailors are almost all believers in their way; though their notions and opinions are unfixed and at loose ends. They say, "God won't be hard upon the poor fellow," and seldom get beyond the common phrase which seems to imply that their sufferings and hard treatment here will be passed to their credit in the books of the Great Captain hereafter—"*To work hard, live hard, die hard, and go to hell after all, would be hard indeed!*" Our cook, a simple-hearted old African, who had been through a good deal in his day, and was rather seriously inclined, always going to church twice a day when on shore, and reading his Bible on a Sunday in the galley, talked to the crew about spending the Lord's-day badly, and told them that they might go as suddenly as George had, and be as little prepared.

Yet a sailor's life is at best but a mixture of a little good with much evil, and a little pleasure with much pain. The beautiful is linked with the revolting, the sublime with the commonplace, and the solemn with the ludicrous.

Not long after we had returned on board with our sad report, an auction was held of the poor man's effects. The captain had first, however, called all hands aft, and asked them if they were satisfied that everything had been done to save the man, and if they thought there was any use in remaining there longer. The crew all said that it was in vain, for the man did not know how to swim, and was very heavily dressed. So we then filed away, and kept the brig off to her course.

The laws regulating navigation make the captain answerable for the effects of a sailor who dies during the voyage, and it is either a law or a custom, established for convenience, that the captain should soon hold an auction of his things, in which they are bid off by the sailors, and the sums which they give are deducted from their wages at the end of the voyage. In this way the trouble and risk of keeping his things through the voyage are avoided, and the clothes are usually sold for more than they would be worth on shore. Accordingly, we had no sooner got the ship before the wind than his chest was brought up upon the forecastle, and the sale began. The jackets and trousers in which we had seen him dressed so lately were exposed and bid off while the life was hardly out of his body, and his chest was taken aft, and used as a store-chest, so that there was nothing left which could be called *his*. Sailors have unwillingness to wear a dead man's clothes during the same voyage, and they seldom do so, unless they are in absolute want.

NATHANIEL HAWTHORNE

From American Notebooks

 1843

Writing in April 1843, in his house in Concord, Massachusetts, Nathaniel Hawthorne (1804–1864) takes note of "winter and spring . . . struggling for . . . mastery"
outside his study window. Hawthorne describes the annual contest with characteristic self-rebuke for allowing exuberance to take over his imagination—as if the tardi-
ness and brevity of a New England spring, that fleeting season squeezed between ice
and heat, have made him wary of crediting its promise of life-renewal.

TUESDAY, APRIL 25TH, [1843].

Spring is advancing, sometimes with sunny days, and sometimes—as is the
case now—with chill, moist, sullen ones. There is an influence in the season
that makes it almost impossible for me to bring my mind down to literary
employment—perhaps because several months' pretty constant work has exhausted that species of energy—perhaps because, in Spring, it is more natural
to labor actively than to think. But my impulse is to be idle altogether;—to lie
in the sun, or wander about and look at the revival of Nature from her death-
like slumber;—or to be borne down the current of the river in my boat. If I
had wings I would gladly fly; yet would prefer to be wafted along by a breeze,
sometimes alighting on a patch of green grass, then gently whirled away to a
still sunnier spot . . . But here I linger upon earth, very happy, it is true, at
bottom, but a good deal troubled with the sense of imbecility—one of the
dismallest sensations, methinks, that mortal can experience—the consciousness of a blunted pen, benumbed figures, and a mind no longer capable of a
vigorous grasp. My torpidity of intellect makes me irritable . . .

Oh, how blest should I be, were there nothing to do! Then I would watch
every inch and hair's breadth of the progress of the season; and not a leaf
should put itself forth, in the vicinity of our old mansion, without my noting
it. But now, with the burthen of a continual task upon me, I have not freedom of mind to make such observations. I merely see what is going on, in a
very general way. The snow, which, two or three weeks ago, covered hill and
valley, is now diminished to one or two solitary specks, in the visible land-

scape; though, doubtless, there are still heaps of it in the shady places of the woods. There have been no violent rains to carry it off; it has diminished gradually, inch by inch, and day after day; and I observed, along the roadside, that the green blades of grass had sometimes sprouted on the very edge of the snow drift, the moment that the earth was uncovered. The pastures and grass-fields have not yet a general effect of green; nor have they that cheerless brown tint, which they wear in latter autumn, when vegetation has entirely ceased. There is now a suspicion of verdure—the faint shadow of it—but not the warm reality. Some tracts, in a happy exposure—there is one such tract across the river; the carefully cultivated mowing-field in front of an old red home-stead—such patches of land wear a beautiful and tender green, which no other season will equal; because, let the grass be green as it may hereafter, it will not be so set off by surrounding barrenness. The trees, in our orchard and elsewhere, have as yet no leaves; yet, to the most careless eye, they appear full of life and vegetable blood. It seems as if, by one magic touch, they might in-stantaneously put forth all their foliage, and that the wind, which now sighs through their naked branches, might all at once find itself impeded by innu-merable leaves. This sudden development would be scarcely more wonderful than the gleam of verdure which often brightens in a moment, as it were, along the slope of a bank, or roadside; it is like a gleam of sunlight. A moment ago, it was brown, like the rest of the scenery; look again, and there is an ap-parition of green grass. The Spring, no doubt, comes onward with fleeter footsteps, because Winter has lingered so long, that, at best, she can hardly re-trieve half the allotted term of her reign.

The river, this season, has encroached farther on the land than it has been known to do for twenty years past. It has formed, along its course, a succes-sion of lakes, with a current through the midst. My boat has lain at the bot-tom of the orchard, in very convenient proximity to the house. It has borne me over stone-fences; and a few days ago, Ellery Channing and I passed through a pair of bars into the great northern road, along which we paddled a considerable distance. The trees have a singular appearance in the midst of waters; the curtailment of their trunks quite destroys the proportions of the whole tree; and we become conscious of a regularity and propriety in the forms of Nature, by the effect of this abbreviation. The waters are now subsid-ing, but gradually;—islands become annexed to the main-land, and other is-lands emerge from the flood, and will soon, likewise, be connected with the continent. We have seen, on a small scale, the process of the deluge, and can now witness that of the reappearance of the earth.

Crows visited us, long before the snow was off; they seem mostly to have departed now; or else to have betaken themselves to remote depths of the woods, which they haunt all summer long. Ducks have come in considerable numbers, and many sportsmen wait in pursuit of them, along the river; but they also have now made themselves scarce. Gulls come up from seaward, and soar high overhead, flapping their broad wings in the upper sunshine. They are among the most picturesque birds that I am acquainted with—indeed, quite the most so—because the manner of their flight makes them almost stationary parts of a landscape; the imagination has time to rest upon them—they have not flitted away in a moment. You go up among the clouds, and lay hold of these soaring gulls, and repose with them upon the sustaining atmosphere. The smaller birds—the birds that build their nests in our trees, and sing for us at morning-red—I leave to my wife to describe. She is birdlike in many things, and loves them as if they were her own kindred. But I must mention the great companies of blackbirds—more than the famous "four-and-twenty," who were baked in a pie—that congregate in the tops of contiguous trees, and vociferate with all the clamor of a turbulent political meeting. Politics must certainly be the occasion of such a tumultuous debate; but still there is a melody in each individual utterance, and a harmony in the general effect. Mr. Thoreau tells me that these noisy assemblages consist of three different species of black-birds—one of them the crow-blackbird—but I forget the other two. Robins have been long among us; and swallows have more recently arrived.

WEDNESDAY, APRIL 26TH, [1843].

Here is another misty day, muffling the sun. The lilac-shrubs, under my study-window, are almost in leaf; in two or three days more, I may put forth my hand and pluck a green bough. These lilacs appear to be very aged, and have lost the luxuriant foliage of their prime. Old age has a singular aspect in lilacs, rose-bushes, and other ornamental shrubs; it seems as if such things, as they grow only for beauty, ought to flourish in immortal youth, or, at least, to die before their decrepitude. They are trees of Paradise, and therefore not naturally subject to decay, but have lost their birthright by being transplanted hither. But there is a kind of ludicrous unfitness in the idea of a venerable rose-bush; and there is something analogous to this in human life. Persons who can only be graceful and ornamental—who can give the world nothing but flowers—should die young, and never be seen with grey hairs and wrinkles, any more than the flower-shrubs with mossy bark and scanty foliage, like the lilacs under my window. Not that beauty is not worthy of immortality—nothing else, indeed, is worthy of it—and thence, perhaps, the sense of impropriety, when we see it triumphed over by time. Apple-trees, on the other hand, grow old without reproach; let them live as long as they may, and con-tort themselves in whatever fashion they please, they are still respectable, even if they afford us only an apple or two in a season, or none at all. Human flower-shrubs, if they will grow old on earth, should, beside their lovely blos-soms, bear some kind of fruit that will satisfy earthly appetites; else men will not be satisfied that the moss should gather on them.

Winter and spring are now struggling for the mastery in my study; and I yield somewhat to each, and wholly to neither. The window is open; and there is a fire in the stove. The day when the window is first thrown open should be an epoch in the year; but I have forgotten to record it. Seventy or eighty springs have visited this old house; and sixty of them found old Dr. Ripley here—not always old, it is true, but gradually getting wrinkles and gray hairs, and looking more and more the picture of winter; but he was no flower-shrub, but one of those fruit trees, or timber trees, that acquire a grace with their old age. Last Spring found the house solitary, for the first time since it was built; and now again she peeps into our open windows, and finds new faces here. Methinks my little wife is twin-sister of the Spring; so they should greet one another tenderly; for they both are fresh and dewy, both full of hope and cheerfulness, both have bird-voices always singing out of their hearts, both are sometimes overcast with flitting mists, which only make the flowers bloom brighter; and both have a power to renew and re-create the weary spirit. I have married the Spring!—I am husband to the month of May!

It is remarkable how much uncleanness Winter brings with it, or leaves be-hind it. My dearest wife has almost toiled herself to death with endeavors to purify her empire within the house; and the yard, garden, and avenue, which should be my department, require a still greater amount of labor. The avenue is strewed with withered leaves—the whole crop, apparently, of last year, some of which my wife has raked into heaps, intending to make a bonfire of them. I wonder what becomes of them, when there is no "neat-handed Phillis" to sweep them away. There are quantities of decayed branches, which one tem-pest after another has flung down, black and rotten. In the garden, are the old cabbages, which we did not think worth gathering, last Autumn; and the dry bean-vines, and the withered stalks of the asparagus bed;—in short, all the wrecks of the departed year—her mouldering relics—her dry bones. It is a pity that the world cannot be really made over anew, every spring. Then in the yard, there are the piles of fire-wood, which I ought to have sawed and thrown into the shed, long since, but which will cumber the earth, I fear, till June at least. Quantities of chips are strewn about; and on removing them, we find the yellow stalks of grass sprouting underneath. Nature does her best to beautify this disarray. The grass springs up most industriously, especially in sheltered and sunny angles of the buildings, or round the door-steps—a locality which seems particularly favorable to its growth; for it is already high enough to bend over, and wave in the wind. I was surprised to observe that some weeds—especially a plant that stains the fingers with its yellow juice—had lived, and retained their freshness and sap as perfectly as in summer—through all the frosts and snows of last winter. I saw them, the last green thing in the Autumn, and here they are again, the first in the summer.

PETER OLIVER

From The History of the Puritan Commonwealth
 1856

In a journal entry of December 1640 long regarded as a classic expression of the Puritan belief that the smallest events and natural phenomena are messages sent by God, John Winthrop noted that copies in his son's library of the Book of Common Prayer (the keystone of the Anglican liturgy, of which Puritans disapproved) had been eaten through by mice while copies of the New Testament and Psalms remained intact. Winthrop's modern editors, Richard Dunn and Letitia Yeandle, remark that "the puritanical mouse was actually not quite so discriminating, for fewer than half of the Anglican Prayer Book leaves are nibbled, and then only at the tips of the lower right-hand corners." Long preceding them, in a remarkable anticipation of modern ideas about the psychological basis of religious belief, the Boston attorney Peter Oliver (1822–1855), who was descended from a distinguished Episcopalian family, wrote in his posthumously published *History of the Puritan Commonwealth* the following withering comment on what he called Puritan "superstition."

It is a curious trait of the human mind, that it seeks refuge from uncertainty in superstition. It is a triumph of imagination over reason. A dream, a comet, the shape of a pebble, are oracles where revelation is forsaken or unknown. A ship without a rudder is at the mercy of the element she was designed to override; and the mind unsteadied by principle, or wandering from the truth, may easily become the slave of superstition. So it was when the despairing Saul endeavored to rend the veil which shielded the gloomy future from his bloodshot eye. So it is whenever the rustic maid crosses with silver the palm of the gipsy vagabond. To sources of a kindred nature, the Puritan Pilgrims applied for excuses to justify their schism. Looking steadfastly in one direction, absorbed by only one interest, they neglected the broad and beaming sun for the specks and motes which floated in his rays. Among the strange noises, the terrible meteors, and the sudden catastrophes, which abound in the early histories of Massachusetts, a more unpretending incident finds place, which exhibits an amusing picture of enmity and superstition, only ten years after Winthrop's fleet had unmoored in the harbor of Southampton. "About this time fell out a thing worthy of observation. One of the magistrates having many books in a chamber where there was corn of divers sorts, had among them one, wherein the Greek Testament, the Psalms, and the Common Prayer were bound together. He found the Common Prayer eaten with mice, every leaf of it, and not any of the two other touched, nor any other of his books, though there were above a thousand." Had Puritanism been certain of a divine mission, it would never have embalmed such a fact as this, dug out of an old store-room, whose only occupants were a few starving mice and a mouldy heap of corn and books. Truth needs no such auxiliaries, and can always afford to be generous.

EMILY DICKINSON

Four Trees upon a Solitary Acre

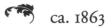 ca. 1863

Emily Dickinson (1830–1886) spent virtually her entire life in Amherst, Massachu-setts, but her imagination was roving and uncontainable. No poet surpassed the precision and power with which she expressed what is conventionally called the nineteenth-century "loss of faith"—as a vast gap opened between the old religious platitudes New Englanders still heard in their churches and the new universe of im-personal forces that science was beginning to disclose. This poem, stark and re-served compared to countless contemporary effusions about the wisdom and solace to be found in nature, is typically poised between dismay at the impenetrability of nature to human understanding and delight at its inviolable remoteness.

Four Trees – upon a solitary Acre –
Without Design
Or Order, or Apparent Action –
Maintain –

The Sun – upon a Morning meets them –
The Wind –
No nearer Neighbor – have they –
But God –

The Acre gives them – Place –
They – Him – Attention of Passer by –
Of Shadow, or of Squirrel, haply –
Or Boy –

What Deed is Theirs unto the General Nature –
What Plan
They severally – retard – or further –
Unknown –

HENRY DAVID THOREAU

From The Maine Woods

 1864

In the late summer of 1846, when he was living in the cabin he had built at Walden Pond, near Concord, Massachusetts, Henry David Thoreau (1817–1862) took a two-month trip in the company of his cousin and two acquaintances from Bangor to the forest of northern Maine. Two years later he published an essay, "Ktaadn," describing the experience of climbing the mile-high mountain now known as Katahdin—a work that, in revised form, ultimately became part of his posthumously published book *The Maine Woods*. As if he were retracing Satan's journey through chaos (the interpolated poetry is from Milton's *Paradise Lost*), Thoreau turns the narrative into a soliloquy on his and the world's destiny. Moving farther and farther beyond all traces of any human presence save his own, he feels himself touching the bedrock of creation: "Talk of mysteries! . . . rocks, trees, wind on our cheeks! the *solid* earth! the *actual* world! . . . *Contact! Contact! Who* are we? *where* are we?" What follows is the great passage in which he describes this encounter with "primeval, untamed, and forever untameable *Nature*"—as, having left his companions for a time, he climbs the mountain alone.

At length we reached an elevation sufficiently bare to afford a view of the summit, still distant and blue, almost as if retreating from us. A torrent, which proved to be the same we had crossed, was seen tumbling down in front, literally from out of the clouds. But this glimpse at our whereabouts was soon lost, and we were buried in the woods again. The wood was chiefly yellow birch, spruce, fir, mountain-ash, or round-wood, as the Maine people call it, and moose-wood. It was the worst kind of travelling; sometimes like the densest scrub-oak patches with us. The cornel, or bunch-berries, were very abundant, as well as Solomon's seal and moose-berries. Blueberries were distributed along our whole route; and in one place the bushes were drooping with the weight of the fruit, still as fresh as ever. It was the 7th of September. Such patches afforded a grateful repast, and served to bait the tired party forward. When any lagged behind, the cry of "blueberries" was most effectual to bring them up. Even at this elevation we passed through a moose-yard, formed by a large flat rock, four or five rods square, where they tread down the snow in winter. At length, fearing that if we held the direct course to the summit, we should not find any water near our camping-ground, we gradually swerved to the west, till, at four o'clock, we struck again the torrent which I have mentioned, and here, in view of the summit, the weary party decided to camp that night.

While my companions were seeking a suitable spot for this purpose, I improved the little daylight that was left, in climbing the mountain alone. We were in a deep and narrow ravine, sloping up to the clouds, at an angle of nearly forty-five degrees, and hemmed in by walls of rock, which were at first covered with low trees, then with impenetrable thickets of scraggy birches and spruce-trees, and with moss, but at last bare of all vegetation but lichens, and almost continually draped in clouds. Following up the course of the torrent which occupied this,—and I mean to lay some emphasis on this word *up,*— pulling myself up by the side of perpendicular falls of twenty or thirty feet, by the roots of firs and birches, and then, perhaps, walking a level rod or two in the thin stream, for it took up the whole road, ascending by huge steps, as it were, a giant's stairway, down which a river flowed, I had soon cleared the trees, and paused on the successive shelves, to look back over the country. The torrent was from fifteen to thirty feet wide, without a tributary, and seemingly not diminishing in breadth as I advanced; but still it came rushing and roaring down, with a copious tide, over and amidst masses of bare rock, from the very clouds, as though a waterspout had just burst over the mountain. Leaving this at last, I began to work my way, scarcely less arduous than Satan's anciently through Chaos, up the nearest, though not the highest peak. At first scrambling on all fours over the tops of ancient black spruce-trees *(Abies nigra),* old as the flood, from two to ten or twelve feet in height, their tops flat and spreading, and their foliage blue, and nipt with cold, as if for centuries they had ceased growing upward against the bleak sky, the solid cold. I walked some good rods erect upon the tops of these trees, which were overgrown with moss and mountain-cranberries. It seemed that in the course of time they had filled up the intervals between the huge rocks, and the cold wind had uniformly levelled all over. Here the principle of vegetation was hard put to it. There was apparently a belt of this kind running quite round the mountain, though, perhaps, nowhere so remarkable as here. Once, slumping through, I looked down ten feet, into a dark and cavernous region, and saw the stem of a spruce, on whose top I stood, as on a mass of coarse basket-work, fully nine inches in diameter at the ground. These holes were bears' dens, and the bears were even then at home. This was the sort of garden I made my way *over,* for an eighth of a mile, at the risk, it is true, of treading on some of the plants, not seeing any path *through* it,—certainly the most treacherous and porous country I ever travelled.

> "Nigh foundered on he fares,
> Treading the crude consistence, half on foot,
> Half flying."

But nothing could exceed the toughness of the twigs,—not one snapped under my weight, for they had slowly grown. Having slumped, scrambled, rolled, bounced, and walked, by turns, over this scraggy country, I arrived upon a side-hill, or rather side-mountain, where rocks, gray, silent rocks, were the flocks and herds that pastured, chewing a rocky cud at sunset. They looked at me with hard gray eyes, without a bleat or a low. This brought me to the skirt of a cloud, and bounded my walk that night. But I had already seen that Maine country when I turned about, waving, flowing, rippling, down below.

When I returned to my companions, they had selected a camping ground on the torrent's edge, and were resting on the ground; one was on the sick list, rolled in a blanket, on a damp shelf of rock. It was a savage and dreary scenery enough; so wildly rough, that they looked long to find a level and open space for the tent. We could not well camp higher, for want of fuel; and the trees here seemed so evergreen and sappy, that we almost doubted if they would acknowledge the influence of fire; but fire prevailed at last, and blazed here, too, like a good citizen of the world. Even at this height we met with frequent traces of moose, as well as of bears. As here was no cedar, we made our bed of coarser feathered spruce; but at any rate the feathers were plucked from the live tree. It was, perhaps, even a more grand and desolate place for a night's lodging than the summit would have been, being in the neighborhood of those wild trees, and of the torrent. Some more aerial and finer-spirited winds rushed and roared through the ravine all night, from time to time arousing our fire, and dispersing the embers about. It was as if we lay in the very nest of a young whirlwind. At midnight, one of my bedfellows, being startled in his dreams by the sudden blazing up to its top of a fir-tree, whose green boughs were dried by the heat, sprang up, with a cry, from his bed, thinking the world on fire, and drew the whole camp after him.

In the morning, after whetting our appetite on some raw pork, a wafer of hard bread, and a dipper of condensed cloud or waterspout, we all together began to make our way up the falls, which I have described; this time choosing the right hand, or highest peak, which was not the one I had approached before. But soon my companions were lost to my sight behind the mountain ridge in my rear, which still seemed ever retreating before me, and I climbed alone over huge rocks, loosely poised, a mile or more, still edging toward the clouds; for though the day was clear elsewhere, the summit was concealed by mist. The mountain seemed a vast aggregation of loose rocks, as if some time it had rained rocks, and they lay as they fell on the mountain sides, nowhere fairly at rest, but leaning on each other, all rocking-stones, with cavities between, but scarcely any soil or smoother shelf. They were the raw materials of a planet dropped from an unseen quarry, which the vast chemistry of nature would anon work up, or work down, into the smiling and verdant plains and valleys of earth. This was an undone extremity of the globe; as in lignite, we see coal in the process of formation.

At length I entered within the skirts of the cloud which seemed forever drifting over the summit, and yet would never be gone, but was generated out of that pure air as fast as it flowed away; and when, a quarter of a mile farther, I reached the summit of the ridge, which those who have seen in clearer weather say is about five miles long, and contains a thousand acres of table-land, I was deep within the hostile ranks of clouds, and all objects were obscured by them. Now the wind would blow me out a yard of clear sunlight, wherein I stood; then a gray, dawning light was all it could accomplish, the cloud-line ever rising and falling with the wind's intensity. Sometimes it seemed as if the summit would be cleared in a few moments, and smile in sunshine: but what was gained on one side was lost on another. It was like sitting in a chimney and waiting for the smoke to blow away. It was, in fact, a cloud-factory,—these were the cloud-works, and the wind turned them off done from the cool, bare rocks. Occasionally, when the windy columns broke in to me, I caught sight of a dark, damp crag to the right or left; the mist driving ceaselessly between it and me. It reminded me of the creations of the old epic and dramatic poets, of Atlas, Vulcan, the Cyclops, and Prometheus. Such was Caucasus and the rock where Prometheus was bound. Æschylus had no doubt visited such scenery as this. It was vast, Titanic, and such as man never inhabits. Some part of the beholder, even some vital part, seems to escape through the loose grating of his ribs as he ascends. He is more lone than you can imagine. There is less of substantial thought and fair understanding in him, than in the plains where men inhabit. His reason is dispersed and shadowy, more thin and subtile, like the air. Vast, Titanic, inhuman Nature has got him at disadvantage, caught him alone, and pilfers him of some of his divine faculty. She does not smile on him as in the plains. She seems to say sternly, why came ye here before your time? This ground is not prepared for you. Is it not enough that I smile in the valleys? I have never made this soil for thy feet, this air for thy breathing, these rocks for thy neighbors. I cannot pity nor fondle thee here, but forever relentlessly drive thee hence to where I *am* kind. Why seek me where I have not called thee, and then complain because you find me but a stepmother? Shouldst thou freeze or starve, or shudder thy life away, here is no shrine, nor altar, nor any access to my ear.

"Chaos and ancient Night, I come no spy
With purpose to explore or to disturb
The secrets of your realm, but . . .
. . . . . as my way
Lies through your spacious empire up to light."

The tops of mountains are among the unfinished parts of the globe, whither it is a slight insult to the gods to climb and pry into their secrets, and try their effect on our humanity. Only daring and insolent men, perchance, go there. Simple races, as savages, do not climb mountains,—their tops are sacred and mysterious tracts never visited by them. Pomola is always angry with those who climb to the summit of Ktaadn.

According to Jackson, who, in his capacity of geological surveyor of the State, has accurately measured it,—the altitude of Ktaadn is 5,300 feet, or a little more than one mile above the level of the sea,—and he adds, "It is then evidently the highest point in the State of Maine, and is the most abrupt granite mountain in New England." The peculiarities of that spacious table-land on which I was standing, as well as the remarkable semi circular precipice or basin on the eastern side, were all concealed by the mist. I had brought my whole pack to the top, not knowing but I should have to make my descent to the river, and possibly to the settled portion of the State alone, and by some other route, and wishing to have a complete outfit with me. But at length, fearing that my companions would be anxious to reach the river before night, and knowing that the clouds might rest on the mountain for days, I was compelled to descend. Occasionally, as I came down, the wind would blow me a vista open, through which I could see the country eastward, boundless forests, and lakes, and streams, gleaming in the sun, some of them emptying into the East Branch. There were also new mountains in sight in that direction. Now and then some small bird of the sparrow family would flit away before me, unable to command its course, like a fragment of the gray rock blown off by the wind.

I found my companions where I had left them, on the side of the peak, gathering the mountain cranberries, which filled every crevice between the rocks, together with blueberries, which had a spicier flavor the higher up they grew, but were not the less agreeable to our palates. When the country is settled, and roads are made, these cranberries will perhaps become an article of commerce. From this elevation, just on the skirts of the clouds, we could overlook the country, west and south, for a hundred miles. There it was, the State of Maine, which we had seen on the map, but not much like that,—immeasurable forest for the sun to shine on, that eastern *stuff* we hear of in Massachusetts. No clearing, no house. It did not look as if a solitary traveller had cut so much as a walking-stick there. Countless lakes,—Moosehead in the southwest, forty miles long by ten wide, like a gleaming silver platter at the end of the table; Chesuncook, eighteen long by three wide, without an island; Millinocket, on the south, with its hundred islands; and a hundred others without a name; and mountains also, whose names, for the most part, are known only to the Indians. The forest looked like a firm grass sward, and the effect of these lakes in its midst has been well compared, by one who has since visited this same spot, to that of a "mirror broken into a thousand fragments, and wildly scattered over the grass, reflecting the full blaze of the sun." It was a large farm for somebody, when cleared. According to the Gazetteer, which was printed before the boundary question was settled, this single Penobscot county, in which we were, was larger than the whole State of Vermont, with its fourteen counties; and this was only a part of the wild lands of Maine. We are concerned now, however, about natural, not political limits. We were about eighty miles, as the bird flies, from Bangor, or one hundred and fifteen, as we had rode, and walked, and paddled. We had to console ourselves with the reflection that this view was probably as good as that from the peak, as far as it went; and what were a mountain without its attendant clouds and mists? Like ourselves, neither Bailey nor Jackson had obtained a clear view from the summit.

Setting out on our return to the river, still at an early hour in the day, we decided to follow the course of the torrent, which we supposed to be Murch Brook, as long as it would not lead us too far out of our way. We thus travelled about four miles in the very torrent itself, continually crossing and recrossing it, leaping from rock to rock, and jumping with the stream down falls of seven or eight feet, or sometimes sliding down on our backs in a thin sheet of water. This ravine had been the scene of an extraordinary freshet in the spring, apparently accompanied by a slide from the mountain. It must have been filled with a stream of stones and water, at least twenty feet above the present level of the torrent. For a rod or two, on either side of its channel, the trees were barked and splintered up to their tops, the birches bent over, twisted, and sometimes finely split, like a stable-broom; some, a foot in diameter, snapped off, and whole clumps of trees bent over with the weight of rocks piled on them. In one place we noticed a rock, two or three feet in diameter, lodged nearly twenty feet high in the crotch of a tree. For the whole four miles, we saw but one rill emptying in, and the volume of water did not seem to be increased from the first. We travelled thus very rapidly with a downward impetus, and grew remarkably expert at leaping from rock to rock, for leap we must, and leap we did, whether there was any rock at the right distance or not. It was a pleasant picture when the foremost turned about and looked up the winding ravine, walled in with rocks and the green forest, to see, at inter-vals of a rod or two, a red-shirted or green-jacketed mountaineer against the white torrent, leaping down the channel with his pack on his back, or pausing upon a convenient rock in the midst of the torrent to mend a rent in his clothes, or unstrap the dipper at his belt to take a draught of the water. At one place we were startled by seeing, on a little sandy shelf by the side of the stream, the fresh print of a man's foot, and for a moment realized how Robin-son Crusoe felt in a similar case; but at last we remembered that we had struck this stream on our way up, though we could not have told where, and one had descended into the ravine for a drink. The cool air above, and the continual bathing of our bodies in mountain water, alternate foot, sitz, douche, and plunge baths, made this walk exceedingly refreshing, and we had travelled only a mile or two, after leaving the torrent, before every thread of our clothes was as dry as usual, owing perhaps to a peculiar quality in the atmosphere.

After leaving the torrent, being in doubt about our course, Tom threw down his pack at the foot of the loftiest spruce tree at hand, and shinned up the bare trunk, some twenty feet, and then climbed through the green tower, lost to our sight, until he held the topmost spray in his hand.* McCauslin, in his younger days, had marched through the wilderness with a body of troops, under General Somebody, and with one other man did all the scouting and spying service. The General's word was, "Throw down the top of that tree," and there was no tree in the Maine woods so high that it did not lose its top in such a case. I have heard a story of two men being lost once in these woods, nearer to the settlements than this, who climbed the loftiest pine they could find, some six feet in diameter at the ground, from whose top they discovered a solitary clearing and its smoke. When at this height, some two hundred feet from the ground, one of them became dizzy, and fainted in his companion's arms, and the latter had to accomplish the descent with him, alternately faint-ing and reviving, as best he could. To Tom we cried, Where away does the summit bear? where the burnt lands? The last he could only conjecture; he descried, however, a little meadow and pond, lying probably in our course, which we concluded to steer for. On reaching this secluded meadow, we found fresh tracks of moose on the shore of the pond, and the water was still

---

* "The spruce-tree," says Springer in '51, "is generally selected, principally for the superior facilities which its numerous limbs afford the climber. To gain the first limbs of this tree, which are from twenty to forty feet from the ground, a smaller tree is undercut and lodged against it, clambering up which the top of the spruce is reached. In some cases, when a very elevated position is desired, the spruce-tree is lodged against the trunk of some lofty pine, up which we ascend to a height twice that of the surrounding forest."

To indicate the direction of pines, he throws down a branch, and a man at the ground takes the bearing.

unsettled as if they had fled before us. A little farther, in a dense thicket, we seemed to be still on their trail. It was a small meadow, of a few acres, on the mountain side, concealed by the forest, and perhaps never seen by a white man before, where one would think that the moose might browse and bathe, and rest in peace. Pursuing this course, we soon reached the open land, which went sloping down some miles toward the Penobscot.

Perhaps I most fully realized that this was primeval, untamed, and forever untameable *Nature,* or whatever else men call it, while coming down this part of the mountain. We were passing over "Burnt Lands," burnt by lightning, perchance, though they showed no recent marks of fire, hardly so much as a charred stump, but looked rather like a natural pasture for the moose and deer, exceedingly wild and desolate, with occasional strips of timber crossing them, and low poplars springing up, and patches of blueberries here and there. I found myself traversing them familiarly, like some pasture run to waste, or partially reclaimed by man; but when I reflected what man, what brother or sister or kinsman of our race made it and claimed it, I expected the proprietor to rise up and dispute my passage. It is difficult to conceive of a region uninhabited by man. We habitually presume his presence and influence everywhere. And yet we have not seen pure Nature, unless we have seen her thus vast and drear and inhuman, though in the midst of cities. Nature was here something savage and awful, though beautiful. I looked with awe at the ground I trod on, to see what the Powers had made there, the form and fashion and material of their work. This was that Earth of which we have heard, made out of Chaos and Old Night. Here was no man's garden, but the unhandselled globe. It was not lawn, nor pasture, nor mead, nor woodland, nor lea, nor arable, nor waste-land. It was the fresh and natural surface of the planet Earth, as it was made for ever and ever,—to be the dwelling of man, we say,—so Nature made it, and man may use it if he can. Man was not to be associated with it. It was Matter, vast, terrific,—not his Mother Earth that we have heard of, not for him to tread on, or be buried in,—no, it were being too familiar even to let his bones lie there,—the home, this, of Necessity and Fate. There was there felt the presence of a force not bound to be kind to man. It was a place for heathenism and superstitious rites,—to be inhabited by men nearer of kin to the rocks and to wild animals than we. We walked over it with a certain awe, stopping, from time to time, to pick the blueberries which grew there, and had a smart and spicy taste. Perchance where *our* wild pines stand, and leaves lie on their forest floor, in Concord, there were once reapers, and husbandmen planted grain; but here not even the surface had been scarred by man, but it was a specimen of what God saw fit to make this world. What is it to be admitted to a museum, to see a myriad of particular things, compared with being shown some star's surface, some hard matter in its home! I stand in awe of my body, this matter to which I am bound has become so strange to me. I fear not spirits, ghosts, of which I am one,—*that* my body might,—but I fear bodies, I tremble to meet them. What is this Titan that has possession of me? Talk of mysteries!—Think of our life in nature,—daily to be shown matter, to come in contact with it,—rocks, trees, wind on our cheeks! the *solid* earth! the *actual* world! the *common sense! Contact! Contact! Who* are we? *where* are we?

Erelong we recognized some rocks and other features in the landscape which we had purposely impressed on our memories, and, quickening our pace, by two o'clock we reached the batteau.* Here we had expected to dine on trout, but in this glaring sunlight they were slow to take the bait, so we were compelled to make the most of the crumbs of our hard bread and our pork, which were both nearly exhausted. Meanwhile we deliberated whether we should go up the river a mile farther, to Gibson's clearing, on the Sowadnchunk, where there was a deserted log-hut, in order to get a half-inch auger, to mend one of our spike-poles with. There were young spruce-trees enough around us, and we had a spare spike, but nothing to make a hole with. But as it was uncertain whether we should find any tools left there, we patched up the broken pole, as well as we could, for the downward voyage, in which there would be but little use for it. Moreover, we were unwilling to lose any time in this expedition, lest the wind should rise before we reached the larger lakes, and detain us; for a moderate wind produces quite a sea on these waters, in which a batteau will not live for a moment; and on one occasion McCauslin had been delayed a week at the head of the North Twin, which is only four miles across. We were nearly out of provisions, and ill prepared in this respect for what might possibly prove a week's journey round by the shore, fording innumerable streams, and threading a trackless forest, should any accident happen to our boat.

It was with regret that we turned our backs on Chesuncook, which McCauslin had formerly logged on, and the Allegash lakes. There were still longer rapids and portages above; among the last the Rippogenus Portage, which he described as the most difficult on the river, and three miles long. The whole length of the Penobscot is two hundred and seventy-five miles, and we are still nearly one hundred miles from its source. Hodge, the assistant State Geologist, passed up this river in 1837, and by a portage of only one mile and three-quarters crossed over into the Allegash, and so went down that into the St. John, and up the Madawaska to the Grand Portage across to the St. Lawrence. His is the only account that I know, of an expedition through to

---

* The bears had not touched things on our possessions. They sometimes tear a batteau to pieces for the sake of the tar with which it is besmeared.

Canada in this direction. He thus describes his first sight of the latter river, which, to compare small things with great, is like Balboa's first sight of the Pacific from the mountains of the Isthmus of Darien. "When we first came in sight of the St. Lawrence," he says, "from the top of a high hill, the view was most striking, and much more interesting to me from having been shut up in the woods for the two previous months. Directly before us lay the broad river, extending across nine or ten miles, its surface broken by a few islands and reefs, and two ships riding at anchor near the shore. Beyond, extended ranges of uncultivated hills, parallel with the river. The sun was just going down behind them, and gilding the whole scene with its parting rays."

About four o'clock, the same afternoon, we commenced our return voyage, which would require but little if any poling. In shooting rapids the boatmen use large and broad paddles, instead of poles, to guide the boat with. Though we glided so swiftly, and often smoothly, down, where it had cost us no slight effort to get up, our present voyage was attended with far more danger: for if we once fairly struck one of the thousand rocks by which we were surrounded the boat would be swamped in an instant. When a boat is swamped under these circumstances, the boatmen commonly find no difficulty in keeping afloat at first, for the current keeps both them and their cargo up for a long way down the stream; and if they can swim, they have only to work their way gradually to the shore. The greatest danger is of being caught in an eddy behind some larger rock, where the water rushes up stream faster than elsewhere it does down, and being carried round and round under the surface till they are drowned. McCauslin pointed out some rocks which had been the scene of a fatal accident of this kind. Sometimes the body is not thrown out for several hours. He himself had performed such a circuit once, only his legs being visible to his companions; but he was fortunately thrown out in season to recover his breath.* In shooting the rapids, the boatman has this problem to solve: to choose a circuitous and safe course amid a thousand sunken rocks, scattered over a quarter or half a mile, at the same time that he is moving steadily on at the rate of fifteen miles an hour. Stop he cannot; the only question is, where will he go? The bow-man chooses the course with all his eyes about him, striking broad off with his paddle, and drawing the boat by main force into her course. The stern-man faithfully follows the bow.

We were soon at the Aboljacarmegus Falls. Anxious to avoid the delay, as well as the labor, of the portage here, our boatmen went forward first to reconnoitre, and concluded to let the batteau down the falls, carrying the bag-

---

* I cut this from a newspaper. "On the 11th (instant?) [May, '49], on Rappogenes Falls, Mr. John Delantee, of Orono, Me., was drowned while running logs. He was a citizen of Orono, and was twenty-six years of age. His companions found his body, enclosed it in bark, and buried it in the solemn woods."

gage only over the portage. Jumping from rock to rock until nearly in the middle of the stream, we were ready to receive the boat and let her down over the first fall, some six or seven feet perpendicular. The boatmen stand upon the edge of a shelf of rock, where the fall is perhaps nine or ten feet perpendicular, in from one to two feet of rapid water, one on each side of the boat, and let it slide gently over, till the bow is run out ten or twelve feet in the air; then, letting it drop squarely, while one holds the painter, the other leaps in, and his companion following, they are whirled down the rapids to a new fall, or to smooth water. In a very few minutes they had accomplished a passage in safety, which would be as foolhardy for the unskilful to attempt as the descent of Niagara itself. It seemed as if it needed only a little familiarity, and a little more skill, to navigate down such falls as Niagara itself with safety. At any rate, I should not despair of such men in the rapids above table-rock, until I saw them actually go over the falls, so cool, so collected, so fertile in resources are they. One might have thought that these were falls, and that falls were not to be waded through with impunity, like a mud-puddle. There was really danger of their losing their sublimity in losing their power to harm us. Familiarity breeds contempt. The boatman pauses, perchance, on some shelf beneath a table-rock under the fall, standing in some cove of back-water two feet deep, and you hear his rough voice come up through the spray, coolly giving directions how to launch the boat this time.

Having carried round Pockwockomus Falls, our oars soon brought us to the Katepskonegan, or Oak Hall carry, where we decided to camp half way over, leaving our batteau to be carried over in the morning on fresh shoulders. One shoulder of each of the boatmen showed a red spot as large as one's hand, worn by the batteau on this expedition; and this shoulder, as it did all the work, was perceptibly lower than its fellow, from long service. Such toil soon wears out the strongest constitution. The drivers are accustomed to work in the cold water in the spring, rarely ever dry; and if one falls in all over he rarely changes his clothes till night, if then, even. One who takes this precaution is called by a particular nickname, or is turned off. None can lead this life who are not almost amphibious. McCauslin said soberly, what is at any rate a good story to tell, that he had seen where six men were wholly under water at once, at a jam, with their shoulders to handspikes. If the log did not start, then they had to put out their heads to breathe. The driver works as long as he can see, from dark to dark, and at night has not time to eat his supper and dry his clothes fairly, before he is asleep on his cedar bed. We lay that night on the very bed made by such a party, stretching our tent over the poles which were still standing, but reshingling the damp and faded bed with fresh leaves.

In the morning we carried our boat over and launched it, making haste lest the wind should rise. The boatmen ran down Passamagamet, and, soon after,

Ambejijis Falls, while we walked round with the baggage. We made a hasty breakfast at the head of Ambejijis Lake, on the remainder of our pork, and were soon rowing across its smooth surface again, under a pleasant sky, the mountain being now clear of clouds, in the northeast. Taking turns at the oars, we shot rapidly across Deep Cove, the foot of Pamadumcook, and the North Twin, at the rate of six miles an hour, the wind not being high enough to disturb us, and reached the Dam at noon. The boatmen went through one of the log sluices in the batteau, where the fall was ten feet at the bottom, and took us in below. Here was the longest rapid in our voyage, and perhaps the running this was as dangerous and arduous a task as any. Shooting down sometimes at the rate, as we judged, of fifteen miles an hour, if we struck a rock we were split from end to end in an instant. Now, like a bait bobbing for some river monster, amid the eddies, now darting to this side of the stream, now to that, gliding swift and smooth near to our destruction, or striking broad off with the paddle and drawing the boat to right or left with all our might, in order to avoid a rock. I suppose that it was like running the rapids of the Saute de St. Marie, at the outlet of Lake Superior, and our boatmen probably displayed no less dexterity than the Indians there do. We soon ran through this mile, and floated in Quakish Lake.

After such a voyage, the troubled and angry waters, which once had seemed terrible and not to be trifled with, appeared tamed and subdued; they had been bearded and worried in their channels, pricked and whipped into submission with the spike-pole and paddle, gone through and through with impunity, and all their spirit and their danger taken out of them, and the most swollen and impetuous rivers seemed but playthings henceforth. I began, at length, to understand the boatman's familiarity with, and contempt for, the rapids. "Those Fowler boys," said Mrs. McCauslin, "are perfect ducks for the water." They had run down to Lincoln, according to her, thirty or forty miles, in a batteau, in the night, for a doctor, when it was so dark that they could not see a rod before them, and the river was swollen so as to be almost a continuous rapid, so that the doctor *cried,* when they brought him up by daylight, "Why, Tom, how did you see to steer?" "We did n't steer much,—only kept her straight." And yet they met with no accident. It is true, the more difficult rapids are higher up than this.

When we reached the Millinocket opposite to Tom's house, and were waiting for his folks to set us over, for we had left our batteau above the Grand Falls, we discovered two canoes, with two men in each, turning up this stream from Shad Pond, one keeping the opposite side of a small island before us, while the other approached the side where we were standing, examining the banks carefully for muskrats as they came along. The last proved to be Louis Neptune and his companion, now, at last, on their way up to Chesuncook after moose; but they were so disguised that we hardly knew them. At a little distance they might have been taken for Quakers, with their broad-brimmed hats, and overcoats with broad capes, the spoils of Bangor, seeking a settlement in this Sylvania,—or, nearer at hand, for fashionable gentlemen the morning after a spree. Met face to face, these Indians in their native woods looked like the sinister and slouching fellows whom you meet picking up strings and paper in the streets of a city. There is, in fact, a remarkable and unexpected resemblance between the degraded savage and the lowest classes in a great city. The one is no more a child of nature than the other. In the progress of degradation the distinction of races is soon lost. Neptune at first was only anxious to know what we "kill," seeing some partridges in the hands of one of the party, but we had assumed too much anger to permit of a reply. We thought Indians had some honor before. But—"Me been sick. O, me unwell now. You make bargain, then me go." They had in fact been delayed so long by a drunken frolic at the Five Islands, and they had not yet recovered from its effects. They had some young musquash in their canoes, which they dug out of the banks with a hoe, for food, not for their skins, for musquash are their principal food on these expeditions. So they went on up the Millinocket, and we kept down the bank of the Penobscot, after recruiting ourselves with a draught of Tom's beer, leaving Tom at his home.

Thus a man shall lead his life away here on the edge of the wilderness, on Indian Millinocket stream, in a new world, far in the dark of a continent, and have a flute to play at evening here, while his strains echo to the stars, amid the howling of wolves; shall live, as it were, in the primitive age of the world, a primitive man. Yet he shall spend a sunny day, and in this century be my contemporary; perchance shall read some scattered leaves of literature, and sometimes talk with me. Why read history, then, if the ages and the generations are now? He lives three thousand years deep into time, an age not yet described by poets. Can you well go further back in history than this? Ay! ay!—for there turns up but now into the mouth of Millinocket stream a still more ancient and primitive man, whose history is not brought down even to the former. In a bark vessel sewn with the roots of the spruce, with hornbeam paddles, he dips his way along. He is but dim and misty to me, obscured by the æons that lie between the bark-canoe and the batteau. He builds no house of logs, but a wigwam of skins. He eats no hot bread and sweet cake, but musquash and moose-meat and the fat of bears. He glides up the Millinocket and is lost to my sight, as a more distant and misty cloud is seen flitting by behind a nearer, and is lost in space. So he goes about his destiny, the red face of man.

After having passed the night, and buttered our boots for the last time, at Uncle George's, whose dogs almost devoured him for joy at his return, we kept on down the river the next day, about eight miles on foot, and then took a batteau, with a man to pole it, to Mattawamkeag, ten more. At the middle of that very night, to make a swift conclusion to a long story, we dropped our buggy over the half-finished bridge at Oldtown, where we heard the confused din and clink of a hundred saws, which never rest, and at six o'clock the next morning one of the party was steaming his way to Massachusetts.

What is most striking in the Maine wilderness is the continuousness of the forest, with fewer open intervals or glades than you had imagined. Except the few burnt-lands, the narrow intervals on the rivers, the bare tops of the high mountains, and the lakes and streams, the forest is uninterrupted. It is even more grim and wild than you had anticipated, a damp and intricate wilderness, in the spring everywhere wet and miry. The aspect of the country, indeed, is universally stern and savage, excepting the distant views of the forest from hills, and the lake prospects, which are mild and civilizing in a degree. The lakes are something which you are unprepared for; they lie up so high, exposed to the light, and the forest is diminished to a fine fringe on their edges, with here and there a blue mountain, like amethyst jewels set around some jewel of the first water,—so anterior, so superior, to all the changes that are to take place on their shores, even now civil and refined, and fair as they can ever be. These are not the artificial forests of an English king,—a royal preserve merely. Here prevail no forest laws but those of nature. The aborigines have never been dispossessed, nor nature disforested.

It is a country full of evergreen trees, of mossy silver birches and watery maples, the ground dotted with insipid, small, red berries, and strewn with damp and moss-grown rocks,—a country diversified with innumerable lakes and rapid streams, peopled with trout and various species of *leucisci,* with salmon, shad, and pickerel, and other fishes; the forest resounding at rare intervals with the note of the chicadee, the blue-jay, and the woodpecker, the scream of the fish-hawk and the eagle, the laugh of the loon, and the whistle of ducks along the solitary streams; at night, with the hooting of owls and howling of wolves; in summer, swarming with myriads of black flies and mosquitoes, more formidable than wolves to the white man. Such is the home of the moose, the bear, the caribou, the wolf, the beaver, and the Indian. Who shall describe the inexpressible tenderness and immortal life of the grim forest, where Nature, though it be mid-winter, is ever in her spring, where the moss-grown and decaying trees are not old, but seem to enjoy a perpetual youth; and blissful, innocent Nature, like a serene infant, is too happy to make a noise, except by a few tinkling, lisping birds and trickling rills?

What a place to live, what a place to die and be buried in! There certainly men would live forever, and laugh at death and the grave. There they could have no such thoughts as are associated with the village graveyard,—that make a grave out of one of those moist evergreen hummocks!

> Die and be buried who will,
> I mean to live here still;
> My nature grows ever more young
> The primitive pines among.

I am reminded by my journey how exceedingly new this country still is. You have only to travel for a few days into the interior and back parts even of many of the old States, to come to that very America which the Northmen, and Cabot, and Gosnold, and Smith, and Raleigh visited. If Columbus was the first to discover the islands, Americus Vespucius and Cabot, and the Puritans, and we their descendants, have discovered only the shores of America. While the republic has already acquired a history world-wide, America is still unsettled and unexplored. Like the English in New Holland, we live only on the shores of a continent even yet, and hardly know where the rivers come from which float our navy. The very timber and boards and shingles of which our houses are made, grew but yesterday in a wilderness where the Indian still hunts and the moose runs wild. New York has her wilderness within her own borders; and though the sailors of Europe are familiar with the soundings of her Hudson, and Fulton long since invented the steamboat on its waters, an Indian is still necessary to guide her scientific men to its headwaters in the Adirondac country.

Have we even so much as discovered and settled the shores? Let a man travel on foot along the coast, from the Passamaquoddy to the Sabine, or to the Rio Bravo, or to wherever the end is now, if he is swift enough to overtake it, faithfully following the windings of every inlet and of every cape, and stepping to the music of the surf,—with a desolate fishing-town once a week, and a city's port once a month to cheer him, and putting up at the light-houses, when there are any,—and tell me if it looks like a discovered and settled country, and not rather, for the most part, like a desolate island, and No-man's Land.

We have advanced by leaps to the Pacific, and left many a lesser Oregon and California unexplored behind us. Though the railroad and the telegraph have been established on the shores of Maine, the Indian still looks out from her interior mountains over all these to the sea. There stands the city of Bangor, fifty miles up the Penobscot, at the head of navigation for vessels of the largest class, the principal lumber depot on this continent, with a population of twelve thousand, like a star on the edge of night, still hewing at the forests of which it is built, already overflowing with the luxuries and refinement of Europe, and sending its vessels to Spain, to England, and to the West Indies for its groceries,—and yet only a few axe-men have gone "up river," into the howling wilderness which feeds it. The bear and deer are still found within its limits; and the moose, as he swims the Penobscot, is entangled amid its shipping, and taken by foreign sailors in its harbor. Twelve miles in the rear, twelve miles of railroad, are Orono and the Indian Island, the home of the Penobscot tribe, and then commence the batteau and the canoe, and the military road; and sixty miles above, the country is virtually unmapped and unexplored, and there still waves the virgin forest of the New World.

MARK TWAIN

The Oldest Inhabitant—
The Weather of New England

 1876

When Mark Twain (1835–1910) addressed the New England Society on "forefathers' day" at its meeting at Delmonico's restaurant in New York City in the winter of 1876, it was early in the phase of his life that belongs to New England. For more than twenty years, beginning in 1871, he spent much of his time halfway between Boston and New York, at Hartford, Connecticut, where he built himself a house at extravagant cost and participated—always with a half-satiric spirit—in local literary life as well as in that of both metropolises. Much in demand as a lecturer and after-dinner speaker, Twain made himself into America's official humorist, and though in this little piece he flirts with a cliché (as the saying goes, if you don't like the weather in New England, just wait an hour), he brings to the subject his inimitable charm and, along with it, a distinctive ability to get behind official pieties about God and nature to the facts of human weakness and the salutary value of laughter.

Address at the New England Society's Seventy-first Annual Dinner, New York City

> The next toast was: "The Oldest Inhabitant—The Weather
>   of New England."
> Who can lose it and forget it?
> Who can have it and regret it?
>
>   "Be interposer 'twixt us Twain."—*Merchant of Venice*.

I reverently believe that the Maker who made us all makes everything in New England but the weather. I don't know who makes that, but I think it must be raw apprentices in the weather-clerk's factory who experiment and learn how, in New England, for board and clothes, and then are promoted to make weather for countries that require a good article, and will take their custom elsewhere if they don't get it. There is a sumptuous variety about the New England weather that compels the stranger's admiration—and regret. The weather is always doing something there; always attending strictly to business; always getting up new designs and trying them on the people to see how they will go. But it gets through more business in spring than in any other season. In the spring I have counted one hundred and thirty-six different kinds of weather inside of four-and-twenty hours. It was I that made the fame and fortune of that man that had that marvellous collection of weather on exhibition at the Centennial, that so astounded the foreigners. He was going to travel all over the world and get specimens from all the climes. I said, "Don't you do it; you come to New England on a favorable spring day." I told him what we could do in the way of style, variety, and quantity. Well, he came and he made his collection in four days. As to variety, why, he confessed that he got hundreds of kinds of weather that he had never heard of before. And as to quantity—well, after he had picked out and discarded all that was blemished in any way, he not only had weather enough, but weather to spare; weather to hire out; weather to sell; to deposit; weather to invest; weather to give to the poor. The people of New England are by nature patient and forbearing, but there are some things which they will not stand. Every year they kill a lot of poets for writing about "Beautiful Spring." These are generally casual visitors, who bring their notions of spring from somewhere else, and cannot, of course, know how the natives feel about spring. And so the first thing they know the opportunity to inquire how they feel has permanently gone by. Old Probabilities has a mighty reputation for accurate prophecy, and thoroughly well deserves it. You take up the paper and observe how crisply and confidently he checks off what to-day's weather is going to be on the Pacific, down South, in the Middle States, in the Wisconsin region. See him sail along in the joy and pride of his power till he gets to New England, and then see his tail drop. *He* doesn't know what the weather is going to be in New England. Well, he mulls over it, and by-and-by he gets out something about like this: Probably northeast to southwest winds, varying to the southward and westward and eastward, and points between, high and low barometer swapping around from place to place; probable areas of rain, snow, hail, and drought, succeeded or preceded by earthquakes, with thunder and lightning. Then he jots down his postscript from his wandering mind, to cover accidents. "But it is possible that the programme may be wholly changed in the mean time." Yes, one of the brightest gems in the New England weather is the dazzling uncertainty of it. There is only one thing certain about it: you are certain there is going to be plenty of it—a perfect grand review; but you never can tell which end of the procession is going to move first. You fix up for the drought; you leave your umbrella in the house and sally out, and two to one you get drowned. You make up your mind that the earthquake is due; you stand from under, and take hold of something to steady yourself, and the first thing you know you get struck by lightning. These are great disappointments; but they can't be helped. The lightning there is peculiar; it is so convincing, that when it strikes a thing it doesn't leave enough of that thing behind for you to tell whether— Well, you'd think it was something valuable, and a Congressman had been there. And the thunder. When the thunder begins to merely tune up and scrape and saw, and key up the instruments for the performance, strangers say, "Why, what awful thunder you have here!" But when the baton is raised and the real concert begins, you'll find that stranger down in the cellar with his head in the ash-barrel. Now as to the *size* of the weather in New England—lengthways, I mean. It is utterly disproportioned to the size of that little country. Half the time, when it is packed as full as it can stick, you will see that New England weather sticking out beyond the edges and projecting around hundreds and hundreds of miles over the neighboring States. She can't hold a tenth part of her weather. You can see cracks all about where she has strained herself trying to do it. I could speak volumes about the inhuman perversity of the New England weather, but I will give but a single specimen. I like to hear rain on a tin roof. So I covered part of my roof with tin, with an eye to that luxury. Well, sir, do you think it ever rains on that tin? No, sir; skips it every time. Mind, in this speech I have been trying merely to do honor to the New England weather—no language could do it justice. But, after all, there is at least one or two things about that weather (or, if you please, effects produced by it) which we residents would not like to part with. If we hadn't our bewitching autumn foliage, we should still have to credit the weather with one feature which compensates for all its bullying vagaries—the ice-storm: when a leafless tree is clothed with ice from the bottom to the top—ice that is as bright and clear as crystal; when every bough and twig is strung with ice-beads, frozen dew-drops, and the whole tree sparkles cold and white, like the Shah of Persia's diamond plume. Then the wind waves the branches and the sun comes out and turns all those myriads of beads and drops to prisms that glow and burn and flash with all manner of colored fires, which change and change again with inconceivable rapidity from blue to red, from red to green, and green to gold—the tree becomes a spraying fountain, a very explosion of dazzling jewels; and it stands there the acme, the climax, the supremest possibility in art or nature, of bewildering, intoxicating, intolerable magnificence. One cannot make the words too strong.

WILLIAM JAMES

What Pragmatism Means

 1907

William James's lectures on the philosophy he called pragmatism (a term borrowed from his Harvard colleague Charles Sanders Peirce) were published in 1907, when James (1842–1910) was sixty-five. All his life James had been haunted, sometimes to the point of crippling depression, by the specter of a meaningless universe—by the possibility that the world described by religion as an emanation or artifact of the divine mind is, in fact, a wasteland in which the only steady principle is the universal tendency toward disintegration and death. James's writings record his struggle toward, and ultimately his attainment of, a modern sort of faith in the vitality of consciousness itself, in the capacity of the human mind to invest the world with meaning and thereby infuse it with love and hope. The second of the eight lectures, "What Pragmatism Means," sets out this saving idea with lucidity and grace.

Some years ago, being with a camping party in the mountains, I returned from a solitary ramble to find everyone engaged in a ferocious metaphysical dispute. The *corpus* of the dispute was a squirrel—a live squirrel supposed to be clinging to one side of a tree-trunk; while over against the tree's opposite side a human being was imagined to stand. This human witness tries to get sight of the squirrel by moving rapidly round the tree, but no matter how fast he goes, the squirrel moves as fast in the opposite direction, and always keeps the tree between himself and the man, so that never a glimpse of him is caught. The resultant metaphysical problem now is this: *Does the man go round the squirrel or not?* He goes round the tree, sure enough, and the squirrel is on the tree; but does he go round the squirrel? In the unlimited leisure of the wilderness, discussion had been worn threadbare. Everyone had taken sides, and was obstinate; and the numbers on both sides were even. Each side, when I appeared, therefore appealed to me to make it a majority. Mindful of the scholastic adage that whenever you meet a contradiction you must make a distinction, I immediately sought and found one, as follows: "Which party is right," I said, "depends on what you *practically mean* by 'going round' the squirrel. If you mean passing from the north of him to the east, then to the south, then to the west, and then to the north of him again, obviously the man does go round him, for he occupies these successive positions. But if on the contrary you mean being first in front of him, then on the right of him, then behind him, then on his left, and finally in front again, it is quite as obvious that the man fails to go round him, for by the compensating movements the squirrel makes, he keeps his belly turned towards the man all the time, and his back turned away. Make the distinction, and there is no occasion for any farther dispute. You are both right and both wrong according as you conceive the verb 'to go round' in one practical fashion or the other."

Altho one or two of the hotter disputants called my speech a shuffling evasion, saying they wanted no quibbling or scholastic hair-splitting, but meant just plain honest English 'round,' the majority seemed to think that the distinction had assuaged the dispute.

I tell this trivial anecdote because it is a peculiarly simple example of what I wish now to speak of as *the pragmatic method.* The pragmatic method is primarily a method of settling metaphysical disputes that otherwise might be interminable. Is the world one or many?—fated or free?—material or spiritual?—here are notions either of which may or may not hold good of the world; and disputes over such notions are unending. The pragmatic method in such cases is to try to interpret each notion by tracing its respective practical consequences. What difference would it practically make to anyone if this notion rather than that notion were true? If no practical difference whatever can be traced, then the alternatives mean practically the same thing, and all dispute is idle. Whenever a dispute is serious, we ought to be able to show some practical difference that must follow from one side or the other's being right.

A glance at the history of the idea will show you still better what pragmatism means. The term is derived from the same Greek word *pragma,* meaning action, from which our words 'practice' and 'practical' come. It was first introduced into philosophy by Mr. Charles Peirce in 1878. In an article entitled 'How to Make Our Ideas Clear,' in the 'Popular Science Monthly' for January of that year* Mr. Peirce, after pointing out that our beliefs are really rules for action, said that, to develope a thought's meaning, we need only determine what conduct it is fitted to produce: that conduct is for us its sole significance. And the tangible fact at the root of all our thought-distinctions, however subtle, is that there is no one of them so fine as to consist in anything but a possible difference of practice. To attain perfect clearness in our thoughts of an object, then, we need only consider what conceivable effects of a practical kind the object may involve—what sensations we are to expect from it, and what reactions we must prepare. Our conception of these effects, whether immedi-

* Translated in the *Revue Philosophique* for January, 1879 (vol. vii).

ate or remote, is then for us the whole of our conception of the object, so far as that conception has positive significance at all.

This is the principle of Peirce, the principle of pragmatism. It lay entirely unnoticed by anyone for twenty years, until I, in an address before Professor Howison's philosophical union at the university of California, brought it forward again and made a special application of it to religion. By that date (1898) the times seemed ripe for its reception. The word 'pragmatism' spread, and at present it fairly spots the pages of the philosophic journals. On all hands we find the 'pragmatic movement' spoken of, sometimes with respect, sometimes with contumely, seldom with clear understanding. It is evident that the term applies itself conveniently to a number of tendencies that hitherto have lacked a collective name, and that it has 'come to stay.'

To take in the importance of Peirce's principle, one must get accustomed to applying it to concrete cases. I found a few years ago that Ostwald, the illustrious Leipzig chemist, had been making perfectly distinct use of the principle of pragmatism in his lectures on the philosophy of science, tho he had not called it by that name.

"All realities influence our practice," he wrote me, "and that influence is their meaning for us. I am accustomed to put questions to my classes in this way: In what respects would the world be different if this alternative or that were true? If I can find nothing that would become different, then the alternative has no sense."

That is, the rival views mean practically the same thing, and meaning, other than practical, there is for us none. Ostwald in a published lecture gives this example of what he means. Chemists have long wrangled over the inner constitution of certain bodies called 'tautomerous.' Their properties seemed equally consistent with the notion that an instable hydrogen atom oscillates inside of them, or that they are instable mixtures of two bodies. Controversy raged; but never was decided. "It would never have begun," says Ostwald, "if the combatants had asked themselves what particular experimental fact could have been made different by one or the other view being correct. For it would then have appeared that no difference of fact could possibly ensue; and the quarrel was as unreal as if, theorizing in primitive times about the raising of dough by yeast, one party should have invoked a 'brownie,' while another insisted on an 'elf' as the true cause of the phenomenon."*

---

* 'Theorie und Praxis,' *Zeitsch. des Oesterreichischen Ingenieur u. Architecten-Vereines,* 1905, Nr. 4 u. 6. I find a still more radical pragmatism than Ostwald's in an address by Professor W. S. Franklin: "I think that the sickliest notion of physics, even if a student gets it, is that it is 'the science of masses, molecules and the ether.' And I think that the healthiest notion, even if a student does not wholly get it, is that physics is the science of the ways of taking hold of bodies and pushing them!" (*Science,* January 2, 1903.)

It is astonishing to see how many philosophical disputes collapse into insignificance the moment you subject them to this simple test of tracing a concrete consequence. There can *be* no difference anywhere that doesn't *make* a difference elsewhere—no difference in abstract truth that doesn't express itself in a difference in concrete fact and in conduct consequent upon that fact, imposed on somebody, somehow, somewhere and somewhen. The whole function of philosophy ought to be to find out what definite difference it will make to you and me, at definite instants of our life, if this world-formula or that world-formula be the true one.

There is absolutely nothing new in the pragmatic method. Socrates was an adept at it. Aristotle used it methodically. Locke, Berkeley and Hume made momentous contributions to truth by its means. Shadworth Hodgson keeps insisting that realities are only what they are 'known-as.' But these forerunners of pragmatism used it in fragments: they were preluders only. Not until in our time has it generalized itself, become conscious of a universal mission, pretended to a conquering destiny. I believe in that destiny, and I hope I may end by inspiring you with my belief.

Pragmatism represents a perfectly familiar attitude in philosophy, the empiricist attitude, but it represents it, as it seems to me, both in a more radical and in a less objectionable form than it has ever yet assumed. A pragmatist turns his back resolutely and once for all upon a lot of inveterate habits dear to professional philosophers. He turns away from abstraction and insufficiency, from verbal solutions, from bad *a priori* reasons, from fixed principles, closed systems, and pretended absolutes and origins. He turns towards concreteness and adequacy, towards facts, towards action, and towards power. That means the empiricist temper regnant and the rationalist temper sincerely given up. It means the open air and possibilities of nature, as against dogma, artificiality and the pretence of finality in truth.

At the same time it does not stand for any special results. It is a method only. But the general triumph of that method would mean an enormous change in what I called in my last lecture the 'temperament' of philosophy. Teachers of the ultra-rationalistic type would be frozen out, much as the courtier type is frozen out in republics, as the ultramontane type of priest is frozen out in protestant lands. Science and metaphysics would come much nearer together, would in fact work absolutely hand in hand.

Metaphysics has usually followed a very primitive kind of quest. You know how men have always hankered after unlawful magic, and you know what a great part, in magic, *words* have always played. If you have his name, or the formula of incantation that binds him, you can control the spirit, genie, afrite, or whatever the power may be. Solomon knew the names of all the spirits, and having their names, he held them subject to his will. So the universe has always appeared to the natural mind as a kind of enigma, of which the key must be sought in the shape of some illuminating or power-bringing word or name. That word names the universe's *principle,* and to possess it is, after a fashion, to possess the universe itself. 'God,' 'Matter,' 'Reason,' 'the Absolute,' 'Energy,' are so many solving names. You can rest when you have them. You are at the end of your metaphysical quest.

But if you follow the pragmatic method, you cannot look on any such word as closing your quest. You must bring out of each word its practical cash-value, set it at work within the stream of your experience. It appears less as a solution, then, than as a program for more work, and more particularly as an indication of the ways in which existing realities may be *changed.*

Theories thus become instruments, not answers to enigmas, in which we can rest. We don't lie back upon them, we move forward, and, on occasion, make nature over again by their aid. Pragmatism unstiffens all our theories, limbers them up and sets each one at work. Being nothing essentially new, it harmonizes with many ancient philosophic tendencies. It agrees with nominalism for instance, in always appealing to particulars; with utilitarianism in emphasizing practical aspects; with positivism in its disdain for verbal solutions, useless questions, and metaphysical abstractions.

All these, you see, are *anti-intellectualist* tendencies. Against rationalism as a pretension and a method, pragmatism is fully armed and militant. But, at the outset, at least, it stands for no particular results. It has no dogmas, and no doctrines save its method. As the young Italian pragmatist Papini has well said, it lies in the midst of our theories, like a corridor in a hotel. Innumerable chambers open out of it. In one you may find a man writing an atheistic volume; in the next someone on his knees praying for faith and strength; in a third a chemist investigating a body's properties. In a fourth a system of idealistic metaphysics is being excogitated; in a fifth the impossibility of metaphysics is being shown. But they all own the corridor, and all must pass through it if they want a practicable way of getting into or out of their respective rooms.

No particular results then, so far, but only an attitude of orientation, is what the pragmatic method means. *The attitude of looking away from first things, principles, 'categories,' supposed necessities; and of looking towards last things, fruits, consequences, facts.*

So much for the pragmatic method! You may say that I have been praising it rather than explaining it to you, but I shall presently explain it abundantly enough by showing how it works on some familiar problems. Meanwhile the word pragmatism has come to be used in a still wider sense, as meaning also a certain *theory of truth.* I mean to give a whole lecture to the statement of that theory, after first paving the way, so I can be very brief now. But brevity is hard to follow, so I ask for your redoubled attention for a quarter of an hour. If much remains obscure, I hope to make it clearer in the later lectures.

One of the most successfully cultivated branches of philosophy in our time is what is called inductive logic, the study of the conditions under which our sciences have evolved. Writers on this subject have begun to show a singular unanimity as to what the laws of nature and elements of fact mean, when formulated by mathematicians, physicists and chemists. When the first mathematical, logical and natural uniformities, the first *laws,* were discovered, men were so carried away by the clearness, beauty and simplification that resulted, that they believed themselves to have deciphered authentically the eternal thoughts of the Almighty. His mind also thundered and reverberated in syllogisms. He also thought in conic sections, squares and roots and ratios, and geometrized like Euclid. He made Kepler's laws for the planets to follow; he made velocity increase proportionally to the time in falling bodies; he made the law of the sines for light to obey when refracted; he established the classes, orders, families and genera of plants and animals, and fixed the distances between them. He thought the archetypes of all things, and devised their variations; and when we rediscover any one of these his wondrous institutions, we seize his mind in its very literal intention.

But as the sciences have developed farther, the notion has gained ground that most, perhaps all, of our laws are only approximations. The laws themselves, moreover, have grown so numerous that there is no counting them; and so many rival formulations are proposed in all the branches of science that investigators have become accustomed to the notion that no theory is absolutely a transcript of reality, but that any one of them may from some point of view be useful. Their great use is to summarize old facts and to lead to new ones. They are only a man-made language, a conceptual shorthand, as someone calls them, in which we write our reports of nature; and languages, as is well known, tolerate much choice of expression and many dialects.

Thus human arbitrariness has driven divine necessity from scientific logic. If I mention the names of Sigwart, Mach, Ostwald, Pearson, Milhaud, Poincaré, Duhem, Ruyssen, those of you who are students will easily identify the tendency I speak of, and will think of additional names.

Riding now on the front of this wave of scientific logic Messrs. Schiller and Dewey appear with their pragmatistic account of what truth everywhere signifies. Everywhere, these teachers say, 'truth' in our ideas and beliefs means the same thing that it means in science. It means, they say, nothing but this, *that ideas (which themselves are but parts of our experience) become true just in so far as they help us to get into satisfactory relation with other parts of our experience,* to summarize them and get about among them by conceptual short-cuts instead of following the interminable succession of particular phenomena. Any idea upon which we can ride, so to speak; any idea that will carry us prosperously from any one part of our experience to any other part, linking things satisfactorily, working securely, simplifying, saving labor; is true for just so much, true in so far forth, true *instrumentally.* This is the 'instrumental' view of truth taught so successfully at Chicago, the view that truth in our ideas means their power to 'work,' promulgated so brilliantly at Oxford.

Messrs. Dewey, Schiller and their allies, in reaching this general conception of all truth, have only followed the example of geologists, biologists and philologists. In the establishment of these other sciences, the successful stroke was always to take some simple process actually observable in operation—as denudation by weather, say, or variation from parental type, or change of dialect by incorporation of new words and pronunciations—and then to generalize it, making it apply to all times, and produce great results by summating its effects through the ages.

The observable process which Schiller and Dewey particularly singled out for generalization is the familiar one by which any individual settles into *new opinions.* The process here is always the same. The individual has a stock of old opinions already, but he meets a new experience that puts them to a strain. Somebody contradicts them; or in a reflective moment he discovers that they contradict each other; or he hears of facts with which they are incompatible; or desires arise in him which they cease to satisfy. The result is an inward trouble to which his mind till then had been a stranger, and from which he seeks to escape by modifying his previous mass of opinions. He saves as much of it as he can, for in this matter of belief we are all extreme conservatives. So he tries to change first this opinion, and then that (for they resist change very variously), until at last some new idea comes up which he can graft upon the ancient stock with a minimum of disturbance of the latter, some idea that mediates between the stock and the new experience and runs them into one another most felicitously and expediently.

This new idea is then adopted as the true one. It preserves the older stock of truths with a minimum of modification, stretching them just enough to make them admit the novelty, but conceiving that in ways as familiar as the case leaves possible. An *outrée* explanation, violating all our preconceptions, would never pass for a true account of a novelty. We should scratch round industriously till we found something less excentric. The most violent revolutions in an individual's beliefs leave most of his old order standing. Time and space, cause and effect, nature and history, and one's own biography remain untouched. New truth is always a go-between, a smoother-over of transitions. It marries old opinion to new fact so as ever to show a minimum of jolt, a maximum of continuity. We hold a theory true just in proportion to its success in solving this 'problem of maxima and minima.' But success in solving this problem is eminently a matter of approximation. We say this theory solves it on the whole more satisfactorily than that theory; but that means more satisfactorily to ourselves, and individuals will emphasize their points of satisfaction differently. To a certain degree, therefore, everything here is plastic.

The point I now urge you to observe particularly is the part played by the older truths. Failure to take account of it is the source of much of the unjust criticism leveled against pragmatism. Their influence is absolutely controlling. Loyalty to them is the first principle—in most cases it is the only principle; for by far the most usual way of handling phenomena so novel that they would make for a serious rearrangement of our preconceptions is to ignore them altogether, or to abuse those who bear witness for them.

You doubtless wish examples of this process of truth's growth, and the only trouble is their superabundance. The simplest case of new truth is of course the mere numerical addition of new kinds of facts, or of new single facts of old kinds, to our experience—an addition that involves no alteration in the old beliefs. Day follows day, and its contents are simply added. The new contents themselves are not true, they simply *come* and *are*. Truth is *what we say about* them, and when we say that they have come, truth is satisfied by the plain additive formula.

But often the day's contents oblige a rearrangement. If I should now utter piercing shrieks and act like a maniac on this platform, it would make many of you revise your ideas as to the probable worth of my philosophy. 'Radium' came the other day as part of the day's content, and seemed for a moment to contradict our ideas of the whole order of nature, that order having come to be identified with what is called the conservation of energy. The mere sight of radium paying heat away indefinitely out of its own pocket seemed to violate that conservation. What to think? If the radiations from it were nothing but an escape of unsuspected 'potential' energy, pre-existent inside of the atoms, the principle of conservation would be saved. The discovery of 'helium' as the radiation's outcome, opened a way to this belief. So Ramsay's view is generally held to be true, because, altho it extends our old ideas of energy, it causes a minimum of alteration in their nature.

I need not multiply instances. A new opinion counts as 'true' just in proportion as it gratifies the individual's desire to assimilate the novel in his experience to his beliefs in stock. It must both lean on old truth and grasp new fact; and its success (as I said a moment ago) in doing this, is a matter for the individual's appreciation. When old truth grows, then, by new truth's addition, it is for subjective reasons. We are in the process and obey the reasons. That new idea is truest which performs most felicitously its function of satisfying our double urgency. It makes itself true, gets itself classed as true, by the way it works; grafting itself then upon the ancient body of truth, which thus grows much as a tree grows by the activity of a new layer of cambium.

Now Dewey and Schiller proceed to generalize this observation and to apply it to the most ancient parts of truth. They also once were plastic. They also were called true for human reasons. They also mediated between still earlier truths and what in those days were novel observations. Purely objective truth, truth in whose establishment the function of giving human satisfaction in marrying previous parts of experience with newer parts played no rôle whatever, is nowhere to be found. The reasons why we call things true is the reason why they *are* true, for 'to be true' *means* only to perform this marriage-function.

The trail of the human serpent is thus over everything. Truth independent; truth that we *find* merely; truth no longer malleable to human need; truth incorrigible, in a word; such truth exists indeed superabundantly—or is supposed to exist by rationalistically minded thinkers; but then it means only the dead heart of the living tree, and its being there means only that truth also has its paleontology and its 'prescription,' and may grow stiff with years of veteran service and petrified in men's regard by sheer antiquity. But how plastic even the oldest truths nevertheless really are has been vividly shown in our day by the transformation of logical and mathematical ideas, a transformation which seems even to be invading physics. The ancient formulas are reinterpreted as special expressions of much wider principles, principles that our ancestors never got a glimpse of in their present shape and formulation.

Mr. Schiller still gives to all this view of truth the name of 'Humanism,' but, for this doctrine too, the name of pragmatism seems fairly to be in the ascendant, so I will treat it under the name of pragmatism in these lectures.

Such then would be the scope of pragmatism—first, a method; and second, a genetic theory of what is meant by truth. And these two things must be our future topics.

What I have said of the theory of truth will, I am sure, have appeared obscure and unsatisfactory to most of you by reason of its brevity. I shall make amends for that hereafter. In a lecture on 'common sense' I shall try to show what I mean by truths grown petrified by antiquity. In another lecture I shall expatiate on the idea that our thoughts become true in proportion as they successfully exert their go-between function. In a third I shall show how hard it is to discriminate subjective from objective factors in Truth's development. You may not follow me wholly in these lectures; and if you do, you may not wholly agree with me. But you will, I know, regard me at least as serious, and treat my effort with respectful consideration.

You will probably be surprised to learn, then, that Messrs. Schiller's and Dewey's theories have suffered a hailstorm of contempt and ridicule. All rationalism has risen against them. In influential quarters Mr. Schiller, in particular, has been treated like an impudent schoolboy who deserves a spanking. I should not mention this, but for the fact that it throws so much sidelight upon that rationalistic temper to which I have opposed the temper of pragmatism. Pragmatism is uncomfortable away from facts. Rationalism is comfortable only in the presence of abstractions. This pragmatist talk about truths in the plural, about their utility and satisfactoriness, about the success with which they 'work,' etc., suggests to the typical intellectualist mind a sort of coarse lame second-rate make-shift article of truth. Such truths are not real truth. Such tests are merely subjective. As against this, objective truth must be something non-utilitarian, haughty, refined, remote, august, exalted. It must be an absolute correspondence of our thoughts with an equally absolute reality. It must be what we *ought* to think, unconditionally. The conditioned ways in which we *do* think are so much irrelevance and matter for psychology. Down with psychology, up with logic, in all this question!

See the exquisite contrast of the types of mind! The pragmatist clings to facts and concreteness, observes truth at its work in particular cases, and generalizes. Truth, for him, becomes a class-name for all sorts of definite working-values in experience. For the rationalist it remains a pure abstraction, to the bare name of which we must defer. When the pragmatist undertakes to show in detail just *why* we must defer, the rationalist is unable to recognize the concretes from which his own abstraction is taken. He accuses us of *denying* truth; whereas we have only sought to trace exactly why people follow it and always ought to follow it. Your typical ultra-abstractionist fairly shudders at concreteness: other things equal, he positively prefers the pale and spectral. If the two universes were offered, he would always choose the skinny outline rather than the rich thicket of reality. It is so much purer, clearer, nobler.

I hope that as these lectures go on, the concreteness and closeness to facts of the pragmatism which they advocate may be what approves itself to you as its most satisfactory peculiarity. It only follows here the example of the sister-sciences, interpreting the unobserved by the observed. It brings old and new harmoniously together. It converts the absolutely empty notion of a static relation of 'correspondence' (what that may mean we must ask later) between our minds and reality, into that of a rich and active commerce (that anyone may follow in detail and understand) between particular thoughts of ours, and the great universe of other experiences in which they play their parts and have their uses.

But enough of this at present? The justification of what I say must be postponed. I wish now to add a word in further explanation of the claim I made at our last meeting, that pragmatism may be a happy harmonizer of empiricist ways of thinking, with the more religious demands of human beings.

Men who are strongly of the fact-loving temperament, you may remember me to have said, are liable to be kept at a distance by the small sympathy with facts which that philosophy from the present-day fashion of idealism offers them. It is far too intellectualistic. Old fashioned theism was bad enough, with its notion of God as an exalted monarch, made up of a lot of unintelligible or preposterous 'attributes'; but, so long as it held strongly by the argument from design, it kept some touch with concrete realities. Since, however, darwinism has once for all displaced design from the minds of the 'scientific,' theism has lost that foothold; and some kind of an immanent or pantheistic deity working *in* things rather than above them is, if any, the kind recommended to our contemporary imagination. Aspirants to a philosophic religion turn, as a rule, more hopefully nowadays towards idealistic pantheism than towards the older dualistic theism, in spite of the fact that the latter still counts able defenders.

But, as I said in my first lecture, the brand of pantheism offered is hard for them to assimilate if they are lovers of facts, or empirically minded. It is the absolutistic brand, spurning the dust and reared upon pure logic. It keeps no connexion whatever with concreteness. Affirming the Absolute Mind, which is its substitute for God, to be the rational presupposition of all particulars of fact, whatever they may be, it remains supremely indifferent to what the particular facts in our world actually are. Be they what they may, the Absolute will father them. Like the sick lion in Esop's fable, all footprints lead into his den, but *nulla vestigia retrorsum.* You cannot redescend into the world of particulars by the Absolute's aid, or deduce any necessary consequences of detail important for your life from your idea of his nature. He gives you indeed the assurance that all is well with *Him,* and for his eternal way of thinking; but thereupon he leaves you to be finitely saved by your own temporal devices.

Far be it from me to deny the majesty of this conception, or its capacity to yield religious comfort to a most respectable class of minds. But from the human point of view, no one can pretend that it doesn't suffer from the faults of remoteness and abstractness. It is eminently a product of what I have ventured to call the rationalistic temper. It disdains empiricism's needs. It substitutes a pallid outline for the real world's richness. It is dapper; it is noble in the bad sense, in the sense in which to be noble is to be inapt for humble service. In this real world of sweat and dirt, it seems to me that when a view of things is 'noble,' that ought to count as a presumption against its truth, and as a philosophic disqualification. The prince of darkness may be a gentleman, as we are told he is, but whatever the God of earth and heaven is, he can surely be no gentleman. His menial services are needed in the dust of our human trials, even more than his dignity is needed in the empyrean.

Now pragmatism, devoted tho she be to facts, has no such materialistic bias as ordinary empiricism labors under. Moreover, she has no objection whatever to the realizing of abstractions, so long as you get about among particulars with their aid and they actually carry you somewhere. Interested in no conclusions but those which our minds and our experiences work out together, she has no *a priori* prejudices against theology. *If theological ideas prove to have a value for concrete life, they will be true, for pragmatism, in the sense of being good for so much. For how much more they are true, will depend entirely on their relations to the other truths that also have to be acknowledged.*

What I said just now about the Absolute of transcendental idealism is a case in point. First, I called it majestic and said it yielded religious comfort to a class of minds, and then I accused it of remoteness and sterility. But so far as it affords such comfort, it surely is not sterile; it has that amount of value; it performs a concrete function. As a good pragmatist, I myself ought to call the Absolute true 'in so far forth,' then; and I unhesitatingly now do so.

But what does *true in so far forth* mean in this case? To answer, we need only apply the pragmatic method. What do believers in the Absolute mean by saying that their belief affords them comfort? They mean that since in the Absolute finite evil is 'overruled' already, we may, therefore, whenever we wish, treat the temporal as if it were potentially the eternal, be sure that we can trust its outcome, and, without sin, dismiss our fear and drop the worry of our finite responsibility. In short, they mean that we have a right ever and anon to take a moral holiday, to let the world wag in its own way, feeling that its issues are in better hands than ours and are none of our business.

The universe is a system of which the individual members may relax their anxieties occasionally, in which the don't-care mood is also right for men, and moral holidays in order—that, if I mistake not, is part, at least, of what the Absolute is 'known-as,' that is the great difference in our particular experiences which his being true makes for us, that is part of his cash-value when he is pragmatically interpreted. Farther than that the ordinary lay-reader in philosophy who thinks favorably of absolute idealism does not venture to sharpen his conceptions. He can use the Absolute for so much, and so much is very precious. He is pained at hearing you speak incredulously of the Absolute, therefore, and disregards your criticisms because they deal with aspects of the conception that he fails to follow.

If the Absolute means this, and means no more than this, who can possibly deny the truth of it? To deny it would be to insist that men should never relax, and that holidays are never in order.

I am well aware how odd it must seem to some of you to hear me say that an idea is 'true' so long as to believe it is profitable to our lives. That it is *good,* for as much as it profits, you will gladly admit. If what we do by its aid is good, you will allow the idea itself to be good in so far forth, for we are the better for possessing it. But is it not a strange misuse of the word 'truth,' you will say, to call ideas also 'true' for this reason?

To answer this difficulty fully is impossible at this stage of my account. You touch here upon the very central point of Messrs. Schiller's, Dewey's and my own doctrine of truth, which I cannot discuss with detail until my sixth lecture. Let me now say only this, that truth is *one species of good,* and not, as is usually supposed, a category distinct from good, and co-ordinate with it. *The true is the name of whatever proves itself to be good in the way of belief, and good, too, for definite, assignable reasons.* Surely you must admit this, that if there were *no* good for life in true ideas, or if the knowledge of them were positively disadvantageous and false ideas the only useful ones, then the current notion that truth is divine and precious, and its pursuit a duty, could never have grown up or become a dogma. In a world like that, our duty would be to *shun* truth, rather. But in this world, just as certain foods are not only agreeable to our taste, but good for our teeth, our stomach and our tissues; so certain ideas are not only agreeable to think about, or agreeable as supporting other ideas that we are fond of, but they are also helpful in life's practical struggles. If there be any life that it is really better we should lead, and if there be any idea which, if believed in, would help us to lead that life, then it would be really *better for us* to believe in that idea, *unless, indeed, belief in it incidentally clashed with other greater vital benefits.*

'What would be better for us to believe'! This sounds very like a definition of truth. It comes very near to saying 'what we *ought* to believe': and in *that* definition none of you would find any oddity. Ought we ever not to believe what it is *better for us* to believe? And can we then keep the notion of what is better for us, and what is true for us, permanently apart?

Pragmatism says no, and I fully agree with her. Probably you also agree, so far as the abstract statement goes, but with a suspicion that if we practically did believe everything that made for good in our own personal lives, we should be found indulging all kinds of fancies about this world's affairs, and all kinds of sentimental superstitions about a world hereafter. Your suspicion here is undoubtedly well founded, and it is evident that something happens when you pass from the abstract to the concrete, that complicates the situation.

I said just now that what is better for us to believe is true *unless the belief incidentally clashes with some other vital benefit.* Now in real life what vital benefits is any particular belief of ours most liable to clash with? What indeed except the vital benefits yielded by *other beliefs* when these prove incompatible with the first ones? In other words, the greatest enemy of any one of our truths may be the rest of our truths. Truths have once for all this desperate instinct of self-preservation and of desire to extinguish whatever contradicts them. My belief in the Absolute, based on the good it does me, must run the gauntlet of all my other beliefs. Grant that it may be true in giving me a moral holiday. Nevertheless, as I conceive it,—and let me speak now confidentially, as it were, and merely in my own private person,—it clashes with other truths of mine whose benefits I hate to give up on its account. It happens to be associated with a kind of logic of which I am the enemy, I find that it entangles me in metaphysical paradoxes that are inacceptable, etc., etc. But as I have enough trouble in life already without adding the trouble of carrying these intellectual inconsistencies, I personally just give up the Absolute. I just *take* my moral holidays; or else as a professional philosopher, I try to justify them by some other principle.

If I could restrict my notion of the Absolute to its bare holiday-giving value, it wouldn't clash with my other truths. But we cannot easily thus restrict our hypotheses. They carry supernumerary features, and these it is that clash so. My disbelief in the Absolute means then disbelief in those other supernumerary features, for I fully believe in the legitimacy of taking moral holidays.

You see by this what I meant when I called pragmatism a mediator and reconciler and said, borrowing the word from Papini, that she 'unstiffens' our theories. She has in fact no prejudices whatever, no obstructive dogmas, no rigid canons of what shall count as proof. She is completely genial. She will entertain any hypothesis, she will consider any evidence. It follows that in the religious field she is at a great advantage both over positivistic empiricism, with its anti-theological bias, and over religious rationalism, with its exclusive interest in the remote, the noble, the simple, and the abstract in the way of conception.

In short, she widens the field of search for God. Rationalism sticks to logic and the empyrean. Empiricism sticks to the external senses. Pragmatism is willing to take anything, to follow either logic or the senses, and to count the humblest and most personal experiences. She will count mystical experiences if they have practical consequences. She will take a God who lives in the very dirt of private fact—if that should seem a likely place to find him.

Her only test of probable truth is what works best in the way of leading us, what fits every part of life best and combines with the collectivity of experience's demands, nothing being omitted. If theological ideas should do this, if the notion of God, in particular, should prove to do it, how could pragmatism possibly deny God's existence? She could see no meaning in treating as 'not true' a notion that was pragmatically so successful. What other kind of truth could there be, for her, than all this agreement with concrete reality?

In my last lecture I shall return again to the relations of pragmatism with religion. But you see already how democratic she is. Her manners are as various and flexible, her resources as rich and endless, and her conclusions as friendly as those of mother nature.

Robert Frost

Out, Out—

 1915

In this harrowing poem, Robert Frost (1874–1963)—born in San Francisco to a New England family that returned east when he was ten—relates a farmyard incident of shock, blood, and death. There is a streak of cruelty in Frost's work (Seamus Heaney calls "Out, Out—" a piece of "cruel reporting") that belies his popular reputation as the New England bard of pretty country scenes and childhood idylls; but, as in the simple word sequence diminishing in scale with which the poet reports the failing of the young boy's pulse, "Little—less—nothing!" there is also fierce compassion.

The buzz saw snarled and rattled in the yard
And made dust and dropped stove-length sticks of wood,
Sweet-scented stuff when the breeze drew across it.
And from there those that lifted eyes could count
Five mountain ranges one behind the other
Under the sunset far into Vermont.
And the saw snarled and rattled, snarled and rattled,
As it ran light, or had to bear a load.
And nothing happened: day was all but done.
Call it a day, I wish they might have said
To please the boy by giving him the half hour
That a boy counts so much when saved from work.
His sister stood beside them in her apron
To tell them 'Supper.' At the word, the saw,
As if to prove saws knew what supper meant,
Leaped out at the boy's hand, or seemed to leap—
He must have given the hand. However it was,
Neither refused the meeting. But the hand!
The boy's first outcry was a rueful laugh,
As he swung toward them holding up the hand
Half in appeal, but half as if to keep
The life from spilling. Then the boy saw all—
Since he was old enough to know, big boy

Doing a man's work, though a child at heart—
He saw all spoiled. 'Don't let him cut my hand off—
The doctor, when he comes. Don't let him, sister!'
So. But the hand was gone already.
The doctor put him in the dark of ether.
He lay and puffed his lips out with his breath.
And then—the watcher at his pulse took fright.
No one believed. They listened at his heart.
Little—less—nothing!—and that ended it.
No more to build on there. And they, since they
Were not the one dead, turned to their affairs.

WALLACE STEVENS

The Snow Man

 1921

Wallace Stevens (1879–1955) lived an inconspicuous life as an executive of an insurance company in Hartford, Connecticut, and did not publish his first book, *Harmonium* (which includes "The Snow Man," first published in *Poetry* magazine), until 1923, when he was in his forties. His poems continually return to the theme of human beings struggling to coax some hint of meaning from recalcitrant nature. Stevens was an allusive writer, and the "bare place" where the wind blows its indecipherable sound in "The Snow Man" may be a conscious echo of the "bare common" where Emerson, as he reports in *Nature,* felt uplifted by "currents of universal being" flowing through him. The contradictory emotions of Stevens's poems—resignation, longing, and a kind of relief or even exhilaration at the clean-sweptness of things—are not so much mutually exclusive as balanced in a way that keeps any one of them from dominating the mood. "The Snow Man" leaves the reader in that state of suspension between horror and wonder that is properly called awe.

One must have a mind of winter
To regard the frost and the boughs
Of the pine-trees crusted with snow;
And have been cold a long time
To behold the junipers shagged with ice,
The spruces rough in the distant glitter

Of the January sun; and not to think
Of any misery in the sound of the wind,
In the sound of a few leaves,

Which is the sound of the land
Full of the same wind
That is blowing in the same bare place

For the listener, who listens in the snow,
And, nothing himself, beholds
Nothing that is not there and the nothing that is.

HENRY BESTON

From The Outermost House

 1928

Born in Quincy, Massachusetts, Henry Sheahan (1888–1968) replaced his surname with the middle name, Beston, that marked his French ancestry. He lived most of his life in Maine, but his book *The Outermost House*, which has become something of an environmental classic, concerns the year he spent living alone in a small house on the beach at Eastham, on Cape Cod. In the tradition of Thoreau's *Walden*, it is a book that registers, with something like a spirit of vindication for the nonhuman world, how elusive nature remains even as it yields a few—very few—of its mysteries to human rationality.

Autumn, Ocean, and Birds

There is a new sound on the beach, and a greater sound. Slowly, and day by day, the surf grows heavier, and down the long miles of the beach, at the lonely stations, men hear the coming winter in the roar. Mornings and evenings grow cold, the northwest wind grows cold; the last crescent of the month's moon, discovered by chance in a pale morning sky, stands north of the sun. Autumn ripens faster on the beach than on the marshes and the dunes. Westward and landward there is colour; seaward, bright space and austerity. Lifted to the sky, the dying grasses on the dune tops' rim tremble and lean seaward in the wind, wraiths of sand course flat along the beach, the hiss of sand mingles its thin stridency with the new thunder of the sea.

I have been spending my afternoons gathering driftwood and observing birds. The skies being clear, noonday suns take something of the bite out of the wind, and now and then a warmish west-sou'westerly finds its way back into the world. Into the bright, vast days I go, shouldering home my sticks and broken boards and driving shore birds on ahead of me, putting up sanderlings and sandpipers, ringnecks and knots, plovers and killdeer, coveys of a dozen, little flocks, great flocks, compact assemblies with a regimented air. For a fortnight past, October 9th to October 23d, an enormous population of the migrants has been "stopping over" on my Eastham sands, gathering, resting, feeding, and commingling. They come, they go, they melt away, they gather again; for actual miles the intricate and inter-crisscross pattern of their feet runs unbroken along the tide rim of Cape Cod.

Yet it is no confused and careless horde through which I go, but an army. Some spirit of discipline and unity has passed over these countless little brains, waking in each flock a conscious sense of its collective self and giving each bird a sense of himself as a member of some migrant company. Lone fliers are rare, and when seen have an air of being in pursuit of some flock which has overlooked them and gone on. Swift as the wind they fly, speeding along the breakers with the directness of a runner down a course, and I read fear in their speed. Sometimes I see them find their own and settle down beside them half a mile ahead, sometimes they melt away into a vista of surf and sky, still speeding on, still seeking.

The general multitude, it would seem, consists of birds who have spent the summer somewhere on the outer Cape and of autumn reinforcements from the north.

I see the flocks best when they are feeding on the edge of a tide which rises to its flood in the later afternoon. No summer blur of breaker mist or glassiness of heat now obscures these outer distances, and as on I stride, keeping to the lower beach when returning with a load, I can see birds and more birds and ever more birds ahead. Every last advance of a dissolved breaker, coursing on, flat and seething, has those who run away before it, turning its flank or fluttering up when too closely pursued; every retreating in-sucked slide has those who follow it back, eagerly dipping and gleaning. Having fed, the birds fly up to the upper beach and sit there for hours in the luke-cold wind, flock by flock, assembly by assembly. The ocean thunders, pale wisps and windy tatters of wintry cloud sail over the dunes, and the sandpipers stand on one leg and dream, their heads tousled deep into their feathers.

I wonder where these thousands spend the night. Waking the other morning just before sunrise, I hurried into my clothes and went down to the beach. North and then south I strolled, along an ebbing tide, and north and south the great beach was as empty of bird life as the sky. Far to the south, I remember now, a frightened pair of semipalmated sandpipers did rise from somewhere on the upper beach and fly toward me swift and voiceless, pass me on the flank, and settle by the water's edge a hundred yards or so behind. They instantly began to run about and feed, and as I watched them an orange sun floated up over the horizon with the speed and solemnity of an Olympian balloon.

The tide being high these days late in the afternoon, the birds begin to muster on the beach about ten o'clock in the morning. Some fly over from the salt meadows, some arrive flying along the beach, some drop from the sky. I startle up a first group on turning from the upper beach to the lower. I walk directly at the birds—a general apprehension, a rally, a scutter ahead, and the birds are gone. Standing on the beach, fresh claw marks at my feet, I watch the lovely sight of the group instantly turned into a constellation of birds, into a fugitive pleiades whose living stars keep their chance positions; I watch the spiralling flight, the momentary tilts of the white bellies, the alternate shows of the clustered, grayish backs. The group next ahead, though wary from the first, continues feeding. I draw nearer; a few run ahead as if to escape me afoot, others stop and prepare to fly; nearer still, the birds can stand no more; another rally, another scutter, and they are following their kin along the surges.

No aspect of nature on this beach is more mysterious to me than the flights of these shorebird constellations. The constellation forms, as I have hinted, in an instant of time, and in that same instant develops its own will. Birds which have been feeding yards away from each other, each one individually busy for his individual body's sake, suddenly fuse into this new volition and, flying, rise as one, coast as one, tilt their dozen bodies as one, and as one wheel off on the course which the new group will has determined. There is no such thing, I may add, as a lead bird or guide. Had I more space I should like nothing better than to discuss this new will and its instant or origin, but I do not want to crowd this part of my chapter, and must therefore leave the problem to all who study the psychic relations between the individual and a surrounding many. My special interest is rather the instant and synchronous obedience of each speeding body to the new volition. By what means, by what methods of communication does this will so suffuse the living constellation that its dozen or more tiny brains know it and obey it in such an instancy of time? Are we to believe that these birds, all of them, are *machina*, as Descartes long ago insisted, mere mechanisms of flesh and bone so exquisitely alike that each cog-wheel brain, encountering the same environmental forces, synchronously lets slip the same mechanic ratchet? or is there some psychic relation between these creatures? Does some current flow through them and between them as they fly? Schools of fish, I am told, make similar mass changes of direction. I saw such a thing once, but of that more anon.

We need another and a wiser and perhaps a more mystical concept of animals. Remote from universal nature, and living by complicated artifice, man in civilization surveys the creature through the glass of his knowledge and sees thereby a feather magnified and the whole image in distortion. We patronize them for their incompleteness, for their tragic fate of having taken form so far below ourselves. And therein we err, and greatly err. For the animal shall not be measured by man. In a world older and more complete than ours they move finished and complete, gifted with extensions of the senses we have lost or never attained, living by voices we shall never hear. They are not

brethren, they are not underlings; they are other nations, caught with ourselves in the net of life and time, fellow prisoners of the splendour and travail
of the earth.

The afternoon sun sinks red as fire; the tide climbs the beach, its foam a
strange crimson; miles out, a freighter goes north, emerging from the shoals.

ROBERT LOWELL

Mr. Edwards and the Spider

 1944

Scion of a distinguished New England family, Robert Lowell (1917–1977) inherited a large capacity for self-torment from his forebears. He was always trying to escape what he called "this planned / Babel of Boston where our money talks"—to Kenyon College after two years at Harvard, to Louisiana, to New York, to a poor immigrant district of Bridgeport, to a new wife after each failed marriage, into a brief embrace of Catholicism, then the United States Army (at the outset of World War II), followed by conscientious objection when he glimpsed the full horror of war. But, as Jean Stafford (to whom he was briefly married) once wrote, one suspects that "in the renegade who has extirpated his New England accent and has espoused the life of the new frontiers, there is still the Puritan within his unalterable bones."

A kind of spiritual rage animates Lowell's best work, as it does this bitter poem (published in his early collection *Lord Weary's Castle*) in which the poet opposes to Edwards's beatific vision images of death and horror: Christ, with nothing to show for his effort to rescue man except thorns and lacerations; Edwards's uncle, Josiah Hawley, who despaired for his soul and cut his own throat; and the beautiful but deadly spider, incinerated in a flash.

> I saw the spiders marching through the air,
> Swimming from tree to tree that mildewed day
>   In latter August when the hay
>   Came creaking to the barn. But where
>   The wind is westerly,
> Where gnarled November makes the spiders fly
> Into the apparitions of the sky,
>   They purpose nothing but their ease and die
> Urgently beating east to sunrise and the sea;
>
> What are we in the hands of the great God?
> It was in vain you set up thorn and briar
>   In battle array against the fire
>   And treason crackling in your blood;

For the wild thorns grow tame
And will do nothing to oppose the flame;
Your lacerations tell the losing game
You play against a sickness past your cure.
How will the hands be strong? How will the heart endure?

A very little thing, a little worm,
Or hourglass-blazoned spider, it is said,
    Can kill a tiger. Will the dead
    Hold up his mirror and affirm
        To the four winds the smell
And flash of his authority? It's well
If God who holds you to the pit of hell,
Much as one holds a spider, will destroy,
Baffle and dissipate your soul. As a small boy

On Windsor Marsh, I saw the spider die
When thrown into the bowels of fierce fire:
    There's no long struggle, no desire
    To get up on its feet and fly—
        It stretches out its feet
And dies. This is the sinner's last retreat;
Yes, and no strength exerted on the heat
Then sinews the abolished will, when sick
And full of burning, it will whistle on a brick.

But who can plumb the sinking of that soul?
Josiah Hawley, picture yourself cast
    Into a brick-kiln where the blast
    Fans your quick vitals to a coal—
        If measured by a glass,
How long would it seem burning! Let there pass
A minute, ten, ten trillion; but the blaze
Is infinite, eternal: this is death,
To die and know it. This is the Black Widow, death.

GALWAY KINNELL

Another Night in the Ruins

 1966, 1968

Galway Kinnell was born in Providence, Rhode Island, in 1927 to immigrant parents—his father came from Scotland, his mother from Ireland—and attended public schools in Pawtucket before going on scholarship to a private academy in Massachusetts, and then to Princeton. Kinnell's poems are often propelled by a frankly exposed fear of death—a panic barely controlled by the patterned sounds and images out of which the poems are built. Raw and stark, but modulated by quiet passages of reflection, they are especially effective when recited aloud by the poet, who is a master reader. Among the most moving are those in which he meditates on the death of his brother in an automobile accident in 1957, as in "Another Night in the Ruins," published in the *Paris Review* in 1966, then revised for his 1968 collection *Body Rags*.

1
In the evening
haze darkening on the hills,
purple
of the eternal, a last bird
crosses over, *'flop flop,'*
adoring
only the instant.

2
Nine years ago,
in a plane that rumbled all night
above the Atlantic,
I could see, lit up
by lightning bolts jumping out of it,
a thunderhead formed like the face
of my brother, looking nostalgically down
on blue,
lightning-flashed moments of the Atlantic.

3
He used to tell me,
"What good is the day?
On some hill of despair
the bonfire
you kindle can light the great sky—
though it's true, of course, to make it burn
you have to throw yourself in . . ."

4
Wind tears itself hollow
in the eaves of my ruins, ghost-flute
of snowdrifts
that build out there in the dark:
upside-down
ravines into which night sweeps
our torn wings, our ink-spattered feathers.

5
I listen.
I hear nothing. Only
the cow, the cow
of nothingness, mooing
down the bones.

6
Is that a
rooster? He
thrashes in the snow
for a grain. Finds
it. Rips
it into
flames. Flaps. Crows.
Flames
bursting out of his brow.

7
How many nights must it take
one such as me to learn
that we aren't, after all, made

from that bird which flies out of its ashes,
that for a man
as he goes up in flames, his one work
is
to open himself, to *be*
the flames?

RICHARD WILBUR

Mayflies

 1998

Richard Wilbur was born in 1921 in the Washington Heights section of Manhattan, and moved as a child to New Jersey. Since his student days at Amherst, he has been a New Englander, teaching for a time at Harvard, and for many years at Wesleyan University in Middletown, Connecticut. Like his younger contemporary John Updike, Wilbur has sometimes been faulted for an excess of elegance and refinement—a mistaken but common charge from the critics. In fact, Wilbur's technique has always been in the service of authentic, if disciplined, emotion, exemplifying his conviction that "poetry, to be vital, does seem to need a periodic acquaintance with the threat of Chaos." That threat seems not far from his consciousness in the recently composed "Mayflies," with its almost wistful invocation of the old faith in a "caller" to whom nature and man are beholden.

In sombre forest, when the sun was low,
I saw from unseen pools a mist of flies
    In their quadrillions rise
And animate a ragged patch of glow
With sudden glittering—as when a crowd
    Of stars appear
Through a brief gap in black and driven cloud,
One arc of their great round-dance showing clear.

It was no muddled swarm I witnessed, for
In entrechats each fluttering insect there
    Rose two steep yards in air,
Then slowly floated down to climb once more,
So that they all composed a manifold
    And figured scene,
And seemed the weavers of some cloth of gold,
Or the fine pistons of some bright machine.

Watching those lifelong dancers of a day
As night closed in, I felt myself alone

      In a life too much my own,
More mortal in my separateness than they—
Unless, I thought, I had been called to be
      Not fly or star
But one whose task is joyfully to see
How fair the fiats of the caller are.

The Examined Self

It may seem a long way from the Puritan demand that every person must root out "the lusts, and deceits, and corruptions" that lurk within one's soul to Emerson's assertion, in his great essay "Self-Reliance," that "nothing is at last sacred but the integrity of your own mind." But the distance may be smaller than it first appears. Common to all the following selections is the conviction that truth—incipient, vestigial, or full-blown—is to be found only through the process of self-discovery, and that the work of searching for it is as compulsory as it is arduous and painful.

Robert Frost in Vermont, 1921

John Cotton

From Christ the Fountain of Life

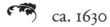 ca. 1630

One of the most eminent leaders of the Puritan movement in England, John Cotton (1584–1652) brought considerable personal prestige to the Massachusetts Bay colony when he emigrated there in 1633. Described by his grandson Cotton Mather as a "walking library," he was renowned not only as a scholar but also as a soul-melting preacher of great spiritual insight and exemplary piety. His sermon series on the first epistle of John, published under the title *Christ the Fountaine of Life* (1651), was first delivered in England but most likely repeated in variant forms from his pulpit in America. Cotton had an incantatory style that beckoned listeners into the mysteries of grace by evoking such paradoxes as the saints' joyful resignation to the overmastering will of God, their unworldly commitment to consecrated action in the world, and, as in this passage about Moses—who, to the Puritan mind, was a prophet and type (in the sense of a foreshadowing) of the Christian hero—the simultaneous gentleness and ferocity that mark the faithful.

It was said of Moses, *He was the meekest man upon earth,* (Numbers 12:3). Take Moses in his own case, and his carriage towards men, as they had respect to himself, and then he was a meek man, soon persuaded. Yet the same Moses, when he saw the matter concerned the cause of God, he is so stiff and unmoveable, as that he will not yield one jot, he will not *leave an hoof behind, of all that appertained to the children of Israel,* (Exodus 10:26). He would not only have men, and women, and children go forth to serve the Lord, but their cattle and their stuff; he will not yield a little here, no not for the king's pleasure's sake. A man would much wonder that such a man, so meek and gentle, and so easy to be persuaded in his own cause, that yet when it comes to a matter of importance, and concerns God, he will not there yield. He is now inflexible; nothing can persuade him to give way to it.

This is a combination of graces that are not wont to be found in men thus mixed together, but it is found in the people of God, that live a sanctified and holy life. I know not better what to instance in, than in the liquid air, of all other things the most easiest to be pierced through. Of itself it gives way to every creature, nor the least fly, or least stone cast into it, but it gives way to it of itself, yet if God say it shall be as a firmament, between the waters above, and the waters below, it then stands like a wall of brass, and yields not. It will not suffer the water in the clouds to fall down, but if it do fall to water the earth, it shall strain through the air as through a sieve. The clouds sometimes are so full that one would think they would burst through the air, and fall upon the earth, but God having set the air to be a firmament, or expulsion between the waters above and the waters below, though of itself a very liquid thing, yet it stands like to a wall of brass.

And truly so is it with a Christian spirit, though of himself he is as liquid as the air, you may easily pass through him, and go an end with him easily; he is easy to be entreated, very gentle, but take him now in anything wherein God hath bid him keep his stand in his course, and there he stands like a wall of brass, that were never such high and great matters put upon him, ready to bear him down, he will not shrink, nor give any way at all. This is another mixture of affections which are found in Christian men, that do enjoy this life of holiness . . .

When [a Christian] looks at earthly things, yea the best of them, his heart is so weaned from them, that he knows not how to have an high thought, weaned even from a kingdom, as a child from the breast, and yet the same soul that is thus weaned, and thus mean in his own eyes, when he comes to spiritual matters, it is [a] wonder to see the height of his spirit . . . He looks at the favor of God, and the blood of Christ, and pardon of sin, the kingdom of glory. He looks at all these high matters as fit objects for his heart to be set upon . . . But *his eyes are not haughty;* he doth not exercise himself in such things as these be, but yet he exerciseth himself in greater matters than these things are, and therefore, when as Christian men are thought to be of shallow weak spirits, and know not how to carry on end matters in this world, yet when they come to spiritual matters, there they can tell how to set their hearts awork about such matters, about the inheritance of the kingdom of heaven, about the favor of God, and the light of God's countenance—these be great matters; when they come to have the eye of God upon them, they can look for the glory of his presence, and the fellowship of the angels, and they can discourse, and tell you of great blessings that God hath layed up for them in Christ . . .

A strange kind of combination in the spirit of grace wrought in such hearts: they can call upon their hearts to be lifted up to the high things of God, nothing then too great for them to exercise themselves in; no mercies, nor judgments too great, no not the unsearchable counsel of God, the depths of the mysteries of God, nothing is too high for them. It will be prying, and looking into the secret counsels of God, and yet both together with most modesty, when the soul is most lifted up in the ways of God. Yet at the same time he looks at himself as nothing, and yet notwithstanding so far forth as God will be pleased to reveal it to him, he will be searching into the deep things of God, and yet all this will he do with a very modest spirit.

Thus you have seen [the] combinations severally of the gracious affections that are not to be found in nature, no not set upon civil objects, much less upon spiritual, but upon civil objects they cannot be so combined together . . .

There is another combination of virtues strangely mixed in every lively holy Christian, and that is diligence in worldly business, and yet deadness to the world; such a mystery as none can read, but they that know it. For a man to *rise early, and go to bed late, and eat the bread of carefulness,* not a sinful, but a provident care, and to avoid idleness, cannot endure to spend any idle time, takes all opportunities to be doing something, early and late, and loseth no opportunity [to] go any way and bestir himself for profit—this will he do most diligently in his calling. And yet be a man dead-hearted to the world, *the diligent hand maketh rich,* (Proverbs 10:4). Now if this be a thing which is so common in the mouth of the Holy Ghost, and you see was the practice of the greatest women then upon the earth, [of] the greatest princes in those times, the more gracious, the more diligent, and laborious in their callings: you see it will well stand with the life of grace, very diligent in worldly business. And yet notwithstanding, the very same souls that are most full of the world's business, the more diligent they be in their callings, yet the same persons are directed to be *dead with Christ,* (Colossians 3:1–3). *Set not your affections upon things below, but on things that are above, for we are dead with Christ.* Meaning dead to all these earthly things, and all the comforts here below; they are not our life, but our *life is bid with Christ in God* and therefore to this world are we dead. And Paul therefore so speaks of it. Galatians 6:14, *The world is crucified to me, and I unto the world,* the very same men that are so crucified to the world, yet the spirits of those men, though their affections be in heaven, yet their labors are in the earth. Philippians 3:20: *Our conversation is in heaven,* but our employments is here upon the earth, diligently taking pains in our callings, ever very busy in outward employments. *Observe the ant, learn her ways, and be wise,* (Proverbs 6). Be busy like ants, morning and evening, early and late, and labor diligently with their hands, and with their wits, and which way soever as may be the best improvement of a man's talent; it must be employed to the best advantage, and yet when a man hath labored thus busily, yet his heart, and mind, and affections are above. He goes about all his business, in obedience to God's commandments, and he intends the glory of God, and he thereby sets himself and his household at more liberty for the service of God in their places, and so, though he labor most diligently in his calling, yet his heart is not set upon these things. He can tell what to do with

his estate when he hath got it. Say not therefore when you see two men laboring very diligently and busily in the world, say not, here is a couple of
worldlings, for two men may do the same business, and have the same success, and yet a marvelous difference between them: the heart of the one may
be dead to these things, he looks at them as they be; indeed, *but crumbs that
fall from the children's table.* He looks not at them as his chiefest good; but *the
bread of life,* the spiritual food of his soul, that is the thing which he chiefly labors after. And another man places his happiness and felicity in them, and
makes them his chiefest good, and so there is a manifest difference between
them . . .

The last virtue is a single one, and that is love of enemies. *I say unto you,
love your enemies,* (Matthew 5:44), *that you may be the children of your heavenly
Father.* Love your enemies. This very grace whereby we do love our enemies, it
hath a contrary work to nature, for naturally, this we shall find to be the frame
of our hearts towards our enemies: We are cold and undisposed to do any
good office unto them, very hard and cold, and frozen towards them. Those
who are our enemies, we take no pleasure in them, but now in such a case as
this, the love of a Christian will come and warm the heart, and thaw this cold
frostiness that is in our souls, whereas before a man was cold toward his enemies, his heart now begins to reflect upon him in pity and compassion. And
instead of hardness, his heart now melts and is made soft within him, to see
what ill measures it could have put upon its enemies. But on the contrary
side, the same hatred in a man that is towards his enemies, it makes a man of
an hot distemper, with boiling in heat of wrath against his enemies, he is all
upon it to do [them] any harm. His heart is full of hot and bitter wrath, so as
that love which was as heat and fire to thaw and warm cold and hard hearts,
when it comes to the fire of wrath, it is as it were cold water, and allays that
heat and bitterness, and harshness, which else our hearts are subject to.

This is the nature of love, as it is the nature of water to cool hot distempers,
and as it is the nature of fire, to thaw and soften hard frozen spirits, and so
though it be but as one entire grace. Yet in the act it puts forth a kind of variety of work, whereby one would think it did cross itself, but it doth not, but
doth all by the life of Christ. Thus you see what the effects of the life of
sanctification is in the heart of a man, after that God hath begun to root the
life of justification in us, and he discerns that God hath wrought a change in
him, and then these several graces, though in themselves, and work, one opposite to another—yet in a Christian heart they can meet and join together.

ANNE BRADSTREET

Before the Birth of One of Her Children

 ca. 1635

Anne Bradstreet (1612–1672)—daughter of the deputy governor of Massachusetts Bay colony, Thomas Dudley, and wife of Simon Bradstreet, governor-to-be—was a reluctant emigrant to New England. "I . . . came into this country," she wrote in a letter to her children, "where I found a new world and new manners, at which my heart rose. But after I was convinced it was the way of God, I submitted to it and joined to the church at Boston." One of the sorrows weighing on her as she made the journey was that "it pleased God to keep me a long time without a child, which was a great grief to me." When a son, Samuel, was born to her, she gave thanks for him as "The Son of Prayers of vowes, of teares, / The child I stay'd for many years."

In 1647, Bradstreet's brother-in-law carried back to London the manuscript of some poems she had been composing in the New World, and arranged for their publication, in 1650, in a volume promotionally entitled *The Tenth Muse, Lately Sprung up in America.* It included several touching love poems addressed to her husband, and, as represented by the poem reprinted below, it was suffused with the knowledge that human beings must expect to live out their days in the absence of those they loved.

> All things within this fading world hath end,
> Adversity doth still our joys attend;
> No ties so strong, no friends so dear and sweet,
> But with death's parting blow is sure to meet.
> The sentence past is most irrevocable,
> A common thing, yet oh, inevitable.
> How soon, my Dear, death may my steps attend,
> How soon't may be thy lot to lose thy friend,
> We both are ignorant, yet love bids me
> These farewell lines to recommend to thee,
> That when that knot's untied that made us one,
> I may seem thine, who in effect am none.
> And if I see not half my days that's due,
> What nature would, God grant to yours and you;

The many faults that well you know I have
Let be interred in my oblivious grave;
If any worth or virtue were in me,
Let that live freshly in thy memory
And when thou feel'st no grief, as I no harms,
Yet love thy dead, who long lay in thine arms.
And when thy loss shall be repaid with gains
Look to my little babes, my dear remains.
And if thou love thyself, or loved'st me,
These O protect from step-dame's injury.
And if chance to thine eyes shall bring this verse,
With some sad sighs honour my absent hearse;
And kiss this paper for thy love's dear sake,
Who with salt tears this last farewell did take.

JONATHAN EDWARDS

Personal Narrative

 ca. 1739

Sometime around his thirty-sixth year, Jonathan Edwards (1703–1758) put into writing his sense of the shape of his own life. The result is a short narrative that in some respects follows the established form of the conversion narrative that was exemplified by Augustine's *Confessions* and routinized by Christians ever after. But Edwards's tale is not easily contained within the standard structure of sin followed by repentance and peace. It gives a glimpse into the restless mind of a man always demanding more of himself, suspicious of his own capacity for self-satisfaction, and eager for the day when his own appetite for beauty and love will have become a worldwide contagion.

I had a variety of concerns and exercises about my soul from my childhood; but had two more remarkable seasons of awakening, before I met with that change, by which I was brought to those new dispositions, and that new sense of things, that I have since had. The first time was when I was a boy, some years before I went to college, at a time of remarkable awakening in my father's congregation. I was then very much affected for many months, and concerned about the things of religion, and my soul's salvation; and was abundant in duties. I used to pray five times a day in secret, and to spend much time in religious talk with other boys; and used to meet with them to pray together. I experienced I know not what kind of delight in religion. My mind was much engaged in it, and had much self-righteous pleasure; and it was my delight to abound in religious duties. I, with some of my schoolmates joined together, and built a booth in a swamp, in a very secret and retired place, for a place of prayer. And besides, I had particular secret places of my own in the woods, where I used to retire by myself; and used to be from time to time much affected. My affections seemed to be lively and easily moved, and I seemed to be in my element, when engaged in religious duties. And I am ready to think, many are deceived with such affections, and such a kind of delight, as I then had in religion, and mistake it for grace.

But in process of time, my convictions and affections wore off; and I entirely lost all those affections and delights, and left off secret prayer, at least as to any constant performance of it; and returned like a dog to his vomit, and went on in ways of sin.

Indeed, I was at some times very uneasy, especially towards the latter part of the time of my being at college. Till it pleased God, in my last year at college, at a time when I was in the midst of many uneasy thoughts about the state of my soul, to seize me with a pleurisy; in which he brought me nigh to the grave, and shook me over the pit of hell.

But yet, it was not long after my recovery, before I fell again into my old ways of sin. But God would not suffer me to go on with any quietness; but I had great and violent inward struggles: till after many conflicts with wicked inclinations, and repeated resolutions, and bonds that I laid myself under by a kind of vows to God, I was brought wholly to break off all former wicked ways, and all ways of known outward sin; and to apply myself to seek my salvation, and practice the duties of religion: but without that kind of affection and delight, that I had formerly experienced. My concern now wrought more by inward struggles and conflicts, and self-reflections. I made seeking my salvation the main business of my life. But yet it seems to me, I sought after a miserable manner: which has made me sometimes since to question, whether ever it issued in that which was saving; being ready to doubt, whether such miserable seeking was ever succeeded. But yet I was brought to seek salvation, in a manner that I never was before. I felt a spirit to part with all things in the world, for an interest in Christ. My concern continued and prevailed, with many exercising things and inward struggles; but yet it never seemed to be proper to express my concern that I had, by the name of terror.

From my childhood up, my mind had been wont to be full of objections against the doctrine of God's sovereignty, in choosing whom he would to eternal life, and rejecting whom he pleased; leaving them eternally to perish, and be everlastingly tormented in hell. It used to appear like a horrible doctrine to me. But I remember the time very well, when I seemed to be convinced, and fully satisfied, as to this sovereignty of God, and his justice in thus eternally disposing of men, according to his sovereign pleasure. But never could give an account, how, or by what means, I was thus convinced; not in the least imagining, in the time of it, nor a long time after, that there was any extraordinary influence of God's Spirit in it: but only that now I saw further, and my reason apprehended the justice and reasonableness of it. However, my mind rested in it; and it put an end to all those cavils and objections, that I had till then abode with me, all the preceding part of my life. And there has been a wonderful alteration in my mind, with respect to the doctrine of God's sovereignty, from that day to this; so that I scarce ever have found so much as the rising of an objection against God's sovereignty, in the most absolute sense, in showing mercy on whom he will show mercy, and hardening and eternally damning whom he will. God's absolute sovereignty, and justice, with respect to salvation and damnation, is what my mind seems to rest assured of, as much as of anything that I see with my eyes; at least it is so at times. But I have oftentimes since that first conviction, had quite another kind of sense of God's sovereignty, than I had then. I have often since, not only had a conviction, but a *delightful* conviction. The doctrine of God's sovereignty has very often appeared, an exceeding pleasant, bright and sweet doctrine to me: and absolute sovereignty is what I love to ascribe to God. But my first conviction was not with this.

The first that I remember that ever I found anything of that sort of inward, sweet delight in God and divine things, that I have lived much in since, was on reading those words, I Tim. 1:17. "Now unto the King eternal, immortal, invisible, the only wise God, be honor and glory forever and ever, Amen." As I read the words, there came into my soul, and was as it were diffused through it, a sense of the glory of the Divine Being; a new sense, quite different from anything I ever experienced before. Never any words of Scripture seemed to me as these words did. I thought with myself, how excellent a Being that was; and how happy I should be, if I might enjoy that God, and be wrapped up to God in heaven, and be as it were swallowed up in him. I kept saying, and as it were singing over these words of Scripture to myself; and went to prayer, to pray to God that I might enjoy him; and prayed in a manner quite different from what I used to do; with a new sort of affection. But it never came into my thought, that there was anything spiritual, or of a saving nature in this.

From about that time, I began to have a new kind of apprehensions and ideas of Christ, and the work of redemption, and the glorious way of salvation by him. I had an inward, sweet sense of these things, that at times came into my heart; and my soul was led away in pleasant views and contemplations of them. And my mind was greatly engaged, to spend my time in reading and meditating on Christ; and the beauty and excellency of his person, and the lovely way of salvation, by free grace in him. I found no books so delightful to me, as those that treated of these subjects. Those words, Cant. 2:1, used to be abundantly with me: "I am the rose of Sharon, the lily of the valleys." The words seemed to me, sweetly to represent, the loveliness and beauty of Jesus Christ. And the whole Book of Canticles used to be pleasant to me; and I used to be much in reading it, about that time. And found, from time to time, an inward sweetness, that used, as it were, to carry me away in my contemplations; in what I know not how to express otherwise, than by a calm, sweet abstraction of soul from all the concerns of this world; and a kind of vision, or fixed ideas and imaginations, of being alone in the mountains, or some solitary wilderness, far from all mankind, sweetly conversing with Christ, and wrapped and swallowed up in God. The sense I had of divine things, would often of a sudden as it were, kindle up a sweet burning in my heart; an ardor of my soul, that I know not how to express.

Not long after I first began to experience these things, I gave an account to my father, of some things that had passed in my mind. I was pretty much affected by the discourse we had together. And when the discourse was ended, I walked abroad alone, in a solitary place in my father's pasture, for contemplation. And as I was walking there, and looked up on the sky and clouds; there came into my mind, a sweet sense of the glorious majesty and grace of God, that I know not how to express. I seemed to see them both in a sweet conjunction: majesty and meekness joined together: it was a sweet and gentle, and holy majesty; and also a majestic meekness; an awful sweetness; a high, and great, and holy gentleness.

After this my sense of divine things gradually increased, and became more and more lively, and had more of that inward sweetness. The appearance of everything was altered: there seemed to be, as it were, a calm, sweet cast, or appearance of divine glory, in almost everything. God's excellency, his wisdom, his purity and love, seemed to appear in everything; in the sun, moon and stars; in the clouds, and blue sky; in the grass, flowers, trees; in the water, and all nature; which used greatly to fix my mind. I often used to sit and view the moon, for a long time; and so in the daytime, spent much time in viewing the clouds and sky, to behold the sweet glory of God in these things: in the meantime, singing forth with a low voice, my contemplations of the Creator and Redeemer. And scarce anything, among all the works of nature, was so sweet to me as thunder and lightning. Formerly, nothing had been so terrible to me. I used to be a person uncommonly terrified with thunder: and it used to strike me with terror, when I saw a thunderstorm rising. But now, on the contrary, it rejoiced me. I felt God at the first appearance of a thunderstorm. And used to take the opportunity at such times, to fix myself to view the clouds, and see the lightnings play, and hear the majestic and awful voice of God's thunder: which oftentimes was exceeding entertaining, leading me to sweet contemplations of my great and glorious God. And while I viewed, used to spend my time, as it always seemed natural to me, to sing or chant forth my meditations; to speak my thoughts in soliloquies, and speak with a singing voice.

I felt then a great satisfaction as to my good estate. But that did not content me. I had vehement longings of soul after God and Christ, and after more holiness; wherewith my heart seemed to be full, and ready to break: which often brought to my mind, the words of the Psalmist, Ps. 119:28, "My soul breaketh for the longing it hath." I often felt a mourning and lamenting in my heart, that I had not turned to God sooner, that I might have had more time to grow in grace. My mind was greatly fixed on divine things; I was almost perpetually in the contemplation of them. Spent most of my time in thinking of divine things, year after year. And used to spend abundance of my time, in walking alone in the woods, and solitary places, for meditation, soliloquy and prayer, and converse with God. And it was always my manner, at such times, to sing forth my contemplations. And was almost constantly in ejaculatory prayer, wherever I was. Prayer seemed to be natural to me; as the breath, by which the inward burnings of my heart had vent.

The delights which I now felt in things of religion, were of an exceeding different kind, from those forementioned, that I had when I was a boy. They were totally of another kind; and what I then had no more notion or idea of, than one born blind has of pleasant and beautiful colors. They were of a more inward, pure, soul-animating and refreshing nature. Those former delights, never reached the heart; and did not arise from any sight of the divine excellency of the things of God; or any taste of the soul-satisfying, and life-giving good, there is in them.

My sense of divine things seemed gradually to increase, till I went to preach at New York; which was about a year and a half after they began. While I was there, I felt them, very sensibly, in a much higher degree, than I had done before. My longings after God and holiness, were much increased. Pure and humble, holy and heavenly Christianity, appeared exceeding amiable to me. I felt in me a burning desire to be in everything a complete Christian; and conformed to the blessed image of Christ: and that I might live in all things, according to the pure, sweet and blessed rules of the gospel. I had an eager thirsting after progress in these things. My longings after it, put me upon pursuing and pressing after them. It was my continual strife day and night, and constant inquiry, how I should be more holy, and live more holily, and more becoming a child of God, and disciple of Christ. I sought an increase of grace and holiness, and that I might live an holy life, with vastly more earnestness, than ever I sought grace, before I had it. I used to be continually examining myself, and studying and contriving for likely ways and means, how I should live holily, with far greater diligence and earnestness, than ever I pursued anything in my life: but with too great a dependence on my own strength; which afterwards proved a great damage to me. My experience had not then taught me, as it has done since, my extreme feebleness and impotence, every manner of way; and the innumerable and bottomless depths of secret corruption and deceit, that there was in my heart. However, I went on with my eager pursuit after more holiness; and sweet conformity to Christ.

The heaven I desired was a heaven of holiness; to be with God, and to spend my eternity in divine love, and holy communion with Christ. My mind was very much taken up with contemplations on heaven, and the enjoyments of those there; and living there in perfect holiness, humility and love. And it used at that time to appear a great part of the happiness of heaven, that there the saints could express their love to Christ. It appeared to me a great clog and hindrance and burden to me, that what I felt within, I could not express to God, and give vent to, as I desired. The inward ardor of my soul, seemed to be hindered and pent up, and could not freely flame out as it would. I used often to think, how in heaven, this sweet principle should freely and fully vent and express itself. Heaven appeared to me exceeding delightful as a world of love. It appeared to me, that all happiness consisted in living in pure, humble, heavenly, divine love.

I remember the thoughts I used then to have of holiness. I remember I then said sometimes to myself, I do certainly know that I love holiness, such as the gospel prescribes. It appeared to me, there was nothing in it but what was ravishingly lovely. It appeared to me, to be the highest beauty and amiableness, above all other beauties: that it was a *divine* beauty; far purer than anything here upon earth; and that everything else, was like mire, filth and defilement, in comparison of it.

Holiness, as I then wrote down some of my contemplations on it, appeared to me to be of a sweet, pleasant, charming, serene, calm nature. It seemed to me, it brought an inexpressible purity, brightness, peacefulness and ravishment to the soul: and that it made the soul like a field or garden of God, with all manner of pleasant flowers; that is all pleasant, delightful and undisturbed; enjoying a sweet calm, and the gently vivifying beams of the sun. The soul of a true Christian, as I then wrote my meditations, appeared like such a little white flower, as we see in the spring of the year; low and humble on the ground, opening its bosom, to receive the pleasant beams of the sun's glory; rejoicing as it were, in a calm rapture; diffusing around a sweet fragrancy; standing peacefully and lovingly, in the midst of other flowers round about; all in like manner opening their bosoms, to drink in the light of the sun.

There was no part of creature-holiness, that I then, and at other times, had so great a sense of the loveliness of, as humility, brokenness of heart and poverty of spirit: and there was nothing that I had such a spirit to long for. My heart as it were panted after this, to lie low before God, and in the dust; that I might be nothing, and that God might be all; that I might become as a little child.

While I was there at New York, I sometimes was much affected with reflections on my past life, considering how late it was, before I began to be truly religious; and how wickedly I had lived till then: and once so as to weep abundantly, and for a considerable time together.

On January 12, 1722–23, I made a solemn dedication of myself to God, and wrote it down; giving up myself, and all that I had to God; to be for the future in no respect my own; to act as one that had no right to himself, in any respect. And solemnly vowed to take God for my whole portion and felicity; looking on nothing else as any part of my happiness, nor acting as if it were: and his law for the constant rule of my obedience: engaging to fight with all my might, against the world, the flesh and the devil, to the end of my life. But have reason to be infinitely humbled, when I consider, how much I have failed of answering my obligation.

I had then abundance of sweet religious conversation in the family where I lived, with Mr. John Smith, and his pious mother. My heart was knit in affection to those, in whom were appearances of true piety; and I could bear the thoughts of no other companions, but such as were holy, and the disciples of the blessed Jesus.

I had great longings for the advancement of Christ's kingdom in the world. My secret prayer used to be in great part taken up in praying for it. If I heard the least hint of any thing that happened in any part of the world, that appeared to me, in some respect or other, to have a favorable aspect on the interest of Christ's kingdom, my soul eagerly catched at it; and it would much animate and refresh me. I used to be earnest to read public newsletters, mainly for that end; to see if I could not find some news favorable to the interest of religion in the world.

I very frequently used to retire into a solitary place, on the banks of Hudson's River, at some distance from the city, for contemplation on divine things, and secret converse with God; and had many sweet hours there. Sometimes Mr. Smith and I walked there together, to converse of the things of God; and our conversation used much to turn on the advancement of Christ's kingdom in the world, and the glorious things that God would accomplish for his church in the latter days.

I had then, and at other times, the greatest delight in the holy Scriptures, of any book whatsoever. Oftentimes in reading it, every word seemed to touch my heart. I felt an harmony between something in my heart, and those sweet and powerful words. I seemed often to see so much light, exhibited by every sentence, and such a refreshing ravishing food communicated, that I could not get along in reading. Used oftentimes to dwell long on one sentence, to see the wonders contained in it; and yet almost every sentence seemed to be full of wonders.

I came away from New York in the month of April 1723, and had a most bitter parting with Madam Smith and her son. My heart seemed to sink within me, at leaving the family and city, where I had enjoyed so many sweet and pleasant days. I went from New York to Wethersfield by water. As I sailed away, I kept sight of the city as long as I could; and when I was out of sight of it, it would affect me much to look that way, with a kind of melancholy mixed with sweetness. However, that night after this sorrowful parting, I was greatly comforted in God at Westchester, where we went ashore to lodge: and had a pleasant time of it all the voyage to Saybrook. It was sweet to me to think of meeting dear Christians in heaven, where we should never part more. At Saybrook we went ashore to lodge on Saturday, and there kept sabbath; where I had a sweet and refreshing season, walking alone in the fields.

After I came home to Windsor, remained much in a like frame of my mind, as I had been in at New York; but only sometimes felt my heart ready to sink, with the thoughts of my friends at New York. And my refuge and support was in contemplations on the heavenly state; as I find in my Diary of May 1, 1723. It was my comfort to think of that state, where there is fullness of joy; where reigns heavenly, sweet, calm and delightful love, without alloy; where there are continually the dearest expressions of this love; where is the enjoyment of the persons loved, without ever parting; where these persons that appear so lovely in this world, will really be inexpressibly more lovely, and full of love to us. And how sweetly will the mutual lovers join together to sing the praises of God and the Lamb! How full will it fill us with joy, to think, that this enjoyment, these sweet exercises will never cease or come to an end; but will last to all eternity!

Continued much in the same frame in the general, that I had been in at New York, till I went to New Haven, to live there as tutor of the College; having one special season of uncommon sweetness: particularly once at Bolton, in a journey from Boston, walking out alone in the fields. After I went to New Haven, I sunk in religion; my mind being diverted from my eager and violent pursuits after holiness, by some affairs that greatly perplexed and distracted my mind.

In September 1725, was taken ill at New Haven; and endeavoring to go home to Windsor, was so ill at the North Village, that I could go no further: where I lay sick for about a quarter of a year. And in this sickness, God was pleased to visit me again with the sweet influences of his Spirit. My mind was greatly engaged there on divine, pleasant contemplations, and longings of soul. I observed that those who watched with me, would often be looking out for the morning, and seemed to wish for it. Which brought to my mind those words of the Psalmist, which my soul with sweetness made its own language. "My soul waiteth for the Lord more than they that watch for the morning: I say, more than they that watch for the morning" [Ps. 130:6]. And when the light of the morning came, and the beams of the sun came in at the windows, it refreshed my soul from one morning to another. It seemed to me to be some image of the sweet light of God's glory.

I remember, about that time, I used greatly to long for the conversion of some that I was concerned with. It seemed to me, I could gladly honor them, and with delight be a servant to them, and lie at their feet, if they were but truly holy.

But some time after this, I was again greatly diverted in my mind, with some temporal concerns, that exceedingly took up my thoughts, greatly to the wounding of my soul: and went on through various exercises, that it would be tedious to relate, that gave me much more experience of my own heart, than ever I had before.

Since I came to [Northampton], I have often had sweet complacency in God in views of his glorious perfections, and the excellency of Jesus Christ. God has appeared to me, a glorious and lovely Being, chiefly on the account of his holiness. The holiness of God has always appeared to me the most lovely of all his attributes. The doctrines of God's absolute sovereignty, and free grace, in showing mercy to whom he would show mercy; and man's abso-lute dependence on the operations of God's Holy Spirit, have very often ap-peared to me as sweet and glorious doctrines. These doctrines have been much my delight. God's sovereignty has ever appeared to me, as great part of his glory. It has often been sweet to me to go to God, and adore him as a sov-ereign God, and ask sovereign mercy of him.

I have loved the doctrines of the gospel: they have been to my soul like green pastures. The gospel has seemed to me to be the richest treasure; the treasure that I have most desired, and longed that it might dwell richly in me. The way of salvation by Christ, has appeared in a general way, glorious and excellent, and most pleasant and beautiful. It has often seemed to me, that it would in a great measure spoil heaven, to receive it in any other way. That text has often been affecting and delightful to me, Is. 32.2, "A man shall be an hid-ing place from the wind, and a covert from the tempest; as rivers of water in a dry place, as the shadow of a great rock in a weary land."

It has often appeared sweet to me, to be united to Christ; to have him for my head, and to be a member of his body: and also to have Christ for my teacher and prophet. I very often think with sweetness and longings and pantings of soul, of being a little child, taking hold of Christ, to be led by him through the wilderness of this world. That text, Matt. 18, at the beginning, has often been sweet to me: "Except ye be converted, and become as little children, ye shall not enter into the kingdom of heaven." I love to think of coming to Christ, to receive salvation of him, poor in spirit, and quite empty of self; humbly exalting him alone; cut entirely off from my own root, and to grow into, and out of Christ: to have God in Christ to be all in all; and to live by faith on the Son of God, a life of humble, unfeigned confidence in him. That Scripture has often been sweet to me, Ps. 115:1, "Not unto us, O Lord, not unto us, but unto thy name give glory, for thy mercy, and for thy truth's sake." And those words of Christ, Luke 10:21, "In that hour Jesus rejoiced in spirit, and said, I thank thee, O Father, Lord of heaven and earth, that thou hast hid these things from the wise and prudent, and hast revealed them unto babes: even so, Father; for so it seemed good in thy sight." That sovereignty of

God that Christ rejoiced in, seemed to me to be worthy to be rejoiced in; and that rejoicing of Christ, seemed to me to show the excellency of Christ, and the Spirit that he was of.

Sometimes only mentioning a single word, causes my heart to burn within me: or only seeing the name of Christ, or the name of some attribute of God. And God has appeared glorious to me, on account of the Trinity. It has made me have exalting thoughts of God, that he subsists in three persons; Father, Son, and Holy Ghost.

The sweetest joys of delights I have experienced, have not been those that have arisen from a hope of my own good estate; but in a direct view of the glorious things of the gospel. When I enjoy this sweetness, it seems to carry me above the thoughts of my own safe estate. It seems at such times a loss that I cannot bear, to take off my eye from the glorious, pleasant object I behold without me, to turn my eye in upon myself, and my own good estate.

My heart has been much on the advancement of Christ's kingdom in the world. The histories of the past advancement of Christ's kingdom, have been sweet to me. When I have read histories of past ages, the pleasantest thing in all my reading has been, to read of the kingdom of Christ being promoted. And when I have expected in my reading, to come to any such thing, I have lotted upon it all the way as I read. And my mind has been much entertained and delighted, with the Scripture promises and prophecies, of the future glorious advancement of Christ's kingdom on earth.

I have sometimes had a sense of the excellent fullness of Christ, and his meetness and suitableness as a Savior; whereby he has appeared to me, far above all, the chief of ten thousands. And his blood and atonement has appeared sweet, and his righteousness sweet; which is always accompanied with an ardency of spirit, and inward strugglings and breathings and groanings, that cannot be uttered, to be emptied of myself, and swallowed up in Christ.

Once, as I rid out into the woods for my health, anno 1737; and having lit from my horse in a retired place, as my manner commonly has been, to walk for divine contemplation and prayer; I had a view, that for me was extraordinary, of the glory of the Son of God; as mediator between God and man; and his wonderful, great, full, pure and sweet grace and love, and meek and gentle condescension. This grace, that appeared to me so calm and sweet, appeared great above the heavens. The person of Christ appeared ineffably excellent, with an excellency great enough to swallow up all thought and conception. Which continued, as near as I can judge, about an hour; which kept me, the bigger part of the time, in a flood of tears, and weeping aloud. I felt withal, an ardency of soul to be, what I know not otherwise how to express, than to be emptied and annihilated; to lie in the dust, and to be full of Christ alone; to love him with a holy and pure love; to trust in him; to live upon him; to serve and follow him, and to be totally wrapped up in the fullness of Christ; and to be perfectly sanctified and made pure, with a divine and heavenly purity. I have several other times, and views very much of the same nature, and that have had the same effects.

I have many times had a sense of the glory of the third person in the Trinity, in his office of sanctifier; in his holy operations communicating divine light and life to the soul. God in the communications of his Holy Spirit, has appeared as an infinite fountain of divine glory and sweetness; being full and sufficient to fill and satisfy the soul: pouring forth itself in sweet communications, like the sun in its glory, sweetly and pleasantly diffusing light and Life.

I have sometimes had an affecting sense of the excellency of the Word of God, as a Word of life; as the light of life; a sweet, excellent, life-giving Word: accompanied with a thirsting after that Word, that it might dwell richly in my heart.

I have often since I lived in this town, had very affecting views of my own sinfulness and vileness; very frequently so as to hold me in a kind of loud weeping, sometimes for a considerable time together: so that I have often been forced to shut myself up. I have had a vastly greater sense of my own wickedness, and the badness of my heart, since my conversion, than ever I had before. It has often appeared to me, that if God should mark iniquity against me, I should appear the very worst of all mankind; of all that have been since the beginning of the world to this time: and that I should have by far the lowest place in hell. When others that have come to talk with me about their soul concerns, have expressed the sense they have had of their own wickedness, by saying that it seemed to them, that they were as bad as the devil himself; I thought their expressions seemed exceeding faint and feeble, to represent my wickedness. I thought I should wonder, that they should content themselves with such expressions as these, if I had any reason to imagine, that their sin bore any proportion to mine. It seemed to me, I should wonder at myself, if I should express *my* wickedness in such feeble terms as they did.

My wickedness, as I am in myself, has long appeared to me perfectly ineffable, and infinitely swallowing up all thought and imagination; like an infinite deluge, or infinite mountains over my head. I know not how to express better, what my sins appear to me to be, than by heaping infinite upon infinite, and multiplying infinite by infinite. I go about very often, for this many years, with these expressions in my mind, and in my mouth, "Infinite upon Infinite. Infinite upon Infinite!" When I look into my heart, and take a view of my wickedness, it looks like an abyss infinitely deeper than hell. And it appears to me, that were it not for free grace, exalted and raised up to the infinite height of all the fullness and glory of the great Jehovah, and the arm of his power and grace stretched forth, in all the majesty of his power, and in all the glory of his sovereignty; I should appear sunk down in my sins infinitely below hell itself, far beyond sight of everything, but the piercing eye of God's grace, that can pierce even down to such a depth, and to the bottom of such an abyss.

And yet, I ben't in the least inclined to think, that I have a greater conviction of sin than ordinary. It seems to me, my conviction of sin is exceeding small, and faint. It appears to me enough to amaze me, that I have no more sense of my sin. I know certainly, that I have very little sense of my sinfulness. That my sins appear to me so great, don't seem to me to be, because I have so much more conviction of sin than other Christians, but because I am so much worse, and have so much more wickedness to be convinced of. When I have had these turns of weeping and crying for my sins, I thought I knew in the time of it, that my repentance was nothing to my sin.

I have greatly longed of late, for a broken heart, and to lie low before God. And when I ask for humility of God, I can't bear the thoughts of being no more humble, than other Christians. It seems to me, that though their degrees of humility may be suitable for them; yet it would be a vile self-exaltation in me, not to be the lowest in humility of all mankind. Others speak of their longing to be humbled to the dust. Though that may be a proper expression for them, I always think for myself, that I ought to be humbled down below hell. 'Tis an expression that it has long been natural for me to use in prayer to God. I ought to lie infinitely low before God.

It is affecting to me to think, how ignorant I was, when I was a young Christian, of the bottomless, infinite depths of wickedness, pride, hypocrisy and deceit left in my heart.

I have vastly a greater sense, of my universal, exceeding dependence on God's grace and strength, and mere good pleasure, of late, than I used formerly to have; and have experienced more of an abhorrence of my own righteousness. The thought of any comfort or joy, arising in me, on any consideration, or reflection on my own amiableness, or any of my performances or experiences, or any goodness of heart or life, is nauseous and detestable to me. And yet I am greatly afflicted with a proud and self-righteous spirit; much more sensibly, than I used to be formerly. I see that serpent rising and putting forth its head, continually, everywhere, all around me.

Though it seems to me, that in some respects I was a far better Christian, for two or three years after my first conversion, than I am now; and lived in a more constant delight and pleasure: yet of late years, I have had a more full and constant sense of the absolute sovereignty of God, and a delight in that sovereignty; and have had more of a sense of the glory of Christ, as a mediator, as revealed in the gospel. On one Saturday night in particular, had a particular discovery of the excellency of the gospel of Christ, above all other doctrines; so that I could not but say to myself; "This is my chosen light, my chosen doctrine": and of Christ, "This is my chosen prophet." It appeared to me to be sweet beyond all expression, to follow Christ, and to be taught and enlightened and instructed by him; to learn of him, and live to him.

Another Saturday night, January 1738–39, had such a sense, how sweet and blessed a thing it was, to walk in the way of duty, to do that which was right and meet to be done, and agreeable to the holy mind of God; that it caused me to break forth into a kind of a loud weeping, which held me some time; so that I was forced to shut myself up, and fasten the doors. I could not but as it were cry out, "How happy are they which do that which is right in the sight of God! They are blessed indeed, they are the happy ones!" I had at the same time, a very affecting sense, how meet and suitable it was that God should govern the world, and order all things according to his own pleasure; and I rejoiced in it, that God reigned, and that his will was done.

Emily Dickinson

I Should Have Been Too Glad, I See

 ca. 1862–1863

With irony that almost, but never quite, descends into bitterness, Emily Dickinson (1830–1886) conveys in this complex poem her relief at being spared the fate of translation from the "little Circuit" of this mortal life to the "new Circumference" of salvation. The beauty of the poem is its painful recognition that what gives to human life its meaning—and what makes poetry possible—is the sense of imminent loss that a confident faith promises to obliterate. Thus, Dickinson's protest that if she were to be "rescued" from this life as the faith of her ancestors promised, her "fluent" voice would be stopped. What makes the poem so powerful is its self-contradictory anger at the retraction of the promise of salvation and at the dehumanizing effect if the promise were to be fulfilled.

I should have been too glad, I see –
Too lifted – for the scant degree
Of Life's penurious Round –
My little Circuit would have shamed
This new Circumference – have blamed –
The homelier time behind –

I should have been too saved – I see –
Too rescued – Fear too dim to me
That I could spell the Prayer
I knew so perfect – yesterday –
That Scalding One – Sabachthani –
Recited fluent – here –

Earth would have been too much – I see –
And Heaven – not enough for me –
I should have had the Joy
Without the Fear – to justify –

The Palm – without the Calvary –
So Savior – Crucify –

Defeat – whets Victory – they say –
The Reefs – in old Gethsemane –
Endear the Coast – beyond!
'Tis Beggars – Banquets – can define –
'Tis parching – vitalizes wine –
"Faith" bleats – to understand!

HENRY ADAMS

From The Education of Henry Adams

 1907

Grandson of one president (John Quincy Adams), great-grandson of another (John Adams), Henry Adams (1838–1918) was born into a family that came as close as any in New England to the status of heritable aristocracy. "Had he been born in Jerusalem under the shadow of the Temple and circumcised in the Synagogue by his uncle the high priest," he wrote at the start of his extraordinary memoir, *The Education of Henry Adams,* "he would scarcely have been more distinctly branded, and not much more heavily handicapped in the races of the coming century." Here was Adams's obsessive theme: the immeasurable gap between the world of his fathers and the vertiginous times in which he came to adulthood—characterized by a ceaseless flood of immigrants, the brutal mechanization of war, the battering of religion by science, and the transformation of time itself by the ever increasing speed of human enterprise under the stimulus of technology.

Nowhere in Adams's writing is this theme better expressed than in the recollected incident of his walk to school with his grandfather. It is a wistful remembrance not merely of John Quincy Adams as the laconic Yankee but of a lost moment when the rules of civilization could be transmitted between the generations without having to be stated at all. It is followed here by a short passage about Boston in which Adams makes clear that New England has never been all about obedient submission.

The atmosphere of education in which he lived was colonial, revolutionary, almost Cromwellian, as though he were steeped, from his greatest grandmother's birth, in the odor of political crime. Resistance to something was the law of New England nature; the boy looked out on the world with the instinct of resistance; for numberless generations his predecessors had viewed the world chiefly as a thing to be reformed, filled with evil forces to be abolished, and they saw no reason to suppose that they had wholly succeeded in the abolition; the duty was unchanged. That duty implied not only resistance to evil, but hatred of it. Boys naturally look on all force as an enemy, and generally find it so, but the New Englander, whether boy or man, in his long struggle with a stingy or hostile universe, had learned also to love the pleasure of hating; his joys were few.

Politics, as a practice, whatever its professions, had always been the systematic organization of hatreds, and Massachusetts politics had been as harsh as the climate. The chief charm of New England was harshness of contrasts and extremes of sensibility,—a cold that froze the blood, and a heat that boiled it,—so that the pleasure of hating—oneself if no better victim offered,—was not its rarest amusement; but the charm was a true and natural child of the soil, not a cultivated weed of the ancients. The violence of the contrast was real and made the strongest motive of education. The double exterior nature gave life its relative values. Winter and summer, cold and heat, town and country, force and freedom, marked two modes of life and thought, balanced like lobes of the brain. Town was winter confinement, school, rule, discipline; straight, gloomy streets, piled with six feet of snow in the middle; frosts that made the snow sing under wheels or runners; thaws when the streets became dangerous to cross; society of uncles, aunts and cousins who expected children to behave themselves, and who were not always gratified; above all else, winter represented the desire to escape and go free. Town was restraint, law, unity. Country, only seven miles away, was liberty, diversity, outlawry, the endless delight of mere sense impressions given by nature for nothing, and breathed by boys without knowing it.

Boys are wild animals, rich in the treasures of sense, but the New England boy had a wider range of emotions than boys of more equable climates. He felt his nature crudely, as it was meant. To the boy Henry Adams, summer was drunken. Among senses, smell was the strongest:—smell of hot pine-woods and sweet-fern in the scorching summer noon; of new-mown hay; of ploughed earth; of box hedges; of peaches, lilacs, seringas; of stables, barns, cow-yards; of salt water and low tide on the marshes; nothing came amiss. Next to smell came taste, and the children knew the taste of everything they saw or touched, from penny-royal and flagroot to the shell of a pignut and the letters of a spelling-book:—the taste of A-B, AB, suddenly revived on the boy's tongue sixty years afterwards. Light, line and color, as sensual pleasures, came later and were as crude as the rest. The New England light is glare, and the atmosphere harshens color. The boy was a full man before he ever knew what was meant by atmosphere; his idea of pleasure in light was the blaze of a New England sun. His idea of color was a peony, with the dew of early morning on its petals. The intense blue of the sea, as he saw it a mile or two away, from the Quincy hills; the cumuli in a June afternoon sky; the strong reds and greens and purples of colored prints and children's picture-books, as the American colors then ran; these were ideals. The opposites or antipathies, were the cold grays of November evenings, and the thick, muddy thaws of Boston winter. With such standards, the Bostonian could not but develop a double nature. Life was a double thing. After a January blizzard, the boy who could look with pleasure into the violent snow-glare of the cold white sun-shine, with its intense light and shade, scarcely knew what was meant by tone. He could reach it only by education.

Winter and summer, then, were two hostile lives, and bred two separate na-tures. Winter was always the effort to live; summer was tropical license. Whether the children rolled in the grass, or waded in the brook, or swam in the salt ocean, or sailed in the bay, or fished for smelts in the creeks, or netted minnows in the salt-marshes, or took to the pine-woods and the granite quar-ries, or chased musk-rats and hunted snapping-turtles in the swamps, or mushrooms or nuts on the autumn hills, summer and country were always sensual living, while winter was always compulsory learning. Summer was the multiplicity of nature; winter was school.

The bearing of the two seasons on the education of Henry Adams was no fancy; it was the most decisive force he ever knew; it ran through life, and made the division between its perplexing, warring, irreconcilable problems, irreducible opposites, with growing emphasis to the last year of study. From earliest childhood the boy was accustomed to feel that, for him, life was dou-ble. Winter and summer, town and country, law and liberty, were hostile, and the man who pretended they were not, was in his eyes a schoolmaster:—that is, a man employed to tell lies to little boys. Though Quincy was but two hours' walk from Beacon Hill, it belonged in a different world. For two hun-dred years, every Adams, from father to son, had lived within sight of State Street, and sometimes had lived in it, yet none had ever taken kindly to the town, or been taken kindly by it. The boy inherited his double nature. He knew as yet nothing about his great-grandfather, who had died a dozen years before his own birth: he took for granted that any great-grandfather of his must have always been good, and his enemies wicked; but he divined his great-grandfather's character from his own. Never for a moment did he con-nect the two ideas of Boston and John Adams; they were separate and antago-nistic; the idea of John Adams went with Quincy. He knew his grandfather John Quincy Adams only as an old man of seventy-five or eighty who was friendly and gentle with him, but except that he heard his grandfather always called "the President," and his grandmother "the Madam," he had no reason to suppose that his Adams grandfather differed in character from his Brooks grandfather who was equally kind and benevolent. He liked the Adams side best, but for no other reason than that it reminded him of the country, the summer and the absence of restraint. Yet he felt also that Quincy was in a way inferior to Boston, and that socially Boston looked down on Quincy. The rea-son was clear enough even to a five-year-old child. Quincy had no Boston style. Little enough style had either; a simpler manner of life and thought could hardly exist, short of cave-dwelling. The flint-and-steel with which his grandfather Adams used to light his own fires in the early morning was still on the mantel-piece of his study. The idea of a livery or even a dress for servants, or of an evening toilette, was next to blasphemy. Bath-rooms, water-supplies, lighting, heating and the whole array of domestic comforts, were unknown at Quincy. Boston had already a bath-room, a water-supply, a furnace, and gas. The superiority of Boston was evident, but a child liked it no better for that.

The magnificence of his grandfather Brooks's house in Pearl Street or South Street has long ago disappeared, but perhaps his country-house at Medford may still remain to show what impressed the mind of a boy in 1845 with the idea of city splendor. The President's place at Quincy was the larger and older and far the more interesting of the two; but a boy felt at once its inferiority in fashion. It showed plainly enough its want of wealth. It smacked of colonial age, but not of Boston style or plush curtains. To the end of his life he never quite overcame the prejudice thus drawn in with his childish breath. He never could compel himself to care for nineteenth century style. He was never able to adopt it, any more than his father or grandfather or great-grandfather had done. Not that he felt it as particularly hostile, for he reconciled himself to much that was worse; but because, for some remote reason, he was born an eighteenth century child. The old house at Quincy was eighteenth century. What style it had was in its Queen Anne mahogany panels and its Louis XVI chairs and sofas. The panels belonged to an old colonial Vassall who built the house; the furniture had been brought back from Paris in 1789 or 1801 or 1817, along with porcelain and books and much else of old diplomatic remnants; and neither of the two eighteenth-century styles—neither English Queen Anne nor French Louis XVI,—was comfortable for a boy, or for anyone else. The dark mahogany had been painted white to suit daily life in winter gloom. Nothing seemed to favor, for a child's objects, the older forms. On the contrary most boys as well as grown-up people, preferred the new, with good reason, and the child felt himself distinctly at a disadvantage for the taste.

Nor had personal preference any share in his bias. The Brooks grandfather was as amiable and as sympathetic as the Adams grandfather. Both were born in 1767, and both died in 1848. Both were kind to children, and both belonged rather to the eighteenth than to the nineteenth centuries. The child knew no difference between them except that one was associated with winter and the other with summer; one with Boston, the other with Quincy. Even with Medford, the association was hardly easier. Once as a very young boy he was taken to pass a few days with his grandfather Brooks under charge of his aunt, but became so violently homesick that within twenty-four hours he was brought back in disgrace. Yet he could not remember ever being seriously homesick again.

The attachment to Quincy was not altogether sentimental or wholly sympathetic. Quincy was not a bed of thornless roses. Even there the curse of Cain set its mark. There as elsewhere a cruel universe combined to crush a child. As though three or four vigorous brothers and sisters, with the best will, were not enough to crush any child, everyone else conspired towards an education which he hated. From cradle to grave this problem of running order through chaos, direction through space, discipline through freedom, unity through multiplicity, has always been, and must always be, the task of education, as it is the moral of religion, philosophy, science, art, politics and economy; but a boy's will is his life, and he dies when it is broken, as the colt dies in harness, taking a new nature in becoming tame. Rarely has the boy felt kindly towards his tamers. Between him and his master has always been war. Henry Adams never knew a boy of his generation to like a master, and the task of remaining on friendly terms with one's own family, in such a relation, was never easy.

All the more singular it seemed afterwards to him that his first serious contact with the President should have been a struggle of will, in which the old man almost necessarily defeated the boy, but instead of leaving, as usual in such defeats, a lifelong sting, left rather an impression of as fair treatment as could be expected from a natural enemy. The boy met seldom with such restraint. He could not have been much more than six years old at the time,—seven at the utmost—and his mother had taken him to Quincy for a long stay with the President during the summer. What became of the rest of the family he quite forgot; but he distinctly remembered standing at the house door one summer-morning in a passionate outburst of rebellion against going to school. Naturally his mother was the immediate victim of his rage; that is what mothers are for, and boys also; but in this case the boy had his mother at unfair disadvantage, for she was a guest, and had no means of enforcing obedience. Henry showed a certain tactical ability by refusing to start, and he met all efforts at compulsion by successful, though too vehement protest. He was in fair way to win, and was holding his own, with sufficient energy, at the bottom of the long staircase which led up to the door of the President's library, when the door opened, and the old man slowly came down. Putting on his hat, he took the boy's hand without a word, and walked with him paralysed by awe, up the road to the town. After the first moments of consternation at this interference in a domestic dispute, the boy reflected that an old gentleman close on eighty would never trouble himself to walk near a mile on a hot summer morning over a shadeless road to take a boy to school, and that it would be strange if a lad imbued with the passion of freedom could not find a corner to dodge around, somewhere before reaching the school-door. Then and always, the boy insisted that this reasoning justified his apparent submission; but the old man did not stop, and the boy saw all his strategical points turned, one after another, until he found himself seated inside the school, and obviously the centre of curious if not malevolent criticism. Not till then did the President release his hand and depart.

The point was that this act, contrary to the inalienable rights of boys, and nullifying the social compact, ought to have made him dislike his grandfather for life. He could not recall that it had this effect even for a moment. With a certain maturity of mind, the child must have recognized that the President, though a tool of tyranny, had done his disreputable work with a certain intelligence. He had shown no temper, no irritation, no personal feeling, and had made no display of force. Above all, he had held his tongue. During their long walk he had said nothing; he had uttered no syllable of revolting cant about the duty of obedience and the wickedness of resistance to law; he had shown no concern in the matter; hardly even a consciousness of the boy's existence. Probably his mind at that moment was actually troubling itself little about his grandson's iniquities, and much about the iniquities of President Polk, but the boy could scarcely at that age feel the whole satisfaction of thinking that President Polk was to be the vicarious victim of his own sins, and he gave his grandfather credit for intelligent silence. For this forbearance he felt instinctive respect. He admitted force as a form of right; he admitted even temper, under protest; but the seeds of a moral education would at that moment have fallen on the stoniest soil in Quincy, which is, as everyone knows, the stoniest glacial and tidal drift known in any Puritan land . . .

Except for politics, Mt. Vernon Street had the merit of leaving the boy-mind supple, free to turn with the world, and if one learned next to nothing, the little one did learn needed not to be unlearned. The surface was ready to take any form that education should cut into it, though Boston, with singular foresight, rejected the old designs. What sort of education was stamped elsewhere, a Bostonian had no idea, but he escaped the evils of other standards by having no standard at all; and what was true of school was true of society. Boston offered none that could help outside. Everyone now smiles at the bad taste of Queen Victoria and Louis Philippe,—the society of the forties,—but the taste was only reflection of the social slack-water between a tide passed, and a tide to come. Boston belonged to neither, and hardly even to America. Neither aristocratic nor industrial nor social, Boston girls and boys were not nearly as unformed as English boys and girls, but had less means of acquiring form as they grew older. Women counted for little as models. Every boy, from the age of seven, fell in love at frequent intervals with some girl,—always more or less the same little girl,—who had nothing to teach him, or he to teach her, except rather familiar and provincial manners, until they married and bore children to repeat the habit. The idea of attaching oneself to a married woman, or of polishing one's manners to suit the standards of women of thirty, could hardly have entered the mind of a young Bostonian, and would have scandalised his parents. From women the boy got the domestic virtues and nothing else. He might not even catch the idea that women had more to give. The garden of Eden was hardly more primitive.

To balance this virtue, the puritan city had always hidden a darker side. Blackguard Boston was only too educational, and to most boys much the more interesting. A successful blackguard must enjoy great physical advantages besides a true vocation, and Henry Adams had neither; but no boy escaped some contact with vice of a very low form. Blackguardism came constantly under boys' eyes, and had the charm of force and freedom and superiority to culture or decency. One might fear it, but no one honestly despised it. Now and then it asserted itself as education more roughly than school ever did. One of the commonest boy-games of winter, inherited directly from the eighteenth-century, was a game of war on Boston Common. In old days the two hostile forces were called North Enders and South Enders. In 1850 the North Enders still survived as a legend, but in practice it was a battle of the Latin School against all comers, and the Latin School, for snow-ball, included all the boys of the west end. Whenever, on a half-holiday the weather was soft enough to soften the snow, the Common was apt to be the scene of a fight, which began in daylight with the Latin School in force, rushing their opponents down to Tremont Street, and which generally ended at dark by the Latin School dwindling in numbers and disappearing. As the Latin School grew weak, the roughs and young blackguards grew strong. As long as snow-balls were the only weapon, no one was much hurt, but a stone may be put in a snow-ball, and in the dark a stick or a slung-shot in the hands of a boy is as effective as a knife. One afternoon the fight had been long and exhausting. The boy Henry, following, as his habit was, his bigger brother Charles, had taken part in the battle, and had felt his courage much depressed by seeing one of his trustiest leaders, Henry Higginson,—"Bully Hig," his school name,—struck by a stone over the eye, and led off the field bleeding in rather a ghastly manner. As night came on, the Latin School was steadily forced back to the Beacon Street Mall where they could retreat no further without disbanding, and by that time only a small band was left, headed by two heroes, Savage and Marvin. A dark mass of figures could be seen below, making ready for the last rush, and rumor said that a swarm of blackguards from the slums, led by a grisly terror called Conky Daniels, with a club and a hideous reputation, were going to put an end to the Beacon Street cowards forever. Henry wanted to run away with the others, but his brother was too big to run away so they stood still and waited immolation. The dark mass set up a shout, and rushed forward. The Beacon Street boys turned and fled up the steps, except Savage and Marvin and the few champions who would not run. The terrible Conky Daniels swaggered up, stopped a moment with his body-guard to swear a few oaths at Marvin, and then swept on and chased the flyers, leaving the few boys untouched who stood their ground. The obvious moral taught that blackguards were not so black as they were painted; but the boy Henry had passed through as much terror as though he were Turenne or Henri IV, and ten or twelve years afterwards when these same boys were fighting and falling on all the battle-fields of Virginia and Maryland, he wondered whether their education on Boston Common had taught Savage and Marvin how to die.

If violence were a part of complete education, Boston was not incomplete. The idea of violence was familiar to the antislavery leaders as well as to their followers. Most of them suffered from it. Mobs were always possible. Henry never happened to be actually concerned in a mob, but he like every other boy, was sure to be on hand wherever a mob was expected, and whenever he heard Garrison or Wendell Phillips speak, he looked for trouble. Wendell Phillips on a platform was a model dangerous for youth. Theodore Parker in his pulpit was not much safer. Worst of all, the execution of the Fugitive Slave Law in Boston,—the sight of Court Square packed with bayonets, and his own friends obliged to line the streets under arms as State militia, in order to return a negro to slavery—wrought frenzy in the brain of a fifteen-year-old, eighteenth-century boy from Quincy, who wanted to miss no reasonable chance of mischief.

W. E. B. Du Bois

From Darkwater

 1920

The amazingly productive life of William Edward Burghardt Du Bois (1868–1963) was too long and rich to summarize. Descended from a white slave-owning great-grandfather who had two sons by a mulatto woman, he was born in Great Barrington, Massachusetts, to a mother of African and Dutch descent who worked as a domestic servant and a Haitian-born father who worked as a barber. Fifteen years after earning the first Ph.D. degree awarded at Harvard to an African American, he became, in 1910, the first black member of the board of directors of the newly organized National Association for the Advancement of Colored People. Such early achievements heralded a life of undiscourageable energy on behalf of the principle that the "color line" dividing American society must be acknowledged and erased. In the short excerpt reprinted here from his 1920 memoir, *Darkwater,* Du Bois recounts his dawning awareness that the insidious idea of racial difference that poisoned the minds of his white peers was coming to inhabit his own.

The Shadow of Years

I was born by a golden river and in the shadow of two great hills, five years after the Emancipation Proclamation. The house was quaint, with clapboards running up and down, neatly trimmed, and there were five rooms, a tiny porch, a rosy front yard, and unbelievably delicious strawberries in the rear. A South Carolinian, lately come to the Berkshire Hills, owned all this—tall, thin, and black, with golden earrings, and given to religious trances. We were his transient tenants for the time.

My own people were part of a great clan. Fully two hundred years before, Tom Burghardt had come through the western pass from the Hudson with his Dutch captor, "Coenraet Burghardt," sullen in his slavery and achieving his freedom by volunteering for the Revolution at a time of sudden alarm. His wife was a little, black, Bantu woman, who never became reconciled to this strange land; she clasped her knees and rocked and crooned:

"Do bana coba—gene me, gene me!
Ben d'nuli, ben d'le—"

Tom died about 1787, but of him came many sons, and one, Jack, who helped in the War of 1812. Of Jack and his wife, Violet, was born a mighty family, splendidly named: Harlow and Ira, Cloë, Lucinda, Maria, and Othello! I dimly remember my grandfather, Othello,—or "Uncle Tallow,"—a brown man, strong-voiced and redolent with tobacco, who sat stiffly in a great high chair because his hip was broken. He was probably a bit lazy and given to wassail. At any rate, grandmother had a shrewish tongue and often berated him. This grandmother was Sarah—"Aunt Sally"—a stern, tall, Dutch-African woman, beak-nosed, but beautiful-eyed and golden-skinned. Ten or more children were theirs, of whom the youngest was Mary, my mother.

Mother was dark shining bronze, with a tiny ripple in her black hair, black-eyed, with a heavy, kind face. She gave one the impression of infinite patience, but a curious determination was concealed in her softness. The family were small farmers on Egremont Plain, between Great Barrington and Sheffield, Massachusetts. The bits of land were too small to support the great families born on them and we were always poor. I never remember being cold or hungry, but I do remember that shoes and coal, and sometimes flour, caused mother moments of anxious thought in winter, and a new suit was an event!

At about the time of my birth economic pressure was transmuting the family generally from farmers to "hired" help. Some revolted and migrated westward, others went cityward as cooks and barbers. Mother worked for some years at house service in Great Barrington, and after a disappointed love episode with a cousin, who went to California, she met and married Alfred Du Bois and went to town to live by the golden river where I was born.

Alfred, my father, must have seemed a splendid vision in that little valley under the shelter of those mighty hills. He was small and beautiful of face and feature, just tinted with the sun, his curly hair chiefly revealing his kinship to Africa. In nature he was a dreamer,—romantic, indolent, kind, unreliable. He had in him the making of a poet, an adventurer, or a Beloved Vagabond, according to the life that closed round him; and that life gave him all too little. His father, Alexander Du Bois, cloaked under a stern, austere demeanor a passionate revolt against the world. He, too, was small, but squarish. I remember him as I saw him first, in his home in New Bedford,—white hair close-cropped; a seamed, hard face, but high in tone, with a gray eye that could twinkle or glare.

Long years before him Louis XIV drove two Huguenots, Jacques and Louis Du Bois, into wild Ulster County, New York. One of them in the third or fourth generation had a descendant, Dr. James Du Bois, a gay, rich bachelor, who made his money in the Bahamas, where he and the Gilberts had plantations. There he took a beautiful little mulatto slave as his mistress, and two sons were born: Alexander in 1803 and John, later. They were fine, straight, clear-eyed boys, white enough to "pass." He brought them to America and put Alexander in the celebrated Cheshire School, in Connecticut. Here he often visited him, but one last time, fell dead. He left no will, and his relations made short shrift of these sons. They gathered in the property, apprenticed grandfather to a shoemaker; then dropped him.

Grandfather took his bitter dose like a thoroughbred. Wild as was his inner revolt against this treatment, he uttered no word against the thieves and made no plea. He tried his fortunes here and in Haiti, where, during his short, restless sojourn, my own father was born. Eventually, grandfather became chief steward on the passenger boat between New York and New Haven; later he was a small merchant in Springfield; and finally he retired and ended his days at New Bedford. Always he held his head high, took no insults, made few friends. He was not a "Negro"; he was a man! Yet the current was too strong even for him. Then even more than now a colored man had colored friends or none at all, lived in a colored world or lived alone. A few fine, strong, black men gained the heart of this silent, bitter man in New York and New Haven. If he had scant sympathy with their social clannishness, he was with them in fighting discrimination. So, when the white Episcopalians of Trinity Parish, New Haven, showed plainly that they no longer wanted black folk as fellow Christians, he led the revolt which resulted in St. Luke's Parish, and was for years its senior warden. He lies dead in the Grove Street Cemetery, beside Jehudi Ashmun.

Beneath his sternness was a very human man. Slyly he wrote poetry,—stilted, pleading things from a soul astray. He loved women in his masterful way, marrying three beautiful wives in succession and clinging to each with a certain desperate, even if unsympathetic, affection. As a father he was, naturally, a failure,—hard, domineering, unyielding. His four children reacted characteristically: one was until past middle life a thin spinster, the mental image of her father; one died; one passed over into the white world and her children's children are now white, with no knowledge of their Negro blood; the fourth, my father, bent before grandfather, but did not break—better if he had. He yielded and flared back, asked forgiveness and forgot why, became the harshly-held favorite, who ran away and rioted and roamed and loved and married my brown mother.

So with some circumstance having finally gotten myself born, with a flood of Negro blood, a strain of French, a bit of Dutch, but, thank God! no "Anglo-Saxon," I come to the days of my childhood.

They were very happy. Early we moved back to Grandfather Burghardt's home,—I barely remember its stone fireplace, big kitchen, and delightful woodshed. Then this house passed to other branches of the clan and we moved to rented quarters in town,—to one delectable place "upstairs," with a wide yard full of shrubbery, and a brook; to another house abutting a railroad, with infinite interests and astonishing playmates; and finally back to the quiet street on which I was born,—down a long lane and in a homely, cozy cottage, with a living-room, a tiny sitting-room, a pantry, and two attic bedrooms. Here mother and I lived until she died, in 1884, for father early began his restless wanderings. I last remember urgent letters for us to come to New Milford, where he had started a barber shop. Later he became a preacher. But mother no longer trusted his dreams, and he soon faded out of our lives into silence.

From the age of five until I was sixteen I went to school on the same grounds,—down a lane, into a widened yard, with a big chokecherry tree and two buildings, wood and brick. Here I got acquainted with my world, and soon had my criterions of judgment.

Wealth had no particular lure. On the other hand, the shadow of wealth was about us. That river of my birth was golden because of the woolen and paper waste that soiled it. The gold was theirs, not ours; but the gleam and glint was for all. To me it was all in order and I took it philosophically. I cordially despised the poor Irish and South Germans, who slaved in the mills, and annexed the rich and well-to-do as my natural companions. Of such is the kingdom of snobs!

Most of our townfolk were, naturally, the well-to-do, shading downward, but seldom reaching poverty. As playmate of the children I saw the homes of nearly every one, except a few immigrant New Yorkers, of whom none of us approved. The homes I saw impressed me, but did not overwhelm me. Many were bigger than mine, with newer and shinier things, but they did not seem to differ in kind. I think I probably surprised my hosts more than they me, for I was easily at home and perfectly happy and they looked to me just like ordinary people, while my brown face and frizzled hair must have seemed strange to them.

Yet I was very much one of them. I was a center and sometimes the leader of the town gang of boys. We were noisy, but never very bad,—and, indeed, my mother's quiet influence came in here, as I realize now. She did not try to make me perfect. To her I was already perfect. She simply warned me of a few things, especially saloons. In my town the saloon was the open door to hell. The best families had their drunkards and the worst had little else.

Very gradually,—I cannot now distinguish the steps, though here and there I remember a jump or a jolt—but very gradually I found myself assuming quite placidly that I was different from other children. At first I think I connected the difference with a manifest ability to get my lessons rather better than most and to recite with a certain happy, almost taunting, glibness, which brought frowns here and there. Then, slowly, I realized that some folks, a few, even several, actually considered my brown skin a misfortune; once or twice I became painfully aware that some human beings even thought it a crime. I was not for a moment daunted,—although, of course, there were some days of secret tears—rather I was spurred to tireless effort. If they beat me at anything, I was grimly determined to make them sweat for it! Once I remember challenging a great, hard farmer-boy to battle, when I knew he could whip me; and he did. But ever after, he was polite.

As time flew I felt not so much disowned and rejected as rather drawn up into higher spaces and made part of a mightier mission. At times I almost pitied my pale companions, who were not of the Lord's anointed and who saw in their dreams no splendid quests of golden fleeces.

Even in the matter of girls my peculiar phantasy asserted itself. Naturally, it was in our town voted bad form for boys of twelve and fourteen to show any evident weakness for girls. We tolerated them loftily, and now and then they played in our games, when I joined in quite as naturally as the rest. It was when strangers came, or summer boarders, or when the oldest girls grew up that my sharp senses noted little hesitancies in public and searchings for possible public opinion. Then I flamed! I lifted my chin and strode off to the mountains, where I viewed the world at my feet and strained my eyes across the shadow of the hills.

I was graduated from high school at sixteen, and I talked of "Wendell Phillips." This was my first sweet taste of the world's applause. There were flowers and upturned faces, music and marching, and there was my mother's smile. She was lame, then, and a bit drawn, but very happy. It was her great day and that very year she lay down with a sigh of content and has not yet awakened. I felt a certain gladness to see her, at last, at peace, for she had worried all her life. Of my own loss I had then little realization. That came only with the after-years. Now it was the choking gladness and solemn feel of wings! At last, I was going beyond the hills and into the world that beckoned steadily.

There came a little pause,—a singular pause. I was given to understand that I was almost too young for the world. Harvard was the goal of my dreams, but my white friends hesitated and my colored friends were silent. Harvard was a mighty conjure-word in that hill town, and even the mill owners' sons had aimed lower. Finally it was tactfully explained that the place for me was in the South among my people. A scholarship had been already arranged at Fisk, and my summer earnings would pay the fare. My relatives grumbled, but after a twinge I felt a strange delight! I forgot, or did not thoroughly realize, the curious irony by which I was not looked upon as a real citizen of my birth-town, with a future and a career, and instead was being sent to a far land among strangers who were regarded as (and in truth were) "mine own people."

ROBERT FROST

To Earthward

 1923

In this exquisite poem published in his 1923 collection *New Hampshire,* Robert Frost (1874–1963) recounts his life as a craving for sensation that grows with his awareness of his senses failing. Fifteen years after composing "To Earthward," Frost described it in a letter to Bernard De Voto as the poetic record of "one of the greatest changes my nature has undergone."

Love at the lips was touch
As sweet as I could bear;
And once that seemed too much;
I lived on air

That crossed me from sweet things
The flow of—was it musk
From hidden grapevine springs
Down hill at dusk?

I had the swirl and ache
From sprays of honeysuckle
That when they're gathered shake
Dew on the knuckle.

I craved strong sweets, but those
Seemed strong when I was young;
The petal of the rose
It was that stung.

Now no joy but lacks salt
That is not dashed with pain
And weariness and fault;
I crave the stain

Of tears, the aftermark
Of almost too much love,
The sweet of bitter bark
And burning clove.

When stiff and sore and scarred
I take away my hand
From leaning on it hard
In grass and sand,

The hurt is not enough:
I long for weight and strength
To feel the earth as rough
To all my length.

ELIZABETH BISHOP

In the Waiting Room

 1971

A few months after Elizabeth Bishop was born in Worcester, Massachusetts, in 1911, her father died. Not long thereafter her mother was committed to a mental institution, and she went to live in Nova Scotia with her maternal grandparents. Upon the demand of her father's family, she returned at the age of six unwillingly to Worcester, "to be saved," as she later put it, "from a life of poverty, provincialism, bare feet, [and] suet puddings." After college at Vassar, and in between intermittent teaching appointments, Bishop traveled for much of her life, spending some of her happiest and most productive years in Brazil with her beloved companion, Lota de Macedo Soares, whose death in 1967 was the greatest devastation in the poet's life since her childhood tragedies. Bishop's life, however peripatetic, remained centered on New England, where she kept an apartment overlooking Boston Harbor, grew close to contemporaries such as Robert Lowell, and spent her summers in North Haven, Maine, until she died suddenly in 1979.

"In the Waiting Room" is a pained reconstruction of a child's incipient awareness that she is being drawn into the adult world—despite her foreboding and resistance.

In Worcester, Massachusetts,
I went with Aunt Consuelo
to keep her dentist's appointment
and sat and waited for her
in the dentist's waiting room.
It was winter. It got dark
early. The waiting room
was full of grown-up people,
arctics and overcoats,
lamps and magazines.
My aunt was inside
what seemed like a long time
and while I waited I read

the *National Geographic*
(I could read) and carefully
studied the photographs:
the inside of a volcano,
black, and full of ashes;
then it was spilling over
in rivulets of fire.
Osa and Martin Johnson
dressed in riding breeches,
laced boots, and pith helmets.
A dead man slung on a pole
—"Long Pig," the caption said.
Babies with pointed heads
wound round and round with string;
black, naked women with necks
wound round and round with wire
like the necks of light bulbs.
Their breasts were horrifying.
I read it right straight through.
I was too shy to stop.
And then I looked at the cover:
the yellow margins, the date.

Suddenly, from inside,
came an *oh!* of pain
—Aunt Consuelo's voice—
not very loud or long.
I wasn't at all surprised;
even then I knew she was
a foolish, timid woman.
I might have been embarrassed,
but wasn't. What took me
completely by surprise
was that it was *me:*
my voice, in my mouth.
Without thinking at all
I was my foolish aunt,
I—we—were falling, falling,
our eyes glued to the cover
of the *National Geographic,*
February, 1918.

         *   *   *

I said to myself: three days
and you'll be seven years old.
I was saying it to stop
the sensation of falling off
the round, turning world
into cold, blue-black space.
But I felt: you are an *I*,
you are an *Elizabeth*,
you are one of *them*.
Why should you be one, too?
I scarcely dared to look
to see what it was I was.
I gave a sidelong glance
—I couldn't look any higher—
at shadowy gray knees,
trousers and skirts and boots
and different pairs of hands
lying under the lamps.
I knew that nothing stranger
had ever happened, that nothing
stranger could ever happen.
Why should I be my aunt,
or me, or anyone?
What similarities—
boots, hands, the family voice
I felt in my throat, or even
the *National Geographic*
and those awful hanging breasts—
held us all together
or made us all just one?
How—I didn't know any
word for it—how "unlikely" . . .
How had I come to be here,
like them, and overhear
a cry of pain that could have
got loud and worse but hadn't?

The waiting room was bright
and too hot. It was sliding
beneath a big black wave,
another, and another.

   * * *

Then I was back in it.
The War was on. Outside,
in Worcester, Massachusetts,
were night and slush and cold,
and it was still the fifth
of February, 1918.

Dorothy West

From The Richer, the Poorer

 1995

In the 1930s, Dorothy West (1907–1998) was a leading member of the literary and artistic movement known as the Harlem Renaissance; but before she became a New Yorker she had been a Bostonian. Her father, born a slave, was emancipated at age seven; her mother came from a poor black family in South Carolina. By dint of her father's modest business success, Dorothy West was raised in Boston's middle-class black community and "summered," as the wealthy set liked to say, in the thriving, if mostly seasonal, black community of the town of Oak Bluffs on the island of Martha's Vineyard. She was the author of memoirs, stories, and two novels separated by nearly fifty years—*The Living Is Easy* (1948) and *The Wedding* (1995); during the Harlem years, she founded the important journal *Challenge*, which Richard Wright joined as associate editor in 1937. Perhaps because she emphasized class more than race as the decisive factor delimiting one's prospects in life, her work was out of favor during the years of black militancy in the 1960s, but she has recently been rediscovered as a significant African American literary voice.

In this chapter from *The Richer, the Poorer* (1995), West recalls the humor and grace with which her family met the consternation of whites and the brassiness of black vacationers from New York, among whom, contrary to her own Bostonian reserve, it was expected that women would wear "dresses . . . cut low," and "high heels on sandy roads."

We were always stared at. Whenever we went outside the neighborhood that knew us, we were inspected like specimens under glass. My mother prepared us. As she marched us down our front stairs, she would say what our smiles were on tiptoe to hear, "Come on, children, let's go out and drive the white folks crazy."

She said it without rancor, and she said it in that outrageous way to make us laugh. She was easing our entry into a world that outranked us and outnumbered us. If she could not help us see ourselves with the humor, however wry, that gives the heart its grace, she would never have forgiven herself for letting our spirits be crushed before we had learned to sheathe them with pride.

When the Ipswich Street trolley screeched to a halt at our car stop, we scrambled aboard and sat in a row on the long seat at one end of the trolley that must have been designed for mothers with broods to keep together. We were thereby in full view. For the rest of that trolley ride into town, we were, in our infinite variety, a total divertissement.

Even my mother on occasion called our family a motley crew. We did not have pointed heads. We were simply a family that ranged in color from the blond child to me, a whim of God's that had gone on over so many generations that we had long since grown accustomed to accepting whatever gift we got. In a world where order is preferred, we were not uniform.

That my mother appeared to highlight the differences by dressing the blond child and me alike did not seem odd to me then, and is now too long ago to seem any odder than anything else that happened in my family. Whether she did it to further confound outsiders or because she was genuinely charmed by pairing the fairest and darkest was no more a cosmic prank on her part than on his.

We were a tribal family, living under a shared roof because that was the way we liked it. My mother was chief mother because nobody challenged her. Her oldest sister, who should have been chief mother, had raised so many of my grandmother's batches of babies that by the time we came along, she had seen enough children to have seen them all, and none of us, including her own, had anything special to delight her.

We gave her the honor that was due her as the senior sister. She carried herself above reproach. She never told lies and was a true Christian. She went to church rain or shine and visited the sick. She read the Bible and could quote it. She gave counsel when asked for it, and was never wrong. We were all in awe of her, even my irreverent mother. She was the soul of starched dignity. We often felt unworthy beside her. We were right to feel unworthy. She would not sit at table with us because we ate too much and upset her digestion. My mother had to take a tray to her in the parlor. If we went to the movies together, she would sit in a different row, so that she would not have to be part of all that candy crunching and reading the titles aloud.

When it was time to go away for the summer and my mother packed a shoebox with sandwiches which we steadily ate between South Station and Woods Hole, that was the time my aunt could have said, "Off with their heads," without thinking twice.

We were black Bostonians on a train full of white ones. Because we were obviously going the same way, laden as we were with all the equipment of a long holiday, children, luggage, last-minute things stuffed in paper bags, a protesting cat in a carton, in addition to the usual battery of disbelieving eyes, we were being subjected to intense speculation as to what people with our unimpressive ancestry were doing on a train that was carrying people with real credentials to a summer sojourn that was theirs by right of birth.

We were among the first blacks to vacation on Martha's Vineyard. It is not unlikely that the Island, in particular Oak Bluffs, had a larger number of vacationing blacks than any other section of the country.

There were probably twelve cottage owners. To us it was an agreeable number. There were enough of us to put down roots, to stake our claim to a summer place, so that the children who came after us would take for granted a style of living that we were learning in stages.

The early blacks were all Bostonians, which is to say they were neither arrogant nor obsequious, they neither overacted nor played ostrich. Though the word was unknown then, in today's connotation they were "cool." It was a common condition of black Bostonians. They were taught very young to take the white man in stride or drown in their own despair. Their survival was proved by their presence on the Island in pursuit of the same goal of happiness.

Every day, the young mothers took their children to a lovely stretch of beach and scattered along it in little pools. They made a point of not bunching together. They did not want the whites to think they knew their place.

There was not much exchange except smiles between the new and the old, no more was needed. Bostonians do not rush into relationships. Sometimes the children took their shovels and pails and built castles together. It was a pretty scene. The blacks in all their beautiful colors, pink and gold and brown and ebony. The whites in summer's bronze.

The days were full. There were berries to pick, a morning's adventure. There were band concerts for an evening's stroll. There were invitations to lemonade and cookies and whist. There was always an afternoon boat to meet, not so much to see who was getting off, but to see and talk to whatever friends had come for that same purpose.

For some years, the black Bostonians, growing in modest numbers, had this idyll to themselves. The flaws were put in perspective because no place is perfection.

And then came the black New Yorkers. They had found a fair land where equality was a working phrase. They joyously tested it. They behaved like New Yorkers because they were not Bostonians. There is nobody like a Bostonian except a man who is one.

The New Yorkers did not talk in low voices. They talked in happy voices. They carried baskets of food to the beach to make the day last. They carried liquor of the best brands. They grouped together in an ever increasing circle because what was the sense of sitting apart?

Their women wore diamonds when the few Bostonians who owned any had left theirs at home. They wore paint and powder when in Boston only a sporting woman bedecked her face in such bold attire. Their dresses were cut low. They wore high heels on sandy roads.

I had a young aunt who would duck behind a hedge and put us children on watch while she rubbed her nose with a chamois when we told her it was shiny. We did not think her performance was unusual. It was the New Yorkers who seemed bizarre, who always seemed to be showing off wherever they gathered together.

The New Yorkers were moving with the times. They had come from a city where they had to shout to be heard. It was a city that offered much, judgeships, professorships, appointments to boards, stardom on stage and more. Whoever wanted them had to push. The New Yorkers wanted them. They were achievers. They worked hard and they played hard.

They would unwind in another generation. They would come to the Island to relax not to posture. They would come to acknowledge that the Bostonians had a certain excellence that was as solid an achievement as money.

But in the meantime they lost the beach for the Bostonians. That beach like no other, that tranquil spot at that tranquil end of the Island. All one summer the Bostonians saw it coming like a wave they could not roll back. It came the next summer. The beach became a private club, with a gate that only dogs could crawl under, and a sign that said, "For members only."

You lose some, and by the same token, you win some. The world was not lost, just a piece of it. And in the intervening years more has been gained than was ever forfeited, more has been fought for and won, more doors have opened as fewer have closed.

Harry T. Burleigh, the composer, who left a priceless legacy in his long research of Negro spirituals—those shouts of grace and suffering and redemption that might have perished forever if he had not given his gifts to preserving them—he was the first to bring back glad tidings of the Island's fair land to his New York friends, who had always thought of Massachusetts as a nice place to come from, but not to go to unless bound and gagged.

Mr. Burleigh had come to stay at Shearer Cottage in the Highlands, a quiet boardinghouse operated by Boston friends, who had recommended the seclusion of the lovely wooded area, where New York's busy lights seemed as remote as the Island stars seemed near.

He was very good to the children of his friends. There were seven or eight of us who were his special favorites. He gave us money every time he saw us. We did not know any better than to spend it in one place. With abundant indulgence he would give us some more to spend in another. He rented cars and took us on tours of the Island. He told us about his trips abroad. To be with him was a learning experience.

There is a snapshot of him in a family album. Under the snapshot, in the handwriting of that aunt who could take us or leave us, there is the caption: "H.T.B., the children's friend." He was rich and well known in important circles at the time. There were a dozen glowing captions that would have applied. I think it is a tribute to him—and perhaps to my aunt—that she chose this simple inscription.

Mr. Burleigh's summers were spent working as well as sunning. Every weekday morning he went to a church in Vineyard Haven where he had use of the piano. Many of the spirituals sung around the world were given arrangements within God's hearing in an Island church.

In the course of time Mr. Burleigh grew to regret the increasing number of New Yorkers who brought their joyous living to his corner of the Highlands. He had extolled this sacred spot, and they were taking over. Who can say they did not share his vision? They simply expressed it in a different way.

Adam Clayton Powell came to summer at Shearer Cottage when he was a boy. He came with his father. His mother stayed home. Adam came to our house to play every day, and every day Adam's father came to ask my mother if his son was somewhere around. We were sorry for Adam that a boy as big as he was had a father who was always following him around. I can see that great tall man, who looked so like Adam was to grow up to look, striding up the road to ask my mother in his mellifluous preacher's voice if she had seen his boy. He would hold her in conversation, and she would turn as pink as a rose. He seemed to make her nervous, and we didn't know why. Sometimes he would come twice a day to see if Adam had lost his way between our house and Shearer Cottage. He never did, but all that summer his father couldn't rest until he had seen for himself.

Judge Watson—the first black man elected to a judgeship in New York City—his wife, and their young children spent several summers on the Island. They were a splendid family. The younger members still return to see the friends of their childhood. They have all achieved much. Barbara Watson is Assistant Secretary of State for Security and Consular Affairs, and the first woman to attain such rank. Grace Watson directs an HEW program for volunteers in education that encompasses nearly two million teaching aides across the country. Douglas Watson is an aeronautical engineer and Chief Project Officer with Republic Aircraft in Jamaica, L. I. James is a judge in the U.S. Customs Court in Manhattan.

Though all of their titles are impressive, they have not changed. Like all who have come to the Island in the years of their innocence, something here has touched them with sweetness and simplicity.

The summer wound down in September. Labor Day came, cottages emptied. Ours stayed open. We were always late returning to school. My mother could not bear to leave. Fall was so lovely. Winter would be so long to wait to see an Oak Bluffs sky again.

We lingered for those magic days until my father wrote, as he wrote every year, "Come on home, there are no more flowers to pick."

Then we packed our shoebox with sandwiches and left.

A Gallery of Portraits

EXEMPLARY LIVES have been a central subject of New England writing at least since Cotton Mather wrote of saintly persons as "patternes of holinesse" through whom God expressed his will. Long after the idea receded that particular men or women are chosen by God as his servant-instruments, the well-lived life remained a spur to emulation, and the defective life a warning and admonition. Over the centuries, New England writers have examined individual lives on the premise that in them one may discern the culture writ small—but also, paradoxically, in the knowledge that gifted individuals are often those who resist or renounce the smothering norms of their time. What follows is a gallery of New England portraits—some factual, some fictional—but all informed by the idea, as Emerson put it in 1841, that "the universal does not attract us until housed in an individual."

John Singer Sargent, Study for a Portrait, 1885

Harriet Beecher Stowe

From Uncle Tom's Cabin

 1852

"Thy love afar is spite at home," Emerson once wrote about those in antebellum New England whom he saw taking up with zealous pride what might be called the vogue of reform—people for whom sin exists exclusively outside their circle and themselves. One representative of this tendency is the fictional Miss Ophelia in the bestselling antislavery novel *Uncle Tom's Cabin,* by Harriet Beecher Stowe (1811–1896), who was born in Litchfield, Connecticut, the daughter of the famous evangelical minister Lyman Beecher.

Called simply "Vermont" by her Louisiana cousin St. Clare, Miss Ophelia exhibits inexhaustible moral indignation on behalf of slaves but little comprehension of the human complexity of those whom she appoints herself to defend—not to mention of their oppressors. Among the implications of Stowe's portrait of this "bondslave of the ought" is what many twentieth-century civil rights activists discovered: that race prejudice can be more deeply rooted and less readily overcome in the North than in the South.

Whoever has travelled in the New England States will remember, in some cool village, the large farm-house, with its clean-swept grassy yard, shaded by the dense and massive foliage of the sugar maple; and remember the air of order and stillness, of perpetuity and unchanging repose, that seemed to breathe over the whole place. Nothing lost, or out of order; not a picket loose in the fence, not a particle of litter in the turfy yard, with its clumps of lilac-bushes growing up under the windows. Within, he will remember wide, clean rooms, where nothing ever seems to be doing or going to be done, where everything is once and forever rigidly in place, and where all household arrangements move with the punctual exactness of the old clock in the corner. In the family "keeping-room," as it is termed, he will remember the staid, respectable old book-case, with its glass doors, where Rollin's History, Milton's Paradise Lost, Bunyan's Pilgrim's Progress, and Scott's Family Bible, stand side by side in decorous order, with multitudes of other books, equally solemn and respectable. There are no servants in the house, but the lady in the snowy cap, with the spectacles, who sits sewing every afternoon among her daughters, as if nothing ever had been done, or were to be done,—she and her girls, in some long-forgotten fore part of the day, *"did up the work,"* and for the rest of the time, probably, at all hours when you would see them, it is *"done up."* The old kitchen floor never seems stained or spotted; the tables, the chairs, and the various cooking utensils, never seem deranged or disordered; though three and sometimes four meals a day are got there, though the family washing and ironing is there performed, and though pounds of butter and cheese are in some silent and mysterious manner there brought into existence.

On such a farm, in such a house and family, Miss Ophelia had spent a quiet existence of some forty-five years, when her cousin invited her to visit his southern mansion. The eldest of a large family, she was still considered by her father and mother as one of "the children," and the proposal that she should go to *Orleans* was a most momentous one to the family circle. The old gray-headed father took down Morse's Atlas out of the book-case, and looked out the exact latitude and longitude; and read Flint's Travels in the South and West, to make up his own mind as to the nature of the country.

The good mother inquired, anxiously, "if Orleans wasn't an awful wicked place," saying, "that it seemed to her most equal to going to the Sandwich Islands, or anywhere among the heathen."

It was known at the minister's and at the doctor's, and at Miss Peabody's milliner shop, that Ophelia St. Clare was "talking about" going away down to Orleans with her cousin; and of course the whole village could do no less than help this very important process of *talking about* the matter. The minister, who inclined strongly to abolitionist views, was quite doubtful whether such a step might not tend somewhat to encourage the southerners in holding on to their slaves; while the doctor, who was a stanch colonizationist, inclined to the opinion that Miss Ophelia ought to go, to show the Orleans people that we don't think hardly of them, after all. He was of opinion, in fact, that southern people needed encouraging. When however, the fact that she had resolved to go was fully before the public mind, she was solemnly invited out to tea by all her friends and neighbors for the space of a fortnight, and her prospects and plans duly canvassed and inquired into. Miss Moseley, who came into the house to help to do the dress-making, acquired daily accessions of importance from the developments with regard to Miss Ophelia's wardrobe which she had been enabled to make. It was credibly ascertained that Squire Sinclare, as his name was commonly contracted in the neighborhood, had counted out fifty dollars, and given them to Miss Ophelia, and told her to buy any clothes she thought best; and that two new silk dresses, and a bonnet, had been sent for from Boston. As to the propriety of this extraordinary outlay, the public mind was divided,—some affirming that it was well enough, all things considered, for once in one's life, and others stoutly affirming that the money had better have been sent to the missionaries; but all parties agreed that there had been no such parasol seen in those parts as had been sent on from New York, and that she had one silk dress that might fairly be trusted to stand alone, whatever might be said of its mistress. There were credible rumors, also, of a hemstitched pocket-handkerchief; and report even went so far as to state that Miss Ophelia had one pocket-handkerchief with lace all around it.—it was even added that it was worked in the corners; but this latter point was never satisfactorily ascertained, and remains, in fact, unsettled to this day.

Miss Ophelia, as you now behold her, stands before you, in a very shining brown linen travelling-dress, tall, square-formed, and angular. Her face was thin, and rather sharp in its outlines; the lips compressed, like those of a person who is in the habit of making up her mind definitely on all subjects; while the keen, dark eyes had a peculiarly searching, advised movement, and travelled over everything, as if they were looking for something to take care of.

All her movements were sharp, decided, and energetic; and, though she was never much of a talker, her words were remarkably direct, and to the purpose, when she did speak.

In her habits, she was a living impersonation of order, method, and exactness. In punctuality, she was as inevitable as a clock, and as inexorable as a railroad engine; and she held in most decided contempt and abomination anything of a contrary character.

The great sin of sins, in her eyes,—the sum of all evils,—was expressed by one very common and important word in her vocabulary—"shiftlessness." Her finale and ultimatum of contempt consisted in a very emphatic pronunciation of the word "shiftless;" and by this she characterized all modes of procedure which had not a direct and inevitable relation to accomplishment of some purpose then definitely had in mind. People who did nothing, or who did not know exactly what they were going to do, or who did not take the most direct way to accomplish what they set their hands to, were objects of her entire contempt,—a contempt shown less frequently by anything she said, than by a kind of stony grimness, as if she scorned to say anything about the matter.

As to mental cultivation,—she had a clear, strong, active mind, was well and thoroughly read in history and the older English classics, and thought with great strength within certain narrow limits. Her theological tenets were all made up, labelled in most positive and distinct forms, and put by, like the bundles in her patch trunk; there were just so many of them, and there were never to be any more. So, also, were her ideas with regard to most matters of practical life,—such as housekeeping in all its branches, and the various political relations of her native village. And, underlying all, deeper than anything else, higher and broader, lay the strongest principle of her being—conscientiousness. Nowhere is conscience so dominant and all-absorbing as with New England women. It is the granite formation, which lies deepest, and rises out, even to the tops of the highest mountains.

Miss Ophelia was the absolute bond-slave of the *"ought."* Once make her certain that the "path of duty," as she commonly phrased it, lay in any given direction, and fire and water could not keep her from it. She would walk straight down into a well, or up to a loaded cannon's mouth, if she were only quite sure that there the path lay. Her standard of right was so high, so all-embracing, so minute, and making so few concessions to human frailty, that, though she strove with heroic ardor to reach it, she never actually did so, and of course was burdened with a constant and often harassing sense of deficiency;—this gave a severe and somewhat gloomy cast to her religious character.

But, how in the world can Miss Ophelia get along with Augustine St. Clare,—gay, easy, unpunctual, unpractical, sceptical,—in short,—walking with impudent and nonchalant freedom over every one of her most cherished habits and opinions? . . .

[*Miss Ophelia now turns her attention to Dinah, St. Clare's cook.*] "Why don't you mix your biscuits on the pastry-table, there?"

"Law, Missis, it gets sot so full of dishes, and one thing and another, der an't no room, noways—"

"But you should *wash* your dishes, and clear them away."

"Wash my dishes!" said Dinah, in a high key, as her wrath began to rise over her habitual respect of manner; "what does ladies know 'bout work, I want to know? When 'd Mas'r ever get his dinner, if I was to spend all my time a washin' and a puttin' up dishes? Miss Marie never told me so, nohow."

"Well, here are these onions."

"Laws, yes!" said Dinah; "thar *is* whar I put 'em, now. I couldn't 'member. Them 's particular onions I was a savin' for dis yer very stew. I'd forgot they was in dat ar old flannel."

Miss Ophelia lifted out the sifting papers of sweet herbs.

"I wish Missis wouldn't touch dem ar. I likes to keep my things where I knows whar to go to 'em," said Dinah, rather decidedly.

"But you don't want these holes in the papers."

"Them 's handy for siftin' on 't out," said Dinah.

"But you see it spills all over the drawer."

"Laws, yes! if Missis will go a tumblin' things all up so, it will. Missis has spilt lots dat ar way," said Dinah, coming uneasily to the drawers. "If Missis only will go up stars till my clarin' up time comes, I'll have everything right; but I can't do nothin' when ladies is round, a henderin'. You, Sam, don't you gib the baby dat ar sugar-bowl! I'll crack ye over, if ye don't mind!"

"I'm going through the kitchen, and going to put everything in order, *once,* Dinah; and then I'll expect you to *keep* it so."

"Lor, now! Miss Phelia; dat ar an't no way for ladies to do. I never did see ladies doin' no sich; my old Missis nor Miss Marie never did, and I don't see no kinder need on 't;" and Dinah stalked indignantly about, while Miss Ophelia piled and sorted dishes, emptied dozens of scattering bowls of sugar into one receptacle, sorted napkins, table-cloths, and towels, for washing; washing, wiping, and arranging with her own hands, and with a speed and alacrity which perfectly amazed Dinah.

"Lor now! if dat ar de way dem northern ladies do, dey an't ladies, nohow," she said to some of her satellites, when at a safe hearing distance. "I has things as straight as anybody, when my clarin' up times comes; but I don't want ladies round, a henderin', and getting my things all where I can't find 'em."

To do Dinah justice, she had, at irregular periods, paroxysms of reformation and arrangement, which she called "clarin' up times," when she would begin with great zeal, and turn every drawer and closet wrong side outward, on to the floor or tables, and make the ordinary confusion seven-fold more confounded. Then she would light her pipe, and leisurely go over her arrangements, looking things over, and discoursing upon them; making all the young fry scour most vigorously on the tin things, and keeping up for several hours a most energetic state of confusion, which she would explain to the satisfaction of all inquirers, by the remark that she was "a clarin' up." "She couldn't hev things a gwine on so as they had been, and she was gwine to make these yer young ones keep better order;" for Dinah herself, somehow, indulged the illusion that she, herself, was the soul of order, and it was only the *young uns,* and the everybody else in the house, that were the cause of anything that fell short of perfection in this respect. When all the tins were scoured, and the tables scrubbed snowy white, and everything that could offend tucked out of sight in holes and corners, Dinah would dress herself up in a smart dress, clean apron, and high, brilliant Madras turban, and tell all marauding "young uns" to keep out of the kitchen, for she was gwine to have things kept nice. Indeed, these periodic seasons were often an inconvenience to the whole household; for Dinah would contract such an immoderate attachment to her scoured tin, as to insist upon it that it shouldn't be used again for any possible purpose,— at least, till the ardor of the "clarin' up" period abated.

Miss Ophelia, in a few days, thoroughly reformed every department of the house to a systematic pattern; but her labors in all departments that depended on the coöperation of servants were like those of Sisyphus or the Danaides. In despair, she one day appealed to St. Clare.

"There is no such thing as getting anything like a system in this family!"

"To be sure, there isn't," said St. Clare.

"Such shiftless management, such waste, such confusion, I never saw!"

"I dare say you didn't."

"You would not take it so coolly, if you were housekeeper."

"My dear cousin, you may as well understand, once for all, that we masters are divided into two classes, oppressors and oppressed. We who are good-natured and hate severity make up our minds to a good deal of inconvenience. If we *will keep* a shambling, loose, untaught set in the community, for our convenience, why, we must take the consequence. Some rare cases I have seen, of persons, who, by a peculiar tact, can produce order and system without severity; but I'm not one of them,—and so I made up my mind, long ago, to let things go just as they do. I will not have the poor devils thrashed and cut to pieces, and they know it,—and, of course, they know the staff is in their own hands."

"But to have no time, no place, no order,—all going on in this shiftless way!"

"My dear Vermont, you natives up by the North Pole set an extravagant value on time! What on earth is the use of time to a fellow who has twice as much of it as he knows what to do with? As to order and system, where there is nothing to be done but to lounge on the sofa and read, an hour sooner or later in breakfast or dinner isn't of much account. Now, there's Dinah gets you a capital dinner,—soup, ragout, roast fowl, dessert, ice-creams and all,—and she creates it all out of chaos and old night down there, in that kitchen. I think it really sublime, the way she manages. But, Heaven bless us! if we are to go down there, and view all the smoking and squatting about, and hurry-scurryation of the preparatory process, we should never eat more! My good cousin, absolve yourself from that! It's more than a Catholic penance, and does no more good. You'll only lose your own temper, and utterly confound Dinah. Let her go her own way."

"But, Augustine, you don't know how I found things."

"Don't I? Don't I know that the rolling-pin is under her bed, and the nutmeg-grater in her pocket with her tobacco,—that there are sixty-five different sugar-bowls, one in every hole in the house,—that she washes dishes with a dinner-napkin one day, and with a fragment of an old petticoat the next? But the upshot is, she gets up glorious dinners, makes superb coffee; and you must judge her as warriors and statesmen are judged, by *her success*."

Elizabeth Stoddard

From The Morgesons

 1862

In this excerpt from Elizabeth Stoddard's novel *The Morgesons,* the appealingly insolent protagonist, Cassandra, who chafes under the regime of her withholding family, recalls her grandfather and the ancestral house that mirrors his proud spartan-
ness. Stoddard (1823–1902), born in a Massachusetts village overlooking Buzzards
Bay, had a minor literary career that has recently been revisited by scholars who see
in her a writer of neglected merits. Many of them are on display in this character
sketch, in which the old man seems to have absorbed the mustiness of the house,
battened as it is against the sun, and the tartness of the fruits in the garden he tends.
That there is a struggle within his soul to keep up the "regularity" and taciturnity
the world expects of him is signified by such deftly drawn details as the "shelly
noise" his fingernails make as he compulsively clicks them together. Like all good
portraitists, Stoddard conveys the distinctness of an individual while also evoking a
type—in this case, a stoic old man suffering uncomplainingly, and, though in the
company of others, ultimately alone.

My life at Grandfather Warren's was one kind of penance and my life in Miss
Black's school another. Both differed from our home-life. My filaments found
no nourishment, creeping between the two; but the fibers of youth are strong,
and they do not perish. Grandfather Warren's house reminded me of the cas-
ket which imprisoned the Genii. I had let loose a Presence I had no power
over—the embodiment of its gloom, its sternness, and its silence.

With feeling comes observation; after that, one reasons. I began to observe.
Aunt Mercy was not the Aunt Merce I had known at home. She wore a mask
before her father. There was constraint between them; each repressed the
other. The result of this relation was a formal, petrifying, unyielding system,—a system which, from the fact of its satisfying neither, was kept up the
more rigidly; on the one side from a morbid conscience, which reiterated its
monitions against the dictates of the natural heart; on the other, out of respect
and timidity.

Grandfather Warren was a little, lean, leather-colored man. His head was
habitually bent, his eyes cast down; but when he raised them to peer about,

their sharpness and clear intelligence gave his face a wonderful vitality. He chafed his small, well-shaped hands continually; his long polished nails clicked together with a shelly noise, like that which beetles make flying against the ceiling. His features were delicate and handsome; gentle blood ran in his veins, as I have said. All classes in Barmouth treated him with invariable courtesy. He was aboriginal in character, not to be moved by antecedent or changed by innovation—a Puritan, without gentleness or tenderness. He scarcely concealed his contempt for the emollients of life, or for those who needed them. He whined over no misfortune, pined for no pleasure. His two sons, who broke loose from him, went into the world, lived a wild, merry life, and died there, he never named. He found his wife dead by his side one morning. He did not go frantic, but selected a text for the funeral sermon; and when he stood by the uncovered grave, took off his hat and thanked his friends for their kindness with a loud, steady voice. Aunt Mercy told me that after her mother's death his habit of chafing his hands commenced; it was all the difference she saw in him, for he never spoke of his trouble or acknowledged his grief by sign or word.

Though he had been frugal and industrious all his life, he had no more property than the old, rambling house we lived in, and a long, narrow garden attached to it, where there were a few plum and quince trees, a row of currant bushes, Aunt Mercy's beds of chamomile and sage, and a few flowers. At the end of the garden was a peaked-roof pigsty; it was cleanly kept, and its inhabitant had his meals served with the regularity which characterized all that Grandfather Warren did. Beautiful pigeons lived in the roof, and were on friendly terms with the occupant on the lower floor. The house was not unpicturesque. It was built on a corner, facing two streets. One front was a story high, with a slanting roof; the other, which was two-storied, sloped like a giraffe's back, down to a wood-shed. Clean cobwebs hung from its rafters, and neat heaps of fragrant chips were piled on the floor.

The house had many rooms, all more or less dark and irregularly shaped. The construction of the chambers was so involved, I could not get out of one without going into another. Some of the ceilings slanted suddenly, and some so gradually that where I could stand erect, and where I must stoop, I never remembered, until my head was unpleasantly grazed, or my eyes filled with flakes of ancient lime-dust. A long chamber in the middle of the house was the shop, always smelling of woolen shreds. At sunset, summer or winter, Aunt Mercy sprinkled water on the unpainted floor, and swept it. While she swept I made my thumb sore, by snipping the bits of cloth that were scattered on the long counter by the window with Grand'ther's shears, or I scrawled figures with gray chalk, where I thought they might catch his eye. When she had finished sweeping she carefully sorted the scraps, and put them into boxes under the counter; then she neatly rolled up the brown-paper curtains, which had been let down to exclude the afternoon sun; shook the old patchwork cushions in the osier-bottomed chairs; watered the rose-geranium and the monthly rose, which flourished wonderfully in that fluffy atmosphere; set every pin and needle in its place, and shut the door, which was opened again at sunrise. Of late years, Grand'ther's occupation had declined. No new customers came. A few, who did not change the fashion of their garb, still patronized him. His income was barely three hundred dollars a year—eked out to this amount by some small pay for offices connected with the church, of which he was a prominent member. From this income he paid his pulpit tithe, gave to the poor, and lived independent and respectable. Mother endeavored in an unobtrusive way to add to his comfort; but he would only accept a few herrings from the Surrey Weir every spring, and a basket of apples every fall. He invariably returned her presents by giving her a share of his plums and quinces.

I had only seen Grand'ther Warren at odd intervals. He rarely came to our house; when he did, he rode down on the top of the Barmouth stagecoach, returning in a few hours. As mother never liked to go to Barmouth, she seldom came to see me.

HENRY JAMES

From The Bostonians

 1886

As one of Henry James's best critics, Frederick Dupee, has written, the portrait of
Miss Birdseye in *The Bostonians*—possibly modeled on that doyenne of Boston reformers, Elizabeth Peabody—is "the bookshop reformer done for all time." In the
long New England tradition of chiding do-gooders for the astringent righteousness
that seems to go with professional charitableness, nothing matches this set-piece by
James (1843–1916) for its combination of clear analysis and warm sympathy.

She had told him before they started that they should be early; she wished to
see Miss Birdseye alone, before the arrival of any one else. This was just for the
pleasure of seeing her—it was an opportunity; she was always so taken up
with others. She received Miss Chancellor in the hall of the mansion, which
had a salient front, an enormous and very high number—756—painted in
gilt on the glass light above the door, a tin sign bearing the name of a doctress
(Mary J. Prance) suspended from one of the windows of the basement, and a
peculiar look of being both new and faded—a kind of modern fatigue—like
certain articles of commerce which are sold at a reduction as shop-worn. The
hall was very narrow; a considerable part of it was occupied by a large hat-tree,
from which several coats and shawls already depended; the rest offered space
for certain lateral demonstrations on Miss Birdseye's part. She sidled about
her visitors, and at last went round to open for them a door of further admission, which happened to be locked inside. She was a little old lady, with an
enormous head; that was the first thing Ransom noticed—the vast, fair, pro-
tuberant, candid, ungarnished brow, surmounting a pair of weak, kind, tired-
looking eyes, and ineffectually balanced in the rear by a cap which had the air
of falling backward, and which Miss Birdseye suddenly felt for while she
talked, with unsuccessful irrelevant movements. She had a sad, soft, pale face,
which (and it was the effect of her whole head) looked as if it had been
soaked, blurred, and made vague by exposure to some slow dissolvent. The
long practice of philanthropy had not given accent to her features; it had
rubbed out their transitions, their meanings. The waves of sympathy, of enthusiasm, had wrought upon them in the same way in which the waves of

time finally modify the surface of old marble busts, gradually washing away their sharpness, their details. In her large countenance her dim little smile scarcely showed. It was a mere sketch of a smile, a kind of instalment, or payment on account; it seemed to say that she would smile more if she had time, but that you could see, without this, that she was gentle and easy to beguile.

She always dressed in the same way: she wore a loose black jacket, with deep pockets, which were stuffed with papers, memoranda of a voluminous correspondence; and from beneath her jacket depended a short stuff dress. The brevity of this simple garment was the one device by which Miss Birdseye managed to suggest that she was a woman of business, that she wished to be free for action. She belonged to the Short-Skirts League, as a matter of course; for she belonged to any and every league that had been founded for almost any purpose whatever. This did not prevent her being a confused, entangled, inconsequent, discursive old woman, whose charity began at home and ended nowhere, whose credulity kept pace with it, and who knew less about her fellow-creatures, if possible, after fifty years of humanitary zeal, than on the day she had gone into the field to testify against the iniquity of most arrangements. Basil Ransom knew very little about such a life as hers, but she seemed to him a revelation of a class, and a multitude of socialistic figures, of names and episodes that he had heard of, grouped themselves behind her. She looked as if she had spent her life on platforms, in audiences, in conventions, in phalansteries, in *séances;* in her faded face there was a kind of reflection of ugly lecture-lamps; with its habit of an upward angle, it seemed turned toward a public speaker, with an effort of respiration in the thick air in which social reforms are usually discussed. She talked continually, in a voice of which the spring seemed broken, like that of an over-worked bell-wire; and when Miss Chancellor explained that she had brought Mr Ransom because he was so anxious to meet Mrs Farrinder, she gave the young man a delicate, dirty, democratic little hand, looking at him kindly, as she could not help doing, but without the smallest discrimination as against others who might not have the good fortune (which involved, possibly, an injustice), to be present on such an interesting occasion. She struck him as very poor, but it was only afterward that he learned she had never had a penny in her life. No one had an idea how she lived; whenever money was given her she gave it away to a negro or a refugee. No woman could be less invidious, but on the whole she preferred these two classes of the human race. Since the Civil War much of her occupation was gone; for before that her best hours had been spent in fancying that she was helping some Southern slave to escape. It would have been a nice question whether, in her heart of hearts, for the sake of this excitement, she did not sometimes wish the blacks back in bondage. She had suffered in the same way by the relaxation of many European despotisms, for in former years much of the romance of her life had been in smoothing the pillow of exile for banished conspirators. Her refugees had been very precious to her; she was always trying to raise money for some cadaverous Pole, to obtain lessons for some shirtless Italian. There was a legend that an Hungarian had once possessed himself of her affections, and had disappeared after robbing her of everything she possessed. This, however, was very apocryphal, for she had never possessed anything, and it was open to grave doubt that she could have entertained a sentiment so personal. She was in love, even in those days, only with causes, and she languished only for emancipations. But they had been the happiest days, for when causes were embodied in foreigners (what else were the Africans?), they were certainly more appealing.

EDWIN ARLINGTON ROBINSON

Miniver Cheevy

 1897

Born in Gardiner, Maine, Edwin Arlington Robinson (1869–1935) is famous for his brief verse portraits of the characters who inhabit the insular town he called Tilbury. They include misers, dandies, jilted lovers, melancholics, and other representative types reminiscent of the stock figures of medieval drama and early Renaissance "character books." Although they sometimes verge on what we would call stereotype, they are always sharply drawn and retain the power to engage a sympathetic imagination. Among the most memorable is Miniver Cheevy, who copes with his present disappointments by living, with the help of alcohol, in a fanciful past.

Miniver Cheevy, child of scorn,
　Grew lean while he assailed the seasons;
He wept that he was ever born,
　And he had reasons.

Miniver loved the days of old
　When swords were bright and steeds were prancing;
The vision of a warrior bold
　Would set him dancing.

Miniver sighed for what was not,
　And dreamed, and rested from his labors;
He dreamed of Thebes and Camelot,
　And Priam's neighbors.

Miniver mourned the ripe renown
　That made so many a name so fragrant;
He mourned Romance, now on the town,
　And Art, a vagrant.

Miniver loved the Medici,
　Albeit he had never seen one;

He would have sinned incessantly
   Could he have been one.

Miniver cursed the commonplace
   And eyed a khaki suit with loathing;
He missed the mediaeval grace
   Of iron clothing.

Miniver scorned the gold he sought,
   But sore annoyed was he without it;
Miniver thought, and thought, and thought,
   And thought about it.

Miniver Cheevy, born too late,
   Scratched his head and kept on thinking;
Miniver coughed, and called it fate,
   And kept on drinking.

WILLIAM DEAN HOWELLS

From Literary Friends and Acquaintance

 1900

Born in Ohio, William Dean Howells (1837–1920) came as an ambitious young writer to Boston, where he was, in effect, anointed by the aging men of letters—Holmes, Lowell, and Emerson himself (Holmes described the event as "the apostolic succession . . . the laying on of hands")—as their successor. By the time Howells wrote *Literary Friends and Acquaintance,* he had been living chiefly in New York City for close to a decade, "having taken the literary center of the country with him," as Alfred Kazin wrote, "from Boston to New York." Much of the book has a valedictory tone toward his adopted, and beloved, New England, as in the following remembrance of the elder Holmes as the embodiment of the spirit of Boston.

Elsewhere we literary folk are apt to be such a common lot, with tendencies here and there to be a shabby lot; we arrive from all sorts of unexpected holes and corners of the earth, remote, obscure; and at the best we do so often come up out of the ground; but at Boston we were of ascertained and noted origin, and good part of us dropped from the skies. Instead of holding horses before the doors of theatres; or capping verses at the plough-tail; or tramping over Europe with nothing but a flute in the pocket; or walking up to the metropolis with no luggage but the MS. of a tragedy; or sleeping in doorways or under the arches of bridges; or serving as apothecaries' 'prentices—we were good society from the beginning. I think this was none the worse for us, and it was vastly the better for good society.

Literature in Boston, indeed, was so respectable, and often of so high a lineage, that to be a poet was not only to be good society, but almost to be good family. If one names over the men who gave Boston her supremacy in literature during that Unitarian harvest-time of the old Puritanic seed-time which was her Augustan age, one names the people who were and who had been socially first in the city ever since the self-exile of the Tories at the time of the Revolution. To say Prescott, Motley, Parkman, Lowell, Norton, Higginson, Dana, Emerson, Channing, was to say patrician, in the truest and often the best sense, if not the largest. Boston was small, but these were of her first citizens, and their primacy, in its way, was of the same quality as that, say, of the chief families of Venice. But these names can never have the effect for the stranger that they had for one to the manner born. I say had, for I doubt whether in Boston they still mean all that they once meant, and that their equivalents meant in science, in law, in politics. The most famous, if not the greatest of all the literary men of Boston, I have not mentioned with them, for Longfellow was not of the place, though by his sympathies and relations he became of it; and I have not mentioned Oliver Wendell Holmes, because I think his name would come first into the reader's thought with the suggestion of social quality in the humanities.

Holmes was of the Brahminical caste which his humorous recognition invited from its subjectivity in the New England consciousness into the light where all could know it and own it, and like Longfellow he was allied to the patriciate of Boston by the most intimate ties of life. For a long time, for the whole first period of his work, he stood for that alone, its tastes, its prejudices, its foibles even, and when he came to stand in his second period, for vastly, for infinitely more, and to make friends with the whole race, as few men have ever done, it was always, I think, with a secret shiver of doubt, a backward look of longing, and an eye askance. He was himself perfectly aware of this at times, and would mark his several misgivings with a humorous sense of the situation. He was essentially too kind to be of a narrow world, too human to be finally of less than humanity, too gentle to be of the finest gentility. But such limitations as he had were in the direction I have hinted, or perhaps more than hinted; and I am by no means ready to make a mock of them, as it would be so easy to do for some reasons that he has himself suggested. To value aright the affection which the old Bostonian had for Boston one must conceive of something like the patriotism of men in the times when a man's city was a man's country, something Athenian, something Florentine. The war that nationalized us liberated this love to the whole country, but its first tenderness remained still for Boston, and I suppose a Bostonian still thinks of himself first as a Bostonian and then as an American, in a way that no New-Yorker could deal with himself. The rich historical background dignifies and ennobles the intense public spirit of the place, and gives it a kind of personality.

E. E. Cummings

The Cambridge Ladies

 1923

In this little spasm of irritation at the chattering matrons of his youth, Edward Estlin Cummings (1894–1962) catches something of the residual small-townishness of Cambridge, where he grew up the son of a Unitarian minister and where, as a student at Harvard, he developed his affinities with the modernist poets and painters among whom he would later be counted a distinguished practitioner.

the Cambridge ladies who live in furnished souls
are unbeautiful and have comfortable minds
(also, with the church's protestant blessings
daughters, unscented shapeless spirited)
they believe in Christ and Longfellow, both dead,
are invariably interested in so many things—
at the present writing one still finds
delighted fingers knitting for the is it Poles?
perhaps.   While permanent faces coyly bandy
scandal of Mrs. N and Professor D
.... the Cambridge ladies do not care, above
Cambridge if sometimes in its box of
sky lavender and cornerless, the
moon rattles like a fragment of angry candy

John P. Marquand

From The Late George Apley

 1937

John P. Marquand's best-known novel, written in the form of letters among friends and family members of a recently deceased Boston gentleman, has achieved the status of a minor classic since it received the Pulitzer Prize in 1937. In this excerpt, we follow the first—and only—episode in which George Apley, by falling in love with an enchanting Irish girl, feels the stirrings of wayward desire to step outside the limits of behavior deemed suitable by his caste. In prose that is deliberately almost suffocating in its reserve, Marquand (1893–1960) captures the sealed atmosphere of upper-crust Boston—and narrates how Apley internalizes the external pressure to "reconcile inclination with obligation." It is the process by which his spark of rebellion is snuffed out and he becomes the proper Bostonian he was born to be.

Interlude

Dealing with a Subject Which Would Not Ordinarily Be Discussed in a Work of This Nature

It should be stated at the outset that nothing which will be published regarding a youthful lapse discussed in this chapter reflects to the discredit of our subject. It serves rather to illustrate that anyone at a certain stage of life may be beset by vagaries which must not be considered seriously. It must be remembered that through it all George Apley remained an outstanding success, not only in his Harvard class, but in society. That he did so, speaks well for his tradition and for his self-control.

As one approaches the age for marriage there are many of both sexes who find it difficult to settle their lives finally in the direction where their real emotions and convictions should lead them. If it is so with George Apley, others of us have faced the same problem. The solicitude of his parents at this time is manifest by the correspondence which was kept intact— . . .

Extract from a Letter from Elizabeth Apley.

You are probably too modest, George darling, and too preoccupied with your Club and your College activities to know what a swathe you are cutting here in Boston. This makes me very proud, within limits, but you must not use that attractiveness, George, as a means of playing fast and loose. I do not need to say any more, because I know that you will be the gallant knight.

I think it is time for you to realize, though, now that you are in the middle of your Senior year, that there is a certain young thing, and a very sweet one, who is taking you quite seriously. Your father and I are very glad and very much approve, because the Bosworths are quite our type of person. Catharine Bosworth has what my dear Jane Austen would call both "sense and sensibility." She has been brought up as you have been, to know that true happiness in life, such as your dear father and I have shared, is not based on external show. I think it would be very nice if you were to pay Catharine some little particular attention the next time you come into town. You and she have so much in common . . .

These beginnings, so intimately connected with George Apley's future happiness, had an unforeseen and erratic interruption . . .

Dear Mary:—

It is eleven o'clock at night. My roommate has gone to bed, so naturally I am sitting writing to you, because my mind keeps going back over every minute we have been together. I believe in fate now, I believe in destiny. Why should I have been in Cambridge Port, and why should you have been there? When I picked up your handkerchief and we looked at each other, I remember every shade of violet in your eyes and every light in the black of your hair. You called me a "Back Bay dude!" Do you remember? You said we shouldn't be seen together but you met me that Sunday on Columbus Avenue. You make me see things as I have never seen them. I am not what you think me, Mary, and now I am going to show you. I am going down to Worcester Square to call on you next Sunday. If your brother Mike doesn't like it, it's time he knew better. I'd be glad to see Mike any time . . .

For reasons too obvious to be specified, any letters which George Apley may have received from the young woman, Mary Monahan, are not at present in existence, but information gathered from conversation and correspondence with members of the family and friends gives one a glimpse of this young woman who appears so abruptly in Apley's life. This glimpse, it must be admitted, reflects favorably on George Apley's taste, granting the impossible elements of this escapade. It appears that the Monahans, in their class, were respectable. The girl's grandfather, a small farmer who held title to his own land in County Galway, left hurriedly for America for political reasons during one of those abortive revolutionary efforts near the middle of the last century. The girl's father, a contractor, who had inherited the family's political proclivities, was in a position regarded as comfortable by many of his nationality in South Boston. There was, it appears, a sufficient amount of attractiveness in this family circle to appeal to some weakness in George Apley's makeup, for there is no doubt that on many occasions he found actual relaxation at this girl's home. It may have been that George Apley's athletic prowess furnished him an additional entrée, in that further correspondence reveals that the Monahans were personal friends of the notorious pugilist John L. Sullivan.

As for the girl herself, she appears to have been superior to her class, even to the extent of being sought after by a young attorney and by a son of a member of the City Council . . . Miss Monahan had many of the externals of a young person of a higher position . . . she was even mistaken once, when George Apley was seen walking with her on Commonwealth Avenue, for a visiting Baltimore belle . . .

Letter to Mary Monahan.

My sweet wild rose:—

I hope your people liked me as much as I liked them. Dearest, I had a very good time. Darling, I love you more than anything in the world. You give me something that makes me feel free for the first time in my life. Nothing, dear, has made me so happy as this sense of freedom. Will you let me read you Browning again sometime? Poetry itself is real when I read to you . . .

Letter to Mary Monahan.

Darling:—

Once and for all I want you to know that I mean every word I tell you. I never knew how dull existence was until I saw you. If your father is worried by my attitude towards you, I think I had better speak to him myself. I shall gladly tell him what I have told you, that I love you and want to marry you, that I shall try all my life to make you happy. If my own family were to see how sweet you are, how unutterably beautiful, they would want it, too. Believe me, believe me, everything I say I mean . . .

Letter to Mary Monahan.

I should not care what they say, there are other places besides Boston and we can go to them. There is the West, for instance . . .

Since this correspondence comes to an abrupt end, it may be assumed that rumors finally reached the ears of Thomas Apley, but the natural reticence of a man of affairs and of a family confronted with such a problem leaves his exact reactions to it, and his methods of dealing with what must have been, to him, a shocking affair, considerably in the dark.

The reactions of the Monahan girl, whom one suspects betrayed better sense than many another in her position and of her connections, lie also behind a blank wall of silence . . .

Very sensibly [George's] family recommended a sea voyage and a change of scene, and thus unexpectedly he entered on an adventure which must always be a bright one in the days of any youth . . .

Letter from Thomas Apley.

Dear George:—

I hope this finds you much better than when I saw you last. A sum of money in the form of a letter of credit has been placed in your uncle's hands for you to draw upon at his discretion. I think it better that we both refrain from discussing various matters until you return . . . You will view matters in quite a different light after a change of scene and will understand your obligations as a member of our family . . .

There are no copies extant of George Apley's answers . . . For a mind as deeply disturbed as his he may quite probably have gone on the New England principle that the least said the soonest mended. He was meeting the severe shock which comes to all of us who must reconcile inclination with obligation. There is no doubt that he struggled with the difficult horns of this dilemma, for his friends on his return from Europe were aware that he had undergone a spiritual change. Much of the irresponsibility which may have endeared him, but had also made him difficult, to many of his associates seems to have left him at this phase of his career. He had departed from New York as a youth; he returned as a man who could thank his own reasonableness, and the watchfulness of his parents, for this change . . .

Letter to his classmate Chickering.

Here I am reaching the end of my trip through Europe. I have seen much of England and not a little of France, but I have been impressed by a similarity existing between almost every scene, the reason for which I think I chanced upon today. It seems to me that all this time a part of Boston has been with me. I am a raisin in a slice of pie which has been conveyed from one plate to another. I have moved; I have seen plate after plate; but all the other raisins have been around me in the same relation to me as they were when we were all baked.

It is strange that instead of gaining much impression of different cultures, we have succeeded in transferring our own culture momentarily upon every place we visited. We had no wish to lose our identity and we did not lose it. We have succeeded in interposing a barrier of polite conversation . . . against the façades of the cathedrals, the collected works of the masters, and the walls of Chinon. When we were not doing this we were quoting from observations made by our own poets and scholars and thus we have seen the world through a local haze. This has had a strange effect on me. This effect is composed of a desire to escape plus an admiration for our tradition.

I taxed my Uncle Horatio with the idea the other night over a bottle of Vouvray . . . This is what he said: "I see nothing astonishing in all this. People of the same tastes and inclinations naturally flock together. As a matter of fact I am quite convinced, and you will be convinced in time, that our own culture and our own morals are a good deal better and finer than those of the people around here. Find a Bostonian and you will find a citizen of the world."

Well, he may be right but I have seen more of Boston than of Europe. By and large, I have seen a great deal of Boston since I was born.

EDWIN O'CONNOR

From The Last Hurrah

 1956

There is a story that when a mischievous editor at the *Boston Globe* asked the four-time Boston Mayor James Michael Curley if he would review Edwin O'Connor's new novel, *The Last Hurrah,* about an Irish pol who bore a striking resemblance to His Honor, Curley shot back a note saying that the matter was in the hands of his lawyers.

The grandson of Irish immigrants, Edwin O'Connor was born in Providence, Rhode Island, in 1918, and died in Boston in 1968. His best-known book is a eulogy for his parents' generation, who fought not only for political power but for the dignity of full citizenship in a once virulently anti-Irish city. It is also, as O'Connor's friend Arthur M. Schlesinger, Jr., has put it, a book about the losses entailed in their victory. "Theirs had been the generation," Schlesinger writes, "that battered down the gates of the old establishment. In many respects they won their fight. The new generation proceeded to rush through the opening—and lost its Irishness along the way."

The Last Hurrah is both a novel of social realism and an allegory of the American immigrant experience. In the passage that follows, the incumbent mayor, Frank Skeffington, tries to explain to his nephew (named Adam, in true allegorical fashion, to denote his callowness) some of the multiple meanings of the wake they have just attended. The dead man is an unpopular cad who bears the wonderfully indicative name Knocko Minihan; his death furnishes the mayor with the opportunity both to show generosity to his widow, for whom he has genuine feeling, and also to earn political points among the mourners.

"You see, what you're up against here is the special local situation. To understand what happened tonight, you have to understand a little bit about that situation, and just a little bit more about my own rather peculiar position in it."

He leaned back, relaxing against the cushions; simply, detachedly, without boast or embellishment, he began to talk about himself. It was an extraordinary procedure; just how extraordinary, Adam did not realize. For while Skeffington had long studied his city and his own relation to it, the results of these studies he had been careful to keep to himself. From the beginning of his career, he had sharply divided the private from the public side of his life. Of the many friends he had made in politics over the years, none—not Gorman, even—had been admitted to the isolated preserve of the private thought, the personal concern. His wife had been his single, ideal confidante; with her death had come a void. Because Skeffington was, literally, a family man, he had tried one day, somewhat against his better judgment, to fill this void with his son. He had talked of himself, his work, his problems and his plans, and as he talked he had gradually become aware of the look upon his son's face: that characteristic, pleasant, glazed half-smile which indicated that somewhere beneath the surface inattention struggled with incomprehension. There had been more than the look; there had been the dancing feet: they had begun an abstracted, rather complicated tapping on the floor of the study, doubtless in anticipation of their evening's work ahead. *I should have been Vernon Castle,* Skeffington had thought bitterly. He had left the room abruptly and the experiment had never been repeated.

And now, as he had one afternoon three weeks before, he talked to his nephew.

"You see," he said, "my position is slightly complicated because I'm not just an elected official of the city; I'm a tribal chieftain as well. It's a necessary kind of dual officeholding, you might say; without the second, I wouldn't be the first."

"The tribe," said Adam, "being the Irish?"

"Exactly. I have heard them called by less winning names: minority pressure group (even though they've been the majority for half a century), immigrant voting bloc (even though many of the said immigrants have been over here for three generations). Still, I don't suppose it makes much difference what you call them; the net result's the same. I won't insult your intelligence by explaining that they're the people who put me in the mayor's chair and keep me there; I think you realize that the body of my support doesn't come from the American Indian. But as a member—at least by birth—of the tribe, you might give a thought to some of the tribal customs. They don't chew betel nut, and as far as I know the women don't beautify themselves by placing saucers in their lower lips. Although now that I come to think of it," he said, "that might not be a bad idea. It might reduce the potential for conversation. However, they do other things, and among them they go to wakes. And so do I."

"Which are and are not political rallies?" Adam asked. "Or was Knocko's case a special one?"

"Not at all special, except that the guest of honor was somewhat less popular than many of his predecessors. But of course when you speak about wakes as being political rallies, that's a little strong. You have to remember something about the history of the wake around here. When I was a boy in this city, a wake was a big occasion, and by no means a sad one. Unless, of course, it was a member of your own family that had died. Otherwise it was a social event. Some of my most vivid memories are of wakes. I remember my poor mother taking me to old Nappy Coughlin's wake. We went into the tenement, and there was Nappy, all laid out in a little coffin which was kept on ice. Embalming was a rather uncertain science in those days. It was a hot day in July and there were no screens on the parlor windows; there were flies in the room. I can still hear the ice dripping into the pans underneath the coffin, and I can still see Nappy. He had one of the old-fashioned shrouds on, and he lay stretched out stiff as a ramrod. And on his head he wore a greasy black cap, which his good wife had lovingly adjusted so that the peak was pulled down over one eye. It gave him a rather challenging look; you had the feeling that at any moment he might spring out of the coffin and offer to go four fast rounds with you. My mother was horrified at the sight, and I remember that she went directly over to the widow and told her she ought to be ashamed of herself, putting her husband in the coffin with his hat on. Whereupon the widow simply said that he'd never had it off; he'd worn it for thirty years, day and night, in bed and out. So naturally she left it on, not wanting to say good-by to a stranger. However, when Father Conroy came in, the hat was whisked off fast enough. I can remember—it was my first wake, by the way—going into the kitchen, where somebody gave me a glass of milk and a piece of cake. And while my mother was in the parlor talking with the other women, I was out there with the men, just sitting around, eating cake, and listening to them talk. I hadn't the faintest notion of what they were talking about, but it didn't matter much. I was in seventh heaven. Everybody seemed to be enjoying themselves, and I knew I was. When my mother came to get me and take me home, I left with the greatest regret; I decided I'd never had a better time. Well," he said, "so much for memories of happy days. I wouldn't imagine it would sound like very much to anyone who'd been brought up today."

JOHN CHEEVER

Reunion

 1962

John Cheever (1912–1982) was born in Quincy, Massachusetts, into an old New England family that lost its dignity when his father, a shoe salesman, went bankrupt in the Great Depression and left his wife, forcing her to support the children by running a gift shop. The theme of betrayal is never far from the heart of Cheever's fiction. After getting himself thrown out of Thayer Academy for repeated and unrepentant smoking, he began writing seriously in the 1930s. In 1935, while living in Greenwich Village, he sold the first of many stories—mostly about family life in New England or New York's Westchester suburbs (to which Cheever soon moved, and where he remained for the rest of his life)—to *The New Yorker* magazine. About his early years in New England, Cheever once remarked, "Calvin played no part at all in my religious education, but his presence seemed to abide in the barns of my childhood and to have left me with some undue bitterness."

The story reprinted below, "Reunion," is amply bitter, but also wickedly funny and suffused with the reproachfulness, as deep as it is controlled, that is a hazard of unrequited love.

The last time I saw my father was in Grand Central Station. I was going from my grandmother's in the Adirondacks to a cottage on the Cape that my mother had rented, and I wrote my father that I would be in New York between trains for an hour and a half, and asked if we could have lunch together. His secretary wrote to say that he would meet me at the information booth at noon, and at twelve o'clock sharp I saw him coming through the crowd. He was a stranger to me—my mother divorced him three years ago and I hadn't been with him since—but as soon as I saw him I felt that he was my father, my flesh and blood, my future and my doom. I knew that when I was grown I would be something like him; I would have to plan my campaigns within his limitations. He was a big, good-looking man, and I was terribly happy to see him again. He struck me on the back and shook my hand. "Hi, Charlie," he said. "Hi, boy. I'd like to take you up to my club, but it's in the Sixties, and if you have to catch an early train I guess we'd better get something to eat around here." He put his arm around me, and I smelled my father the way my mother sniffs a rose. It was a rich compound of whiskey, after-shave lotion, shoe polish, woolens, and the rankness of a mature male. I hoped that someone would see us together. I wished that we could be photographed. I wanted some record of our having been together.

We went out of the station and up a side street to a restaurant. It was still early, and the place was empty. The bartender was quarreling with a delivery boy, and there was one very old waiter in a red coat down by the kitchen door. We sat down, and my father hailed the waiter in a loud voice. *"Kellner!"* he shouted. *"Garçon! Cameriere! You!"* His boisterousness in the empty restaurant seemed out of place. "Could we have a little service here!" he shouted. "Chop-chop." Then he clapped his hands. This caught the waiter's attention, and he shuffled over to our table.

"Were you clapping your hands at me?" he asked.

"Calm down, calm down, *sommelier,*" my father said. "If it isn't too much to ask of you—if it wouldn't be too much above and beyond the call of duty, we would like a couple of Beefeater Gibsons."

"I don't like to be clapped at," the waiter said.

"I should have brought my whistle," my father said. "I have a whistle that is audible only to the ears of old waiters. Now, take out your little pad and your little pencil and see if you can get this straight: two Beefeater Gibsons. Repeat after me: two Beefeater Gibsons."

"I think you'd better go somewhere else," the waiter said quietly.

"That," said my father, "is one of the most brilliant suggestions I have ever heard. Come on, Charlie, let's get the hell out of here."

I followed my father out of that restaurant and into another. He was not so boisterous this time. Our drinks came, and he cross-questioned me about the baseball season. He then struck the edge of his empty glass with his knife and began shouting again. *"Garçon! Kellner! Cameriere! You!* Could we trouble you to bring us two more of the same."

"How old is the boy?" the waiter asked.

"That," my father said, "is none of your God-damned business."

"I'm sorry, sir," the waiter said, "but I won't serve the boy another drink."

"Well, I have some news for you," my father said. "I have some very interesting news for you. This doesn't happen to be the only restaurant in New York. They've opened another on the corner. Come on, Charlie."

He paid the bill, and I followed him out of that restaurant into another. Here the waiters wore pink jackets like hunting coats, and there was a lot of horse tack on the walls. We sat down, and my father began to shout again. "Master of the hounds! Tallyhoo and all that sort of thing. We'd like a little something in the way of a stirrup cup. Namely, two Bibson Geefeaters."

"Two Bibson Geefeaters?" the waiter asked, smiling.

"You know damned well what I want," my father said angrily. "I want two Beefeater Gibsons, and make it snappy. Things have changed in jolly old England. So my friend the duke tells me. Let's see what England can produce in the way of a cocktail."

"This isn't England," the waiter said.

"Don't argue with me," my father said. "Just do as you're told."

"I just thought you might like to know where you are," the waiter said.

"If there is one thing I cannot tolerate," my father said, "it is an impudent domestic. Come on, Charlie."

The fourth place we went to was Italian. *"Buon giorno,"* my father said. *"Per favore, possiamo avere due cocktail americani, forti, forti. Molto gin, poco vermut."*

"I don't understand Italian," the waiter said.

"Oh, come off it," my father said. "You understand Italian, and you know damned well you do. *Vogliamo due cocktail americani. Subito."*

The waiter left us and spoke with the captain, who came over to our table and said, "I'm sorry, sir, but this table is reserved."

"All right," my father said. "Get us another table."

"All the tables are reserved," the captain said.

"I get it," my father said. "You don't desire our patronage. Is that it? Well, the hell with you. *Vada all' inferno.* Let's go, Charlie."

"I have to get my train," I said.

"I'm sorry, sonny," my father said. "I'm terribly sorry." He put his arm around me and pressed me against him. "I'll walk you back to the station. If there had only been time to go up to my club."

"That's all right, Daddy," I said.

"I'll get you a paper," he said. "I'll get you a paper to read on the train."

Then he went up to a newsstand and said, "Kind sir, will you be good enough to favor me with one of your God-damned, no-good, ten-cent afternoon papers?" The clerk turned away from him and stared at a magazine cover. "Is it asking too much, kind sir," my father said, "is it asking too much for you to sell me one of your disgusting specimens of yellow journalism?"

"I have to go, Daddy," I said. "It's late."

"Now, just wait a second, sonny," he said. "Just wait a second. I want to get a rise out of this chap."

"Goodbye, Daddy," I said, and I went down the stairs and got my train, and that was the last time I saw my father.

JOHN UPDIKE

Plumbing

 1972

Born in 1932 to a Lutheran family in the small town of Shillington, Pennsylvania, John Updike came to New England on a scholarship to Harvard; after a year in London studying drawing, and two years as a staff writer for *The New Yorker*, he moved with his first wife to Ipswich, Massachusetts. He has lived near or in Boston ever since. Updike's wit and prodigious verbal inventiveness have sometimes been almost resented by critics, as if his remarkable fluency with the language somehow marks him as a frivolous or showy writer. But few writers in our time face so squarely such issues as moral responsibility, guilt, and the fear of death. In "Plumbing," Updike muses on the terrifying transience of human life, and, in a spiritual echo of Thoreau and Emerson ("He knows my plumbing; I merely own it"), celebrates a man who seems to have found some solid footing in the world.

The old plumber bends forward tenderly, in the dusk of the cellar of my new house, to show me a precious, antique joint. "They haven't done them like this for thirty years," he tells me. His thin voice is like a trickle squeezed through rust. "Thirty, forty years. When I began with my father, we did them like this. It's an old lead joint. You wiped it on. You poured it hot with a ladle and held a wet rag in the other hand. There were sixteen motions you had to make before it cooled. Sixteen distinct motions. Otherwise you lost it and ruined the joint. You had to chip it away and begin again. That's how we had to do it when I started out. A boy of maybe fifteen, sixteen. This joint here could be fifty years old."

He knows my plumbing; I merely own it. He has known it through many owners. We think we are what we think and see when in truth we are upright bags of tripe. We think we have bought living space and a view when in truth we have bought a maze, a history, an archeology of pipes and cut-ins and traps and valves. The plumber shows me some stout dark pipe that follows a diagonal course into the foundation wall. "See that line along the bottom there?" A line of white, a whisper of frosting on the dark pipe's underside—pallid oxidation. "Don't touch it. It'll start to bleed. See, they cast this old soil pipe in two halves. They were supposed to mount them so the seams were on the sides.

But sometimes they mounted them so the seam is on the bottom." He demonstrates with cupped hands; his hands part so the crack between them widens. I strain to see between his dark palms and become by his metaphor water
seeking the light. "Eventually, see, it leaks."

With his flashlight beam he follows the telltale pale line backward. "Four,
five new sections should do it." He sighs, wheezes; his eyes open wider than
other men's, from a life spent in the dusk. He is a poet. Where I see only a
flaw, a vexing imperfection that will cost me money, he gazes fondly, musing
upon the eternal presences of corrosion and flow. He sends me magnificent
ironical bills, wherein catalogues of tiny parts—

1 1¼ × 1″ galv bushing	58¢
1 ⅜″ brass pet cock	90¢
3 ½″ blk nipple	23¢

—itemized with an accountancy so painstaking as to seem mad are in the
end offset and swallowed by a torrential round figure attributed merely to
"Labor":

Labor	$550.

I suppose that his tender meditations with me now, even the long pauses
when his large eyes blink, are Labor.

The old house, the house we left, a mile away, seems relieved to be rid of our
furniture. The rooms where we lived, where we staged our meals and ceremonies and self-dramatizations and where some of us went from infancy to adolescence, rooms and stairways so imbued with our daily motions that their
irregularities were bred into our bones and could be traversed in the dark,
do not seem to mourn, as I had thought they would. The house exults in its
sudden size, in the reach of its empty corners. Floor boards long muffled
by carpets shine as if freshly varnished. Sun pours unobstructed through
the curtainless windows. The house is young again. It, too, had a self, a life,
which for a time was eclipsed by our lives; now, before its new owners come
to burden it, it is free. Now only moonlight makes the floor creak. When,
some mornings, I return, to retrieve a few final oddments—andirons, picture
frames—the space of the house greets me with virginal impudence. Opening
the front door is like opening the door to the cat who comes in with the
morning milk, who mews in passing on his way to the beds still warm with
our night's sleep, his routine so tenuously attached to ours, by a single mew
and a shared roof. Nature is tougher than ecologists admit. Our house forgot
us in a day.

I feel guilty that we occupied it so thinly, that a trio of movers and a day's breezes could so completely clean us out. When we moved in, a dozen years ago, I was surprised that the house, though its beams and fireplaces were three hundred years old, was not haunted. I had thought, it being so old, it would be. But an amateur witch my wife had known at college tapped the bedroom walls, sniffed the attic, and assured us—like my plumber, come to think of it, she had unnaturally distended eyes—that the place was clean. Puritan hay-farmers had built it. In the nineteenth century, it may have served as a tavern; the pike to Newburyport ran right by. In the nineteen-thirties, it had been a tenement, the rooms now so exultantly large then subdivided by plasterboard partitions that holes were poked through, so the tenants could trade sugar and flour. Rural days, poor days. Chickens had been kept upstairs for a time; my children at first said that when it rained they could smell feathers, but I took this to be the power of suggestion, a myth. Digging in the back yard, we did unearth some pewter spoons and chunks of glass bottles from a lost era of packaging. Of ourselves, a few plastic practice golf balls in the iris and a few dusty little Superballs beneath the radiators will be all for others to find. The ghosts we have left only we can see.

I see a man in a tuxedo and a woman in a long white dress stepping around the back yard, in a cold drizzle that makes them laugh, at two o'clock on Easter morning. They are hiding chocolate eggs in tinfoil and are drunk. In the morning, they will have sickly-sweet headaches, and children will wake them with the shrieks and quarrels of the hunt, and come to their parents' bed with chocolate-smeared mouths and sickening sweet breaths; but it is the apparition of early morning I see, from the perspective of a sober conscience standing in the kitchen, these two partygoers tiptoeing in the muddy yard, around the forsythia bush, up to the swing set and back. Easter bunnies.

A man bends above a child's bed; his voice and a child's voice murmur prayers in unison. They have trouble with "trespasses" versus "debts," having attended different Sunday schools. Weary, slightly asthmatic (the ghost of chicken feathers?), anxious to return downstairs to a book and a drink, he passes into the next room. The child there, a bigger child, when he offers to bow his head with her, cries softly, "Daddy, no, don't!" The round white face, dim in the dusk of the evening, seems to glow with tension, embarrassment, appeal. Embarrassed himself, too easily embarrassed, he gives her a kiss, backs off, closes her bedroom door, leaves her to the darkness.

In the largest room, its walls now bare but for phantasmal rectangles where bookcases stood and pictures hung, people are talking, gesturing dramatically. The woman, the wife, throws something—it had been about to be an ashtray, but even in her fury, which makes her face rose-red, she prudently switched to a book. She bursts into tears, perhaps at her Puritan inability to throw the ashtray, and runs into another room, not forgetting to hop over the little raised threshold where strangers to the house often trip. Children sneak quietly up and down the stairs, pale, guilty, blaming themselves, in the vaults of their innocent hearts, for this disruption. Even the dog curls her tail under, ashamed. The man sits slumped on a sofa that is no longer there. His ankles are together, his head is bowed, as if shackles restrict him. He is dramatizing his conception of himself, as a prisoner. It seems to be summer, for a little cabbage butterfly irrelevantly alights on the window screen, where hollyhocks rub and tap. The woman returns, pink in the face instead of red, and states matters in a formal, deliberated way; the man stands and shouts. She hits him; he knocks her arm away and punches her side, startled by how pleasant, how spongy, the sensation is. A sack of guts. They flounce among the furniture, which gets in their way, releasing whiffs of dust. The children edge one step higher on the stairs. The dog, hunched as if being whipped, goes to the screen door and begs to be let out. The man embraces the woman and murmurs. She is pink and warm with tears. He discovers himself weeping; what a good feeling it is!—like vomiting, like sweat. What are they saying, what are these violent, frightened people discussing? They are discussing change, natural process, the passage of time, death.

Feeble ghosts. They fade like breath on glass. In contrast I remember the potent, powerful, numinous Easter eggs of my childhood, filled solid with moist coconut, heavy as ingots, or else capacious like theatres, populated by paper silhouettes—miniature worlds generating their own sunlight. These eggs arose, in their nest of purple excelsior, that certain Sunday morning, from the same impossible-to-plumb well of mystery where the stars swam, and old photographs predating my birth were snapped, and God listened. At night, praying, I lay like a needle on the surface of this abyss, in a house haunted to the shadowy corners by Disneyesque menaces with clutching fingernails, in a town that boasted a funeral parlor at its main intersection and that was ringed all around its outskirts by barns blazoned with hex signs. On the front-parlor rug was a continent-shaped stain where as a baby I had vomited. Myth upon myth: now I am three or four, a hungry soul, eating dirt from one of the large parlor pots that hold strange ferns—feathery, cloudy, tropical presences. One of my grandmother's superstitions is that a child must eat a pound of dirt a year to grow strong. And then later, at nine or ten, I am lying on my belly, in the same spot, reading the newspaper to my blind grandfather—first the obituaries, then the rural news, and lastly the front-page headlines about Japs and Roosevelt. The paper has a deep smell, not dank like the smell of comic books but fresher, less sweet than doughnut bags but spicy, an exciting smell that has the future in it, a smell of things stacked and crisp and faintly warm, the smell of the *new.* Each day, I realize, this smell arrives and fades. And then I am thirteen and saying goodbye to the front parlor. We are moving. Beside the continent-shaped stain on the carpet are the round stains of the fern flowerpots. The uncurtained sunlight on these stains is a revelation. They are stamped deep, like dinosaur footprints.

Did my children sense the frivolity of our Easter priesthoods? The youngest used to lie in her bed in the smallest of the upstairs rooms and suck her thumb and stare past me at something in the dark. Our house, in her, did surely possess the dimension of dread that imprints every surface on the memory, that makes each scar on the paint a clue to some terrible depth. She was the only child who would talk about death. Tomorrow was her birthday. "I don't want to have a birthday. I don't want to be nine."

"But you must grow. Everybody grows. The trees grow."

"I don't want to."

"Don't you want to be a big girl like Judith?"

"No."

"Then you can wear lipstick, and a bra, and ride your bicycle even on Central Street."

"I don't want to ride on Central Street."

"Why not?"

"Because then I will get to be an old old lady and die."

And her tears well up, and the man with her is dumb, as all the men ever with her will be on this point dumb, in this little room where nothing remains of us but scuffmarks and a half-scraped Snoopy decal on the window frame. If we still lived here, it would be time to put the screens in the windows.

Crocuses are up at the old house; daffodils bloom at the new. The children who lived here before us left Superballs under the radiators for us to find. In the days of appraisal and purchase, we used to glimpse them skulking around their house, behind bushes and bannisters, gazing at us, the usurpers of their future. In the days after they moved out but before our furniture moved in, we played hilarious games in the empty rooms—huge comic ricochets and bounces. Soon the balls became lost again. The rooms became crowded.

Tenderly, musingly, the plumber shows me a sawed-off section of the pipe that leads from the well to our pressure tank. The inside diameter of the pipe is reduced to the size of his finger by mineral accretions—a circle of stony layers thin as paper. It suggests a book seen endwise, but one of those books not meant to be opened, that priests wisely kept locked. "See," he says, "this has built up over forty, fifty years. I remember my dad and me putting in the pump, but this pipe was here then. Nothing you can do about it, minerals in the water. Nothing you can do about it but dig it up and replace it with inch-and-a-quarter, inch-and-a-half new."

I imagine my lawn torn up, the great golden backhoe trampling my daffo-dils, my dollars flooding away. Ineffectually, I protest.

The plumber sighs, as poets do, with an eye on the audience. "See, keep on with it like this, you'll burn out your new pump. It has to work too hard to draw the water. Replace it now, you'll never have to worry with it again. It'll outlast your time here."

My time, his time. His eyes open wide in the unspeaking presences of cor-rosion and flow. We push out through the bulkhead; a blinding piece of sky slides into place above us, fitted with temporary, timeless clouds. All around us, we are outlasted.

TIMOTHY LEWONTIN

From Parsons' Mill

 1989

Born in Raleigh, North Carolina, in 1955, Timothy Lewontin spent much of his childhood in Marlboro, Vermont, and returned to the area as a young man to take a job at a local sawmill. In *Parsons' Mill*, written with Thoreauvian economy and understated wit, Lewontin engages the old theme of a young man's initiation into men's work. In the selections presented here, he catches the tone and rituals of the mill: in "Floored," feeling shunned, he discovers how to talk back to his comrades in a pantomime that, much better than words, can be understood above the hum of the machines. In "The Two Fountains," he learns the local meaning of redundancy.

The Two Fountains

For reasons I did not understand, the mill had two drinking fountains in immediate proximity to each other. One was an attachment to the old porcelain sink just outside Parsons' door; the other was a modern institutional water cooling machine, located directly inside Parsons' office. The old-fashioned device rotated at its point of attachment so that it could be swung out over the sink when in use and pushed back when the sink was needed for some other purpose. Its water flow was controlled by applying pressure to a little porcelain button that at one time had been marked with the word "press"; now the worn instruction could only be deciphered by a logic so obvious as to make one wonder why the word had been printed there in the first place. When pressed, that hard little button elicited an impressive six-inch arc of water and took some getting used to before one could determine the exact amount of pressure required for a safe and steady flow.

The newer machine—the institutional water bubbler inside Parsons' office—was contained in a drab gray metal box, which offered the supplicant sipper a choice of hand and foot actuated controls. This variety of control must have been by way of compensation for the fact that regardless of the pressure applied to the controls, the machine would only emit the most minimal and controlled arc of water, forcing its operator to bring his lips dangerously close to the spout. Of course in summer the institutional water-drinking machine had the advantage that it provided a consistently cooler drink than its old-fashioned counterpart. But otherwise there was no obvious reason why two machines of this type should be in such close proximity.

At first the matter brought to mind the Jim Crow practices of the South, where "separate-but-equal" drinking fountains were the theory, while "separate" was the more distinct practice. Yet in this part of Vermont there were very few blacks, and to my knowledge none of them had ever labored in Parsons' mill. There was certainly a distinction between worker and boss, but it had not been formalized into one of rights to specific drinking fountains. At Parsons' mill the boss and his workers had equal access to the drinking fountain of their choice.

However, there could be no doubt that Parsons showed a particular proclivity toward drinking from the older machine, while the rest of us preferred its modern counterpart. In fact it made for a very interesting study in contrasts. Parsons might be busy in his office with lunch but would go to the trouble of stepping outside for a drink from his favorite drinking fountain, while we had to go to the trouble of stepping into his office to get a drink from our favorite machine. These differences in preference were not always clear-cut. Sometimes Parsons could be seen bending stiffly over the water-drinking machine, slurping water with the same peculiar precision with which he did everything, while we would sometimes indulge in the tepid effluvia from the old sink. Still, the divisions were clear: Parsons had no need of these modern contrivances and their artificially modified product. Tepid water was good enough for him, and it was a point of moral triumph over us that we were so soft as to require cool water. For our part, there was no little triumph in being able to traipse into the boss's office whenever we felt like it and partake of the waters there.

The issue became of particular interest to me that week when I'd been left alone, because I had the run of the place and no one to demonstrate my loyalties to. I tested both fountains, enjoyed their individual characters, and considered the aesthetics of drinking tepid water from an unreliable stream, when water was available in a perfectly cooled and modulated flow. I had just finished with a round of fountain sampling, and was leaning on a large push broom in contemplation that Wednesday morning when a knock came on the door leading from the office to the outside stairs. As I opened it, I was greeted by the slightly apprehensive, partially distrustful, and wholly unshaven countenance of an older man in red suspenders.

"Is Mr. Pahsuns here?"

"Uuh, no. The mill is closed for vacation."

His look remained suspicious, and I felt compelled to account for my presence. "I'm cleaning up this week."

"Oh . . . I'm Mr. Jorgenson, I live across the way, in that house thaya." He took some seconds of maneuvering to point the exact house out to me.

"Yea-ahs?" I said, unintentionally mimicking his accent.

"Well, I keep an eye on the place for Mr. Pahsuns, and I seen it dark in here, and then the lights come on, so I figure I'll take a look."

"Oh . . . well," I said mustering a smile, "he's got me cleaning out the whole place."

"Oh my." He looked about. "Never seen it this clean. Bad sign when a saw-mill's this clean."

"Oh?" My voice dropped.

"Lots of sawdust means good business." He still looked around distract-edly.

"Well there was lots of sawdust before, and I expect we'll produce some more pretty soon."

"Oh!" He brightened, and turned his attention back to me. "So you work for Mr. Pahsuns then." I nodded uncertainly. Who did he think I worked for?

"I seen lots a' hands come and go. He can't hold 'em long." He paused to scratch his unshaven face. "He pays me to cut grass in summer, watch the sprinklers when he's not here, and I stoke the boiler for him in winter. You know, I just keep an eye on the place for him."

"Tough guy to work for!" I said, trying to sound cheerful about it.

"Oh yes. He once asked me: 'Why don't you come work for me?' 'No,' I says, 'I want no part of that.' You know, I keep busy. Take care of my house, shovelin' the walks, cuttin' the grass, rakin', trimmin' bushes. I'm fixin' storm doors right now.

"My daughter . . . she works up at the hospital. She's got three little girls. Two of 'em goes off to school early with their mother. But the little one, she goes later. I fix her breakfast, and see she gets to school."

Having summed up his existence so simply, and seeming so content with it, I felt at that moment that it might almost be worth trading off the thirty-five years which separated us in order to exchange places. But I was still thinking about those water fountains, and since he'd been watching the sprinklers ev-ery day for so long, I asked him if the mill had ever run out of water during a dry summer.

"Oh no. He's got two water systems here. A few years back they put 'im on town water, but he don't like town water. Me neither. No, we got a spring here." He paused to twist around and point up out the window. "You see that mountain thaya? Well we got a spring up thaya that's been piped right down here for years. Comes right off the mountain . . . right into the mill here. Clearest, sweetest water you ever see. Beautiful water." His eyes seemed to light up at the mere mention of it.

I knew that if I didn't get back to work, this old codger would be talking to me all day, and despite feeling rude, started to push my broom around. "Well," he said looking a little hurt, "I'll be seein' you around I expect," and again pointing out his house added, "I live right over thaya." He turned to go, but before slipping out, he edged over to the old-fashioned drinking fountain and took a good long slurp at it, furtively eyeing me from the side to see if I minded or not.

Floored

By nature I am a shy person, and as the next few days of work went by, and I became more and more practiced in the art of trimming dowels, I began to concentrate on the problem of how to break the ice with my fellow employees. Aside from a few bits of mumbled advice from Craig on the qualities of this or that particular dowel rod, there had been virtually no communication between us. Craig was quite young, only eighteen or nineteen I guessed, but he enjoyed the advantage of experience in the ways of the mill and used that advantage to maintain an aura of aloof superiority over me that was nearly suffocating. Charlie was much older and more ragged, but he had a kind of forbidding dignity about him. At break I would make a few attempts at eye contact with him, hoping for the exchange of a word or two. But he just sat there on his upturned bucket, staring fixedly at the floor, taking long hard drags at his cigarette, studiously ignoring me.

It was Craig and Charlie's habit to sit outside in warm weather in order to more fully enjoy their lunches, while Parsons remained sequestered in his office, listening to the noon news on an ancient tube radio. I chose to eat outside but spent the first couple of days in depressed isolation on a large pile of railroad ties well out of sight of Craig and Charlie. By the third day, as I sat there munching away at an apple, I began to berate myself for not trying hard enough, thinking that perhaps I appeared to be the unfriendly one. After finishing my lunch, I strolled over to the others, just as casual as you please, and hovered there for a moment waiting for an invitation to join their company. No such invitation was forthcoming, so after a few moments of uncomfortable silence, I volunteered a weak, "Hi!" They both nodded in return and continued about the business of consuming their lunches.

"God, it's a beautiful day," I ventured.

"Yeah," said Craig.

And then, as often happens in such circumstances, my mind went blank, and I could think of absolutely nothing else to say. Or, if I could think of anything, it seemed so totally banal that I simply could not muster the courage to make myself speak. Apparently they had nothing to say either, and the renewed silence became as deadly as ever. I was by now completely convinced that these two despised me for some as yet unspecified reason. What had I done? Had I taken someone else's job? Was I some kind of a scab? Or was there something in my appearance that offended them? The entire matter remained a mystery to me until I gave up and began to shuffle off.

"Fag!" one of them cursed under his breath.

I stopped dead in my tracks and turned to face my accuser. But the two of them continued to avoid looking directly at me, shooting sly, resentful little sidelong glances at me instead.

"Lord!" I thought. I had certainly faced this one before, but I was burning. I turned on my heel and muttering obscenities headed back into the mill's cool darkness. Back at work, trimming dowels, I grew angrier and angrier at the thought of such closed mindedness. Why did people always have to categorize others? Why did one always have to prove one's loyalties? My pace picked up. Lost in thought, and by now completely used to the task, I lost all awareness of the world beyond me and my trimmer. The others were no longer creating new dowels for me to trim, and I worked with a grim determination to empty the remaining cart and get on to some other task, or get the hell out of that place altogether. Parsons had other ideas. After two-and-a-half days of standing at the trim saw, I had come to the end of the work. Parsons led me "downcellar" to show me several more carts filled to the brim with untrimmed dowels and asked me if I "wouldn't mind" doing these as well. It looked as though there were more dowels on these carts than on those I had already tackled. I was flabbergasted. I could not believe that the old man really meant it and kept looking at his face for some sign that perhaps this was just a little joke that he liked to play on newcomers. But despite the little touches of humor to be seen playing at the corners of his mouth, he appeared to be absolutely serious.

Arriving on the main floor with my new burden, I was starting to boil. Charlie looked up from his work across the mill and shot me a sympathetic glance. "Save it!" I tried to say with a look and pushed the cart off the freight elevator with all the power I could muster. Its wheels clattered and banged as they struck the floor, and it rumbled along uneven floorboards, giving force to my feelings. "Just let anyone get in the way and I'll run 'em right over," I thought.

Although the mill was a noisy place, it was always possible to make yourself heard when you wanted. The trim saw was nearly inaudible as it ran, mixing in with the generalized *shhhh* of many other running blades. But when a dowel was forced, the trim saw had a high pitched shriek that was all its own. If you were gentle in the way you fed it, the sound was gentle also, but to push a dowel through its blades with full force was to make a statement that nobody could miss. As I worked, and my anger increased, my automatized motion took on a savage emphasis. The others now started to regard me with some alarm. But now that I had gotten their attention, I returned it with a defiant and fixed glare.

At first Parsons seemed to enjoy my predicament. He shuffled about, busying himself with this or that, a kind of reddish humor decorating his face. It was becoming clear that this was the old man's idea of fun. Inadvertently, I had run into a contest with him. Either he was going to fire me, or I was going to quit, but I was determined to get the better of the old bastard. Defiant looks had no visible effect, so I started muttering at him from under my breath, punctuating each insult with the thrust of the arms in the motion of my work. The place was much too noisy for my words to be heard, but Parsons could see my lips moving, and he was obviously a man of some imagination.

After a while the treatment began to work. He no longer smiled, the red in his face began to deepen, and I was encouraged to increase the force of my motions and the depth of my obscenities. Parsons now began to strut about with great urgency, making little beelines past me, harassing me, trying to break my spell of anger. Finally he stopped and stood directly behind me so that I was unable to see him. He might have been preparing to bring a hammer crashing down on my skull for all I knew, but I continued my forced pace. On my periphery, I could see that he had decided to sort through my finished cart, looking for mistakes. With an angry and erratic motion he pawed through dowels, sending them clattering to and fro. I slowed a bit, concerned that he might find the evidence he needed to justify his anger against me, and straightened my back, feeling that a confrontation was imminent.

To my surprise, he stopped his impatient search for faulty work, threw a dowel aside, and wheeled around my machine, heading for some distant point across the mill. But no sooner had he cleared my machine than he caught his foot on a looped handle attached to one of the cull baskets and came tumbling to the floor with a mighty crash.

An old person falling is a terrible sight to see. Their bodies no longer have the spring with which the young can defend themselves against the tricks of gravity. Instead they collapse, and fall inwards, their bodies seeming as vulnerable as some grand old building undergoing instant demolition. Despite my anger, my first instinct was to see that Parsons was alive and well. Despite a look of shock that momentarily crossed his face, no serious damage appeared to have occurred. Stunned, and sitting there on his seventy-year-old butt with his legs stretched before him, he looked like some absurd and overaged child playing in the sand at the beach. Looking around as if to find his bearing, he fixed his gaze on the offending basket loop, and withdrawing an unpleasant-looking pocket knife, he focused all his fury against the offending handle as he slashed and tore it away.

It was clear that I could just as easily have been the intended victim of Parsons' slashing fury, and my body tensed instinctually. But with the trim saw and its spinning blades between us, and him still sitting foolishly on the floor, I felt safe. That brief sense of critical danger passed almost as soon as it had come. And though I am not a person prone to violence and am ill-equipped to handle it, I felt a little giddy with triumph. My ears told me the mill had hesitated in its labors, and as I looked up I could see that Craig and Charlie were both watching me with wide-open eyes from across the floor. I gave them an even and prideful look, and then indicating with my eyes the man on the floor, who was by now folding up his knife, I tried to say without words that I was the one who had put him there.

Education

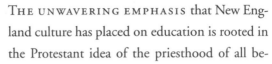

THE UNWAVERING EMPHASIS that New England culture has placed on education is rooted in the Protestant idea of the priesthood of all believers—the idea that the fate of the individual soul, and therefore of Christian society, requires an educated laity able to read Scripture and to respond in an informed way to the teachings of the ministry. "Here the mind / Learn'd to expand its wing, and stretch its flight / Through truth's broad fields," wrote Timothy Dwight, grandson of Jonathan Edwards and president of Yale, in 1794. "Hence Education opens, spreading far / Through the bold yeomanry . . . / Views more expanded, generous, just, refin'd, / Than other nations know." This commitment to education began in hope linked to fear. The Puritan founders feared that without the discipline of educated minds, the destructive impulses of human beings would go unchecked. Yet they harbored the compensatory hope that all human beings contain within themselves dormant truths that can be awakened by the right kind of teacher.

View of Harvard College, 1726

HARVARD COLLEGE

From New England's First Fruits

 1643

In 1641, when the infant colony of Massachusetts Bay was suffering through economic depression and the Puritan party had risen to power in England, the Massachusetts General Court arranged for several leading ministers and gentlemen to undertake a journey "home." It was, as Samuel Eliot Morison put it, a "begging mission," one of whose purposes was to launch "the first concerted 'drive' to obtain income and endowment for the College" that had been established at Cambridge a few years earlier. Among its results was what might be called the first campaign statement in the history of American fundraising—a document that sets out the motives and aspirations of Harvard College for the consideration of potential benefactors.

In respect of the College, and the proceedings of *Learning* therein.

1. After God had carried us safe to *New England,* and we had builded our houses, provided necessaries for our livelihood, reared convenient places for God's worship, and settled the Civil Government, one of the next things we longed for and looked after was to advance *Learning* and perpetuate it to Posterity, dreading to leave an illiterate Ministery to the Churches, when our present Ministers shall lie in the Dust. And as we were thinking and consulting how to effect this great Work, it pleased God to stir up the heart of one Mr. *Harvard* (a godly Gentleman, and a lover of Learning, there living amongst us) to give the one half of his Estate (it being in all about 1700£) towards the erecting of a College, and all his Library. After him another gave 300£. Others after them cast in more, and the public hand of the State added the rest. The College was, by common consent, appointed to be at *Cambridge* (a place very pleasant and accommodate) and is called (according to the name of the first founder) *Harvard College.*

The Edifice is very fair and comely within and without, having in it a spacious Hall (where they daily meet at Commons, Lectures, Exercises), and a large Library with some Books to it, the gifts of diverse of our friends; their Chambers and studies also fitted for and possessed by the Students, and all other rooms of Office necessary and convenient, with all needful Offices thereto belonging. And by the side of the College a fair *Grammar* School for the training up of young Scholars and fitting of them for *Academical Learning,* that still as they are judged ripe, they may be received into the College of this School. Master *Corlet* is the Mr., who hath very well approved himself for his abilities, dexterity, and painfulness in teaching and education of the youth under him.

Over the College is master *Dunster* placed as President, a learned conscionable and industrious man, who hath so trained up his Pupils in the tongues and Arts, and so seasoned them with principles of Divinity and Christianity, that we have to our great comfort, (and in truth) beyond our hopes, beheld their progress in Learning and godliness also; the former of these hath appeared in their public declamations in *Latin* and *Greek,* and Disputations Logical and Philosophical, which they have been wonted (besides their ordinary Exercises in the College-Hall) in the audience of the Magistrates, Ministers, and other Scholars, for the probation of their growth in Learning, upon set days, constantly once every month to make and uphold. The latter hath been manifested in sundry of them, by the savoury breathings of their Spirits in their godly conversation. Insomuch that we are confident, if these early blossoms may be cherished and warmed with the influence of the friends of Learning and lovers of this pious work, they will by the help of God come to happy maturity in a short time.

Over the College are twelve Overseers chosen by the general Court, six of them are of the Magistrates, the other six of the Ministers, who are to promote the best good of it and (having a power of influence into all persons in it) are to see that every one be diligent and proficient in his proper place.

2. *Rules and Precepts that are observed in the College.*

1. When any Scholar is able to understand *Tully,* or such like classical Latin Author *extempore,* and make and speak true Latin in Verse and Prose, *suo ut aiunt Marte,* and decline perfectly the Paradigms of *Nouns* and *Verbs* in the *Greek* tongue, let him then and not before be capable of admission into the College.

2. Let every Student be plainly instructed, and earnestly pressed to consider well, the main end of his life and studies is *to know God and Jesus Christ which is eternal life,* Joh. 17.3. and therefore to lay *Christ* in the bottom, as the only foundation of all sound knowledge and Learning.

And seeing the Lord only giveth wisdom, let every one seriously set himself by prayer in secret to seek it of him *Prov* 2, 3.

3. Every one shall so exercise himself in reading the Scriptures twice a day, that he shall be ready to give such an account of his proficiency therein, both in *Theoretical* observations of the Language and *Logic,* and in *Practical* and spiritual truths, as his Tutor shall require, according to his ability—seeing *the entrance of the word giveth light, it giveth understanding to the simple,* Psalm. 119.130.

4. That they eschewing all profanation of God's Name, Attributes, Word, Ordinances, and times of Worship, do study with good conscience, carefully to retain God, and the love of his truth in their minds, else let them know, that (notwithstanding their Learning) God may give them up to *strong delusions* and in the end *to a reprobate mind,* 2 Thes. 2.11, 12. Rom. 1. 28.

5. That they studiously redeem the time, observe the general hours appointed for all the Students, and the special hours for their own *Classes,* and then diligently attend the Lectures, without any disturbance by word or gesture. And if in any thing they doubt, they shall inquire, as of their fellows, so, (in case of *Non Satisfaction*) modestly of their Tutors.

6. None shall under any pretence whatsoever frequent the company and society of such men as lead an unfit and dissolute life.

Nor shall any without his Tutor's leave, or (in his absence) the call of Parents or Guardians, go abroad to other Towns.

7. Every Scholar shall be present in his Tutor's chamber at the 7th hour in the morning, immediately after the sound of the Bell, at his opening the Scripture and prayer. So also at the 5th hour at night, and then give account of his own private reading, as aforesaid in Particular the third, and constantly attend Lectures in the Hall at the hours appointed. But if any (without necessary impediment) shall absent himself from prayer or Lectures, he shall be liable to Admonition, if he offend above once a week.

8. If any Scholar shall be found to transgress any of the Laws of God, or the School, after twice Admonition, he shall be liable, if not *adultus,* to correction; if *adultus,* his name shall be given up to the Overseers of the College, that he may be admonished at the public monthly Act.

3. *The times and order of their Studies, unless experience shall show cause to alter.*

The second and third day of the week, read Lectures, as followeth:

To the first year, at 8th of the clock in the morning, *Logic,* the first three quarters, *Physics* the last quarter.

To the second year, at the 9th hour, *Ethics and Politics,* at convenient distances of time.

To the third year, at the 10th, *Arithmetic* and *Geometry,* the three first quarters, *Astronomy* the last . . .

All things in the College are, at present, like to proceed even as we can wish, may it but please the Lord to go on with his blessing in Christ, and stir up the hearts of his faithful, and able Servants in our own Native Country, and here (as he hath graciously begun) to advance this Honourable and most hopeful work. The beginnings whereof and progress hitherto (generally) do fill our hearts with comfort, and raise them up to much more expectation of the Lord's goodness for hereafter, for the good of prosperity and the Churches of Christ Jesus.

Benjamin Franklin

Dogood Papers, No. 4

 1722

Some eighty years after *New England's First Fruits* had announced to the world the scope and mission of Harvard College, a sixteen-year-old Boston printer's apprentice named Benjamin Franklin (1706–1790) published an essay in his brother's broadside newspaper, *The New England Courant,* that gave the college considerably less respect. Imitating the acid style of the famous London magazine *The Spectator,* young Franklin wrote in the persona of Silence Dogood, the widow of a country clergyman who had outspoken views on every conceivable subject. The piece was typical fare for the *Courant,* which became so obnoxious to the established Boston authorities (notably the venerable Cotton Mather) that a few weeks later, James Franklin was banned from publishing it. Undefeated, he kept the paper going by turning it over to his precocious brother.

(FROM MONDAY MAY 7. TO MONDAY MAY 14. 1722.)

An sum etiam nunc vel Graecè loqui vel Latinè docendus?—Cicero.

To the Author of the New-England Courant.

Sir,

Discoursing the other Day at Dinner with my Reverend Boarder, formerly mention'd, (whom for Distinction sake we will call by the Name of *Clericus,*) concerning the Education of Children, I ask'd his Advice about my young Son *William,* whether or no I had best bestow upon him Academical Learning, or (as our Phrase is) *bring him up at our College:* He perswaded me to do it by all Means, using many weighty Arguments with me, and answering all the Objections that I could form against it; telling me withal, that he did not doubt but that the Lad would take his Learning very well, and not idle away his Time as too many there now-a-days do. These words of *Clericus* gave me a Curiosity to inquire a little more strictly into the present Circumstances of that famous Seminary of Learning; but the Information which he gave me, was neither pleasant, nor such as I expected.

As soon as Dinner was over, I took a solitary Walk into my Orchard, still ruminating on *Clericus's* Discourse with much Consideration, until I came to my usual Place of Retirement under the *Great Apple-Tree;* where having seated my self, and carelessly laid my Head on a verdant Bank, I fell by Degrees into a soft and undisturbed Slumber. My waking Thoughts remained with me in my Sleep, and before I awak'd again, I dreamt the following DREAM.

I fancy'd I was travelling over pleasant and delightful Fields and Meadows, and thro' many small Country Towns and Villages; and as I pass'd along, all Places resounded with the Fame of the Temple of LEARNING: Every Peasant, who had wherewithal, was preparing to send one of his Children at least to this famous Place; and in this Case most of them consulted their own Purses instead of their Childrens Capacities: So that I observed, a great many, yea, the most part of those who were travelling thither, were little better than Dunces and Blockheads. Alas! Alas!

At length I entred upon a spacious Plain, in the Midst of which was erected a large and stately Edifice: It was to this that a great Company of Youths from all Parts of the Country were going; so stepping in among the Crowd, I passed on with them, and presently arrived at the Gate.

The Passage was Kept by two sturdy Porters named *Riches* and *Poverty,* and the latter obstinately refused to give Entrance to any who had not first gain'd the Favour of the former; so that I observed, many who came even to the very Gate, were obliged to travel back again as ignorant as they came, for want of this necessary Qualification. However, as a Spectator I gain'd Admittance, and with the rest entred directly into the Temple.

In the Middle of the great Hall stood a stately and magnificent Throne, which was ascended to by two high and difficult Steps. On the Top of it sat LEARNING in awful State; she was apparelled wholly in Black, and surrounded almost on every Side with innumerable Volumes in all Languages. She seem'd very busily employ'd in writing something on half a Sheet of Paper, and upon Enquiry, I understood she was preparing a Paper, call'd, *The New-England Courant.* On her Right Hand sat *English,* with a pleasant smiling Countenance, and handsomely attir'd; and on her left were seated several *Antique Figures* with their Faces vail'd. I was considerably puzzl'd to guess who they were, until one informed me, (who stood beside me,) that those Figures on her left Hand were *Latin, Greek, Hebrew,* &c. and that they were very much reserv'd, and seldom or never unvail'd their Faces here, and then to few or none, tho' most of those who have in this Place acquir'd so much Learning as to distinguish them from *English,* pretended to an intimate Acquaintance with them. I then enquir'd of him, what could be the Reason why they continued vail'd, in this Place especially: He pointed to the Foot of the Throne, where I saw *Idleness,* attended with *Ignorance,* and these (he informed me) were they, who first vail'd them, and still kept them so.

Now I observed, that the whole Tribe who entred into the Temple with me, began to climb the Throne; but the Work proving troublesome and difficult to most of them, they withdrew their Hands from the Plow, and contented themselves to sit at the Foot, with Madam *Idleness* and her Maid *Ignorance*, until those who were assisted by Diligence and a docible Temper, had well nigh got up the first Step: But the Time drawing nigh in which they could no way avoid ascending, they were fain to crave the Assistance of those who had got up before them, and who, for the Reward perhaps of a *Pint of Milk*, or a *Piece of Plumb-Cake*, lent the Lubbers a helping Hand, and sat them in the Eye of the World, upon a Level with themselves.

The other Step being in the same Manner ascended, and the usual Ceremonies at an End, every Beetle-Scull seem'd well satisfy'd with his own Portion of Learning, tho' perhaps he was *e'en just* as ignorant as ever. And now the Time of their Departure being come, they march'd out of Doors to make Room for another Company, who waited for Entrance: And I, having seen all that was to be seen, quitted the Hall likewise, and went to make my Observations on those who were just gone out before me.

Some I perceiv'd took to Merchandizing, others to Travelling, some to one Thing, some to another, and some to Nothing; and many of them from henceforth, for want of Patrimony, liv'd as poor as church Mice, being unable to dig, and asham'd to beg, and to live by their Wits it was impossible. But the most Part of the Crowd went along a large beaten Path, which led to a Temple at the further End of the Plain, call'd, *The Temple of Theology*. The Business of those who were employ'd in this Temple being laborious and painful, I wonder'd exceedingly to see so many go towards it; but while I was pondering this Matter in my Mind, I spy'd *Pecunia* behind a Curtain, beckoning to them with her Hand, which Sight immediately satisfy'd me for whose Sake it was, that a great Part of them (I will not say all) travel'd that Road. In this Temple I saw nothing worth mentioning, except the ambitious and fraudulent Contrivances of *Plagius*, who (notwithstanding he had been severely reprehended for such Practices before) was diligently transcribing some eloquent Paragraphs out of *Tillotson's* Works, &c. to embellish his own.

Now I bethought my self in my Sleep, that it was Time to be at Home, and as I fancy'd I was travelling back thither, I reflected in my Mind on the extream Folly of those Parents, who, blind to their Childrens Dulness, and insensible of the Solidity of their Skulls, because they think their Purses can afford it, will needs send them to the Temple of Learning, where, for want of a suitable Genius, they learn little more than how to carry themselves handsomely, and enter a Room genteely, (which might as well be acquir'd at a Dancing-School,) and from whence they return, after Abundance of Trouble and Charge, as great Blockheads as ever, only more proud and self-conceited.

While I was in the midst of these unpleasant Reflections, *Clericus* (who with a Book in his Hand was walking under the Trees) accidentally awak'd me; to him I related my Dream with all its Particulars, and he, without much Study, presently interpreted it, assuring me, *That it was a lively Representation of* HARVARD COLLEGE, *Etcetera.*

> *I remain, Sir,*
> *Your Humble Servant,*
> SILENCE DOGOOD.

ELIZABETH PALMER PEABODY AND
A. BRONSON ALCOTT

From Conversations with Children

 1835, 1836

From 1834 to 1836, Elizabeth Palmer Peabody (1804–1894) assisted Bronson Alcott (1799–1888)—a "tall, mild, milky man," as Van Wyck Brooks once described him, who lived in "Plato's cloudland"—at his experimental Temple Street School in Boston. She recorded his "Conversations" with the pupils, who ranged in age from four to twelve years old, dialogues between teacher and students that mark a decisive shift in the history of American education from recitation of memorized texts to what we would call discussion. The premise of the new method—taken for granted today—is that "education . . . is *Self-Realization*," that children harbor truths within themselves that can be coaxed into articulate expression by a teacher with sufficient patience and skill. Alcott's topics (the selection below records a discussion of childbirth) stirred public outrage in Boston and beyond. When he admitted a black student to the school, the remaining support from the local community collapsed.

Explanatory Preface

To contemplate Spirit in the Infinite Being, has ever been acknowledged to be the only ground of true Religion. To contemplate Spirit in External nature, is universally allowed to be the only true Science. To contemplate Spirit in ourselves and in our fellow men, is obviously the only means of understanding social duty, and quickening within ourselves a wise Humanity.—In general terms, Contemplation of Spirit is the first principle of Human Culture; the foundation of Self-education.

This principle, Mr. Alcott begins with applying to the education of the youngest children . . .

Instead, therefore, of making it his aim to make children investigate External nature, after Spirit, Mr. Alcott leads them in the first place, to the contemplation of Spirit as it unveils itself within themselves. He thinks there is no intrinsic difficulty in doing this, inasmuch as a child can as easily perceive and name pleasure, pain, love, anger, hate and any other exercises of soul, to which himself is subjected, as he can see the objects before his eyes, and thus a living knowledge of that part of language, which expresses intellectual and moral ideas, and involves the study of his own consciousness of feelings and moral law, may be gained, External nature being only made use of, as imagery, to express the inward life which he experiences. Connected with this self contemplation, and constantly checking any narrowing effect of egotism, or self complacency, which it may be supposed to engender, is the contemplation of God . . .

The first object of investigation is also in the highest degree fruitful for the intellect. Spirit, as it appears within themselves, whether in the form of feeling, law, or thought, is universally interesting. No subject interests children so much as self-analysis . . . all are conscious of something within themselves which moves, thinks, and feels; and as a mere subject of curiosity and investigation, for the sake of knowledge, it may take place of all others. In order to investigate it, a great many things must be done, which are in themselves very agreeable. Mr. Alcott reads, and tells stories, calculated to excite various moral emotions. On these stories, he asks questions, in order to bring out from each, in words, the feelings which have been called forth. These feelings receive their name, and history, and place in the moral scale. Then books, and passages from books are read, calculated to exercise various intellectual faculties, such as Perception, Imagination, Judgment, Reason (both in apprehension and comprehension); and these various exercises of mind are discriminated and named. There can be no intellectual action more excellent than this . . .

Plans

Mr. Alcott re-commenced his school in Boston, after four years' interval, September, 1834, at the Masonic Temple, No. 7 . . .

About twenty children came the first day. They were all under ten years of age, excepting two or three girls. I became his assistant, to teach Latin to such as might desire to learn.

Mr. Alcott sat behind his table, and the children were placed in chairs, in a large arc around him; the chairs so far apart, that they could not easily touch each other. He then asked each one separately, what idea he or she had of the purpose of coming to school? To learn; was the first answer. To learn what? By pursuing this question, all the common exercises of school were brought up by the children themselves; and various subjects of art, science, and philosophy. Still Mr. Alcott intimated that this was not all; and at last some one said "to behave well," and in pursuing this expression into its meanings, they at last decided that they came to learn to feel rightly, to think rightly, and to act rightly. A boy of seven years old suggested, and all agreed, that the most important of these three, was right action.

Simple as all this seems, it would hardly be believed what an evident exercise it was to the children, to be led of themselves to form and express these conceptions and few steps of reasoning. Every face was eager and interested. From right actions, the conversation naturally led into the means of bringing them out. And the necessity of feeling in earnest, of thinking clearly, and of school discipline, was talked over. School discipline was very carefully considered; both Mr. Alcott's duty, and the children's duties, also various means of producing attention, self-control, perseverance, faithfulness. Among these means, punishment was mentioned; and after a consideration of its nature and issues, they all very cheerfully agreed, that it was necessary; and that they preferred Mr. Alcott should punish them, rather than leave them in their faults, and that it was his duty to do so. Various punishments were mentioned, and hurting the body was decided upon, as necessary and desirable in some instances. It was universally admitted that it was desirable, whenever words were found insufficient to command the memory of conscience . . . In many of the punishments, . . . the innocent were obliged to suffer with the guilty. Mr. Alcott wished both parties to feel that this was the inevitable con sequence of moral evil in this world; and that the good, in proportion to the depth of their principle, always feel it to be worth while to share the suffering, in order to bring the guilty to rectitude and moral sensibility . . .

It was very striking to see how much nearer the kingdom of heaven (if by this expression is meant the felt authority of moral principles,) were the little children, than were those who had begun to pride themselves on knowing something. We could not but often remark to each other, how unworthy the name of knowledge was that superficial acquirement, which has nothing to do with self-knowledge; and how much more susceptible to the impressions of genius, as well as how much more apprehensive of general truths, were those who had not been hackneyed by a false education . . .

February 2 . . . *Birth* was the first word. Mr. Alcott remarked that we had once before talked of birth, and their ideas had been brought out. Now I am going to speak of it again, and we shall read Mr. Wordsworth's Ode. He then asked the youngest child present, how old he was, and found he was four. The oldest was twelve. He said, that little boy, in four years, has not had time to make that comparison of thoughts and feelings which makes up conscious life. He asked those who understood him, to hold up their hands. Several held up their hands. Those who do not understand these words, may hold up their hands. A great many of the younger ones held up their hands . . .

Mr. Wordsworth had lived, when he wrote this ode, many years, and consequently had felt changes, and he expresses this in the lines I am about to read . . .

> It is not now as it has been of yore,
> > Turn whereso'er I may,
> > > By night or day
> The things which I have seen I now can see no more.

He here stopped, and asked why Mr. Wordsworth could not see the things which he had seen before; had they changed, or had he changed? He had changed, said a boy of ten. Have you had any degree of this change? Yes, and more in this last year, than in all my life before. Mr. Alcott said he thought that there were periods in life, when great changes took place: he had experienced it himself.

He then said: but let us all look back six months; how many of you look at things, and feel about them differently from what you did six months ago? How many of you feel that this school-room is a different place from what it was the first week you were here? Almost every one, immediately, with great animation, held up his hand. He then asked those who knew why this was, to hold up their hands. Many did. And when called on to answer, they severally said, because we know more, because we think more, because we understand you, because you know us, because you have looked inside of us. Mr. Alcott said, the place is very different to me; and why? They give similar answers; but he said they had not hit it. At last one said: because we behave better. Yes, said he, you have it now; knowledge is chaff of itself; but you have taken the knowledge and used it to govern yourselves, and to make yourselves better. If I thought I gave you knowledge only, and could not lead you to use it, to make yourselves better, I would never enter this school-room again! . . .

Analysis of a Human Being. General Survey of the Analysis

Mr. Alcott called the class to analysis, for the last time . . .

We began with Love; and then went to Faith; and then to Conscience, speaking of Obedience, Temptation, and Will; and then to the Appetites, Affections, and Aspirations of the Soul; and then we went to Mind, and spoke of Imagination, Judgment, and Insight . . .

He here stopped and said that one of the boys in this school had said that he did not know before he came to this school, that he had inward eyes; but now he felt that they were open. They began to guess who it was, but they did not guess the right one. Mr. Alcott said that many of them, when they came, were blind, were in midnight. And then he went on reading different passages of the Gospels. He ended with, the light of the body is the eye; what eye? This eye, said a little boy of five. That is the body's eye; what is the spirit's eye? That eye which can see every thing that it wants to see, and which can see God; the body's eye cannot see what it wants to, but the spirit's eye can; and Mr. Alcott, I think that when we are asleep, the spirit goes out of the body, and leaves the body dead; and bye and bye it goes back again, and makes the body alive again. But is the body entirely dead, in sleep? said Mr. Alcott. Why, perhaps a little spirit stays in the body to keep it alive. But almost all the spirit goes out, and sees and hears with its inward eyes and ears, and that is dreaming . . .

Who think that we must know ourselves, in order to know God? All. Who thinks he cannot know God, till he knows himself a great deal? All. Who think that they can know God by studying outward things? None. What are outward things? Shadows of inward things, said the little girl, who was generally the subject of analysis. The Representation of Mind, said a boy of nine. Who was called the Image of God? Jesus Christ, said the whole school. Yes, the outward world is the image of the perfect Mind; and Jesus Christ was the Image of God; or his nature was all Spirit, as he said. Who think that until we study ourselves, we cannot study outward things to much advantage? Many. . . .

Conclusion

It may seem to some persons rather out of place, to bring philosophy to bear upon taking care of babies. But here is the starting point of education . . . The principles growing out of the few primal facts of human nature which are stated above, carried out into the whole education—this is Mr. Alcott's system. He would teach children to discriminate spiritual happiness from that bodily ease and enjoyment, which too often takes its place; to cherish the principle of love, by feeding it on beauty and good, and not on illusion; and to clarify and strengthen faith, by getting knowledge in the right way; not by accumulation, but by growth; for there is something at the foundation of the human soul, analogous to the organization of a plant, which does indeed feed on the earth from which it springs, the air in which it flourishes, the light of heaven which comes upon it from afar; but which admits nothing that it cannot assimilate to itself. We may assist a plant, if we will study its nature, but there are things which might be put round one plant, which would destroy another. And so we may assist a soul; but there is only one way. We must study its nature; we must offer the individual those elements alone, which it needs, and at the time it needs them, and never too much, and always enough. Then we shall find that each soul has a form, a beauty, a purpose of its own. And we shall also find, that there are a few general conditions never to be shut out: that, as the light of heaven, the warmth of earth, and space to expand, are necessary to the plants; so knowledge of God, the sympathy of human love, and liberty to act from within outward, are indispensable to the soul.

Editor's Preface

The work now presented to the reader, forms the introduction to a course of conversations with children, on the Life of Christ, as recorded in the Gospels. It is the Record of an attempt to unfold the Idea of Spirit from the Consciousness of Childhood; and to trace its Intellectual and Corporeal Relations, its Temptations and Disciplines; its Struggles and Conquests, while in the flesh. To this end, the character of Jesus has been presented to the consideration of children, as the brightest Symbol of Spirit; and they have been encouraged to express their views regarding it. The Conductor of these conversations has reverently explored their consciousness, for the testimony which it might furnish in favor of the truth of Christianity . . .

Conversation VIII. Nativity of Spirit. Family Relation

Birth

MR. ALCOTT. I should like to hear all your pictures, but as I have not time, you may tell me now what interested you most?

CHARLES. The prophecy of Zacharias.

LUCIA. Elisabeth's saying the child's name must be John.

LUCY. Zacharias finding his speech again.

ANDREW. The birth of the child.

MR. ALCOTT. How was it?

ANDREW. I thought, one night, as Elisabeth was sleeping, an angel brought her a child, and made her dream she had one, and she awoke and it was lying at her side.

WILLIAM B. I think he was born like other children except that Elisabeth had visions.

GEORGE K. I thought God sent an angel to give her a child. It cried as soon as it came and waked up its mother to give it something to eat.

LUCIA. When John was first born, his mother did not know it, for he was born in the night; but she found it by her side in the morning.

CHARLES. Elisabeth must have had some vision as well as Zacharias, or how could she know the child was theirs? Zacharias could not speak.

NATHAN. I don't see why John came in the night. All other children come in the day.

Sacredness of Birth

MR. ALCOTT. No; more frequently in the night. God draws a veil over these sacred events, and they ought never to be thought of except with reverence. The coming of a spirit is a great event. It is greater than death. It should free us from all wrong thoughts. (See Note 85.)

NOTE 85

MR. ALCOTT. And now I don't want you to speak; but to hold up your hands, if you have ever heard any disagreeable or vulgar things about birth. *(None raised hands.)*

Men have been brought before Courts of Justice for saying vulgar things about the birth of Christ; and all birth is sacred as Jesus Christ's. And I have heard of children saying very profane things about it; and have heard fathers and mothers do so. I hope that none of us will ever violate the sacredness of this subject.

Travail of Body with Spirit

MR. ALCOTT . . . What is meant by "delivered"?
WILLIAM B. She delivered her child to Zacharias.
OTHERS. No; God delivered the child to Elisabeth.
CHARLES. Elisabeth's thoughts made the child's soul, and when it was fairly born she was delivered from the anxiety of the thought.*
*MR. ALCOTT. Yes, the deliverance of the spirit is the first thing. And I am glad to find, that you have so strong an impression of that. The physiological facts, sometimes referred to, are only a sign of the spiritual birth. You have seen the rose opening from the seed with the assistance of the atmosphere; this is the birth of the rose. It typifies the bringing forth of the spirit, by pain, and labor, and patience. (See Note 86.)

NOTE 86

MR. ALCOTT. Edward B., it seems, had some profane notions of birth, connected with some physiological facts; but they were corrected here. Did you ever hear this line,

"The throe of suffering is the birth of bliss"?

GEORGE K. Yes; it means that Love, and Joy, and Faith, lead you to have suffering, which makes more happiness for you.

MR. ALCOTT. Yes; you have the thought. And a mother suffers when she has a child. When she is going to have a child, she gives up her body to God, and he works upon it, in a mysterious way, and with her aid, brings forth the Child's Spirit in a little Body of its own, and when it has come, she is blissful. But I have known some mothers who are so timid that they are not willing to bear the pain; they fight against God, and suffer much more.

CHARLES. I should think it ought to be the father, he is so much stronger.

MR. ALCOTT. He suffers because it is his part to see the suffering in order to relieve it. But it is thought, and with good reason, that if there were no wrong doing there would be no suffering attending this mysterious act. When Adam and Eve did wrong, it was said that Adam should earn bread by the sweat of his brow, and Eve have pain in bringing her children into the world. We never hear of trees groaning to put forth their leaves.

CHARLES. They have no power to do wrong.

MR. ALCOTT. True; God only gives them power to put forth, and they do it without pain. A rose has no pain in being born.

Emblems of Birth

MR. ALCOTT. You may give me some emblems of birth.

ALEXANDER. Birth is like the rain. It comes from heaven.

LUCIA. I think it is like a small stream coming from a great sea; and it runs back every night, and so becomes larger and larger every day, till at last it is large enough to send out other streams.

LEMUEL. Lives streamed from the ocean first; now smaller streams from the larger ones, and so on.

SAMUEL R. Birth is like the rising light of the sun; the setting is death.

ANDREW. God's wind came upon the ocean of life, and washed up the waters a little into a channel, and that is birth. They run up farther, and that is living.

MR. ALCOTT. I should like to have all your emblems but have not time. There is no adequate sign of birth in the outward world, except the physiological facts that attend it, with which you are not acquainted . . .

HORACE BUSHNELL

From Christian Nurture

 1847

One of the ironies of American history is that contemporary culture, in which the ideal of protected childhood seems in full retreat before the forces of technology, advertising, and the general sexual frankness that marks modernity, finds a precedent in Puritan New England, where the distinction between children and adults was, in some respects, no sharper than it is today. Children in early New England were granted no exemption from adult obligations. They were expected to be on watch for saving signs of conversion within themselves—and were taught that without the transforming grace of God they were doomed to damnation. Preachers held up examples of childhood piety and virtue as means to inspire (and shame) children who were as yet untouched by God's spiritual fire. God did his saving work chiefly through sermons, Bible reading, and catechistic teaching. In matters of moral responsibility, youth was no excuse.

By the time Horace Bushnell (1802–1876) completed his education at Yale, these doctrines had settled into an inflexible orthodoxy, all the more rigid in the face of the challenge implicit in the Enlightenment view that environment and circumstance had as much to do with forming character as did the spirit implanted in the soul by God. In his famous treatise on *Christian Nurture,* attacking the old dogmas as pretexts for parental negligence, Bushnell shifted the burden from God to parents in the sacred work of child rearing. He put forth a much more interconnected ideal of spiritual, mental, and physical growth, which parents were responsible for encouraging and supporting in their children. In stressing family rather than church as the key locus of spiritual development, Bushnell was a precursor and pioneer of modern notions about childhood; his ideas are closer to those of John Dewey and Sigmund Freud than to those of Cotton Mather and Jonathan Edwards. The selection that follows—on the significance of early childhood for the development of adult character—discloses one of the first distinctively modern educational sensibilities in America.

Where and how early does the work of nurture begin? . . . The true, and only true answer is, that the nurture of the soul and character is to begin just when the nurture of the body begins. It is first to be infantile nurture—as such,

Christian; then to be a child's nurture; then to be a youth's nurture—advancing by imperceptible gradations, if possible, according to the gradations and stages of the growth, or progress toward maturity.

There is, of course, no absolute classification to be made here, because there are no absolute lines of distinction. A kind of proximate and partly ideal distinction may be made, and I make it simply to serve the convenience of my subject—otherwise impossible to be handled, so as to secure any right practical conviction respecting it. It is the distinction between the age of *impressions* and the age of *tuitional influences;* or between the age of *existence in the will of the parent,* and the age of *will and personal choice in the child.* If the distinction were laid, between the age previous to language and the age of language, it would amount to nearly the same thing; for the time of personal and responsible choice depends on the measure of intelligence attained to, and the measure of intelligence is well represented, outwardly, by the degree of development in language. Of course it will be understood that we speak, in this distinction, of that which is not sharply defined, and is passed at no precise date or age. The transition is gradual, and it will even be doubtful, when it is passed. No one can say just where a given child passes out of the field of mere impression into the field of responsible action. It will be doubtful, in about the same degree, when it can be said to have come into the power of language. We do not even know that there is not some infinitesimal development of will in the child's first cry, and some instinct of language struggling in that cry. Our object in the distinction is not to assume any thing in respect to such matters, but simply to accommodate our own ignorance, by raising a distribution that enables us to speak of times and characteristics truly enough to serve the conditions of general accuracy, and to assist in that manner, the purposes of our discussion.

Now the very common assumption is that, in what we have called the age of impressions, there is really nothing done, or to be done, for the religious character. The lack of all genuine apprehensions, in respect to this matter, among people otherwise intelligent and awake, is really wonderful; it amounts even to a kind of coarseness. Full of all fondness, and all highest expectation respecting their children, and having also many Christian desires for their welfare, they seem never to have brought their minds down close enough to the soul of infancy, to imagine that any thing of consequence is going on with it. What can they do, till they can speak to it? what can it do, till it speaks? As if there were no process going on to bring it forward into language; or as if that process had itself nothing to do with the bringing on of intelligence, and no deep, seminal working toward a character, unfolding and to be unfolded in it. The child, in other words, is to come into intelligence through perfect unintelligence! to get the power of words out of words themselves, and without any experience whereby their meaning is developed! to be taught responsibility under moral and religious ideas, when the experience has unfolded no such ideas! In this first stage, therefore, which I have called the stage of impressions, how very commonly will it be found that the parents, even Christian parents, discharge themselves, in the most innocently unthinking way possible, of so much as a conception of responsibility. The child can not talk, what then can it know? So they dress it in all fineries, practice it in shows and swells and all the petty airs of foppery and brave assumption, act it into looks and manners not fit to be acted anywhere, provoking the repetition of its bad tricks by laughing at them, indulging freely every sort of temper towards it, or, it may be, filling the house with a din of scolding between the parents—all this in simple security, as if their child were only a thing, or an ape! What hurt can the simple creature get from any thing done before it, toward it, or upon it, when it can talk of nothing, and will not so much as remember any thing it has seen or heard? Doubtless there is a wise care to be had of it, when it is old enough to be taught and commanded, but till then there is nothing to be done, but simply to foster the plaything kindly, enjoy it freely, or abuse it pettishly, at pleasure!

Just contrary to this, I suspect, and I think it can also be shown by sufficient evidence, that more is done to affect, or fix, the moral and religious character of children, before the age of language than after; that the age of impressions, when parents are commonly waiting, in idle security, or trifling away their time in mischievous indiscretions, or giving up their children to the chance of such keeping as nurses and attendants may exercise, is in fact their golden opportunity; when more is likely to be done for their advantage or damage than in all the instruction and discipline of their minority afterward.

And something like this I think we should augur beforehand, from the peculiar, full-born intensity of the maternal affection, at the moment when it first embraces the newly arrived object. It scarcely appears to grow, never to grow tender and self-sacrificing in its care. It turns itself to its charge, with a love that is boundless and fathomless, at the first. As if just then and there some highest and most sacred office of motherhood were required to begin. Is it only that the child demands her physical nurture and carefulness? That is not the answer of her consciousness. Her maternity scorns all comparison with that of the mere animals. Her love, as she herself feels, looks through the body into the inborn personality of her child,—the man or woman to be. Nay, more than that, if she could sound her consciousness deeply enough, she would find a certain religiousness in it, measurable by no scale of mere earthly and temporal love. Here springs the secret of her maternity, and its semi-divine proportions. It is the call and equipment of God, for a work on the impressional and plastic age of a soul. Christianized as it should be, and wrought in by the grace of the Spirit, the minuteness of its care, its gentleness, its patience, its almost divine faithfulness, are prepared for the shaping of a soul's immortality. And, to make the work a sure one, the intrusted soul is allowed to have no will as yet of its own, that this motherhood may more certainly plant the angel in the man, uniting him to all heavenly goodness by predispositions from itself, before he is united, as he will be, by choices of his own. Nothing but this explains and measures the wonderful proportions of maternity.

It will be seen at once, and will readily be taken as a confirmation of the transcendent importance of what is done, or possible to be done, for children, in their impressional and plastic age, that whatever is impressed or inserted here, at this early point, must be profoundly seminal, as regards all the future developments of the character. And though it can not, by the supposition, amount to character, in the responsible sense of that term, it may be the seed, in some very important sense, of all the future character to be unfolded; just as we familiarly think of sin itself, as a character in blame when the will is ripe, though prepared, in still another view, by the seminal damages and misaffections derived from sinning ancestors. So when a child, during the whole period of impressions, or passive recipiencies, previous to the development of his responsible will, lives in the life and feeling of his parents, and they in the molds of the Spirit, they will, of course, be shaping themselves in him, or him in themselves, and the effects wrought in him will be preparations of what he will by-and-by do from himself . . .

CHARLES SUMNER

From Equality before the Law

 1849

One of New England's most eloquent and unyielding opponents of slavery in the years leading up to the Civil War, Charles Sumner (1811–1874) was a man simultaneously revered and reviled. To those who sympathized with the antislavery movement, he was its most determined soldier: relentless, undiscouraged, and contemptuous of all who would compromise with evil or evildoers. To others, his measureless indignation made him a reckless man—a "statesman doctrinaire," as Charles Francis Adams, Jr., once called him—for whom nothing could moderate his zeal for, or deter him from, his cause.

In 1849, two years before his election to the United States Senate, Sumner combined his legal training and moral passion in arguing before the Massachusetts Supreme Judicial Court in the Sarah Roberts case—a suit brought against the city of Boston on behalf of a five-year-old African American child, claiming that segregated schools violated the child's constitutional right to equal treatment by the state. The suit was denied, but Sumner's brief anticipates the arguments about the psychological damage inflicted on excluded children that eventually prevailed 105 years later in the case of *Brown v. Board of Education*. Six years after the Roberts case, legal segregation of the city's schools was terminated by an act of the state legislature. More than 100 years later, Boston was rocked by violent conflict over school integration, and public schools in many New England cities remain virtually segregated as a consequence of residential separation between the races, if no longer as a matter of law.

According to the Constitution of Massachusetts, *all men, without distinction of race or color, are equal before the law* . . .

Equality as a sentiment was early cherished by generous souls. It showed itself in dreams of ancient philosophy, and was declared by Seneca, when, in a letter of consolation on death, he said, *Prima enim pars Aequitatis est Aequalitas:* "The chief part of Equity is Equality." But not till the truths of the Christian Religion was it enunciated with persuasive force. Here we learn that God is no respecter of persons,—that he is the Father of all,—and that we are all his children, and brethren to each other. When the Saviour gave us the

Lord's Prayer, he taught the sublime doctrine of Human Brotherhood, enfold-
ing the equality of men . . .

Obviously, men are not born equal in physical strength or in mental capacity, in beauty of form or health of body. Diversity or inequality in these respects is the law of creation. From this difference springs divine harmony. But
this inequality is in no particular inconsistent with complete civil and political equality.

The equality declared by our fathers in 1776, and made the fundamental
law of Massachusetts in 1780, was *Equality before the Law.* Its object was to ef-
face all political or civil distinctions, and to abolish all institutions founded
upon *birth.* "All men are *created* equal," says the Declaration of Independence.
"All men are *born* free and equal," says the Massachusetts Bill of Rights. These
are not vain words. Within the sphere of their influence, no person can be *created,* no person can be *born,* with civil or political privileges not enjoyed
equally by all his fellow-citizens; nor can any institution be established, recognizing distinction of birth. Here is the Great Charter of every human being
drawing vital breath upon this soil, whatever may be his condition, and whoever may be his parents. He may be poor, weak, humble, or black,—he may
be of Caucasian, Jewish, Indian, or Ethiopian race,—he may be of French,
German, English, or Irish extraction; but before the Constitution of Massachusetts all these distinctions disappear. He is not poor, weak, humble, or
black; nor is he Caucasian, Jew, Indian, or Ethiopian; nor is he French, German, English, or Irish; he is a MAN, the equal of all his fellow-men. He is one
of the children of the State, which, like an impartial parent, regards all its off-
spring with an equal care. To some it may justly allot higher duties, according
to higher capacities; but it welcomes all to its equal hospitable board. The
State, imitating the divine justice, is no respecter of persons . . .

Separate Schools Inconsistent with Equality.

It is easy to see that the exclusion of colored children from the Public Schools
is a constant inconvenience to them and their parents, which white children
and white parents are not obliged to bear. Here the facts are plain and unan-
swerable, showing a palpable violation of Equality. *The black and white are not
equal before the law.* I am at a loss to understand how anybody can assert that
they are.

Among the regulations of the Primary School Committee is one to this effect. "Scholars to go to the school nearest their residences." . . . The exception
here is "of those for whom special provision has been made" in separate
schools,—that is, colored children . . .

It may . . . be the boast of our Common Schools, that, through the multitude of schools, education in Boston is brought to every *white* man's door. But it is not brought to every *black* man's door. He is obliged to go for it, to travel for it, to walk for it,—often a great distance . . . [In the present case,] the little child, only five years old, is compelled, if attending the nearest African School, to go a distance of two thousand one hundred feet from her home, while the nearest Primary School is only nine hundred feet, and, in doing this, she passes by no less than five different Primary Schools, forming part of our Common Schools, and open to white children, all of which are closed to her. Surely this is not *Equality before the Law* . . .

If a colored person, yielding to the necessities of position, removes to a distant part of the city, his children may be compelled daily, at an inconvenience which will not be called trivial, to walk a long distance for the advantages of the school. In our severe winters this cannot be disregarded, in the case of children so tender in years as those of the Primary Schools. There is a peculiar instance of hardship which has come to my knowledge. A respectable colored parent became some time since a resident of East Boston, separated from the mainland by water. Of course there are Common Schools at East Boston, but none open to colored children. This parent was obliged to send his children, three in number, daily across the ferry to the distant African School. The tolls amounted to a sum which formed a severe tax upon a poor man, while the long way to travel was a daily tax upon the time and strength of his children. Every toll paid by this parent, as every step taken by the children, testifies to that inequality which I now arraign . . .

The separation of children in the Schools, on account of race or color, is in the nature of *Caste,* and, on this account, a violation of Equality . . . a recent political and juridical writer of France uses the same term to denote not only the distinctions in India, but those of our own country, especially referring to the exclusion of colored children from the Common Schools as among "the humiliating and brutal distinctions" by which their caste is characterized. It is, then, on authority and reason alike that we apply this term to the hereditary distinction on account of color now established in the schools of Boston.

Boston is set on a hill, and her schools have long been the subject of observation, even in this respect. As far back as the last century, the French Consul here made a report on our "separate" school; and De Tocqueville, in his masterly work, testifies, with evident pain, that the same schools do not receive the children of the African and European . . . Strange that here, under a State Constitution declaring the Equality of all men, we should follow the worst precedents and establish among us a Caste . . . here, the black child who goes to sit on the same benches with the white is banished, not indeed from the country, but from the school . . . it is the triumph of Caste . . .

But the words Caste and Equality are contradictory. They mutually exclude each other. Where Caste is, there cannot be Equality; where Equality is, there cannot be Caste.

Unquestionably there is a distinction between the Ethiopian and the Caucasian. Each received from the hand of God certain characteristics of color and form. The two may not readily intermingle, although we are told by Homer that Jupiter did not

> "disdain to grace
> The feasts of Ethiopia's blameless race."

One may be uninteresting or offensive to the other, precisely as individuals of the same race and color may be uninteresting or offensive to each other. But this distinction can furnish no ground for any discrimination before the law.

We abjure nobility of all kinds; but here is a nobility of the skin. We abjure all hereditary distinctions; but here is an hereditary distinction, founded, not on the merit of the ancestor, but on his color. We abjure all privileges of birth; but here is a privilege which depends solely on the accident whether an ancestor is black or white. We abjure all inequality before the law; but here is an inequality which touches not an individual, but a race. We revolt at the relation of Caste; but here is a Caste which is established under a Constitution declaring that all men are born equal . . .

But it is said that these separate schools are for the benefit of both colors, and of the Public Schools. In similar spirit Slavery is sometimes said to be for the benefit of master and slave, and of the country where it exists. There is a mistake in the one case as great as in the other. This is clear. Nothing unjust, nothing ungenerous, can be for the benefit of any person or any thing. From some seeming selfish superiority, or from the gratified vanity of class, shortsighted mortals may hope to draw permanent good; but even-handed justice rebukes these efforts and redresses the wrong. The whites themselves are injured by the separation. Who can doubt this? With the Law as their monitor, they are taught to regard a portion of the human family, children of God, created in his image, coequals in his love, as a separate and degraded class; they are taught practically to deny that grand revelation of Christianity, the Brotherhood of Man. Hearts, while yet tender with childhood, are hardened, and ever afterward testify to this legalized uncharitableness. Nursed in the sentiments of Caste, receiving it with the earliest food of knowledge, they are unable to eradicate it from their natures, and then weakly and impiously charge upon our Heavenly Father the prejudice derived from an unchristian school. Their characters are debased, and they become less fit for the duties of citizenship.

The Helots of Sparta were obliged to intoxicate themselves, that by example they might teach the deformity of intemperance. Thus sacrificing one class to the other, both were injured,—the imperious Spartan and the abased Helot. The School Committee of Boston act with similar double-edged injustice in sacrificing the colored children to the prejudice or fancied advantage of the white.

A child should be taught to shun wickedness, and, as he is yet plastic under impressions, to shun wicked men. Horace was right, when, speaking of a person morally wrong, false, and unjust, he calls him black, and warns against him:—

"Hic niger est: hunc tu, Romane, caveto."

The Boston Committee adopt the warning, but apply it not to the black in heart, but the black in skin. They forget the admonition addressed to the prophet: "The Lord said unto Samuel, *Look not on his countenance:* . . . . for the Lord seeth not as man seeth; for man looketh on the outward appearance, *but the Lord looketh on the heart.*" The Committee look on the outward appearance, without looking on the heart, and thus fancy that they are doing right! . . .

Duty of the Court.

May it please your Honors: Such are some of the things which I feel it my duty to say in this important cause. I have occupied much time, but the topics are not yet exhausted. Still, which way soever we turn, we are brought back to one single proposition,—*the Equality of men before the Law.* This stands as the mighty guardian of the colored children in this case. It is the constant, ever-present, tutelary genius of this Commonwealth, frowning upon every privilege of birth, every distinction of race, every institution of Caste. You cannot slight it or avoid it. You cannot restrain it. God grant that you may welcome it! Do this, and your words will be a "charter and freehold of rejoicing" to a race which by much suffering has earned a title to much regard. Your judgment will become a sacred landmark, not in jurisprudence only, but in the history of Freedom, giving precious encouragement to the weary and heavy-laden wayfarers in this great cause. Massachusetts, through you, will have fresh title to respect, and be once more, as in times past, an example to the whole land.

Already you have banished Slavery from this Commonwealth. I call upon you now to obliterate the last of its footprints, and to banish the last of the hateful spirits in its train. The law interfering to prohibit marriage between blacks and whites has been abolished by the Legislature. Railroads, which, im-

itating the Boston schools, placed colored people apart by themselves, are
compelled, under the influence of an awakened public sentiment, to abandon
this regulation, and to allow them the privileges of other travellers. Only recently I have read that his Excellency, our present Governor [George Briggs]
took his seat in a train by the side of a negro. In the Caste Schools of Boston
the prejudice of color seeks its final refuge. It is for you to drive it forth. You
do well, when you rebuke and correct individual offences; but it is a higher office to rebuke and correct a vicious institution. Each individual is limited in
influence; but an institution has the influence of numbers organized by law.
The charity of one man may counteract or remedy the uncharitableness of another; but no individual can counteract or remedy the uncharitableness of an
organized injury. Against it private benevolence is powerless. It is a monster to
be hunted down by the public and the constituted authorities. And such is
the institution of Caste in the Common Schools of Boston, which now awaits
a just condemnation from a just Court . . . Hesitate not, I pray you, to strike
it down. Let the blow fall which shall end its domination here in Massachusetts . . .

The Christian spirit, then, I . . . invoke. Where this prevails, there is neither
Jew nor Gentile, Greek nor Barbarian, bond nor free, but all are alike. From
this we derive new and solemn assurance of the Equality of Men, as an ordinance of God. Human bodies may be unequal in beauty or strength; these
mortal cloaks of flesh may differ, as do these worldly garments; these intellectual faculties may vary, as do opportunities of action and advantages of position; but amid all unessential differences there is essential agreement and
equality. Dives and Lazarus are equal in the sight of God: they must be equal
in the sight of all human institutions.

This is not all. The vaunted superiority of the white race imposes corre-
sponding duties. The faculties with which they are endowed, and the advantages they possess, must be exercised for the good of all. If the colored people
are ignorant, degraded, and unhappy, then should they be especial objects of
care. From the abundance of our possessions must we seek to remedy their
lot. And this Court, which is parent to all the unfortunate children of the
Commonwealth, will show itself most truly parental, when it reaches down,
and, with the strong arm of Law, elevates, encourages, and protects our colored fellow-citizens.

Charles W. Eliot

Inaugural Address

 1869

Today, few American colleges require students to follow a prescribed curriculum. To the extent that compulsory learning survives at all, it has been reduced to a "core" of recommended courses to be taken before students are released to pursue their individual interests. Until the late nineteenth century, this idea of "electives" was unknown. In his inaugural address as President of Harvard University in 1869, Charles W. Eliot (1834–1926) set out, against strong faculty opposition, what we now take for granted as the normative structure—the "elective" system—of modern undergraduate education.

Only a few years ago, all students who graduated at this College passed through one uniform curriculum. Every man studied the same subjects in the same proportions, without regard to his natural bent or preference. The individual student had no choice of either subject or teachers. This system is still the prevailing system among American colleges, and finds vigorous defenders. It has the merit of simplicity. So had the school methods of our grandfathers—one primer, one catechism, one rod for all children. On the whole, a single common course of studies, tolerably well selected to meet the average needs, seems to most Americans a very proper and natural thing, even for grown men.

As a people, we do not apply to mental activities the principle of division of labor; and we have but a halting faith in special training for high professional employments. The vulgar conceit that a Yankee can turn his hand to anything we insensibly carry into high places where it is preposterous and criminal. We are accustomed to seeing men leap from farm or shop to court-room or pulpit, and we half believe that common men can safely use the seven-league boots of genius. What amount of knowledge and experience do we habitually demand of our lawgivers? What special training do we ordinarily think necessary for our diplomatists?—although in great emergencies the nation has known where to turn. Only after years of the bitterest experience did we come to believe the professional training of a soldier to be of value in war. This lack of faith in the prophecy of a natural bent, and in the value of a discipline concentrated upon a single object, amounts to a national danger.

In education, the individual traits of different minds have not been sufficiently attended to. Through all the period of boyhood the school studies should be representative; all the main fields of knowledge should be entered upon. But the young man of nineteen or twenty ought to know what he likes best and is most fit for. If his previous training has been sufficiently wide, he will know by that time whether he is most apt at language or philosophy or natural science or mathematics. If he feels no loves, he will at least have his hates. At that age the teacher may wisely abandon the school-dame's practice of giving a copy of nothing but zeros to the child who alleges that he cannot make that figure. When the revelation of his own peculiar taste and capacity comes to a young man, let him reverently give it welcome, thank God, and take courage. Thereafter he knows his way to happy, enthusiastic work, and, God willing, to usefulness and success. The civilization of a people may be inferred from the variety of its tools. There are thousands of years between the stone hatchet and the machine-shop. As tools multiply, each is more ingeniously adapted to its own exclusive purpose. So with the men that make the State. For the individual, concentration, and the highest development of his own peculiar faculty, is the only prudence. But for the State, it is variety, not uniformity, of intellectual product, which is needful.

These principles are the justification of the system of elective studies which has been gradually developed in this College during the past forty years. At present the Freshman year is the only one in which there is a fixed course prescribed for all. In the other three years, more than half the time allotted to study is filled with subjects chosen by each student from lists which comprise six studies in the Sophomore year, nine in the Junior year, and eleven in the Senior year. The range of elective studies is large, though there are some striking deficiencies. The liberty of choice of subject is wide, but yet has very rigid limits. There is a certain framework which must be filled; and about half the material of the filling is prescribed. The choice offered to the student does not lie between liberal studies and professional or utilitarian studies. All the studies which are open to him are liberal and disciplinary, not narrow or special. Under this system the College does not demand, it is true, one invariable set of studies of every candidate for the first degree in Arts; but its requisitions for this degree are nevertheless high and inflexible, being nothing less than four years devoted to liberal culture.

It has been alleged that the elective system must weaken the bond which unites members of the same class. This is true; but in view of another much more efficient cause of the diminution of class intimacy, the point is not very significant. The increased size of the college classes inevitably works a great change in this respect. One hundred and fifty young men cannot be so intimate with each other as fifty used to be. This increase is progressive. Taken in connection with the rising average age of the students, it would compel the adoption of methods of instruction different from the old, if there were no better motive for such change. The elective system fosters scholarship, because it gives free play to natural preferences and inborn aptitudes, makes possible enthusiasm for a chosen work, relieves the professor and the ardent disciple of the presence of a body of students who are compelled to an unwelcome task, and enlarges instruction by substituting many and various lessons given to small, lively classes, for a few lessons many times repeated to different sections of a numerous class. The College therefore proposes to persevere in its efforts to establish, improve, and extend the elective system. Its administrative difficulties, which seem formidable at first, vanish before a brief experience.

There has been much discussion about the comparative merits of lectures and recitations. Both are useful—lectures, for inspiration, guidance, and the comprehensive methodizing which only one who has a view of the whole field can rightly contrive; recitations, for securing and testifying a thorough mastery on the part of the pupil of the treatise or author in hand, for conversational comment and amplification, for emulation and competition. Recitations alone readily degenerate into dusty repetitions, and lectures alone are too often a useless expenditure of force. The lecturer pumps laboriously into sieves. The water may be wholesome, but it runs through. A mind must work to grow. Just as far, however, as the student can be relied on to master and appreciate his author without the aid of frequent questioning and repetitions, so far is it possible to dispense with recitations. Accordingly, in the later College years there is a decided tendency to diminish the number of recitations, the faithfulness of the student being tested by periodical examinations. This tendency is in a right direction, if prudently controlled.

The discussion about lectures and recitations has brought out some strong opinions about text-books and their use. Impatience with text-books and manuals is very natural in both teachers and taught. These books are indeed, for the most part, very imperfect, and stand in constant need of correction by the well-informed teacher. Stereotyping, in its present undeveloped condition, is in part to blame for their most exasperating defects. To make the metal plates keep pace with the progress of learning is costly. The manifest deficiencies of text-books must not, however, drive us into a too sweeping condemnation of their use. It is a rare teacher who is superior to all manuals in his subject. Scientific manuals are, as a rule, much worse than those upon language, literature, or philosophy; yet the main improvement in medical education in this country during the last twenty years has been the addition of systematic recitations from text-books to the lectures which were formerly the principal means of theoretical instruction. The training of a medical student, inadequate as it is, offers the best example we have of the methods and fruits of an education mainly scientific. The transformation which the average student of a good medical school undergoes in three years is strong testimony to the efficiency of the training he receives.

There are certain common misapprehensions about colleges in general, and this College in particular, to which I wish to devote a few moments' attention. And, first, in spite of the familiar picture of the moral dangers which environ the student, there is no place so safe as a good college during the critical passage from boyhood to manhood. The security of the college commonwealth is largely due to its exuberant activity. Its public opinion, though easily led astray, is still high in the main. Its scholarly tastes and habits, its eager friendships and quick hatreds, its keen debates, its frank discussions of character and of deep political and religious questions, all are safeguards against sloth, vulgarity, and depravity. Its society and, not less, its solitudes are full of teaching. Shams, conceit, and fictitious distinctions get no mercy. There is nothing but ridicule for bombast and sentimentality. Repression of genuine sentiment and emotion is indeed, in this College, carried too far. Reserve is more respectable than any undiscerning communicativeness; but neither Yankee shamefacedness nor English stolidity is admirable. This point especially touches you, young men, who are still undergraduates. When you feel a true admiration for a teacher, a glow of enthusiasm for work, a thrill of pleasure at some excellent saying, give it expression. Do not be ashamed of these emotions. Cherish the natural sentiment of personal devotion to the teacher who calls out your better powers. It is a great delight to serve an intellectual master. We Americans are but too apt to lose this happiness. German and French students get it. If ever in after years you come to smile at the youthful reverence you paid, believe me, it will be with tears in your eyes.

Many excellent persons see great offense in any system of college rank; but why should we expect more of young men than we do of their elders? How many men and women perform their daily tasks from the highest motives alone—for the glory of God and the relief of man's estate? Most people work for bare bread, a few for cake. The college rank-list reinforces higher motives. In the campaign for character, no auxiliaries are to be refused. Next to despising the enemy, it is dangerous to reject allies. To devise a suitable method of estimating the fidelity and attainments of college students is, however, a problem which has long been under discussion, and has not yet received a satisfactory solution. The worst of rank as a stimulus is the self-reference it implies in the aspirants. The less a young man thinks about the cultivation of his mind, about his own mental progress,—about himself, in short,—the better.

The petty discipline of colleges attracts altogether too much attention from both friends and foes. It is to be remembered that the rules concerning decorum, however necessary to maintain the high standard of manners and conduct which characterizes this College, are nevertheless justly described as petty. What is technically called a quiet term cannot be accepted as the acme of university success. This success is not to be measured by the frequency or rarity of college punishments. The criteria of success or failure in a high place of learning are not the boyish escapades of an insignificant minority, nor the exceptional cases of ruinous vice. Each year must be judged by the added opportunities of instruction, by the prevailing enthusiasm in learning, and by the gathered wealth of culture and character. The best way to put boyishness to shame is to foster scholarship and manliness. The manners of a community cannot be improved by main force any more than its morals. The Statutes of the University need some amendment and reduction in the chapters on crimes and misdemeanors. But let us render to our fathers the justice we shall need from our sons. What is too minute or precise for our use was doubtless wise and proper in its day. It was to inculcate a reverent bearing and due consideration for things sacred that the regulations prescribed a black dress on Sunday. Black is not the only decorous wear in these days; but we must not seem, in ceasing from this particular mode of good manners, to think less of the gentle breeding of which only the outward signs, and not the substance, have been changed.

John Jay Chapman

The Function of a University

 1900

Perhaps the best-known fact about John Jay Chapman (1862–1933) is that he thrashed an acquaintance with a cane for making advances to the woman Chapman intended to marry and then, in an act of penance after learning that his suspicions were unfounded, thrust his own hand into a coal fire, burning it so badly it was useless for the rest of his life. Chapman was not a moderate man. He was bristling, impatient, often manic, sometimes brutally depressed—attributes that converge in his writing into a ferocious directness that makes him one of those rare critics whose work remains fresh long after he wrote it. Descended from New England luminaries, and very much a part of the Cambridge-Harvard orbit even after he settled in upstate New York, Chapman was not conventionally liberal or humane, and certainly not consistent in his views. He could be inflamed to outrage by racial injustice but was not above giving vent to anti-Catholic and anti-Semitic sentiments. In "The Function of a University," he sets out his college ideal at a time when, like his similarly disaffected contemporary Thorstein Veblen, he regarded the academy as the target of a hostile takeover by big business.

Youth is not sordid; and the use of a university is that it adds a few years to a man's boyhood, during which his relations to others are not sordid. The problems of life boil down to the question whether one shall be of service to people or shall make use of them; and it makes a great difference whether a man gets his first taste of the issue at the age of 18 or of 22. It makes a great difference, too, whether the intervening years are spent in a counting house, where the very clocks measure nothing but interest, and where the duty to self is preached and practiced at the young man till he feels his nature stiffening into an heroic determination to master this grim and terrible religion of money, or whether those years shall be spent amid surroundings that may awaken the youth to a noble ambition. You may refuse to send your son to a university, you may refuse to have a library in your house, but you cannot greatly disparage the instructive wisdom of mankind which maintains both. There is a utility in them deeper than your cavil. They are perpetual fonts of inspiration for such as know how to use them.

The college buildings, the professors, the games, the societies and the library are a palace of vision. Nothing is spared that can assist vision. The grounds are studded with camerae obscurae showing views of life. But the meaning of these sights is to come afterwards.

If a man is a student while in college he learns to value the accomplishments of valor and intellect; but the cost of them cannot be learned here. The cost remains as unknown as the other side of the moon; language cannot express it. And whether he is a student or not, he lives in an atmosphere of generosity while his bones are setting, and goes out from the place with an integrity which he can, perhaps, never entirely unlearn.

Any one who visits a university feels the influence of a delightful and slightly enervating calm which creeps over him as he crosses the campus. Here are peaceful days and early hours, precision, routine, social happiness. The pictures which the instructors are putting into the slide seem too bright. The instructors themselves appear not to know what tragedies they are handling. The visitor feels he must take the rod from the proctor's hand and give a lecture on the almost imperceptible vestiges of pain still shown on the plate. But the bell rings and it is lunch time. The class in algebra goes on at two.

The lack of vigor in the air of a university comes from the professors. It is impossible for a man to remain at the top of his bent while he is doing anything else but wrestle with new truth; and the temptation of a teacher towards lassitude is overwhelming. He is beyond the reach of new experience, except as he makes it himself in contact with his students and his Faculty; and the man who can make spiritual progress with this outfit is a rare man. The consequence is that most professors go on thinking and teaching the same thing year after year. Give a professor a false thesis in early life, and he will teach it till he dies. He has no way of correcting it.

The rise and progress of new ideas is somewhat as follows: A man makes a discovery; he divulges a theology, or a theory of science or government. If his theory falls into harmony with the current thought of the age, it becomes popular and is taken up on all sides. Years may elapse before a man's theory is adopted by the world at large as being in harmony with accepted notions, and altogether a plausible thing. But when the day of its popularity arrives and no one is any longer afraid of the doctrine, when it is recognized as useful and at any rate as innocuous, then it is adopted by the learned, and professors are established to teach it in the universities, where it smolders and dies away unless it is reinforced from the world. The master minds of the world, whose thoughts have survived change, thus get set before the young of each generation and together with this valuable heritage of thought, mixed in with it, accepted with the same reverence and transmitted with the same zeal, we find all the not-yet-exploded dogmas of contemporary politics, society and trade.

Such were the reflections that passed through my mind as I turned over the journals on a book stall, and noted the flood of essays upon international politics which the professors in our fresh water colleges have recently been pouring upon the world. It is a striking fact that our college professors of economics have been furnishing the arguments for the imperialists. The learning of the land seems to be given over to a crude and bloodthirsty materialism. It is impossible not to be shocked at the heartless rubbish put forth in the name of science, and embellished with absurd technical terms, by men who know as much about war and government as the spinsters and knitters in the sun who weave their thread with bones. The ferocity of these professors puzzled me greatly till I remembered the explanation of it, and then I perceived that these dominies were the mouthpieces of an academic dogma, and were no more to be blamed than their predecessors who had preached infant damnation, no-faith-with-heretics, or any other orthodoxy that was once so canonized by the world as to be regarded as science by a university.

The cause in all such cases must be sought in history. The early formulation of Darwin's discoveries was coeval with an era of great commercial progress. The phrase "struggle for existence," could be understood by everyone, and seemed to justify any form of self-interest. It became popular at once, was labeled science, was widely accepted, and finally it sifted through into the universities where it is taught to-day. It represents a misapprehension of 1850.

The ideal of a university is to encourage thought. But it is a law of nature that thought cannot move forward except through action. Therefore, a university is no sifting place, but only a treasury. It preserves so much that is really sacred that we can forgive the sanctity it sheds on some ever-changing dross that is shoveled into it and out of it by every passing age. Scientific and prophetic light reaches the university mind thirty years late. Successive dogmas shine down through the elm trees upon leisure and breed pedantry. The pleasant lanes are charged with latent death that makes our pulse beat slower: the lotus is in bloom. We enjoy it for an afternoon and then we cry out "Certainly, this is no place for a grown man." And yet certainly there are no places where grown men are more needed than at the colleges, for the difficulty with these pools of life is to keep open the channels by which the thoughts and feelings of the current world shall run into them.

A thousand new faiths are now forming in the people of the United States; new religions, new forms of spiritual force, and yet such is the constitution of society that they must have passed through the experimental stage before the learned can take note of them. This is due in part to that hiatus in the history of culture which left the mediaeval world at the mercy of the past, and which still stamps all our minds with the instinct that what is of value must be old. It is due in part to the hiatus in our own thought which makes us divide the process of learning from the process of teaching, as if a teacher could have anything more valuable to impart than his own passion to learn the truth. To get professors into your university who want to learn and who have nothing to teach is the way to bring the students as near as possible to the best influences they will meet when they leave your doors. Our western universities have taken a most notable step in filling their chairs of sociology with the younger kind of experimenters. It is true that the torch of the prophet is apt to go out if brought into carbonic acid gas, but on the other hand, the prophet is apt to throw open windows and impart oxygen by which he and all his colleagues may be kept alive. A university ought to be the mere residence of a lot of men who are excited about various aspects of life and history, and who lecture as a means of expressing themselves and of developing their own thought. Their chief corporate bond should be a distrust of each other's society, lest that society come between them and the world. Their great danger is the fixity of their salary and of their entourage, the danger lest this fixity extend itself imperceptibly over their minds. Where such men lived no poppy would bloom, no nerves would grow limp, and the pictures they showed to the young would have in them some tinge of effort and of pain which would imprint them indelibly, and make them hold their own beside the sombre originals which the youth are sure to see at no distant time.

DOROTHY CANFIELD FISHER

Sex Education

 1945

Migration from New England to the territory known in the early nineteenth century as the Western Reserve gave a Yankee flavor to towns and villages from Ohio to Kansas, but, like that of Howells, the life of Dorothy Canfield Fisher (1879–1958) followed the reverse direction. Born in Nebraska, she moved as a student and fledgling writer to New York City and then, with her husband, to the southern Vermont town of Arlington, where she committed herself to a writing career while raising two children. Proficient in five languages, Fisher did distinguished work as a translator, a historian of her adopted state, and a prolific writer of fiction. While working for relief agencies in France during World War I, she founded a children's hospital and a Braille press for soldiers who had been blinded in combat; in later years she made important contributions to American literature by championing such writers as Anzia Yezierska and, as one of the original members of the Board of Selection of the Book-of-the-Month Club, Richard Wright.

The beautifully wrought story reprinted below, "Sex Education," has at its center a thrice-told tale about the bewildering mix of desire and fear a young girl discovers within herself during a summer spent away from her closely guarded life in Vermont.

It was three times—but at intervals of many years—that I heard my Aunt Minnie tell about an experience of her girlhood that had made a never-to-be-forgotten impression on her. The first time she was in her thirties, still young. But she had then been married for ten years, so that to my group of friends, all in the early teens, she seemed quite of another generation.

The day she told us the story, we had been idling on one end of her porch as we made casual plans for a picnic supper in the woods. Darning stockings at the other end, she paid no attention to us until one of the girls said, "Let's take blankets and sleep out there. It'd be fun."

"No," Aunt Minnie broke in sharply, "you mustn't do that."

"Oh, for goodness' sakes, why not!" said one of the younger girls, rebelliously, "the boys are always doing it. Why can't we, just once?"

Aunt Minnie laid down her sewing. "Come here, girls," she said, "I want you should hear something that happened to me when I was your age."

Her voice had a special quality which, perhaps, young people of today would not recognize. But we did. We knew from experience that it was the dark voice grownups used when they were going to say something about sex.

Yet at first what she had to say was like any dull family anecdote; she had been ill when she was fifteen; and afterwards she was run down, thin, with no appetite. Her folks thought a change of air would do her good, and sent her from Vermont out to Ohio—or was it Illinois? I don't remember. Anyway, one of those places where the corn grows high. Her mother's Cousin Ella lived there, keeping house for her son-in-law.

The son-in-law was the minister of the village church. His wife had died some years before, leaving him a young widower with two little girls and a baby boy. He had been a normally personable man then, but the next summer, on the Fourth of July when he was trying to set off some fireworks to amuse his children, an imperfectly manufactured rocket had burst in his face. The explosion had left one side of his face badly scarred. Aunt Minnie made us see it, as she still saw it, in horrid detail: the stiffened, scarlet scar tissue distorting one cheek, the lower lip turned so far out at one corner that the moist red mucous-membrane lining always showed, one lower eyelid hanging loose, and watering.

After the accident, his face had been a long time healing. It was then that his wife's elderly mother had gone to keep house and take care of the children. When he was well enough to be about again, he found his position as pastor of the little church waiting for him. The farmers and village people in his congregation, moved by his misfortune, by his faithful service and by his unblemished character, said they would rather have Mr. Fairchild, even with his scarred face, than any other minister. He was a good preacher, Aunt Minnie told us, "and the way he prayed was kind of exciting. I'd never known a preacher, not to live in the same house with him, before. And when he was in the pulpit, with everybody looking up at him, I felt the way his children did, kind of proud to think we had just eaten breakfast at the same table. I liked to call him 'Cousin Malcolm' before folks. One side of his face was all right, anyhow. You could see from that that he *had* been a good-looking man. In fact, probably one of those ministers that all the women—" Aunt Minnie paused, drew her lips together, and looked at us uncertainly.

Then she went back to the story as it happened—as it happened that first time I heard her tell it. "I thought he was a saint. Everybody out there did. That was all *they* knew. Of course, it made a person sick to look at that awful scar—the drooling corner of his mouth was the worst. He tried to keep that side of his face turned away from folks. But you always knew it was there. That was what kept him from marrying again, so Cousin Ella said. I heard her say lots of times that he knew no woman would touch any man who looked the way he did, not with a ten-foot pole.

"Well, the change of air did do me good. I got my appetite back, and ate a lot and played outdoors a lot with my cousins. They were younger than I (I had my sixteenth birthday there) but I still liked to play games. I got taller and laid on some weight. Cousin Ella used to say I grew as fast as the corn did. Their house stood at the edge of the village. Beyond it was one of those big cornfields they have out west. At the time when I first got there, the stalks were only up to a person's knee. You could see over their tops. But it grew like lightning, and before long, it was the way thick woods are here, way over your head, the stalks growing so close together it was dark under them.

"Cousin Ella told us youngsters that it was lots worse for getting lost in than woods, because there weren't any landmarks in it. One spot in a corn-field looked just like any other. 'You children keep out of it,' she used to tell us almost every day, '*especially you girls.* It's no place for a decent girl. You could easy get so far from the house nobody could hear you if you hollered. There are plenty of men in this town that wouldn't like anything better than—' She never said what.

"In spite of what she said, my little cousins and I had figured out that if we went across one corner of the field, it would be a short cut to the village, and sometimes, without letting on to Cousin Ella, we'd go that way. After the corn got really tall, the farmer stopped cultivating, and we soon beat down a path in the loose dirt. The minute you were inside the field it was dark. You felt as if you were miles from anywhere. It sort of scared you. But in no time the path turned and brought you out on the far end of Main Street. Your breath was coming fast, maybe, but that was what made you like to do it.

"One day I missed the turn. Maybe I didn't keep my mind on it. Maybe it had rained and blurred the tramped-down look of the path. I don't know what. All of a sudden, I knew I was lost. And the minute I knew that, I began to run, just as hard as I could run. I couldn't help it, any more than you can help snatching your hand off a hot stove. I didn't know what I was scared of, I didn't even know I *was* running, till my heart was pounding so hard I had to stop.

"The minute I stood still, I could hear Cousin Ella saying 'There are plenty of men in this town that wouldn't like anything better than—' I didn't know, not really, what she meant. But I knew she meant something horrible. I opened my mouth to scream. But I put both hands over my mouth to keep the scream in. If I made any noise, one of those men would hear me. I thought I heard one just behind me, and whirled around. And then I thought another one had tiptoed up behind me, the other way, and I spun around so fast I almost fell over. I stuffed my hands hard up against my mouth. And then—I couldn't help it—I ran again—but my legs were shaking so I soon had to stop. There I stood, scared to move for fear of rustling the corn and letting the men know where I was. My hair had come down, all over my face. I kept pushing it back and looking around, quick, to make sure one of the men hadn't found out where I was. Then I thought I saw a man coming towards me, and I ran away from him—and fell down, and burst some of the buttons off my dress, and was sick to my stomach—and thought I heard a man close to me and got up and staggered around, knocking into the corn because I couldn't even see where I was going.

"And then, off to one side, I saw Cousin Malcolm. Not a man. The minister. He was standing still, one hand up to his face, thinking. He hadn't heard me.

"I was so *terrible* glad to see him, instead of one of those men, I ran as fast as I could and just flung myself on him, to make myself feel how safe I was."

Aunt Minnie had become strangely agitated. Her hands were shaking, her face was crimson. She frightened us. We could not look away from her. As we waited for her to go on, I felt little spasms twitch at the muscles inside my body. "And what do you think that *saint,* that holy minister of the Gospel, did to an innocent child who clung to him for safety? The most terrible look came into his eyes—you girls are too young to know what he looked like. But once you're married, you'll find out. He grabbed hold of me—that dreadful face of his was *right on mine*—and began clawing the clothes off my back."

She stopped for a moment, panting. We were too frightened to speak. She went on, "He had torn my dress right down to the waist before I—then I *did* scream—all I could—and pulled away from him so hard I almost fell down, and ran and all of a sudden I came out of the corn, right in the back yard of the Fairchild house. The children were staring at the corn, and Cousin Ella ran out of the kitchen door. They had heard me screaming. Cousin Ella shrieked out, 'What is it? What happened? Did a man scare you?' And I said, 'Yes, yes, yes, a man—I ran—!' And then I fainted away. I must have. The next thing I knew I was on the sofa in the living room and Cousin Ella was slapping my face with a wet towel."

She had to wet her lips with her tongue before she could go on. Her face was gray now. "There! that's the kind of thing girls' folks ought to tell them about—so they'll know what men are like."

She finished her story as if she were dismissing us. We wanted to go away, but we were too horrified to stir. Finally one of the youngest girls asked in a low trembling voice, "Aunt Minnie, did you tell on him?"

"No, I was ashamed to," she said briefly. "They sent me home the next day anyhow. Nobody ever said a word to me about it. And I never did either. Till now."

By what gets printed in some of the modern child-psychology books, you would think that girls to whom such a story had been told would never develop normally. Yet, as far as I can remember what happened to the girls in that group, we all grew up about like anybody. Most of us married, some happily, some not so well. We kept house. We learned—more or less—how to live with our husbands, we had children and struggled to bring them up right—we went forward into life, just as if we had never been warned not to.

Perhaps, young as we were that day, we had already had enough experience of life so that we were not quite blank paper for Aunt Minnie's frightening story. Whether we thought of it then or not, we couldn't have failed to see that at this very time, Aunt Minnie had been married for ten years or more, comfortably and well married, too. Against what she tried by that story to brand into our minds stood the cheerful home life in that house, the good-natured, kind, hard-working husband, and the children—the three rough-and-tumble, nice little boys, so adored by their parents, and the sweet girl baby who died, of whom they could never speak without tears. It was such actual contact with adult life that probably kept generation after generation of girls from being scared by tales like Aunt Minnie's into a neurotic horror of living.

Of course, since Aunt Minnie was so much older than we, her boys grew up to be adolescents and young men while our children were still little enough so that our worries over them were nothing more serious than whooping cough and trying to get them to make their own beds. Two of our aunt's three boys followed, without losing their footing, the narrow path which leads across adolescence into normal adult life. But the middle one, Jake, repeatedly fell off into the morass. "Girl trouble," as the succinct family phrase put it. He was one of those boys who have "charm," whatever we mean by that, and was always being snatched at by girls who would be "all wrong" for him to marry. And once, at nineteen, he ran away from home, whether with one of these girls or not we never heard, for through all her ups and downs with this son, Aunt Minnie tried fiercely to protect him from scandal that might cloud his later life.

Her husband had to stay on his job to earn the family living. She was the one who went to find Jake. When it was gossiped around that Jake was in "bad company" his mother drew some money from the family savings-bank account, and silent, white-cheeked, took the train to the city where rumor said he had gone.

Some weeks later he came back with her. With no girl. She had cleared him of that entanglement. As of others, which followed, later. Her troubles seemed over when, at a "suitable" age, he fell in love with a "suitable" girl, married her and took her to live in our shire town, sixteen miles away, where he had a good position. Jake was always bright enough.

Sometimes, idly, people speculated as to what Aunt Minnie had seen that time she went after her runaway son, wondering where her search for him had taken her—very queer places for Aunt Minnie to be in, we imagined. And how could such an ignorant, homekeeping woman ever have known what to say to an errant willful boy to set him straight?

Well, of course, we reflected, watching her later struggles with Jake's erratic ways, she certainly could not have remained ignorant, after seeing over and over what she probably had; after talking with Jake about the things which, a good many times, must have come up with desperate openness between them.

She kept her own counsel. We never knew anything definite about the facts of those experiences of hers. But one day she told a group of us—all then married women—something which gave us a notion about what she had learned from them.

We were hastily making a layette for a not especially welcome baby in a poor family. In those days, our town had no such thing as a district-nursing service. Aunt Minnie, a vigorous woman of fifty-five, had come in to help. As we sewed, we talked, of course; and because our daughters were near or in their teens, we were comparing notes about the bewildering responsibility of bringing up girls.

After a while, Aunt Minnie remarked, "Well, I hope you teach your girls some *sense*. From what I read, I know you're great on telling them 'the facts,' facts we never heard of when we were girls. Like as not, some facts I don't know, now. But knowing the facts isn't going to do them any more good than *not* knowing the facts ever did, unless they have some sense taught them, too."

"What do you mean, Aunt Minnie?" one of us asked her uncertainly.

She reflected, threading a needle, "Well, I don't know but what the best way to tell you what I mean is to tell you about something that happened to me, forty years ago. I've never said anything about it before. But I've thought about it a good deal. Maybe—"

She had hardly begun when I recognized the story—her visit to her Cousin Ella's Midwestern home, the widower with his scarred face and saintly reputation and, very vividly, her getting lost in the great cornfield. I knew every word she was going to say—to the very end, I thought.

But no, I did not. Not at all.

She broke off, suddenly, to exclaim with impatience, "Wasn't I the big ninny? But not so big a ninny as that old cousin of mine. I could wring her neck for getting me in such a state. Only she didn't know any better, herself. That was the way they brought young people up in those days, scaring them out of their wits about the awfulness of getting lost, but not telling them a thing about how *not* to get lost. Or how to act, if they did.

"If I had had the sense I was born with, I'd have known that running my legs off in a zigzag was the worst thing I could do. I couldn't have been more than a few feet from the path when I noticed I wasn't on it. My tracks in the loose plow dirt must have been perfectly plain. If I'd h' stood still, and collected my wits, I could have looked down to see which way my footsteps went and just walked back over them to the path and gone on about my business.

"Now I ask you, if I'd been told how to do that, wouldn't it have been a lot better protection for me—if protection was what my aunt thought she wanted to give me—than to scare me so at the idea of being lost that I turned deef-dumb-and-blind when I thought I was?

"And anyhow that patch of corn wasn't as big as she let on. And she knew it wasn't. It was no more than a big field in a farming country. I was a well-grown girl of sixteen, as tall as I am now. If I couldn't have found the path, I could have just walked along one line of cornstalks—*straight*—and I'd have come out somewhere in ten minutes. Fifteen at the most. Maybe not just where I wanted to go. But all right, safe, where decent folks were living."

She paused, as if she had finished. But at the inquiring blankness in our faces, she went on, "Well, now, why isn't teaching girls—and boys, too, for the Lord's sake don't forget they need it as much as the girls—about this man-and-woman business, something like that? If you give them the idea—no matter whether it's *as* you tell them the facts, or as you *don't* tell them the facts, that it is such a terribly scary thing that if they take a step into it, something's likely to happen to them so awful that you're ashamed to tell them what—well, they'll lose their heads and run around like crazy things, first time they take one step away from the path.

"For they'll be trying out the paths, all right. You can't keep them from it. And a good thing too. How else are they going to find out what it's like? Boys' and girls' going together is a path across one corner of growing up. And when they go together, they're likely to get off the path some. Seems to me, it's up to their folks to bring them up so when they do, they don't start screaming and running in circles, but stand still, right where they are, and get their breath and figure out how to get back.

"And anyhow, you don't tell 'em the truth about sex" (I was astonished to hear her use the actual word, taboo to women of her generation) "if they get the idea from you that it's all there is to living. It's not. If you don't get to where you want to go in it, well, there's a lot of landscape all around it a person can have a good time in.

"D'you know, I believe one thing that gives girls and boys the wrong idea is the way folks *look!* My old cousin's face, I can see her now, it was as red as a rooster's comb when she was telling me about men in that cornfield. I believe now she kind of *liked* to talk about it."

(Oh, Aunt Minnie—and yours! I thought.)

Someone asked, "But how *did* you get out, Aunt Minnie?"

She shook her head, laid down her sewing. "More foolishness. That minister my mother's cousin was keeping house for—her son-in-law—I caught sight of him, down along one of the aisles of cornstalks, looking down at the ground, thinking, the way he often did. And I was so glad to see him I rushed right up to him, and flung my arms around his neck and hugged him. He hadn't heard me coming. He gave a great start, put one arm around me and turned his face full towards me—I suppose for just a second he had forgotten how awful one side of it was. His expression, his eyes—well, you're all married women, you know how he looked, the way any able-bodied man thirty-six or -seven, who'd been married and begotten children, would look—for a minute anyhow, if a full-blooded girl of sixteen, who ought to have known better, flung herself at him without any warning, her hair tumbling down, her dress half unbuttoned, and hugged him with all her might.

"I was what they called innocent in those days. That is, I knew just as little about what men are like as my folks could manage I should. But I was old enough to know all right what that look meant. And it gave me a start. But of course the real thing of it was that dreadful scar of his, so close to my face— that wet corner of his mouth, his eye drawn down with the red inside of the lower eyelid showing—

"It turned me so sick, I pulled away with all my might, so fast that I ripped one sleeve nearly loose, and let out a screech like a wildcat. And ran. Did I run? And in a minute, I was through the corn and had come out in the back yard of the house. I hadn't been more than a few feet from it, probably, any of the time. And then I fainted away. Girls were always fainting away; it was the way our corset strings were pulled tight, I suppose, and then—oh, a lot of fuss.

"But anyhow," she finished, picking up her work and going on, setting neat, firm stitches with steady hands, "there's one thing, I never told anybody it was Cousin Malcolm I had met in the cornfield. I told my old cousin that 'a man had scared me.' And nobody said anything more about it to me, not ever. That was the way they did in those days. They thought if they didn't let on about something, maybe it wouldn't have happened. I was sent back to Vermont right away and Cousin Malcolm went on being minister of the church. I've always been," said Aunt Minnie moderately, "kind of proud that I didn't go and ruin a man's life for just one second's slip-up. If you could have called it that. For it *would* have ruined him. You know how hard as stone people are about other folks' letdowns. If I'd have told, not one person in that town would have had any charity. Not one would have tried to understand. One slip, *once,* and they'd have pushed him down in the mud. If I had told, I'd have felt pretty bad about it, later—when I came to have more sense. But I declare, I can't see how I came to have the decency, dumb as I was then, to know that it wouldn't be fair."

It was not long after this talk that Aunt Minnie's elderly husband died, mourned by her, by all of us. She lived alone then. It was peaceful October weather for her, in which she kept a firm roundness of face and figure, as quiet-living country-women often do, on into her late sixties.

But then Jake, the boy who had had girl trouble, had wife trouble. We heard he had taken to running after a young girl, or was it that she was running after him? It was something serious. For his nice wife left him and came back with the children to live with her mother in our town. Poor Aunt Minnie used to go to see her for long talks which made them both cry. And she went to keep house for Jake, for months at a time.

She grew old, during those years. When finally she (or something) managed to get the marriage mended so that Jake's wife relented and went back to live with him, there was no trace left of her pleasant brisk freshness. She was stooped and slow-footed and shrunken. We, her kins-people, although we would have given our lives for any one of our own children, wondered whether Jake was worth what it had cost his mother to—well, steady him, or reform him. Or perhaps just understand him. Whatever it took.

She came of a long-lived family and was able to go on keeping house for herself well into her eighties. Of course we and the other neighbors stepped in often to make sure she was all right. Mostly, during those brief calls, the talk turned on nothing more vital than her geraniums. But one midwinter afternoon, sitting with her in front of her cozy stove, I chanced to speak in rather hasty blame of someone who had, I thought, acted badly. To my surprise this brought from her the story about the cornfield which she had evidently quite forgotten telling me twice before.

This time she told it almost dreamily, swaying to and fro in her rocking chair, her eyes fixed on the long slope of snow outside her window. When she came to the encounter with the minister she said, looking away from the distance and back into my eyes, "I know now that I had been, all along, kind of *interested* in him, the way any girl as old as I was would be in any youngish man living in the same house with her. And a minister, too. They have to have the gift of gab so much more than most men, women get to thinking they are more alive than men who can't talk so well. I *thought* the reason I threw my arms around him was because I had been so scared. And I certainly had been scared, by my old cousin's horrible talk about the cornfield being full of men waiting to grab girls. But that wasn't all the reason I flung myself at Malcolm Fairchild and hugged him. I know that now. Why in the world shouldn't I have been taught *some* notion of it then? 'Twould do girls good to know that they are just like everybody else—human nature *and* sex, all mixed up together. I didn't have to hug him. I wouldn't have, if he'd been dirty or fat and old, or chewed tobacco."

I stirred in my chair, ready to say, "But it's not so simple as all that to tell girls—" and she hastily answered my unspoken protest. "I know, I know, most of it can't be put into words. There just aren't any words to say something that's so both-ways-at-once all the time as this man-and-woman business. But look here, you know as well as I do that there are lots more ways than in words to teach young folks what you want 'em to know."

The old woman stopped her swaying rocker to peer far back into the past with honest eyes. "What was in my mind back there in the cornfield—partly anyhow—was what had been there all the time I was living in the same house with Cousin Malcolm—that he had long straight legs, and broad shoulders, and lots of curly brown hair, and was nice and flat in front, and that one side of his face was goodlooking. But most of all, that he and I were really alone, for the first time, without anybody to see us.

"I suppose, if it hadn't been for that dreadful scar, he'd have drawn me up, tight, and—most any man would—kissed me. I know how I must have looked, all red and hot and my hair down and my dress torn open. And, used as he was to big cornfields, he probably never dreamed that the reason I looked that way was because I was scared to be by myself in one. He may have thought—you know what he may have thought.

"Well—if his face had been like anybody's—when he looked at me the way he did, the way a man does look at a woman he wants to have, it would have scared me—some. But I'd have cried, maybe. And probably he'd have kissed me again. You know how such things go. I might have come out of the cornfield halfway engaged to marry him. Why not? I was old enough, as people thought then. That would have been nature. That was probably what he thought of, in that first instant.

"But what did I do? I had one look at his poor, horrible face, and started back as though I'd stepped on a snake. And screamed and ran.

"What do you suppose *he* felt, left there in the corn? He must have been sure that I would tell everybody he had attacked me. He probably thought that when he came out and went back to the village he'd already be in disgrace and put out of the pulpit.

"But the worst must have been to find out, so rough, so plain from the way I acted—as if somebody had hit him with an ax—the way he would look to any woman he might try to get close to. That must have been—" she drew a long breath, "well, pretty hard on him."

After a silence, she murmured pityingly, "Poor man!"

Louis Auchincloss, John McPhee, and Geoffrey Wolff

Schoolmasters

🌿 1964, 1966, 1978

In our era of overtime fundraising and the corporatization of everything, the figure of the frank, magnetic, belligerently authoritative, much loved (and sometimes hated) prep school headmaster has receded into myth—along with his classroom deputy, the proverbially crusty teacher whose pedagogic passion expressed itself as contempt for philistinism and sloth. In the following passages from *The Rector of Justin* (1964), by Louis Auchincloss (b. 1917); *The Headmaster* (1966), by John McPhee (b. 1931), and *The Duke of Deception* (1978), by Geoffrey Wolff (b. 1937), these characters—who tend in the hands of lesser writers to become stock or caricatured—come vividly to life. They are, respectively, the fictional headmaster Rev. Francis Prescott of Justin Martyr School (modeled on Endicott Peabody of Groton), Frank Boyden of Deerfield Academy (who taught McPhee chemistry when he was a student there), and Mr. Pratt, an extravagant English teacher with whom Wolff had had a memorably funny encounter at Choate. Each sketch is an exercise in memorial portraiture that catches a lost, or fast-fading, force in New England culture whose effect on generations of those we would now call the "elite" was large and enlarging.

Louis Auchincloss

From *The Rector of Justin*

🌿 To an egotist of fourteen the mighty events across the Atlantic hardly existed. The holocaust that was ending in Europe was dwarfed by the difficulties of adjusting to the school hierarchy. I was the only "new kid" in my form and ranked socially with those in the two below. What was the agony of the trenches, sublimated as it must have been, according to my wishfully thinking mother, by the wonderful comradeship engendered by shared dangers, to one of my Byronic pride who had to endure alone the indignities of hazing? The ultimate humiliation was my family's assumption that I was homesick. There was surely a difference between homesickness, to which morbid malady I was always a stranger, and a natural, healthy detestation of Justin Martyr!

My first important discovery was that Dr. Prescott was a master and my father a mere amateur in the great nineteenth century art of making life uncomfortable. "Fun" was defined in terms of group activity, such as football or singing or even praying; the devil lay in wait for the boy alone, or worse, for two boys alone. The headmaster believed that adolescence should be passed in an organized crowd, that authority should never avert its eyes unless the boys were engaged in fighting or hazing or some other activity savage enough to be classified as "manly." Life beyond the campus was universally suspect: the drugstores, with their sodas and lurid magazines, the slatternly country girls, the very woods and streams that encouraged boys to take long walks and wax sentimental about nature and perhaps each other.

Where Prescott excelled above all was in his intuition as to where temptation lay. As a young man and an Oxford dandy, he had strolled by the Thames reading Baudelaire and Rossetti. He was widely, and I think justly, reputed to have a perfect ear for music and a fine tongue for wine, and he could actually speak Greek and Latin. Had it not been for the perverted violence of his puritan conscience, he might have been a great artist or at least a great voluptuary. But he had crushed the joy in his own nature, and so far as he could, in those of others, pleading with his angry God to help him, his hands tightly clasped, his eyes squeezed tightly shut, waiting as much as thirty seconds between the prayer that he recited at the end of chapel, and his own thundering "Amen," knowing, the old ham, that the congregation was reverently watching his silent communion. He would have been a glorious repertory actor of the Henry Irving school, playing Iago one night and Tamburlaine the next.

Yet he got away with it. My own father is proof of that. If you want to be taken seriously in this life, you must start by taking yourself seriously. Prescott was surrounded with an atmosphere of almost incredible awe, to which the parents, trustees and faculty all contributed. I do not think that many of the boys liked him, but they respected and feared him, which was much more fun, both for them and for him.

JOHN MCPHEE

From *The Headmaster*

People seeing the headmaster for the first time often find him different from what they expected. Those who stay in the Deerfield community for any length of time quickly become aware that they are living in a monarchy and that the small man in the golf cart is the king, but visitors who have heard of him and know what a great man he is seem to insist that he ought to be a tall, white-haired patriarch. People see him picking up papers and assume it is his job. Coming upon a group of women outside one of his old houses a few years ago, he took them in and led them through its ancient rooms. On the way out, one lady gave him a quarter. People walk right by him sometimes without seeing him. Someone once stopped, turned around, and said, "I'm sorry, Mr. Boyden. I didn't notice you."

"That's all right," he said. "No one ever does."

He loves such stories, perhaps in part because they help to fake out the faculty and the boys. How else, after all, could an inconspicuous man like that hold an entire community in the palm of his hand? When the stories come back to him, he lights up with pleasure. He has one way of judging everything: If it's good for the academy, it's good. He was once walking with an impressive-looking Deerfield faculty member when someone, a stranger, said, "Who was that?"

"That was the headmaster."

"Yes, but who was that little man with him?"

Boyden looked old when he was four, older when he was in college, and older still in the nineteen-twenties, but now he doesn't look particularly old at all. His hair is not white but slate-gray, and his demeanor, which hasn't changed in forty years, still suggests a small, grumpy Labrador. He sometimes dresses in gray trousers, a dark-blue jacket, and brown cordovan shoes—choices that are somewhat collegiate and could be taken as a mild sign of age, because for decades he wore dark-blue worsted suits and maroon ties almost exclusively, winter and summer, hanging on to each excessive suit until it fell off him in threads. One of his jacket pockets today has a four-inch rip that has been bound with black thread. He doesn't care. He is an absolutely unselfconscious man. Let one scuff mark appear on a stair riser in his academy and he will quickly find a janitor and report it, but this kind of concern is entirely projected onto the school. He once got up on a cool July morning and put on an old leather coat covered with cracks and lined with sheepskin that was coming loose; he went off to New York in it and obviously wore it all day in the sweltering city. After eighty-six years, his only impairment is bad hearing. "My ears are gone," he will say, and then he will walk into a roomful of people and pretend that there isn't a syllable he can't catch. He indulges himself in nothing. He will eat anything, and he usually doesn't notice the components of his meals, unless they happen to be root beer and animal crackers, which he occasionally eats for breakfast. He has been given honorary degrees by Harvard, Yale, Princeton, and seventeen other colleges and universities, but he apparently has not even a trace of desire to be called Dr. Boyden, and no one calls him that except eraser salesmen and strangers whose sons are applying to the school . . .

A new boy at Deerfield cannot have been there very long before the idea is impressed upon him that he is a part of something that won't work unless he does his share. The headmaster is able to create this kind of feeling in his boys to a greater degree than most parents are. All boys are given an equal footing from which to develop their own positions. There are no special responsibilities for scholarship boys, such as waiting on tables. Everyone does that. In fact, the headmaster insists that scholarship boys not be told that they have scholarships, since that might injure the sense of equality he tries to build. His school, which grew so phenomenally out of almost nothing, has frequently been visited by curious educational theorists. One researcher spent a few days at the academy and finally said, "Well, there isn't any system here, but it works." Such people perplex Frank Boyden almost as much as he perplexes them. "People come here thinking we have some marvelous method," he says. "We just treat the boys as if we expect something of them, and we keep them busy. So many of our things simply exist. They're not theory. They're just living life. I expect most of our boys want to do things the way we want them done. We drive with a light rein, but we can pull it up just like that, if we need to. We just handle the cases as they come up." . . .

All discipline ultimately becomes a private matter between each boy and the headmaster. Most of the boys feel guilty if they do something that offends his sensibilities. Unlike his great predecessor Arnold of Rugby, he does not believe that schoolboys are his natural enemies; on the contrary, he seems to convince them that although he is infallible, he badly needs their assistance. A local farmer who was in the class of 1919 says, "When you thought of doing something wrong, you would know that you would hurt him deeply, so you wouldn't do it. He had twenty-four-hour control." A 1928 alumnus says, "It didn't matter what you did as long as you told him the truth." And 1940: "Whatever it was, you didn't do it, because you might drop a little in his eyes." He will give a problem boy a second, third, fourth, fifth, and sixth chance, if necessary. The rest of the student body sometimes becomes cynical about the case, but the headmaster refuses to give up. "I would have kicked me out," says one alumnus who had a rather defiant senior year in the early nineteen-fifties. The headmaster had reason enough to expel him, and almost any other school would have dropped him without a thought, but Boyden graduated him, sent him to Princeton, and, today, does not even recall that the fellow was ever a cause of trouble. Boyden is incapable of bearing grudges. He wants to talk things out and forget them. He is sensitive to the potential effect of his forbearance, so he has sometimes taken the risk of calling the student body together and asking for its indulgence. A boy once drank the better part of a fifth of whiskey in a bus returning from another school, reeled in the aisle, fell on his face, and got sick. The headmaster called the school together and said that for the sake of discipline in the academy at large he would have to let the boy go unless they would guarantee him that no episode of the kind would happen again. The headmaster was beyond being thought of as weak, so he got away with it. People often wonder what on earth could make him actually drop a boy, and the five cases in which he has done so are therefore of particular interest. All have a common factor: the offender was unremorseful. One of them was guilty of nineteen different offenses, including arson. Nevertheless, if he had told the headmaster that he was wrong, he could have stayed in school.

A boy of considerable talent once told the headmaster that he could write his English papers only between midnight and dawn. His muse, the boy claimed, refused to appear at any other time of day. The difficulty was that after the boy's inspiration ran out he invariably fell asleep and missed his morning classes. Like all geniuses, this boy was likely to attract imitators. The headmaster addressed the student body. "Are you willing to let Mac Farrell stay up all night writing his English papers?" he said. "Mac Farrell alone?" The boys agreed.

The headmaster has often put himself in an uncomfortable corner for a boy who is different. He once had two students—artistic cousins of Mac Farrell—who liked to paint and particularly liked to go out at night and do nocturnes. They did the cemetery by moonlight and the old houses in the edge of the glow of street lamps. The headmaster knew that this was going on, but he overlooked it. His own favorites have always been responsible, uncomplicated, outstanding athletes, and he cares even less about art than he knows about it, but, in his way, he was just the right headmaster for these two boys. "With a person as unDeerfield as myself," remembers one of them, who is now Curator of Graphic Arts at Princeton University, "he was sympathetic and understanding. He was patient and—what can I say?—incredibly wise in the way that he handled me."

Certain boys at Deerfield in earlier years would commit long series of petty crimes and believe that all had gone undetected. Then, finally, the headmaster would stop such a boy, pull out a small notebook, and read off to him everything he had done wrong since the first day of school. For years, the headmaster roved the campus late at night, like a watchman. Until the late nineteen-thirties, he made rounds to every room in every dormitory during study hours every night. Since then, he has made spot visits. He never gives a boy bad news at night. He never threatens. He uses shame privately. He more often trades favors than gives them. If a boy asks something of him, he asks something in return. There is no student government, nor are there faculty committees, helping to run Deerfield. The headmaster holds himself distant from that sort of thing. Senior class presidents are elected on the eve of Commencement. Students who are in the school now say they would not want student government anyway, because they feel that it is a mockery elsewhere.

GEOFFREY WOLFF

From *The Duke of Deception: Memories of My Father*

🐿 Once before I had felt this, coming through. Every Choate boy was required to endure Public Speaking, the province of Mr. Pratt, a theatrical character who wore a cape, carried a cane and said the most abusive things I have ever heard a human being say to another human being. The boys hated and feared him, till they left Choate, when they agreed to revere him. We would sit thirty at a time once a week in the basement of the chapel; Mr. Pratt would call on five of us in turn, according to a system of his own devising, so that five times a year, perhaps five weeks in a row, each of us would speak for five minutes on a subject of his choice. If he didn't like what he heard Mr. Pratt would beat his cane and scream; he seldom liked what he heard. My first year I sat trembling week after week for seven weeks before he called on me. I wanted to tell him I stammered, but I didn't want to tell him I stammered. What I wanted most was not to stammer.

Mr. Pratt called on a slow-witted bully, a Lake Forest boy who elected to disarm the ogre with low wit. He began his speech smirking: "Doctor Frood, the infamous" (he said it *in-fay-muss*) "Hun, tells us there is a war between the supernegro and the yid. I'd like to explore . . ."

Two words into this monologue I heard Pratt mumble; then a sound like a death rattle came from behind us, and rose. We scrunched down as the words rumbled past us, hitting the silly, blushing boy at the lectern:

"You vile thing! You cur of a child. Where do you think you are?"

As the boy considered a response to this bewildering question, and perhaps developed an alternate presentation—on The Greatness of Napoleon, or Why I'm Proud to Be a Midwesterner—Pratt bowled down the aisle with his cane raised and his cape spread out behind him, showing its blood-red silk lining. He climbed the dais stage left as the boy exited weeping stage right, as though pursued by a bear. Mr. Pratt spoke:

"WOLFF! NEXT! TALK TO ME!"

I stammered an exposition of powerboat racing. I had committed to memory three double-spaced pages, and twenty minutes after I began, shaking my head wildly from side to side to force the words out, *forcing* them out, every word, no substitutes, no cheating on the sadistic plosives, no tricks to push off to a new sentence *(let's see, the fastest hydroplane in the world is, let's see, let's see, Slo-Mo-Shun, let's see),* just getting it done . . . after twenty minutes I knew something I had not known before. Doing it is never as bad as not doing it. Before I reached the end of my speech Mr. Pratt held up his hand:

"We have to eat, Wolff. That's enough. Well done."

Dissident Dreamers

IT IS SOMETIMES THOUGHT that the doctrines of God's sovereignty and man's dependence led early New Englanders to regard the world as a vale of suffering to be passively endured; and there is, indeed, much felt awareness in their writing of the fleetingness and unmasterable pain of life. But Puritanism was a religion of action, a call to reform, resistance, and sacrifice; and implicit in it was the idea that apprehending the imperfections of the human world was the first step toward changing it. The life of sanctification began, in other words, with a change in perception—an event, or process, that Puritans called conversion.

The writers in this section inherited this restless discontent with the world as they found it. They refused the idea, as William James put it, that "reality . . . stands ready-made and complete, and our intellects supervene with the one simple duty of describing it as it is already." Instead, with James, they regarded the universe as "unfinished, growing in all sorts of places, especially in the places where thinking beings are at work." They believed that what can be imagined can be made actual—and that human beings are most alive when they are full of determined yearning.

Carlton Fisk in the 1975 World Series

JOHN WINTHROP

Letter to His Wife

 1630

With a favorable wind finally blowing and the crew of the *Arbella* preparing to set sail in the morning, John Winthrop (1588–1649) wrote this tender letter to his wife, confirming their plan to "meet in spirit" on Mondays and Fridays at 5:00 until God saw fit to let them rejoin in person in the New World.

John Winthrop to His Wife
To M. W. the Elder at Groton

My faithful and dear wife,

It pleaseth God that thou shouldest once again hear from me before our departure, and I hope this shall come safe to thy hands. I know it will be a great refreshing to thee. And blessed be his mercy, that I can write thee so good news, that we are all in very good health, and having tried our ship's entertainment now more than a week, we find it agrees very well with us. Our boys are well and cheerful, and have no mind of home. They lie both with me and sleep as soundly in a rug (for we use no sheets here) as ever they did at Groton, and so I do myself (I praise God). The wind hath been against us this week and more, but this day it is come fair to the North. So as we are preparing (by God's assistance) to set sail in the morning, we have only 4 ships ready, and 2 or 3 hollands go along with us, the rest of our fleet (being 7 ships) will not be ready this senight. We have spent now 2 Sabbaths on shipboard, very comfortably (God be praised) and are daily more and more encouraged to look for the Lord's presence to go along with us. Hen Kingesburye hath a child or 2 in the Talbott sick of the measles, but like to do well; one of my men had them at Hampton, but he was soon well again. We are in all our 11 ships, about 700 persons passengers, and 240 cows, and about 60 horses. The ship which went from Plimouth carried about 140 persons, and the ship which goes from Bristowe, carrieth about 80 persons.

And now (my sweet soul), I must once again take my last farewell of thee in old England. It goeth very near to my heart to leave thee, but I know to whom I have committed thee, even to him, who loves thee much better than any husband can, who hath taken account of the hairs of thy head, and puts all thy tears in his bottle, who can, and (if it be for his glory) will bring us together again with peace and comfort. Oh, how it refresheth my heart to think that I shall yet again see thy sweet face in the land of the living, that lovely countenance that I have so much delighted in, and beheld with so great content!

I have hitherto been so taken up with business, as I could seldom look back to my former happiness, but now when I shall be at some leisure, I shall not avoid the remembrance of thee, nor the grief for thy absence. Thou hast thy share with me, but I hope the course we have agreed upon will be some ease to us both. Mondays and Fridays at 5 o'clock at night, we shall meet in spirit till we meet in person. Yet if all these hopes should fail, blessed be our God, that we are assured we shall meet one day, if not as husband and wife, yet in a better condition. Let that stay and comfort thy heart. Neither can the sea drown thy husband, nor enemies destroy, nor any adversity deprive thee of thy husband or children.

Therefore I will only take thee now and my sweet children in mine arms, and kiss and embrace you all, and so leave you with my God. Farewell, farewell. I bless you all in the name of the Lord Jesus. I salute my daughter Winth., Matt, Nan and the rest, and all my good neighbors and friends, pray all for us. Farewell.

Commend my blessing to my son John. I cannot now write to him, but tell him I have committed thee and thine to him. Labor to draw him yet nearer to God, and he will be the surer staff of comfort to thee. I cannot name the rest of my good friends, but thou canst supply it. I wrote a week since to thee and Mr. Leigh and diverse others.

> Thine wheresoever
> Jo. Winthrop
> From Aboard the Arbella riding at the
> Cowes, March 28, 1630.

I would have written to my brother and sister Gostlinge, but is near midnight. Let this excuse, and commend my love to them and all theirs.

James Otis

From The Rights of the British Colonies
Asserted and Proved

 1764

An attorney known for his fire and fury, James Otis (1725–1783) first became a publicly recognized enemy of the Massachusetts colonial government in 1760, when he argued before the Superior Judicial Court against the "writs of assistance" that authorized customs officials to search at their discretion for smuggled goods. Otis was accused by some (in his own time and since) of harboring animus against the royal government based on personal resentment rather than principle. Whatever his private motives, he emerged as one of the most eloquent opponents in eighteenth-century New England of unchecked government power. The 1764 pamphlet excerpted below was written after the passage of the Sugar Act, a tax imposed by the British Parliament that provoked bitter opposition from New England merchants as well as growing popular discontent. But Otis reaches beyond the specific issues of the day. In language that mixes religious piety (as a young man, he had participated eagerly in a religious revival) with indignation on behalf of people denied their political rights, he anticipates the Revolution and introduces the problem that would haunt the future American republic: in a nation dedicated to liberty, some people remained enslaved.

Property cannot be the foundation of dominion as synonymous with government; for on the supposition that property has a precarious existence antecedent to government, and though it is also admitted that the security of property is one end of government but that of little estimation even in the view of a *miser* when life and liberty of locomotion and further accumulation are placed in competition, it must be a very absurd way of speaking to assert that *one* end of government is the foundation of government. If the ends of government are to be considered as its foundation, it cannot with truth or propriety be said that government is founded on any *one* of those ends; and therefore government is not founded on property or its security *alone,* but at least on something else in conjunction. It is however true in fact and *experience,* as the great, the incomparable *Harrington* has most abundantly demonstrated in his *Oceana* and other divine writings, that empire follows the balance of *property*. 'Tis also certain that *property* in fact generally *confers* power, though the possessor of it may not have much more wit than a mole or a musquash: and this is too often the cause that riches are sought after without the least concern about the right application of them. But is the fault in the riches, or the general law of nature, or the unworthy possessor? It will never follow from all this that government is *rightfully* founded on *property* alone. What shall we say then? Is not government founded on *grace?* No. Nor on *force?* No. Nor on *compact?* Nor *property?* Not altogether on either. Has it *any* solid foundation, any chief cornerstone but what accident, chance, or confusion may lay one moment and destroy the next? I think it has an everlasting foundation in the *unchangeable will of* God, the author of nature, whose laws never vary. The same omniscient, omnipotent, infinitely good and gracious Creator of the universe who has been pleased to make it necessary that what we call matter should *gravitate* for the celestial bodies to roll round their axes, dance their orbits, and perform their various revolutions in that beautiful order and concert which we all admire has made it *equally* necessary that from *Adam* and *Eve* to these degenerate days the different sexes should sweetly *attract* each other, form societies of *single* families, of which *larger* bodies and communities are as naturally, mechanically, and necessarily combined as the dew of heaven and the soft distilling rain is collected by the all-enlivening heat of the sun. *Government* is therefore most evidently founded *on the necessities of our nature.* It is by no means an *arbitrary* thing depending merely on *compact* or *human will* for its existence.

We come into the world forlorn and helpless; and if left alone and to ourselves at any one period of our lives, we should soon die in want, despair, or distraction. So kind is that hand, though little known or regarded, which feeds the rich and the poor, the blind and the naked, and provides for the safety of infants by the principle of parental love, and for that of men by government! We have a King who neither slumbers nor sleeps, but eternally watches for our good, whose rain falls on the just and on the unjust: yet while they live, move, and have their being in Him, and cannot account for either or for anything else, so stupid and wicked are some men as to deny his existence, blaspheme his most evident government, and disgrace their nature.

Let no man think I am about to commence advocate for *despotism* because I affirm that government is founded on the necessity of our natures and that an original supreme, sovereign, absolute, and uncontrollable *earthly* power *must* exist in and preside over every society, from whose final decisions there can be no appeal but directly to Heaven. It is therefore *originally* and *ultimately* in the people. I say this supreme absolute power is *originally* and *ultimately* in the people; and they never did in fact *freely,* nor can they *rightfully* make an absolute, unlimited renunciation of this divine right.* It is ever in the nature of the thing given in *trust* and on a condition the performance of which no mortal can dispense with, namely, that the person or persons on whom the sovereignty is conferred by the people shall *incessantly* consult *their* good. Tyranny of all kinds is to be abhorred, whether it be in the hands of one or of the few or of the many. And though "in the last age a generation of men sprung up that would flatter princes with an opinion that *they* have a *divine right* to absolute power," yet "slavery is so vile and miserable an estate of man and so directly opposite to the generous temper and courage of our nation that 'tis hard to be conceived that an *Englishman,* much less a *gentleman,* should plead for it,"† especially at a time when the finest writers of the most polite nations on the continent of *Europe* are enraptured with the beauties of the civil constitution of *Great Britain,* and envy her no less for the *freedom* of her sons than for her immense *wealth* and *military* glory.

But let the *origin* of government be placed where it may, the *end* of it is manifestly the good of *the whole. Salus populi suprema lex esto* is of the law of nature and part of that grand charter given the human race (though too many of them are afraid to assert it) by the only monarch in the universe who has a clear and indisputable right to *absolute* power, because he is the *only* One who is *omniscient* as well as *omnipotent.*

It is evidently contrary to the first principles of reason that supreme *unlimited* power should be in the hands of *one* man. It is the greatest "*idolatry* begotten by *flattery* on the body of *pride*" that could induce one to think that a *single mortal* should be able to hold so great a power if ever so well inclined. Hence the origin of *deifying* princes: it was from the trick of gulling the vulgar into a belief that their tyrants were *omniscient,* and that it was therefore right that they should be considered as *omnipotent.* Hence the *dii majorum et minorum gentium,* the great, the monarchical, the little, provincial, subordinate, and subaltern gods, demigods, and semidemigods, ancient and modern. Thus deities of all kinds were multiplied and increased in *abundance,* for every devil incarnate who could enslave a people acquired a title to *divinity;* and thus the "rabble of the skies" was made up of locusts and caterpillars, lions, tigers, and harpies, and other devourers translated from plaguing the earth!‡

---

* The power of GOD Almighty is the power that can properly and strictly be called supreme and absolute. In the order of nature immediately under him comes the power of a simple *democracy* or the power of the whole over the whole. Subordinate to both these are all other political powers, from that of the French monarch to a petty constable.
† Mr. Locke
‡ Kingcraft and priestcraft have fallen out so often that 'tis a wonder this grand and ancient alliance is not broken off forever. Happy for mankind will it be when such a separation shall take place.

The *end* of government being the *good* of mankind points out its great duties: it is above all things to provide for the security, the quiet, and happy enjoyment of life, liberty, and property. There is no one act which a government can have a *right* to make that does not tend to the advancement of the security, tranquillity, and prosperity of the people. If life, liberty, and property could be enjoyed in as great perfection in *solitude* as in *society* there would be no need of government. But the experience of ages has proved that such is the nature of man, a weak, imperfect being, that the valuable ends of life cannot be obtained without the union and assistance of many. Hence 'tis clear that men cannot live apart or independent of each other. In solitude men would perish, and yet they cannot live together without contests. These contests require some arbitrator to determine them. The necessity of a common, indifferent, and impartial judge makes all men seek one, though few find him in the *sovereign power* of their respective states or anywhere else in *subordination* to it.

Government is founded *immediately* on the necessities of human nature and *ultimately* on the will of God, the author of nature, who has not left it to men in general to choose whether they will be members of society or not, but at the hazard of their senses if not of their lives. Yet it is left to every man as he comes of age to choose *what society* he will continue to belong to. Nay, if one has a mind to turn *hermit,* and after he has been born, nursed, and brought up in the arms of society, and acquired the habits and passions of social life is willing to run the risk of starving alone, which is generally most unavoidable in a state of hermitage, who shall hinder him? I know of no human law founded on the law of *nature* to restrain him from separating himself from all the species if he can find it in his heart to leave them, unless it should be said it is against the great law of *self-preservation:* but of this every man will think himself *his own judge.*

The few *hermits* and *misanthropes* that have ever existed show that those states are *unnatural.* If we were to take out from them those who have made great *worldly* gain of their *godly* hermitage and those who have been under the madness of *enthusiasm* or *disappointed* hopes in their *ambitious* projects for the detriment of mankind, perhaps there might not be left ten from *Adam* to this day.

The form of government is by *nature* and by *right* so far left to the *individuals* of each society that they may alter it from a simple democracy or government of all over all to any other form they please. Such alteration may and ought to be made by express compact. But how seldom this right has been asserted, history will abundantly show. For once that it has been fairly settled by compact, *fraud, force,* or *accident* have determined it an hundred times. As the people have gained upon tyrants, these have been obliged to relax *only* till a fairer opportunity has put it in their power to encroach again.

But if every prince since *Nimrod* had been a tyrant, it would not prove a *right* to tyrannize. There can be no prescription old enough to supersede the law of nature and the grant of GOD Almighty, who has given to all men a natural right to be *free*, and they have it ordinarily in their power to make themselves so if they please.

Government having been proved to be necessary by the law of nature, it makes no difference in the thing to call it from a certain period *civil*. This term can only relate to form, to additions to or deviations from the substance of government: this being founded in nature, the superstructures and the whole administration should be conformed to the law of universal reason. A supreme legislative and a supreme executive power must be placed *somewhere* in every commonwealth. Where there is no other positive provision or compact to the contrary, those powers remain in the *whole body of the people*. It is also evident there can be but *one* best way of depositing those powers; but what that way is, mankind have been disputing in peace and in war more than five thousand years. If we could suppose the individuals of a community met to deliberate whether it were best to keep those powers in *their own* hands or dispose of them in *trust*, the following questions would occur:—Whether those two great powers of *legislation* and *execution* should remain united? If so, whether in the hands of the many or jointly or severally in the hands of a few, or jointly in some one individual? If both those powers are retained in the hands of the many, where nature seems to have placed them originally, the government is a simple *democracy* or a government of all over all. This can be administered only by establishing it as a first principle that the votes of the majority shall be taken as the voice of the whole. If those powers are lodged in the hands of a few, the government is an *aristocracy* or *oligarchy.** Here too the first principles of a practicable administration is that the majority rules the whole. If those great powers are both lodged in the hands of one man, the government is a *simple monarchy*, commonly though falsely called *absolute* if by that term is meant a right to do as one pleases.—*Sic volo, sic jubeo, stet pro ratione voluntas* belongs not of right to any mortal man.

The same law of nature and of reason is equally obligatory on a *democracy*, an *aristocracy*, and a *monarchy*: whenever the administrators in any of those forms deviate from truth, justice, and equity, they verge towards tyranny, and are to be opposed; and if they prove incorrigible they will be *deposed* by the people, if the people are not rendered too abject. Deposing the administrators of a *simple democracy* may sound oddly, but it is done every day and in almost every vote. A, B, and C, for example, make a *democracy*. Today A and B are for

* For the sake of the unlettered reader 'tis noted that monarchy means the power of one great man, aristocracy and oligarchy that of a few, and democracy that of all men.

so vile a measure as a standing army. Tomorrow B and C vote it out. This is as really deposing the former administrators as setting up and making a new King is deposing the old one. *Democracy* in the one case and *monarchy* in the other still remain; all that is done is to change the administration . . .

'Tis well known that the first American grants were by the bulls of the popes. The Roman pontiffs had for ages usurped the most abominable power over princes: they granted away the kingdoms of the earth with as little ceremony as a man would lease a sheepcote. Now according to Dr. Strahan's logic it may be inferred that the canon law and the pope's bulls must be of *service likewise for determining any controversy that may arise touching the duties or forfeitures of the proprietors of lands in the British colonies.* And indeed it must be owned, if we were to judge of some late proceedings* by this rule, we must allow that they savor more of modern Rome and the Inquisition than of the common law of England and the constitution of Great Britain.

In order to form an idea of the natural rights of the colonists, I presume it will be granted that they are men, the common children of the same Creator with their brethren of Great Britain. Nature has placed all such in a state of equality and perfect freedom to act within the bounds of the laws of nature and reason without consulting the will or regarding the humor, the passions, or whims of any other man, unless they are formed into a society or body politic. This it must be confessed is rather an abstract way of considering men than agreeable to the real and general course of nature. The truth is, as has been shown, men come into the world and into society at the same instant. But this hinders not but that the natural and original rights of each individual may be illustrated and explained in this way better than in any other. We see here, by the way, a probability that this abstract consideration of men, which has its use in reasoning on the principles of government, has insensibly led some of the greatest men to imagine some real general state of nature agreeable to this abstract conception, antecedent to and independent of society. This is certainly not the case in general, for most men become members of society from their birth, though separate independent states are really in the condition of perfect freedom and equality with regard to each other, and so are any number of individuals who separate themselves from a society of which they have formerly been members, for ill treatment or other good cause, with express design to found another. If in such case there is a real interval between the separation and the new conjunction, during such interval the individuals are as much detached and under the law of nature only as would be two men who should chance to meet on a desolate island.

---

* Of some American courts of admiralty, if the reader pleases.

The colonists are by the law of nature freeborn, as indeed all men are, white or black. No better reasons can be given for enslaving those of any color than such as Baron Montesquieu has humorously given as the foundation of that cruel slavery exercised over the poor Ethiopians, which threatens one day to reduce both Europe and America to the ignorance and barbarity of the darkest ages. Does it follow that 'tis right to enslave a man because he is black? Will short curled hair like wool instead of Christian hair, as 'tis called by those whose hearts are as hard as the nether millstone, help the argument? Can any logical inference in favor of slavery be drawn from a flat nose, a long or a short face? Nothing better can be said in favor of a trade that is the most shocking violation of the law of nature, has a direct tendency to diminish the idea of the inestimable value of liberty, and makes every dealer in it a tyrant, from the director of an African company to the petty chapman in needles and pins on the unhappy coast. It is a clear truth that those who every day barter away other men's liberty will soon care little for their own. To this cause must be imputed that ferocity, cruelty, and brutal barbarity that has long marked the general character of the sugar islanders. They can in general form no idea of government but that which in person or by an overseer, the joint and several proper representative of a creole* and of the d——l, is exercised over ten thousand of their fellow men, born with the same right to freedom and the sweet enjoyments of liberty and life as their unrelenting taskmasters, the overseers and planters.

Is it to be wondered at if when people of the stamp of a creolean planter get into power they will not stick for a little present gain at making their own posterity, white as well as black, worse slaves if possible than those already mentioned?

There is nothing more evident, says Mr. Locke, than "that creatures of the same species and rank, promiscuously born to all the same advantages of nature and the use of the same faculties, should also be equal one among another without subordination and subjection, unless the master of them all should by any manifest declaration of his will set one above another and confer on him by an evident and clear appointment an undoubted right to dominion and sovereignty." "The natural liberty of man is to be free from any superior power on earth, and not to be under the will or legislative authority of man, but only to have the law of nature for his rule." This is the liberty of independent states; this is the liberty of every man out of society and who has

---

* Those in England who borrow the terms of the Spaniards, as well as their notions of government, apply this term to all Americans of European extract; but the northern colonists apply it only to the islanders and others of such extract, under the Torrid Zone.

a mind to live so; which liberty is only abridged in certain instances, not lost to those who are born in or voluntarily enter into society; this gift of God cannot be annihilated.

The colonists, being men, have a right to be considered as equally entitled to all the rights of nature with the Europeans, and they are not to be restrained in the exercise of any of these rights but for the evident good of the whole community.

By being or becoming members of society they have not renounced their natural liberty in any greater degree than other good citizens, and if 'tis taken from them without their consent they are so far enslaved.

Abigail Adams and John Adams
Letters
 1776

In this famous exchange of letters, Abigail Adams (1744–1818) urges her husband John (1735–1826)—who, as a member of the Continental Congress meeting in Philadelphia, was working to establish a new republic with specified rights for its citizens—to "remember the ladies." In John Adams's jocular reply there is evidence of the warmth and mutual intellectual respect that characterized their marriage. He could not have known that, for later generations, his wife's phrase would come to signify the serious unfinished business of securing equal rights for women in the democracy of America.

Abigail Adams to John Adams

BRAINTREE MARCH 31 1776

I wish you would ever write me a Letter half as long as I write you; and tell me if you may where your Fleet are gone? What sort of Defence Virginia can make against our common Enemy? Whether it is so situated as to make an able Defence? Are not the Gentery Lords and the common people vassals, are they not like the uncivilized Natives Brittain represents us to be? I hope their Riffel Men who have shewen themselves very savage and even Blood thirsty; are not a specimen of the Generality of the people.

I am willing to allow the Colony great merrit for having produced a Washington but they have been shamefully duped by a Dunmore.

I have sometimes been ready to think that the passion for Liberty cannot be Eaqually Strong in the Breasts of those who have been accustomed to deprive their fellow Creatures of theirs. Of this I am certain that it is not founded upon that generous and christian principal of doing to others as we would that others should do unto us.

Do not you want to see Boston; I am fearfull of the small pox, or I should have been in before this time. I got Mr. Crane to go to our House and see what state it was in. I find it has been occupied by one of the Doctors of a Regiment, very dirty, but no other damage has been done to it. The few things which were left in it are all gone. Cranch has the key which he never deliverd up. I have wrote to him for it and am determined to get it cleand as soon as possible and shut it up. I look upon it a new acquisition of property, a property which one month ago I did not value at a single Shilling, and could with pleasure have seen it in flames.

The Town in General is left in a better state than we expected, more oweing to a percipitate flight than any Regard to the inhabitants, tho some individuals discoverd a sense of honour and justice and have left the rent of the Houses in which they were, for the owners and the furniture unhurt, or if damaged sufficent to make it good.

Others have committed abominable Ravages. The Mansion House of your President is safe and the furniture unhurt whilst both the House and Furniture of the Solisiter General have fallen a prey to their own merciless party. Surely the very Fiends feel a Reverential awe for Virtue and patriotism, whilst they Detest the paricide and traitor.

I feel very differently at the approach of spring to what I did a month ago. We knew not then whether we could plant or sow with safety, whether when we had toild we could reap the fruits of our own industery, whether we could rest in our own Cottages, or whether we should not be driven from the sea coasts to seek shelter in the wilderness, but now we feel as if we might sit under our own vine and eat the good of the land.

I feel a gaieti de Coar to which before I was a stranger. I think the Sun looks brighter, the Birds sing more melodiously, and Nature puts on a more chearfull countanance. We feel a temporary peace, and the poor fugitives are returning to their deserted habitations.

Tho we felicitate ourselves, we sympathize with those who are trembling least the Lot of Boston should be theirs. But they cannot be in similar circumstances unless pusilanimity and cowardise should take possession of them. They have time and warning given them to see the Evil and shun it.—I long to hear that you have declared an independancy—and by the way in the new Code of Laws which I suppose it will be necessary for you to make I desire you would Remember the Ladies, and be more generous and favourable to them than your ancestors. Do not put such unlimited power into the hands of the Husbands. Remember all Men would be tyrants if they could. If perticuliar care and attention is not paid to the Ladies we are determined to foment a Rebelion, and will not hold ourselves bound by any Laws in which we have no voice, or Representation.

That your Sex are Naturally Tyrannical is a Truth so thoroughly established as to admit of no dispute, but such of you as wish to be happy willingly give up the harsh title of Master for the more tender and endearing one of Friend. Why then, not put it out of the power of the vicious and the Lawless to use us with cruelty and indignity with impunity. Men of Sense in all Ages abhor those customs which treat us only as the vassals of your Sex. Regard us then as Beings placed by providence under your protection and in immitation of the Supreem Being make use of that power only for our happiness.

John Adams to Abigail Adams

AP. 14. 1776

You justly complain of my short Letters, but the critical State of Things and the Multiplicity of Avocations must plead my Excuse.—You ask where the Fleet is. The inclosed Papers will inform you. You ask what Sort of Defence Virginia can make. I believe they will make an able Defence. Their Militia and minute Men have been some time employed in training them selves, and they have Nine Battallions of regulars as they call them, maintained among them, under good Officers, at the Continental Expence. They have set up a Number of Manufactories of Fire Arms, which are busily employed. They are tolerably supplied with Powder, and are succcessfull and assiduous, in making Salt Petre. Their neighbouring Sister or rather Daughter Colony of North Carolina, which is a warlike Colony, and has several Battallions at the Continental Expence, as well as a pretty good Militia, are ready to assist them, and they are in very good Spirits, and seem determined to make a brave Resistance.—The Gentry are very rich, and the common People very poor. This Inequality of Property, gives an Aristocratical Turn to all their Proceedings, and occasions a strong Aversion in their Patricians, to Common Sense. But the Spirit of these Barons, is coming down, and it must submit.

It is very true, as you observe they have been duped by Dunmore. But this is a Common Case. All the Colonies are duped, more or less, at one Time and another. A more egregious Bubble was never blown up, than the Story of Commissioners coming to treat with the Congress. Yet it has gained Credit like a Charm, not only without but against the clearest Evidence. I never shall forget the Delusion, which seized our best and most sagacious Friends the dear Inhabitants of Boston, the Winter before last. Credulity and the Want of Foresight, are Imperfections in the human Character, that no Politician can sufficiently guard against.

You have given me some Pleasure, by your Account of a certain House in Queen Street. I had burned it, long ago, in Imagination. It rises now to my View like a Phœnix.—What shall I say of the Solicitor General? I pity his pretty Children, I pity his Father, and his sisters. I wish I could be clear that it is no moral Evil to pity him and his Lady. Upon Repentance they will certainly have a large Share in the Compassions of many. But let Us take Warning and give it to our Children. Whenever Vanity, and Gaiety, a Love of Pomp and Dress, Furniture, Equipage, Buildings, great Company, expensive Diversions, and elegant Entertainments get the better of the Principles and Judgments of Men or Women there is no knowing where they will stop, nor into what Evils, natural, moral, or political, they will lead us.

Your Description of your own Gaiety de Coeur, charms me. Thanks be to God you have just Cause to rejoice—and may the bright Prospect be obscured by no Cloud.

As to Declarations of Independency, be patient. Read our Privateering Laws, and our Commercial Laws. What signifies a Word.

As to your extraordinary Code of Laws, I cannot but laugh. We have been told that our Struggle has loosened the bands of Government every where. That Children and Apprentices were disobedient—that schools and Colledges were grown turbulent—that Indians slighted their Guardians and Negroes grew insolent to their Masters. But your Letter was the first Intimation that another Tribe more numerous and powerfull than all the rest were grown discontented.—This is rather too coarse a Compliment but you are so saucy, I wont blot it out.

Depend upon it, We know better than to repeal our Masculine systems. Altho they are in full Force, you know they are little more than Theory. We dare not exert our Power in its full Latitude. We are obliged to go fair, and softly, and in Practice you know We are the subjects. We have only the Name of Masters, and rather than give up this, which would compleatly subject Us to the Despotism of the Peticoat, I hope General Washington, and all our brave Heroes would fight. I am sure every good Politician would plot, as long as he would against Despotism, Empire, Monarchy, Aristocracy, Oligarchy, or Ochlocracy.—A fine Story indeed. I begin to think the Ministry as deep as they are wicked. After stirring up Tories, Landjobbers, Trimmers, Bigots, Canadians, Indians, Negroes, Hanoverians, Hessians, Russians, Irish Roman Catholicks, Scotch Renegadoes, at last they have stimulated the [women] to demand new Priviledges and threaten to rebell.

George Ripley,
Ralph Waldo Emerson,
and Nathaniel Hawthorne
Letters concerning Brook Farm
 1840, 1841

From the Plymouth Pilgrims to the messianic cults of our own time, there has been an impulse in American culture to secede from the world and start anew and alone. One famous (and, to some, notorious) experiment in utopian living in antebellum America was Brook Farm, conceived in the late 1830s by a group of leading Transcendentalists, including George and Sophia Ripley, and (though he stayed on the periphery) Ralph Waldo Emerson himself. "I wished to be convinced," Emerson wrote in his journal about his friends' heady plans, "to be thawed, to be made nobly mad by the kindlings before my eye of a new dawn of human piety . . . [but] not once could I be inflamed."

The goals of the Brook Farm dreamers were dear to Emerson's heart. But he never fully embraced their plan to establish a self-sufficient and all-sufficient communal farm where everything from manual labor to financial decisions would be equally shared by all members of the community, and all conventional distinctions—between thinkers and workers, between labor and leisure—would be obliterated. Beginning in 1841, several families tried to realize this egalitarian vision on a plot of land just to the northwest of Dedham and West Roxbury, Massachusetts. Their experiment lasted from 1841 until 1847, during which time it went through several reorganizations. For stays of varying lengths of time it attracted the interest of such luminaries as Theodore Parker and Orestes Brownson (though neither joined) and Nathaniel Hawthorne (who served for a time as treasurer). For some who visited or heard about it, Brook Farm was utter folly; for others it was, as Ripley put it, "a light over this country and this age." For still others—as it seemed to be for Hawthorne, who made it the basis for his psychological novel *The Blithedale Romance* (1852)—it was a laboratory in which the human capacity for selfless action and self-knowledge could be put to the test. In the three letters that follow, Ripley and Emerson (writing to each other), and Hawthorne (writing to his future wife, Sophia, during his sojourn at the farm), give voice to very different estimates of the prospect that Brook Farm would open the way toward human perfection.

George Ripley to R. W. Emerson

My dear Sir: Our conversation in Concord was of such a general nature that I do not feel as if you were in complete possession of the idea of the association which I wish to see established. As we have now a prospect of carrying it into effect, at an early period, I wish to submit the plan more distinctly to your judgment, that you may decide whether it is one that can have the benefit of your aid and cooperation.

Our objects, as you know, are to insure a more natural union between intellectual and manual labor than now exists; to combine the thinker and the worker, as far as possible, in the same individual; to guarantee the highest mental freedom by providing all with labor adapted to their tastes and talents, and securing to them the fruits of their industry; to do away with the necessity of menial services by opening the benefits of education and the profits of labor to all; and thus to prepare a society of liberal, intelligent, and cultivated persons whose relations with each other would permit a more simple and wholesome life than can be led amidst the pressure of our competitive institutions.

To accomplish these objects, we propose to take a small tract of land, which, under skillful husbandry, uniting the garden and the farm, will be adequate to the subsistence of the families, and to connect with this a school or college in which the most complete instruction shall be given, from the first rudiments to the highest culture. Our farm would be a place for improving the race of men that lived on it; thought would preside over the operations of labor, and labor would contribute to the expansion of thought; we should have industry without drudgery, and true equality without its vulgarity.

An offer has been made to us of a beautiful estate, on very reasonable terms, on the borders of Newton, West Roxbury, and Dedham. I am very familiar with the premises, having resided on them a part of last summer, and we might search the country in vain for anything more eligible. Our proposal now is for three or four families to take possession on the first of April next, to attend to the cultivation of the farm and the erection of buildings, to prepare for the coming of as many more in the autumn, and thus to commence the institution in the simplest manner, and with the smallest number with which it can go into operation at all. It would thus be not less than two or three years before we should be joined by all who mean to be with us; we should not fall to pieces by our own weight; we should grow up slowly and strong; and the attractiveness of our experiment would win to us all whose society we should want.

The step now to be taken at once is the procuring of funds for the necessary capital. According to the present modification of our plan, a much less sum will be required than that spoken of in our discussion at Concord. We thought then $50,000 would be needed; I find now, after a careful estimate, that $30,000 will purchase the estate and buildings for ten families, and give the required surplus for carrying on the operations for one year.

We propose to raise this sum by a subscription to a joint stock company among the friends of the institution, the payment of a fixed interest being guaranteed to the subscribers, and the subscription itself secured by the real estate. No man then will be in danger of losing; he will receive as fair an interest as he would from any investment, while at the same time he is contributing toward an institution in which, while the true use of money is retained, its abuses are done away. The sum required cannot come from rich capitalists; their instinct would protest against such an application of their coins; it must be obtained from those who sympathize with our ideas, and who are willing to aid their realization with their money, if not by their personal cooperation. There are some of this description on whom I think we can rely; among ourselves we can produce perhaps $10,000; the remainder must be subscribed for by those who wish us well, whether they mean to unite with us or not.

I can imagine no plan which is suited to carry into effect so many divine ideas as this. If wisely executed, it will be a light over this country and this age. If not the sunrise, it will be the morning star. As a practical man, I see clearly that we must have some such arrangement, or all changes less radical will be nugatory. I believe in the divinity of labor; I wish to "harvest my flesh and blood from the land"; but to do this, I must either be insulated and work to disadvantage, or avail myself of the services of hirelings who are not of my order and whom I can scarce make friends, for I must have another to drive the plow which I hold. I cannot empty a cask of lime upon my grass alone. I wish to see a society of educated friends, working, thinking, and living together, with no strife except that of each to contribute the most to the benefit of all.

Personally, my tastes and habits would lead me in another direction. I have a passion for being independent of the world and of every man in it. This I could do easily on the estate which is now offered, and which I could rent at a rate that, with my other resources, would place me in a very agreeable condition as far as my personal interests were involved. I should have a city of God on a small scale of my own; and please God, I should hope one day to drive my own cart to market and sell greens. But I feel bound to sacrifice this private feeling in the hope of a great social good. I shall be anxious to hear from you. Your decision will do much toward settling the question with me, whether the time has come for the fulfillment of a high hope or whether the work belongs to a future generation. All omens now are favorable; a singular union of diverse talents is ready for the enterprise; everything indicates that we ought to arise and build; and if we let slip this occasion, the unsleeping

Nemesis will deprive us of the boon we seek. For myself, I am sure that I can never give so much thought to it again; my mind must act on other objects, and I shall acquiesce in the course of fate, with grief that so fair a light is put out. A small pittance of the wealth which has been thrown away on ignoble objects during this wild contest for political supremacy would lay the corner-stone of a house which would ere long become the desire of nations . . .

George Ripley.

P.S. I ought to add that in the present stage of the enterprise no proposal is considered as binding. We wish only to know what can probably be relied on, provided always that no pledge will be accepted until the articles of association are agreed on by all parties.

I recollect you said that if you were sure of compeers of the right stamp, you might embark yourself in the adventure: as to this, let me suggest the inquiry, whether our association should not be composed of various classes of men? If we have friends whom we love and who love us, I think we should be content to join with others with whom our personal sympathy is not strong, but whose general ideas coincide with ours, and whose gifts and abilities would make their services important. For instance, I should like to have a good washerwoman in my parish admitted into the plot. She is certainly not a Minerva or a Venus, but we might educate her two children to wisdom and varied accomplishments, who otherwise will be doomed to drudge through life. The same is true of some farmers and mechanics whom we should like with us.

Ralph Waldo Emerson to George Ripley

CONCORD, 15 DECEMBER, 1840.

My dear Sir,
It is quite time I made an answer to your proposition that I should join you in your new enterprise. The design appears to me so noble & humane, proceeding, as I plainly see, from a manly & expanding heart & mind that it makes me & all men its friends & debtors It becomes a matter of conscience to entertain it friendly & to examine what it has for us.

I have decided not to join it & yet very slowly & I may almost say penitentially. I am greatly relieved by learning that your coadjutors are now so many that you will no longer ascribe that importance to the defection of individuals which you hinted in your letter to me. it might attach to mine.

The ground of my decision is almost purely personal to myself. I have some remains of skepticism in regard to the general practicability of the plan, but these have not much weighed with me. That which determines me is the conviction that the Community is not good for me. Whilst I see it may hold out many inducements for others it has little to offer me which with resolution I cannot procure for myself. It seems to me that it would not be worth my while to make the difficult exchange of my property in Concord for a share in the new Household. I am in many respects suitably placed. in an agreeable neighborhood, in a town which I have many reasons to love & which has respected my freedom so far that I may presume it will indulge me farther if I need it. Here I have friends & kindred. Here I have builded & planted: & here I have greater facilities to prosecute such practical enterprizes as I may cherish, than I could probably find by any removal. I cannot accuse my townsmen or my social position of my domestic grievances:—only my own sloth & conformity. It seems to me a circuitous & operose way of relieving myself of any irksome circumstances, to put on your community the task of my emancipation which I ought to take on myself.

The principal particulars in which I wish to mend my domestic life are in acquiring habits of regular manual labor, and in ameliorating or abolishing in my house the condition of hired menial service. I should like to come one step nearer to nature than this usage permits. I desire that my manner of living may be honest and agreeable to my imagination. But surely I need not sell my house & remove my family to Newton in order to make the experiment of labor & self help. I am already in the act of trying some domestic & social experiments which my present position favors. And I think that my present position has even greater advantages than yours would offer me for testing my improvements in those small private parties into which men are all set off already throughout the world.

But I own I almost shrink from making any statement of my objections to our ways of living because I see how slowly I shall mend them. My own health & habits & those of my wife & my mother are not of that robustness which should give any pledge of enterprize & ability in reform. And whenever I am engaged in literary composition I find myself not inclined to insist with heat on new methods. Yet I think that all I shall solidly do, I must do alone. I do not think I should gain anything—I who have little skill to converse with people—by a plan of so many parts and which I comprehend so slowly & imperfectly as the proposed Association.

If the community is not good for me neither am I good for it. I do not look on myself as a valuable member to any community which is not either very large or very small & select I fear that yours would not find me as profitable & pleasant an associate as I should wish to be and as so important a project seems imperatively to require in all its constituents Moreover I am so ignorant

& uncertain in my improvements that I would fain hide my attempts & fail-
ures in solitude where they shall perplex none or very few beside myself The
result of our secretest improvements will certainly have as much renown as
shall be due to them.

In regard to the plan as far as it respects the formation of a School or College, I have more hesitation, inasmuch as a concentration of scholars in one
place seems to me to have certain great advantages. Perhaps as the school
emerges to more distinct consideration out of the Farm, I shall yet find it attractive And yet I am very apt to relapse into the same skepticism as to modes
& arrangements the same magnifying of the men—the men alone. According
to your ability & mine, you & I do now keep school for all comers, & the energy of our thought & will measures our influence. In the community we
shall utter not a word more—not a word less.

Whilst I refuse to be an active member of your company I must yet declare
that of all the philanthropic projects of which I have heard yours is the most
pleasing to me and if it is prosecuted in the same spirit in which it is begun, I
shall regard it with lively sympathy & with a sort of gratitude.

Yours affectionately
R W Emerson

Nathaniel Hawthorne to Sophia Peabody

OAK HILL, APRIL 13TH, 1841

Ownest love,
Here is thy poor husband in a polar Paradise! I know not how to interpret this
aspect of Nature—whether it be of good or evil omen to our enterprise. But I
reflect that the Plymouth pilgrims arrived in the midst of storm and stept
ashore upon mountain snow-drifts; and nevertheless they prospered, and became a great people—and doubtless it will be the same with us. I laud my
stars, however, that thou wilt not have thy first impressions of our future
home from such a day as this. Thou wouldst shiver all thy life afterwards, and
never realize that there could be bright skies, and green hills and meadows,
and trees heavy with foliage, where now the whole scene is a great snow-bank,
and the sky full of snow likewise. Through faith, I persist in believing that
spring and summer will come in due season; but the unregenerated man shiv-
ers within me, and suggests a doubt whether I may not have wandered within
the precincts of the Arctic circle, and chosen my heritage among everlasting
snows. Dearest, provide thyself with a good stock of furs; and if thou canst
obtain the skin of a polar bear, thou wilt find it a very suitable summer dress

for this region. Thou must not hope ever to walk abroad, except upon snow-shoes, nor to find any warmth, save in thy husband's heart.

Belovedest, I have not yet taken my first lesson in agriculture, as thou mayest well suppose—except that I went to see our cows foddered, yesterday afternoon. We have eight of our own; and the number is now increased by a transcendental heifer, belonging to Miss Margaret Fuller. She is very fractious, I believe, and apt to kick over the milk pail. Thou knowest best, whether, in these traits of character, she resembles her mistress. Thy husband intends to convert himself into a milk-maid, this evening; but I pray heaven that Mr. Ripley may be moved to assign him the kindliest cow in the herd—otherwise he will perform his duty with fear and trembling.

Ownest wife, I like my brethren in affliction very well; and couldst thou see us sitting round our table, at meal-times, before the great kitchen-fire, thou wouldst call it a cheerful sight. Mrs. Barker is a most comfortable woman to behold; she looks as if her ample person were stuffed full of tenderness—indeed, as if she were all one great, kind heart. Wert thou but here, I should ask for nothing more—not even for sunshine and summer weather; for thou wouldst be both, to thy husband. And how is that cough of thine, my belovedest? Hast thou thought of me, in my perils and wanderings? Thou must not think how I longed for thee, when I crept into my cold bed last night,—my bosom remembered thee,—and refused to be comforted without thy kisses. I trust that thou dost muse upon me with hope and joy, not with repining. Think that I am gone before, to prepare a home for my Dove, and will return for her, all in good time.

Thy husband has the best chamber in the house, I believe; and though not quite so good as the apartment I have left, it will do very well. I have hung up thy two pictures; and they give me a glimpse of summer and of thee. The vase I intended to have brought in my arms; but could not very conveniently do it yesterday; so that it still remains at Mrs. Hillards, together with my carpet. I shall bring them the next opportunity.

Now farewell, for the present, most beloved. I have been writing this in my chamber; but the fire is getting low, and the house is old and cold; so that the warmth of my whole person has retreated to my heart, which burns with love for thee. I must run down to the kitchen or parlor hearth, where thy image shall sit beside me—yea be pressed to my breast. At bed-time, thou shalt have a few lines more. Now I think of it, dearest, wilt thou give Mrs. Ripley a copy of Grandfather's Chair and Liberty Tree; she wants them for some boys here. I have several copies of Famous Old People.

April 14th. 10 A.M. Sweetest, I did not milk the cows last night, because Mr. Ripley was afraid to trust them to my hands, or me to their horns—I know not which. But this morning, I have done wonders. Before breakfast, I went out to the barn, and began to chop hay for the cattle; and with such "righteous vehemence" (as Mr. Ripley says) did I labor, that, in the space of ten minutes, I broke the machine. Then I brought wood and replenished the fires; and finally sat down to breakfast and ate up a huge mound of buckwheat cakes. After breakfast, Mr. Ripley put a four-pronged instrument into my hands, which he gave me to understand was called a pitch-fork; and he and Mr. Farley being armed with similar weapons, we all three commenced a gallant attack upon a heap of manure. This affair being concluded, and thy husband having purified himself, he sits down to finish this letter to his most beloved wife. Dearest, I will never consent that thou come within a half a mile of me, after such an encounter as that of this morning. Pray Heaven that this letter retain none of the fragrance with which the writer was imbued. As for thy husband himself, he is peculiarly partial to the odor; but that whimsical little nose of thine might chance to quarrel with it.

Belovedest, Miss Fuller's cow hooks the other cows, and has made herself ruler of the herd, and behaves in a very tyrannical manner. Sweetest, I know not when I shall see thee; but I trust it will not be longer than till the end of next week. I love thee! I love thee! I would thou wert with me; for then would my labor be joyful—and even now, it is not sorrowful. Dearest, I shall make an excellent husbandman. I feel the original Adam reviving within me.

John Quincy Adams

Argument before the Supreme Court in the *Amistad* Case

 1841

In March 1841, former President John Quincy Adams (1767–1848) stood before the United States Supreme Court and argued successfully for the release of several dozen African mutineers who had seized a Spanish slave ship, the *Amistad,* off the coast of Cuba. The rebels, led by a charismatic young African named Cinque, had been captured by American naval forces in Long Island Sound just east of the Connecticut shore while trying to sail back to Africa. Famous in its day, the case became well known again recently when the popular movie *Amistad* presented it as a prelude to emancipation.

The *Amistad* case was such a precedent in only a limited sense. Slavery continued to flourish in the United States for more than two decades after the *Amistad* captives won their freedom. The main issue of the case, as Chief Justice Joseph Story put it, was whether the United States government had proven that the rebellious Africans were, in fact, the legitimate property of the two Spanish owners, Ruiz and Montes, who survived the mutiny and who were demanding return of their "property" under Article 9 of a 1795 treaty concerning international obligations. The problem for them was that the international slave trade had long been illegal, though the domestic slave trade remained lawful in much of the United States. And so the case turned on the question of whether the Africans in custody, as the Spaniards claimed, had been born into servitude in Cuba and were being legally transported from one point to another within that Spanish colony when they mutinied, or whether, as the Africans and their abolitionist defenders countered, they had been kidnapped from their native continent and were thus free persons. Adams's arguments are largely technical and historical, having to do with the force of the documents presented by Ruiz and Montes to prove the identity of their "property."

Yet there are passages in Adams's brief that rise to a level of eloquent outrage—mixed with a certain haughty pride in his own history of personal righteousness. In his diary, as he prepared for the task of transforming the oral arguments he had made in court into the published text excerpted here, he wrote, "The world, the flesh, and all the devils in hell are arrayed against any man who now in this North

American Union shall dare to join the standard of Almighty God to put down the African slave-trade; and what can I, upon the verge of my seventy-fourth birthday, with a shaking hand, a darkening eye, a drowsy brain, and with all my faculties dropping from me one by one, as the teeth are dropping from my head—what can I do for the cause of God and man, for the progress of human emancipation, for the suppression of the African slave-trade? Yet my conscience presses me on; let me but die upon the breach." What follows is as pure an expression of the "New England conscience" as any in this book.

For I inquire by what *right,* all this sympathy, from Lieut. Gedney to the Secretary of State, and from the Secretary of State, *as it were,* to the nation, was extended to the two Spaniards from Cuba exclusively, and utterly denied to the fifty-two victims of *their* lawless violence? By what *right* was it denied to the men who had restored themselves to freedom, and secured their oppressors to abide the consequences of the acts of violence perpetrated by them, and why was it extended to the perpetrators of those acts of violence themselves? When the Amistad first came within the territorial jurisdiction of the United States, acts of violence had passed between the two parties, the Spaniards and Africans on board of her, but on which side these acts were *lawless,* on which side were the *oppressors,* was a question of right and wrong, for the settlement of which, if the government and people of the United States interfered at all, they were bound in duty to extend their sympathy to them all; and if they intervened at all *between* them, the duty incumbent upon this intervention was not of favor, but of impartiality—not of sympathy, but of JUSTICE, dispensing to every individual *his own right* . . .

M. Calderon de la Barca then refers to several treaty stipulations in support of his demand, and particularly the 8th, 9th, and 10th articles of the treaty of 1795, continued in force by the treaty of 1819 . . .

"ART. 9. All ships and merchandise, of what nature soever, which shall be rescued out of the hands of any pirates or robbers on the high seas, shall be brought into some port of either state, and shall be delivered to the custody of the officers of that port, in order to be taken care of, and restored entire to the true proprietor, as soon as due and sufficient proof shall be made concerning the property thereof."

Was this ship rescued out of the hands of pirates and robbers? Is this Court competent to declare it? The Courts below have decided that they have no authority to try, criminally, what happened on board the vessel. They have then no right to regard those who forcibly took possession of the vessel as pirates and robbers. If the sympathies of Lieutenant Gedney, which the Secretary of State says had become national, had been felt for all the parties, in due proportion to their sufferings and their deserts, who were the pirates and robbers?

Were they the Africans? When they were brought from Lomboko, in the Tecora, against the laws of Spain, against the laws of the United States, and against the law of nations, so far as the United States, and Spain, and Great Britain, are concerned, who were the robbers and pirates? And when the same voyage, in fact, was continued in the Amistad, and the Africans were in a perishing condition in the hands of Ruiz, dropping dead from day to day under his treatment, were *they* the pirates and robbers? This honorable Court will observe from the record that there were fifty-four Africans who left the Havana. Ruiz says in his libel that nine had died before they reached our shores. The marshal's return shows that they were dying day after day from the effects of their sufferings. One died before the Court sat at New London. Three more died before the return was made to the Court at Hartford—only seventeen days—and three more between that and November. Sixteen fell victims before November, and from that time not one has died. Think only of the relief and benefit of being restored to the absolute wants of human nature. Although placed in a condition which, if applied to forty citizens of the United States, we should call cruel, shut up eighteen months in a prison, and enjoying only the tenderness which our laws provide for the worst of criminals, so great is the improvement of their condition from what it was in the hands of Ruiz, that they have perfectly recovered their health, and not one has died; when, before that time, they were perishing from hour to hour.

At the great day of accounts, may it please the Court, who is to be responsible for those sixteen souls that died? Ruiz claims those sixteen as his property, as merchandise. How many of them, at his last hour, will pass before him and say, "Let me sit heavy on thy soul to-morrow!"

Who, then, are the tyrants and oppressors against whom our laws are invoked? Who are the innocent sufferers, for whom we are called upon to protect this ship against enemies and robbers? . . .

Was ever such a scene of Liliputian trickery enacted by the rulers of a great, magnanimous, and Christian nation? Contrast it with that act of self-emancipation by which the savage, heathen barbarians Cinque and Grabeau liberated themselves and their fellow suffering countrymen from Spanish slave-traders, and which the Secretary of State, by communion of sympathy with Ruiz and Montes, denominates *lawless violence.* Cinque and Grabeau are uncouth and barbarous names. Call them Harmodius and Aristogiton, and go back for moral principle three thousand years to the fierce and glorious democracy of Athens. They too resorted to *lawless violence,* and slew the tyrant to redeem the freedom of their country. For this heroic action they paid the forfeit of their lives: but within three years the Athenians expelled their tyrants themselves, and in gratitude to their self-devoted deliverers decreed, that thenceforth no slave should ever bear either of their names. Cinque and Grabeau are not slaves. Let them bear in future history the names of Harmodius and Aristogiton . . .

I will now make a few observations on the passport, or permit, as it has been called, which is relied on as of authority sufficient to bind this Court and Government to deliver up my clients irrevocably as slaves, on a claim of property by Ruiz and Montes. Here we have what appears to be a blank passport, filled up with forty-nine Spanish names of persons, who are described as *ladinos,* and as being the property of Don José Ruiz. Now, this on the face of it is an imposture. It is not a passport, that can be inspected as such by this Court, or by any tribunal. It appears on the face of it to be a passport designed for one person, a man, as there are blanks in the margin, to be filled up with a description of the person, as to his height, age, complexion, hair, forehead, eyebrows, eyes, nose, mouth, beard, and particular marks. This particular description of the person is the very essence of a passport, as it is designed to identify the individual by the conformity of his person to the marks given; and a passport is nothing, and is good for nothing, if it does not accord with the marks given. The man who presents it must show by this accordance that he is the person named. Every body who has ever had occasion to use passports knows this. We are not in the habit of using passports in this country; you may go through the country from State to State, freely, without any passport to show who and what you are and what is your business. But throughout the continent of Europe, passports are everywhere necessary. At every town you show your passport to a public officer, who instantly compares your person with the description, and if it corresponds, you proceed, but if the description varies from the reality, you cannot pass. That is the nature of a passport. It says, let the person who bears these marks pass the custom-house, or the guard, as the case may be. And its validity depends on the accuracy of the description.

I once had occasion, many years ago, to see the operation of these things in a very remarkable case. I was a passenger in a merchant vessel, bound to the north of Europe. In passing through the Sound, at Elsinore, we were arrested by a British squadron, who brought us to, and sent a lieutenant on board to examine our crew. He ordered all the men to be mustered on deck, and the captain had no alternative but to comply. It was a most mortifying scene to an American. Every American seaman was obliged to show his protection, the same thing at sea as a passport on the land, to secure him from impressment by British cruisers. The officer examined every man carefully, to see whether his person corresponded with the description in his protection. He finally found one young man, who was a native of Charlestown, Massachusetts, within ten miles of where I was born; but his description was not correct, whether through the blunder of the man who wrote it, or because he had taken another man's protection, I do not know, but the officer said he had a good mind to take him, and if I had not been on board, as the bearer of a public commission in the service of the Government, I have no doubt that man would have been taken, and compelled to serve on board a British man of war, solely for the want of correspondence of the description with his person. I mention this to show that the value of a passport, according to the rules of those countries where such things are used, depends on the description of the person, and this is all left blank in the paper here presented us as a passport. There is not a particle of description by which even a single individual named could be identified. It is not worth a cent. I do not say it is a forgery, but I say its incompetency to answer the purpose of a passport is apparent on the face of it. Who knows, or how is this Court to ascertain, that the persons named in this paper are the same with those taken in the Amistad? No court, no tribunal, no officer, would accept such a document as a passport. And will this Court grant its decree in a case affecting both liberty and life on that paper? It is impossible.

NATHANIEL PARKER WILLIS

The Lady in the White Dress, Whom I Helped into the Omnibus

 1844

Born in Portland, Maine, Nathaniel Parker Willis (1806–1867) was educated at the Boston Latin School and Yale before becoming a magazine editor in Boston. Like Bryant before him and Howells later in the century, he left New England to pursue a literary career in New York, where he became known as something of a dandy and man-about-town. "For one day we list to the pastor," he wrote about his adopted city, "For six days we list to the band!" In our own time, Willis has fallen into obscurity, but his writing remains a lively record of struggle between New England restraint and big-city freedom. In this poem about what today we would call a sexual fantasy, he catches the poignance of a missed chance for intimacy.

I know her not! Her hand has been in mine,
And the warm pressure of her taper arm
Has thrill'd upon my fingers, and the hem
Of her white dress has lain upon my feet,
Till my hush'd pulse, by the caressing folds,
Was kindled to a fever! I, to her,
Am but the undistinguishable leaf
Blown by upon the breeze—yet I have sat,
And in the blue depths of her stainless eyes,
(Close as a lover in his hour of bliss,
And steadfastly as look the twin stars down
Into unfathomable wells,) have gazed!
And I have felt from out its gate of pearl
Her warm breath on my cheek, and while she sat
Dreaming away the moments, I have tried
To count the long dark lashes in the fringe
Of her bewildering eyes! The kerchief sweet
That enviably visits her red lip
Has slumber'd, while she held it, on my knee,—

And her small foot has crept between mine own—
And yet, she knows me not!

     Now, thanks to heaven
For blessings chainless in the rich man's keeping—
Wealth that the miser cannot hide away!
Buy, if they will, the invaluable flower—
They cannot store its fragrance from the breeze!
Wear, if they will, the costliest gem of Ind—
It pours its light on every passing eye!
And he who on this beauty sets his name—
Who dreams, perhaps, that for his use alone
Such loveliness was first of angels born—
Tell him, oh whisperer at his dreaming ear,
That I too, in her beauty, sun my eye,
And, unrebuked, may worship her in song—
Tell him that heaven, along our darkling way,
Hath set bright lamps with loveliness alight—
And all may in their guiding beams rejoice;
But he—as 'twere a watcher by a lamp—
Guards but this bright one's shining.

DANIEL WEBSTER

Speech in the United States Senate

 1850

Daniel Webster (1782–1852) was a leading lawyer and the greatest orator in antebellum America. He served as a representative from his native New Hampshire, as a representative and senator from Massachusetts, and twice as Secretary of State. His eloquent and winning arguments before the United States Supreme Court in the landmark cases of *Dartmouth College v. Woodward* and *McCulloch v. Maryland* greatly strengthened, respectively, the legal autonomy of corporations and the immunity of federal laws to state nullification.

Like all statesmen of his time, Webster could not escape the rising contention over slavery. Once regarded by the founding fathers (including the Virginians) as a tragic inheritance from the colonists who had brought unfree labor to these shores, slavery—because of the irresistible profitability of cotton—had been rehabilitated in the minds of many southerners. John C. Calhoun pronounced it a "positive good," as did some New Englanders. Webster was no friend of slavery. Yet in the face of the sad evidence that "exigent interests" underlay ideas of right and wrong, Webster lamented slavery but "expressed no opinion of the mode of its extinguishment or amelioration." On March 7, 1850, in the midst of a national crisis that seemed a prelude to civil war, he tried to propose a way that slavery and Union might continue to coexist.

Even as he spoke, Webster's Whig party was being torn apart by the conflicting interests of its several constituencies: New England manufacturers who favored high import tariffs that were odious to southern planters, merchants who disliked slavery but were afraid of a business collapse should the South secede, impassioned abolitionists (like Charles Sumner), and "cotton Whigs" with investments in the textile industry that depended on the supply of slave-grown cotton. Although Webster's great opponent, John C. Calhoun, was dying of tuberculosis, the senator from South Carolina had dragged himself to the Senate chamber to hear the much-anticipated speech. Three days earlier, Calhoun had been too weak to stand and read his own remarks, and was now known to be working on a plan that would split the United States presidency into two, one for the North and one for the South, each with veto power over Congress.

Under these tense conditions, in which the fate of the Union seemed bleaker than it had ever been, Webster delivered a speech that was immediately recognized as a great achievement of American oratory—a performance that, according to observers, began quietly and rose to a crescendo in which gesture, voice, and rhetoric were perfectly harmonized in the service of a quasi-religious celebration of the sacred Union. Webster makes concessions to both sides, granting the justice of southerners' resentment at the failure of northerners to enforce existing fugitive slave laws while defending the dignity of northern working men in the face of the growing southern cry that slavery was the more efficient, and more moral, system of labor.

In the aftermath of his speech, Webster was greeted in some quarters as a selfless compromiser who had put aside regional loyalty for the sake of the nation. But Calhoun, looking haunted and barely able to whisper his prophecy, had objected, "No, sir, the Union can be broken." In the view of antislavery New Englanders, Webster had sold his soul. Harriet Beecher Stowe portrayed him, in the figure of Senator Bird in *Uncle Tom's Cabin,* as an unfeeling, amoral temporizer. And Emerson, who had once admired him as a mighty force for truth, now counted him among the "half-villains" of history.

Mr. President,—I wish to speak to-day, not as a Massachusetts man, nor as a Northern man, but as an American, and a member of the Senate of the United States. It is fortunate that there is a Senate of the United States; a body not yet moved from its propriety, not lost to a just sense of its own dignity and its own high responsibilities, and a body to which the country looks, with confidence, for wise, moderate, patriotic, and healing counsels. It is not to be denied that we live in the midst of strong agitations, and are surrounded by very considerable dangers to our institutions and government. The imprisoned winds are let loose. The East, the North, and the stormy South combine to throw the whole sea into commotion, to toss its billows to the skies, and disclose its profoundest depths. I do not affect to regard myself, Mr. President, as holding, or as fit to hold, the helm in this combat with the political elements; but I have a duty to perform, and I mean to perform it with fidelity, not without a sense of existing dangers, but not without hope. I have a part to act, not for my own security or safety, for I am looking out for no fragment upon which to float away from the wreck, if wreck there must be, but for the good of the whole, and the preservation of all; and there is that which will keep me to my duty during this struggle, whether the sun and the stars shall appear, or shall not appear for many days. I speak to-day for the preservation of the Union. "Hear me for my cause." I speak to-day, out of a solicitous and anxious heart, for the restoration to the country of that quiet and that harmony which make the blessings of this Union so rich, and so dear to us all. These are the topics that I propose to myself to discuss; these are the motives, and the sole motives, that influence me in the wish to communicate my opinions to the Senate and the country; and if I can do any thing, however little, for the promotion of these ends, I shall have accomplished all that I expect . . .

Mr. President, in the excited times in which we live, there is found to exist a state of crimination and recrimination between the North and South. There are lists of grievances produced by each; and those grievances, real or supposed, alienate the minds of one portion of the country from the other, exasperate the feelings, and subdue the sense of fraternal affection, patriotic love, and mutual regard. I shall bestow a little attention, Sir, upon these various grievances existing on the one side and on the other. I begin with complaints of the South. I will not answer, further than I have, the general statements of the honorable Senator from South Carolina, that the North has prospered at the expense of the South in consequence of the manner of administering this government, in the collecting of its revenues, and so forth. These are disputed topics, and I have no inclination to enter into them. But I will allude to other complaints of the South, and especially to one which has in my opinion just foundation; and that is, that there has been found at the North, among individuals and among legislators, a disinclination to perform fully their constitutional duties in regard to the return of persons bound to service who have escaped into the free States. In that respect, the South, in my judgment, is right, and the North is wrong. Every member of every Northern legislature is bound by oath, like every other officer in the country, to support the Constitution of the United States; and the article of the Constitution which says to these States that they shall deliver up fugitives from service is as binding in honor and conscience as any other article. No man fulfils his duty in any legislature who sets himself to find excuses, evasions, escapes from this constitutional obligation . . .

Then, Sir, there are the Abolition societies, of which I am unwilling to speak, but in regard to which I have very clear notions and opinions. I do not think them useful. I think their operations for the last twenty years have produced nothing good or valuable. At the same time, I believe thousands of their members to be honest and good men, perfectly well-meaning men. They have excited feelings; they think they must do something for the cause of liberty; and, in their sphere of action, they do not see what else they can do than to contribute to an Abolition press, or an Abolition society, or to pay an Abolition lecturer. I do not mean to impute gross motives even to the leaders of these societies, but I am not blind to the consequences of their proceedings. I cannot but see what mischiefs their interference with the South has produced . . .

Well, in all this I see no solid grievance, no grievance presented by the South, within the redress of the government, but the single one to which I have referred; and that is, the want of a proper regard to the injunction of the Constitution for the delivery of fugitive slaves.

There are also complaints of the North against the South. I need not go over them particularly. The first and gravest is, that the North adopted the Constitution, recognizing the existence of slavery in the States, and recognizing the right, to a certain extent, of the representation of slaves in Congress, under a state of sentiment and expectation which does not now exist; and that, by events, by circumstances, by the eagerness of the South to acquire territory and extend her slave population, the North finds itself, in regard to the relative influence of the South and the North, of the free States and the slave States, where it never did expect to find itself when they agreed to the compact of the Constitution. They complain, therefore, that, instead of slavery being regarded as an evil, as it was then, an evil which all hoped would be extinguished gradually, it is now regarded by the South as an institution to be cherished, and preserved, and extended; an institution which the South has already extended to the utmost of her power by the acquisition of new territory.

Well, then, passing from that, every body in the North reads; and every body reads whatsoever the newspapers contain; and the newspapers, some of them, especially those presses to which I have alluded, are careful to spread about among the people every reproachful sentiment uttered by any Southern man bearing at all against the North; every thing that is calculated to exasperate and to alienate; and there are many such things, as every body will admit, from the South, or some portion of it, which are disseminated among the reading people; and they do exasperate, and alienate, and produce a most mischievous effect upon the public mind at the North. Sir, I would not notice things of this sort appearing in obscure quarters; but one thing has occurred in this debate which struck me very forcibly. An honorable member from Louisiana addressed us the other day on this subject. I suppose there is not a more amiable and worthy gentleman in this chamber, nor a gentleman who would be more slow to give offence to any body, and he did not mean in his remarks to give offence. But what did he say? Why, Sir, he took pains to run a contrast between the slaves of the South and the laboring people of the North, giving the preference, in all points of condition, and comfort, and happiness, to the slaves of the South. The honorable member, doubtless, did not suppose that he gave any offence, or did any injustice. He was merely expressing his opinion. But does he know how remarks of that sort will be received by the laboring people of the North? Why, who are the laboring people of the North? They are the whole North. They are the people who till their own farms with their own hands; freeholders, educated men, independent men. Let me say, Sir, that five sixths of the whole property of the North is in the hands of the laborers of the North; they cultivate their farms, they educate their children, they provide the means of independence. If they are not freeholders, they earn wages; these wages accumulate, are turned into capital, into new freeholds, and small capitalists are created. Such is the case, and such the course of things, among the industrious and frugal. And what can these people think when so respectable and worthy a gentleman as the member from Louisiana undertakes to prove that the absolute ignorance and the abject slavery of the South are more in conformity with the high purposes and destiny of immortal, rational human beings, than the educated, the independent free labor of the North?

There is a more tangible and irritating cause of grievance at the North. Free blacks are constantly employed in the vessels of the North, generally as cooks or stewards. When the vessel arrives at a Southern port, these free colored men are taken on shore, by the police or municipal authority, imprisoned, and kept in prison till the vessel is again ready to sail. This is not only irritating, but exceedingly unjustifiable and oppressive. Mr. Hoar's mission, some time ago, to South Carolina, was a well-intended effort to remove this cause of complaint. The North thinks such imprisonments illegal and unconstitutional; and as the cases occur constantly and frequently, they regard it as a great grievance.

Now, Sir, so far as any of these grievances have their foundation in matters of law, they can be redressed, and ought to be redressed; and so far as they have their foundation in matters of opinion, in sentiment, in mutual crimination and recrimination, all that we can do is to endeavor to allay the agitation, and cultivate a better feeling and more fraternal sentiments between the South and the North.

Mr. President, I should much prefer to have heard from every member on this floor declarations of opinion that this Union could never be dissolved, than the declaration of opinion by any body, that, in any case, under the pressure of any circumstances, such a dissolution was possible. I hear with distress and anguish the word "secession," especially when it falls from the lips of those who are patriotic, and known to the country, and known all over the world, for their political services. Secession! Peaceable secession! Sir, your eyes and mine are never destined to see that miracle. The dismemberment of this vast country without convulsion! The breaking up of the fountains of the great deep without ruffling the surface! Who is so foolish, I beg every body's pardon, as to expect to see any such thing? Sir, he who sees these States, now revolving in harmony around a common centre, and expects to see them quit their places and fly off without convulsion, may look the next hour to see the heavenly bodies rush from their spheres, and jostle against each other in the realms of space, without causing the wreck of the universe. There can be no such thing as a peaceable secession. Peaceable secession is an utter impossibility. Is the great Constitution under which we live, covering this whole country, is it to be thawed and melted away by secession, as the snows on the mountain melt under the influence of a vernal sun, disappear almost unobserved, and run off? No, Sir! No, Sir! I will not state what might produce the disruption of the Union; but, Sir, I see as plainly as I see the sun in heaven what that disruption itself must produce; I see that it must produce war, and such a war as I will not describe, *in its twofold character.*

Peaceable secession! Peaceable secession! The concurrent agreement of all the members of this great republic to separate! A voluntary separation, with alimony on one side and on the other. Why, what would be the result? Where is the line to be drawn? What States are to secede? What is to remain American? What am I to be? An American no longer? Am I to become a sectional man, a local man, a separatist, with no country in common with the gentlemen who sit around me here, or who fill the other house of Congress? Heaven forbid! Where is the flag of the republic to remain? Where is the eagle still to tower? or is he to cower, and shrink, and fall to the ground? Why, Sir, our ancestors, our fathers and our grandfathers, those of them that are yet living amongst us with prolonged lives, would rebuke and reproach us, and our children and our grandchildren would cry out shame upon us, if we of this generation should dishonor these ensigns of the power of the government and the harmony of that Union which is every day felt among us with so much joy and gratitude. What is to become of the army? What is to become of the navy? What is to become of the public lands? How is each of the thirty States to defend itself? I know, although the idea has not been stated distinctly, there is to be, or it is supposed possible that there will be, a Southern Confederacy. I do not mean, when I allude to this statement, that any one seriously contemplates such a state of things. I do not mean to say that it is true, but I have heard it suggested elsewhere, that the idea has been entertained, that, after the dissolution of this Union, a Southern Confederacy might be formed. I am sorry, Sir, that it has ever been thought of, talked of, or dreamed of, in the wildest flights of human imagination. But the idea, so far as it exists, must be of a separation, assigning the slave States to one side and the free States to the other. Sir, I may express myself too strongly, perhaps, but there are impossibilities in the natural as well as in the physical world, and I hold the idea of a separation of these States, those that are free to form one government, and those that are slave-holding to form another, as such an impossibility. We could not separate the States by any such line, if we were to draw it. We could not sit down here to-day and draw a line of separation that would satisfy any five men in the country. There are natural causes that would keep and tie us together, and there are social and domestic relations which we could not break if we would, and which we should not if we could.

Sir, nobody can look over the face of this country at the present moment, nobody can see where its population is the most dense and growing, without being ready to admit, and compelled to admit, that ere long the strength of America will be in the Valley of the Mississippi. Well, now, Sir, I beg to inquire what the wildest enthusiast has to say on the possibility of cutting that river in two, and leaving free States at its source and on its branches, and slave States down near its mouth, each forming a separate government? Pray, Sir, let me say to the people of this country, that these things are worthy of their pondering and of their consideration. Here, Sir, are five millions of freemen in the free States north of the river Ohio. Can any body suppose that this population can be severed, by a line that divides them from the territory of a foreign and an alien government, down somewhere, the Lord knows where, upon the lower banks of the Mississippi? What would become of Missouri? Will she join the *arrondissement* of the slave States? Shall the man from the Yellow Stone and the Platte be connected, in the new republic, with the man who lives on the southern extremity of the Cape of Florida? Sir, I am ashamed to pursue this line of remark. I dislike it, I have an utter disgust for it. I would rather hear of natural blasts and mildews, war, pestilence, and famine, than to hear gentlemen talk of secession. To break up this great government! to dismember this glorious country! to astonish Europe with an act of folly such as Europe for two centuries has never beheld in any government or any people! No, Sir! no, Sir! There will be no secession! Gentlemen are not serious when they talk of secession.

Sir, I hear there is to be a convention held at Nashville. I am bound to believe that, if worthy gentlemen meet at Nashville in convention, their object will be to adopt conciliatory counsels; to advise the South to forbearance and moderation, and to advise the North to forbearance and moderation; and to inculcate principles of brotherly love and affection, and attachment to the Constitution of the country as it now is. I believe, if the convention meet at all, it will be for this purpose; for certainly, if they meet for any purpose hostile to the Union, they have been singularly inappropriate in their selection of a place. I remember, Sir, that, when the treaty of Amiens was concluded between France and England, a sturdy Englishman and a distinguished orator, who regarded the conditions of the peace as ignominious to England, said in the House of Commons, that, if King William could know the terms of that treaty, he would turn in his coffin! Let me commend this saying of Mr. Windham, in all its emphasis and in all its force, to any persons who shall meet at Nashville for the purpose of concerting measures for the overthrow of this Union over the bones of Andrew Jackson!

Sir, I wish now to make two remarks, and hasten to a conclusion. I wish to say, in regard to Texas, that if it should be hereafter, at any time, the pleasure of the government of Texas to cede to the United States a portion, larger or smaller, of her territory which lies adjacent to New Mexico, and north of 36°

30′ of north latitude, to be formed into free States, for a fair equivalent in money or in the payment of her debt, I think it an object well worthy the consideration of Congress, and I shall be happy to concur in it myself, if I should have a connection with the government at that time.

I have one other remark to make. In my observations upon slavery as it has existed in this country, and as it now exists, I have expressed no opinion of the mode of its extinguishment or melioration. I will say, however, though I have nothing to propose, because I do not deem myself so competent as other gentlemen to take any lead on this subject, that if any gentleman from the South shall propose a scheme, to be carried on by this government upon a large scale, for the transportation of free colored people to any colony or any place in the world, I should be quite disposed to incur almost any degree of expense to accomplish that object. Nay, Sir, following an example set more than twenty years ago by a great man, then a Senator from New York, I would return to Virginia, and through her to the whole South, the money received from the lands and territories ceded by her to this government, for any such purpose as to remove, in whole or in part, or in any way to diminish or deal beneficially with, the free colored population of the Southern States. I have said that I honor Virginia for her cession of this territory. There have been received into the treasury of the United States eighty millions of dollars, the proceeds of the sales of the public lands ceded by her. If the residue should be sold at the same rate, the whole aggregate will exceed two hundred millions of dollars. If Virginia and the South see fit to adopt any proposition to relieve themselves from the free people of color among them, or such as may be made free, they have my full consent that the government shall pay them any sum of money out of the proceeds of that cession which may be adequate to the purpose.

And now, Mr. President, I draw these observations to a close. I have spoken freely, and I meant to do so. I have sought to make no display. I have sought to enliven the occasion by no animated discussion, nor have I attempted any train of elaborate argument. I have wished only to speak my sentiments, fully and at length, being desirous, once and for all, to let the Senate know, and to let the country know, the opinions and sentiments which I entertain on all these subjects. These opinions are not likely to be suddenly changed. If there be any future service that I can render to the country, consistently with these sentiments and opinions, I shall cheerfully render it. If there be not, I shall still be glad to have had an opportunity to disburden myself from the bottom of my heart, and to make known every political sentiment that therein exists.

And now, Mr. President, instead of speaking of the possibility or utility of secession, instead of dwelling in those caverns of darkness, instead of groping with those ideas so full of all that is horrid and horrible, let us come out into the light of day; let us enjoy the fresh air of Liberty and Union; let us cherish those hopes which belong to us; let us devote ourselves to those great objects that are fit for our consideration and our action; let us raise our conceptions to the magnitude and the importance of the duties that devolve upon us; let our comprehension be as broad as the country for which we act, our aspirations as high as its certain destiny; let us not be pigmies in a case that calls for men. Never did there devolve on any generation of men higher trusts than now devolve upon us, for the preservation of this Constitution and the harmony and peace of all who are destined to live under it. Let us make our generation one of the strongest and brightest links in that golden chain which is destined, I fondly believe, to grapple the people of all the States to this Constitution for ages to come. We have a great, popular, constitutional government, guarded by law and by judicature, and defended by the affections of the whole people. No monarchical throne presses these States together, no iron chain of military power encircles them; they live and stand under a government popular in its form, representative in its character, founded upon principles of equality, and so constructed, we hope, as to last for ever. In all its history it has been beneficent; it has trodden down no man's liberty; it has crushed no State. Its daily respiration is liberty and patriotism; its yet youthful veins are full of enterprise, courage, and honorable love of glory and renown. Large before, the country has now, by recent events, become vastly larger. This republic now extends, with a vast breadth, across the whole continent. The two great seas of the world wash the one and the other shore. We realize, on a mighty scale, the beautiful description of the ornamental border of the buckler of Achilles:—

> Now, the broad shield complete, the artist crowned
> With his last hand, and poured the ocean round;
> In living silver seemed the waves to roll,
> And beat the buckler's verge, and bound the whole.

THEODORE PARKER

From Three Sermons
 1849, 1854

Theodore Parker (1810–1860) was pastor of the Unitarian congregation in West Roxbury, Massachusetts, a passionate advocate of abolition who supported John Brown and harbored fugitive slaves in his own home. In the excerpts from three sermons reprinted here, his talent for inflammatory oratory is on full display. More than any other figure in nineteenth-century New England, Parker exemplifies how the old religious faith, moderated by Enlightenment rationality and softened by romantic feeling, remained a powerful force for animating collective human action.

In the sermon on conscience (delivered in September 1850), Parker puts into sharp focus the moral issue raised by the passage of the Fugitive Slave Law—odious to him even as it was being defended by such New England luminaries as Senator Daniel Webster and Judge Lemuel Shaw, Chief Justice of the Massachusetts Supreme Judicial Court. He broaches the same issue that Thoreau addressed in the famous essay "Resistance to Civil Government" (1849; generally known as "Civil Disobedience"), and anticipates the dilemma between conscience and law that Shaw's son-in-law, Herman Melville, would pose unforgettably in his late life masterpiece, *Billy Budd.*

In the sermons on poverty (preached in January 1849) and prosperity (November 1854), Parker confronts issues that, a century and a half later, remain vividly with us. His insights into how poverty begets disease, discouragement, and dependence and how prosperity discourages both individual initiative and the sense of human fellowship do not fall easily into the categories—liberal vs. conservative or left vs. right—through which we sometimes try, fruitlessly, to comprehend the American past.

Conscience

Let me suppose a case which may happen here, and before long. A woman flies from South Carolina to Massachusetts to escape from bondage. Mr. Greatheart aids her in her escape, harbors and conceals her, and is brought to trial for it. The punishment is a fine of one thousand dollars and imprisonment for six months. I am drawn to serve as a juror, and pass upon this offense. I may refuse to serve, and be punished for that, leaving men with no scruples to take my place, or I may take the juror's oath to give a verdict according to the law and the testimony. The law is plain, let us suppose, and the testimony conclusive. Greatheart himself confesses that he did the deed alleged, saving one ready to perish. The judge charges, that if the jurors are satisfied of that fact, then they must return that he is guilty. This is a nice matter. Here are two questions. The one, put to me in my official capacity as juror, is this: "Did Greatheart aid the woman?" The other, put to me in my natural character as man, is this: "Will you help punish Greatheart with fine and imprisonment for helping a woman obtain her unalienable rights?" I am to answer both. If I have extinguished my manhood by my juror's oath, then I shall do my official business and find Greatheart guilty, and I shall seem to be a true man; but if I value my manhood, I shall answer after my natural duty to love a man and not hate him, to do him justice, not injustice, to allow him the natural rights he has not alienated, and shall say "Not guilty." Then foolish men, blinded by the dust of courts, may call me forsworn and a liar; but I think human nature will justify the verdict.

In cases of this kind, when justice is on one side and the court on the other, it seems to me a conscientious man must either refuse to serve as a juror, or else return a verdict at variance with the facts and what courts declare to be his official business as juror; but the eyes of some men have been so long blinded by what the court declares is the law, and by its notion of the juror's function, that they will help inflict such a punishment on their brother, and the judge decree the sentence, in a case where the arrest, the verdict, and the sentence are the only wrong in which the prisoner is concerned. It seems to me it is time this matter should be understood, and that it should be known that no official oath can take a man out of the jurisdiction of God's natural law of the universe.

A case may be brought before a commissioner or judge of the United States, to determine whether Daniel is a slave, and therefore to be surrendered up. His official business, sanctioned by his oath, enforced by the law of the land, demands the surrender; his natural duty, sanctioned by his conscience, enforced by absolute justice, forbids the surrender. What shall he do? There is no serving of God and Mammon both. He may abandon his commission and refuse to remain thus halting between two opposites. But if he keeps his office, I see not how he can renounce his nature and send back a fugitive slave, and do as great a wrong as to make a freeman a slave!

Suppose the Constitution had been altered, and Congress had made a law, making it the business of the United States' commissioners to enslave and sell at public outcry all the red-haired men in the nation, and forbid us to aid and abet their escape, to harbor and conceal them, under the same penalties just now mentioned; do you think any commissioner would be justified before God by his oath in kidnapping the red-haired men, or any person in punishing such as harbored or concealed them, such as forcibly took the victims out of the hand of officials who would work mischief by statute? Will the color of a hair make right wrong, and wrong right?

Suppose a man has sworn to keep the Constitution of the United States, and the Constitution is found to be wrong in certain particulars: then his oath is not morally binding, for before his oath, by his very existence, he is morally bound to keep the law of God as fast as he learns it. No oath can absolve him from his natural allegiance to God. Yet I see not how a man can knowingly, and with a good conscience, swear to keep what he deems wrong to keep, and will not keep, and does not intend to keep.

It seems to me very strange that men so misunderstand the rights of conscience and their obligations to obey their country. Not long ago, an eminent man taunted one of his opponents, telling him he had better adhere to the "higher law." The newspapers echoed the sneer, as if there were no law higher than the Constitution. Latterly, the Democratic party, even more completely than the Whig party, seems to have forgotten that there is any law higher than the Constitution, any rights above vested rights.

Poverty

Boston is a strange place; here is energy enough to conquer half the continent in ten years; power of thought to seize and tame the Connecticut and the Merrimac; charity enough to send missionaries all over the world; but not justice enough to found a high school for her own daughters, or to forbid her richest citizens from letting bar-rooms as nurseries of poverty and crime, from opening wide gates which lead to the almshouse, the jail, the gallows, and earthly hell!

Such are the causes of poverty, organic, political, social. You may see families pass from the comfortable to the miserable class, by intemperance, idleness, wastefulness, even by feebleness of body and of mind; yet, while it is common for the rich to descend into the comfortable class, solely by lack of the eminent thrift which raised their fathers thence, or because they lack the common stimulus to toil and save, it is not common for the comfortable to fall into the pit of misery in New England, except through wickedness, through idleness, or intemperance.

It is not easy to study poverty in Boston. But take a little inland town, which few persons migrate into, you will find the miserable families have commonly been so for a hundred years; that many of them are descended from the "servants," or white slaves, brought here by our fathers; that such as fall from the comfortable classes are commonly made miserable by their own fault, sometimes by idleness, which is certainly a sin: for any man who will not work, and persists in living, eats the bread of some other man, either begged or stolen—but chiefly by intemperance. Three-fourths of the poverty of this character is to be attributed to this cause.

Now there is a tendency in poverty to drive the ablest men to work, and so get rid of the poverty; and this I take it is the providential design thereof. Poverty, like an armed man, stalks in the rear of the social march, huge and haggard, and gaunt and grim, to scare the lazy, to goad the idle with his sword, to trample and slay the obstinate sluggard. But he treads also the feeble under his feet, for no fault of theirs, only for the misfortune of being born in the rear of society. But in poverty there is also a tendency to intimidate, to enfeeble, to benumb. The poverty of the strong man compels him to toil; but with the weak, the destruction of the poor is his poverty. An active man is awakened from his sleep by the cold; he arises and seeks more covering; the indolent, or the feeble, shiver on till the morning, benumbed and enfeebled by the cold. So weakness begets weakness; poverty, poverty; intemperance, intemperance; crime, crime.

Everything is against the poor man; he pays the dearest tax, the highest rent for his house, the dearest price for all he eats or wears. The poor cannot watch their opportunity, and take advantage of the markets, as other men. They have the most numerous temptations to intemperance and crime; they have the poorest safeguards from these evils. If the chief value of wealth, as a rich man tells us, be this—that "it renders its owner independent of others," then on what shall the poor men lean, neglected and despised by others, looked on as loathsome, and held in contempt, shut out even from the sermons and the prayers of respectable men? It is no marvel if they cease to respect themselves.

The poor are the most obnoxious to disease; their children are not only most numerous, but most unhealthy. More than half of the children of that class perish at the age of five. Amongst the poor, infectious diseases rage with frightful violence. The mortality in that class is amazing. If things are to continue as now, I thank God it is so. If Death is their only guardian, he is at least powerful, and does not scorn his work.

In addition to the poor, whom these causes have made and kept in poverty, the needy of other lands flock hither. The nobility of old England, so zealous in pursuing their game, in keeping their entails unbroken, and primogeniture safe, have sent their beggary to New England, to be supported by the crumbs that fall from our table. So, in the same New England city, the extremes of society are brought together. Here is health, elegance, cultivation, sobriety, decency, refinement—I wish there was more of it; there is poverty, ignorance, drunkenness, violence, crime, in most odious forms—starvation! We have our

St. Giles's and St. James's; our nobility, not a whit less noble than the noblest of other lands, and our beggars, both in a Christian city. Amid the needy population, misery and death have found their parish. Who shall dare stop his ears, when they preach their awful denunciation of want and woe?

Good men ask, "What shall we do?" Foreign poverty has had this good effect; it has shamed or frightened the American beggar into industry and thrift.

Poverty will not be removed till the causes thereof are removed. There are some who look for a great social revolution. So do I; only I do not look for it to come about suddenly, or by mechanical means. We are in a social revolution, and do not know it. While I cannot accept the peculiar doctrines of the Associationists, I rejoice in their existence. I sympathize with their hope. They point out the evils of society, and that is something. They propose a method of removing its evils. I do not believe in that method, but mankind will probably make many experiments before we hit upon the right one. For my own part, I confess I do not see any way of removing poverty wholly or entirely, in one or two, or in four or five generations. I think it will linger for some ages to come. Like the snow, it is to be removed by a general elevation of the temperature of the air, not all at once; and will long hang about the dark and cold places of the world. But I do think it will at last be overcome, so that a man who cannot subsist will be as rare as a cannibal. "Ye have the poor with you always," said Jesus; and many who remember this, forget that he also said, "And whensoever ye will ye may do them good." I expect to see a mitigation of poverty in this country, and that before long . . .

But now something can be done directly to remove the causes of poverty, something to mitigate their effects; we need both the palliative charity, and the remedial justice. Tenements for the poor can be provided at a cheap rent, that shall yet pay their owner a reasonable income. This has been proved by actual experiment, and, after all that has been said about it, I am amazed that no more is done. I will not exhort the churches to this in the name of religion—they have other matters to attend to; but if capitalists will not, in a place like Boston, it seems to me the city should see that this class of the population is provided with tenements, at a rate not ruinous. It would be good economy to do it, in the pecuniary sense of good economy; certainly to hire money at six per cent., and rent the houses built therewith at eight per cent., would cost less than to support the poor entirely in almshouses, and punish them in jails.

Something yet more may be done, in the way of furnishing them with work, or of directing them to it; something towards enabling them to purchase food and other articles cheap.

Something might be done to prevent street beggary, and begging from house to house, which is rather a new thing in this town. The indiscriminate charity, which it is difficult to withhold from a needy and importunate beggar, does more harm than good . . .

Something can be done for the children of the poor—to promote their education, to find them employment, to snatch these little ones from underneath the feet of that grim poverty. It is not less than awful to think, while there are more children born in Boston of Catholic parents than of Protestant, that yet more than three-fifths thereof die before the sun of their fifth year shines on their luckless heads. I thank God that thus they die. If there be not wisdom enough in society, nor enough justice there to save them from their future long-protracted suffering, than I thank God that Death comes down betimes, and moistens his sickle while his crop is green. I pity not the miserable babes who fall early before that merciful arm of Death. They are at rest. Poverty cannot touch them. Let the mothers who bore them rejoice, but weep only for those that are left—left to ignorance, to misery, to intemperance, to vice that I shall not name; left to the mercies of the jail, and perhaps the gallows at the last. Yet Boston is a Christian city—and it is eighteen hundred years since one great Son of man came to seek and to save that which was lost!

I see not what more can be done directly, and I see not why these things should not be done. Still some will suffer; the idle, the lazy, the proud who will not work, the careless who will voluntarily waste their time, their strength, or their goods—they must suffer, they ought to suffer. Want is the only schoolmaster to teach them industry and thrift. Such as are merely unable, who are poor not by their fault—we do wrong to let them suffer; we do wickedly to leave them to perish. The little children who survive—are they to be left to become barbarians in the midst of our civilization?

Want is not an absolutely needful thing, but very needful for the present distress, to teach us industry, economy, thrift, and its creative arts. There is nature—the whole material world—waiting to serve. "What would you have thereof?" says God. "Pay for it and take it, as you will; only pay as you go!" There are hands to work, heads to think; strong hands, hard heads. God is an economist; He economizes suffering; there is never too much of it in the world for the purpose it is to serve, though it often falls where it should not fall. It is here to teach us industry, thrift, justice. It will be here no more when we have learned its lesson. Want is here on sufferance; misery on sufferance; and mankind can eject them if we will. Poverty, like all evils, is amenable to suppression.

Can we not end this poverty—the misery and crime it brings? No, not today. Can we not lessen it? Soon as we will. Think how much ability there is in this town—cool, far-sighted talent. If some of the ablest men directed their thoughts to the reform of this evil, how much might be done in a single generation; and in a century—what could not they do in a hundred years? What better work is there for able men? I would have it written on my tombstone: "This man had but little wit, and less fame, yet he helped remove the causes of poverty, making men better off and better;" rather by far than this: "Here lies a great man; he had a great place in the world, and great power, and great fame, and made nothing of it, leaving the world no better for his stay therein, and no man better off." . . .

Prosperity

Because they have no changes, therefore they fear not God.—Psalm lv. 19.

By prosperity I mean the present success of schemes which we form for our material purposes. The ambitious man wants power; the acquisitive, money; the vain, admiration; the nation wants numbers, riches, wide territory, commercial and military power. When they succeed in these desires, they attain prosperity. It is the effect of this condition of success on the formation of a moral character which I ask you to consider.

The human race does not thrive very well under circumstances where nature does too much for us: man becomes an animal, or a plant; not also to the same extent a self-directing spirit, with the power to do, to be, and to suffer what becomes a man. In physical geography, there are two extremes equally unfavorable for the higher development of man; namely, the equatorial region, where nature does too much; and the polar region, where she does too little. No high civilization adorns the equatorial day; none such blooms in the polar night. And so there are two analogous extremes in the geography of human condition; polar misfortune, equatorial prosperity. To the eye of man, very little lofty manhood ever comes from the frozen ring wherein are hedged the beggar and the thief, where

"To be born and die
Makes up the sum of human history."

And little comes also from the tropic zone of excessive affluence. I say it is so to the mind of man; but the mind of God takes in alike the circumstances of both, and allows for such as perish on hills of gold, or hills of snow, and doubtless has a compensation somewhere for all that is anywhere suffered by success or by disappointment.

It is a very wise prayer, in the Book of Proverbs—suiting either latitude— "Give me neither poverty nor riches; feed me with food convenient for me; lest I be full, and deny Thee, and say, Who is the Lord? or lest I be poor, and steal, and take the name of my God in vain."

It seems comparatively easy to understand the peril of want, of distress, of cold and hunger. Yet it is difficult, adequately, to appreciate all these—the squalidness of want, the misery of human life, when reduced to its lowest terms of physical misfortune and material barrenness. But that is far easier than to calculate the effects of continual success. Prosperity is not a good schoolmaster to produce the higher forms of character. For that end life must be discipline even more than it is delight. Give a man all that he asks for, and he ruins himself. So under God's providence we are often thwarted and checked by the material and the human world, while we learn the use and beauty of both. Contrary to the wishes of the town and the family, some angel is always troubling the water, that impotent folk may be healed thereby. If continually successful, we grow rash, heedless, vain-glorious, and over-confident. It is stormy seas which breed good sailors, who in stout ships outride the tempest. What a sad world it would be if there were no winter, never a storm! Man would be a mere butterfly, and no more. Adam was turned out of Eden, says the Hebrew mythology, and the Christians mourn thereat. It was his first step towards heaven. He "fell through sin," did he? He fell upward, and by his proper motion has been ever since ascending in laborious flight. It was the tree of spiritual life,

> "Whose mortal taste
> Brought death into the world, and all our woe."

It is amazing how much we need the continual check of failure and disappointment. When the body is over-fed, leanness devours the soul; there is sleekness of flesh, but no great growth of character; the mouth stops the mind. With too many favors we are not thankful. Gratitude is one of the rarest of virtues; the boy does not think so; the man knows it. She comes rather late to the feast of Christian graces, after all that sweet sisterhood have sat down to meat. Gratitude is a nice touch of beauty added last of all to the countenance, giving a classic beauty, an angelic loveliness, to the character. But in our present stage of growth, gratitude to men for their services is by no means common; and thankfulness to God is oftener expressed by the fasting than the feasted. We have a lively sense of favors to come, but humanity is not yet rich enough, nor well enough bred, to be very thankful for what we have in hand. It is only when the well is dry that we appreciate the worth of water, and the first return thereof brings thanks,—which soon dry up and perish. How grateful we should be if we could get the bird in the bush; that in the hand is an old thing not worth thinking of. In jail, Pharaoh's chief butler courts Joseph; but when restored to honor, it is written, "Neither did the chief butler remember Joseph; but forgat him." The boy at college—prosperous, high in his class, welcomed to the society of rich men's sons, and often associating with their daughters—soon forgets the plain-clad sister at Manchester or Lowell, whose toil gave the poor boy his scanty outfit; he feels small gratitude for that tender hand which pushed his little shallop from the shore, and set him afloat on the academic sea, whether her nightly prayer and daily toil attend his now thoughtless voyaging. But when sick, deserted by the gilded, fickle butterfly, which drew his puerile eyes and idle thought, he falls back on the sisterly heart which beats so self-denyingly for him. The Hebrews, settled in their land of hills and valleys, forgot the high hand and outstretched arm which brought them forth from the house of bondage in Egypt, whose unleavened bread and bitter herbs were a healthier sacrament than Canaan's milk and honey. How strange it seems! but look through any village or family, and you see in brief what the world's history has writ on its vast pages, blazoned in luxury and in war . . .

JULIA WARD HOWE

Battle-Hymn of the Republic
 1861

Born in New York City, Julia Ward Howe (1819–1910) moved to Boston with her husband, Samuel Gridley Howe, with whom she maintained a household frequented by intellectuals and reformers. In late 1861, at the suggestion of her friend and fellow abolitionist James Freeman Clarke, Howe set new words to the tune of "John Brown's Body," a song that Union troops were singing on the march in that early stage of the Civil War when the great bloodletting had barely begun. Howe later recalled that as she lay in bed, "the long lines of the desired poem began to twine themselves in my mind," and in order not to forget them, she rose "in the dimness" to write them out with "an old stump of a pen." The result was a work that, unlike most that pass into legend, remains a living part of the culture.

Mine eyes have seen the glory of the coming of the Lord:
He is trampling out the vintage where the grapes of wrath are stored;
He hath loosed the fateful lightning of his terrible swift sword:
    His truth is marching on.

I have seen Him in the watch-fires of a hundred circling camps;
They have builded Him an altar in the evening dews and damps;
I can read His righteous sentence by the dim and flaring lamps.
    His day is marching on.

I have read a fiery gospel, writ in burnished rows of steel:
"As ye deal with my contemners, so with you my grace shall deal;
Let the Hero, born of woman, crush the serpent with his heel,
    Since God is marching on."

He has sounded forth the trumpet that shall never call retreat;
He is sifting out the hearts of men before his judgment-seat:
Oh! be swift, my soul, to answer Him! be jubilant, my feet!
    Our God is marching on.

In the beauty of the lilies Christ was born across the sea,
With a glory in his bosom that transfigures you and me:
As he died to make men holy, let us die to make men free,
    While God is marching on.

LOUISA MAY ALCOTT

Transcendental Wild Oats

 1873

In this mocking but affectionate sketch, Louisa May Alcott (1832–1888) looks back nearly thirty years to the utopian community Fruitlands, for which her father enlisted his wife and daughters in 1843, when Louisa was barely eleven. Bronson Alcott was a man of large vision and small competence, in both the nineteenth-century sense of the word (having little money) and in the more modern sense of possessing none of the practical skills needed for making a farm prosper. Writing about him as the bumbling dreamer Abel Lamb, who turns his family into helpless utopians, his daughter notes in her lightly fictionalized account that "no one knew how" to make candles from vegetable wax—and so, forbidden to burn animal oil in their lamps, they were forced to live largely in the dark.

On the first day of June, 184-, a large wagon, drawn by a small horse and containing a motley load, went lumbering over certain New England hills, with the pleasing accompaniments of wind, rain, and hail. A serene man with a serene child upon his knee was driving, or rather being driven, for the small horse had it all his own way. A brown boy with a William Penn style of countenance sat beside him, firmly embracing a bust of Socrates. Behind them was an energetic-looking woman, with a benevolent brow, satirical mouth, and eyes brimful of hope and courage. A baby reposed upon her lap, a mirror leaned against her knee, and a basket of provisions danced about at her feet, as she struggled with a large, unruly umbrella. Two blue-eyed little girls, with hands full of childish treasures, sat under one old shawl, chatting happily together.

In front of this lively party stalked a tall, sharp-featured man, in a long blue cloak; and a fourth small girl trudged along beside him through the mud as if she rather enjoyed it.

The wind whistled over the bleak hills; the rain fell in a despondent drizzle, and twilight began to fall. But the calm man gazed as tranquilly into the fog as if he beheld a radiant bow of promise spanning the gray sky. The cheery woman tried to cover every one but herself with the big umbrella. The brown boy pillowed his head on the bald pate of Socrates and slumbered peacefully.

The little girls sang lullabies to their dolls in soft, maternal murmurs. The sharp-nosed pedestrian marched steadily on, with the blue cloak streaming out behind him like a banner; the lively infant splashed through the puddles with a duck-like satisfaction pleasant to behold.

Thus these modern pilgrims journeyed hopefully out of the old world, to found a new one in the wilderness.

The editors of *The Transcendental Tripod* had received from Messrs. Lion & Lamb (two of the aforesaid pilgrims) a communication from which the following statement is an extract:

"We have made arrangements with the proprietor of an estate of about a hundred acres which liberates this tract from human ownership. Here we shall prosecute our effort to initiate a Family in harmony with the primitive instincts of man.

"Ordinary secular farming is not our object. Fruit, grain, pulse, herbs, flax, and other vegetable products, receiving assiduous attention, will afford ample manual occupation, and chaste supplies for the bodily needs. It is intended to adorn the pastures with orchards, and to supersede the labor of cattle by the spade and the pruning-knife.

"Consecrated to human freedom, the land awaits the sober culture of devoted men. Beginning with small pecuniary means, this enterprise must be rooted in a reliance on the succors of an ever-bounteous Providence, whose vital affinities being secured by this union with uncorrupted field and unworldly persons, the cares and injuries of a life of gain are avoided.

"The inner nature of each member of the Family is at no time neglected. Our plan contemplates all such disciplines, cultures, and habits as evidently conduce to the purifying of the inmates.

"Pledged to the spirit alone, the founders anticipate no hasty or numerous addition to their numbers. The kingdom of peace is entered only through the gates of self-denial; and felicity is the test and the reward of loyalty to the unswerving law of Love."

This prospective Eden at present consisted of an old red farm-house, a dilapidated barn, many acres of meadow-land, and a grove. Ten ancient apple trees were all the "chaste supply" which the place offered as yet; but, in the firm belief that plenteous orchards were soon to be evoked from their inner consciousness, these sanguine founders had christened their domain Fruitlands.

Here Timon Lion intended to found a colony of Latter Day Saints, who, under his patriarchal sway, should regenerate the world and glorify his name for ever. Here Abel Lamb, with the devoutest faith in the high ideal which was to him a living truth, desired to plant a Paradise, where Beauty, Virtue, Justice, and Love might live happily together, without the possibility of a serpent

entering in. And here his wife, unconverted but faithful to the end, hoped, after many wanderings over the face of the earth, to find rest for herself and a
home for her children.

"There is our new abode," announced the enthusiast, smiling with a satisfaction quite undamped by the drops dripping from his hatbrim, as they
turned at length into a cart-path that wound along a steep hillside into a bar-
ren-looking valley.

"A little difficult of access," observed his practical wife, as she endeavored to
keep her various household gods from going overboard with every lurch of
the laden ark.

"Like all good things. But those who earnestly desire and patiently seek will
soon find us," placidly responded the philosopher from the mud, through
which he was now endeavoring to pilot the much-enduring horse.

"Truth lies at the bottom of a well, Sister Hope," said Brother Timon,
pausing to detach his small comrade from a gate, whereon she was perched for
a clearer gaze into futurity.

"That's the reason we so seldom get at it, I suppose," replied Mrs. Hope,
making a vain clutch at the mirror, which a sudden jolt sent flying out of her
hands.

"We want no false reflections here," said Timon, with a grim smile, as he
crunched the fragments under foot in his onward march.

Sister Hope held her peace, and looked wistfully through the mist at her
promised home. The old red house with a hospitable glimmer at its windows
cheered her eyes; and considering the weather, was a fitter refuge than the syl-
van bowers some of the more ardent souls might have preferred.

The newcomers were welcomed by one of the elect precious—a regenerate
farmer, whose idea of reform consisted chiefly in wearing white cotton raiment and shoes of untanned leather. This costume, with a snowy beard, gave
him a venerable, and at the same time a somewhat bridal appearance.

The goods and chattels of the Society not having arrived, the weary family
reposed before the fire on blocks of wood, while Brother Moses White regaled
them with roasted potatoes, brown bread and water, in two plates, a tin pan,
and one mug—his table service being limited. But, having cast the forms and
vanities of a depraved world behind them, the elders welcomed hardship with
the enthusiasm of new pioneers, and the children heartily enjoyed this fore-
taste of what they believed was to be a sort of perpetual picnic.

During the progress of this frugal meal, two more brothers appeared. One a
dark, melancholy man, clad in homespun, whose particular mission was to
turn his name hind part before and use as few words as possible. The other
was a bland, bearded Englishman, who expected to be saved by eating uncooked food and going without clothes. He had not yet adopted the primitive

costume, however; but contented himself with meditatively chewing dry beans out of a basket.

"Every meal should be a sacrament, and the vessels used beautiful and symbolical," observed Brother Lamb, mildly, righting the tin pan slipping about on his knees. "I priced a silver service when in town, but it was too costly; so I got some graceful cups and vases of Britannia ware."

"Hardest things in the world to keep bright. Will whiting be allowed in the community?" inquired Sister Hope, with a housewife's interest in labor-saving institutions.

"Such trivial questions will be discussed at a more fitting time," answered Brother Timon, sharply, as he burnt his fingers with a very hot potato. "Neither sugar, molasses, milk, butter, cheese, nor flesh are to be used among us, for nothing is to be admitted which has caused wrong or death to man or beast."

"Our garments are to be linen till we learn to raise our own cotton or some substitute for woollen fabrics," added Brother Abel, blissfully basking in an imaginary future as warm and brilliant as the generous fire before him.

"Haou abaout shoes?" asked Brother Moses, surveying his own with interest.

"We must yield that point till we can manufacture an innocent substitute for leather. Bark, wood, or some durable fabric will be invented in time. Meanwhile, those who desire to carry out our idea to the fullest extent can go barefooted," said Lion, who liked extreme measures.

"I never will, nor let my girls," murmured rebellious Sister Hope, under her breath.

"Haou do you cattle'ate to treat the ten-acre lot? Ef things ain't 'tended to right smart, we shan't hev no crops," observed the practical patriarch in cotton.

"We shall spade it," replied Abel, in such perfect good faith that Moses said no more, though he indulged in a shake of the head as he glanced at hands that had held nothing heavier than a pen for years. He was a paternal old soul and regarded the younger men as promising boys on a new sort of lark.

"What shall we do for lamps, if we cannot use any animal substance? I do hope light of some sort is to be thrown upon the enterprise," said Mrs. Lamb, with anxiety, for in those days kerosene and camphene were not, and gas unknown in the wilderness.

"We shall go without till we have discovered some vegetable oil or wax to serve us," replied Brother Timon, in a decided tone, which caused Sister Hope to resolve that her private lamp should always be trimmed, if not burning.

"Each member is to perform the work for which experience, strength, and taste best fit him," continued Dictator Lion. "Thus drudgery and disorder will be avoided and harmony prevail. We shall arise at dawn, begin the day by bathing, followed by music, and then a chaste repast of fruit and bread. Each one finds congenial occupation till the meridian meal; when some deep-searching conversation gives rest to the body and development to the mind. Healthful labor again engages us till the last meal, when we assemble in social communion, prolonged till sunset, when we retire to sweet repose, ready for the next day's activity."

"What part of the work do you incline to yourself?" asked Sister Hope, with a humorous glimmer in her keen eyes.

"I shall wait till it is made clear to me. Being in preference to doing is the great aim, and this comes to us rather by a resigned willingness than a willful activity, which is a check to all divine growth," responded Brother Timon.

"I thought so." And Mrs. Lamb sighed audibly, for during the year he had spent in her family Brother Timon had so faithfully carried out his idea of "being, not doing," that she had found his "divine growth" both an expensive and unsatisfactory process.

Here her husband struck into the conversation, his face shining with the light and joy of the splendid dreams and high ideals hovering before him.

"In these steps of reform, we do not rely so much on scientific reasoning or physiological skill as on the spirit's dictates. The greater part of man's duty consists in leaving alone much that he now does. Shall I stimulate with tea, coffee, or wine? No. Shall I consume flesh? Not if I value health. Shall I subjugate cattle? Shall I claim property in any created thing? Shall I trade? Shall I adopt a form of religion? Shall I interest myself in politics? To how many of these questions—could we ask them deeply enough and could they be heard as having relation to our eternal welfare—would the response be 'Abstain'?"

A mild snore seemed to echo the last word of Abel's rhapsody, for brother Moses had succumbed to mundane slumber and sat nodding like a massive ghost. Forest Absalom, the silent man, and John Pease, the English member, now departed to the barn; and Mrs. Lamb led her flock to a temporary fold, leaving the founders of the "Consociate Family" to build castles in the air till the fire went out and the symposium ended in smoke.

The furniture arrived next day, and was soon bestowed; for the principal property of the community consisted in books. To this rare library was devoted the best room in the house, and the few busts and pictures that still survived many flittings were added to beautify the sanctuary, for here the family was to meet for amusement, instruction, and worship.

Any housewife can imagine the emotions of Sister Hope, when she took possession of a large, dilapidated kitchen, containing an old stove and the peculiar stores out of which food was to be evolved for her little family of eleven.

Cakes of maple sugar, dried peas and beans, barley and hominy, meal of all sorts, potatoes, and dried fruit. No milk, butter, cheese, tea, or meat. appeared. Even salt was considered a useless luxury and spice entirely forbidden by these lovers of Spartan simplicity. A ten years' experience of vegetarian vagaries had been good for training for this new freak, and her sense of the ludicrous supported her through many trying scenes.

Unleavened bread, porridge, and water for breakfast; bread, vegetables, and water for dinner; bread, fruit, and water for supper was the bill of fare ordained by the elders. No teapot profaned that sacred stove, no gory steak cried aloud for vengeance from her chaste gridiron; and only a brave woman's taste, time, and temper were sacrificed on that domestic altar.

The vexed question of light was settled by buying a quantity of bayberry wax for candles; and, on discovering that no one knew how to make them, pine knots were introduced, to be used when absolutely necessary. Being summer, the evenings were not long, and the weary fraternity found it no great hardship to retire with the birds. The inner light was sufficient for most of them. But Mrs. Lamb rebelled. Evening was the only time she had to herself, and while the tired feet rested the skilful hands mended torn frocks and little stockings, or anxious heart forgot its burden in a book.

So "mother's lamp" burned steadily, while the philosophers built a new heaven and earth by moonlight; and through all the metaphysical mists and philanthropic pyrotechnics of that period Sister Hope played her own little game of "throwing light," and none but the moths were the worse for it.

Such farming probably was never seen before since Adam delved. The band of brothers began by spading garden and field; but a few days of it lessened their ardor amazingly. Blistered hands and aching backs suggested the expediency of permitting the use of cattle till the workers were better fitted for noble toil by a summer of the new life.

Brother Moses brought a yoke of oxen from his farm—at least, the philosophers thought so till it was discovered that one of the animals was a cow; and Moses confessed that he "must be let down easy, for he couldn't live on garden sarse entirely."

Great was Dictator Lion's indignation at this lapse from virtue. But time pressed, the work must be done; so the meek cow was permitted to wear the yoke and the recreant brother continued to enjoy forbidden draughts in the barn, which dark proceeding caused the children to regard him as one set apart for destruction.

The sowing was equally peculiar, for, owing to some mistake, the three brethren, who devoted themselves to this graceful task, found when about half through the job that each had been sowing a different sort of grain in the same field; a mistake which caused much perplexity, as it could not be remedied; but, after a long consultation and a good deal of laughter, it was decided to say nothing and see what would come of it.

The garden was planted with a generous supply of useful roots and herbs; but, as manure was not allowed to profane the virgin soil, few of these vegetable treasures ever came up. Purslane reigned supreme, and the disappointed planters ate it philosophically, deciding that Nature knew what was best for them, and would generously supply their needs, if they could only learn to digest her "sallets" and wild roots.

The orchard was laid out, a little grafting done, new trees and vines set, regardless of the unfit season and entire ignorance of the husbandmen, who honestly believed that in the autumn they would reap a bounteous harvest.

Slowly things got into order, and rapidly rumors of the new experiment went abroad, causing many strange spirits to flock thither, for in those days communities were the fashion and transcendentalism raged wildly. Some came to look on and laugh, some to be supported in poetic idleness, a few to believe sincerely and work heartily. Each member was allowed to mount his favorite hobby and ride it to his heart's content. Very queer were some of these riders, and very rampant some of the hobbies.

One youth, believing that language was of little consequence if the spirit was only right, startled newcomers by blandly greeting them with "good morning, damn you," and other remarks of an equally mixed order. A second irrepressible being held that all the emotions of the soul should be freely expressed, and illustrated his theory by antics that would have sent him to a lunatic asylum, if, as an unregenerate wag said, he had not already been in one. When his spirit soared, he climbed trees and shouted; when doubt assailed him, he lay upon the floor and groaned lamentably. At joyful periods, he raced, leaped, and sang; when sad, he wept aloud; and when a great thought burst upon him in the watches of the night, he crowed like a jocund cockerel, to the great delight of the children and the great annoyance of the elders. One musical brother fiddled whenever so moved, sang sentimentally to the four little girls, and put a music-box on the wall when he hoed corn.

Brother Pease ground away at his uncooked food, or browsed over the farm on sorrel, mint, green fruit, and new vegetables. Occasionally he took his walks abroad, airily attired in an unbleached cotton *poncho,* which was the nearest approach to the primeval costume he was allowed to indulge in. At midsummer he retired to the wilderness, to try his plan where the woodchucks were without prejudices and huckleberry bushes were hospitably full. A sunstroke unfortunately spoilt his plan, and he returned to semi-civilization a sadder and wiser man.

Forest Absalom preserved his Pythagorean silence, cultivated his fine dark locks, and worked like a beaver, setting an excellent example of brotherly love, justice, and fidelity by his upright life. He it was who helped overworked Sister Hope with her heavy washes, kneaded the endless succession of batches of bread, watched over the children, and did the many tasks left undone by the brethren, who were so busy discussing and defining great duties that they forgot to perform the small ones.

Moses White placidly plodded about, "chorin' raound," as he called it, looking like an old-time patriarch, with his silver hair and flowing beard, and saving the community from many a mishap by his thrift and Yankee shrewdness.

Brother Lion domineered over the whole concern; for, having put the most money into the speculation, he was resolved to make it pay—as if anything founded on an ideal basis could be expected to do so by any but enthusiasts.

Abel Lamb simply revelled in the Newness, firmly believing that his dream was to be beautifully realized, and in time not only little Fruitlands, but the whole earth, be turned into a Happy Valley. He worked with every muscle of his body, for *he* was in deadly earnest. He taught with his whole head and heart; planned and sacrificed, preached and prophesied, with a soul full of the purest aspirations, most unselfish purposes, and desires for a life devoted to God and man, too high and tender to bear the rough usage of this world.

It was a little remarkable that only one woman ever joined this community. Mrs. Lamb merely followed wheresoever her husband led—"as ballast for his balloon," as she said, in her bright way.

Miss Jane Gage was a stout lady of mature years, sentimental, amiable, and lazy. She wrote verses copiously, and had vague yearnings and graspings after the unknown, which led her to believe herself fitted for a higher sphere than any she had yet adorned.

Having been a teacher, she was set to instructing the children in the common branches. Each adult member took a turn at the infants; and, as each taught in his own way, the result was a chronic state of chaos in the minds of these much-afflicted innocents.

Sleep, food, and poetic musings were the desires of dear Jane's life, and she shirked all duties as clogs upon her spirit's wings. Any thought of lending a hand with the domestic drudgery never occurred to her; and when to the question, "Are there any beasts of burden on the place?" Mrs. Lamb answered, with a face that told its own tale, "Only one woman!" the buxom Jane took no shame to herself, but laughed at the joke, and let the stout-hearted sister tug on alone.

Unfortunately, the poor lady hankered after the fleshpots, and endeavored to stay herself with private sips of milk, crackers, and cheese, and on one dire occasion she partook of fish at a neighbor's table.

One of the children reported this sad lapse from virtue, and poor Jane was publicly reprimanded by Timon.

"I only took a little bit of the tail," sobbed the penitent poetess.

"Yes, but the whole fish had to be tortured and slain that you might tempt your carnal appetite with that one taste of the tail. Know ye not, consumers of flesh meat, that ye are nourishing the wolf and tiger in your bosoms?"

At this awful question and the peal of laughter which arose from some of the younger brethren, tickled by the ludicrous contrast between the stout sinner, the stern judge, and the naughty satisfaction of the young detective, poor Jane fled from the room to pack her trunk, and return to a world where fishes' tails were not forbidden fruit.

Transcendental wild oats were sown broadcast that year, and the fame thereof has not yet ceased in the land; for, futile as this crop seemed to outsiders, it bore an invisible harvest, worth much to those who planted in earnest. As none of the members of this particular community have ever recounted their experiences before, a few of them may not be amiss, since the interest in these attempts has never died out and Fruitlands was the most ideal of all these castles in Spain.

A new dress was invented, since cotton, silk, and wool were forbidden as the product of slave-labor, worm-slaughter, and sheep-robbery. Tunics and trowsers of brown linen were the only wear. The women's skirts were longer, and their straw hat-brims wider than the men's and this was the only difference. Some persecution lent a charm to the costume, and the long-haired, linen-clad reformers quite enjoyed the mild martyrdom they endured when they left home.

Money was abjured, as the root of all evil. The produce of the land was to supply most of their wants, or be exchanged for the few things they could not grow. This idea had its inconveniences; but self-denial was the fashion, and it was surprising how many things one can do without. When they desired to travel, they walked, if possible, begged the loan of a vehicle, or boldly entered car or coach, and, stating their principles to the officials, took the consequences. Usually their dress, their earnest frankness, and gentle resolution won them a passage; but now and then they met with hard usage, and had the satisfaction of suffering for their principles.

On one of these penniless pilgrimages they took passage on a boat, and, when fare was demanded, artlessly offered to talk, instead of pay. As the boat was well under way and they actually had not a cent, there was no help for it. So Brothers Lion and Lamb held forth to the assembled passengers in their most eloquent style. There must have been something effective in this conversation, for the listeners were moved to take up a contribution for these inspired lunatics, who preached peace on earth and goodwill to man so earnestly, with empty pockets. A goodly sum was collected; but when the captain presented it the reformers proved that they were consistent even in their madness, for not a penny would they accept, saying, with a look at the group about them, whose indifference or contempt had changed to interest and respect, "You see how well we get on without money;" and so went serenely on their way, with their linen blouses flapping airily, in the cold October wind.

They preached vegetarianism everywhere and resisted all temptations of the flesh, contentedly eating apples and bread at well-spread tables, and much afflicting hospitable hostesses by denouncing their food and taking away their appetites, discussing the "horrors of shambles," the "incorporation of the brute in man," and "on elegant abstinence the sign of a pure soul." But, when the perplexed or offended ladies asked what they should eat, they got in reply a bill of fare consisting of "bowls of sunrise for breakfast," "solar seeds of the sphere," "dishes from Plutarch's chaste table," and other viands equally hard to find in any modern market.

Reform conventions of all sorts were haunted by these brethren, who said many wise things and did many foolish ones. Unfortunately, these wanderings interfered with their harvest at home; but the rule was to do what the spirit moved, so they left their crops to Providence and went a-reaping in wider and, let us hope, more fruitful fields than their own.

Luckily, the earthly providence who watched over Abel Lamb was at hand to glean the scanty crop yielded by the "uncorrupted land," which, "consecrated to human freedom," had received "the sober culture of devout men."

About the same time the grain was ready to house, some call of the Oversoul wafted all the men away. An easterly storm was coming up and the yellow stacks were sure to be ruined. Then Sister Hope gathered her forces. Three little girls, one boy (Timon's son), and herself, harnessed to clothes-baskets and Russia-linen sheets, were the only teams she could command; but with these poor appliances the indomitable woman got in the grain and saved food for her young, with the instinct and energy of a mother-bird with a brood of hungry nestlings to feed.

This attempt at regeneration had its tragic as well as comic side, though the world only saw the former.

With the first frosts, the butterflies, who had sunned themselves in the new light through the summer, took flight, leaving the few bees to see what honey they had stored for winter use. Precious little appeared beyond the satisfaction of a few months of holy living.

At first it seemed as if a chance to try holy dying was also to be offered them. Timon, much disgusted with the failure of the scheme, decided to retire to the Shakers, who seemed to be the only successful community going.

"What is to become of us?" asked Mrs. Hope, for Abel was heartbroken at the bursting of his lovely bubble.

"You can stay here, if you like, till a tenant is found. No more wood must be cut, however, and no more corn ground. All I have must be sold to pay the debts of the concern, as the responsibility is mine," was the cheering reply.

"Who is to pay us for what we have lost? I gave all I had—furniture, time, strength, six months of my children's lives—and all are wasted. Abel gave himself body and soul, and is almost wrecked by hard work and disappointment. Are we to have no return for this, but leave to starve and freeze in an old house, with winter at hand, no money, and hardly a friend left, for this wild scheme has alienated nearly all we had? You talk much about justice. Let us have a little, since there is nothing else left."

But the woman's appeal met with no reply but the old one: "It was an experiment. We all risked something, and must bear our losses as we can."

With this cold comfort, Timon departed with his son, and was absorbed into the Shaker brotherhood, where he soon found that the order of things was reversed, and it was all work and no play.

Then the tragedy began for the forsaken little family. Desolation and despair fell upon Abel. As his wife said, his new beliefs had alienated many friends. Some thought him mad, some unprincipled. Even the most kindly thought him a visionary, whom it was useless to help till he took more practical views of life. All stood aloof, saying: "Let him work out his own ideas, and see what they are worth."

He had tried, but it was a failure. The world was not ready for Utopia yet, and those who attempted to found it only got laughed at for their pains. In other days, men could sell all and give to the poor, lead lives devoted to holiness and high thought, and after the persecution was over, find themselves honored as saints or martyrs. But in modern times these things are out of fashion. To live for one's principles, at all costs, is a dangerous speculation; and the failure of an ideal, no matter how humane and noble, is harder for the world to forgive and forget than bank robbery or the grand swindles of corrupt politicians.

Deep waters now for Abel, and for a time there seemed no passage through. Strength and spirits were exhausted by hard work and too much thought. Courage failed when, looking about for help, he saw no sympathizing face, no hand outstretched to help him, no voice to say cheerily:

"We all make mistakes, and it takes many experiences to shape a life. Try again, and let us help you."

Every door was closed, every eye averted, every heart cold, and no way open whereby he might earn bread for his children. His principles would not permit him to do many things that others did; and in the few fields where conscience would allow him to work, who would employ a man who had flown in the face of society, as he had done?

Then this dreamer, whose dream was the life of his life, resolved to carry out his idea to the bitter end. There seemed no place for him here—no work, no friend. To go begging conditions was as ignoble as to go begging money. Better perish of want than sell one's soul for the sustenance of his body. Silently he lay down upon his bed, turned his face to the wall, and waited with pathetic patience for death to cut the knot which he could not untie. Days and nights went by, and neither food nor water passed his lips. Soul and body were dumbly struggling together, and no word of complaint betrayed what either suffered.

His wife, when tears and prayers were unavailing, sat down to wait the end with a mysterious awe and submission; for in this entire resignation of all things there was an eloquent significance to her who knew him as no other human being did.

"Leave all to God," was his belief; and in this crisis the loving soul clung to his faith, sure that the All-wise Father would not desert this child who tried to live so near to Him. Gathering her children about her, she waited the issue of the tragedy that was being enacted in that solitary room, while the first snow fell outside, untrodden by the footprints of a single friend.

But the strong angels who sustain and teach perplexed and troubled souls came and went, leaving no trace without, but working miracles within. For, when all other sentiments had faded into dimness, all other hopes died utterly; when the bitterness of death was nearly over, when the body was past any pang of hunger or thirst, and soul stood ready to depart, the love that outlives all else refused to die. Head had bowed to defeat, hand had grown weary with too heavy tasks, but heart could not grow cold to those who live in its tender depths, even when death touched it.

"My faithful wife, my little girls—they have not forsaken me, they are mine by ties that none can break. What right have I to leave them alone? What right to escape from the burden and the sorrow I have helped to bring? This duty remains to me, and I must do it manfully. For their sakes, the world will forgive me in time; for their sakes, God will sustain me now."

Too feeble to rise, Abel groped for the food that always lay within his reach, and in the darkness and solitude of that memorable night ate and drank what was to him the bread and wine of a new communion, a new dedication of heart and life to the duties that were left him when the dreams fled.

In the early dawn, when that sad wife crept fearfully to see what change had come to the patient face on the pillow, she found it smiling at her, saw a wasted hand outstretched to her, and heard a feeble voice cry bravely, "Hope!"

What passed in that little room is not to be recorded except in the hearts of those who suffered and endured much for love's sake. Enough for us to know that soon the wan shadow of a man came forth, leaning on the arm that never failed him, to be welcomed and cherished by the children, who never forgot the experiences of that time.

"Hope" was the watchword now; and, while the last logs blazed on the hearth, the last bread and apples covered the table, the new commander, with recovered courage, said to her husband:

"Leave all to God—and me. He has done his part; now I will do mine."

"But we have no money, dear."

"Yes, we have. I sold all we could spare, and have enough to take us away from this snowbank."

"Where can we go?"

"I have engaged four rooms at our good neighbor, Lovejoy's. There we can live cheaply till spring. Then for new plans and a home of our own, please God."

"But, Hope, your little store won't last long, and we have no friends."

"I can sew and you can chop wood. Lovejoy offers you the same pay as he gives his other men; my old friend, Mrs. Truman, will send me all the work I want; and my blessed brother stands by us to the end. Cheer up, dear heart, for while there is work and love in the world we shall not suffer."

"And while I have my good angel Hope, I shall not despair, even if I wait another thirty years before I step beyond the circle of the sacred little world in which I still have a place to fill."

So one bleak December day, with their few possessions piled on an ox-sled, the rosy children perched atop, and the parents trudging arm in arm behind, the exiles left their Eden and faced the world again.

"Ah, me! my happy dream. How much I leave behind that never can be mine again," said Abel, looking back at the lost Paradise, lying white and chill in its shroud of snow.

"Yes, dear; but how much we bring away," answered brave-hearted Hope, glancing from husband to children.

"Poor Fruitlands! The name was as great a failure as the rest!" continued Abel, with a sigh, as a frost-bitten apple fell from a leafless bough at his feet.

But the sigh changed to a smile as his wife added, in a half-tender, half-satirical tone:

"Don't you think Apple Slump would be a better name for it, dear?"

WILLIAM GRAHAM SUMNER

From What Social Classes Owe to Each Other

 1883

In 1883 William Graham Sumner (1840–1910) published a book under the provocative title *What Social Classes Owe to Each Other.* Many years later, the renowned economist George Stigler is said to have summed up the answer Sumner gave to his own question: "Not a damn thing."

From his post at Yale (where he held that university's first chair in political and social science), Sumner issued a flood of writings attacking what he perceived to be the soft-minded cant of progressive critics of industrial society. Son of an English immigrant who had worked as a railroad machinist (the family was no relation to that of the abolitionist Charles Sumner), Sumner attended Yale, where he studied theology as well as economics. He belongs in the present book as a dissenter from the dissidents—a corrective to the supposition that New England intellectuals were uniformly liberal in their political attitudes. Sumner had contempt for those who saw the world as a battleground between vulnerable workers and predatory employers, and who thought that the state owed the former protection from the latter. In the chapter reprinted here, his implicit targets include Henry George, who had recently proposed a tax on landed wealth, and Charles Francis Adams, Jr., who had written a series of outraged articles about the piratical practices of railroad tycoons.

In some respects, Sumner (who is often described over-simply as a "Social Darwinist") can be understood as a doctrinaire believer in the virtues of the marketplace. He scorns as merely sentimental and squeamish the belief that there is such a thing as too much profit or too much wealth—a venerable New England idea that goes back to the early Puritans, whose proto-modern business ethic never quite displaced the medieval principle that, regardless of consumer demand, goods should not be sold above a "just price." Yet Sumner had a sentimentality of his own that also had roots in an older New England idea: a quasi-providential view of history that regarded raw, unregulated human competition as ultimately directed by some superhuman force toward collectively beneficial ends.

That it is not wicked to be rich; nay, even, that it is not wicked to be richer than one's neighbor

I have before me a newspaper slip on which a writer expresses the opinion that no one should be allowed to possess more than one million dollars' worth of property. Alongside of it is another slip, on which another writer expresses the opinion that the limit should be five millions. I do not know what the comparative wealth of the two writers is, but it is interesting to notice that there is a wide margin between their ideas of how rich they would allow their fellow-citizens to become, and of the point at which they ("the State," of course) would step in to rob a man of his earnings. These two writers only represent a great deal of crude thinking and declaiming which is in fashion. I never have known a man of ordinary common-sense who did not urge upon his sons, from earliest childhood, doctrines of economy and the practice of accumulation. A good father believes that he does wisely to encourage enterprise, productive skill, prudent self-denial, and judicious expenditure on the part of his son. The object is to teach the boy to accumulate capital. If, however, the boy should read many of the diatribes against "the rich" which are afloat in our literature; if he should read or hear some of the current discussion about "capital"; and if, with the ingenuousness of youth, he should take these productions at their literal sense, instead of discounting them, as his father does, he would be forced to believe that he was on the path of infamy when he was earning and saving capital. It is worth while to consider which we mean or what we mean. Is it wicked to be rich? Is it mean to be a capitalist? If the question is one of degree only, and it is right to be rich up to a certain point and wrong to be richer, how shall we find the point? Certainly, for practical purposes, we ought to define the point nearer than between one and five millions of dollars.

There is an old ecclesiastical prejudice in favor of the poor and against the rich. In days when men acted by ecclesiastical rules these prejudices produced waste of capital, and helped mightily to replunge Europe into barbarism. The prejudices are not yet dead, but they survive in our society as ludicrous contradictions and inconsistencies. One thing must be granted to the rich: they are good-natured. Perhaps they do not recognize themselves, for a rich man is even harder to define than a poor one. It is not uncommon to hear a clergyman utter from the pulpit all the old prejudice in favor of the poor and against the rich, while asking the rich to do something for the poor; and the rich comply, without apparently having their feelings hurt at all by the invidious comparison. We all agree that he is a good member of society who works his way up from poverty to wealth, but as soon as he has worked his way up we begin to regard him with suspicion, as a dangerous member of society. A newspaper starts the silly fallacy that "the rich are rich because the poor are industrious," and it is copied from one end of the country to the other as if it were a brilliant apothegm. "Capital" is denounced by writers and speakers who have never taken the trouble to find out what capital is, and who use the word in two or three different senses in as many pages. Labor organizations are formed, not to employ combined effort for a common object, but to indulge in declamation and denunciation, and especially to furnish an easy living to some officers who do not want to work. People who have rejected dogmatic religion, and retained only a residuum of religious sentimentalism, find a special field in the discussion of the rights of the poor and the duties of the rich. We have denunciations of banks, corporations, and monopolies, which denunciations encourage only helpless rage and animosity, because they are not controlled by any definitions or limitations, or by any distinctions between what is indispensably necessary and what is abuse, between what is established in the order of nature and what is legislative error. Think, for instance, of a journal which makes it its special business to denounce monopolies, yet favors a protective tariff, and has not a word to say against trades-unions or patents! Think of public teachers who say that the farmer is ruined by the cost of transportation, when they mean that he cannot make any profits because his farm is too far from the market, and who denounce the railroad because it does not correct for the farmer, at the expense of its stockholders, the disadvantage which lies in the physical situation of the farm! Think of that construction of this situation which attributes all the trouble to the greed of "moneyed corporations!" Think of the piles of rubbish that one has read about corners, and watering stocks, and selling futures!

Undoubtedly there are, in connection with each of these things, cases of fraud, swindling, and other financial crimes; that is to say, the greed and selfishness of men are perpetual. They put on new phases, they adjust themselves to new forms of business, and constantly devise new methods of fraud and robbery, just as burglars devise new artifices to circumvent every new precaution of the lock-makers. The criminal law needs to be improved to meet new forms of crime, but to denounce financial devices which are useful and legitimate because use is made of them for fraud, is ridiculous and unworthy of the age in which we live. Fifty years ago good old English Tories used to denounce all joint-stock companies in the same way, and for similar reasons.

All the denunciations and declamations which have been referred to are made in the interest of "the poor man." His name never ceases to echo in the halls of legislation, and he is the excuse and reason for all the acts which are passed. He is never forgotten in poetry, sermon, or essay. His interest is invoked to defend every doubtful procedure and every questionable institution. Yet where is he? Who is he? Who ever saw him? When did he ever get the benefit of any of the numberless efforts in his behalf? When, rather, were his name and interest ever invoked, when, upon examination, it did not plainly appear that somebody else was to win—somebody who was far too "smart" ever to be poor, far too lazy ever to be rich by industry and economy?

A great deal is said about the unearned increment from land, especially with a view to the large gains of landlords in old countries. The unearned increment from land has indeed made the position of an English land-owner, for the last two hundred years, the most fortunate that any class of mortals ever has enjoyed; but the present moment, when the rent of agricultural land in England is declining under the competition of American land, is not well chosen for attacking the old advantage. Furthermore, the unearned increment from land appears in the United States as a gain to the first comers, who have here laid the foundations of a new State. Since the land is a monopoly, the unearned increment lies in the laws of Nature. Then the only question is, Who shall have it?—the man who has the ownership by prescription, or some or all others? It is a beneficent incident of the ownership of land that a pioneer who reduces it to use, and helps to lay the foundations of a new State, finds a profit in the increasing value of land as the new State grows up. It would be unjust to take that profit away from him, or from any successor to whom he has sold it. Moreover, there is an unearned increment on capital and on labor, due to the presence, around the capitalist and the laborer, of a great, industrious, and prosperous society. A tax on land and a succession or probate duty on capital might be perfectly justified by these facts. Unquestionably capital accumulates with a rapidity which follows in some high series the security, good government, peaceful order of the State in which it is employed; and if the State steps in, on the death of the holder, to claim a share of the inheritance, such a claim may be fully justified. The laborer likewise gains by carrying on his labor in a strong, highly civilized, and well-governed State far more than he could gain with equal industry on the frontier or in the midst of anarchy. He gains greater remuneration for his services, and he also shares in the enjoyment of all that accumulated capital of a wealthy community which is public or semipublic in its nature.

It is often said that the earth belongs to the race, as if raw land was a boon, or gift. Raw land is only a *chance* to prosecute the struggle for existence, and the man who tries to earn a living by the subjugation of raw land makes that attempt under the most unfavorable conditions, for land can be brought into use only by great hardship and exertion. The boon, or gift, would be to get some land after somebody else had made it fit for use. Any one in the world today can have raw land by going to it; but there are millions who would regard it simply as "transportation for life," if they were forced to go and live on new land and get their living out of it. Private ownership of land is only division of labor. If it is true in any sense that we all own the soil in common, the best use we can make of our undivided interests is to vest them all gratuitously (just as we now do) in any who will assume the function of directly treating the soil, while the rest of us take other shares in the social organization. The reason is, because in this way we all get more than we would if each one owned some land and used it directly. Supply and demand now determine the distribution of population between the direct use of land and other pursuits; and if the total profits and chances of land-culture were reduced by taking all the "unearned increment" in taxes, there would simply be a redistribution of industry until the profits of land-culture, less taxes and without chances from increasing value, were equal to the profits of other pursuits under exemption from taxation.

It is remarkable that jealousy of individual property in land often goes along with very exaggerated doctrines of tribal or national property in land. We are told that John, James, and William ought not to possess part of the earth's surface because it belongs to all men; but it is held that Egyptians, Nicaraguans, or Indians have such right to the territory which they occupy, that they may bar the avenues of commerce and civilization if they choose, and that it is wrong to override their prejudices or expropriate their land. The truth is, that the notion that the race own the earth has practical meaning only for the latter class of cases.

The great gains of a great capitalist in a modern state must be put under the head of wages of superintendence. Anyone who believes that any great enterprise of an industrial character can be started without labor must have little experience of life. Let anyone try to get a railroad built, or to start a factory and win reputation for its products, or to start a school and win a reputation for it, or to found a newspaper and make it a success, or to start any other enterprise, and he will find what obstacles must be overcome, what risks must be taken, what perseverance and courage are required, what foresight and sagacity are necessary. Especially in a new country, where many tasks are waiting, where resources are strained to the utmost all the time, the judgment, courage, and perseverance required to organize new enterprizes and carry them to success are sometimes heroic. Persons who possess the necessary qualifications obtain great rewards. They ought to do so. It is foolish to rail at them. Then, again, the ability to organize and conduct industrial, commercial, or financial enterprises is rare; the great captains of industry are as rare as great generals. The great weakness of all co-operative enterprises is in the matter of supervision. Men of routine or men who can do what they are told are not hard to find; but men who can think and plan and tell the routine men what to do are very rare. They are paid in proportion to the supply and demand of them.

If Mr. A. T. Stewart made a great fortune by collecting and bringing dry-goods to the people of the United States, he did so because he understood how to do that thing better than any other man of his generation. He proved it, because he carried the business through commercial crises and war, and kept increasing its dimensions. If, when he died, he left no competent successor, the business must break up, and pass into new organization in the hands of other men. Some have said that Mr. Stewart made his fortune out of those who worked for him or with him. But would those persons have been able to come together, organize themselves, and earn what they did earn without him? Not at all. They would have been comparatively helpless. He and they together formed a great system of factories, stores, transportation, under his guidance and judgment. It was for the benefit of all; but he contributed to it what no one else was able to contribute—the one guiding mind which made the whole thing possible. In no sense whatever does a man who accumulates a fortune by legitimate industry exploit his employés, or make his capital "out of" anybody else. The wealth which he wins would not be but for him.

The aggregation of large fortunes is not at all a thing to be regretted. On the contrary, it is a necessary condition of many forms of social advance. If we should set a limit to the accumulation of wealth, we should say to our most valuable producers, "We do not want you to do us the services which you best understand how to perform, beyond a certain point." It would be like killing off our generals in war. A great deal is said, in the cant of a certain school about "ethical views of wealth," and we are told that some day men will be found of such public spirit that, after they have accumulated a few millions, they will be willing to go on and labor simply for the pleasure of paying the taxes of their fellow-citizens. Possibly this is true. It is a prophecy. It is as impossible to deny it as it is silly to affirm it. For if a time ever comes when there are men of this kind, the men of that age will arrange their affairs accordingly. There are no such men now, and those of us who live now cannot arrange our affairs by what men will be a hundred generations hence.

There is every indication that we are to see new developments of the power of aggregated capital to serve civilization, and that the new developments will be made right here in America. Joint-stock companies are yet in their infancy, and incorporated capital, instead of being a thing which can be overturned, is a thing which is becoming more and more indispensable. I shall have something to say in another chapter about the necessary checks and guarantees, in a political point of view, which must be established. Economically speaking, aggregated capital will be more and more essential to the performance of our social tasks. Furthermore, it seems to me certain that all aggregated capital will fall more and more under personal control. Each great company will be known as controlled by one master mind. The reason for this lies in the great superiority of personal management over management by boards and committees. This tendency is in the public interest, for it is in the direction of more satisfactory responsibility. The great hindrance to the development of this continent has lain in the lack of capital. The capital which we have had has been wasted by division and dissipation, and by injudicious applications. The waste of capital, in proportion to the total capital, in this country between 1800 and 1850, in the attempts which were made to establish means of communication and transportation, was enormous. The waste was chiefly due to ignorance and bad management, especially to State control of public works. We are to see the development of the country pushed forward at an unprecedented rate by an aggregation of capital, and a systematic application of it under the direction of competent men. This development will be for the benefit of all, and it will enable each one of us, in his measure and way, to increase his wealth. We may each of us go ahead to do so, and we have every reason to rejoice in each other's prosperity. There ought to be no laws to guarantee property against the folly of its possessors. In the absence of such laws, capital inherited by a spendthrift will be squandered and re-accumulated in the hands of men who are fit and competent to hold it. So it should be, and under such a state of things there is no reason to desire to limit the property which any man may acquire.

OLIVER WENDELL HOLMES, JR.

Natural Law

 1918

Oliver Wendell Holmes, Jr. (1841–1935) inherited not only his name but also a tradition of public-spiritedness from his eminent father (1809–1894), a leading member of the New England intellectual scene for most of the nineteenth century. Before completing his senior year at Harvard, the younger Holmes enlisted in the Union army, and during his service was repeatedly and seriously wounded. His youthful idealism seemed never to wane—and he made himself over his long life into the pre-eminent legal authority in the English-speaking world.

His conception of law is perhaps best expressed in his classic 1897 lecture delivered at Boston University, "The Path of the Law" (too long to reprint here), in which he argued that though the law is "the witness and external deposit of our moral life," it is best understood as an always evolving series of constraints whose power resides in the threat of penalty. The virtue of particular laws must be judged not according to some abstract principle but by their consequences for society at large. Thus, law necessarily must change as society changes.

Holmes's irreverence and iconoclasm were construed by some as cynicism. In fact, he was a latter-day exemplar of an old New England impatience with those who revere established forms for their own sake. "It is revolting," he writes, "to have no better reason for a rule of law than that so it was laid down in the time of Henry IV. It is still more revolting if the grounds upon which it was laid down have vanished long since, and the rule simply persists from blind imitation of the past."

At roughly the midpoint of his service as an Associate Justice of the United States Supreme Court (he was appointed by President Theodore Roosevelt in 1902, and retired upon the election of Franklin Roosevelt in 1932), he published this brilliant short essay, "Natural Law," in the *Harvard Law Review*. It makes short work of the notion that the norms of our local society have any claim on us as transcendent truths, but it puts forth a bracing and capacious vision of history as the process by which society pushes past provincial boundaries to embrace the "common wants and ideals that we find in man."

It is not enough for the knight of romance that you agree that his lady is a very nice girl—if you do not admit that she is the best that God ever made or will make, you must fight. There is in all men a demand for the superlative, so much so that the poor devil who has no other way of reaching it attains it by getting drunk. It seems to me that this demand is at the bottom of the philosopher's effort to prove that truth is absolute and of the jurist's search for criteria of universal validity which he collects under the head of natural law.

I used to say, when I was young, that truth was the majority vote of that nation that could lick all others. Certainly we may expect that the received opinion about the present war will depend a good deal upon which side wins (I hope with all my soul it will be mine), and I think that the statement was correct in so far as it implied that our test of truth is a reference to either a present or an imagined future majority in favor of our view. If, as I have suggested elsewhere, the truth may be defined as the system of any (intellectual) limitations, what gives it objectivity is the fact that I find my fellow man to a greater or less extent (never wholly) subject to the same *Can't Helps.* If I think that I am sitting at a table I find that the other persons present agree with me; so if I say that the sum of the angles of a triangle is equal to two right angles. If I am in a minority of one they send for a doctor or lock me up; and I am so far able to transcend the to me convincing testimony of my senses or my reason as to recognize that if I am alone probably something is wrong with my works.

Certitude is not the test of certainty. We have been cock-sure of many things that were not so. If I may quote myself again, property, friendship, and truth have a common root in time. One can not be wrenched from the rocky crevices into which one has grown for many years without feeling that one is attacked in one's life. What we most love and revere generally is determined by early associations. I love granite rocks and barberry bushes, no doubt because with them were my earliest joys that reach back through the past eternity of my life. But while one's experience thus makes certain preferences dogmatic for oneself, recognition of how they came to be so leaves one able to see that others, poor souls, may be equally dogmatic about something else. And this again means scepticism. Not that one's belief or love does not remain. Not that we would not fight and die for it if important—we all, whether we know it or not, are fighting to make the kind of a world that we should like— but that we have learned to recognize that others will fight and die to make a different world, with equal sincerity or belief. Deep-seated preferences can not be argued about—you can not argue a man into liking a glass of beer— and therefore, when differences are sufficiently far reaching, we try to kill the other man rather than let him have his way. But that is perfectly consistent with admitting that, so far as appears, his grounds are just as good as ours.

The jurists who believe in natural law seem to me to be in that naïve state of mind that accepts what has been familiar and accepted by them and their neighbors as something that must be accepted by all men everywhere. No doubt it is true that, so far as we can see ahead, some arrangements and the rudiments of familiar institutions seem to be necessary elements in any society that may spring from our own and that would seem to us to be civilized— some form of permanent association between the sexes—some residue of property individually owned—some mode of binding oneself to specified future conduct—at the bottom of all, some protection for the person. But without speculating whether a group is imaginable in which all but the last of these might disappear and the last be subject to qualifications that most of us would abhor, the question remains as to the *Ought* of natural law.

It is true that beliefs and wishes have a transcendental basis in the sense that their foundation is arbitrary. You can not help entertaining and feeling them, and there is an end of it. As an arbitrary fact people wish to live, and we say with various degrees of certainty that they can do so only on certain conditions. To do it they must eat and drink. That necessity is absolute. It is a necessity of less degree but practically general that they should live in society. If they live in society, so far as we can see, there are further conditions. Reason working on experience does tell us, no doubt, that if our wish to live continues, we can do it only on those terms. But that seems to me the whole of the matter. I see no *a priori* duty to live with others and in that way, but simply a statement of what I must do if I wish to remain alive. If I do live with others they tell me that I must do and abstain from doing various things or they will put the screws on to me. I believe that they will, and being of the same mind as to their conduct I not only accept the rules but come in time to accept them with sympathy and emotional affirmation and begin to talk about duties and rights. But for legal purposes a right is only the hypostasis of a prophecy—the imagination of a substance supporting the fact that the public force will be brought to bear upon those who do things said to contravene it—just as we talk of the force of gravitation accounting for the conduct of bodies in space. One phrase adds no more than the other to what we know without it. No doubt behind these legal rights is the fighting will of the subject to maintain them, and the spread of his emotions to the general rules by which they are maintained; but that does not seem to me the same thing as the supposed *a priori* discernment of a duty or the assertion of a preëxisting right. A dog will fight for his bone.

The most fundamental of the supposed preëxisting rights—the right of life—is sacrificed without a scruple not only in war, but whenever the interest of society, that is, of the predominant power in the community, is thought to demand it. Whether that interest is the interest of mankind in the long run no one can tell, and as, in any event, to those who do not think with Kant and Hegel it is only an interest, the sanctity disappears. I remember a very tender-hearted judge being of opinion that closing a hatch to stop a fire and the destruction of a cargo was justified even if it was known that doing so would stifle a man below. It is idle to illustrate further, because to those who agree with me I am uttering commonplaces and to those who disagree I am ignoring the necessary foundations of thought. The *a priori* men generally call the dissentients superficial. But I do agree with them in believing that one's attitude on these matters is closely connected with one's general attitude toward the universe. Proximately, as has been suggested, it is determined largely by early associations and temperament, coupled with the desire to have an absolute guide. Men to a great extent believe what they want to—although I see in that no basis for a philosophy that tells us what we should want to want.

Now when we come to our attitude toward the universe I do not see any rational ground for demanding the superlative—for being dissatisfied unless we are assured that our truth is cosmic truth, if there is such a thing—that the ultimates of a little creature on this little earth are the last word of the unimaginable whole. If a man sees no reason for believing that significance, consciousness and ideals are more than marks of the finite, that does not justify what has been familiar in French sceptics; getting upon a pedestal and professing to look with haughty scorn upon a world in ruins. The real conclusion is that the part can not swallow the whole—that our categories are not, or may not be, adequate to formulate what we cannot know. If we believe that we come out of the universe, not it out of us, we must admit that we do not know what we are talking about when we speak of brute matter. We do know that a certain complex of energies can wag its tail and another can make syllogisms. These are among the powers of the unknown, and if, as may be, it has still greater powers that we can not understand, as Fabre in his studies of instinct would have us believe, studies that gave Bergson one of the strongest strands for his philosophy and enabled Maeterlinck to make us fancy for a moment that we heard a clang from behind phenomena—if this be true, why should we not be content? Why should we employ the energy that is furnished to us by the cosmos to defy it and shake our fist at the sky? It seems to me silly.

That the universe has in it more than we understand, that the private soldiers have not been told the plan of campaign, or even that there is one, rather than some vaster unthinkable to which every predicate is an impertinence, has no bearing upon our conduct. We still shall fight—all of us because we want to live, some, at least, because we want to realize our spontaneity and prove our powers, for the joy of it, and we may leave to the unknown the supposed final valuation of that which in any event has value to us. It is enough for us that the universe has produced us and has within it, as less than it, all that we believe and love. If we think of our existence not as that of a little god outside, but as that of a ganglion within, we have the infinite behind us. It gives us our only but our adequate significance. A grain of sand has the same, but what competent person supposes that he understands a grain of sand? That is as much beyond our grasp as man. If our imagination is strong enough to accept the vision of ourselves as parts inseverable from the rest, and to extend our final interest beyond the boundary of our skins, it justifies the sacrifice even of our lives for ends outside of ourselves. The motive, to be sure, is the common wants and ideals that we find in man. Philosophy does not furnish motives, but it shows men that they are not fools for doing what they already want to do. It opens to the forlorn hopes on which we throw ourselves away, the vista of the farthest stretch of human thought, the chords of a harmony that breathes from the unknown.

John F. Kennedy

Broadcast Address

 1963

In early June 1963, as public tension rose over the national civil rights crisis, political maneuvering became fast and furious. Brutal police attacks on blacks demonstrating against segregation in Birmingham, Alabama, and more recently in Danville, Virginia, were fresh in the memory. Governor George Wallace had staged a piece of political theater by allowing two black students to enroll at the University of Alabama while, on national television, he stood "in the schoolhouse door," symbolically defying the Assistant United States Attorney General with words about Alabamians being "God-fearing people, not government-fearing people." Pressure was mounting on President John F. Kennedy (1917–1963)—whose Boston Irish roots and patrician Harvard finish made his sincerity on the issue of racial justice suspect to many blacks—to proclaim his commitment to the civil rights legislation that Congress was about to consider. Dr. Martin Luther King, Jr., made it clear to the President that the strategy of nonviolence might not hold the allegiance of black Americans much longer.

On the morning of Tuesday, June 11, President Kennedy told his advisors that he was going to go on television and radio that night to speak about civil rights. They scrambled to produce a draft speech, which the President found stiff and which he proceeded to revise by dictating changes to his secretary virtually up to the moment he went on the air. The result, as King wrote to Kennedy immediately after the broadcast that night, "was one of the most eloquent, profound, and unequivocal pleas for Justice and the Freedom of all men ever made by any President." It was a signal moment in the process—to be accelerated by President Lyndon Johnson after Kennedy's assassination five months later—by which the United States government put its full force behind the principle of racial equality. And though it was the work of several hands (Theodore Sorensen and Louis Martin were its chief contributors), Kennedy's speech expressed a personal passion on the issue previously unheard from a sitting president. The depth of the crisis to which he had spoken was confirmed a few hours later when, in Jackson, Mississippi, the civil rights leader Medgar Evers was shot to death outside his house while his wife and children waited for him to come home.

Good evening, my fellow citizens:

This afternoon, following a series of threats and defiant statements, the presence of Alabama National Guardsmen was required on the University of Alabama to carry out the final and unequivocal order of the United States District Court of the Northern District of Alabama. That order called for the admission of two clearly qualified young Alabama residents who happened to have been born Negro.

That they were admitted peacefully on the campus is due in good measure to the conduct of the students of the University of Alabama, who met their responsibilities in a constructive way.

I hope that every American, regardless of where he lives, will stop and examine his conscience about this and other related incidents. This Nation was founded by men of many nations and backgrounds. It was founded on the principle that all men are created equal, and that the rights of every man are diminished when the rights of one man are threatened.

Today we are committed to a worldwide struggle to promote and protect the rights of all who wish to be free. And when Americans are sent to Viet-Nam or West Berlin, we do not ask for whites only. It ought to be possible, therefore, for American students of any color to attend any public institution they select without having to be backed up by troops.

It ought to be possible for American consumers of any color to receive equal service in places of public accommodation, such as hotels and restaurants and theaters and retail stores, without being forced to resort to demonstrations in the street, and it ought to be possible for American citizens of any color to register and to vote in a free election without interference or fear of reprisal.

It ought to be possible, in short, for every American to enjoy the privileges of being American without regard to his race or his color. In short, every American ought to have the right to be treated as he would wish to be treated, as one would wish his children to be treated. But this is not the case.

The Negro baby born in America today, regardless of the section of the Nation in which he is born, has about one-half as much chance of completing a high school as a white baby born in the same place on the same day, one-third as much chance of completing college, one-third as much chance of becoming a professional man, twice as much chance of becoming unemployed, about one-seventh as much chance of earning $10,000 a year, a life expectancy which is 7 years shorter, and the prospects of earning only half as much.

This is not a sectional issue. Difficulties over segregation and discrimination exist in every city, in every State of the Union, producing in many cities a rising tide of discontent that threatens the public safety. Nor is this a partisan issue. In a time of domestic crisis men of good will and generosity should be able to unite regardless of party or politics. This is not even a legal or legislative issue alone. It is better to settle these matters in the courts than on the streets, and new laws are needed at every level, but law alone cannot make men see right.

We are confronted primarily with a moral issue. It is as old as the scriptures and is as clear as the American Constitution.

The heart of the question is whether all Americans are to be afforded equal rights and equal opportunities, whether we are going to treat our fellow Americans as we want to be treated. If an American, because his skin is dark, cannot eat lunch in a restaurant open to the public, if he cannot send his children to the best public school available, if he cannot vote for the public officials who represent him, if, in short, he cannot enjoy the full and free life which all of us want, then who among us would be content to have the color of his skin changed and stand in his place? Who among us would then be content with the counsels of patience and delay?

One hundred years of delay have passed since President Lincoln freed the slaves, yet their heirs, their grandsons, are not fully free. They are not yet freed from the bonds of injustice. They are not yet freed from social and economic oppression. And this Nation, for all its hopes and all its boasts, will not be fully free until all its citizens are free.

We preach freedom around the world, and we mean it, and we cherish our freedom here at home, but are we to say to the world, and much more importantly, to each other that this is a land of the free except for the Negroes; that we have no second-class citizens except Negroes; that we have no class or caste system, no ghettoes, no master race except with respect to Negroes?

Now the time has come for this Nation to fulfill its promise. The events in Birmingham and elsewhere have so increased the cries for equality that no city or State or legislative body can prudently choose to ignore them.

The fires of frustration and discord are burning in every city, North and South, where legal remedies are not at hand. Redress is sought in the streets, in demonstrations, parades, and protests which create tensions and threaten violence and threaten lives.

We face, therefore, a moral crisis as a country and as a people. It cannot be met by repressive police action. It cannot be left to increased demonstrations in the streets. It cannot be quieted by token moves or talk. It is a time to act in the Congress, in your State and local legislative body and, above all, in all of our daily lives.

It is not enough to pin the blame on others, to say this is a problem of one section of the country or another, or deplore the fact that we face. A great change is at hand, and our task, our obligation, is to make that revolution, that change, peaceful and constructive for all.

Those who do nothing are inviting shame as well as violence. Those who act boldly are recognizing right as well as reality.

Next week I shall ask the Congress of the United States to act, to make a commitment it has not fully made in this century to the proposition that race has no place in American life or law. The Federal judiciary has upheld that proposition in a series of forthright cases. The executive branch has adopted that proposition in the conduct of its affairs, including the employment of Federal personnel, the use of Federal facilities, and the sale of federally financed housing.

But there are other necessary measures which only the Congress can provide, and they must be provided at this session. The old code of equity law under which we live commands for every wrong a remedy, but in too many communities, in too many parts of the country, wrongs are inflicted on Negro citizens and there are no remedies at law. Unless the Congress acts, their only remedy is in the street.

I am, therefore, asking the Congress to enact legislation giving all Americans the right to be served in facilities which are open to the public—hotels, restaurants, theaters, retail stores, and similar establishments.

This seems to me to be an elementary right. Its denial is an arbitrary indignity that no American in 1963 should have to endure, but many do.

I have recently met with scores of business leaders urging them to take voluntary action to end this discrimination and I have been encouraged by their response, and in the last 2 weeks over 75 cities have seen progress made in desegregating these kinds of facilities. But many are unwilling to act alone, and for this reason, nationwide legislation is needed if we are to move this problem from the streets to the courts.

I am also asking Congress to authorize the Federal Government to participate more fully in lawsuits designed to end segregation in public education. We have succeeded in persuading many districts to desegregate voluntarily. Dozens have admitted Negroes without violence. Today a Negro is attending a State-supported institution in every one of our 50 States, but the pace is very slow.

Too many Negro children entering segregated grade schools at the time of the Supreme Court's decision 9 years ago will enter segregated high schools this fall, having suffered a loss which can never be restored. The lack of an adequate education denies the Negro a chance to get a decent job.

The orderly implementation of the Supreme Court decision, therefore, cannot be left solely to those who may not have the economic resources to carry the legal action or who may be subject to harassment.

Other features will be also requested, including greater protection for the right to vote. But legislation, I repeat, cannot solve this problem alone. It must be solved in the homes of every American in every community across our country.

In this respect, I want to pay tribute to those citizens North and South who have been working in their communities to make life better for all. They are acting not out of a sense of legal duty but out of a sense of human decency.

Like our soldiers and sailors in all parts of the world they are meeting freedom's challenge on the firing line, and I salute them for their honor and their courage.

My fellow Americans, this is a problem which faces us all—in every city of the North as well as the South. Today there are Negroes unemployed, two or three times as many compared to whites, inadequate in education, moving into the large cities, unable to find work, young people particularly out of work without hope, denied equal rights, denied the opportunity to eat at a restaurant or lunch counter or go to a movie theater, denied the right to a decent education, denied almost today the right to attend a State university even though qualified. It seems to me that these are matters which concern us all, not merely Presidents or Congressmen or Governors, but every citizen of the United States.

This is one country. It has become one country because all of us and all the people who came here had an equal chance to develop their talents.

We cannot say to 10 percent of the population that you can't have that right; that your children can't have the chance to develop whatever talents they have; that the only way that they are going to get their rights is to go into the streets and demonstrate. I think we owe them and we owe ourselves a better country than that.

Therefore, I am asking for your help in making it easier for us to move ahead and to provide the kind of equality of treatment which we would want ourselves; to give a chance for every child to be educated to the limit of his talents.

As I have said before, not every child has an equal talent or an equal ability or an equal motivation, but they should have the equal right to develop their talent and their ability and their motivation, to make something of themselves.

We have a right to expect that the Negro community will be responsible, will uphold the law, but they have a right to expect that the law will be fair, that the Constitution will be color blind, as Justice Harlan said at the turn of the century.

This is what we are talking about and this is a matter which concerns this country and what it stands for, and in meeting it I ask the support of all our citizens.

Thank you very much.

A. Bartlett Giamatti

The Green Fields of the Mind

 1977

"From the beginning of the world," Jonathan Edwards wrote in 1747, "the state of the church has appeared most dark . . . before some remarkable deliverance and advancement." Since the last World Series victory by the Boston Red Sox, in 1918, this creed has given comfort to those still waiting for the day of deliverance for their beloved team—a team amazingly adept at "snatching defeat," as the saying goes, "from the jaws of victory." While serving as President of Yale University, A. Bartlett Giamatti (1938–1989), who went on to become Commissioner of Baseball (and died just a week after banishing Pete Rose from the game for his gambling activities), turned the experience of a lifelong Red Sox fan into this lyrical meditation on hope.

It breaks your heart. It is designed to break your heart. The game begins in the spring, when everything else begins again, and it blossoms in the summer, filling the afternoons and evenings, and then as soon as the chill rains come, it stops and leaves you to face the fall alone. You count on it, rely on it to buffer the passage of time, to keep the memory of sunshine and high skies alive, and then just when the days are all twilight, when you need it most, it stops. Today, October 2, a Sunday of rain and broken branches and leaf-clogged drains and slick streets, it stopped, and summer was gone.

Somehow, the summer seemed to slip by faster this time. Maybe it wasn't this summer, but all the summers that, in this my fortieth summer, slipped by so fast. There comes a time when every summer will have something of autumn about it. Whatever the reason, it seemed to me that I was investing more and more in baseball, making the game do more of the work that keeps time fat and slow and lazy. I was counting on the game's deep patterns, three strikes, three outs, three times three innings, and its deepest impulse, to go out and back, to leave and to return home, to set the order of the day and to organize the daylight. I wrote a few things this last summer, this summer that did not last, nothing grand but some things, and yet that work was just camouflage. The real activity was done with the radio—not the all-seeing, all-falsifying television—and was the playing of the game in the only place it will last, the enclosed green field of the mind. There, in that warm, bright place, what the old poet called Mutability does not so quickly come.

But out here, on Sunday, October 2, where it rains all day, Dame Mutability never loses. She was in the crowd at Fenway yesterday, a gray day full of bluster and contradiction, when the Red Sox came up in the last of the ninth trailing Baltimore 8–5, while the Yankees, rain-delayed against Detroit, only needing to win one or have Boston lose one to win it all, sat in New York washing down cold cuts with beer and watching the Boston game. Boston had won two, the Yankees had lost two, and suddenly it seemed as if the whole season might go to the last day, or beyond, except here was Boston losing 8–5, while New York sat in its family room and put its feet up. Lynn, both ankles hurting now as they had in July, hits a single down the right-field line. The crowd stirs. It is on its feet. Hobson, third baseman, former Bear Bryant quarterback, strong, quiet, over 100 RBIs, goes for three breaking balls and is out. The goddess smiles and encourages her agent, a canny journeyman named Nelson Briles.

Now comes a pinch hitter, Bernie Carbo, onetime Rookie of the Year, erratic, quick, a shade too handsome, so laid-back he is always, in his soul, stretched out in the tall grass, one arm under his head, watching the clouds and laughing; now he looks over some low stuff unworthy of him and then, uncoiling, sends one out, straight on a rising line, over the center-field wall, no cheap Fenway shot, but all of it, the physics as elegant as the arc the ball describes.

New England is on its feet, roaring. The summer will not pass. Roaring, they recall the evening, late and cold, in 1975, the sixth game of the World Series, perhaps the greatest baseball game played in the last fifty years, when Carbo, loose and easy, had uncoiled to tie the game that Fisk would win. It is 8–7, one out, and school will never start, rain will never come, sun will warm the back of your neck forever. Now Bailey, picked up from the National League recently, big arms, heavy gut, experienced, new to the league and the club; he fouls off two and then, checking, tentative, a big man off balance, he pops a soft liner to the first baseman. It is suddenly darker and later, and the announcer doing the game coast to coast, a New Yorker who works for a New York television station, sounds relieved. His little world, well-lit, hot-combed, split-second-timed, had no capacity to absorb this much gritty, grainy, contrary reality.

Cox swings a bat, stretches his long arms, bends his back, the rookie from Pawtucket who broke in two weeks earlier with a record six straight hits, the kid drafted ahead of Fred Lynn, rangy, smooth, cool. The count runs two and two, Briles is cagey, nothing too good, and Cox swings, the ball beginning toward the mound and then, in a jaunty, wayward dance, skipping past Briles, fainting to the right, skimming the last of the grass, finding the dirt, moving now like some small, purposeful marine creature negotiating the green deep, easily avoiding the jagged rock of second base, traveling steady and straight now out into the dark, silent recesses of center field.

The aisles are jammed, the place is on its feet, the wrappers, the programs, the Coke cups and peanut shells, the doctrines of an afternoon; the anxieties, the things that have to be done tomorrow, the regrets about yesterday, the accumulation of a summer: all forgotten, while hope, the anchor, bites and takes hold where a moment before it seemed we would be swept out with the tide. Rice is up. Rice whom Aaron had said was the only one he'd seen with the ability to break his records. Rice the best clutch hitter on the club, with the best slugging percentage in the league. Rice, so quick and strong he once checked his swing halfway through and snapped the bat in two. Rice the Hammer of God sent to scourge the Yankees, the sound was overwhelming, fathers pounded their sons on the back, cars pulled off the road, households froze, New England exulted in its blessedness, and roared its thanks for all good things, for Rice and for a summer stretching halfway through October. Briles threw, Rice swung, and it was over. One pitch, a fly to center, and it stopped. Summer died in New England and like rain sliding off a roof, the crowd slipped out of Fenway, quickly, with only a steady murmur of concern for the drive ahead remaining of the roar. Mutability had turned the seasons and translated hope to memory once again. And, once again, she had used baseball, our best invention to stay change, to bring change on. That is why it breaks my heart, that game—not because in New York they could win because Boston lost; in that, there is a rough justice, and a reminder to the Yankees of how slight and fragile are the circumstances that exalt one group of human beings over another. It breaks my heart because it was meant to, because it was meant to foster in me again the illusion that there was something abiding, some pattern and some impulse that could come together to make a reality that would resist the corrosion; and because, after it had fostered again that most hungered-for illusion, the game was meant to stop, and betray precisely what it promised.

Of course, there are those who learn after the first few times. They grow out of sports. And there are others who were born with the wisdom to know that nothing lasts. These are the truly tough among us, the ones who can live without illusion, or without even the hope of illusion. I am not that grown-up or up-to-date. I am a simpler creature, tied to more primitive patterns and cycles. I need to think something lasts forever, and it might as well be that state of being that is a game; it might as well be that, in a green field, in the sun.

Strangers in the Promised Land

EARLY NEW ENGLAND developed as a land of closely knit villages that were, at least according to myth, ideal communities fostering virtuous citizenship through open institutions such as the town meeting. But New England has also been brutally hostile to immigrants, outsiders, or anyone deemed deviant according to prevailing norms. One strategy adopted by those who have endured the searing experience of exclusion has been to hold New England accountable to its own proclaimed standards of equity and justice. Several of the following selections do so with great eloquence. Others belong to the rich literature of what is conventionally called assimilation, the wrenching process by which newcomers—half-willingly, half-coerced—accommodate themselves to their new world.

African Meeting House, Boston, around 1860

The Salem Court

Examination of Susanna Martin

 1692

The infamous events at Salem, Massachusetts, in 1692 can be briefly summarized. In the winter of 1691–92, erratic behavior—"fits" and "foolish speeches," as one observer described them—was noticed among a few young girls, and "witchcraft" began to be murmured as an explanation. When "natural" causes for the girls' behavior could not be found, and when a West Indian slave named Tituba confessed to taking girls into the woods for nighttime revels with the devil, the murmur became a full hue and cry. By spring, the jails were jammed with women, men, and children accused of participating in witchcraft, and a special court was appointed by the governor to proceed with interrogations and prosecutions—which it did with flagrant disregard of basic rules of evidence. This shameful episode in the history of New England did not close before nineteen persons were hanged and one pressed to death by stones.

Ultimately, those on the side of the prosecutors (notably Cotton Mather) suffered damage to their contemporary and historical reputations, and a number of participants, including Samuel Sewall, publicly asked forgiveness from the families of the victims. Among them, Susanna Martin, whose interrogation follows as recorded in the court deposition, was particularly brave and unyielding. In her bristling defiance we encounter not only a courageous woman but also the general dilemma in which New England found itself (and which Arthur Miller, some 260 years later, made the theme of *The Crucible*): since confession was the only chance for acquittal, innocent people were being tempted to admit crimes they had not committed, and to implicate others. Faced with a choice between accepting mercy and preserving self-respect, Susanna Martin chose the latter. A few weeks later, she was hanged.

As soon as she came in many had fits.

"Do you know this woman?"

Abigail Williams saith, "It is Goody Martin; she hath hurt me often." Others by fits were hindered from speaking. Elizabeth Hubbard said she hath not been hurt by her. John Indian said he hath not seen her. Mercy Lewis pointed to her and fell into a little fit. Ann Putnam threw her glove in a fit at her. The examinant laughed.

"What, do you laugh at it?"

"Well I may at such folly."

"Is this folly? The hurt of these persons?"

"I never hurt man, woman, or child."

Mercy Lewis cried out, "She hath hurt me a great many times and pulls me down."

Then Martin laughed again.

Mary Walcott saith, "This woman hath hurt me a great many times." Susan Sheldon also accused her of afflicting her.

"What do you say to this?"

"I have no hand in witchcraft."

"What did you do? Did not you give your consent?"

"No, never in my life."

"What ails this people?"

"I do not know."

"But what do you think?"

"I do not desire to spend my judgment upon it."

"Do not you think they are bewitched?"

"No, I do not think they are."

"Tell me your thoughts about them?"

"Why, my thoughts are my own when they are in; but when they are out they are another's."

"You said 'their master'—who do you think is their master?"

"If they be dealing in the black art you may know as well as I."

"Well, what have you done towards this?"

"Nothing."

"Why, it is you or your appearance."

"I cannot help it."

"That may be your master."

"I desire to lead myself according to the word of God."

"Is this according to God's word?"

"If I were such a person I would tell you the truth."

"How comes your appearance just now to hurt these?"

"How do I know?"

"Are not you willing to tell the truth?"

"I cannot tell: he that appeared in Samuel [the] shape [of] a glorified saint can appear in anyone's shape."

"Do you believe these do not say true?"

"They may lie for aught I know."

"May not you lie?"

"I dare not tell a lie if it would save my life."

"Then you will speak the truth."

"I have spoke nothing else. I would do them any good."

"I do not think you have such affections for them whom just now you insinuated had the devil for their master."

Elizabeth Hubbard was afflicted and then the marshall who was by her said she [Martin] pinched her hand.

Several of the afflicted cried out they saw her upon the beam.

"Pray God discover you, if you be guilty."

"Amen, amen. A false tongue will never make a guilty person."

"You have been a long time coming to the court today; you can come fast enough in the night," said Mercy Lewis.

"No, sweetheart," said the examinant, and then Mercy Lewis and all or many of the rest were afflicted.

John Indian fell into a violent fit and said, "It was that woman, she bites, she bites," and then she was biting her lips.

"Have you not compassion for these afflicted?"

"No, I have none."

Some cried out there was the black man with her, and Goody Vibber, who had not accused her before, confirmed it.

Abigail Williams upon trial could not come near her, nor Goody Vibber, nor Mary Walcott. John Indian cried he would kill her if he came near her, but he was flung down in his approach to her.

"What is the reason these cannot come near you?"

"I cannot tell: it may be the devil bears me more malice than another."

"Do not you see how God evidently discovers you?"

"No. Not a bit for that."

"All the congregation think so."

"Let them think what they will."

"What is the reason these cannot come near you?"

"I do not know but they can if they will, or else if you please I will come to them."

"What is the black man whispering to you?"

"There was none whispered to me."

WILLIAM APESS

From Eulogy on King Philip

 1836

In an often quoted remark, the German Jewish writer Walter Benjamin—a man intimately acquainted with both the glories and horrors of European civilization (he committed suicide while fleeing the Nazis)—wrote "there is no cultural document that is not at the same time a record of barbarism." The salience of this comment for New England should be obvious, for the great achievements of New England culture came at an incalculable price: the subjugation and virtual elimination by disease, expulsion, and assimilation of the native peoples that the English encountered when they emigrated to America.

One of the leading spokesmen for the dispossessed was William Apess. Born in Colrain, Massachusetts, in 1798, he knew his family heritage only by way of fragmentary stories recounted by relatives who believed themselves descended from the great Pokunoket chief Metacom, known to the English as King Philip. Apess's mother, who may have been of mixed Native American and African American heritage, was a domestic servant, and his father an itinerant shoemaker. Their marriage was stormy, and Apess was left as a child with his mother's parents in southeastern Connecticut, where his Pequot Indian ancestors had lived for generations. When it became clear that the child was being beaten by his grandparents, a neighbor intervened and took him into his own home. For seven years, Apess lived as an indentured servant in his benefactor's household, where he received some formal schooling and was touched by its atmosphere of Christian piety. From his early teens, he lived a wandering life as a cook, a laborer, and a soldier in the War of 1812. After experiencing religious conversion, he became a Methodist "exhorter" and eventually an ordained preacher, working mainly in the region where he had lived as a child. He came to prominence, and notoriety, toward the end of his life—he died in 1838—when, having joined the Mashpee Indian community on Cape Cod, he led its efforts to win independence from its white overseers.

Until the recent resurgence of interest in the history of minority peoples in the United States, Apess had been largely forgotten. But recent scholarship has restored him to our awareness; and no anthology of New England writing would be complete without him. This is true especially because he did not speak from outside New England's religious and political traditions. He was a critic from within who deployed against New England's insouciant triumphalism the very techniques and ideas of which New Englanders were most proud: the tradition of pulpit chastisement that goes back to the Puritan founders, and the Christian imperative of subjecting oneself to unflinching introspection.

In 1675 Apess's supposed ancestor King Philip had led an alliance of tribes in a bloody uprising against the white settlers of New England. Speaking in Boston 160 years later, Apess attained in the *Eulogy on King Philip* a remarkable synthesis of irony ("they are so pious [in Connecticut] that they kill the cats for killing rats") and indignation ("O Savage, where art thou to weep over the Christian's crimes?") as he spoke to those who would have preferred to forget the darkest aspect of the New England past—the dispossession of its native peoples.

I do not arise to spread before you the fame of a noted warrior, whose natural abilities shone like those of the great and mighty Philip of Greece, or of Alexander the Great, or like those of Washington—whose virtues and patriotism are engraven on the hearts of my audience. Neither do I approve of war as being the best method of bowing to the haughty tyrant, Man, and civilizing the world. No, far from me be such a thought. But it is to bring before you beings made by the God of Nature, and in whose hearts and heads he has planted sympathies that shall live forever in the memory of the world, whose brilliant talents shone in the display of natural things, so that the most cultivated, whose powers shone with equal luster, were not able to prepare mantles to cover the burning elements of an uncivilized world. What, then? Shall we cease to mention the mighty of the earth, the noble work of God?

Yet those purer virtues remain untold. Those noble traits that marked the wild man's course lie buried in the shades of night; and who shall stand? I appeal to the lovers of liberty. But those few remaining descendants who now remain as the monument of the cruelty of those who came to improve our race and correct our errors—and as the immortal Washington lives endeared and engraven on the hearts of every white in America, never to be forgotten in time—even such is the immortal Philip honored, as held in memory by the degraded but yet grateful descendants who appreciate his character; so will every patriot, especially in this enlightened age, respect the rude yet all-accomplished son of the forest, that died a martyr to his cause, though unsuccessful, yet as glorious as the *American* Revolution. Where, then, shall we place the hero of the wilderness?

Justice and humanity for the remaining few prompt me to vindicate the character of him who yet lives in their hearts and, if possible, melt the prejudice that exists in the hearts of those who are in the possession of his soil, and only by the right of conquest—is the aim of him who proudly tells you, the blood of a denominated savage runs in his veins. It is, however, true that there are many who are said to be honorable warriors, who, in the wisdom of their civilized legislation, think it no crime to wreak their vengeance upon whole nations and communities, until the fields are covered with blood and the rivers turned into purple fountains, while groans, like distant thunder, are heard from the wounded and the tens of thousands of the dying, leaving helpless families depending on their cares and sympathies for life; while a loud response is heard floating through the air from the ten thousand Indian children and orphans, who are left to mourn the honorable acts of a few—civilized men.

Now, if we have common sense and ability to allow the difference between the civilized and the uncivilized, we cannot but see that one mode of warfare is as just as the other; for while one is sanctioned by authority of the enlightened and cultivated men, the other is an agreement according to the pure laws of nature, growing out of natural consequences; for nature always has her defense for every beast of the field; even the reptiles of the earth and the fishes of the sea have their weapons of war. But though frail man was made for a nobler purpose—to live, to love, and adore his God, and do good to his brother—for this reason, and this alone, the God of heaven prepared ways and means to blast anger, man's destroyer, and cause the Prince of Peace to rule, that man might swell those blessed notes. My image is of God; I am not a beast.

But as all men are governed by animal passions who are void of the true principles of God, whether cultivated or uncultivated, we shall now lay before you the true character of Philip, in relation to those hostilities between himself and the whites; and in so doing, permit me to be plain and candid.

The first inquiry is: Who is Philip? He was the descendant of one of the most celebrated chiefs in the known world, for peace and universal benevolence toward all men; for injuries upon injuries, and the most daring robberies and barbarous deeds of death that were ever committed by the American Pilgrims, were with patience and resignation borne, in a manner that would do justice to any Christian nation or being in the world—especially when we realize that it was voluntary suffering on the part of the good old chief. His country extensive, his men numerous, so as the wilderness was enlivened by them, say, a thousand to one of the white men, and they also sick and feeble—where, then, shall we find one nation submitting so tamely to another, with such a host at their command? For injuries of much less magnitude have the people called Christians slain their brethren, till they could sing, like Samson: With a jawbone of an ass have we slain our thousands and laid them in heaps. It will be well for us to lay those deeds and depredations committed by whites upon Indians before the civilized world, and then they can judge for themselves . . .

How inhuman it was in those wretches, to come into a country where nature shone in beauty, spreading her wings over the vast continent, sheltering beneath her shades those natural sons of an Almighty Being, that shone in grandeur and luster like the stars of the first magnitude in the heavenly world; whose virtues far surpassed their more enlightened foes, notwithstanding their pretended zeal for religion and virtue. How they could go to work to enslave a free people and call it religion is beyond the power of my imagination and outstrips the revelation of God's word. O thou pretended hypocritical Christian, whoever thou art, to say it was the design of God that we should murder and slay one another because we have the power. Power was not given us to abuse each other, but a mere power delegated to us by the King of heaven, a weapon of defense against error and evil; and when abused, it will turn to our destruction. Mark, then, the history of nations throughout the world . . .

December 1620, the Pilgrims landed at Plymouth, and without asking liberty from anyone they possessed themselves of a portion of the country, and built themselves houses, and then made a treaty, and commanded them to accede to it. This, if now done, it would be called an insult, and every white man would be called to go out and act the part of a patriot, to defend their country's rights; and if every intruder were butchered, it would be sung upon every hilltop in the Union that victory and patriotism was the order of the day. And yet the Indians (though many were dissatisfied), without the shedding of blood or imprisoning anyone, bore it. And yet for their kindness and resignation toward the whites, they were called savages and made by God on purpose for them to destroy . . . Now let us see who the greatest savages were; . . . Another act of humanity for Christians, as they call themselves, that one Captain Standish, gathering some fruit and provisions, goes forward with a black and hypocritical heart and pretends to prepare a feast for the Indians; and when they sit down to eat, they seize the Indians' knives hanging about their necks, and stab them to the heart. The white people call this stabbing, feasting the savages. We suppose it might well mean themselves, their conduct being more like savages than Christians. They took one Wittumumet, the chief's head, and put it upon a pole in their fort and, for aught we know, gave praise to their God for success in murdering a poor Indian; for we know it was their usual course to give praise to God for this kind of victory, believing it was God's will and command for them to do so. We wonder if these same Christians do not think it the command of God that they should lie, steal, and get drunk, commit fornication and adultery. The one is as consistent as the other. What say you, judges, is it not so, and was it not according as they did? Indians think it is . . .

But there is still more. In 1619 a number of Indians went on board of a ship, by order of their chief, and the whites set upon them and murdered them without mercy; says Mr. Dermer, "without the Indians giving them the least provocation whatever." Is this insult to be borne, and not a word to be said? Truly, Christians would never bear it; why, then, think it strange that the denominated savages do not? O thou white Christian, look at acts that honored your countrymen, to the destruction of thousands, for much less insults than that. And who, my dear sirs, were wanting of the name of savages—whites, or Indians? Let justice answer . . .

Only look for a few moments at the abuses the son of Massasoit received. Alexander being sent for with armed men, and while he and his men were breaking their fast in the morning, they were taken immediately away, by order of the governor, without the least provocation but merely through suspicion . . . Alexander was a man of strong passion and of a firm mind; and this insulting treatment of him caused him to fall sick of a fever, so that he never recovered. Some of the Indians were suspicious that he was poisoned to death. He died in the year 1662. "After him," says that eminent divine, Dr. Mather, "there rose up one Philip, of cursed memory." Perhaps if the Doctor was present, he would find that the memory of Philip was as far before his, in the view of sound, judicious men, as the sun is before the stars at noonday. But we might suppose that men like Dr. Mather, so well versed in Scripture, would have known his work better than to have spoken evil of anyone, or have cursed any of God's works. He ought to have known that God did not make his red children for him to curse; but if he wanted them cursed, he could have done it himself. But, on the contrary, his suffering Master commanded him to love his enemies and to pray for his persecutors, and to do unto others as he would that men should do unto him. Now, we wonder if the sons of the Pilgrims would like to have us, poor Indians, come out and curse the Doctor, and all their sons, as we have been by many of them. And suppose that, in some future day, our children should repay all these wrongs, would it not be doing as we, poor Indians, have been done to? But we sincerely hope there is more humanity in us than that . . .

The history of New England writers say that our tribes were large and respectable. How, then, could it be otherwise, but their safety rested in the hands of friendly Indians? In 1647, the Pilgrims speak of large and respectable tribes. But let us trace them for a few moments. How have they been destroyed? Is it by fair means? No. How then? By hypocritical proceedings, by being duped and flattered; flattered by informing the Indians that their God was going to speak to them, and then place them before the cannon's mouth in a line, and then putting the match to it and kill thousands of them. We might suppose that meek Christians had better gods and weapons than cannon; weapons that were not carnal, but mighty through God, to the pulling down of strongholds. These are the weapons that modern Christians profess to have; and if the Pilgrims did not have them, they ought not to be honored as such. But let us again review their weapons to civilize the nations of this soil. What were they? Rum and powder and ball, together with all the diseases, such as the smallpox and every other disease imaginable, and in this way sweep off thousands and tens of thousands. And then it has been said that these men who were free from these things, that they could not live among civilized people. We wonder how a virtuous people could live in a sink of diseases, a people who had never been used to them.

And who is to account for those destructions upon innocent families and helpless children? It was said by some of the New England writers that living babes were found at the breast of their dead mothers. What an awful sight! And to think, too, that these diseases were carried among them on purpose to destroy them. Let the children of the Pilgrims blush, while the son of the forest drops a tear and groans over the fate of his murdered and departed fathers . . . For be it remembered, although the Gospel is said to be glad tidings to all people, yet we poor Indians never have found those who brought it as messengers of mercy, but contrawise . . .

Why, my brethren, the poor missionaries want money to go and convert the poor heathen, as if God could not convert them where they were but must first drive them out. If God wants the red men converted, we should think that he could do it as well in one place as in another. But must I say, and shall I say it, that missionaries have injured us more than they have done us good, by degrading us as a people, in breaking up our governments and leaving us without any suffrages whatever, or a legal right among men? Oh, what cursed doctrine is this! It most certainly is not fit to civilize men with, much more to save their souls; and we poor Indians want no such missionaries around us. But I would suggest one thing, and that is, let the ministers and people use the colored people they have already around them like human beings, before they go to convert any more; and let them show it in their churches; and let them proclaim it upon the housetops; and I would say to the benevolent, withhold your hard earnings from them, unless they do do it, until they can stop laying their own wickedness to God, which is blasphemy . . .

But we have another dark and corrupt deed for the sons of Pilgrims to look at, and that is the fight and capture of Philip's son and wife and many of his warriors, in which Philip lost about 130 men killed and wounded; this was in August 1676. But the most horrid act was in taking Philip's son, about ten years of age, and selling him to be a slave away from his father and mother . . . He that will advocate slavery is worse than a beast, is a being devoid of shame, and has gathered around him the most corrupt and debasing principles in the world; and I care not whether he be a minister or member of any church in the world—no, not excepting the head men of the nation. And he that will not set his face against its corrupt principles is a coward and not worthy of being numbered among men and Christians—and conduct, too, that libels the laws of the country, and the word of God, that men profess to believe in . . .

I do not hesitate to say that through the prayers, preaching, and examples of those pretended pious has been the foundation of all the slavery and degradation in the American colonies toward colored people. Experience has taught me that this has been a most sorry and wretched doctrine to us poor ignorant Indians. I will mention two or three things to amuse you a little; that is, as I was passing through Connecticut, about 15 years ago, where they are so pious that they kill the cats for killing rats, and whip the beer barrels for working upon the Sabbath, that in a severe cold night, when the face of the earth was one glare of ice, dark and stormy, I called at a man's house to know if I could not stay with him, it being about nine miles to the house where I then lived, and knowing him to be a rich man, and withal very pious, knowing if he had a mind he could do it comfortably, and withal we were both members of one church. My reception, however, was almost as cold as the weather, only he did not turn me out-of-doors; if he had, I know not but I should have frozen to death. My situation was a little better than being out, for he allowed a little wood but no bed, because I was an Indian. Another Christian asked me to dine with him and put my dinner behind the door; I thought this a queer compliment indeed.

About two years ago, I called at an inn in Lexington; and a gentleman present, not spying me to be an Indian, began to say they ought to be exterminated. I took it up in our defense, though not boisterous but coolly; and when we came to retire, finding that I was an Indian, he was unwilling to sleep opposite my room for fear of being murdered before morning. We presume his conscience pled guilty. These things I mention to show that the doctrines of the Pilgrims has grown up with the people.

But not to forget Philip . . . that put an enlightened nation to flight and won so many battles. It was a son of nature, with nature's talents alone. And who did he have to contend with? With all the combined arts of cultivated talents of the Old and New World. It was like putting one talent against a thousand. And yet Philip, with that, accomplished more than all of them. Yea, he outdid the well-disciplined forces of Greece, under the command of Philip, the Grecian emperor; for he never was enabled to lay such plans of allying the tribes of the earth together, as Philip of Mount Hope did. And even Napoleon patterned after him, in collecting his forces and surprising the enemy. Washington, too, pursued many of his plans in attacking the enemy and thereby enabled him to defeat his antagonists and conquer them. What, then, shall we say? Shall we not do right to say that Philip, with his one talent, outstrips them all with their ten thousand? No warrior, of any age, was ever known to pursue such plans as Philip did . . .

How deep, then, was the thought of Philip, when he could look from Maine to Georgia, and from the ocean to the lakes, and view with one look all his brethren withering before the more enlightened to come; and how true his prophecy, that the white people would not only cut down their groves but would enslave them. Had the inspiration of Isaiah been there, he could not have been more correct. Our groves and hunting grounds are gone, our dead are dug up, our council fires are put out, and a foundation was laid in the first Legislature to enslave our people, by taking from them all rights, which has been strictly adhered to ever since. Look at the disgraceful laws, disfranchising us as citizens. Look at the treaties made by Congress, all broken. Look at the deep-rooted plans laid, when a territory becomes a state, that after so many years the laws shall be extended over the Indians that live within their boundaries. Yea, every charter that has been given was given with the view of driving the Indians out of the states, or dooming them to become chained under desperate laws, that would make them drag out a miserable life as one chained to the galley; and this is the course that has been pursued for nearly two hundred years. A fire, a canker, created by the Pilgrims from across the Atlantic, to burn and destroy my poor unfortunate brethren, and it cannot be denied. What, then, shall we do? Shall we cease crying and say it is all wrong, or shall we bury the hatchet and those unjust laws and Plymouth Rock together and become friends? And will the sons of the Pilgrims aid in putting out the fire and destroying the canker that will ruin all that their fathers left behind them to destroy? (By this we see how true Philip spoke.) If so, we hope we shall not hear it said from ministers and church members that we are so good no other people can live with us, as you know it is a common thing for them to say Indians cannot live among Christian people; no, even the president of the United States tells the Indians they cannot live among civilized people, and we want your lands and must have them and will have them. As if he had said to them, "We want your land for our use to speculate upon; it aids us in paying off our national debt and supporting us in Congress to drive you off.

"You see, my red children, that our fathers carried on this scheme of getting your lands for our use, and we have now become rich and powerful; and we have a right to do with you just as we please; we claim to be your fathers. And we think we shall do you a great favor, my dear sons and daughters, to drive you out, to get you away out of the reach of our civilized people, who are cheating you, for we have no law to reach them, we cannot protect you although you be our children. So it is no use, you need not cry, you must go, even if the lions devour you, for we promised the land you have to somebody else long ago, perhaps twenty or thirty years; and we did it without your consent, it is true. But this has been the way our fathers first brought us up, and it is hard to depart from it; therefore, you shall have no protection from us." Now, while we sum up this subject, does it not appear that the cause of all wars from beginning to end was and is for the want of good usage? That the whites have always been the aggressors, and the wars, cruelties, and bloodshed is a job of their own seeking, and not the Indians? Did you ever know of Indians hurting those who was kind to them? No. We have a thousand witnesses to the contrary. Yea, every male and female declare it to be the fact. We often hear of the wars breaking out upon the frontiers, and it is because the same spirit reigns there that reigned here in New England; and wherever there are any Indians, that spirit still reigns; and at present, there is no law to stop it. What, then, is to be done? Let every friend of the Indians now seize the mantle of Liberty and throw it over those burning elements that has spread with such fearful rapidity, and at once extinguish them forever. It is true that now and then a feeble voice has been raised in our favor. Yes, we might speak of distinguished men, but they fall so far short in the minority that it is heard but at a small distance. We want trumpets that sound like thunder, and men to act as though they were going at war with those corrupt and degrading principles that robs one of all rights, merely because he is ignorant and of a little different color. Let us have principles that will give everyone his due; and then shall wars cease, and the weary find rest. Give the Indian his rights, and you may be assured war will cease.

But by this time you have been enabled to see that Philip's prophecy has come to pass; therefore, as a man of natural abilities, I shall pronounce him the greatest man that was ever in America; and so it will stand, until he is proved to the contrary, to the everlasting disgrace of the Pilgrims' fathers . . .

Do not then wonder, my dear friends, at my bold and unpolished statements, though I do not believe that truth wants any polishing whatever. And I can assure you that I have no design to tell an untruth, but facts alone. Oft have I been surprised at the conduct of those who pretend to be Christians, to see how they were affected toward those who were of a different cast, professing one faith. Yes, the spirit of degradation has always been exercised toward us poor and untaught people. If we cannot read, we can see and feel; and we find no excuse in the Bible for Christians conducting toward us as they do.

It is said that in the Christian's guide, God is merciful, and they that are his followers are like him. How much mercy do you think has been shown toward Indians, their wives, and their children? Not much, we think. No. And ye fathers, I will appeal to you that are white. Have you any regard for your wives and children, for those delicate sons and daughters? Would you like to see them slain and lain in heaps, and their bodies devoured by the vultures and wild beasts of prey, and their bones bleaching in the sun and air, till they molder away or were covered by the falling leaves of the forest, and not resist? No. Your hearts would break with grief, and with all the religion and knowledge you have, it would not impede your force to take vengeance upon your

foe that had so cruelly conducted thus, although God has forbid you in so doing. For he has said, "Vengeance is mine, and I will repay." What, then, my
dear affectionate friends, can you think of those who have been so often betrayed, routed, and stripped of all they possess, of all their kindred in the
flesh? Can or do you think we have no feeling? . . . Our affections for each
other are the same as yours; we think as much of ourselves as you do of yourselves. When our children are sick, we do all we can for them; they lie buried
deep in our affections; if they die, we remember it long and mourn in after
years. Children also cleave to their parents; they look to them for aid; they do
the best they know how to do for each other; and when strangers come
among us, we use them as well as we know how; we feel honest in whatever
we do; we have no desire to offend anyone. But when we are so deceived, it
spoils all our confidence in our visitors. And although I can say that I have
some dear, good friends among white people, yet I eye them with a jealous
eye, for fear they will betray me. Having been deceived so much by them,
how can I help it? Being brought up to look upon white people as being enemies and not friends, and by the whites treated as such, who can wonder? Yes,
in vain have I looked for the Christian to take me by the hand and bid me
welcome to his cabin, as my fathers did them, before we were born; and if
they did, it was only to satisfy curiosity and not to look upon me as a man and
a Christian. And so all of my people have been treated, whether Christians or
not. I say, then, a different course must be pursued, and different laws must
be enacted, and all men must operate under one general law. And while you
ask yourselves, "What do they, the Indians, want?" you have only to look at
the unjust laws made for them and say, "They want what I want," in order to
make men of them, good and wholesome citizens. And this plan ought to be
pursued by all missionaries or not pursued at all. That is not only to make
Christians of us, but men, which plan as yet has never been pursued. And
when it is, I will then throw my might upon the side of missions and do what
I can to favor it. But this work must begin here first, in New England.

FREDERICK DOUGLASS

From My Bondage and My Freedom

 1855

On the persistent American problem of race, New England has often been divided against itself. Antebellum Boston was the headquarters of abolitionism; but it was also a banking city that financed the slave trade and the mills that turned slave-harvested cotton into finished goods. In Boston, according to Walt Whitman in the 1850s, "at the eating houses, a black, when he wants his dinner, comes in and takes a vacant seat wherever he finds one—and nobody minds it." But the great African American leader Frederick Douglass (1817–1895), who had better grounds for knowing, tells us that when he tried to sit down next to a white man on a train traveling near Boston, he caused an uproar over what many deemed his act of insolent transgression.

Some people will have it that there is a natural, an inherent, and an invincible repugnance in the breast of the white race toward dark-colored people; and some very intelligent colored men think that their proscription is owing solely to the color which nature has given them. They hold that they are rated according to their color, and that it is impossible for white people ever to look upon dark races of men, or men belonging to the African race, with other than feelings of aversion. My experience, both serious and mirthful, combats this conclusion. Leaving out of sight, for a moment, grave facts, to this point, I will state one or two, which illustrate a very interesting feature of American character as well as American prejudice. Riding from Boston to Albany, a few years ago, I found myself in a large car, well filled with passengers. The seat next to me was about the only vacant one. At every stopping place we took in new passengers, all of whom, on reaching the seat next to me, cast a disdainful glance upon it, and passed to another car, leaving me in the full enjoyment of a whole form. For a time, I did not know but that my riding there was prejudicial to the interest of the railroad company. A circumstance occurred, however, which gave me an elevated position at once. Among the passengers on this train was Gov. George N. Briggs. I was not acquainted with him, and had no idea that I was known to him. Known to him, however, I was, for upon observing me, the governor left his place, and making his way toward me, respectfully asked the privilege of a seat by my side; and upon introducing himself, we entered into a conversation very pleasant and instructive to me. The despised seat now became honored. His excellency had removed all the prejudice against sitting by the side of a negro; and upon his leaving it, as he did, on reaching Pittsfield, there were at least one dozen applicants for the place. The governor had, without changing my skin a single shade, made the place respectable which before was despicable.

A similar incident happened to me once on the Boston and New Bedford railroad, and the leading party to it has since been governor of the state of Massachusetts. I allude to Col. John Henry Clifford. Lest the reader may fancy I am aiming to elevate myself, by claiming too much intimacy with great men, I must state that my only acquaintance with Col. Clifford was formed while I was *his hired servant* during the first winter of my escape from slavery. I owe it him to say, that in that relation I found him always kind and gentlemanly. But to the incident. I entered a car at Boston, for New Bedford, which, with the exception of a single seat, was full, and found I must occupy this, or stand up, during the journey. Having no mind to do this, I stepped up to the man having the next seat, and who had a few parcels on the seat, and gently asked leave to take a seat by his side. My fellow-passenger gave me a look made up of reproach and indignation, and asked me why I should come to that particular seat. I assured him, in the gentlest manner, that of all others this was the seat for me. Finding that I was actually about to sit down, he sang out, "O! stop, stop! and let me get out!" Suiting the action to the word, up the agitated man got, and sauntered to the other end of the car, and was compelled to stand for most of the way thereafter. Half-way to New Bedford, or more, Col. Clifford, recognizing me, left his seat, and not having seen me before since I had ceased to wait on him, (in everything except hard arguments against his pro-slavery position,) apparently forgetful of his rank, manifested, in greeting me, something of the feeling of an old friend. This demonstration was not lost on the gentleman whose dignity I had, an hour before, most seriously offended. Col. Clifford was known to be about the most aristocratic gentleman in Bristol county; and it was evidently thought that I must be somebody, else I should not have been thus noticed, by a person so distinguished. Sure enough, after Col. Clifford left me, I found myself surrounded with friends; and among the number, my offended friend stood nearest, and with an apology for his rudeness, which I could not resist, although it was one of the lamest ever offered. With such facts as these before me—and I have many of them—I am inclined to think that pride and fashion have much to do with the treatment commonly extended to colored people in the United States. I once heard a very plain man say, (and he was cross-eyed, and awkwardly flung together in other respects,) that he should be a handsome man when public opinion shall be changed.

Henry Wadsworth Longfellow

The Jewish Cemetery at Newport

 1858

Coming at first from the Dutch colonies of Barbados and Curaçao, and later from Portugal, Spain, and England, Jewish emigrants began arriving in Newport, Rhode Island, as early as 1658, drawn by that colony's atmosphere of religious toleration. When Henry Wadsworth Longfellow (1807–1882) composed his poem on the Newport cemetery, whose earliest extant tombstone dates from 1677, he doubtless had in mind parallels between the Jewish experience of persecution and that of enslaved African Americans in his own time. Longfellow was the author of such popular epic and commemorative works as "The Song of Hiawatha" and "The Village Blacksmith"—once found on lists of poems to be memorized by schoolchildren. His verses may not convey to readers today the "ghostly melancholy" (J. D. McClatchy's phrase) they once evoked, but this meditation on how a once vital people leave behind markers that, after a small span of time, become no more meaningful to posterity than weathered rocks or paving stones remains quietly affecting.

> How strange it seems! These Hebrews in their graves,
>   Close by the street of this fair seaport town,
> Silent beside the never-silent waves,
>   At rest in all this moving up and down!
>
> The trees are white with dust, that o'er their sleep
>   Wave their broad curtains in the south-wind's breath,
> While underneath such leafy tents they keep
>   The long, mysterious Exodus of Death.
>
> And these sepulchral stones, so old and brown,
>   That pave with level flags their burial-place,
> Seem like the tablets of the Law, thrown down
>   And broken by Moses at the mountain's base.
>
> The very names recorded here are strange,
>   Of foreign accent, and of different climes;

Alvares and Rivera interchange
   With Abraham and Jacob of old times.

"Blessed be God! for he created Death!"
   The mourners said, "and Death is rest and peace";
Then added, in the certainty of faith,
   "And giveth Life that never more shall cease."

Closed are the portals of their Synagogue,
   No Psalms of David now the silence break,
No Rabbi reads the ancient Decalogue
   In the grand dialect the Prophets spake.

Gone are the living, but the dead remain,
   And not neglected; for a hand unseen,
Scattering its bounty, like a summer rain,
   Still keeps their graves and their remembrance green.

How came they here? What burst of Christian hate,
   What persecution, merciless and blind,
Drove o'er the sea—that desert desolate—
   These Ishmaels and Hagars of mankind?

They lived in narrow streets and lanes obscure,
   Ghetto and Judenstrass, in mirk and mire;
Taught in the school of patience to endure
   The life of anguish and the death of fire.

All their lives long, with the unleavened bread
   And bitter herbs of exile and its fears,
The wasting famine of the heart they fed,
   And slaked its thirst with marah of their tears.

Anathema maranatha! was the cry
   That rang from town to town, from street to street;
At every gate the accursed Mordecai
   Was mocked and jeered, and spurned by Christian feet.

Pride and humiliation hand in hand
   Walked with them through the world where'er they went
Trampled and beaten were they as the sand,
   And yet unshaken as the continent.

For in the background figures vague and vast
    Of patriarchs and of prophets rose sublime,
And all the great traditions of the Past
    They saw reflected in the coming time.

And thus for ever with reverted look
    The mystic volume of the world they read,
Spelling it backward, like a Hebrew book,
    Till life became a Legend of the Dead.

But ah! what once has been shall be no more!
    The groaning earth in travail and in pain
Brings forth its races, but does not restore,
    And the dead nations never rise again.

MARY ANTIN

From The Promised Land

 1912

Born in Russia, Mary Antin (1881–1949) came to America with her mother and sisters in 1894 to rejoin her father, who three years earlier had fled the Czarist pogroms for Boston. In the public school in Chelsea, Massachusetts, she proved herself to be a precocious student and attracted the attention of a teacher who encouraged her writing. Some of her letters to relatives in Russia, written in Yiddish, were translated and published and she was welcomed into the circle of progressive Boston intellectuals—one of whom, a midwesterner of German descent who was studying geology at Harvard, she married. In 1901 Antin moved with her husband to New York so that he could take up a position at Columbia University, thus abandoning her plan to attend Radcliffe College. In New York, Antin became well known as the author of stories and essays, culminating in her memoir, *The Promised Land,* which testified to and exemplified the willing assimilation of immigrants at a time when xenophobia and nativism were running high.

Having made such good time across the ocean, I ought to be able to proceed no less rapidly on *terra firma,* where, after all, I am more at home. And yet here is where I falter. Not that I hesitated, even for the space of a breath, in my first steps in America. There was no time to hesitate. The most ignorant immigrant, on landing, proceeds to give and receive greetings, to eat, sleep, and rise, after the manner of his own country; wherein he is corrected, admonished, and laughed at, whether by interested friends or the most indifferent strangers; and his American experience is thus begun . . . So I am bound to unravel, as well as I can, the tangle of events, outer and inner, which made up the first breathless years of my American life.

During his three years of probation, my father had made a number of false starts in business. His history for that period is the history of thousands who come to America, like him, with pockets empty, hands untrained to the use of tools, minds cramped by centuries of repression in their native land. Dozens of these men pass under your eyes every day, my American friend, too absorbed in their honest affairs to notice the looks of suspicion which you cast at them, the repugnance with which you shrink from their touch. You see them shuffle from door to door with a basket of spools and buttons, or bending over the sizzling irons in a basement tailor shop, or rummaging in your ash can, or moving a pushcart from curb to curb, at the command of the burly policeman. "The Jew peddler!" you say, and dismiss him from your premises and from your thoughts, never dreaming that the sordid drama of his days may have a moral that concerns you. What if the creature with the untidy beard carries in his bosom his citizenship papers? What if the cross-legged tailor is supporting a boy in college who is one day going to mend your state constitution for you? What if the ragpicker's daughters are hastening over the ocean to teach your children in the public schools? Think, every time you pass the greasy alien on the street, that he was born thousands of years before the oldest native American; and he may have something to communicate to you, when you two shall have learned a common language. Remember that his very physiognomy is a cipher the key to which it behooves you to search for most diligently.

By the time we joined my father, he had surveyed many avenues of approach toward the coveted citadel of fortune. One of these, heretofore untried, he now proposed to essay, armed with new courage, and cheered on by the presence of his family. In partnership with an energetic little man who had an English chapter in his history, he prepared to set up a refreshment booth on Crescent Beach. But while he was completing arrangements at the beach we remained in town, where we enjoyed the educational advantages of a thickly populated neighborhood; namely, Wall Street, in the West End of Boston.

Anybody who knows Boston knows that the West and North Ends are the wrong ends of that city. They form the tenement district, or, in the newer phrase, the slums of Boston. Anybody who is acquainted with the slums of any American metropolis knows that that is the quarter where poor immigrants foregather, to live, for the most part, as unkempt, half-washed, toiling, unaspiring foreigners; pitiful in the eyes of social missionaries, the despair of boards of health, the hope of ward politicians, the touchstone of American democracy. The well-versed metropolitan knows the slums as a sort of house of detention for poor aliens, where they live on probation till they can show a certificate of good citizenship.

He may know all this and yet not guess how Wall Street, in the West End, appears in the eyes of a little immigrant from Polotzk. What would the sophisticated sight-seer say about Union Place, off Wall Street, where my new home waited for me? He would say that it is no place at all, but a short box of an alley. Two rows of three-story tenements are its sides, a stingy strip of sky is its lid, a littered pavement is the floor, and a narrow mouth its exit.

But I saw a very different picture on my introduction to Union Place. I saw two imposing rows of brick buildings, loftier than any dwelling I had ever lived in. Brick was even on the ground for me to tread on, instead of common earth or boards. Many friendly windows stood open, filled with uncovered heads of women and children. I thought the people were interested in us, which was very neighborly. I looked up to the topmost row of windows, and my eyes were filled with the May blue of an American sky!

In our days of affluence in Russia we had been accustomed to upholstered parlors, embroidered linen, silver spoons and candlesticks, goblets of gold, kitchen shelves shining with copper and brass. We had featherbeds heaped halfway to the ceiling; we had clothes presses dusky with velvet and silk and fine woollen. The three small rooms into which my father now ushered us, up one flight of stairs, contained only the necessary beds, with lean mattresses; a few wooden chairs; a table or two; a mysterious iron structure, which later turned out to be a stove; a couple of unornamental kerosene lamps; and a scanty array of cooking-utensils and crockery. And yet we were all impressed with our new home and its furniture. It was not only because we had just passed through our seven lean years, cooking in earthen vessels, eating black bread on holidays and wearing cotton; it was chiefly because these wooden chairs and tin pans were American chairs and pans that they shone glorious in our eyes. And if there was anything lacking for comfort or decoration we expected it to be presently supplied—at least, we children did. Perhaps my mother alone, of us newcomers, appreciated the shabbiness of the little apartment, and realized that for her there was as yet no laying down of the burden of poverty.

Our initiation into American ways began with the first step on the new soil. My father found occasion to instruct or correct us even on the way from the pier to Wall Street, which journey we made crowded together in a rickety cab. He told us not to lean out of the windows, not to point, and explained the word "greenhorn." We did not want to be "greenhorns," and gave the strictest attention to my father's instructions . . .

The first meal was an object lesson of much variety. My father produced several kinds of food, ready to eat, without any cooking, from little tin cans that had printing all over them. He attempted to introduce us to a queer, slippery kind of fruit, which he called "banana," but had to give it up for the time being. After the meal, he had better luck with a curious piece of furniture on runners, which he called "rocking-chair." There were five of us newcomers, and we found five different ways of getting into the American machine of perpetual motion, and as many ways of getting out of it. One born and bred to the use of a rocking-chair cannot imagine how ludicrous people can make themselves when attempting to use it for the first time. We laughed immoderately over our various experiments with the novelty, which was a wholesome way of letting off steam after the unusual excitement of the day.

In our flat we did not think of such a thing as storing the coal in the bathtub. There was no bathtub. So in the evening of the first day my father conducted us to the public baths. As we moved along in a little procession, I was delighted with the illumination of the streets. So many lamps, and they burned until morning, my father said, and so people did not need to carry lanterns. In America, then, everything was free, as we had heard in Russia. Light was free; the streets were as bright as a synagogue on a holy day. Music was free; we had been serenaded, to our gaping delight, by a brass band of many pieces, soon after our installation on Union Place.

Education was free. That subject my father had written about repeatedly, as comprising his chief hope for us children, the essence of American opportunity, the treasure that no thief could touch, not even misfortune or poverty. It was the one thing that he was able to promise us when he sent for us; surer, safer than bread or shelter. On our second day I was thrilled with the realization of what this freedom of education meant. A little girl from across the alley came and offered to conduct us to school. My father was out, but we five between us had a few words of English by this time. We knew the word school. We understood. This child, who had never seen us till yesterday, who could not pronounce our names, who was not much better dressed than we, was able to offer us the freedom of the schools of Boston! No application made, no questions asked, no examinations, rulings, exclusions; no machinations, no fees. The doors stood open for every one of us. The smallest child could show us the way.

This incident impressed me more than anything I had heard in advance of the freedom of education in America. It was a concrete proof—almost the thing itself. One had to experience it to understand it.

It was a great disappointment to be told by my father that we were not to enter upon our school career at once. It was too near the end of the term, he said, and we were going to move to Crescent Beach in a week or so. We had to wait until the opening of the schools in September. What a loss of precious time—from May till September!

Not that the time was really lost. Even the interval on Union Place was crowded with lessons and experiences. We had to visit the stores and be dressed from head to foot in American clothing; we had to learn the mysteries of the iron stove, the washboard, and the speaking-tube; we had to learn to trade with the fruit peddler through the window, and not to be afraid of the policeman; and, above all, we had to learn English.

The kind people who assisted us in these important matters form a group by themselves in the gallery of my friends. If I had never seen them from those early days till now, I should still have remembered them with gratitude. When I enumerate the long list of my American teachers, I must begin with those who came to us on Wall Street and taught us our first steps. To my mother, in her perplexity over the cookstove, the woman who showed her how to make the fire was an angel of deliverance. A fairy godmother to us children was she who led us to a wonderful country called "uptown," where, in a dazzlingly beautiful palace called a "department store," we exchanged our hateful home-made European costumes, which pointed us out as "greenhorns" to the children on the street, for real American machine-made garments, and issued forth glorified in each other's eyes.

With our despised immigrant clothing we shed also our impossible Hebrew names. A committee of our friends, several years ahead of us in American experience, put their heads together and concocted American names for us all. Those of our real names that had no pleasing American equivalents they ruthlessly discarded, content if they retained the initials. My mother, possessing a name that was not easily translatable, was punished with the undignified nickname of Annie. Fetchke, Joseph, and Deborah issued as Frieda, Joseph, and Dora, respectively. As for poor me, I was simply cheated. The name they gave me was hardly new. My Hebrew name being Maryashe in full, Mashke for short, Russianized into Marya *(Mar-ya)*, my friends said that it would hold good in English as *Mary;* which was very disappointing, as I longed to possess a strange-sounding American name like the others.

I am forgetting the consolation I had, in this matter of names, from the use of my surname, which I have had no occasion to mention until now. I found on my arrival that my father was "Mr. Antin" on the slightest provocation, and not, as in Polotzk, on state occasions alone. And so I was "Mary Antin," and I felt very important to answer to such a dignified title. It was just like America that even plain people should wear their surnames on week days.

As a family we were so diligent under instruction, so adaptable, and so clever in hiding our deficiencies, that when we made the journey to Crescent Beach, in the wake of our small wagon-load of household goods, my father had very little occasion to admonish us on the way, and I am sure he was not ashamed of us. So much we had achieved toward our Americanization during the two weeks since our landing.

Crescent Beach is a name that is printed in very small type on the maps of the environs of Boston, but a life-size strip of sand curves from Winthrop to Lynn; and that is historic ground in the annals of my family. The place is now a popular resort for holiday crowds, and is famous under the name of Revere Beach. When the reunited Antins made their stand there, however, there were no boulevards, no stately bath-houses, no hotels, no gaudy amusement places, no illuminations, no showmen, no tawdry rabble. There was only the bright clean sweep of sand, the summer sea, and the summer sky. At high tide the whole Atlantic rushed in, tossing the seaweeds in his mane; at low tide he rushed out, growling and gnashing his granite teeth. Between tides a baby might play on the beach, digging with pebbles and shells, till it lay asleep on the sand. The whole sun shone by day, troops of stars by night, and the great moon in its season.

Into this grand cycle of the seaside day I came to live and learn and play. A few people came with me, as I have already intimated; but the main thing was that *I* came to live on the edge of the sea—I, who had spent my life inland . . . I lay stretched out in the sun, my eyes level with the sea, till I seemed to be absorbed bodily by the very materials of the world around me; till I could not feel my hand as separate from the warm sand in which it was buried. Or I crouched on the beach at full moon, wondering, wondering, between the two splendors of the sky and the sea. Or I ran out to meet the incoming storm, my face full in the wind, my being a-tingle with an awesome delight to the tips of my fog-matted locks flying behind; and stood clinging to some stake or upturned boat, shaken by the roar and rumble of the waves. So clinging, I pretended that I was in danger, and was deliciously frightened; I held on with both hands, and shook my head, exulting in the tumult around me, equally ready to laugh or sob. Or else I sat, on the stillest days, with my back to the sea, not looking at all, but just listening to the rustle of the waves on the sand; not thinking at all, but just breathing with the sea.

Thus courting the influence of sea and sky and variable weather, I was bound to have dreams, hints, imaginings . . . it was the growing time, that idle summer by the sea, and I grew all the faster because I had been so cramped before . . .

Let no one suppose that I spent my time entirely, or even chiefly, in inspired solitude. By far the best part of my day was spent in play—frank, hearty, boisterous play, such as comes natural to American children. In Polotzk I had already begun to be considered too old for play, excepting set games or organized frolics. Here I found myself included with children who still played, and I willingly returned to childhood. There were plenty of playfellows. My father's energetic little partner had a little wife and a large family. He kept them in the little cottage next to ours; and that the shanty survived the tumultuous presence of that brood is a wonder to me to-day. The young Wilners included an assortment of boys, girls, and twins, of every possible variety of age, size, disposition, and sex. They swarmed in and out of the cottage all day long, wearing the door-sill hollow, and trampling the ground to powder. They swung out of windows like monkeys, slid up the roof like flies, and shot out of trees like fowls . . .

I managed to retain my identity in this multitude somehow, and while I was very much impressed with their numbers, I even dared to pick and choose my friends among the Wilners. One or two of the smaller boys I liked best of all, for a game of hide-and-seek or a frolic on the beach. We played in the water like ducks, never taking the trouble to get dry. One day I waded out with one of the boys, to see which of us dared go farthest. The tide was extremely low, and we had not wet our knees when we began to look back to see if familiar objects were still in sight. I thought we had been wading for hours, and still the water was so shallow and quiet. My companion was marching straight ahead, so I did the same. Suddenly a swell lifted us almost off our feet, and we clutched at each other simultaneously. There was a lesser swell, and little waves began to run, and a sigh went up from the sea. The tide was turning—perhaps a storm was on the way—and we were miles, dreadful miles from dry land.

Boy and girl turned without a word, four determined bare legs ploughing through the water, four scared eyes straining toward the land. Through an eternity of toil and fear they kept dumbly on, death at their heels, pride still in their hearts. At last they reach high-water mark—six hours before full tide.

Each has seen the other afraid, and each rejoices in the knowledge. But only the boy is sure of his tongue.

"You was scared, war n't you?" he taunts.

The girl understands so much, and is able to reply:—

"You can schwimmen, I not."

"Betcher life I can schwimmen," the other mocks.

And the girl walks off, angry and hurt.

"An' I can walk on my hands," the tormentor calls after her. "Say, you greenhorn, why don'tcher look?"

The girl keeps straight on, vowing that she would never walk with that rude boy again, neither by land nor sea, not even though the waters should part at his bidding.

I am forgetting the more serious business which had brought us to Crescent Beach. While we children disported ourselves like mermaids and mermen in the surf, our respective fathers dispensed cold lemonade, hot peanuts, and pink popcorn, and piled up our respective fortunes, nickel by nickel, penny by penny. I was very proud of my connection with the public life of the beach. I admired greatly our shining soda fountain, the rows of sparkling glasses, the pyramids of oranges, the sausage chains, the neat white counter, and the bright array of tin spoons. It seemed to me that none of the other refreshment stands on the beach—there were a few—were half so attractive as ours. I thought my father looked very well in a long white apron and shirt sleeves. He dished out ice cream with enthusiasm, so I supposed he was getting rich. It never occurred to me to compare his present occupation with the position for which he had been originally destined; or if I thought about it, I was just as well content, for by this time I had by heart my father's saying, "America is not Polotzk." All occupations were respectable, all men were equal, in America.

If I admired the soda fountain and the sausage chains, I almost worshipped the partner, Mr. Wilner. I was content to stand for an hour at a time watching him make potato chips. In his cook's cap and apron, with a ladle in his hand and a smile on his face, he moved about with the greatest agility, whisking his raw materials out of nowhere, dipping into his bubbling kettle with a flourish, and bringing forth the finished product with a caper. Such potato chips were not to be had anywhere else on Crescent Beach. Thin as tissue paper, crisp as dry snow, and salt as the sea—such thirst-producing, lemonade-selling, nickel-bringing potato chips only Mr. Wilner could make. On holidays, when dozens of family parties came out by every train from town, he could hardly keep up with the demand for his potato chips. And with a waiting crowd around him our partner was at his best. He was as voluble as he was skilful, and as witty as he was voluble; at least so I guessed from the laughter that frequently drowned his voice. I could not understand his jokes, but if I could get near enough to watch his lips and his smile and his merry eyes, I was happy. That any one could talk so fast, and in English, was marvel enough, but that this prodigy should belong to *our* establishment was a fact to thrill me. I had never seen anything like Mr. Wilner, except a wedding jester; but then he spoke common Yiddish. So proud was I of the talent and good taste displayed at our stand that if my father beckoned to me in the crowd and sent me on an errand, I hoped the people noticed that I, too, was connected with the establishment.

And all this splendor and glory and distinction came to a sudden end. There was some trouble about a license—some fee or fine—there was a storm in the night that damaged the soda fountain and other fixtures—there was talk and consultation between the houses of Antin and Wilner—and the promising partnership was dissolved. No more would the merry partner gather the crowd on the beach; no more would the twelve young Wilners gambol like mermen and mermaids in the surf. And the less numerous tribe of Antin must also say farewell to the jolly seaside life; for men in such humble business as my father's carry their families, along with their other earthly goods, wherever they go, after the manner of gypsies. We had driven a feeble stake into the sand. The jealous Atlantic, in conspiracy with the Sunday law, had torn it out. We must seek our luck elsewhere.

In Polotzk we had supposed that "America" was practically synonymous with "Boston." When we landed in Boston, the horizon was pushed back, and we annexed Crescent Beach. And now, espying other lands of promise, we took possession of the province of Chelsea, in the name of our necessity.

In Chelsea, as in Boston, we made our stand in the wrong end of the town. Arlington Street was inhabited by poor Jews, poor Negroes, and a sprinkling of poor Irish. The side streets leading from it were occupied by more poor Jews and Negroes. It was a proper locality for a man without capital to do business. My father rented a tenement with a store in the basement. He put in a few barrels of flour and of sugar, a few boxes of crackers, a few gallons of kerosene, an assortment of soap of the "save the coupon" brands; in the cellar, a few barrels of potatoes, and a pyramid of kindling-wood; in the showcase, an alluring display of penny candy. He put out his sign, with a gilt-lettered warning of "Strictly Cash," and proceeded to give credit indiscriminately. That was the regular way to do business on Arlington Street. My father, in his three years' apprenticeship, had learned the tricks of many trades. He knew when and how to "bluff." The legend of "Strictly Cash" was a protection against notoriously irresponsible customers; while none of the "good" customers, who had a record for paying regularly on Saturday, hesitated to enter the store with empty purses.

If my father knew the tricks of the trade, my mother could be counted on to throw all her talent and tact into the business. Of course she had no English yet, but as she could perform the acts of weighing, measuring, and mental computation of fractions mechanically, she was able to give her whole attention to the dark mysteries of the language, as intercourse with her customers gave her opportunity. In this she made such rapid progress that she soon lost all sense of disadvantage, and conducted herself behind the counter very much as if she were back in her old store in Polotzk. It was far more cosey than Polotzk—at least, so it seemed to me; for behind the store was the kitchen, where, in the intervals of slack trade, she did her cooking and washing. Arlington Street customers were used to waiting while the storekeeper salted the soup or rescued a loaf from the oven.

Once more Fortune favored my family with a thin little smile, and my father, in reply to a friendly inquiry, would say, "One makes a living," with a shrug of the shoulders that added "but nothing to boast of." It was characteristic of my attitude toward bread-and-butter matters that this contented me, and I felt free to devote myself to the conquest of my new world . . . My early letters to my Russian friends were filled with boastful descriptions of [the] glories of my new country. No native citizen of Chelsea took such pride and delight in its institutions as I did. It required no fife and drum corps, no Fourth of July procession, to set me tingling with patriotism. Even the common agents and instruments of municipal life, such as the letter carrier and the fire engine, I regarded with a measure of respect. I know what I thought of people who said that Chelsea was a very small, dull, unaspiring town, with no discernible excuse for a separate name or existence.

The apex of my civic pride and personal contentment was reached on the bright September morning when I entered the public school. That day I must always remember, even if I live to be so old that I cannot tell my name. To most people their first day at school is a memorable occasion. In my case the importance of the day was a hundred times magnified, on account of the years I had waited, the road I had come, and the conscious ambitions I entertained . . .

Your immigrant inspectors will tell you what poverty the foreigner brings in his baggage, what want in his pockets. Let the overgrown boy of twelve, reverently drawing his letters in the baby class, testify to the noble dreams and high ideals that may be hidden beneath the greasy caftan of the immigrant. Speaking for the Jews, at least, I know I am safe in inviting such an investigation . . .

Father himself conducted us to school. He would not have delegated that mission to the President of the United States. He had awaited the day with impatience equal to mine, and the visions he saw as he hurried us over the sun-flecked pavements transcended all my dreams. Almost his first act on landing on American soil, three years before, had been his application for naturalization. He had taken the remaining steps in the process with eager promptness, and at the earliest moment allowed by the law, he became a citizen of the United States. It is true that he had left home in search of bread for his hungry family, but he went blessing the necessity that drove him to America. The boasted freedom of the New World meant to him far more than the right to reside, travel, and work wherever he pleased; it meant the freedom to speak his thoughts, to throw off the shackles of superstition, to test his own fate, un-hindered by political or religious tyranny. He was only a young man when he landed—thirty-two; and most of his life he had been held in leading-strings. He was hungry for his untasted manhood.

Three years passed in sordid struggle and disappointment. He was not prepared to make a living even in America, where the day laborer eats wheat instead of rye. Apparently the American flag could not protect him against the pursuing Nemesis of his limitations; he must expiate the sins of his fathers who slept across the seas. He had been endowed at birth with a poor constitution, a nervous, restless temperament, and an abundance of hindering prejudices. In his boyhood his body was starved, that his mind might be stuffed with useless learning. In his youth this dearly gotten learning was sold, and the price was the bread and salt which he had not been trained to earn for himself. Under the wedding canopy he was bound for life to a girl whose features were still strange to him; and he was bidden to multiply himself, that sacred learning might be perpetuated in his sons, to the glory of the God of his fathers. All this while he had been led about as a creature without a will, a chattel, an instrument. In his maturity he awoke, and found himself poor in health, poor in purse, poor in useful knowledge, and hampered on all sides. At the first nod of opportunity he broke away from his prison, and strove to atone for his wasted youth by a life of useful labor; while at the same time he sought to lighten the gloom of his narrow scholarship by freely partaking of modern ideas. But his utmost endeavor still left him far from his goal. In business, nothing prospered with him. Some fault of hand or mind or temperament led him to failure where other men found success. Wherever the blame for his disabilities be placed, he reaped their bitter fruit. "Give me bread!" he cried to America. "What will you do to earn it?" the challenge came back. And he found that he was master of no art, of no trade; that even his precious learning was of no avail, because he had only the most antiquated methods of communicating it.

So in his primary quest he had failed. There was left him the compensation of intellectual freedom. That he sought to realize in every possible way. He had very little opportunity to prosecute his education, which, in truth, had never been begun. His struggle for a bare living left him no time to take advantage of the public evening school; but he lost nothing of what was to be learned through reading, through attendance at public meetings, through exercising the rights of citizenship. Even here he was hindered by a natural inability to acquire the English language. In time, indeed, he learned to read, to follow a conversation or lecture; but he never learned to write correctly, and his pronunciation remains extremely foreign to this day.

If education, culture, the higher life were shining things to be worshipped from afar, he had still a means left whereby he could draw one step nearer to them. He could send his children to school, to learn all those things that he knew by fame to be desirable. The common school, at least, perhaps high school; for one or two, perhaps even college! His children should be students, should fill his house with books and intellectual company; and thus he would walk by proxy in the Elysian Fields of liberal learning. As for the children themselves, he knew no surer way to their advancement and happiness.

So it was with a heart full of longing and hope that my father led us to school on that first day. He took long strides in his eagerness, the rest of us running and hopping to keep up.

At last the four of us stood around the teacher's desk; and my father, in his impossible English, gave us over in her charge, with some broken word of his hopes for us that his swelling heart could no longer contain. I venture to say that Miss Nixon was struck by something uncommon in the group we made, something outside of Semitic features and the abashed manner of the alien. My little sister was as pretty as a doll, with her clear pink-and-white face, short golden curls, and eyes like blue violets when you caught them looking up. My brother might have been a girl, too, with his cherubic contours of face, rich red color, glossy black hair, and fine eyebrows. Whatever secret fears were in his heart, remembering his former teachers, who had taught with the rod, he stood up straight and uncringing before the American teacher, his cap respectfully doffed. Next to him stood a starved-looking girl with eyes ready to pop out, and short dark curls that would not have made much of a wig for a Jewish bride.

All three children carried themselves rather better than the common run of "green" pupils that were brought to Miss Nixon. But the figure that challenged attention to the group was the tall, straight father, with his earnest face and fine forehead, nervous hands eloquent in gesture, and a voice full of feeling. This foreigner, who brought his children to school as if it were an act of consecration, who regarded the teacher of the primer class with reverence, who spoke of visions, like a man inspired, in a common schoolroom, was not like other aliens, who brought their children in dull obedience to the law; was not like the native fathers, who brought their unmanageable boys, glad to be relieved of their care. I think Miss Nixon guessed what my father's best English could not convey. I think she divined that by the simple act of delivering our school certificates to her he took possession of America.

FELIX FRANKFURTER

From The Case of Sacco and Vanzetti

 1927

On an April afternoon in 1920, a paymaster and a security guard employed by a shoe manufacturer in South Braintree, Massachusetts, were robbed and shot to death by two men who escaped in a car driven by accomplices. Several weeks later, two Italian immigrants—a fish peddler in Plymouth named Bartolomeo Vanzetti, and a laborer in a Stoughton shoe factory named Nicola Sacco—were arrested on charges of murder. Indicted in September, they went on trial the following spring in the courthouse in Dedham, a wealthy Boston suburb that, as Felix Frankfurter (1882–1965) wryly put it in the March 1927 issue of *The Atlantic Monthly*, "furnished a striking contrast to the background and antecedents of the prisoners." After their conviction, several motions for a new trial—based both on claims of improper procedures and on the emergence of new evidence—were filed and denied. In June 1927, in the face of public outcry, Governor Alvin T. Fuller of Massachusetts appointed a special commission, including the presidents of Harvard and M.I.T., to advise him with respect to appeals for clemency. The appeals were denied and in August 1927 the defendants were executed by electrocution.

The case of Sacco and Vanzetti has become a symbolic instance of how, in our supposedly classless society, the American judicial system sometimes moves without mercy, through the instrumentalities of hostile judges and juries, against defendants whose right to due process is wholly or partially denied. While all the facts may never be known, and the guilt or innocence of each defendant may never be conclusively proven, Felix Frankfurter makes a powerful case that Sacco and Vanzetti were identified by unreliable witnesses who were "casual observers of men they had never seen before, men of foreign race, under circumstances of unusual confusion," and convicted on the dubious basis of the defendants' "consciousness of guilt" as indicated, according to the prosecution, by their nervous and inconsistent accounts of their actions on the day of the crime.

With controlled outrage at what he considered a flagrant miscarriage of justice, Frankfurter, a professor at Harvard who was to be appointed a few years later by Franklin Roosevelt to the U.S. Supreme Court, argues against the legitimacy of such evidence and, in a long quotation from Vanzetti's own testimony, lets us hear one of the accused speaking for himself. The result is both a landmark essay on a historically important criminal trial and a vivid account of New England divided against itself.

Innocent men, it is suggested, do not lie when picked up by the police. But Sacco and Vanzetti knew they were not innocent of the charge on which they supposed themselves arrested, and about which the police interrogated them. For, when apprehended, Sacco and Vanzetti were not confronted with the charge of murder; they were not accused of banditry; they were not given the remotest intimation that the murders of Parmenter and Berardelli were laid at their door. They were told they were arrested as "suspicious characters," and the meaning which that carried to their minds was rendered concrete by the questions that were put to them.

Q. Tell us all you recall that Stewart, the chief, asked of you?
A. He asked me why we were in Bridgewater, how long I knew Sacco, if I am a radical, if I am an anarchist or Communist, and he asked me if I believe in the government of the United States.
Q. Did either Chief Stewart at the Brockton police station or Mr. Katzmann tell you that you were suspected of robberies and murder?
A. No.
Q. Was there any question asked of you or any statement made to you to indicate to you that you were charged with that crime on April 15?
A. No.
Q. What did you understand, in view of the questions asked of you, what did you understand you were being detained for at the Brockton police station?
A. I understand they arrested me for a political matter . . .
Q. . . . Why did you feel you were being detained for political opinions?
A. Because I was asked if I was a Socialist. I said, "Well—"
Q. You mean by reason of the questions asked of you?
A. Because I was asked if I am a Socialist, if I am I.W.W., if I am a Communist, if I am a Radical, if I am a Black Hand.

Plainly their arrest meant to Sacco and Vanzetti arrest for radicalism.

Boston was one of the worst centres of the lawlessness and hysteria that characterized the campaign of the Department of Justice for the wholesale arrest and deportation of Reds. Its proximity to industrial communities having a large proportion of foreign labor and a history of past industrial conflicts lent to the lawless activities of the government officials the widespread support of influential public opinion. Mr. John F. Moors, himself a banker, has called attention to the fact that "the hysteria against 'the reds' was so great, at the time when these men were convicted, that even the most substantial bankers in this city [Boston] were carried away to the extent of paying for full-page advertisements about the red peril." Sacco and Vanzetti were notorious Reds. They were associates of leading radicals; they had for some time been on the list of suspects of the Department of Justice; and they were especially obnoxious because they were draft-dodgers.

The terrorizing methods of the Government had very specific meaning for the two Italians. Two of their friends had already been deported. The arrest of the New York radical Salsedo, and his detention incommunicado by the Department of Justice, had been for some weeks a source of great concern to them. Vanzetti was sent to New York to confer with a committee having charge of the case of Salsedo and other Italian political prisoners. On his return, May 2, he reported to his Boston friends the advice which had been given him: namely, to dispose of their radical literature and thus eliminate the most damaging evidence in the deportation proceedings they feared. The urgency of acting on this advice was intensified by the tragic news of Salsedo's death after Vanzetti's return from New York. Though Salsedo's death was unexplained, to Sacco and Vanzetti it conveyed only one explanation. It was a symbol of their fears and an omen of their own fate.

On the witness stand Sacco and Vanzetti accounted for their movements on April 15. They also accounted for their ambiguous behavior on May 5. Up to the time that Sacco and Vanzetti testified to their radical activities, their pacifism, their flight to Mexico to avoid the draft, the trial was a trial for murder and banditry; with the cross-examination of Sacco and Vanzetti patriotism and radicalism became the dominant emotional issues. Outside the courtroom the Red hysteria was rampant; it was allowed to dominate within. The prosecutor systematically played on the feelings of the jury by exploiting the unpatriotic and despised beliefs of Sacco and Vanzetti, and the judge allowed him thus to divert and pervert the jury's mind.

The opening question in the cross-examination of Vanzetti by the District Attorney discloses a motif that he persistently played upon:—

Q. (by Mr. Katzmann) So you left Plymouth, Mr. Vanzetti, in May, 1917, to dodge the draft, did you?
A. Yes, sir.
Q. When this country was at war, you ran away, so you would not have to fight as a soldier?
A. Yes.

This method was elaborated when Sacco took the stand:—

Q. (by Mr. Katzmann) Did you say yesterday you love a free country?
A. Yes, sir.

Q. Did you love this country in the month of May, 1917?

A. I did not say—I don't want to say I did not love this country.

Q. Did you go to Mexico to avoid being a soldier for this country that you loved?

A. Yes.

Q. And would it be your idea of showing your love for your wife that, when she needed you, you ran away from her?

A. I did not run away from her.

Q. Don't you think going away from your country is a vulgar thing to do when she needs you?

A. I don't believe in war.

Q. You don't believe in war?

A. No, sir.

Q. Do you think it is a cowardly thing to do what you did?

A. No, sir.

Q. Do you think it is a brave thing to do what you did?

A. Yes, sir.

Q. Do you think it would be a brave thing to go away from your own wife?

A. No.

Q. When she needed you?

A. No.

THE COURT. All I ask is this one question, and it will simplify matters very much. Is it your claim that in the collection of the literature and the books and papers that that was done in the interest of the United States?

MR. JEREMIAH MCANARNEY. I make no such broad claim as that . . .

MR. KATZMANN. Well, he [Sacco] stated in his direct examination yesterday that he loved a free country, and I offer it to attack that statement made in his examination by his own counsel.

THE COURT. That is what I supposed, and that is what I supposed that remark meant when it was introduced in this cross-examination, but counsel now say they don't make that claim.

MR. KATZMANN. They say they don't make the claim that gathering up the literature on May 5 at West Bridgewater was for the purpose of helping the country, but that is a different matter, not released [sic] to May 5.

THE COURT. I will let you inquire further first as to what he meant by the expression.

Q. What did you mean when you said yesterday you loved a free country?

A. Give me a chance to explain.

Q. I am asking you to explain now.

A. When I was in Italy, a boy, I was a Republican, so I always thinking Republican has more chance to manage education, develop, to build some day his family, to raise the child and education, if you could. But that was my opinion; so when I came to this country I saw there was not what I was thinking before, but there was all the difference, because I been working in Italy not so hard as I been work in this country. I could live free there just as well. Work in the same condition but not so hard, about seven or eight hours a day, better food. I mean genuine. Of course, over here is good food, because it is bigger country, to any those who got money to spend, not for the working and laboring class, and in Italy is more opportunity to laborer to eat vegetable, more fresh, and I came in this country. When I been started work here very hard and been work thirteen years, hard worker, I could not been afford much a family the way I did have the idea before. I could not put any money in the bank; I could no push my boy some to go to school and other things. I teach over here men who is with me. The free idea gives any man a chance to profess his own idea, not the supreme idea, not to give any person, not to be like Spain in position, yes, about twenty centuries ago, but to give a chance to print and education, literature, free speech, that I see it was all wrong. I could see the best men, intelligent, education, they been arrested and sent to prison and died in prison for years and years without getting them out, and Debs, one of the great men in his country, he is in prison, still away in prison, because he is a Socialist. He wanted the laboring class to have better conditions and better living, more education, give a push his son if he could have a chance some day, but they him in prison. Why? Because the capitalist class, they know, they are against that, because the capitalist class, they don't want our child to go to high school or college or Harvard College. There would be no chance, there would not be no—they don't want the working class educationed; they want the working class to be a low all the times, be underfoot, and not to be up with the head. So, sometimes, you see, the Rockefellers, Morgans, they give fifty—I mean they give five hundred thousand dollars to Harvard College, they give a million dollars for another school. Every day say, 'Well, D. Rockefeller is a great man, the best man in the country.' I want to ask him who is going to Harvard College? What benefit the working class they will get by those million dollars they give by Rockefeller, D. Rockefellers. They won't get, the poor class, they won't have no chance to go to Harvard College because men who is getting $21 a week or $30 a week, I don't care if he gets $80 a week, if he gets a family of five children he can't live and send his child and go to Harvard College if he wants to eat everything nature will give him. If he wants to eat like a cow, and that is the best thing, but I want men to live like men. I like men to get everything that nature will give best, because they belong—we are not the friend of any other place, but we are belong to nations. So that is why my idea has been changed. So that is why I love people who labor and work and see better conditions every day develop, makes no more war. We no want fight by the gun, and we don't want to destroy young men. The mother has been suffering for building the young man. Some day need a little more bread, so when the time the mother get some bread or profit out of that boy, the Rockefellers, Morgans, and some of the peoples, high class, they send to war. Why? What is war? The war is not shoots like Abraham Lincoln's and Abe Jefferson, to fight for the free country, for the better education to give chance to any other peoples, not the white people but the black and the others, because they believe and know they are mens like the rest, but they are war for the great millionaire. No war for the civilization of men. They are war for business, million dollars come on the side. What right we have to kill each other? I been work for the Irish. I have been working with the German fellow, with the French, many other peoples. I love them people just as I could love my wife, and my people for that did receive me. Why should I go kill them men? What he done to me? He never done anything, so I don't believe in no war. I want to destroy those guns. All I can say, the Government put the literature, give us educations. I remember in Italy, a long time ago, about sixty years ago, I should say, yes, about sixty years ago, the Government they could not control very much those two— devilment went on, and robbery, so one of the government in the cabinet he says, 'If you want to destroy those devilments, if you want to take off all those criminals, you ought to give a chance to Socialist literature, education of people, emancipation. That is why I destroy government, boys.' That is why my idea I love Socialists. That is why I like people who want education and living, building, who is good, just as much as they could. That is all.

Q. And that is why you love the United States of America?

A. Yes.

Q. She is back more than twenty centuries like Spain, is she?

A. At the time of the war they do it.

Q. So without the light of knowledge on that subject, you are condemning even Harvard University, are you, as being a place for rich men? . . .

Q. Did you intend to condemn Harvard College? (Objection overruled.)

A. No, sir.

Q. Were you ready to say none but the rich could go there without knowing about offering scholarships? (Objection overruled.)

Q. The question is this: As far as you understood Fruzetti's views, were yours the same? (Objection overruled.)

Q. Answer, please.

A. (through the interpreter) I cannot say yes or no.

Q. Is it because you can't or because you don't want to?

A. (through the interpreter) Because it is a very delicate question.

Q. It is very delicate, isn't it, because he was deported for his views?

Q. Do you know why Fruzetti was deported?

A. (through the interpreter) Yes.

Q. Was it because he was of anarchistic opinions?

THE INTERPRETER. He says he understands it now.

Q. Was it because Fruzetti entertained anarchistic opinions?

A. One reason, he was an anarchist. Another reason, Fruzetti been writing all the time on the newspapers, and I am not sure why the reason he been deported.

Q. And the books which you intended to collect were books relating to anarchy, weren't they?

A. Not all of them.

Q. How many of them?

A. Well, all together. We are Socialists, democratic, any other socialistic information, Socialists, Syndicalists, Anarchists, any paper.

Q. Bolshevist?

A. I do not know what Bolshevism means.

Q. Soviet?

A. I do not know what Soviet means.

Q. Communism?

A. Yes. I got some on astronomy, too.

Q. You weren't going to destroy them?

A. I was going to keep them.

Q. You were going to keep them and when the time was over, you were going to bring them out again, weren't you?

A. Yes.

In the Anglo-American system of criminal procedure the role of a public prosecutor is very different from that of an advocate in a private cause. In the words of a leading New York case:—

> Language which might be permitted to counsel in summing up a civil action cannot with propriety be used by a public prosecutor, who is a quasi-judicial officer, representing the people of the state, and presumed to act impartially in the interest only of justice. If he lays aside the impartiality that should characterize his official action to become a heated partisan, and by vituperation of the prisoner and appeals to prejudice seeks to procure a conviction at all hazards, he ceases to properly repre-

sent the public interest, which demands no victim, and asks no conviction through the aid of passion, sympathy, or resentment.

In 1921 the temper of the times made it the special duty of a prosecutor and a
court engaged in trying two Italian radicals before a jury of native New Englanders to keep the instruments of justice free from the infection of passion or
prejudice. In the case of Sacco and Vanzetti no such restraints were respected.
By systematic exploitation of the defendents' alien blood, their imperfect
knowledge of English, their unpopular social views, and their opposition to
the war, the District Attorney invoked against them a riot of political passion
and patriotic sentiment; and the trial judge connived at—one had almost
written, cooperated in—the process.

F. O. MATTHIESSEN
Journal Letters
 1939

Francis Otto Matthiessen (1902–1950) was the leading scholar of classic American literature of his time; indeed it was his book *American Renaissance* (1941) that made it intelligible to speak of American literary works as "classic." As a student at Yale, he had been a member of the exclusive Skull and Bones Society, and he went on to become a professor at Harvard, where he was especially known for the attention he gave to teaching undergraduates. Although he lived on Beacon Hill, Matthiessen never felt fully at home among the Brahmins. He had strong leftist sympathies and, more costly to his ability to "fit in," he led a semi-secret life as the lover of the painter Russell Cheney, who was exiled to the periphery of Matthiessen's conventional social circle in Cambridge and Boston. In the two "journal letters" reprinted here (written for Cheney's eyes as well as his own), Matthiessen describes the depression that gripped him in the winter of 1939, when he committed himself to McLean Hospital for psychiatric treatment. These extraordinary letters were efforts to write himself out of madness and, in some measure, they may have helped. He overcame his mental paralysis for a time; in 1940, he finished *American Renaissance.* But in their articulate anguish one glimpses the deadly mixture of fear and guilt (and, according to his doctors, self-directed rage) that eventually cost him his life. In 1950, five years after Cheney's death, Matthiessen leapt to his death from the window of a high-floor room he had taken in Boston's North Station Hotel.

McLean Hospital
Waverly [Mass.]
[Jan. 4, 1939]

I don't know how to begin a record of this experience since it is so irrational, and when its power is upon me, so beyond the scope of my comprehension. I can trace, and have traced to various friends the genesis of my condition. At Kittery, this fall, instead of riding my work, it began without precedent to ride me. I couldn't seem to turn off the pressure and relax. I lost sleep and that made me more strained; and that strain cost me more sleep and I was caught in an increasingly vicious circle. Was I tired to begin with after so many years of high pressure? Perhaps, though I was hardly aware of it. But certainly the readjustment to leisure was hard. With the external tensions relaxed, the mind may have fallen limp and flaccid like a released rubber band. (Jan 4, evening, physically relaxed for the first time, having been absorbed into a rhythm of routine which I have managed to create for myself after nine days here.)

At any rate as the fall advanced, though I continued to write, and though given sections seemed good to my acutest critics, I found less satisfaction and less control. The worst trouble was that having tried to shape something one way and not being content with it, I didn't seem to have the resilience to start it anew, but would feel bogged down before it. The range of memory and reference that I counted on became clogged and dull. I began questioning my talent, questioning my knowledge, questioning my maturity. I don't want to question them further at this point, for when and if I come out of this experience, I want to start anew with fresh and vigorous assumptions.

About the middle of December the jagged rhythm of going to bed, dropping off to sleep as usual but being dragged back after an hour or two into the monotony of nervous thoughts about my work, of taking nembutal, of lasting through until four-thirty or five, and then being awake for good, began to wear me down. It hardly seemed serious, but to someone so used to sleeping through the night, so without a technique for handling this obtrusion, it seemed sensible to talk to a doctor about it. So I called on Dr. Maurice Fremont-Smith, and he gave me very sensible advice, hints of how to relax, of how to think of something else, not to worry about nembutal since it was not habit-forming, not to be anxious if the book [American Renaissance] was not getting written since I was gaining knowledge and experience through it, indeed primarily not to worry at all since loss of sleep was not dangerous. These scattered quick notes do not do justice to his quiet consideration during the hour and a half I talked with him. He hardly told me things that I didn't already know, since I am also sensitive and considerate, but he reinforced me with the authority of the man in white and that was necessary for me.

But that very night at the Murdocks (after the Eliot House play) I was hauled out of sleep by the fantasy that it would be better if I jumped out the window. And during the succeeding week in Kittery I was recurrently filled with the desire to kill myself. Why? That is what is so baffling, so unfathomed. Because my talent was less than I thought? Because, on the first onset, I couldn't write the book I wanted? Such reasons seem preposterous to anyone reasonable, and certainly they do to me as I sit here this evening listening to Mozart's Quintet in A Major. For even though it should turn out that I am an enthusiast trying to be a critic, a Platonic rhapsode trying to be an Aristotelian, that means a fairly hard period of readjustment, but scarcely grounds for death for a man of thirty-six. But what if you found out you couldn't write any book at all? But why introduce that phantom when you have already written three? Must it be aut Caesar aut nullus? Must everything meet you on your first terms? As Dr. Barrett said a couple of days ago, "No one kills himself over a book." And I answered, "Nobody but a goddamned fool, and I'm not a goddamned fool."

Towards the end of my session with Dr. Fremont-Smith he dwelt on the danger of fear, and perhaps intuitively introduced the fear of the death of someone you loved. At once I raised the question of whether I could face life without Russell, and saw again the fear that gripped me so fiercely at that moment in the fall, in September when he had gone home after the hurricane, and had gotten caught by drink, as I knew he would, and had finally called from the Copley and I had gone down and brought him back, and lying on the bed the next morning his hands still shaking desperately from the nervous shock, he had said that he had wanted to die. That moment stunned me. It brought out what has probably been latent for a long time. I have not been given at all to worry or to fear, and now I am tangled in them. Having built my life so simply and wholly with Russell's, having had my eyes opened by him to so much beauty, my heart filled by such richness, my pulse beating steadily in time with his in intimate daily companionship, I am shocked at the thought of life without him. How would it be possible? How go on from day to day? Again my questions are not reasonable. Russell is not dead, and my present confused misery can only serve to dishearten and bring nearer the very event that I fear. And why must I cross the bridge of being alone again before I am, why try to settle a situation that does not exist? I don't think that has been my practice with situations in the past. Mitch [Russell Davenport] said last spring that the clarity of my thought sometimes bothered him in being more definite than life. Bruno [Kollar] once remarked on how conscious I was. The American mind terribly aware of itself. Has its bright scrutiny, the self-knowledge which I have believed to be my sureness in making my life an integrated one, shut off more than I am aware, has it left nine-tenths of the iceberg hidden?

A week after my session with Dr. Fremont-Smith,—though it seemed a much longer interval, since having once glimpsed the image of suicide, my mind and emotions galloped so violently down the corridors of that temptation—I was back in Boston again, on our way through to New York and to the Hydes for Christmas. Kenneth [Murdock] knows better than I do what my exact condition was then. I was very depressed, nervously worn down by having these gray clouds day after day around my head and shoulders with no rift in them. I no longer had poise. I sat and talked to him several hours, while he was nursing a cold, and covered much of the history that I have given so shortly here. He was very balanced and wise. He tried to make me see that even if I couldn't swing this book for some reason, still there was so much I could give as a teacher, as a vital member participating in shaping the life around me. His words were simpler, more charged than those, as mine have been when I was doing those very things. He also reasoned with me that I was strong, and when the time came would find resources to face Russell's death. He kept urging upon me how many friends I have and how much I meant to them. God knows I am aware how much they mean to me. At one point in our talk I broke into tears, and said that I loved life, that I had felt myself in contact with so many sides of American society and believed there was so much work to be done, absorbing it, helping to direct it intelligently. And now I felt a film of unreality between me and everything that had seemed most real, that I had to find some way to break through it. We discussed alternatives which I presented: going to New Mexico for a complete change (but I would take myself with me), going to some healthy place to get my sleep steady first, coming to Boston with an apartment where Russell could paint and where I would see more people and perhaps even take up part time work at Harvard, going to see a psychiatrist or analyst. The latter alternative being the one wholly unknown, it seemed sensible to investigate where it might lead. Dr. Fremont-Smith recommended me to Dr. Barrett. I urged upon his secretary an appointment for that very afternoon. I summarized for him, as honestly and intensely as I could my dilemma as I saw it: work vitiated by lack of sleep, real fear (or unreal? obsessive at any rate) for the first time in my life, and now this desire to jump out of a window.

[*McLean Hospital*]
[*Waverly, Mass.*]
[Jan. 8, 1939]

I resume this some days later (Sunday, January 8). I grew so sick of stewing over myself that I had no heart to prolong the discussion in ink. Barrett was quiet and impressive, assumed my relationship with Russell at once. The remark that he made that clicked was, "You may remember the sentence from Freud that every man is entitled to one neurosis when his father dies." He had previously asked when my father had died, and I had told him that he was still alive but that mother had separated from him when I was five. The element of my search for a father in Russell had not been specially conscious for me, as it had been in my feeling for Bruno [Kollar] and for Harry Dorman. But Barrett's remark brought a flash of perception to me. I had a glimpse of understanding my incomprehensible state. For that evening [about December 23rd], going down to Pomfret and staying with the Putnams', Coriolanus was himself again. The external world was real and exciting again. I could almost have cried with joy, for instance, at being able to *see* once more a street light flooding over a policeman's heavy jaw and blue shoulder, and not being caught fast in the miasmatic film of my incessant thoughts.

I write this somewhat at random, since, though more relaxed, I am fairly tired. The narrative needs little further extension of outline. I saw Mitch in NY, in his Fortune office, in between telephone conversations with Sumner Welles, et al. He was salutary, if impersonally cool, in his detachment. He had just lived through the experience of having a woman with whom he was in love kill herself, of having had to fight down the desire for himself. He said that he no longer asked his friends not to commit suicide, but not to do it without a reason that he could respect. He agreed that analysis was dynamite, but that if you admired wisdom it could be a great experience, even if it was to be your last.

Louis, who was the final one to be plagued by the tired insistence of my story, was unfailingly gentle and reassuring. I asked him if what I needed was a swift kick to shake me out of my obsession. He answered, only on the grounds of demanding too much of myself, of gearing my notion of this book too high. He kept saying that he was sure that my energy would carry me through this.

I returned to Boston, saw Barrett, decided to come out to McLean for one-two-or three weeks, to get rested, and to start an analysis. I have been here two weeks now and plan to leave on Jan. 13. These days have contained some of the most searing hours I have known. Misery, melancholy, almost despair have settled around me like clouds through which I could not see a rift in the morning. Then each day by early afternoon, after lunch and a short sleep, I have struggled back to some poise, to late afternoons and evenings when the bars on the windows seemed absurd. But then the descent through sleep to finding at 5 a.m. that none of the problem had been solved, and to be swept again by gusts of hot dry futility.

What are some of the things that have shaken me most? The first days were a nightmare that had to be constantly fought back to keep it from becoming me. I had never before been surrounded by the mentally deranged, young men quite out of touch with reality, old men with softened wits, the vacant faces much less horrible than the suffering ones. I had to wrestle with the dread that having gotten in here I wouldn't be able to get out, that I too would be faced with years of soothing baths, shuffling feet and disintegration. I knew that death would be better than being kept alive on those terms. If I could convey the full intensity of the horror of those days, it would take me deep into misery.

Step after step of humiliation has brought me a new understanding of humility. I have hated imaginary illnesses in tweed coats and costly sanitariums, and here I am. I have prided myself most on clarity and control, and have been confused, without self-understanding or any mastery. My great resource, books, has become meaningless. I have tried to read and though I recognize the individual words, the debate with myself obtrudes between me and them, the paragraph slides away and seems not worth pursuing. And even words that I know suddenly look strange,—what is *ramify?*—and I have no resilience to pursue them. My steel-trap memory is blurred. I have had a distressing time with the names of the attendants. (I can recognize that I am better, however, for I am considerably clearer now.) I who was sure have become unsure, unable to make decisions, unable to see my way from *a* to *b*, most agonizingly unable to get out of the sterile round of my own miserable thoughts, to see the shapes and colors of the world, to feel the values of society or any meaning to God.

The death wish took agonizingly vivid images of jumping out of a window during those first tortured days. But that image is much less insistent now. By living with it I may have built up an anti-toxin. But I am living with it: that is the fact I face. I have every reason to live that can be enumerated: work that I believe to be important, an interest, no a zest for understanding and participating in shaping the society of which I am part, more generous and devoted friends than ordinarily fall to the lot of any man. And none of the more usual pressures: I have money in the bank, a good job, no physical illness. Where has this fear come from to engulf one who has never even been bothered by anxiety or worry before? If I dread life without Russell, the fact is that he is alive, buoyant, rich, and I am merely hastening by my melancholy the event that might lie far in the future, for this strain is very hard for him. It hasn't heretofore been my habit, has it, to leap across bridges long before they were in sight? The nub of the problem is here. When you give yourself entirely to love, you cannot demand that it last forever. For then fear intrudes, and there I am.

This obviously doesn't state the whole problem. Much of the iceberg lies hidden. Barrett talks of the aggression that I am now turning against myself, and God knows I have been knifing my confidence, rubbing salt into the wounds of my self-esteem.

What I know is that I am living with the phantom of death, and I have resolved to fight it. I cannot die because it would kill Russell. And to keep from jumping I must cast out this fear of Russell's death. Many times in these past weeks I have felt possessed with a devil. I pray now for strength of nerve and courage to resist the temptation of violent unreason.

(10 p.m. Jan. 8 Sunday)

JEAN STAFFORD

From Boston Adventure

 1944

Jean Stafford's best-selling novel *Boston Adventure* is a revealing window into the clannish world of upper-crust Boston. Stafford (1915–1979), who was born in California, brought an outsider's mix of enchantment and revulsion to her subject of Beacon Hill society as seen through the eyes of the daughter of immigrants. The tale is told in the voice of Sonie Marburg, whose Russian mother is in a mental asylum—a fate toward which she began to descend after Sonie's German father deserted the family. Sonie, who is eighteen, has been taken in as secretary-companion by Miss Lucy Pride, an aging Boston blue-blood who had spent summers in a resort hotel where Sonie's mother once worked as a chambermaid. Through her meticulous description of the furnishings, rituals, and rhythms of Miss Pride's household, Stafford captures its atmosphere of strained heartiness and underlying decay as only an outsider could have felt it.

Some afternoons, I stepped across the threshold and wandered about the drawing-room for a quarter of an hour, musing on how it would be when it was occupied by Miss Pride's friends. At first I had thought of the room as altogether Victorian, but after a few investigations, I saw that its objects were disparate and that the only really Victorian part of the room was the bay-window, furnished with an uncushioned love-seat of some stony black wood, the arms carved and embossed and curled; the feet of a stunted lion had been calcified and grafted on to the slender ankles of the seat's well-developed legs. On either side, stationed on the floor where presumably they got the morning light, were a variety of house-plants, no one of which laid claim to beauty. They were kept there and were replaced when they died (this happened rarely, their chief virtue being longevity) because they had been there forever just as a Pride or a tributary to the family had always lived in the house. Miss Pride detested them but would not have dreamed of having them removed; she was especially offended by one species which had large flat dusky leaves chased with pink striations. She did not know its name but called it after a kind of cookie it reminded her of, "Aunt Alice's Birthday Trifle" which had figured in her childhood. Evidently some former owner of the house had been a Francophile and another had fancied Oriental handiwork, for upon the ormolu top of a tulip-wood commode there sat a golden Buddha and above him on the white New England wall hung two Japanese prints of long ladies, long herons, and long sprays of wisteria. Yet at the Buddha's feet, as if to confirm the nationality of the commode, lay aimlessly an ivory-handled dagger of which the blade was inlaid with slate-blue *fleur-de-lis*. The sofas, high and stuffed with an inelastic substance, and the slipper chairs, low, velvety, resilient, had, like Aunt Alice's Birthday Trifle, grown up with the house and their removal was unthinkable although even Miss Pride admitted that they were hideous. Cluttered and inarticulate as it was, I preferred this room to the library, for it was lighter, being at the front of the house and carpeted with a buff rug sprinkled with rich, blue flowers, and its anachronisms imparted to it an atmosphere of geniality as if each heir had accepted the vagaries of the one who preceded him with good will and added his own in the same spirit. The library, on the other hand, was a formidable, masculine province, dominated by Mr. Pride and by several umbrageous ancestral portraits. The furniture was plain, solid, useful. Miss Pride had told me that on Christmas Eve when the revelers and carolers thronged Beacon Hill and one's door-bell rang a hundred times whether or not one had intended to hold open house, her father had read aloud to the servants from the Gospel according to Saint Matthew while in the drawing-room his daring wife, trembling with fear at her own importunity, served sillabub and *lebkuchen* to the visitors. In the library, too, President Eliot had been in the habit of spending two or three evenings a month playing chess with Mr. Pride. His daughter described to me one such evening. "My mother sent me down to ask Papa if they would have some Brazil nuts with their sherry. She was never content to let well enough alone. She was a regular doter. The gentlemen were in the midst of their game and my father, very much annoyed at the disturbance, put his finger to his lips and motioned to me not to move a step nearer the table. President Eliot looked up and through me; my father finished a play and said, 'Sir, for your sake, I regret the brilliance of my rook's performance, for it has won the game for me.' 'You apologized too soon, sir,' said Mr. Eliot and bending forward with a smile like the Cheshire cat's, he captured the rook and checkmated Papa. Then, without any further talk, they set up the men again and to my question would they like some Brazil nuts with their sherry, Papa curtly replied, 'No.' But President Eliot, without looking at me though he glared at my father, said, 'Speak for yourself, Mr. Pride. I, for my part, would relish Brazil nuts as a reward for my triumph.'" . . .

One Friday night [Miss Pride] requested me to come downstairs at tea time the following afternoon to be, as she said, "broken in," an unfortunate phrase since it was also the one she used in speaking of servants whom she had trained . . . A dozen people were already drinking tea when I went into the drawing-room and were deep in conversation . . .

"Take charge [of the tea-table] for a while," [Miss Pride] said when I came to her. "I must speak to someone." Then, bending over as if to inspect the plate of lemon slices, she said in a much lower voice, "I think you should be more sparing of lip rouge." This was by no means the first reproof I had received since I had been in Boston. She had taken it upon herself to civilize me, or, as she called it, to "caulk" me, for, she said, not even the sturdiest vessel could weather such storms as I had without some damage. The "storms" were not so much the facts of my father's desertion, my brother's death, my mother's calamity, as they were the omissions in my upbringing . . .

[Miss Pride] was moving in and out amongst her guests . . . As she halted before each of the little groups, I observed that she treated her friends with very little more warmth than she did me or her chauffeur. She did not bend towards them, but stood erect, looking down upon the interrupted talkers and perhaps rewarding them with a cool smile. Her smile had about it the same economy that had her speech and her eating habits and her apparel. I do not mean that she lacked either cordiality or humor and no doubt she was genuinely fond of many of the people gathered here. But she was never, so to speak, surprised into a smile, and she allowed her smile to last only so long as it was justified by the nature of its provocation. I noticed, however, that she was not the only one who husbanded her responses, for often one of her guests cracked open and resealed his mouth as perfunctorily as she. I admired their abstention, regarding it as a kind of hallmark of the Puritans, like the haemophilia of the Bourbons. I had noticed, from the beginning, that Miss Pride was extremely frugal of her laughter. Now and again, she was amused enough to emit two muted barks of the same volume and duration, as if she were actually saying "Ha! ha!" . . .

I could not evaluate accurately the aspects of this select world: whether the personal connection of these people with the immortals, or their poised arrogance in regard to such issues as the contemptible political machine of Boston, or their stylish language, or their blue-blooded ugliness was the more impressive. The roots of Miss Pride's guests were so deep and tough that I thought they were eternal . . . It was not, I concluded, that what they said and the judgments they passed were of any profundity or of any insight (on the contrary, they often sprang from a primitive and passionate ignorance of the opinions of the rest of the world but which, despite their egotism, contained a measure of self-distrust) but that the manner of these pilgrims' heirs was so fearless and direct that one was not struck with their fatuity . . .

I rose, intending to make my way to the bay-window and try covertly to close it for I was suffering acutely from the cold. Miss Pride detained me. "I want you to talk with Amy Brooks, who is over there by the fire. She's about your age and a very suitable person." . . .

My appointed interlocutor was ruinously plain, wanting both an adequate nose and chin, but having, for compensation, large square glossy teeth and hyperthyroid eyes. She was small and nervous and given to giggling as well as to sudden fits of seriousness when her whole organism tensed to apparently agonizing statements like, "I have been reading Eugene O'Neill!" or "Last week I went to T Wharf and spent an afternoon sketching!" Then for a few seconds she would stare at me with her high, blue, mammiform eyes . . .

This girl, so inferior to my ideal conception of a Bostonian, and yet, with all her cordiality, so aloof, unwilling even to inquire what my business might be in that drawing-room (For how could she have failed to sense immediately that I was an outsider?) had, when she began to speak of Hopestill Mather, changed her tone from nervousness to calm, as if she were held in check by a powerful emotion which had put a stop to the vertigo of her introspection and had made her temporarily critical. I said, "Do you know Miss Mather well?"

"Oh, of course," she replied. "She's my cousin."

In the course of that day, I discovered a Bostonian general principle: namely, that everyone was related to everyone else, or if blood kinship did not obtain, something else almost as binding did; people had gone to dancing school together or their fathers had been law-partners or their mothers had been Red Cross nurses in the same village in France. But this kinship, even that of blood (perhaps actually it was true more of this than of the other kind) was so taken for granted that it was almost uninteresting. It was important to know who had married into what family and who were the forebears of the bride and groom and whether the bride's mother were the Martha Endicott who had gone to Winsor School with Priscilla Bradley but had married into Philadelphia. All of this was of vital concern, but half the time, the performers of that drama, coiled about itself innumerable times, were known most vaguely to their commentators. And the relation of twigs to the trees had become so complicated that no one could straighten it out immediately: the whole rigamarole must be gone through each time.

SHIRLEY JACKSON

The Lottery

 1948

Shirley Jackson (1916–1965) grew up in an affluent suburb of San Francisco, moved east with her parents during her teens, and eventually settled in North Bennington, Vermont, when her husband, the critic Stanley Edgar Hyman, took a position at Bennington College in 1945. Subjected to a lifetime of wounding reproaches by her mother—who told her as a child that she had tried to abort the pregnancy that produced her and, in later years, commented on her figure by sending her corsets—Jackson was as psychologically fragile as she was brilliant. When she moved with her brash, philandering, Brooklyn-born husband to Vermont, she found the townfolk at odds with the avant-garde college on their doorstep, and though she had little use for the college herself (especially for the young women who sported with her husband) she felt immediately unwelcome.

The story that made Jackson famous, "The Lottery," was published in *The New Yorker* in the summer of 1948. In it she concentrated a number of complementary themes and feelings, including her interest in witchcraft practices and persecutions, her horror at the anti-Semitism she discovered in her own family when she married Hyman, and certain anthropological ideas about ritual scapegoating, which both she and her husband were studying at the time. At the heart of the tale is her personal revulsion at small-town xenophobia—an emotion that both appealed to and appalled her gothic imagination.

The morning of June 27th was clear and sunny, with the fresh warmth of a full-summer day; the flowers were blossoming profusely and the grass was richly green. The people of the village began to gather in the square, between the post office and the bank, around ten o'clock; in some towns there were so many people that the lottery took two days and had to be started on June 26th, but in this village, where there were only about three hundred people, the whole lottery took less than two hours, so it could begin at ten o'clock in the morning and still be through in time to allow the villagers to get home for noon dinner.

The children assembled first, of course. School was recently over for the summer, and the feeling of liberty sat uneasily on most of them; they tended to gather together quietly for a while before they broke into boisterous play, and their talk was still of the classroom and the teacher, of books and reprimands. Bobby Martin had already stuffed his pockets full of stones, and the other boys soon followed his example, selecting the smoothest and roundest stones; Bobby and Harry Jones and Dickie Delacroix—the villagers pronounced this name "Dellacroy"—eventually made a great pile of stones in one corner of the square and guarded it against the raids of the other boys. The girls stood aside, talking among themselves, looking over their shoulders at the boys, and the very small children rolled in the dust or clung to the hands of their older brothers or sisters.

Soon the men began to gather, surveying their own children, speaking of planting and rain, tractors and taxes. They stood together, away from the pile of stones in the corner, and their jokes were quiet and they smiled rather than laughed. The women, wearing faded house dresses and sweaters, came shortly after their menfolk. They greeted one another and exchanged bits of gossip as they went to join their husbands. Soon the women, standing by their husbands, began to call to their children, and the children came reluctantly, having to be called four or five times. Bobby Martin ducked under his mother's grasping hand and ran, laughing, back to the pile of stones. His father spoke up sharply, and Bobby came quickly and took his place between his father and his oldest brother.

The lottery was conducted—as were the square dances, the teen-age club, the Halloween program—by Mr. Summers, who had time and energy to devote to civic activities. He was a round-faced, jovial man and he ran the coal business, and people were sorry for him, because he had no children and his wife was a scold. When he arrived in the square, carrying the black wooden box, there was a murmur of conversation among the villagers, and he waved and called, "Little late today, folks." The postmaster, Mr. Graves, followed him, carrying a three-legged stool, and the stool was put in the center of the square and Mr. Summers set the black box down on it. The villagers kept their distance, leaving a space between themselves and the stool, and when Mr. Summers said, "Some of you fellows want to give me a hand?" there was a hesitation before two men, Mr. Martin and his oldest son, Baxter, came forward to hold the box steady on the stool while Mr. Summers stirred up the papers inside it.

The original paraphernalia for the lottery had been lost long ago, and the black box now resting on the stool had been put into use even before Old Man Warner, the oldest man in town, was born. Mr. Summers spoke frequently to the villagers about making a new box, but no one liked to upset even as much tradition as was represented by the black box. There was a story that the present box had been made with some pieces of the box that had preceded it, the one that had been constructed when the first people settled down to make a village here. Every year, after the lottery, Mr. Summers began talking again about a new box, but every year the subject was allowed to fade off without anything's being done. The black box grew shabbier each year; by now it was no longer completely black but splintered badly along one side to show the original wood color, and in some places faded or stained.

Mr. Martin and his oldest son, Baxter, held the black box securely on the stool until Mr. Summers had stirred the papers thoroughly with his hand. Because so much of the ritual had been forgotten or discarded, Mr. Summers had been successful in having slips of paper substituted for the chips of wood that had been used for generations. Chips of wood, Mr. Summers had argued, had been all very well when the village was tiny, but now that the population was more than three hundred and likely to keep on growing, it was necessary to use something that would fit more easily into the black box. The night before the lottery, Mr. Summers and Mr. Graves made up the slips of paper and put them in the box, and it was then taken to the safe of Mr. Summers' coal company and locked up until Mr. Summers was ready to take it to the square next morning. The rest of the year, the box was put away, sometimes one place, sometimes another; it had spent one year in Mr. Graves's barn and another year underfoot in the post office, and sometimes it was set on a shelf in the Martin grocery and left there.

There was a great deal of fussing to be done before Mr. Summers declared the lottery open. There were the lists to make up—of heads of families, heads of households in each family, members of each household in each family. There was the proper swearing-in of Mr. Summers by the postmaster, as the official of the lottery; at one time, some people remembered, there had been a recital of some sort, performed by the official of the lottery, a perfunctory, tuneless chant that had been rattled off duly each year; some people believed that the official of the lottery used to stand just so when he said or sang it, others believe that he was supposed to walk among the people, but years and years ago this part of the ritual had been allowed to lapse. There had been, also, a ritual salute, which the official of the lottery had had to use in addressing each person who came up to draw from the box, but this also had changed with time, until now it was felt necessary only for the official to speak to each person approaching. Mr. Summers was very good at all this; in his clean white shirt and blue jeans, with one hand resting carelessly on the black box, he seemed very proper and important as he talked interminably to Mr. Graves and the Martins.

Just as Mr. Summers finally left off talking and turned to the assembled villagers, Mrs. Hutchinson came hurriedly along the path to the square, her sweater thrown over her shoulders, and slid into place in the back of the crowd. "Clean forgot what day it was," she said to Mrs. Delacroix, who stood next to her, and they both laughed softly. "Thought my old man was out back stacking wood," Mrs. Hutchinson went on, "and then I looked out the window and the kids were gone, and then I remembered it was the twenty-seventh and came a-running." She dried her hands on her apron, and Mrs. Delacroix said, "You're in time, though. They're still talking away up there."

Mrs. Hutchinson craned her neck to see through the crowd and found her husband and children standing near the front. She tapped Mrs. Delacroix on the arm as a farewell and began to make her way through the crowd. The people separated good-humoredly to let her through; two or three people said, in voices just loud enough to be heard across the crowd, "Here comes your Missus, Hutchinson," and "Bill, she made it after all." Mrs. Hutchinson reached her husband, and Mr. Summers, who had been waiting, said cheerfully, "Thought we were going to have to get on without you, Tessie." Mrs. Hutchinson said, grinning, "Wouldn't have me leave m'dishes in the sink, now, would you, Joe?" and soft laughter ran through the crowd as the people stirred back into position after Mrs. Hutchinson's arrival.

"Well, now," Mr. Summers said soberly, "guess we better get started, get this over with, so's we can go back to work. Anybody ain't here?"

"Dunbar," several people said. "Dunbar, Dunbar."

Mr. Summers consulted his list. "Clyde Dunbar," he said. "That's right. He's broke his leg, hasn't he? Who's drawing for him?"

"Me, I guess," a woman said, and Mr. Summers turned to look at her. "Wife draws for her husband," Mr. Summers said. "Don't you have a grown boy to do it for you, Janey?" Although Mr. Summers and everyone else in the village knew the answer perfectly well, it was the business of the official of the lottery to ask such questions formally. Mr. Summers waited with an expression of polite interest while Mrs. Dunbar answered.

"Horace's not but sixteen yet," Mrs. Dunbar said regretfully. "Guess I gotta fill in for the old man this year."

"Right," Mr. Summers said. He made a note on the list he was holding. Then he asked, "Watson boy drawing this year?"

A tall boy in the crowd raised his hand. "Here," he said. "I'm drawing for m'mother and me." He blinked his eyes nervously and ducked his head as several voices in the crowd said things like "Good fellow, Jack," and "Glad to see your mother's got a man to do it."

"Well," Mr. Summers said, "guess that's everyone. Old Man Warner make it?"

"Here," a voice said, and Mr. Summers nodded.

A sudden hush fell on the crowd as Mr. Summers cleared his throat and looked at the list. "All ready?" he called. "Now, I'll read the names—heads of families first—and the men come up and take a paper out of the box. Keep the paper folded in your hand without looking at it until everyone has had a turn. Everything clear?"

The people had done it so many times that they only half listened to the directions; most of them were quiet, wetting their lips, not looking around. Then Mr. Summers raised one hand high and said, "Adams." A man disengaged himself from the crowd and came forward. "Hi, Steve," Mr. Summers said, and Mr. Adams said, "Hi, Joe." They grinned at one another humorlessly and nervously. Then Mr. Adams reached into the black box and took out a folded paper. He held it firmly by one corner as he turned and went hastily back to his place in the crowd, where he stood a little apart from his family, not looking down at his hand.

"Allen," Mr. Summers said. "Anderson. . . . Bentham."

"Seems like there's no time at all between lotteries any more," Mrs. Delacroix said to Mrs. Graves in the back row. "Seems like we got through with the last one only last week."

"Time sure goes fast," Mrs. Graves said.

"Clark. . . . Delacroix."

"There goes my old man," Mrs. Delacroix said. She held her breath while her husband went forward.

"Dunbar," Mr. Summers said, and Mrs. Dunbar went steadily to the box while one of the women said, "Go on, Janey," and another said, "There she goes."

"We're next," Mrs. Graves said. She watched while Mr. Graves came around from the side of the box, greeted Mr. Summers gravely, and selected a slip of paper from the box. By now, all through the crowd there were men holding the small folded papers in their large hands, turning them over and over nervously. Mrs. Dunbar and her two sons stood together, Mrs. Dunbar holding the slip of paper.

"Harburt. . . . Hutchinson."

"Get up there, Bill," Mrs. Hutchinson said, and the people near her laughed.

"Jones."

"They do say," Mr. Adams said to Old Man Warner, who stood next to him, "that over in the north village they're talking of giving up the lottery."

Old Man Warner snorted. "Pack of crazy fools," he said. "Listening to the young folks, nothing's good enough for *them*. Next thing you know, they'll be wanting to go back to living in caves, nobody work any more, live *that* way for a while. Used to be a saying about 'Lottery in June, corn be heavy soon.' First thing you know, we'll all be eating stewed chickweed and acorns. There's *always* been a lottery," he added petulantly. "Bad enough to see young Joe Summers up there joking with everybody."

"Some places have already quit lotteries," Mrs. Adams said.

Nothing but trouble in *that*," Old Man Warner said stoutly. "Pack of young fools."

"Martin." And Bobby Martin watched his father go forward. "Over-dyke. . . . Percy."

"I wish they'd hurry," Mrs. Dunbar said to her older son. "I wish they'd hurry."

"They're almost through," her son said.

"You get ready to run tell Dad," Mrs. Dunbar said.

Mr. Summers called his own name and then stepped forward precisely and selected a slip from the box. Then he called, "Warner."

"Seventy-seventh year I been in the lottery," Old Man Warner said as he went through the crowd. "Seventy-seventh time."

"Watson." The tall boy came awkwardly through the crowd. Someone said, "Don't be nervous, Jack," and Mr. Summers said, "Take your time, son."

"Zanini."

After that, there was a long pause, a breathless pause, until Mr. Summers, holding his slip of paper in the air, said, "All right, fellows." For a minute, no one moved, and then all the slips of paper were opened. Suddenly, all the women began to speak at once, saying, "Who is it?" "Who's got it?" "Is it the Dunbars?" "Is it the Watsons?" Then the voices began to say, "It's Hutchinson. It's Bill," "Bill Hutchinson's got it."

"Go tell your father," Mrs. Dunbar said to her older son.

People began to look around to see the Hutchinsons. Bill Hutchinson was standing quiet, staring down at the paper in his hand. Suddenly, Tessie Hutchinson shouted to Mr. Summers, "You didn't give him time enough to take any paper he wanted. I saw you. It wasn't fair."

"Be a good sport, Tessie," Mrs. Delacroix called, and Mrs. Graves said, "All of us took the same chance."

"Shut up, Tessie," Bill Hutchinson said.

"Well, everyone," Mr. Summers said, "that was done pretty fast, and now we've got to be hurrying a little more to get done in time." He consulted his next list. "Bill," he said, "you draw for the Hutchinson family. You got any other households in the Hutchinsons."

"There's Don and Eva," Mrs. Hutchinson yelled. "Make *them* take their chance!"

"Daughters draw with their husbands' families, Tessie," Mr. Summers said gently. "You know that as well as anyone else."

"It wasn't *fair*," Tessie said.

"I guess not, Joe," Bill Hutchinson said regretfully. "My daughter draws with her husband's family, that's only fair. And I've got no other family except the kids."

"Then, as far as drawing for families is concerned, it's you," Mr. Summers said in explanation, "and as far as drawing for households is concerned, that's you, too. Right?"

"Right," Bill Hutchinson said.

"How many kids, Bill?" Mr. Summers asked formally.

"Three," Bill Hutchinson said. "There's Bill, Jr., and Nancy, and little Dave. And Tessie and me."

"All right, then," Mr. Summers said. "Harry, you got their tickets back?"

Mr. Graves nodded and held up the slips of paper. "Put them in the box, then," Mr. Summers directed. "Take Bill's and put it in."

"I think we ought to start over," Mrs. Hutchinson said, as quietly as she could. "I tell you it wasn't *fair*. You didn't give him time enough to choose. *Everybody* saw that."

Mr. Graves had selected the five slips and put them in the box, and he dropped all the papers but those onto the ground, where the breeze caught them and lifted them off.

"Listen, everybody," Mrs. Hutchinson was saying to the people around her.

"Ready, Bill?" Mr. Summers asked, and Bill Hutchinson, with one quick glance around at his wife and children, nodded.

"Remember," Mr. Summers said, "take the slips and keep them folded until each person has taken one. Harry, you help little Dave." Mr. Graves took the hand of the little boy, who came willingly with him up to the box. "Take a paper out of the box, Davy," Mr. Summers said. Davy put his hand into the box and laughed. "Take just *one* paper," Mr. Summers said. "Harry, you hold it for him." Mr. Graves took the child's hand and removed the folded paper from the tight fist and held it while little Dave stood next to him and looked up at him wonderingly.

"Nancy next," Mr. Summers said. Nancy was twelve, and her school friends breathed heavily as she went forward, switching her skirt, and took a slip daintily from the box. "Bill, Jr.," Mr. Summers said, and Billy, his face red and his feet over-large, nearly knocked the box over as he got a paper out. "Tessie," Mr. Summers said. She hesitated for a minute, looking around defiantly, and then set her lips and went up to the box. She snatched a paper out and held it behind her.

"Bill," Mr. Summers said, and Bill Hutchinson reached into the box and felt around, bringing his hand out at last with the slip of paper in it.

The crowd was quiet. A girl whispered, "I hope it's not Nancy," and the sound of the whisper reached the edges of the crowd.

"It's not the way it used to be," Old Man Warner said clearly. "People ain't the way they used to be."

"All right," Mr. Summers said. "Open the papers. Harry, you open little Dave's."

Mr. Graves opened the slip of paper and there was a general sigh through the crowd as he held it up and everyone could see that it was blank. Nancy and Bill, Jr., opened theirs at the same time, and both beamed and laughed, turning around to the crowd and holding their slips of paper above their heads.

"Tessie," Mr. Summers said. There was a pause, and then Mr. Summers looked at Bill Hutchinson, and Bill unfolded his paper and showed it. It was blank.

"It's Tessie," Mr. Summers said, and his voice was hushed. "Show us her paper, Bill."

Bill Hutchinson went over to his wife and forced the slip of paper out of her hand. It had a black spot on it, the black spot Mr. Summers had made the night before with the heavy pencil in the coal-company office. Bill Hutchinson held it up, and there was a stir in the crowd.

"All right, folks," Mr. Summers said. "Let's finish quickly."

Although the villagers had forgotten the ritual and lost the original black box, they still remembered to use stones. The pile of stones the boys had made earlier was ready; there were stones on the ground with the blowing scraps of paper that had come out of the box. Mrs. Delacroix selected a stone so large she had to pick it up with both hands and turned to Mrs. Dunbar. "Come on," she said. "Hurry up."

Mrs. Dunbar had small stones in both hands, and she said, gasping for breath, "I can't run at all. You'll have to go ahead and I'll catch up with you."

The children had stones already, and someone gave little Davy Hutchinson a few pebbles.

Tessie Hutchinson was in the center of a cleared space by now, and she held her hands out desperately as the villagers moved in on her. "It isn't fair," she said. A stone hit her on the side of the head.

Old Man Warner was saying, "Come on, come on, everyone." Steve Adams was in the front of the crowd of villagers, with Mrs. Graves beside him.

"It isn't fair, it isn't right," Mrs. Hutchinson screamed, and then they were upon her.

ROBERT LOWELL

For the Union Dead

 1960

Robert Lowell's best-known poem, "For the Union Dead," was given its first public reading by the poet at the Boston Arts Festival in the Public Garden in the summer of 1960. Nearby, in the shadow of the gilded State House, stood Saint-Gaudens's bronze frieze commemorating the young hero Colonel Robert Gould Shaw and the scores of black Union soldiers who died beside him when he led them in the bloody assault on Fort Wagner, near Charleston, South Carolina, in 1863. Lowell (1917–1977), a descendant of Boston Brahmins who was related by marriage to the family of Colonel Shaw, felt a personal connection to the subject of the sculpture, which he renders as a betrayed symbol of the New England past. The impact of Lowell's disciplined rage has doubtless faded with time, and today's reader must work to reconstruct the startling effect of his juxtaposed childhood memories set against the image of the parking-garage excavation, likened to an open wound in the body of the town. But "For the Union Dead" remains a powerful personal and civic poem—a blue-blood's howl on behalf of a lost world.

"Relinquunt Omnia Servare Rem Publicam."

The old South Boston Aquarium stands
in a Sahara of snow now. Its broken windows are boarded.
The bronze weathervane cod has lost half its scales.
The airy tanks are dry.

Once my nose crawled like a snail on the glass;
my hand tingled
to burst the bubbles
drifting from the noses of the cowed, compliant fish.

My hand draws back. I often sigh still
for the dark downward and vegetating kingdom
of the fish and reptile. One morning last March,
I pressed against the new barbed and galvanized

fence on the Boston Common. Behind their cage,
yellow dinosaur steamshovels were grunting
as they cropped up tons of mush and grass
to gouge their underworld garage.

Parking spaces luxuriate like civic
sandpiles in the heart of Boston.
A girdle of orange, Puritan-pumpkin colored girders
braces the tingling Statehouse,

shaking over the excavations, as it faces Colonel Shaw
and his bell-cheeked Negro infantry
on St. Gaudens' shaking Civil War relief,
propped by a plank splint against the garage's earthquake.

Two months after marching through Boston,
half the regiment was dead;
at the dedication,
William James could almost hear the bronze Negroes breathe.

Their monument sticks like a fishbone
in the city's throat.
Its Colonel is as lean
as a compass-needle.

He has an angry wrenlike vigilance,
a greyhound's gentle tautness;
he seems to wince at pleasure,
and suffocate for privacy.

He is out of bounds now. He rejoices in man's lovely,
peculiar power to choose life and die—
when he leads his black soldiers to death,
he cannot bend his back.

On a thousand small town New England greens,
the old white churches hold their air
of sparse, sincere rebellion; frayed flags
quilt the graveyards of the Grand Army of the Republic.

The stone statues of the abstract Union Soldier
grow slimmer and younger each year—
wasp-waisted, they doze over muskets
and muse through their sideburns . . .

Shaw's father wanted no monument
except the ditch,
where his son's body was thrown
and lost with his "niggers."

The ditch is nearer.
There are no statues for the last war here;
on Boylston Street, a commercial photograph
shows Hiroshima boiling

over a Mosler Safe, the "Rock of Ages"
that survived the blast. Space is nearer.
When I crouch to my television set,
the drained faces of Negro school-children rise like balloons.

Colonel Shaw
is riding on his bubble,
he waits
for the blessèd break.

The Aquarium is gone. Everywhere,
giant finned cars nose forward like fish;
a savage servility
slides by on grease.

Malcolm X and Alex Haley

From The Autobiography of Malcolm X

 1965

Malcolm X (1925–1965) was born Malcolm Little, the son of a Nebraska Baptist minister who had sympathy for Marcus Garvey's black separatist movement. It seems clear that Malcolm's father was killed by a white mob after the family had moved to Michigan, an event that precipitated the mental breakdown of his mother and the dispersion of the children into foster homes. The remarkable story of Malcolm's life—from his early days as a petty criminal, to his years as the stern deputy of the Black Muslim leader Elijah Muhammad, to his emergence as a national leader increasingly moved by a spirit of reconciliation—is told in *The Autobiography of Malcolm X,* the result of interviews and collaboration with the writer Alex Haley (b. 1921). The pages reprinted below describe Malcolm's discovery, in Boston, of new possibilities of freedom and degradation.

The very week I finished the eighth grade, I . . . boarded the Greyhound bus for Boston.

I've thought about that time a lot since then. No physical move in my life has been more pivotal or profound in its repercussions.

If I had stayed on in Michigan, I would probably have married one of those Negro girls I knew and liked in Lansing. I might have become one of those state capitol building shoeshine boys, or a Lansing Country Club waiter, or gotten one of the other menial jobs which, in those days, among Lansing Negroes, would have been considered "successful"—or even become a carpenter.

Whatever I have done since then, I have driven myself to become a success at it. I've often thought that if [my eighth-grade English teacher] had encouraged me to become a lawyer, I would today probably be among some city's professional black bourgeoisie, sipping cocktails and palming myself off as a community spokesman for and leader of the suffering black masses, while my primary concern would be to grab a few more crumbs from the groaning board of the two-faced whites with whom they're begging to "integrate."

All praise is due to Allah that I went to Boston when I did. If I hadn't, I'd probably still be a brainwashed black Christian.

* * *

I looked like Li'l Abner. Mason, Michigan, was written all over me. My kinky, reddish hair was cut hick style, and I didn't even use grease in it. My green suit's coat sleeves stopped above my wrists, the pants legs showed three inches of socks. Just a shade lighter green than the suit was my narrow-collared, three-quarter length Lansing department store topcoat. My appearance was too much for even Ella. But she told me later she had seen countrified members of the Little family come up from Georgia in even worse shape than I was.

Ella had fixed up a nice little upstairs room for me. And she was truly a Georgia Negro woman when she got into the kitchen with her pots and pans. She was the kind of cook who would heap up your plate with such as ham hock, greens, black-eyed peas, fried fish, cabbage, sweet potatoes, grits and gravy, and cornbread. And the more you put away, the better she felt. I worked out at Ella's kitchen table like there was no tomorrow.

Ella still seemed to me as big, black, outspoken and impressive a woman as she had been in Mason and Lansing. Only about two weeks before I arrived, she had split up with her second husband—the soldier, Frank, whom I had met there the previous summer; but she was taking it right in stride. I could see, though I didn't say, how any average man would find it almost impossible to live for very long with a woman whose every instinct was to run everything and everybody she had anything to do with—including me. About my second day there in Roxbury, Ella told me that she didn't want me to start hunting for a job right away, like most newcomer Negroes did. She said that she had told all those she'd brought North to take their time, to walk around, to travel the buses and the subway, and get the feel of Boston, before they tied themselves down working somewhere, because they would never again have the time to really see and get to know anything about the city they were living in. Ella said she'd help me find a job when it was time for me to go to work.

So I went gawking around the neighborhood—the Waumbeck and Humboldt Avenue Hill section of Roxbury, which is something like Harlem's Sugar Hill, where I'd later live. I saw those Roxbury Negroes acting and living differently from any black people I'd ever dreamed of in my life. This was the snooty-black neighborhood; they called themselves the "Four Hundred," and looked down their noses at the Negroes of the black ghetto, or so-called "town" section where Mary, my other half-sister, lived.

What I thought I was seeing there in Roxbury were high-class, educated, important Negroes, living well, working in big jobs and positions. Their quiet homes sat back in their mowed yards. These Negroes walked along the sidewalks looking haughty and dignified, on their way to work, to shop, to visit, to church. I know now, of course, that what I was really seeing was only a big-city version of those "successful" Negro bootblacks and janitors back in Lansing. The only difference was that the ones in Boston had been brainwashed even more thoroughly. They prided themselves on being incomparably more "cultured," "cultivated," "dignified," and better off than their black brethren down in the ghetto, which was no further away than you could throw a rock. Under the pitiful misapprehension that it would make them "better," these Hill Negroes were breaking their backs trying to imitate white people.

Any black family that had been around Boston long enough to own the home they lived in was considered among the Hill elite. It didn't make any difference that they had to rent out rooms to make ends meet. Then the native-born New Englanders among them looked down upon recently migrated Southerner homeowners who lived next door, like Ella. And a big percentage of the Hill dwellers were in Ella's category—Southern strivers and scramblers, and West Indian Negroes, whom both the New Englanders and the Southerners called "Black Jews." Usually it was the Southerners and the West Indians who not only managed to own the places where they lived, but also at least one other house which they rented as income property. The snooty New Englanders usually owned less than they.

In those days on the Hill, any who could claim "professional" status— teachers, preachers, practical nurses—also considered themselves superior. Foreign diplomats could have modeled their conduct on the way the Negro postmen, Pullman porters, and dining car waiters of Roxbury acted, striding around as if they were wearing top hats and cutaways.

I'd guess that eight out of ten of the Hill Negroes of Roxbury, despite the impressive-sounding job titles they affected, actually worked as menials and servants. "He's in banking," or "He's in securities." It sounded as though they were discussing a Rockefeller or a Mellon—and not some grayheaded, dignity-posturing bank janitor, or bond-house messenger. "I'm with an old family" was the euphemism used to dignify the professions of white folks' cooks and maids who talked so affectedly among their own kind in Roxbury that you couldn't even understand them. I don't know how many forty- and fifty-year-old errand boys went down the Hill dressed like ambassadors in black suits and white collars, to downtown jobs "in government," "in finance," or "in law." It has never ceased to amaze me how so many Negroes, then and now, could stand the indignity of that kind of self-delusion.

Soon I ranged out of Roxbury and began to explore Boston proper. Historic buildings everywhere I turned, and plaques and markers and statues for famous events and men. One statue in the Boston Commons astonished me: a Negro named Crispus Attucks, who had been the first man to fall in the Boston Massacre. I had never known anything like that.

I roamed everywhere. In one direction, I walked as far as Boston University. Another day, I took my first subway ride. When most of the people got off, I followed. It was Cambridge, and I circled all around in the Harvard University campus. Somewhere, I had already heard of Harvard—though I didn't know much more about it. Nobody that day could have told me I would give an address before the Harvard Law School Forum some twenty years later.

I also did a lot of exploring downtown . . . On Massachusetts Avenue . . . was the huge, exciting Roseland State Ballroom. Big posters out in front advertised the nationally famous bands, white and Negro, that had played there. "COMING NEXT WEEK," when I went by that first time, was Glenn Miller. I remember thinking how nearly the whole evening's music at Mason High School dances had been Glenn Miller's records. What wouldn't that crowd have given, I wondered, to be standing where Glenn Miller's band was actually going to play? I didn't know how familiar with Roseland I was going to become.

Ella began to grow concerned, because even when I had finally had enough sight-seeing, I didn't stick around very much on the Hill . . . I didn't want to disappoint or upset Ella, but despite her advice, I began going down into the town ghetto section. That world of grocery stores, walk-up flats, cheap restaurants, poolrooms, bars, storefront churches, and pawnshops seemed to hold a natural lure for me.

Not only was this part of Roxbury much more exciting, but I felt more relaxed among Negroes who were being their natural selves and not putting on airs. Even though I did live on the Hill, my instincts were never—and still aren't—to feel myself any better than any other Negro.

I spent my first month in town with my mouth hanging open. The sharp-dressed young "cats" who hung on the corners and in the poolrooms, bars and restaurants, and who obviously didn't work anywhere, completely entranced me. I couldn't get over marveling at how their hair was straight and shiny like white men's hair; Ella told me this was called a "conk." I had never tasted a sip of liquor, never even smoked a cigarette, and here I saw little black children, ten and twelve years old, shooting craps, playing cards, fighting, getting grown-ups to put a penny or a nickel on their number for them, things like that. And these children threw around swear words I'd never heard before, even, and slang expressions that were just as new to me, such as "stud" and "cat" and "chick" and "cool" and "hip." Every night as I lay in bed I turned these new words over in my mind. It was shocking to me that in town, especially after dark, you'd occasionally see a white girl and a Negro man strolling arm in arm along the sidewalk, and mixed couples drinking in the neon-lighted bars—not slipping off to some dark corner, as in Lansing. I wrote Wilfred and Philbert about that, too.

I wanted to find a job myself, to surprise Ella. One afternoon, something told me to go inside a poolroom whose window I was looking through. I had looked through that window many times. I wasn't yearning to play pool; in fact, I had never held a cue stick. But I was drawn by the sight of the cool-looking "cats" standing around inside, bending over the big, green, felt-topped tables, making bets and shooting the bright-colored balls into the holes. As I stared through the window this particular afternoon, something made me decide to venture inside and talk to a dark, stubby, conk-headed fellow who racked up balls for the pool-players, whom I'd heard called "Shorty." One day he had come outside and seen me standing there and said "Hi, Red," so that made me figure he was friendly.

As inconspicuously as I could, I slipped inside the door and around the side of the poolroom, avoiding people, and on to the back, where Shorty was filling an aluminum can with the powder that pool players dust on their hands. He looked up at me. Later on, Shorty would enjoy teasing me about how with that first glance he knew my whole story. "Man, that cat still *smelled* country!" he'd say, laughing. "Cat's legs was so long and his pants so short his knees showed—an' his head looked like a briar patch!"

But that afternoon Shorty didn't let it show in his face how "country" I appeared when I told him I'd appreciate it if he'd tell me how could somebody go about getting a job like his.

"If you mean racking up balls," said Shorty, "I don't know of no pool joints around here needing anybody. You mean you just want any slave you can find?" A "slave" meant work, a job.

He asked what kind of work I had done. I told him that I'd washed restaurant dishes in Mason, Michigan. He nearly dropped the powder can. "My homeboy! Man, gimme some skin! I'm from Lansing!"

I never told Shorty—and he never suspected—that he was about ten years older than I. He took us to be about the same age. At first I would have been embarrassed to tell him, later I just never bothered. Shorty had dropped out of first-year high school in Lansing, lived a while with an uncle and aunt in Detroit, and had spent the last six years living with his cousin in Roxbury. But when I mentioned the names of Lansing people and places, he remembered many, and pretty soon we sounded as if we had been raised in the same block. I could sense Shorty's genuine gladness, and I don't have to say how lucky I felt to find a friend as hip as he obviously was.

"Man, this is a swinging town if you dig it," Shorty said. "You're my homeboy—I'm going to school you to the happenings." I stood there and grinned like a fool. "You got to go anywhere now? Well, stick around until I get off."

One thing I liked immediately about Shorty was his frankness. When I told him where I lived, he said what I already knew—that nobody in town could stand the Hill Negroes. But he thought a sister who gave me a "pad," not charging me rent, not even running me out to find "some slave," couldn't be all bad. Shorty's slave in the poolroom, he said, was just to keep ends together while he learned his horn. A couple of years before, he'd hit the numbers and bought a saxophone. "Got it right in there in the closet now, for my lesson tonight." Shorty was taking lessons "with some other studs," and he intended one day to organize his own small band. "There's a lot of bread to be made gigging right around here in Roxbury," Shorty explained to me. "I don't dig joining some big band, one-nighting all over just to say I played with Count or Duke or somebody." I thought that was smart. I wished I had studied a horn; but I never had been exposed to one.

All afternoon, between trips up front to rack balls, Shorty talked to me out of the corner of his mouth: which hustlers—standing around, or playing at this or that table—sold "reefers," or had just come out of prison, or were "second-story men." Shorty told me that he played at least a dollar a day on the numbers. He said as soon as he hit a number, he would use the winnings to organize his band.

I was ashamed to have to admit that I had never played the numbers. "Well, you ain't never had nothing to play with," he said, excusing me, "but you start when you get a slave, and if you hit, you got a stake for something."

He pointed out some gamblers and some pimps. Some of them had white whores, he whispered. "I ain't going to lie—I dig them two-dollar white chicks," Shorty said. "There's a lot of that action around here, nights; you'll see it." I said I already had seen some. "You ever had one?" he asked.

My embarrassment at my inexperience showed. "Hell, man," he said, "don't be ashamed. I had a few before I left Lansing—them Polack chicks that used to come over the bridge. Here, they're mostly Italians and Irish. But it don't matter what kind, they're something else! Ain't no different nowhere— there's nothing they love better than a black stud."

Through the afternoon, Shorty introduced me to players and loungers. "My homeboy," he'd say, "he's looking for a slave if you hear anything." They all said they'd look out.

At seven o'clock, when the night ball-racker came on, Shorty told me he had to hurry to his saxophone lesson. But before he left, he held out to me the six or seven dollars he had collected that day in nickel and dime tips. "You got enough bread, homeboy?"

I was okay, I told him—I had two dollars. But Shorty made me take three more. "Little fattening for your pocket," he said. Before we went out, he opened his saxophone case and showed me the horn. It was gleaming brass against the green velvet, an alto sax. He said, "Keep cool, homeboy, and come back tomorrow. Some of the cats will turn you up a slave."

*   *   *

When I got home, Ella said there had been a telephone call from somebody
named Shorty. He had left a message that over at the Roseland State Ballroom, the shoeshine boy was quitting that night, and Shorty had told him to
hold the job for me.

"Malcolm, you haven't had any experience shining shoes," Ella said. Her
expression and tone of voice told me she wasn't happy about my taking that
job. I didn't particularly care, because I was already speechless thinking about
being somewhere close to the greatest bands in the world. I didn't even wait to
eat any dinner.

The ballroom was all lighted when I got there. A man at the front door was
letting in members of Benny Goodman's band. I told him I wanted to see the
shoeshine boy, Freddie.

"You're going to be the new one?" he asked. I said I thought I was, and he
laughed, "Well, maybe you'll hit the numbers and get a Cadillac, too." He
told me that I'd find Freddie upstairs in the men's room on the second floor.

But downstairs before I went up, I stepped over and snatched a glimpse inside the ballroom. I just couldn't believe the size of that waxed floor! At the far
end, under the soft, rose-colored lights, was the bandstand with the Benny
Goodman musicians moving around, laughing and talking, arranging their
horns and stands.

A wiry, brown-skinned, conked fellow upstairs in the men's room greeted
me. "You Shorty's homeboy?" I said I was, and he said he was Freddie. "Good
old boy," he said. "He called me, he just heard I hit the big number, and he
figured right I'd be quitting." I told Freddie what the man at the front door
had said about a Cadillac. He laughed and said, "Burns them white cats up
when you get yourself something. Yeah, I told them I was going to get me
one—just to bug them."

Freddie then said for me to pay close attention, that he was going to be
busy and for me to watch but not get in the way, and he'd try to get me ready
to take over at the next dance, a couple of nights later.

As Freddie busied himself setting up the shoeshine stand, he told me, "Get
here early . . . your shoeshine rags and brushes by this footstand . . . your polish bottles, paste wax, suede brushes over here . . . everything in place, you get
rushed, you never need to waste motion. . . ."

While you shined shoes, I learned, you also kept watch on customers inside, leaving the urinals. You darted over and offered a small white hand
towel. "A lot of cats who ain't planning to wash their hands, sometimes you
can run up with a towel and shame them. Your towels are really your best hustle in here. Cost you a penny apiece to launder—you always get at least a
nickel tip."

The shoeshine customers, and any from the inside rest room who took a towel, you whiskbroomed a couple of licks. "A nickel or a dime tip, just give 'em that," Freddie said. "But for two bits, Uncle Tom a little—white cats especially like that. I've had them to come back two, three times a dance."

From down below, the sound of the music had begun floating up. I guess I stood transfixed. "You never seen a big dance?" asked Freddie. "Run on awhile, and watch."

There were a few couples already dancing under the rose-colored lights. But even more exciting to me was the crowd thronging in. The most glamorous-looking white women I'd ever seen—young ones, old ones, white cats buying tickets at the window, sticking big wads of green bills back into their pockets, checking the women's coats, and taking their arms and squiring them inside.

Freddie had some early customers when I got back upstairs. Between the shoeshine stand and thrusting towels to men just as they approached the wash basin, Freddie seemed to be doing four things at once. "Here, you can take over the whiskbroom," he said, "just two or three licks—but let 'em feel it."

When things slowed a little, he said, "You ain't seen nothing tonight. You wait until you see a spooks' dance! Man, our own people carry *on!*" Whenever he had a moment, he kept schooling me. "Shoelaces, this drawer here. You just starting out, I'm going to make these to you as a present. Buy them for a nickel a pair, tell cats they need laces if they do, and charge two bits."

Every Benny Goodman record I'd ever heard in my life, it seemed, was filtering faintly into where we were. During another customer lull, Freddie let me slip back outside again to listen. Peggy Lee was at the mike singing. Beautiful! She had just joined the band and she was from North Dakota and had been singing with a group in Chicago when Mrs. Benny Goodman discovered her, we had heard some customers say. She finished the song and the crowd burst into applause. She was a big hit.

"It knocked me out, too, when I first broke in here," Freddie said, grinning, when I went back in there. "But, look, you ever shined any shoes?" He laughed when I said I hadn't, excepting my own. "Well, let's get to work. I never had neither." Freddie got on the stand and went to work on his own shoes. Brush, liquid polish, brush, paste wax, shine rag, lacquer sole dressing . . . step by step, Freddie showed me what to do.

"But you got to get a whole lot faster. You can't waste time!" Freddie showed me how fast on my own shoes. Then, because business was tapering off, he had time to give me a demonstration of how to make the shine rag pop like a firecracker. "Dig the action?" he asked. He did it in slow motion. I got down and tried it on his shoes. I had the principle of it. "Just got to do it faster," Freddie said. "It's a jive noise, that's all. Cats tip better, they figure you're knocking yourself out!"

By the end of the dance, Freddie had let me shine the shoes of three or four stray drunks he talked into having shines, and I had practiced picking up my speed on Freddie's shoes until they looked like mirrors. After we had helped the janitors to clean up the ballroom after the dance, throwing out all the paper and cigarette butts and empty liquor bottles, Freddie was nice enough to drive me all the way home to Ella's on the Hill in the secondhand maroon Buick he said he was going to trade in on his Cadillac. He talked to me all the way. "I guess it's all right if I tell you, pick up a couple of dozen packs of rubbers, two-bits apiece. You notice some of those cats that came up to me around the end of the dance? Well, when some have new chicks going right, they'll come asking you for rubbers. Charge a dollar, generally you'll get an extra tip."

He looked across at me. "Some hustles you're too new for. Cats will ask you for liquor, some will want reefers. But you don't need to have nothing except rubbers—until you can dig who's a cop.

"You can make ten, twelve dollars a dance for yourself if you work everything right," Freddie said, before I got out of the car in front of Ella's. "The main thing you got to remember is that everything in the world is a hustle. So long, Red."

The next time I ran into Freddie I was downtown one night a few weeks later. He was parked in his pearl gray Cadillac, sharp as a tack, "cooling it."

"Man, you sure schooled me!" I said, and he laughed; he knew what I meant. It hadn't taken me long on the job to find out that Freddie had done less shoeshining and towel-hustling than selling liquor and reefers, and putting white "Johns" in touch with Negro whores. I also learned that white girls always flocked to the Negro dances—some of them whores whose pimps brought them to mix business and pleasure, others who came with their black boy friends, and some who came in alone, for a little freelance lusting among a plentiful availability of enthusiastic Negro men.

At the white dances, of course, nothing black was allowed, and that's where the black whores' pimps soon showed a new shoeshine boy what he could pick up on the side by slipping a phone number or address to the white Johns who came around the end of the dance looking for "black chicks."

Most of Roseland's dances were for whites only, and they had white bands only. But the only white band ever to play there at a Negro dance to my recollection, was Charlie Barnet's. The fact is that very few white bands could have satisfied the Negro dancers. But I know that Charlie Barnet's "Cherokee" and his "Redskin Rhumba" drove those Negroes wild. They'd jampack that ballroom, the black girls in way-out silk and satin dresses and shoes, their hair done in all kinds of styles, the men sharp in their zoot suits and crazy conks, and everybody grinning and greased and gassed.

Some of the bandsmen would come up to the men's room at about eight o'clock and get shoeshines before they went to work. Duke Ellington, Count Basie, Lionel Hampton, Cootie Williams, Jimmie Lunceford were just a few of those who sat in my chair. I would really make my shine rag sound like someone had set off Chinese firecrackers. Duke's great alto saxman, Johnny Hodges—he was Shorty's idol—still owes me for a shoeshine I gave him. He was in the chair one night, having a friendly argument with the drummer, Sonny Greer, who was standing there, when I tapped the bottom of his shoes to signal that I was finished. Hodges stepped down, reaching his hand in his pocket to pay me, but then snatched his hand out to gesture, and just forgot me, and walked away. I wouldn't have dared to bother the man who could do what he did with "Daydream" by asking him for fifteen cents.

I remember that I struck up a little shoeshine-stand conversation with Count Basie's great blues singer, Jimmie Rushing. (He's the one famous for "Sent For You Yesterday, Here You Come Today" and things like that.) Rushing's feet, I remember, were big and funny-shaped—not long like most big feet, but they were round and roly-poly like Rushing. Anyhow, he even introduced me to some of the other Basie cats, like Lester Young, Harry Edison, Buddy Tate, Don Byas, Dickie Wells, and Buck Clayton. They'd walk in the rest room later, by themselves. "Hi, Red." They'd be up there in my chair, and my shine rag was popping to the beat of all of their records, spinning in my head. Musicians never have had, anywhere, a greater shoeshine-boy fan than I was. I would write to Wilfred and Hilda and Philbert and Reginald back in Lansing, trying to describe it.

I never got any decent tips until the middle of the Negro dances, which is when the dancers started feeling good and getting generous. After the white dances, when I helped to clean out the ballroom, we would throw out perhaps a dozen empty liquor bottles. But after the Negro dances, we would have to throw out cartons full of empty fifth bottles—not rotgut, either, but the best brands, and especially Scotch.

During lulls up there in the men's room, sometimes I'd get in five minutes of watching the dancing. The white people danced as though somebody had trained them—left, one, two; right, three, four—the same steps and patterns over and over, as though somebody had wound them up. But those Negroes—nobody in the world could have choreographed the way they did whatever they felt—just grabbing partners, even the white chicks who came to the Negro dances. And my black brethren today may hate me for saying it, but a lot of black girls nearly got run over by some of those Negro males scrambling to get at those white women; you would have thought God had lowered some of his angels. Times have sure changed; if it happened today, those same black girls would go after those Negro men—and the white women, too.

Anyway, some couples were so abandoned—flinging high and wide, improvising steps and movements—that you couldn't believe it. I could feel the beat in my bones, even though I had never danced.

"*Showtime!*" people would start hollering about the last hour of the dance. Then a couple of dozen really wild couples would stay on the floor, the girls changing to low white sneakers. The band now would really be blasting, and all the other dancers would form a clapping, shouting circle to watch that wild competition as it began, covering only a quarter or so of the ballroom floor. The band, the spectators and the dancers, would be making the Roseland Ballroom feel like a big rocking ship. The spotlight would be turning, pink, yellow, green, and blue, picking up the couples lindy-hopping as if they had gone mad. "*Wail, man, wail!*" people would be shouting at the band; and it *would* be wailing, until first one and then another couple just ran out of strength and stumbled off toward the crowd, exhausted and soaked with sweat. Sometimes I would be down there standing inside the door jumping up and down in my gray jacket with the whiskbroom in the pocket, and the manager would have to come and shout at me that I had customers upstairs.

The first liquor I drank, my first cigarettes, even my first reefers, I can't specifically remember. But I know they were all mixed together with my first shooting craps, playing cards, and betting my dollar a day on the numbers, as I started hanging out at night with Shorty and his friends. Shorty's jokes about how country I had been made us all laugh. I still was country, I know now, but it all felt so great because I was accepted. All of us would be in somebody's place, usually one of the girls', and we'd be turning on, the reefers making everybody's head light, or the whisky aglow in our middles. Everybody understood that my head had to stay kinky a while longer, to grow long enough for Shorty to conk it for me. One of these nights, I remarked that I had saved about half enough to get a zoot.

"*Save?*" Shorty couldn't believe it. "Homeboy, you never heard of credit?" He told me he'd call a neighborhood clothing store the first thing in the morning, and that I should be there early.

A salesman, a young Jew, met me when I came in. "You're Shorty's friend?" I said I was; it amazed me—all of Shorty's contacts. The salesman wrote my name on a form, and the Roseland as where I worked, and Ella's address as where I lived. Shorty's name was put down as recommending me. The salesman said, "Shorty's one of our best customers."

I was measured, and the young salesman picked off a rack a zoot suit that was just wild: sky-blue pants thirty inches in the knee and angle-narrowed down to twelve inches at the bottom, and a long coat that pinched my waist and flared out below my knees.

As a gift, the salesman said, the store would give me a narrow leather belt with my initial "L" on it. Then he said I ought to also buy a hat, and I did—

blue, with a feather in the four-inch brim. Then the store gave me another present: a long, thick-linked, gold-plated chain that swung down lower than my coat hem. I was sold forever on credit.

When I modeled the zoot for Ella, she took a long look and said, "Well, I guess it had to happen." I took three of those twenty-five-cent sepia-toned, while-you-wait pictures of myself, posed the way "hipsters" wearing their zoots would "cool it"—hat angled, knees drawn close together, feet wide apart, both index fingers jabbed toward the floor. The long coat and swinging chain and the Punjab pants were much more dramatic if you stood that way. One picture, I autographed and airmailed to my brothers and sisters in Lansing, to let them see how well I was doing. I gave another one to Ella, and the third to Shorty, who was really moved: I could tell by the way he said, "Thanks, homeboy." It was part of our "hip" code not to show that kind of affection.

Shorty soon decided that my hair was finally long enough to be conked. He had promised to school me in how to beat the barbershops' three- and four-dollar price by making up congolene, and then conking ourselves.

I took the little list of ingredients he had printed out for me, and went to a grocery store, where I got a can of Red Devil lye, two eggs, and two medium-sized white potatoes. Then at a drugstore near the poolroom, I asked for a large jar of vaseline, a large bar of soap, a large-toothed comb and a fine-toothed comb, one of those rubber hoses with a metal spray-head, a rubber apron and a pair of gloves.

"Going to lay on that first conk?" the drugstore man asked me. I proudly told him, grinning, "Right!"

Shorty paid six dollars a week for a room in his cousin's shabby apartment. His cousin wasn't at home. "It's like the pad's mine, he spends so much time with his woman," Shorty said. "Now, you watch me—"

He peeled the potatoes and thin-sliced them into a quart-sized Mason fruit jar, then started stirring them with a wooden spoon as he gradually poured in a little over half the can of lye. "Never use a metal spoon; the lye will turn it black," he told me.

A jelly-like, starchy-looking glop resulted from the lye and potatoes, and Shorty broke in the two eggs, stirring real fast—his own conk and dark face bent down close. The congolene turned pale-yellowish. "Feel the jar," Shorty said. I cupped my hand against the outside, and snatched it away. "Damn right, it's hot, that's the lye," he said. "So you know it's going to burn when I comb it in—it burns *bad.* But the longer you can stand it, the straighter the hair."

He made me sit down, and he tied the string of the new rubber apron tightly around my neck, and combed up my bush of hair. Then, from the big vaseline jar, he took a handful and massaged it hard all through my hair and into the scalp. He also thickly vaselined my neck, ears and forehead. "When I get to washing out your head, be sure to tell me anywhere you feel any little stinging," Shorty warned me, washing his hands, then pulling on the rubber gloves, and tying on his own rubber apron. "You always got to remember that any congolene left in burns a sore into your head."

The congolene just felt warm when Shorty started combing it in. But then my head caught fire.

I gritted my teeth and tried to pull the sides of the kitchen table together. The comb felt as if it was raking my skin off.

My eyes watered, my nose was running. I couldn't stand it any longer; I bolted to the washbasin. I was cursing Shorty with every name I could think of when he got the spray going and started soap-lathering my head.

He lathered and spray-rinsed, lathered and spray-rinsed, maybe ten or twelve times, each time gradually closing the hot-water faucet, until the rinse was cold, and that helped some.

"You feel any stinging spots?"

"No," I managed to say. My knees were trembling.

"Sit back down, then. I think we got it all out okay."

The flame came back as Shorty, with a thick towel, started drying my head, rubbing hard. "*Easy,* man, *easy!*" I kept shouting.

"The first time's always worst. You get used to it better before long. You took it real good, homeboy. You got a good conk."

When Shorty let me stand up and see in the mirror, my hair hung down in limp, damp strings. My scalp still flamed, but not as badly; I could bear it. He draped the towel around my shoulders, over my rubber apron, and began again vaselining my hair.

I could feel him combing, straight back, first the big comb, then the fine-toothed one.

Then, he was using a razor, very delicately, on the back of my neck. Then, finally, shaping the sideburns.

My first view in the mirror blotted out the hurting. I'd seen some pretty conks, but when it's the first time, on your *own* head, the transformation, after the lifetime of kinks, is staggering.

The mirror reflected Shorty behind me. We both were grinning and sweating. And on top of my head was this thick, smooth sheen of shining red hair—real red—as straight as any white man's.

How ridiculous I was! Stupid enough to stand there simply lost in admiration of my hair now looking "white," reflected in the mirror in Shorty's room. I vowed that I'd never again be without a conk, and I never was for many years.

This was my first really big step toward self-degradation: when I endured all of that pain, literally burning my flesh with lye, in order to cook my natural hair until it was limp, to have it look like a white man's hair. I had joined that multitude of Negro men and women in America who are brainwashed into believing that the black people are "inferior"—and white people "superior"—that they will even violate and mutilate their God-created bodies to try to look "pretty" by white standards.

Look around today, in every small town and big city, from two-bit catfish and soda-pop joints into the "integrated" lobby of the Waldorf-Astoria, and you'll see conks on black men. And you'll see black women wearing these green and pink and purple and red and platinum-blonde wigs. They're all more ridiculous than a slapstick comedy. It makes you wonder if the Negro has completely lost his sense of identity, lost touch with himself.

You'll see the conk worn by many, many so-called "upper class" Negroes, and, as much as I hate to say it about them, on all too many Negro entertainers. One of the reasons that I've especially admired some of them, like Lionel Hampton and Sidney Poitier, among others, is that they have kept their natural hair and fought to the top. I admire any Negro man who has never had himself conked, or who has had the sense to get rid of it—as I finally did.

I don't know which kind of self-defacing conk is the greater shame—the one you'll see on the heads of the black so-called "middle class" and "upper class," who ought to know better, or the one you'll see on the heads of the poorest, most downtrodden, ignorant black men. I mean the legal-minimum-wage ghetto-dwelling kind of Negro, as I was when I got my first one. It's generally among these poor fools that you'll see a black kerchief over the man's head, like Aunt Jemima; he's trying to make his conk last longer, between trips to the barbershop. Only for special occasions is this kerchief-protected conk exposed—to show off how "sharp" and "hip" its owner is. The ironic thing is that I have never heard any woman, white or black, express any admiration for a conk. Of course, any white woman with a black man isn't thinking about his hair. But I don't see how on earth a black woman with any race pride could walk down the street with any black man wearing a conk—the emblem of his shame that he is black.

To my own shame, when I say all of this I'm talking first of all about myself—because you can't show me any Negro who ever conked more faithfully than I did. I'm speaking from personal experience when I say of any black man who conks today, or any white-wigged black woman, that if they gave the brains in their heads just half as much attention as they do their hair, they would be a thousand times better off.

ANNE SEXTON

Her Kind

 1960

Born in 1928, Anne Sexton traced her roots to *Mayflower* ancestors and lived virtually all her life in Massachusetts. Suffering from depression and alcoholism, she un-
dertook poetry at the suggestion of her therapist and studied for a time with Robert
Lowell at Boston University. The following poem went through several drafts between late 1957 and midsummer of 1959; first entitled "Night Voyage on a Broom-
stick," it became "Witch," and finally "Her Kind"—a poem, as her biographer Di-
ane Middlebrook has put it, that "finds a way to represent a condition symbolized
not in words but in symptoms that yearn to be comprehended." The poem has a
frantic quality kept barely in check by rhyme and refrain as it reviews, in the form of
a New England nightmare, the life of a woman whose subject was often her suffocating sense of constriction in conventional life. Anne Sexton died by her own hand
in 1974.

I have gone out, a possessed witch,
haunting the black air, braver at night;
dreaming evil, I have done my hitch
over the plain houses, light by light:
lonely thing, twelve-fingered, out of mind.
A woman like that is not a woman, quite.
I have been her kind.

I have found the warm caves in the woods,
filled them with skillets, carvings, shelves,
closets, silks, innumerable goods;
fixed the suppers for the worms and the elves:
whining, rearranging the disaligned.
A woman like that is misunderstood.
I have been her kind.

I have ridden in your cart, driver,
waved my nude arms at villages going by,

learning the last bright routes, survivor
where your flames still bite my thigh
and my ribs crack where your wheels wind.
A woman like that is not ashamed to die.
I have been her kind.

JONATHAN KOZOL

From Death at an Early Age

 1967

Jonathan Kozol's *Death at an Early Age* describes a young idealist's year spent teaching poor black children in the Boston public schools. Kozol was born in 1936 into a prosperous Jewish family in Brookline, Massachusetts (his father was a neurologist), and educated at an elite private school and at Harvard, where he won a Rhodes Scholarship to attend Oxford. In 1964, back in Boston, he was moved by the civil rights crisis to volunteer to help in a Roxbury public school, and was shocked and outraged by the conditions he found there. He became a fourth-grade teacher, and the resulting book about his experience, which had a major effect on public opinion during the school busing crisis in Boston (also the subject of J. Anthony Lukas's *Common Ground*), has become a classic of American writing devoted to social reform.

In the passage that follows, Kozol narrates the technique and effect of extracting confession and apology from a child—a circumstance eerily reminiscent of the examination of Susanna Martin with which this section began.

Eliciting the confession of lies out of children who didn't lie and hadn't lied can easily become one of the most highly developed practices within a segregated school. An assumption of prior guilt is often so overwhelming and so absorbing that even a new teacher with strong affiliations to the Negro community, and sometimes even a teacher who is Negro, will be surprised to discover the extent to which he shares it. It seems at moments to require an almost muscular effort of the imagination to consider the possibility in a particular case that the Negro child might actually *not* have done it, that he might *not* be telling any lie. I remember several incidents of this kind when a pupil whom I knew for certain to be innocent was actually brought around to the point of saying, "Yes I did it" or "Yes I was lying," simply from the force of a white adult's accusation.

There was an example of this in the middle of the winter. One morning the Mathematics Teacher came into the Fourth Grade across the stairs from mine when the regular teacher was not present and when I was taking his class while somebody else was filling in with mine. The children had done an arithmetic assignment the day before. All but two had had it graded and passed back. The two who didn't get it back insisted to me that they had done it but that the substitute teacher who had been with them the day before must have thrown it aside or lost it. I had been in and out of that room long enough to know those two boys and to believe what they were saying. I also knew that in the chaos of substitute changes there was a continual loss and mislaying of homework and of papers of all sorts. Despite this, the Math Teacher came into the room in a mood of anger, delivered a withering denunciation to the whole class on their general performance, then addressed herself to the two boys whose papers had not been given back. She called them to the front and, without questioning or qualifications, she *told* them that they were lying and that she knew they were lying and, furthermore, that she did not want contradictions from them because she knew them too well to be deceived. The truth is that she did not know them at all and probably did not even know their names or who they were. What she meant that she knew was "children who are like them"—in this case, "Negro nine-year-old boys who like to tell lies." Knowing them or not, however, she descended upon them in her manner and she told them that they were liars and did it with so much vigor that she virtually compelled them to believe it must be so. She wasn't the only one in our school who could break down a child by that method, but she was one of the most effective at it.

A somewhat different incident of this sort concerned another boy and involved one of the male teachers in our school. One day while I was working I saw this teacher coming toward me and holding a boy named Anthony rather firmly by the arm. I asked my class to sit still a moment while I went out behind the portable blackboard to find out what was going on. The teacher continued to hold Anthony firmly by the arm. He stood Anthony before me. Anthony looked down at the floor: a common focus at our school for the intimidated eyes of Negro boys. I knew him only slightly. He was one of the slow readers who met with me for extra work from time to time. In this case, I had not seen him for a number of days.

"ANTHONY," said the teacher, "I WANT YOU TO TELL MR. KOZOL NOW THE SAME THING THAT YOU TOLD ME."

It was spaced out like that, exactly, with a caesura of intensity and measured judgment and of persuasive intelligence in between every parceled word: "I WANT YOU TO GO ON NOW AND SAY TO MR. KOZOL WHAT YOU WANT TO TELL HIM AND I WANT YOU TO SAY IT IN A VOICE WHICH IS LOUD AND CLEAR AND I WANT YOU TO LOOK UP AT MR. KOZOL."

When he spoke this way it was as if every child, or every person, in the whole world might be an isolated idiot and that, if the words did not come out so slow and careful, nobody in the world might ever truly find out what any other person believed. Sometimes I think that many teachers in these schools make the mistake of attributing their own obtuseness or sense of isolation to the children they are teaching and that, having little faith in the communication of man to man themselves, they do not really believe you can get through to children either unless you spell everything out in these awful singsong terms.

"Anthony," the teacher continued, "Mr. Kozol is a very busy man. Mr. Kozol has a whole class of children waiting. Now we don't want to keep Mr. Kozol standing here and waiting for you, Anthony, do we? And we wouldn't want Mr. Kozol to think that we were afraid to speak up and apologize to him when we have done something wrong. Would we want Mr. Kozol to think that, Anthony?"

Anthony kept his eyes on the floor. My students poked and peered and stared and craned their necks around from behind the broken blackboard. At last I could see that Anthony had decided to give in. With one of the most cynical yet thoroughly repentant looks of confession that I have ever seen in any person's eyes, he looked up first at the teacher, then at me, and said decently: "I'm sorry." And the teacher said to him: "I'm sorry—who?" And Anthony said nicely: "I'm sorry, Mr. Kozol." And the teacher said: "Good boy, Anthony!" or something of that sort and he touched him in a nice way on the arm. Now the truth is: He *had* been a good boy. He had been a very good boy indeed. He had been a good boy in exactly this regard: that he had gone along with the assumption of one white man about one Negro, had done nothing at all to contradict or to topple that conception, and he even had acted out and executed agreeably a quite skillful little confessional vignette to reinforce it. To this day, I have not the slightest idea of what he had done wrong, or whether he had even done anything at all.

When something as crazy as this happens, I think that it is important to find out how it could be possible. How can an adult so easily, so heedlessly and so unhesitatingly attribute to a child the blame for a misdemeanor about which he has so little information and about which, in fact, he may know nothing? I am sure some of the reasons are the same as those for the frequent use of the rattan: haste and hurry, fear on the part of teachers, animosity and resentment and the potentiality for some sort of sudden insurrection on the parts of certain children. The atmosphere at times becomes so threatening to many teachers that they dare not risk the outbreak of disorder which might occur if they should take time to ascertain gently and carefully and moderately the actual nature of what is really going on. It always seems more practical and less risky to pretend to know more than you do and to insist on your omniscience. When you assume a child is lying and tell him so without reservations, he is almost inclined to agree with you, and furthermore it is often to his advantage to do so since in this way he is likely to minimize his punishment. A child, of course, who begins by pretending to accept blame may end up by *really* accepting it. If you pretend something well, and if that pretense becomes a habit, and if that habit in time becomes the entire style and strategy with which you deal with the white world, then probably it is not surprising if at last it gets into your bloodstream too and begins to feed your body. Naturally all children don't react in the same way and, among the children at my school, there were many different degrees of blame-acceptance or resignation or docility. There were also children who did not give in at all. It was not these—not the defiant ones—but the children who gave in to their teachers most easily and utterly who seemed the saddest.

I noticed this one day while I was out in the auditorium doing reading with some children: Classes were taking place on both sides of us. The Glee Club and the sewing classes were taking place at the same time in the middle. Along with the rest, there was a Fifth Grade remedial math group, comprising six pupils, and there were several other children whom I did not know about simply walking back and forth. Before me were six Fourth Graders, most of them from the disorderly Fourth Grade and several of them children who had had substitute teachers during much of the previous two years. It was not their fault; they had done nothing to deserve substitute teachers. And it was not their fault now if they could not hear my words clearly since it also was true that I could barely hear theirs. Yet the way that they dealt with this dilemma, at least on the level at which I could observe it, was to blame, not the school but themselves. Not one of those children would say to me: "Mr. Kozol, it's too noisy." Not one of them would say: "Mr. Kozol, what's going on here? This is a crazy place to learn."

This instead is what I heard:

"Mr. Kozol, I'm trying as hard as I can but I just can't even hear a word you say."

"Mr. Kozol, please don't be angry. It's so hard—I couldn't hear you."

"Mr. Kozol—please would you read it to me one more time?"

J. ANTHONY LUKAS

From Common Ground

 1976

Although J. Anthony Lukas (1933–1997) was not a New Englander by blood or birth (he was born in New York), his masterful book *Common Ground,* about racial strife in Boston during the 1960s and 1970s, shows that he thought long and deeply about the experience of ordinary New Englanders thrown by history into conflict with one another. The chapter reprinted here introduces Alice McGoff of Charlestown, one of a cast of characters whose interwoven experiences during the crisis over school desegregation constitute the substance of the book. With a novelist's gift for portraiture and narrative, Lukas reveals through her eyes one local meaning of what is sometimes called the Kennedy mystique and detects the gathering storm over what he calls "compensatory rights"—better known today as affirmative action—that would tear apart the old Democratic stronghold of James Michael Curley and Honey Fitz.

McGoff

It was the moment she liked best, the vegetables spread out before her in voluptuous profusion: squeaky stalks of celery, damp lettuce, succulent tomatoes, chilled radishes. From the sink rose the earthy smells of wet roots and peels, and from all about her the clamor and fracas of a busy kitchen, gearing up for dinner only minutes away.

Three nights a week, Alice McGoff served as salad chef at the Officers Club of the Charlestown Navy Yard, a break from her usual job as the club's hatcheck girl. Taking coats and hats was more rewarding—tips could run nearly $200 a week—but Alice liked the sounds and smells and breezy camaraderie of the kitchen. That April night she was cheerfully tossing her greens when she noticed a commotion across the room. A black busboy was in tears. Eventually someone told her that Martin Luther King had been killed in a Southern city.

Through her mind flashed a memory five years old, a solemn television announcer reporting the President's assassination in another Southern city. She'd mourned that night as never before, an anguish so acute it might have been for her husband or brother.

She didn't feel that way about Martin Luther King. You had to admit he'd done one hell of a job for his people; if she were black, she would have been the first one in line behind him. And you had to support his crusade down South. No right-minded person wanted blacks to sit in the back of the bus, eat at separate lunch counters, or use different toilets. That sort of thing was just plain wrong. But when King turned northward, Alice had grown skeptical. When King held his big rally on the Boston Common, Alice had asked, "What the hell is he doing up here?" As far as she could see, Boston wasn't prejudiced against blacks—nobody rode the back of the bus, nobody was kept out of restaurants; Boston wasn't Birmingham or Selma. King was getting a bit above himself. So while his assassination was a terrible thing, she couldn't bring herself to grieve for him.

When dinner at the Officers Club was over and the kitchen had been scoured clean, Alice walked up Decatur Street to her apartment in the Bunker Hill housing project. Her husband, Danny, was still tending bar at the Point Tavern, but their seven children were home, huddled around the television set, watching the riots that had broken out in dozens of American cities. For more than an hour, Alice and her kids watched young blacks racing through the nation's streets—burning, looting, battling the police. Her daughters, Lisa and Robin, seemed terrified by the violent images flickering across the screen, but her sons, Danny Jr., Billy, Kevin, Tommy, and Bobby, sat openmouthed, absorbing the action as avidly as they did their weekly police dramas. Well past midnight, Billy took her outside and pointed toward the horizon, where the fires of Blue Hill Avenue cast a dull red glow.

What did the blacks think they were doing? Alice wondered. They acted as though they were the only people who'd ever had it tough in this world. Poor was poor, hungry was hungry. The housing project where the McGoffs lived wasn't any better than those across town in the ghetto. The widow upstairs who had to get by on social security and food stamps didn't have any more than those black welfare mothers the newspapers were always writing about. The discrimination which blacks had confronted over the years was no worse than the arrogance and indifference which the Irish had faced when they came to this country.

The difference between the blacks and the Irish, she thought, was that the blacks had tried to advance through the civil rights movement—sit-ins, marches, demonstrations, ultimately riots—while the Irish had used politics. Alice believed in politics—it was the American way of getting ahead. And for a long while it had paid off. No district in the country had produced a more potent roster of pols than the storied "Old Eleventh," of which Charlestown was part.

As early as 1894, in a race marked by bogus "mattress" voters, street brawls, and bully-boy raids on polling places, a tough little mick named John Francis Fitzgerald had won election to Congress from the Eleventh. "Honey Fitz" promptly repaid Charlestown's support by getting the Navy Yard reopened, bringing hundreds of jobs back to town. But his stock in trade was an appeal to Irish rage against the "blue-nosed Yankee bigots." In 1905, he rode that anger into the Mayor's office.

Eventually, Fitzgerald's old congressional seat passed to an even more aggressive young Irishman, James Michael Curley, who also exploited Irish resentments against the Yankee nabobs. The very term "codfish aristocracy," he once said, was "an insult to the fish." His style was flamboyant, even demagogic, but both as congressman and later as Boston's mayor he appealed less to narrow Irish ethnocentrism than to the poor of all races. Nowhere was he more popular than in Charlestown and no neighborhood received more of his largesse. One of the most consistently Democratic wards in the nation—Democrats routinely defeated Republicans there by margins of five or six to one—Charlestown did well under the New Deal, receiving one of the country's first public housing projects (the very one where the McGoffs now lived), relief assistance for 1,200 of its 30,000 residents, and a staggering 400 federal jobs.

As late as 1942, at age sixty-eight, Jim Curley was returned to Congress from the Eleventh District. Even his subsequent indictment by a federal grand jury for mail fraud didn't dampen Charlestown's enthusiasm for the old scoundrel. Reelected in 1944, he withdrew only after winning his fourth term as mayor. That left his congressional seat to be filled by special election in 1946. One of the candidates was Honey Fitz's grandson—John Fitzgerald Kennedy.

At first, the notion seemed preposterous. Kennedy was virtually a stranger to Boston, having spent the best part of his twenty-nine years in New York, Hyannis Port, and the South Pacific. His "residence" in the district was the Bellevue Hotel on Beacon Hill. "You're a carpetbagger," one politician in the district told him bitterly. "You don't belong here." Moreover, his patrician gloss, the elegant ease acquired at Choate and Harvard and cultivated in London and Palm Beach, was not calculated to go down well in the waterfront saloons of Charlestown, the clammy tenements of the North End, or the bleak three-deckers of East Boston, Brighton, Somerville, and Cambridge. True, his family's roots went deep in the district: not only had Honey Fitz represented it in Congress for six years, but Jack's paternal grandfather, Patrick J. Kennedy, had been born and raised in East Boston and served as its Democratic ward leader for many years. But those roots could be as much a hindrance as an asset. Boston's Irish were notoriously resentful of the "two toilet" Irish who had betrayed their heritage by moving to the suburbs and sending their sons to Harvard.

One who shared those feelings was Alice McGoff's father, Bernie Kirk. A second-generation Irish-American, Bernie had worked for decades at a South End ink factory, where he served as a union shop steward. "The little man has to unite to get anyplace," he would tell his daughter Alice, and that turn of mind was reflected in his stalwart Democratic politics, his unwavering support for Al Smith, David I. Walsh, and Franklin Roosevelt. But he had no use whatsoever for Joe Kennedy, the patriarch of the Kennedy clan, whom he regarded as a womanizer, a high liver, an incurable conniver. "That man's forgotten where he came from," he'd tell Alice, "he's no longer one of us." Moreover, Kennedy was simply too close to Richard Cardinal Cushing, Boston's venerable archbishop. There was a touch of the anticlerical in Bernie; priests were okay when they stuck to the Church's business, he thought, but their writ didn't extend to public life. Cushing and Kennedy were both overreachers, too eager to steal a march on their countrymen. There was an old Charlestown saying, "Up to me, up to me, but never above me." No son of Joe Kennedy's was going to clamber over Bernie's head.

Moreover, Bernie was committed to Charlestown's own candidate for Congress, John F. "Fish" Cotter, a popular figure who had served as secretary to Curley and before that to Congressman John P. Higgins. When Higgins resigned his congressional seat, Cotter had been appointed to fill out his unexpired term. During his years in Washington, he had dispensed countless favors to his fellow "Townies." The Kirks had received more than a few of them, and now Bernie Kirk was determined to return the favor.

Among the Townies who had committed themselves to Fish Cotter was a young Air Force veteran named Dave Powers. One night in January 1946 there was a knock at the door of the three-decker that Dave shared with his widowed sister and her eight children. When he opened it, there stood a gangly fellow who stuck out his hand and said, "My name's Jack Kennedy. I'm a candidate for Congress." Sitting at the kitchen table, Powers explained that he was working for one of Kennedy's opponents. But he liked his young visitor, and when Kennedy mentioned that he was speaking the next week to Gold Star Mothers at Charlestown's American Legion Hall, Powers agreed to go with him.

The next Tuesday, Dave stood at the back of the hall as Kennedy gave what seemed like "the world's worst speech"—halting, awkward, clumsily worded. But then the candidate looked out across the phalanx of women, all of whom had lost sons in the war, and said, "I think I know how you feel, because my mother is a Gold Star Mother too." (Jack's older brother, Joe, had been shot down over Germany.) In the back of the room, Powers could hear some women weeping and others turn to their neighbors and say, "He reminds me of my boy." When the speech was over, the young aristocrat was mobbed by dozens of working-class women, ardently promising him their support. Powers was convinced.

A few denounced him for deserting Cotter, but working with other veteran operatives, Dave mounted a crisply efficient campaign. On a routine day in Charlestown, Kennedy started at 7:00 a.m., shaking hands outside the Navy Yard, then rang doorbells at every three-decker along Bunker Hill Street. In the afternoon he dropped into grocery stores and barbershops, ending up back at the Navy Yard, where he shook the hands he'd missed that morning. In the evening there'd be a rally at the American Legion Hall or a get-together in somebody's parlor.

Meanwhile, Jack set out to acquire the more formal badges of Irish Catholic orthodoxy, starting with membership in the Knights of Columbus. Shrewdly, his aides directed him to the Bunker Hill Council, oldest in the state, much honored among Boston's Celts. Appropriately enough, induction in the Third Degree took place on St. Patrick's Day. The ceremony began with fifty "candidates" marching through Charlestown's streets to the Knights Hall, each with a "relic"—an oversized key, cross, or candle—to lug along the three-mile route. Jack was assigned a special burden—a live, frisky billy goat which the future President hauled on a leash past hundreds of amused spectators. A powerful symbol in Knights ritual, the goat was intended to teach humility: the candidate might think he was leading it, but as would eventually become clear, the goat was leading him. After the initiation, Jack adjourned with his fellow Knights to Sully's Cafe on Union Street for the traditional hoisting of the brew. It was a moment that would remain sacred to all those who stood that night at Sully's beer-stained bar.

But the climax of the Charlestown campaign was the annual Bunker Hill Day parade on June 17. The night before, Townies and their guests celebrated at a half dozen banquets and balls. Jack addressed no fewer than five, then went on with Powers to an after-hours joint called the Stork Club, where he stayed until 2:00 a.m.

Hours later, he was back in town for the traditional round of house calls before the afternoon parade. With the primary only hours away, each candidate sought to make a final splash. Seeking to exploit his image as a war hero, Kennedy marched that day under the glittering new banners of the Lieutenant Joseph P. Kennedy Post of the Veterans of Foreign Wars, named after Jack's late brother. Hatless, dressed in a dark gray flannel suit, he strode up Bunker Hill Street with more than a hundred supporters marching three abreast behind him. Every few steps, someone broke from the crowd to pump his hand or ask for an autograph.

The Kirks watched the parade from a friend's stoop on Monument Square. As Kennedy went by, Bernie stood stonily with arms folded; he was sticking with Cotter. But his wife, Gertrude, and his three daughters had long since succumbed to Jack's charms. Alice, then only nine, was desolate that she couldn't cast a vote for the dashing young candidate.

The next day, Kennedy lost Charlestown to Cotter by only 337 votes, and elsewhere in the Eleventh District he outpolled his nearest competitor by nearly two to one. That night at a victory party, eighty-three-year-old Honey Fitz clambered up on a table and croaked out his famous rendition of "Sweet Adeline."

Almost overnight Jack Kennedy had become an honorary Townie. Charlestown voted overwhelmingly for his return to Congress in 1948 and 1950, for his election to the Senate in 1952 and 1958, and to put him in the White House in 1960. And Kennedy returned the attention. He appointed Bob Morey, his Townie driver, to be U.S. Marshal for Massachusetts, and he brought Dave Powers into the White House as boon companion. Powers took pains to see that loyal Charlestown supporters received appropriate recognition. In April 1961, the President received some three hundred members of the Bunker Hill Council of the Knights of Columbus—*his* council. For nearly an hour, the proud Knights milled across the White House lawn, jawing with *their* President.

The substance of Kennedy's policies did nothing to alienate Charlestown. In foreign policy, he was perceived as a tough guy, a battle-hardened veteran, not unlike the thousands of Charlestown men who had fought in the two world wars and Korea (there is a legend that Charlestown sent more boys into World War II than any community of its size in the country). Charlestown's vets thrilled to Kennedy's rhetorical flourishes, applauded his firm resistance to international Communism, cheered the attempted invasion of Cuba and the brinksmanship of the Missile Crisis.

In domestic matters, Kennedy suited the Townies nearly as well. For although he came to be considered a liberal, he was deeply suspicious of the conventional pieties. One strain in him, to be sure, rang with lofty purpose, summoning the nation to live up to its highest aspirations ("No problem of human destiny is beyond human beings"). But another side was ironic, intensely aware of man's limitations ("Life is unfair," he liked to say). Something deep in Kennedy's Irish soul bespoke a tragic view of life; the Kirks and their neighbors responded to that.

On civil rights, Kennedy's stance was deliberate and intensely political. Convinced that he didn't have the votes in Congress to enact significant rights legislation—and afraid that the attempt would cost him Southern support for the remainder of his legislative program—he was determined to move in this area only by executive order. Yet even here he was laggard, delaying more than two years in signing an order to ban discrimination in federal housing programs, something which, during the campaign, he had airily declared "the President could do by a stroke of his pen." With this delay, Martin Luther King said, Kennedy had "undermined confidence in his intentions." Summing up the President's first year in office, King found it "essentially cautious and defensive"; Kennedy had the understanding and political skill, but "the moral passion is missing." Even when Kennedy finally introduced a civil rights bill in February 1963, black leaders bemoaned its lack of teeth.

It took the Birmingham crisis of late spring 1963—with Bull Connor's cops using nightsticks, dogs, and fire hoses on King's marchers—to create a sense of national urgency to which the President could respond. And respond he did in a nationally televised address that June, in which he said the country confronted "a moral issue . . . as old as the scriptures and as clear as the American Constitution." That night, the President announced that he would bring in a new, stronger civil rights bill, embodying "the proposition that race has no place in American life and law." To support the bill, a quarter million Americans marched on Washington on August 28. That evening, Kennedy received ten black leaders at the White House, greeting them with the very words King had used at the Lincoln Memorial just hours before—"I have a dream." At last, it seemed, the dreams of Martin Luther King and the political exigencies of John F. Kennedy were about to converge. Less than three months later, the President was dead.

When Lyndon Johnson capitalized on the nation's grief to push Kennedy's civil rights bill through Congress, Alice McGoff and her neighbors concurred. But before long they detected a not so subtle shift in the rhetoric of civil rights. No longer were politicians, professors, and editorial writers talking merely about giving Negroes an equal shot at life, liberty, and the pursuit of happiness. By the mid-sixties, they were proposing to take real things—money, jobs, housing, and schools—away from whites and give them to blacks.

This notion of preferential treatment for blacks originated with a young Irish-American, Assistant Secretary of Labor Daniel Patrick Moynihan. When Lyndon Johnson agreed to deliver the commencement address at Howard University on June 4, 1965, Moynihan drafted the text. "Freedom is not enough," the President said that day. "You do not take a person who, for years, has been hobbled by chains and liberate him, bring him up to the starting line of a race, and then say, 'You are free to compete with all the others,' and still justly believe that you have been completely fair. We seek not just freedom but opportunity. We seek not just legal equity, not just equality as a right and a theory, but equality as a fact and equality as a result."

The more Alice McGoff heard about this doctrine, the less she liked it. The government picked several races and called them minorities, but the Irish, they weren't a minority; the government was saying the Irish were well off, they'd never had a hard life. Sure, slavery had been a great injustice, but she didn't see why whites who weren't even alive during slave times should be penalized for it. How could you make slaves of the majority to free the minority? Was that justice?

Moreover, she knew full well which whites would pay the price for all of this. It wouldn't be those who worked in the big corporate and law offices downtown, the ones who dined in those Back Bay clubs and lived in the comfortable, all-white suburbs. No, as usual it would be the working-class whites who shared the inner city with blacks, competed with them for schools and jobs and housing, and jostled with them on the street corners.

Before long, the issue of compensatory rights had helped to drive a wedge between the Townies and the remaining Kennedy brothers. Nobody proved a more impassioned advocate of the new doctrine than Robert Kennedy. And Bobby was among the first to point his finger at Northern cities like Boston. "In the North," he told one reporter, "I think you have had *de facto* segregation which in some areas is as bad or even more extreme than in the South. Everybody in those communities, including my own state of Massachusetts, concentrated on what was happening in Birmingham, Alabama, or Jackson, Mississippi, and didn't look at what needed to be done in our own home, our own town, our own city."

For Alice McGoff, that was sheer political posturing, designed to curry favor with Martin Luther King and the "limousine liberals" at the expense of working-class whites. But Bobby was an increasingly remote figure in Massachusetts. To Alice, the Kennedy survivor who really mattered was Ted.

When Ted first ran for Jack's old Senate seat in 1962, there were those who regarded him as grossly unqualified for the job and resented the Kennedys' "arrogance" in forwarding his candidacy. But Alice and most other Townies had no such reservations. Indeed, so fierce was Charlestown's loyalty to the President that it gave his brother a whopping 86.8 percent of its vote, the highest of any neighborhood in the city. Two years later—with JFK's assassination fresh in most minds and Ted in the hospital after a near-fatal air crash—the Townies tendered him an incredible 94.8 percent.

But Alice's enthusiasm waned as Ted took up the cudgels for minority rights. In June 1965—just months after the Selma march and Martin Luther King's address on the Boston Common—Ted put himself squarely behind efforts in the Massachusetts legislature to withhold state funds from cities and towns with racially segregated schools. Receiving an honorary degree from Northeastern University, he told a throng at Boston Garden, "We in the Northeast say we have given opportunity to each wave of immigrants that has come to our shores, but if this is our tradition, why have we failed so far to offer similar opportunity to Negro citizens who have come from other states? It should be clear that a Negro child in Massachusetts has as much of a right to an integrated education as a Negro child in Mississippi or Alabama."

Jerry Doherty, a Townie ally of Ted's, warned that such positions would cost him heavily in Charlestown. And indeed they did, for Teddy had never been so much an object of Charlestown's affections as the beneficiary of its special relationship with Jack. And if Jack's advance to the White House had released the Boston Irish from their anxiety about being only half American, so it had made them secure enough to reject an Irishman as well. Ultimately, many blue-collar Irish unloaded on Ted the pent-up envy and resentment they'd never dared to direct at Jack.

By the spring of 1968, at age thirty-one, Alice McGoff was beginning to feel some of her father's sense of grievance at the Kennedy clan. She was still a committed Democrat; she couldn't imagine herself voting for a Republican. But she found herself wondering whether the Kennedys were genuine Democrats any longer, whether they really had the interests of the white working class at heart.

Hours after Martin Luther King's death, Ted Kennedy delivered an impassioned eulogy to the fallen prophet. "He was a noble man, eloquent, patient, and brave," the Senator told reporters. "He loved his fellow man, white and black. He died because he was willing to go throughout this country, as a leader and a symbol, in an effort to bring them together."

Watching the Senator on television, Alice felt a rush of anger at his smug, preachy tone. As usual, Ted seemed to care more about blacks than he did about his own people. The Kennedys had never had it tough in their lives—who were they to sit down there at Hyannis Port and tell her what to do for the minorities? As fires stained the night sky over Roxbury, Alice turned off the set and went to bed.

The Abiding Sense of Place

JOHN CROWE RANSOM, born in Tennessee, once expounded a theory to explain the evolving relation of a people to their land. While "the first settlers in a region are occupied with its conquest," he wrote, "physical nature, being harried and torn up by violence, looks raw." But over time, as "nature . . . yield[s] to man's solicitations [and] displays her charm," the conquerors come to "represent it lovingly in their arts." This idea that culture moves from opposition to union with the nurturing land is as serviceable for New England as for Ransom's native South—except that during their own distinctive phase of conquest, New Englanders disregarded their Indian predecessors and viewed the land not as raw and resistant but through eyes already accustomed by Scripture to see it, lovingly, as a new Canaan.

New England literary culture has long expressed this kind of grateful reverence: when Daniel Webster, the most famous orator of his time, stood in 1820 at the site in Plymouth (or as near to it as legend could guide him) where the Pilgrims had landed 200 years earlier, he invoked "the genius of the place" as if it sang undiminished in the sound of the wind and the sea. In the selections that follow, a range of writers give voice to this feeling of proprietary intimacy with—and sometimes mischievous affection for—the land of New England and its enduring "genius."

Chapel at Biddeford Pool, Maine, 1880s

RALPH WALDO EMERSON

Hamatreya

 1846

Emerson (1803–1882) owned a copy of *The Vishnu Purana,* a collection of Hindu mythology, in a translation by H. H. Wilson (published in 1840), from which he copied into his notebook the following passage chanted by the earth to Hamatreya (Emerson's variant name for the Buddhist god Maitreya, the Buddha of the future): "Those who said 'the earth is mine,—it is my son's—it belongs to my dynasty,'— have all passed away . . . Earth laughs, as if smiling with autumnal flowers to behold her kings unable to effect the subjugation of themselves." Emerson's poem "Hamatreya" echoes this theme (which he had broached ten years earlier in *Nature*) of human presumption and earth's abiding.

> Minott, Lee, Willard, Hosmer, Meriam, Flint
> Possessed the land which rendered to their toil
> Hay, corn, roots, hemp, flax, apples, wool, and wood.
> Each of these landlords walked amidst his farm,
> Saying, "'Tis mine, my children's, and my name's.
> How sweet the west wind sounds in my own trees!
> How graceful climb those shadows on my hill!
> I fancy these pure waters and the flags
> Know me, as does my dog: we sympathize;
> And, I affirm, my actions smack of the soil.'
> Where are these men? Asleep beneath their grounds;
> And strangers, fond as they, their furrows plough.
> Earth laughs in flowers, to see her boastful boys
> Earth-proud, proud of the earth which is not theirs;
> Who steer the plough, but cannot steer their feet
> Clear of the grave.
> They added ridge to valley, brook to pond,
> And sighed for all that bounded their domain.
> 'This suits me for a pasture; that's my park;
> We must have clay, lime, gravel, granite-ledge,
> And misty lowland, where to go for peat.

The land is well,—lies fairly to the south.
'Tis good, when you have crossed the sea and back,
To find the sitfast acres where you left them.'
Ah! the hot owner sees not Death, who adds
Him to his land, a lump of mould the more.
Hear what the Earth says:—

EARTH-SONG.

'Mine and yours;
Mine, not yours.
Earth endures;
Stars abide—
Shine down in the old sea;
Old are the shores;
But where are old men?
I who have seen much,
Such have I never seen.

'The lawyer's deed
Ran sure,
In tail,
To them, and to their heirs
Who shall succeed,
Without fail,
Forevermore.

'Here is the land,
Shaggy with wood,
With its old valley,
Mound, and flood.
But the heritors?
Fled like the flood's foam,—
The lawyer, and the laws,
And the kingdom,
Clean swept herefrom.

'They called me theirs,
Who so controlled me;
Yet every one
Wished to stay, and is gone.

How am I theirs,
If they cannot hold me,
But I hold them?'

When I heard the Earth-song,
I was no longer brave;
My avarice cooled
Like lust in the chill of the grave.

SARAH ORNE JEWETT

A White Heron

 1886

Often associated with the New England branch of the literary movement known as "local color," Sarah Orne Jewett (1849–1909) divided her time between her native village of South Berwick, Maine, and the literary salons of Boston, where she lived for nearly thirty years in a "Boston marriage" with Annie Fields, widow of the founder of the *Atlantic Monthly,* James T. Fields. In Jewett's delicately suspenseful story "A White Heron" one encounters the elements that made her novella *The Country of the Pointed Firs* (1896) a minor classic: village life imperiled by invaders who regard nature as a storehouse of collectibles ready for the taking, and the resilient stoicism of country women, who, accustomed to death and desertion, have a melancholy dignity. In the background of Jewett's fictional world one hears the low but rising roar of industrialization; and there is a sense of peace imperiled, childhood fleeting, and sexual desire suppressed or on the wane even as it first stirs.

I

The woods were already filled with shadows one June evening, just before eight o'clock, though a bright sunset still glimmered faintly among the trunks of the trees. A little girl was driving home her cow, a plodding, dilatory, provoking creature in her behavior, but a valued companion for all that. They were going away from the western light, and striking deep into the dark woods, but their feet were familiar with the path, and it was no matter whether their eyes could see it or not.

There was hardly a night the summer through when the old cow could be found waiting at the pasture bars; on the contrary, it was her greatest pleasure to hide herself away among the high huckleberry bushes, and though she wore a loud bell she had made the discovery that if one stood perfectly still it would not ring. So Sylvia had to hunt for her until she found her, and call Co'! Co'! with never an answering Moo, until her childish patience was quite spent. If the creature had not given good milk and plenty of it, the case would have seemed very different to her owners. Besides, Sylvia had all the time there was, and very little use to make of it. Sometimes in pleasant weather it was a consolation to look upon the cow's pranks as an intelligent attempt to play hide and seek, and as the child had no playmates she lent herself to this amusement with a good deal of zest. Though this chase had been so long that the wary animal herself had given an unusual signal of her whereabouts, Sylvia had only laughed when she came upon Mistress Moolly at the swampside, and urged her affectionately homeward with a twig of birch leaves. The old cow was not inclined to wander farther, she even turned in the right direction for once as they left the pasture, and stepped along the road at a good pace. She was quite ready to be milked now, and seldom stopped to browse. Sylvia wondered what her grandmother would say because they were so late. It was a great while since she had left home at half past five o'clock, but everybody knew the difficulty of making this errand a short one. Mrs. Tilley had chased the hornéd torment too many summer evenings herself to blame any one else for lingering, and was only thankful as she waited that she had Sylvia, nowadays, to give such valuable assistance. The good woman suspected that Sylvia loitered occasionally on her own account; there never was such a child for straying about out-of-doors since the world was made! Everybody said that it was a good change for a little maid who had tried to grow for eight years in a crowded manufacturing town, but, as for Sylvia herself, it seemed as if she never had been alive at all before she came to live at the farm. She thought often with wistful compassion of a wretched dry geranium that belonged to a town neighbor.

"'Afraid of folks,'" old Mrs. Tilley said to herself, with a smile, after she had made the unlikely choice of Sylvia from her daughter's houseful of children, and was returning to the farm. "'Afraid of folks,' they said! I guess she won't be troubled no great with 'em up to the old place!" When they reached the door of the lonely house and stopped to unlock it, and the cat came to purr loudly, and rub against them, a deserted pussy, indeed, but fat with young robins, Sylvia whispered that this was a beautiful place to live in, and she never should wish to go home.

The companions followed the shady woodroad, the cow taking slow steps, and the child very fast ones. The cows stopped long at the brook to drink, as if the pasture were not half a swamp, and Sylvia stood still and waited, letting her bare feet cool themselves in the shoal water, while the great twilight moths struck softly against her. She waded on through the brook as the cow moved away, and listened to the thrushes with a heart that beat fast with pleasure. There was a stirring in the great boughs overhead. They were full of little birds and beasts that seemed to be wide-awake, and going about their world, or else saying goodnight to each other in sleepy twitters. Sylvia herself felt sleepy as she walked along. However, it was not much farther to the house, and the air was soft and sweet. She was not often in the woods so late as this, and it made her feel as if she were a part of the gray shadows and the moving leaves. She was just thinking how long it seemed since she first came to the farm a year ago, and wondering if everything went on in the noisy town just the same as when she was there; the thought of the great red-faced boy who used to chase and frighten her made her hurry along the path to escape from the shadow of the trees.

Suddenly this little woods-girl is horror-stricken to hear a clear whistle not very far away. Not a bird's whistle, which would have a sort of friendliness, but a boy's whistle, determined, and somewhat aggressive. Sylvia left the cow to whatever sad fate might await her, and stepped discreetly aside into the bushes, but she was just too late. The enemy had discovered her, and called out in a very cheerful and persuasive tone, "Halloa, little girl, how far is it to the road?" and trembling Sylvia answered almost inaudibly, "A good ways."

She did not dare to look boldly at the tall young man, who carried a gun over his shoulder, but she came out of her bush and again followed the cow, while he walked alongside.

"I have been hunting for some birds," the stranger said kindly, "and I have lost my way, and need a friend very much. Don't be afraid," he added gallantly. "Speak up and tell me what your name is, and whether you think I can spend the night at your house, and go out gunning early in the morning."

Sylvia was more alarmed than before. Would not her grandmother consider her much to blame? But who could have foreseen such an accident as this? It did not appear to be her fault, and she hung her head as if the stem of it were broken, but managed to answer "Sylvy," with much effort when her companion again asked her name.

Mrs. Tilley was standing in the doorway when the trio came into view. The cow gave a loud moo by way of explanation.

"Yes, you'd better speak up for yourself, you old trial! Where'd she tuck herself away this time, Sylvy?" Sylvia kept an awed silence; she knew by instinct that her grandmother did not comprehend the gravity of the situation. She must be mistaking the stranger for one of the farmer-lads of the region.

The young man stood his gun beside the door, and dropped a heavy game-bag beside it; then he bade Mrs. Tilley good-evening, and repeated his wayfarer's story, and asked if he could have a night's lodging.

"Put me anywhere you like," he said. "I must be off early in the morning, before day; but I am very hungry, indeed. You can give me some milk at any rate, that's plain."

"Dear sakes, yes," responded the hostess, whose long slumbering hospitality seemed to be easily awakened. "You might fare better if you went out on the main road a mile or so, but you're welcome to what we've got. I'll milk right off, and you make yourself at home. You can sleep on husks or feathers," she proffered graciously. "I raised them all myself. There's good pasturing for geese just below here towards the ma'sh. Now step round and set a plate for the gentleman, Sylvy!" And Sylvia promptly stepped. She was glad to have something to do, and she was hungry herself.

It was a surprise to find so clean and comfortable a little dwelling in this New England wilderness. The young man had known the horrors of its most primitive housekeeping, and the dreary squalor of that level of society which does not rebel at the companionship of hens. This was the best thrift of an old-fashioned farmstead, though on such a small scale that it seemed like a hermitage. He listened eagerly to the old woman's quaint talk, he watched Sylvia's pale face and shining gray eyes with ever growing enthusiasm, and insisted that this was the best supper he had eaten for a month; then, afterward, the new-made friends sat down in the doorway together while the moon came up.

Soon it would be berry-time, and Sylvia was a great help at picking. The cow was a good milker, though a plaguy thing to keep track of, the hostess gossiped frankly, adding presently that she had buried four children, so that Sylvia's mother, and a son (who might be dead) in California were all the children she had left. "Dan, my boy, was a great hand to go gunning," she explained sadly. "I never wanted for pa'tridges or gray squer'ls while he was to home. He's been a great wand'rer, I expect, and he's no hand to write letters. There, I don't blame him, I'd ha' seen the world myself if it had been so I could.

"Sylvia takes after him," the grandmother continued affectionately, after a minute's pause. "There ain't a foot o' ground she don't know her way over, and the wild creatur's counts her one o' themselves. Squer'ls she'll tame to come an' feed right out o' her hands, and all sorts o' birds. Last winter she got the jay-birds to bangeing here, and I believe she'd 'a' scanted herself of her own meals to have plenty to throw out amongst 'em, if I hadn't kep' watch. Anything but crows, I tell her, I'm willin' to help support,—though Dan he went an' tamed one o' them that did seem to have reason same as folks. It was round here a good spell after he went away. Dan an' his father they didn't hitch,—but he never held up his head ag'in after Dan had dared him an' gone off."

The guest did not notice this hint of family sorrows in his eager interest in something else.

"So Sylvy knows all about birds, does she?" he exclaimed, as he looked round at the little girl who sat, very demure but increasingly sleepy, in the moonlight. "I am making a collection of birds myself. I have been at it ever since I was a boy." (Mrs. Tilley smiled.) "There are two or three very rare ones

I have been hunting for these five years. I mean to get them on my own ground if they can be found."

"Do you cage 'em up?" asked Mrs. Tilley doubtfully, in response to this enthusiastic announcement.

"Oh, no, they're stuffed and preserved, dozens and dozens of them," said the ornithologist, "and I have shot or snared every one myself. I caught a glimpse of a white heron three miles from here on Saturday, and I have followed it in this direction. They have never been found in this district at all. The little white heron, it is," and he turned again to look at Sylvia with the hope of discovering that the rare bird was one of her acquaintances.

But Sylvia was watching a hop-toad in the narrow footpath.

"You would know the heron if you saw it," the stranger continued eagerly. "A queer tall white bird with soft feathers and long thin legs. And it would have a nest perhaps in the top of a high tree, made of sticks, something like a hawk's nest."

Sylvia's heart gave a wild beat; she knew that strange white bird, and had once stolen softly near where it stood in some bright green swamp grass, away over at the other side of the woods. There was an open place where the sunshine always seemed strangely yellow and hot, where tall, nodding rushes grew, and her grandmother had warned her that she might sink in the soft black mud underneath and never be heard of more. Not far beyond were the salt marshes and beyond those was the sea, the sea which Sylvia wondered and dreamed about, but never had looked upon, though its great voice could often be heard above the noise of the woods on stormy nights.

"I can't think of anything I should like so much as to find that heron's nest," the handsome stranger was saying. "I would give ten dollars to anybody who could show it to me," he added desperately, "and I mean to spend my whole vacation hunting for it if need be. Perhaps it was only migrating, or had been chased out of its own region by some bird of prey."

Mrs. Tilley gave amazed attention to all this, but Sylvia still watched the toad, not divining, as she might have done at some calmer time, that the creature wished to get to its hole under the doorstep, and was much hindered by the unusual spectators at that hour of the evening. No amount of thought, that night, could decide how many wished-for treasures the ten dollars, so lightly spoken of, would buy.

The next day the young sportsman hovered about the woods, and Sylvia kept him company, having lost her first fear of the friendly lad, who proved to be most kind and sympathetic. He told her many things about the birds and what they knew and where they lived and what they did with themselves. And he gave her a jack-knife, which she thought as great a treasure as if she were a desert-islander. All day long he did not once make her troubled or afraid except when he brought down some unsuspecting singing creature from its bough. Sylvia would have liked him vastly better without his gun; she could not understand why he killed the very birds he seemed to like so much. But as the day waned, Sylvia still watched the young man with loving admiration. She had never seen anybody so charming and delightful; the woman's heart, asleep in the child, was vaguely thrilled by a dream of love. Some premonition of that great power stirred and swayed these young foresters who traversed the solemn woodlands with soft-footed silent care. They stopped to listen to a bird's song; they pressed forward again eagerly, parting the branches,—speaking to each other rarely and in whispers; the young man going first and Sylvia following, fascinated, a few steps behind, with her gray eyes dark with excitement.

She grieved because the longed-for white heron was elusive, but she did not lead the guest, she only followed, and there was no such thing as speaking first. The sound of her own unquestioned voice would have terrified her,—it was hard enough to answer yes or no when there was need of that. At last evening began to fall, and they drove the cow home together, and Sylvia smiled with pleasure when they came to the place where she heard the whistle and was afraid only the night before.

2

Half a mile from home, at the farther edge of the woods, where the land was highest, a great pine-tree stood, the last of its generation. Whether it was left for a boundary mark, or for what reason, no one could say; the woodchoppers who had felled its mates were dead and gone long ago, and a whole forest of sturdy trees, pines and oaks and maples, had grown again. But the stately head of this old pine towered above them all and made a landmark for sea and shore miles and miles away. Sylvia knew it well. She had always believed that whoever climbed to the top of it could see the ocean; and the little girl had often laid her hand on the great rough trunk and looked up wistfully at those dark boughs that the wind always stirred, no matter how hot and still the air might be below. Now she thought of the tree with a new excitement, for why, if one climbed it at break of day, could not one see all the world, and easily discover whence the white heron flew, and mark the place, and find the hidden nest?

What a spirit of adventure, what wild ambition! What fancied triumph and delight and glory for the later morning when she could make known the secret! It was almost too real and too great for the childish heart to bear.

All night the door of the little house stood open, and the whippoorwills came and sang upon the very step. The young sportsman and his old hostess were sound asleep, but Sylvia's great design kept her broad awake and watching. She forgot to think of sleep. The short summer night seemed as long as the winter darkness, and at last when the whippoorwills ceased, and she was afraid the morning would after all come too soon, she stole out of the house and followed the pasture path through the woods, hastening toward the open ground beyond, listening with a sense of comfort and companionship to the drowsy twitter of a half-awakened bird, whose perch she had jarred in passing. Alas, if the great wave of human interest which flooded for the first time this dull little life should sweep away the satisfactions of an existence heart to heart with nature and the dumb life of the forest!

There was the huge tree asleep yet in the paling moonlight, and small and hopeful Sylvia began with utmost bravery to mount to the top of it, with tingling, eager blood coursing the channels of her whole frame, with her bare feet and fingers, that pinched and held like bird's claws to the monstrous ladder reaching up, up, almost to the sky itself. First she must mount the white oak tree that grew alongside, where she was almost lost among the dark branches and the green leaves heavy and wet with dew; a bird fluttered off its nest, and a red squirrel ran to and fro and scolded pettishly at the harmless housebreaker. Sylvia felt her way easily. She had often climbed there, and knew that higher still one of the oak's upper branches chafed against the pine trunk, just where its lower boughs were set close together. There, when she made the dangerous pass from one tree to the other, the great enterprise would really begin.

She crept out along the swaying oak limb at last, and took the daring step across into the old pine-tree. The way was harder than she thought; she must reach far and hold fast, the sharp dry twigs caught and held her and scratched her like angry talons, the pitch made her thin little fingers clumsy and stiff as she went round and round the tree's great stem, higher and higher upward. The sparrows and robins in the woods below were beginning to wake and twitter to the dawn, yet it seemed much lighter there aloft in the pine-tree, and the child knew that she must hurry if her project were to be of any use.

The tree seemed to lengthen itself out as she went up, and to reach farther and farther upward. It was like a great main-mast to the voyaging earth; it must truly have been amazed that morning through all its ponderous frame as it felt this determined spark of human spirit creeping and climbing from higher branch to branch. Who knows how steadily the least twigs held themselves to advantage this light, weak creature on her way! The old pine must have loved his new dependent. More than all the hawks, and bats, and moths, and even the sweet-voiced thrushes, was the brave, beating heart of the solitary gray-eyed child. And the tree stood still and held away the winds that June morning while the dawn grew bright in the east.

Sylvia's face was like a pale star, if one had seen it from the ground, when the last thorny bough was past, and she stood trembling and tired but wholly triumphant, high in the tree-top. Yes, there was the sea with the dawning sun making a golden dazzle over it, and toward that glorious east flew two hawks with slow-moving pinions. How low they looked in the air from that height when before one had only seen them far up, and dark against the blue sky. Their gray feathers were as soft as moths; they seemed only a little way from the tree, and Sylvia felt as if she too could go flying away among the clouds. Westward, the woodlands and farms reached miles and miles into the distance; here and there were church steeples, and white villages; truly it was a vast and awesome world.

The birds sang louder and louder. At last the sun came up bewilderingly bright. Sylvia could see the white sails of ships out at sea, and the clouds that were purple and rose-colored and yellow at first began to fade away. Where was the white heron's nest in the sea of green branches, and was this wonderful sight and pageant of the world the only reward for having climbed to such a giddy height? Now look down again, Sylvia, where the green marsh is set among the shining birches and dark hemlocks; there where you saw the white heron once you will see him again; look, look! a white spot of him like a single floating feather comes up from the dead hemlock and grows larger, and rises, and comes close at last, and goes by the landmark pine with steady sweep of wing and outstretched slender neck and crested head. And wait! wait! do not move a foot or a finger, little girl, do not send an arrow of light and consciousness from your two eager eyes, for the heron has perched on a pine bough not far beyond yours, and cries back to his mate on the nest, and plumes his feathers for the new day!

The child gives a long sigh a minute later when a company of shouting catbirds comes also to the tree, and vexed by their fluttering and lawlessness the solemn heron goes away. She knows his secret now, the wild, light, slender bird that floats and wavers, and goes back like an arrow presently to his home in the green world beneath. Then Sylvia, well satisfied, makes her perilous way down again, not daring to look far below the branch she stands on, ready to cry sometimes because her fingers ache and her lamed feet slip. Wondering over and over again what the stranger would say to her, and what he would think when she told him how to find his way straight to the heron's nest.

"Sylvy, Sylvy!" called the busy old grandmother again and again, but nobody answered, and the small husk bed was empty, and Sylvia had disappeared.

The guest waked from a dream, and remembering his day's pleasure hurried to dress himself that it might sooner begin. He was sure from the way the shy little girl looked once or twice yesterday that she had at least seen the white heron, and now she must really be persuaded to tell. Here she comes now, paler than ever, and her worn old frock is torn and tattered, and smeared with pine pitch. The grandmother and the sportsman stand in the door together and question her, and the splendid moment has come to speak of the dead hemlock-tree by the green marsh.

But Sylvia does not speak after all, though the old grandmother fretfully rebukes her, and the young man's kind appealing eyes are looking straight in her own. He can make them rich with money; he has promised it, and they are poor now. He is so well worth making happy, and he waits to hear the story she can tell.

No, she must keep silence! What is it that suddenly forbids her and makes her dumb? Has she been nine years growing, and now, when the great world for the first time puts out a hand to her, must she thrust it aside for a bird's sake? The murmur of the pine's green branches is in her ears, she remembers how the white heron came flying through the golden air and how they watched the sea and the morning together, and Sylvia cannot speak; she cannot tell the heron's secret and give its life away.

Dear loyalty, that suffered a sharp pang as the guest went away disappointed later in the day, that could have served and followed him and loved him as a dog loves! Many a night Sylvia heard the echo of his whistle haunting the pasture path as she came home with the loitering cow. She forgot even her sorrow at the sharp report of his gun and the piteous sight of thrushes and sparrows dropping silent to the ground, their songs hushed and their pretty feathers stained and wet with blood. Were the birds better friends than their hunter might have been,—who can tell? Whatever treasures were lost to her, woodlands and summer-time, remember! Bring your gifts and graces and tell your secrets to this lonely country child!

HENRY JAMES

From The American Scene

 1907

In 1904, after an absence of twenty years, Henry James (1843–1916) sailed for America from his adopted country, England, in order to visit the scenes of his youth and to make a westward lecture tour. One of James's first stops was a stay of several weeks at his brother William's summer home in New Hampshire. In the typically gnarled and wonderfully reflective prose of *The American Scene,* James considers how, over the years of his self-exile, rural New England seems to have been transformed from farmland to a playground for "summer people."

Written over the great New Hampshire region at least, and stamped, in particular, in the shadow of the admirable high-perched cone of Chocorua, which rears itself, all granite, over a huge interposing shoulder, quite with the *allure* of a minor Matterhorn—everywhere legible was the hard little historic record of agricultural failure and defeat. It had to pass for the historic background, that traceable truth that a stout human experiment had been tried, had broken down. One was in presence, everywhere, of the refusal to consent to history, and of the consciousness, on the part of every site, that this precious compound is in no small degree being insolently made, on the other side of the continent, at the expense of such sites. The touching appeal of nature, as I have called it therefore, the "Do something kind for me," is not so much a "Live upon me and thrive by me" as a "Live *with* me, somehow, and let us make out together what we may do for each other—something that is not merely estimable in more or less greasy greenbacks. See how 'sympathetic' I am," the still voice seemed everywhere to proceed, "and how I am therefore better than my fate; see how I lend myself to poetry and sociability—positively to æsthetic use: give me that consolation." The appeal was thus not only from the rude absence of the company that had gone, and the still ruder presence of the company left, the scattered families, of poor spirit and loose habits, who had feared the risk of change; it was to a listening ear, directly—that of the "summer people," to whom, in general, one soon began to figure so much of the country, in New England, as looking for its future; with the consequence in fact that, from place to place, the summer people themselves almost promised to glow with a reflected light. It was a clue, at any rate, in the maze of contemplation, for this vision of the relation so established, the disinherited, the impracticable land throwing itself, as for a finer argument, on the non-rural, the intensely urban class, and the class in question throwing itself upon the land for reasons of its own. What would come of such an *entente,* on the great scale, for both parties?—that special wonderment was to strike me everywhere as in order. How populations with money to spare may extract a vulgar joy from "show" sections of the earth, like Switzerland and Scotland, we have seen abundantly proved, so that this particular lesson has little more to teach us; in America, however, evidently, the difference in the conditions, and above all in the scale of demonstration, is apt to make lessons new and larger . . .

E. B. WHITE

Maine Speech

 1940

Author of the children's classic *Charlotte's Web,* Elwyn Brooks White (1899–1985) was born in suburban New York. In 1938, he turned down an offer to succeed Harold Ross, the founding editor of *The New Yorker* magazine, in order to move full-time to the Maine seacoast, where he had spent his summers since childhood. This affectionate piece on "Maine Speech" is organized around two long-standing principles central to New England literary practice: that good speech and writing must adhere to what Puritans called the "plain style" (White coauthored the famous handbook *The Elements of Style,* which condemns all forms of circumlocution and verbosity), and that "country talk is alive . . . and contains more pictures and images than city talk." In the second respect, if not the first, White was a true disciple of Emerson—who, a century earlier, had celebrated the "piquancy [in] the conversation of the strong-minded farmer or backwoodsman, which all men relish."

I find that, whether I will or no, my speech is gradually changing, to conform to the language of the country. The tongue spoken here in Maine is as different from the tongue spoken in New York as Dutch is from German. Part of this difference is in the meaning of words, part in the pronunciation, part in the grammar. But the difference is very great. Sometimes when a child is talking it is all one can do to translate until one has mastered the language. Our boy came home from school the first day and said the school was peachy but he couldn't understand what anybody was saying. This lasted only a couple of days.

For the word "all" you use the phrase "the whole of." You ask, "Is that the whole of it?" And whole is pronounced hull. Is that the hull of it? It sounds as though you might mean a ship.

For lift, the word is heft. You heft a thing to see how much it weighs. When you are holding a wedge for somebody to tap with a hammer, you say: "Tunk it a little." I've never heard the word tap used. It is always tunk.

Baster (pronounced bayster) is a popular word with boys. All the kids use it. He's an old baster, they say, when they pull an eel out of an eel trap. It probably derives from bastard, but it sounds quite proper and innocent when you hear it, and rather descriptive. I regard lots of things now (and some people) as old basters.

A person who is sensitive to cold is spleeny. We have never put a heater in our car, for fear we might get spleeny. When a pasture is sparse and isn't providing enough feed for the stock, you say the pasture is pretty snug. And a man who walks and talks slowly or lazily is called mod'rate. He's a powerful mod'rate man, you say.

When you're prying something with a pole and put a rock under the pole as a fulcrum, the rock is called a bait. Few people use the word "difference." When they want to say it makes no difference, they say it doesn't make any odds.

If you have enough wood for winter but not enough to carry you beyond that, you need wood "to spring out on." And when a ewe shows an udder, she "bags out." Ewe is pronounced yo.

This ewe and yo business had me licked at first. It seemed an affectation to say yo when I was talking about a female sheep. But that was when I was still thinking of them as yews. After a while I thought of them as yos, and then it seemed perfectly all right. In fact, yo is a better-sounding word, all in all, than yew. For a while I tried to pronounce it half way between yew and yo. This proved fatal. A man has to make up his mind and then go boldly ahead. A ewe can't stand an umlaut any more than she can a terrier.

Hunting or shooting is called gunning. Tamarack is always hackmatack. Tackle is pronounced taykle. You rig a block and taykle.

If one of your sheep is tamer than the others, and the others follow her, you say she will "toll" the others in. The chopped clams which you spread upon the waters to keep the mackerel schooling around your boat, are called toll bait. Or chum bait. A windy day is a "rough" day, whether you are on land or sea. Mild weather is "soft." And there is a distinction between weather overhead and weather underfoot. Lots of times, in spring when the ground is muddy, you will have a "nice day overhead."

Manure is always dressing, never manure. I think, although I'm not sure, that manure is considered a nasty word, not fit for polite company. The word dung is used some but not as much as dressing. But a manure fork is always a dung fork.

Wood that hasn't properly seasoned is dozy. The lunch hour is one's nooning. A small cove full of mud and eelgrass is a gunkhole. When a pullet slips off and lays in the blackberry bushes she "steals away a nest." If you get through the winter without dying or starving you "wintered well."

Persons who are not native to this locality are "from away." We are from away ourselves, and always shall be, even if we live here the rest of our lives. You've got to be born here—otherwise you're from away.

People get born, but lambs and calves get dropped. This is literally true of course. The lamb actually does get dropped. (It doesn't hurt it any—or at any rate it never complains.) When a sow has little ones, she "pigs." Mine pigged on a Sunday morning, the ol' baster.

The road is often called "the tar." And road is pronounced rud. The other day I heard someone call President Roosevelt a "war mongrel." Statute is called Statue. Lawyers are busy studying the statues. Library is liberry. Chimney is chimley.

Fish weir is pronounced fish ware. Right now they're not getting anything in the wares.

Hoist is pronounced hist. I heard a tall story the other day about a man who was histed up on the end of a derrick boom while his companions accused him of making free with another man's wife. "Come on, confess!" they shouted. "Isn't it true you went with her all last year?" For a while he swung at the end of the boom and denied the charges. But he got tired finally. "You did, didn't you?" they persisted. "Well, once, boys," he replied. "Now hist me down."

The most difficult sound is the "a." I've been in Maine, off and on, all my life, but I still have to pause sometimes when somebody asks me something with an "a" in it. The other day a friend met me in front of the store, and asked, "How's the famine comin' along?" I had to think fast before I got the word "farming" out of his famine.

The word dear is pronounced dee-ah. Yet the word deer is pronounced deer. All children are called dee-ah, by men and women alike.

The final "y" of a word becomes "ay." Our boy used to call our dog Freddie. Now he calls him Fredday. Sometimes he calls him Fredday dee-ah; other times he calls him Fredday you ol' baster.

Country talk is alive and accurate, and contains more pictures and images than city talk. It usually has an unmistakable sincerity which gives it distinction. I think there is less talking merely for the sound which it makes. At any rate, I seldom tire listening to even the most commonplace stuff, directly and sincerely spoken; and I still recall with dread the feeling that occasionally used to come over me at parties in town when the air was crowded with loud intellectual formations—the feeling that there wasn't a remark in the room that couldn't be brought down with a common pin.

FRED ALLEN

Letter to *The Cape Codder*

 1950

No less an authority than Henry Adams doubted that "New England Calvinists ever laughed." Apart from a minor satirical vein that runs through New England literature from the Puritan pamphleteer Nathaniel Ward to the late eighteenth-century poets known as the Connecticut Wits, it is hard to furnish much evidence to contradict Adams's judgment. In the nineteenth century, Thoreau mixed mordant humor with high moral seriousness, and James Russell Lowell brought a new kind of humane wit to literary criticism. Some readers of Transcendental utterances such as Bronson Alcott's "Orphic Sayings" found them so (unintentionally) funny that one responded with a series of "Gastric Sayings," and his own daughter Louisa parodied him in *Transcendental Wild Oats*. Yet any anthology devoted to New England humor would be a slim book.

Fred Allen (1894–1956), born in North Cambridge as John Florence Sullivan and best known as a radio comedian, belongs on any short list of New England writers who retain beyond their own moment the power to amuse—as Allen certainly does in this charming, and, in its way, loving, letter to his local Cape Cod newspaper.

july
12
1950

dear editor—
    you are the editor of The Cape Codder. i am a subscriber.
when a subscriber writes to an editor it is usually to complain about the paper's editorial policy, the small-sized print used in the help-wanted columns that is keeping nearsighted people, who are out of work and have no glasses, from finding jobs or to berate the editor for misspelling the name of the subscriber's wife in the news story that told how the subscriber's wife fell off a stool at a howard johnson stand and spilled 26 kinds of ice cream on her burlap ensemble.
    my purpose in writing this letter is not to condemn. i have no desire to add

another gray hair to your editorial cowlick. i merely want to despatch a kind word to you and to your little gazette.

to me The Cape Codder is a friend who comes to my door each week bearing tidings from the cape. the affairs of the outside world find no place in its columns. The Cape Codder chronicles only the happenings on the cape and the gossip and matters of moment to its denizens.

what other weekly gives you news and items such as these? (i quote from recent issues)

"now is the time to protect pine trees from the destructive turpentine bark beetles."

"albino woodchuck shot by frank hinckley in cummaquid."

"the striped bass struck in at pochot beach, orleans, sunday."

"cranberry clinic to be held july 12 and july 18. cranberry growers will meet to discuss bog problems."

"mildewed sails can now be prevented easily and inexpensively."

what other journal gives its readers pieces comparable to "orchard twilight," "the june woods" and "campin' on the island" by somebody who signs himself l.r.j.—colorful memories of happy yesterdays and tributes to fauna, flora and secluded nooks and crannies discovered by l.r.j. in strolls about the cape?

what other paper comes out on thursday to enable you to finish its contents and have its pages ready to wrap up a fish on friday? the answer is—no other paper.

until i subscribed to The Cape Codder i thought that a cranberry was a cherry with an acid condition. i thought that a seagull was a thyroid pigeon. i thought the mayor of cotuit was an oyster. today, thanks to The Cape Codder, i know why the pilgrim fathers, who had the entire continent available for their purposes, chose to land on cape cod.

enclosed please find check for another year's subscription. may you and The Cape Codder trudge along down through the years enjoying the success you merit for a job well done.

sincerely—

> fred allen
> the belmont
> west harwich
> massachusetts

DONALD HALL

Scenic View

 1986

Refusing to be placed in any category, including the one (New England) to which
the present anthology implicitly assigns him, Donald Hall (b. 1928) once told an in-
terviewer, "I want to be a poet by myself, not a New England poet or a deep image
poet or what have you." Fair enough. Hall is a poet of imaginative and geographical
mobility, whose suburban Connecticut upbringing and Harvard education were followed by a distinguished career in the Midwest at the University of Michigan. But
his heart has always been in New England—especially the hills of New Hampshire,
where he now lives on the farm that once belonged to his grandfather. "Scenic
View" is a native's witty retort to the tourists.

Every year the mountains
get paler and more distant—
trees less green, rock piles
disappearing—as emulsion
from a billion Kodaks
sucks color out.
In fifteen years
Monadnock and Kearsarge,
the Green Mountains
and the White, will turn
invisible, all
tint removed
atom by atom to albums
in Medford and Greenwich,
while over the valleys
the still intractable granite
rears with unseeable peaks
fatal to airplanes.

ACKNOWLEDGMENTS

A number of friends and colleagues made helpful suggestions while I was working on this book—among them, Nicholas and Elena Delbanco, Michael Elliott, Robert Ferguson, Rachel Hadas, John Hildebidle, Mary Holland, Jonathan Levin, Henry Moses, and especially Charles Capper, whose prodigious knowledge of New England history and literature is matched by his generosity. At Harvard University Press, I am grateful to Elizabeth Suttell and Gail Graves for their energy and good humor, and to Jennifer Snodgrass, who combines tact with precision in just the way one hopes for from one's editor. As the book neared completion, Robert Battistini responded quickly, cheerfully, and with great resourcefulness to a burst of research questions and fact-checking requests. I owe a large debt to Yael Schacher, a talented young scholar who did an outstanding job of tracking down hard-to-find materials and whose extensive work on the chronology was indispensable. As always, the person who worked with me most closely has been my wife, Dawn, who, with her usual grace and forbearance, helped me to choose, and to edit, roughly a hundred selections from what sometimes seemed a thousand candidates.

This volume was first imagined several years ago by Aida Donald, who asked me to undertake it, waited patiently for it, and when I had completed a first version of the manuscript, subjected it to the incisive and demanding criticism for which she is well known. The present book is the fourth on which I have worked with Aida over more than fifteen years. When I was starting out as a writer, I was buoyed by her belief in me, and I have been touched by her support ever since.

For permission to reprint materials in this book, I am grateful to the following:

"Four Trees upon a Solitary Acre," reprinted by permission of the publishers and the Trustees of Amherst College from *The Poems of Emily Dickinson*, Ralph W. Franklin, ed., Cambridge, Mass.: The Belknap Press of Harvard University Press, Copyright © 1998 by the President and Fellows of Har-

mings, edited by George J. Firmage. Used by permission of Liveright Publishing Corporation.

Excerpt from *The Late George Apley* by J. P. Marquand. Copyright © 1937 by John P. Marquand; copyright © renewed 1964 by John P. Marquand. By permission of Little, Brown and Company (Inc.) and James Marquand.

Excerpt from *The Last Hurrah* by Edwin O'Connor. Originally published in 1956 by Little, Brown. Reprinted by permission of Mrs. Barbara O'Connor Burrell.

"Reunion," from *The Stories of John Cheever.* Copyright © 1978 by John Cheever. Copyright © 2000 by Mary Cheever. Reprinted by permission of Alfred A. Knopf, a Division of Random House, Inc., and by the Wylie Agency.

"Plumbing," from *Museums and Women and Other Stories* by John Updike. Copyright © 1972 by John Updike. Reprinted by permission of Alfred A. Knopf, a Division of Random House, Inc., and by Penguin Books, Ltd., UK.

Excerpts from chapters 4 and 13, *Parsons' Mill*, © 1989 by Timothy Lewontin, reprinted by permission of University Press of New England.

"Sex Education" by Dorothy Canfield Fisher. Originally published 1945. Copyright 1973 by Sarah Fisher Scott. Reprinted from *A Harvest of Stories* published by Harcourt Brace Jovanovich, Inc., by permission of Vivian Scott Hixson.

Excerpt from *The Rector of Justin* by Louis Auchincloss. Copyright © 1956, 1964 by Louis Auchincloss. Reprinted by permission of Houghton Mifflin Company and Curtis Brown, Ltd.

Excerpts from *The Headmaster* by John McPhee. Copyright © 1966, renewed 1994 by John McPhee. Reprinted by permission of Farrar, Straus and Giroux, LLC, and Macfarlane Walter & Ross.

Excerpt from *The Duke of Deception: Memories of My Father* by Geoffrey Wolff. Copyright © 1979 by Geoffrey Wolff. Reprinted by permission of Random House, Inc., and Lescher & Lescher Ltd.

Excerpt from *The Rights of the British Colonies Asserted and Proved,* by James Otis, reprinted by permission of the publisher from *Pamphlets of the American Revolution, 1750–1776,* ed. Bernard Bailyn, Cambridge, Mass.: The Belknap Press of Harvard University Press, Copyright © 1965 by the President and Fellows of Harvard College.

"The Green Fields of the Mind" by A. Bartlett Giamatti, reprinted by permission of the *Yale Alumni Magazine*

Excerpt from "The Case of Sacco and Vanzetti" by Felix Frankfurter. Originally published in the March 1927 issue of *The Atlantic Monthly.* Reprinted by arrangement with *The Atlantic Monthly.*

Illustrations

The Founding Idea: Augustus Saint-Gaudens, *The Puritan*. Virginia Museum of Fine Arts, Richmond. The Charles G. Thalhimer Family Fund. © Virginia Museum of Fine Arts.

God Speaks to the Rain: Jonathan Edwards, page from "The Spider Letter" of October 31, 1723. Misc. manuscripts, no. 73091. © Collection of The New-York Historical Society.

The Examined Self: Robert Frost on his farm in South Saftsbury, Vermont, 1921. The Blackington Collection; Paul Waitt, photographer. Yankee Publishing, Inc., Dublin, N.H.

A Gallery of Portraits: John Singer Sargent, Study for a Portrait of Mrs. Albert Vickers (Edith Foster), charcoal on paper, ca. 1885. Courtesy of the Fogg Art Museum, Harvard University Art Museums. Gift of Miss Emily Sargent and Mrs. Francis Ormond in memory of their brother, John Singer Sargent.

Education: "A Prospect of the Colledges in Cambridge in New England," engraving attributed to John Harris after William Burgis, 1726. Massachusetts Historical Society.

Dissident Dreamers: Carlton Fisk waving his home run into fair territory during the sixth game of the 1975 World Series. AP Photo/Harry Cabluck.

Strangers in the Promised Land: African Meeting House, Boston. Photograph by Halliday Historic Photograph Co., ca. 1860. The Society for the Preservation of New England Antiquities.

The Abiding Sense of Place: Chapel at Biddeford Pool. Photograph by Baldwin Coolidge, 1880s. The Society for the Preservation of New England Antiquities.

Index